HARRAP'S
ILLUSTRATED DICTIONARY OF
MUSIC & MUSICIANS

First published in Great Britain 1989
by Harrap Books Ltd
19–23 Ludgate Hill, London EC4M 7PD

ISBN 0 245 54693 6

Copy preparation by Clark Robinson Ltd, London
Typeset by August Filmsetting, Haydock, St Helens
Printed in Great Britain at The Bath Press, Avon

SHREWSBURY COLLEGE
056758

HARRAP'S
ILLUSTRATED DICTIONARY OF
MUSIC & MUSICIANS

HARRAP'S *REFERENCE*

CONTRIBUTORS AND CONSULTANTS

Ian Bartlett

Roger Clegg, G.R.S.M, A.R.C.M.

William Gould

Richard Langham Smith

Steve Stanton, B.A., D.Phil., A.R.C.M.

Roy Teed, F.R.A.M.

ACKNOWLEDGEMENTS

Clark Robinson Limited would like to acknowledge the help of all those who have contributed to the creation of this dictionary. In particular, we would like to thank Donald Binney, Alan Blackwood, Katy Guess, Stephen Luck, Lawrence Norfolk, Victoria Ramsay and Mark Trewin for their editorial contributions, and Janet Tanner at Colin Lewis Associates for her illustrations.

Preface

Harrap's Illustrated Dictionary of Music and Musicians is both a beginner's guide and an expert's companion to the rich and diverse world of music and musicians. To novices and the initiated alike, this is a fascinating yet often mysterious world, although access to it today is arguably easier than at any time in history.

During this century, in Western music, interest has been developing in 'authentic' performances of historical works – especially of the Baroque period. Concurrently, modern music has undergone a sequence of revolutions that have taken it to rarefied intellectual extremes, and a host of new combinations of sounds have been made possible by the use of electronic equipment. Coupled with this, there is a growing interest in the music of the East, which has led to the inclusion of Eastern music in some school and college syllabuses.

Anyone interested in a broad spectrum of musical experience is inundated with the names of musicians, orchestras, composition types and technicalities. To enable the general listener or the student to get to grips with the intricacies of this huge subject, the *Harrap's Illustrated Dictionary of Music and Musicians* concentrates on people, modes of composition, technical terms and instruments, with a comprehensive cross-referencing system which helps the reader to find related subjects.

Composers, conductors and performers are discussed in terms of their importance in the history of music, and the names of their best-known or most important works and specialisms are given. Most of the technical terms related to the theory of music are illustrated, to clarify what could otherwise seem jargon-ridden and ultimately confusing.

Above all, the compilers have tried to be concise and up-to-date, and to provide information in an easily accessible form, on all aspects of music as it is today.

L. B. – Clark Robinson Limited, London 1989

A

A Name of the note that lies one tone above G and one tone below B. The scale of A major has three sharps in the key-signature.

aak (Korea) Court orchestral music of Chinese origin, mainly associated with Confucian ritual music. Literally, 'elegant music'. Two orchestras are used alternately – *tŭngga* (orchestra on the terrace) and *hŏn'ga* (orchestra on the ground) – distinguished by their repertory and instrumentation. Both, however, include stone-chimes, bell-chimes, a wooden clapper and scraper, bamboo flutes, a clay **ocarina** and barrel drums. See also **hyangak; tangak**.

abandonné (Fr.) Free or abandoned, indicating that a passage or piece should not be played too strictly; it applies mainly to **rhythm**.

Abbado, Claudio (1933-) Italian conductor, born in Milan, who studied at the Milan Conservatoire and with Hans Swarowsky at the Vienna Academy of Music, 1956-1958. After winning the Koussevitsky Competition (1958) and the Mitropoulos Prize (1963), he soon had many impressive debuts: La Scala in 1967 (where he subsequently became principal conductor and, later, artistic director) and

Claudio Abbado

Covent Garden in 1968. He became principal conductor of the London Symphony Orchestra in 1979 and principal guest conductor of the Chicago Symphony Orchestra in 1982.

Although noted mainly for his performances of late 19th- and early 20th-century works, particularly the operas of **Verdi**, Abbado is also an enthusiastic exponent of the music of such contemporary composers as **Berio, Ligeti, Nono, Penderecki** and **Stockhausen**.

abbandono (It.) Abandoned. See **abandonné**.

abdämpfen (Ger.) Indication to apply a **mute** to an instrument.

Abel, Carl Friedrich (1723-1787) German composer and viola da **gamba** player. He moved to England during the late 1750s and in 1763 established an association with J.C. **Bach**, performing in an annual series of public concerts which were to introduce many notable continental musicians to London. Although he received popular acclaim as a performer, Abel is chiefly remembered as a composer of lively and lighthearted instrumental music. His works include symphonies, overtures, numerous concerti for various instruments, and sonatas for the viola da gamba.

abendlied (Ger.) Evening song; sometimes used by composers as a title for a song or instrumental piece.

abendmusik (Ger.) Originally a type of concert held in the Marienkirche, Lübeck, during the 17th and 18th centuries, but now refers concerts held in any church. The Lübeck concerts probably began in the mid-17th century. They were financed by local businessmen and admission to the church was free. The earliest were organ recitals, organized by the organist at the Marienkirche, Franz **Tunder**. Later, vocal and instrumental soloists were included. Dietrich **Buxtehude**, Tunder's successor, added orchestra and chorus and composed **oratorios** for these concerts, some of which were in several parts, presumably to be performed on successive Sundays. In 1752 the practice of charging admission to the Friday dress rehearsals was introduced and these performances eventually assumed greater importance than the Sunday ones. Sunday performances were abolished in 1800 and Friday concerts ceased in 1810 as a result of the Napoleonic wars.

abnehmend (Ger.) Taking away; it implies taking away volume, and hence is the same as **diminuendo**.

Absil, Jean (1893-1974) Belgian composer who trained as an organist but went on to study composition with **Gilson**, winning national prizes with his Symphony No. 1 and his **cantata**, *La guerre*. With other young Belgian composers he founded *La Sirène*, a series of concerts to promote new music in Brussels and abroad. In 1937 he published his *Postulats de la musique contemporaine*, declaring that the distinction between consonance and dissonance is meaningless. Absil's own style began to evolve in his chamber music after 1934. He wrote polyphonically and with irregular metric divisions, often superimposing different metres, but used conventional and straightforward forms. After 1938 he tried to make his work more accessible, making use of folk material, and later he concentrated almost entirely on instrumental music.

absolute music Concept of music subject to many different shades of interpretation. Broadly speaking, it denotes music that is understood purely on its own terms and without reference to external factors. This excludes music with words, because the words determine the musical structure to some extent, and the music in turn contributes to the sense of the words. It also excludes dramatic music and **programme music** (such as the symphonies and symphonic poems of Liszt and Berlioz), which rely on external scenes or events for their meaning. It has even been argued that art music of a definite emotional character is not absolute music. On the other hand, it has also been argued that any music is absolute only insofar as it reveals the divine in nature; in this view, liturgical music is the purest of all.

The idea of absolute music appears in medieval writings, but aroused much interest in the 19th century when it became a controversial issue, argued by philosophers, critics and composers such as Liszt and **Wagner**. Many of the compositional techniques of the 20th century are based on a concept of absolute music understandable purely through structure.

An alternative term for absolute music is abstract music.

absolute pitch Ability to recognize and name a sounded note, or to sing a named note. The facility for absolute pitch is quite rare, although some say it can be taught.

abstract music Alternative term for **absolute music**.

Abt, Franz Wilhelm (1819-1885) German composer who studied theology and music in Leipzig, where he was a friend of **Mendelssohn** and **Schumann**.

From his post as *Kapellmeister* at Bernburg, Abt went to Zurich to embark upon an immensely successful career as a choral conductor. From 1855 until his retirement in 1882, he was *Kapellmeister* at the Court Theatre in Brunswick. During this time he conducted in many cities in Europe, and toured the United States (1872). He composed more than 3,000 works, mostly songs and partsongs in a popular and simple style, often close to folksong. His work also included two operas and some piano pieces.

Academy of Ancient Music Name given to an 18th-century society of music and to a present-day orchestra.

In the 18th century, the Academy of Ancient Music was an influential London society of aristocratic amateur and eminent professional musicians. It was apparently a continuation of the Academy of Vocal Music, established in 1726 "in an attempt to restore ancient church music", changing its name after a schism in 1731. It met regularly at the Crown and Anchor tavern in the Strand until 1781, and thereafter at Freemasons Hall until its disbanding in 1792. Pepusch was its first director. **Handel** and Geminiani are among the musicians who played at its meetings.

The orchestra of this name was founded in 1973 by Christopher Hogwood and was one of the first English professional groups to perform Baroque music on period instruments or copies of them. Since its formation its repertory has extended into Classical and Romantic music.

Academy of Music, New York New York theatre, opened in 1854; at the time it contained the largest stage in the world. Until the opening of the Metropolitan Opera House in 1883, it was the only theatre in the city devoted exclusively to concerts and opera.

Academy of St Martin-in-the-Fields English orchestra formed in 1959, which was originally a string ensemble directed by the leader. The orchestra's name derives from the church in Trafalgar Square, London, where its concerts were first given. Under its founder and principal conductor, Sir Neville **Marriner**, the orchestra has established an international reputation, particularly in performances of music of the **Baroque** period.

a cappella See **cappella**

Accardo, Salvatore (1941-) Italian violinist and conductor. Accardo graduated from the Naples Conservatoire in 1956, although he had already won international competitions at Vercelli in 1955 and Geneva in 1956, and in 1958 won both the Italian Radio Spring Trophy and the Paganini International Prize at Genoa. Accardo is considered a fine interpreter of Paganini, although his repertory ranges from the music of Vivaldi to contemporary works.

accelerando (It.) Direction indicating that the music should get faster.

acciaccatura (It.) Type of **grace note** found especially in music of the Classical and Romantic periods. It is written in the form of a small quaver with a stroke through the tail. It should occupy only a small amount of time – it is a 'crushed' note – and may be sounded on or just before the beat on which the succeeding note occurs.

Acciaccatura

accidental In Western musical notation, any symbol of **chromatic** alteration other than in the key-signature. Should a note, during the course of a piece, require such an alteration, the accidental is placed immediately before the note to be altered on the same line or space. The five accidentals in common use are:

The sharp (♯), raising the natural note by a semitone.

The flat (♭), lowering the natural note by a semitone.

The natural (♮), restoring a note which has been altered by the key-signature or by a previous accidental, to its natural pitch.

The double sharp (♯♯), raising the natural note by a tone.

The double flat (♭♭), lowering the natural note by a tone.

By convention, if a note has been altered by an accidental, the accidental holds for any subsequent repetition of that note within the same bar unless such a repetition is preceded by another accidental, although some 20th-century composers have adopted a system in which accidentals apply only to the notes they immediately precede. Any accidental is cancelled by a bar-line. To clarify any possible confusion arising from this, and also as an occasional reminder of an alteration required by the key-signature, cautionary accidentals are sometimes added before the relevant notes.

accompaniment Feature of any music that has a tune or musical line standing out from the other musical lines in interest or importance. These other musical lines are collectively known as the accompaniment. A song may have a piano or guitar accompaniment, for example, although a solo piano or guitar piece may equally have a "tune" and an "accompaniment" (both played by one and the same player on the same instrument). A player of separate accompaniments is called an accompanist.

accordion Portable instrument popularly known as the squeezebox. It consists of large rectangular bellows, which push air through two sets of reeds which sound on both inspiration and expiration. The tune is played on a **keyboard** on the right side, and buttons operated by the left hand provide accompanying chords.

Accordion

On the simplest instruments (e.g. the **melodeon**), the right hand control buttons give a **diatonic scale**, usually of D or C. Later models add one or two extra rows of buttons, each tuned a semitone higher than the preceding row so that all the notes of the **chromatic scale** may be obtained.

The piano accordion has a piano-style keyboard for the right hand, rather than buttons. In French Canadian music the accordion may be heard at its most virtuosic, but it is also commonly used in most Western European folk music.

accoupler (Fr.) To couple. Instruction in organ music to join two **keyboards** together or one keyboard to the **pedalboard**, by using a **coupler**. This enables music played on one keyboard to be heard as if it were played on both.

Ackermann, Otto (1909-1960) Swiss conductor. Having studied in Bucharest and Berlin, his first post was as *Kapellmeister* at Dusseldorf Opera House. He subsequently held posts in theatres and opera houses at Brno, Berne, Zurich and Cologne, and gave guest performances in Vienna, Monaco and Italy. Ackermann gained international fame as an opera conductor, especially for his interpretations of Johann **Strauss**'s operettas and **Mozart**'s operas.

Ackté, Aïno (1876-1944) Finnish **soprano**. She studied with her mother and at the Paris Conservatoire and made her debut at the Paris Opéra in 1897, singing Marguerite in **Gounod**'s *Faust*. She went on to sing at the Metropolitan Opera in New York and at Covent Garden in London, taking the title role in the first English performances of **Strauss**'s *Salomé* under Sir Thomas **Beecham**. Most of the later part of her career was spent in Finland, where she helped to found the Finnish Opera and was its director from 1938 to 1939.

acoustics Branch of physics that deals with the properties, production, propagation and behaviour of sounds. The subject treats of the various ways in which sounds are obtained from all musical instruments and provides instrument-makers and musicians with the information they need to get the best results from the instruments concerned.

Sound is produced by a vibrating object (in the case of a musical instrument this may for example be a string, reed, drumhead, air column or piece of ringing metal), which causes the air molecules near it to vibrate as well. The air molecules moving rapidly from side to side set up localized contractions and expansions of the surrounding air like a ripple or wave, and in this way the vibration is carried to a listener whose eardrum is made to vibrate at the same rate as the original vibration. The movement of the eardrum is interpreted by the brain as sound. Sound vibrations are subject to modifications: the speed or frequency of the vibration (**pitch**) may be increased to make the sound higher or reduced to make it lower; the amplitude (extent) of each cycle of movement as the air vibrates may be large if the sound is loud, or small if the sound is quiet. A sound has a discernible pitch if the bulk of its vibrations sustain a constant rate or frequency. Such a sound in music is called a note or **tone**.

Depending on its means of production, a note will have a number of less audible notes associated with it. This is best explained by the example of a guitar string. When the string is plucked its whole length vibrates to give the fundamental (principal) note; but at the same time fractions of its length vibrate too. These fractional vibrations (known as **overtone**s or partials) are much less audible than the fundamental, but their presence provides the guitar, or any other instruments, with its special tone colour, or timbre. All vibrating objects, apart from the **tuning fork**, produce a fundamental with its partials, and instruments are engineered to make the best use of this feature.

Overtones or partials are also known as harmonics. Those with frequencies that are integral multiples of that of a given fundamental constitute a set of notes called the **harmonic series**. This feature is vital to brass players who use their lips to change the effective vibrating length of the air column in their instruments and without **valves** can only play notes from this series. Valves are in fact used to lengthen the instrument's tube and provide the player with a new harmonic series.

The term is also used to describe the general capabilities of a concert hall, recital room, church or other venue for music for allowing the sound of a musical performance to be heard to its best advantage. A building that allows the sound to be transmitted without interruption to all parts of the auditorium is said to have good acoustics, whereas one that does not has poor acoustics. Soft furnishings and heavy curtains and wall coverings muffle sounds and may cause the softest passages in a piece to be almost inaudible to listeners at the back of the room. A high, vaulted ceiling is likely to cause considerable reverberation, and notes may continue to echo long after they have been played or sung, producing an unpleasant 'mush' of sound. The most satisfactory acoustics are to be found in venues where the surfaces of walls and ceilings are broken up by panelling to cut down, but not to eliminate, sound reflection; where the floor is raked to allow audience seating to be tiered so that those in front do not block out the sound from those behind; and where furnishings provide a means of controlling excessive reverberation rather than 'deadening' sound.

action Term with three meanings.

First, it is the operation of mechanical devices used in the construction of musical instruments. For example, the direct mechanical link between striking a piano key and the hammer striking the string. Actions are usually given trade names and are often patented, or they may be described under general categories such as the various organ actions: tracker action, pneumatic action, electric action, etc.

Second, in the orchestral harp, it is a mechanism that alters the pitch of the strings when a pedal is depressed.

Third, it describes the distance between the strings and fretboard on an instrument such as a guitar (the greater the distance, the 'higher' the action).

acute High-pitched or shrill **note**.

adagio, adagietto (It.) At ease. It is often used at the head of a slow piece or movement (and that movement called an adagio), in which case it should not be taken as slowly as **largo**.

When it occurs during the course of a piece of Baroque music it does not necessarily mean a slowing down of tempo, but it certainly indicates more relaxation.

A piece or movement marked adagietto is not so slow as adagio.

Adam, Adolphe Charles (1803-1856) French composer. He studied at the Conservatoire in Paris, where he eventually became professor in 1849. He produced his first operetta, *Pierre et Catherine*, at the Opéra-Comique in 1829 and his first opera, *Danilowa*, the following year.

He was a prolific composer of operas but is probably best known for *Giselle* (1841), which has become one of the best loved of all ballets. Among his other compositions are choral and sacred music.

Adami, Giuseppe (1878-1946) Italian librettist. He is best remembered for his libretti for operas by such composers as **Puccini**, Vittadini and **Zandonai**. His association with Puccini included texts for *La Rondine* and *Il Tabarro* and, with Simoni, *Turandot*.

Adamis, Michael (1929-) Greek composer and musicologist, who studied at Athens and Brandeis Universities. He taught neo-Byzantine music at the Holy Cross Theological Academy, Boston, Massachusetts, and was appointed head of the music department at Pierce College, Athens in 1968. His career as a composer began in the late 1950s mainly with instrumental pieces. Later he began to work more particularly with electronic media, often turning to Byzantine chant for source material. Adamis is best known for employing new techniques within old forms, such as the *Byzantine Passion* (1971).

Adam, Theo (1926-) German bass-baritone. He studied in Dresden and Weimar before making his debut at the Dresden Staatsoper in 1952. During the same year he played his first role at Bayreuth, where he was later to form his reputation as a **Wagner** singer. The role with which he is particularly associated is Wotan, but he has produced excellent portrayals of many roles in the works of Wagner and other composers.

added sixth **Chord** formed by adding the **sixth** from the **root** to the major or minor **triad**. In Classical **harmony** it usually occurs on the **subdominant** chord, resolving to the **dominant** or the **tonic**. In later music it was freely used for its colour, without any strict rules governing its **resolution**. It has been much used by jazz musicians, especially as the last chord of a piece.

Addinsell, Richard (1904-1977) English composer who studied at Oxford, the Royal College of Music, Berlin and Vienna. In 1941 he became composer and accompanist to Joyce Grenfell, writing music for her one-woman shows such as *I'm going to see you today*. His greatest success was a one-movement piano concerto in the style of **Rachmaninov** called the *Warsaw Concerto*, composed for the film *Dangerous Moonlight* (1941). As a composer of light music he wrote many film scores, musical revues and songs.

additional accompaniments Additional orchestral parts written for 17th- and 18th-century vocal works with orchestral accompaniment, to make them more suitable for performance in large 19th-century concert halls. Often they were written without any real understanding of the Baroque style, resulting in stylistically inappropriate arrangements. The works of **Bach** and **Handel** were commonly rearranged in this way.

The practice of writing additional accompaniments has now fallen out of favour, and the performance practice movement in the second half of the 20th century has led to a growing understanding of Baroque music and a demand for authentic performances using the forces intended by the composer, often on reproductions of period instruments.

Adler, Kurt Herbert (1905-1977) American conductor and opera director who was born in Austria and studied in Vienna, where he made his conducting debut in 1925. He went on to conduct at opera houses throughout Europe, assisting **Toscanini** at Salzburg in 1936. In the same year he went to the United States, first to Chicago and then to San Francisco in 1943. He became director of the San Francisco Opera in 1956, where he introduced new repertory, engaged untried singers and implemented modern staging techniques. Adler has been honoured by the governments of Italy, Germany, Austria and the Soviet Union.

Adler, Larry (1914-) American virtuoso harmonica player, the first to achieve recognition by Classical musicians and to raise the status of the harmonica to that of a concert instrument. **Vaughan Williams**, **Milhaud**, Gordon **Jacob** and Malcolm **Arnold** are among those who have written works for him. He has toured extensively, broadcast in many countries and been much concerned with teaching the harmonica; he has also written a number of film scores, most notably *Genevieve* (1953).

Adler, Peter Herman (1899-) American conductor, born in Czechoslovakia. Having studied composition and conducting in Prague, he held conducting posts in Bremen and Kiev and gave guest performances throughout Europe. In 1939 he went to the United States, working alongside **Toscanini** in television opera from 1949 to 1959. He was musical director of the Baltimore Symphony Orchestra (1959-1968) and director of the American Opera Center at the Juilliard School (1973-1981). Adler was a pioneer director of television opera in the United States, for which he commissioned many new productions.

ad lib Direction in written music allowing the player the freedom to improvise with the written notes, for example to vary the tempo or to include a **cadenza** of his or her own invention.

Aeolian harp Instrument comprising a long narrow box, with six or more gut strings stretched inside it over two bridges. The strings are of various thicknesses and hence have different tensions although they are tuned in unison. Named after Aeolos, the

Aeolian harp

Greek god of the winds, the strings 'sing' when the harp is placed in a free current of air, producing a variety of harmonics, all with the same **fundamental**. First known in ancient China and India and then in Europe during the middle ages, the Aeolian harp underwent a surge of popularity in the Romantic period. See also **acoustics**.

Aeolian mode One of the modes that emerged in the 8th century modal system used for **Gregorian chant**, now extensively employed in jazz improvisation and in modern compositions. The note structure of the mode can be obtained by playing the white notes on the piano from A to A, the note acting as a quasi **tonic**. See also **mode**.

affettuoso (It.) Tender.

affrettando (It.) Hurrying. An indication to increase the tempo with an added sense of nervous energy.

Agazzari, Agostino (1578-1640) Italian composer and organist, chiefly remembered as the author of one of the first and most influential treatises on the basso **continuo**, first published in Siena in 1607. Its value lies in its lists of contemporary continuo instruments (which include harp, lute, guitar and violin), its description of their roles, and its introductions on how to play from an unfigured bass. Agazzari also published five volumes of madrigals and much sacred music, being one of the first composers to use the basso continuo in this idiom.

agitato (It.) Agitated or restless. Often used to qualify other terms, as in allegro agitato, it may also imply an increase in tempo.

Agnus Dei (Lat.) Final movement of a musical setting of the Roman Catholic mass. When sung liturgically it accompanies the breaking and sharing of the bread, or the sharing of the peace. The text reads "*Agnus Dei qui tollis peccata mundi*" ("O Lamb of God that takest away the sins of the world"), with alternative endings "*miserere nobis*" ("have mercy upon us"), and, on the last repeat, "*dona nobis pacem*" ("grant us peace") or, as during the **requiem** mass, "*dona eis requiem*" ("grant them rest"). See also **mass; plainsong**.

Agricola, Alexander (*c*1446-1506) Franco-Netherlands composer. He composed eight complete mass cycles, and other sacred music and secular music with French, Flemish and Italian texts. His large body of instrumental music is particularly important – often extremely intricate and of great rhythmical complexity. The wide-ranging parts suggest that these may be rare written examples of early virtuoso string music.

Ahle, Johann Rudolf (1625-1673) German composer, organist and poet. Born in Mulhausen, he studied theology at the University of Ehrfurt, at the same time serving as cantor at the Andreaskirche. Returning from Ehrfurt to Mulhausen in 1650, he held the post of organist at the Blausiuskirche from 1654 to 1673. Ahle composed much sacred music, including some popular chorales, among which were the hymns *Es ist genug* and *Liebster Jesu, wir sind hier*, both used in works by J. S. **Bach**. He also wrote a set of dances and a singing tutor for use in elementary schools. Active in local politics, he became burgomaster of Mulhausen in 1673, shortly before his death.

Ahle, Tomas Giovanni (1671-1751) German composer, organist and poet. He was born in Mulhausen and succeeded his father Johann Rudolf **Ahle** as organist of the Blasiuskirche there in 1673. A gifted poet, he was awarded the laurel crown by Emperor Leopold I. He was succeeded as organist of the Blasiuskirche by J.S. **Bach**.

air Term first used in 16th-century England and France to denote a simple song or melody. In England it was frequently known as an **ayre**, particularly to describe a song of a light nature. After the decline of the lute ayre in the 17th century, the word air was used in a much more general sense. In 16th-century France, air was used to describe many forms of lute songs, such as the *air de cour* and the *air à boire*. From the early part of the 17th century the word also regularly applied to instrumental pieces, the most well known example being the air from **Bach**'s Suite No.3 in D – the so-called *Air on the G string*.

Alain, Jehan (1911-1940) French organist and composer. He wrote chamber music, songs and several pieces for organ and piano, although little of it was published during his lifetime. While drawing influences from **Satie**, **Debussy** and **Messiaen**, Alain's music is full of individual charm and picturesque imagery. A skilful organist and brilliant performer, he was killed in action during World War II.

Alain, Marie-Claire (1926-) French organist who studied harmony under Duruflé and organ with Dupré at the Paris Conservatoire, subsequently winning several prizes. She specializes in 17th- and 18th-century music, and is concerned with the recreation of historical authenticity in her performances. Also notable among her many recordings are the complete works of her brother Jehan **Alain**.

ālāp/ālāpana (India) Improvised prelude in various classical genres of northern Indian music in which the melodic features of a **raga** are introduced. It is characterized by unmeasured rhythm, slow tempo and serene mood, it is one of the most expressive forms of Indian music, regarded by some musicians as a religious invocation.

Albéniz, Isaac (1860-1909) Spanish pianist and composer. He was a child prodigy, making his first public appearance at the age of four. He studied for a while at the Madrid Conservatoire and then, at the age of 12, stowed away on a ship to the United States, where he supported himself as a pianist. On returning to Europe he studied at the Leipzig Conservatoire, the Brussels Conservatoire (with **Liszt**) and in Paris (with **d'Indy** and **Dukas**). He was persuaded to set the opera librettos of the English banker Francis Burdett Money-Coutts, but although he worked on several of these, the only successful opera was *Pepita Jimenez* (1896). From 1893 he lived for some years in Paris, where he became well known as a composer. He was one of a number of late 19th-century composers to draw his inspiration from Spanish idioms in music, for example in his orchestral works *Rapsodia española* and *Catalonia*. He is probably best known for his four sets of *Iberia* for the piano.

Albéniz, Mateo Perez de (*c*1755-1831) Spanish composer, active in San Sebastián. He wrote primarily for the church (masses, motets, etc.) but also composed some piano music and a theoretical work on ancient and modern music. An admirer of **Haydn** and **Mozart**, he was among the first to introduce their works into Spain.

Albert, Eugène (1816-1890) Belgian maker of woodwind instruments, whose high reputation was established by designing models for individual players. Specializing in clarinets, he was also influential in the development of bass and contrabass clarinets. His most notable contribution was the addition of an extra C♯′ on the clarinet, created around 1860, and now known as the Albert System. His business, established in 1846, was awarded the gold medal for clarinets and saxophones at the Paris Exhibition of 1889, and still continues in Brussels today.

Alberti bass Type of accompaniment to a melody that consists of a series of arpeggios and appears most often in keyboard music. It was named after Domenico Alberti (*c*1710-1740), an early composer of keyboard sonatas. The Alberti bass was frequently used by such composers as **Haydn** and **Mozart**. See also **figured bass**.

Albinoni, Tomaso Giovanni (1671-1751) Italian composer, violinist and singing teacher. Born the son of a Venetian paper merchant, he first came to light as a composer in 1694 with the staging of his first opera *Zenobia* and the publication of a set of 12 trio-sonatas. He had a brilliantly successful career as a composer for the stage, producing more than 70 operas, although few appear to have survived. Modern critics prize his instrumental works, notably his concerti for strings, his concerti grossi and his concerti for trumpet and for oboe. A contemporary of **Vivaldi**, he was one of the earliest composers to write concerti featuring wind instruments. **Bach** borrowed some of Albinoni's themes and used his bass parts for practice in **figured bass**. The popular Albinoni *Adagio* for organ and strings owes little to him; it was composed by the 20th-century Italian musicologist Remo Giazotto, who used an authentic Albinoni bass line from an unidentifiable work as the foundation for his highly romanticized composition.

alborada (Sp.) Type of Spanish music, played on the dulzaina (rustic oboe) and tamboril (small drum), originally a morning song. **Ravel**'s *Alborada del gracioso* (*The Jester's Morning Song*, 1905) derives certain features from the Spanish alborada.

Albrechtsberger, Johann Georg (1736-1809) Austrian composer and organist. After securing various positions as court organist, he eventually became *Kapellmeister* at St Stephen's Cathedral, Vienna, in 1793. A prolific composer – he wrote 284 church compositions (oratorios, cantatas, masses and motets), 278 keyboard works (preludes and fugues) and 193 works for other instruments – he perpetuated the Baroque tradition of **counterpoint** at a time when the Classical style was taking root. He is best remembered as a teacher and theorist: **Haydn** praised him highly and **Beethoven** was numbered among his many pupils.

albumblatt (Ger.) Album leaf. Originally, a composition written in the album of a friend or patron and usually dedicated to him or her. It came to be used as a convenient title for any such short, simple piece (later entitled simply *blatt*). Collections were published under the title *album*, sometimes by one composer (e.g. **Schumann**'s *Album für die Jugend*) or sometimes by several composers. Such pieces were usually for piano solo, although **Beethoven** wrote a song with accompaniment for piano duet, and **Wagner** wrote an *albumblatt* for violin and piano.

Alcock, John (1715-1806) British organist and composer. He was born in London and served as a choirboy at St Paul's Cathedral. He went on to hold several positions as organist at churches throughout England. He was also organist at Lichfield Cathedral. Alcock is particularly noted as a composer of church music and of glees, popular choral part songs written in a largely homophonic style. Alcock's son, also called John Alcock (1740-1791), was also an organist and composer of church music.

Aldeburgh Festival Major annual fesival of music and the arts founded by the composer Benjamin **Britten** and the singer Peter **Pears** in 1948 and centred upon the Suffolk fishing town of Aldeburgh and the surrounding district. The festival is held each June and features operas, concerts and some non-musical events. Several of Britten's works have been premiered at the festival, including his operas *A Midsummer Night's Dream* (1960) and *Death in Venice* (1973). Many concerts take place in the Maltings at nearby Snape, a purpose-built concert hall completed in 1970 on the site of an earlier brick building that was part of an old barley-importing complex. The building, which had been converted and used as a concert venue by the festival since 1967, had burned down in 1969. Its rapid 'resurrection' moved Britten to celebrate the fact by writing a grand overture, *The Building of the House*, for the start of the 1970 festival. Following the deaths of Britten in 1976 and Pears in 1986, artistic direction of the festival was carried on by a group of Britten's friends, including the cellist **Rostropovich** and the pianist Murray Perahia.

Aldrich, Henry (1647-1710) British writer on musical theory and composer of music for the church. He was also a notable composer of catches. Born in London, Aldrich went on both to study and teach at Oxford University, where he became dean of Christ church and was twice elected vice chancellor of the University. In addition to his musical achievements, he was also a classical scholar, theologian, architect and expert on heraldry.

aleatory Piece in which the composer has deliberately withdrawn control of some parameter of its performance or composition. Commonly recognized aleatory techniques include (1) the use of random procedures in the composition of a work (e.g. *Music of Changes* by John **Cage**), (2) the choice of a number of performance alternatives as stipulated by the composer, and (3) the use of an abstract notation system (e.g. *Intersection and Projection* by Morton **Feldman**).

Alfano, Franco (1875-1954) Italian composer who began his career as a professional pianist but subsequently took on numerous teaching and administrative roles throughout Italy. He is known principally as the composer who, after **Puccini**'s death in 1924, completed the unfinished opera *Turandot* from the composer's autograph sketches. Alfano was, however, a prolific composer in his own right; his numerous operas include *Risurrezione*, written largely in the style of Pucinni, and *La leggenda di Sakuntala*, which demonstrates a growing and less conformist, personal style. Among his other works are two symphonies, a piano concerto, several ballets and various chamber works.

Alfvén, Hugo (1872-1960) Swedish composer, violinist and choral and orchestral conductor. He studied at the Stockholm Conservatoire and spent some years as a violinist in the Royal Opera Orchestra, while studying composition. A state scholarship allowed him to train in Brussls under the violinist César Thomson (1857-1931). He wrote the first of his five symphonies in 1897. The second (1898) won him the Jenny Lind prize. In 1904, after studying conducting in Dresden, he became director of the Siljan Choir, a mixed choir based at Dalecarlia, western Sweden. He held this post for 53 years. From 1910 to 1939 he served as music director of Uppsala University and also directed the Initiates of Orpheus, another mixed choir, from 1910 to 1947. Apart from his symphonies, Alfvén is noted for his choral works, although few are known outside Sweden. He has also written much orchestral music, including film scores. He is probably best known for the first of his three *Swedish Rhapsodies*, which is subtitled 'Summer Vigil'.

Alison, Richard (1592-1606) English composer, mainly of sacred music. He composed metrical psalms for voices with chamber ensemble and published two such collections. He also wrote some solo pieces for **lute**.

Alkan, (Charles-) Valentin (1813-1888) French pianist and composer. He was a child prodigy, winning the *premier prix* for *solfège* at the Paris Conservatoire at the age of seven, and publishing his first piano piece at the age of 14. He was regarded as one of the leading virtuoso pianists of his day. He composed works for piano and pedal-piano, exploiting the technical resources of the fast-developing 19th-century instrument. He was a close friend of **Chopin**, and was greatly valued by **Liszt, Busoni** and others.

alla breve (It.) Popularly, the time-signature of 2/2, or two minim beats per bar, the symbol C often being used in place of the 2/2 on the stave. In older music, however, the same term and symbol may also indicate 4/2, or four minim beats per bar. The symbol dates back to before the widespread introduction of bar lines, when

Alla breve

it simply indicated that each successively smaller note value was to be one half (as opposed to one-third) of the length of the preceding one.

allant (Fr.) Going. Direction for tempo, as in *plus allant*, to go faster. It may also mean going on, as in *allant grandissant*, continuing to grow.

allargando (It.) Broadening or spreading. Direction that the piece should slow down and be played more majestically.

Allegri, Gregorio (1582-1652) Italian singer and composer, whose most popular work is his setting of the *Miserere* (Psalm 51). This setting has traditionally been sung in the Sistine Chapel in Holy Week every year since its composition, and so closely did the choir guard it that for many years no copy of the music was allowed to leave the Chapel. This monopoly was supposedly broken only by the 14-year-old **Mozart**, who wrote it down from memory after only one hearing.

Allegri sang at the Cathedrals of Fermo and Tivoli and became *maestro di cappella* at Santo Spirito in Sassia, Rome. He published four masses and many motets, chiefly in the old Roman style of **Palestrina**.

allegro, allegretto (It.) Lively or happy, often used at the head of a fast movement or piece, but not to be taken as fast as **presto**. *Allegretto* generally means a little slower and more lighthearted. Both are often qualified by other words, as in *allegro agitato*.

alleluia Praise Yaweh, a term that occurs in many Biblical texts, especially psalms, and is retained untranslated in many liturgies. The word therefore appears, often repeated many times for effect, in a great deal of sacred music of joyful character, in whatever language. In the Roman Catholic liturgy the third item of the proper is the alleluia, which consists of a verse of scripture preceded and followed by the word 'alleluia'.

In the early Middle Ages extra texts and music (known as **tropes**) were added to the 'ia' syllable (known as the *jubilus*). Because this was the earliest type of free-composed music condoned by the Western Church, the *jubilus* is regarded as the birthplace of Western composition.

allemande (Fr.) German. Used to describe two types of dance, which both probably originated in Germany. One was a dignified dance of moderate tempo in quadruple or duple time that was used as the first or second movement of the Classical suite. The other, still in use in Germany and Switzerland, is a rustic dance in triple time and has the character of a waltz or *laendler*. Alternative spellings are allemand, almand, almain, almayn.

Allen, Thomas (1944-) English baritone. A graduate of the Royal College of Music (1964-1968), he sang in the chorus of Glyndebourne Opera before joining the Welsh National Opera, where he made his debut as Figaro in **Rossini**'s opera *The Barber of Seville* in 1969. He joined Covent Garden in 1972 and, while maintaining frequent visits to Cardiff, he established an international reputation through extensive freelance engagements. By the mid-1980s he had become an established principal at most major opera houses, including the Metropolitan Opera House in New York.

In addition to his operatic repertory, Allen is admired as a recitalist and oratorio soloist. He has a wide and even-toned vocal range and possesses an impressive dramatic presence. He is equally at ease in the portrayal of tragedy, *bravura* or comedy.

Allende, Humberto (1885-1959) Chilean composer, ethnomusicologist and teacher.

His studies in France and Spain (1910-1911) are evident in his mature compositional style, which combines the techniques of French **impressionism** with the native rhythms and melodies of Chile. His output is varied and includes works written specifically for children, choral pieces, songs, chamber music and orchestral compositions such as his violin concerto (1942) and award winning symphony (1910).

alpenhorn (Ger.) Swiss peasant wind instrument, made of wood and varying in length up to 12 feet. It has a cup-shaped mouthpiece and can only produce to notes of the **harmonic series**. The French equivalent term is *cor des Alpes*.

al rovescio (It.) Equivalent of the Latin **recte et retro**.

alto Second highest of the four categories into which the human voice is generally divided in Western music. From the late 18th to early 20th centuries this part was generally sung by women or boys, but before that time it was more often sung by men. This practice has been revived in recent years. Male altos are often referred to as counter-tenors, whereas the term contralto is now generally used to distinguish a female alto.

Alva, Luigi (1927-) Peruvian tenor who studied in Lima and at La Scala, Milan. He made his professional debut in Lima and his European debut in Milan in 1954, singing Alfredo in **Verdi**'s *La Traviata*. In 1955 he sang for the opening of La Piccola Scala in Milan. Since the 1960s Alva has performed at Covent Garden, London, and the Metropolitan Opera, New York, in addition to regular appearances in Milan. He is best known for his interpretation of **Mozart** and **Rossini**, and is generally at his most secure when performing the works of pre-Romantic composers.

Alwyn, William (1905-1985) British composer, flautist and teacher who studied at the Royal Academy of Music in London. He earned his living by teaching and playing the flute in theatre orchestras and in 1926 took a post at the Royal Academy of Music, teaching composition. His early works, including a piano concerto and an oratorio (*The Marriage of Heaven and Hell*, after William Blake), were highly successful but in 1939 he rejected all his early work and began to concentrate on technical perfection. His concern with both the nature of artistic experience and craftmanship is shown in his long essay poem, *Daphne, or the Pursuit of Beauty* (1972).

Alwyn's artistic development is marked by constant self-assessment and the search for new creative stimuli. In several works (1955-1962) he used a tonal form of twelve-note technique based on Indian music. He has written more than 60 film scores and was a founder-member of the Composer's Guild of Great Britain.

Alypius Greek musicologist who lived around the 3rd century AD. He is remembered for his treatise *Eisagoge mousike* (Introduction to Music), which gives information on Greek scales and **modes** and their system of transposition. It represents the most comprehensive and authoritative surviving survey of the musical notation of Ancient Greece. Published in Italy in 1616, it proved highly significant to the studies of humanist scholars of music.

Amati family Family of violin makers who worked in Cremona, Italy, during the 16th century. The most famous was Nicolo Amati, who taught both **Stradivari** and **Guarneri**, all of these names being associated with the finest violins in the world, still highly prized by today's virtuoso players.

Ambrosian chant Type of **plainsong** peculiar to the rite of the Milanese or Ambrosian Church. It is the only corpus of Western chant to have survived other than **Gregorian chant**, and like the latter has its origin in Eastern chants which may have reached Milan in the 5th-7th centuries.

In chants that derive from a common root, the Milanese is often the least changed from the original, and is longer and more melismatic than the Gregorian version. The oldest surviving manuscript sources date from 11th-12th centuries.

Ameling, Elly (1938-) Dutch soprano. The most influential of her several teachers was Pierre **Bernac**, who encouraged her to study French song. Since the firm establishment of her reputation as a recitalist, she has become known for her highly personal interpretation of works from such diverse composers as **Bach, Britten, Handel, Mozart, Ravel, Satie, Schubert** and **Stravinsky**.

amoroso (It.) In an amorous or loving style.

Amy, Gilbert (1936-) French composer and conductor. He began learning the piano at the age of six and studied at the Paris Conservatoire from 1955 to 1960. **Milhaud** and **Messiaen** were among his teachers, but he was most influenced by Pierre **Boulez**, whom he met at Darmstadt. He took up conducting in 1962 and succeeded Boulez as conductor of the Domaine Musical concerts in 1967, retaining the post until the concerts were discontinued in 1973. Since 1973 Amy has combined an international conducting career with the duties of music adviser to the French broadcasting organization ORTF. As a composer, he has progressed from an affinity with **Webern** to an increasingly experimental style. His works include: a piano sonata (1957-1960); *Diaphonies* (1962) for two chamber orchestras; *D'un éspace déployé* for orchestra and soprano (a work almost in the style of a concerto grosso); and *Sonata pian' e forte* (1974) for soprano, mezzo-soprano and 12 players. His later works, such as *Messe* (1982-1983) for soloists, chorus and orchestra, with optional children's choir, has moved away from the strictures of Boulez to the mysticism of Messiaen.

ancora (It.) Equivalent of the French *encore*, meaning again.

andante (It.) Walking. Indication of tempo (at a walking pace), generally interpreted as being a moderate speed, lying between **allegretto** and **adagio**. There is no real agreement among musicians as to whether it is a quick or slow category of tempo.

andantino (It.) Diminutive of **andante**, usually used to define a piece of andante tempo or character. If used as a tempo mark it means a slight moderation of andante. Whether this modification should be faster or slower is a matter of debate, but the concensus among modern musicians is that it indicates a somewhat quicker tempo.

Anderson, Marian (1902-) American contralto who studied with Giuseppe Boghetti in New York, and went to Europe in 1930. She sang in England, Germany and Scandinavia, winning high praise from **Toscanini**. Her recital debut was at Town Hall, New York, in 1935 and she made her opera debut as Ulric in **Verdi**'s *Un ballo in maschera* at the Metropolitan Opera, being the first black soloist to appear there. Anderson was mainly known as a fine singer of **spirituals**, to which her large voice was admirably suited. She gave her last recital at Carnegie Hall in 1965.

André, Maurice (1933-) French trumpeter who, after studying with Sabarich at the Paris Conservatoire, quickly established himself as the leading trumpeter of his generation, achieving particular success through his use of a four-valve piccolo trumpet. He has recorded the complete trumpet repertory and has had compositions written for him by, among others, Jolivet, Tomasi and Blacher.

Andriessen, Hendrik (1892-1981) Dutch composer, organist and teacher, brother of Willem **Andriessen**. He studied at the Amsterdam Conservatoire and held positions as organist in Haarlem and Utrecht between 1916 and 1938. In 1926 he combined his duties as organist with a teaching post at the Roman Catholic School for Church Music in Utrecht. He was director of the Utrecht Conservatoire from 1937 to 1949, and of the Royal Conservatoire in The Hague from 1949 to 1957. He was professor of music history at Nijmegen University from 1952 to 1962. He wrote several masses with organ accompaniment and secular vocal and choral music. His orchestral works include five symphonies and the fine *Hymus in Pentecostem*, written during his 84th year.

Andriessen, Juriaan (1925-) Son of the Dutch composer Hendrik Andriessen and brother of Louis Andriessen, and composer of incidental and film music. More recently he has worked in television. Andriessen's music displays a skilful absorption of various styles rather than striking individuality.

Andriessen, Willem (1887-1964) Dutch composer and pianist, brother of Hendrik **Andriessen**. He studied at Amsterdam. He rose to be director of the Amsterdam Conservatoire from 1937 to 1953. He composed mainly choral and orchestral works.

Anerio, Felice (*c*1560-1614) Italian church composer, brother of Giovanni **Anerio**. He succeeded **Palestrina** as composer to the Papal court at Rome and with Francesco Soriano (1549-1620) completed Palestrina's task of revising and modernizing the plainsong of the Gradual, Antiphonal and Psalter. The first edition of the new and revised plainsong melodies was published in 1614-1615. He composed four masses, spiritual madrigals and lively secular canzonettas.

Anerio, Giovanni Francesco (*c*1567-1630) Italian composer and priest, brother of Felice **Anerio**. After holding major musical posts in Rome and Verona, he went to Warsaw in about 1624 as director of music to Sigismund III, King of Poland. After handing over this post in 1628 to his pupil Marco Scacchi, he decided to return to Italy. As a composer of sacred music, Anerio wrote very much in the old style epitomized by **Palestrina**. He made a four-part version of Palestrina's *Missa Pappae Marcelli*. But he also composed secular madrigals in which he embraced many aspects of the new style that was sweeping Italy at the start of the 17th century.

Anfossi, Pasquale (1727-1797) Italian composer who, after studying the violin in Naples and playing in a theatre orchestra, began to study composition with **Piccini**. He worked in Rome and Venice, and between 1781 and 1783 was employed as the director of the King's Theatre, London, where among the numerous operas staged were several of his own compositions. Anfossi is chiefly remembered for his operatic works such as *L'incognita perseguitata* (1773), but in his later career he also wrote a large number of sacred pieces, both on Italian and Latin texts.

angklung (Indonesia) Tuned bamboo rattle instrument which consists of two or more tubes tuned an octave apart, suspended over a slotted resonator tube. The term is also used as the collective name for a group of the rattles tuned at different pitches, one for each pitch in the melody.

anglaise, anglois, angloise (Fr.) Loosely applied in the late Baroque era to any of the English dance types. More particularly it refers to a fast dance movement in an orchestral **suite**, typically in **duple time**; the anglaise is usually simple and heavily accented.

Anglican chant Method of choral singing of psalms and canticles evolved by the Anglican Church (and later adopted by other reformed churches). An Anglican chant consists of a short sequence of chords to which the words of each verse (in a single chant or pair of verses in a double chant) are fitted by means of a system of pointing (i.e. special punctuation marks in the text indicating the position of the bar-lines in the chant). There are several thousand chants in the Anglican repertory, the main period of their composition being the 19th century, although the origins of the system go back to **plainsong** and the Festal psalm settings of the Tudor composers. Psalms are generally chanted antiphonally, that is, alternate verses are sung by alternate sides of the choir.

animato (It.) Animated, an indication to enliven or quicken the tempo.

Animuccia, Giovanni (*c*1500-1571) Italian composer who, after an early training in Florence until 1550, worked in Rome, where he was later appointed head of the Cappella Giulia. He is now known principally for his association with the oratory of Filippo Neri, for which he wrote many *laudi*; these sacred compositions consist of vernacular texts with several voice parts set in a simple homophonic style, and are noted for the clarity of their word setting.

Ansermet, Ernst (1883-1969) Swiss conductor who studied with **Bloch**. He joined Diaghilev's *Ballets Russes* in 1915 as conductor and toured extensively and in 1819 founded L'Orchestre de la Suisse Romande. He is most famous for his interpretations of the works of such composers as **Stravinsky** and **Debussy** and conducted the premiere performance of **Britten**'s *The Rape of Lucretia* at Glyndebourne in 1946.

answer Statement of a **theme**, usually in a fugal exposition, which answers the opening statement. This is normally pitched a **fifth** higher or a **fourth** lower (that is, **dominant** answer to **tonic** statement) than the initial statement. Where the answer exactly reproduces the theme, it is called a real answer; if it is altered it is called a tonal answer. Alterations are usually made to ensure that the dominant note in the opening statement is answered by the tonic note in the answer, so that the sense of **key** is preserved. The term may also be applied to the second of any subsequent pair of entries that stand in a tonic-dominant relationship, or to the second of any pair of **phrases** that balance each other in a musical structure.

antarā (India) Second section of a composition, of which the first part is the *sthāyī*, set in a particular mode (**rāga**) and rhythm (**tāla**) and often used as a basis for subsequent improvisation.

Antheil, George (1900-1959) American composer who is best known for his contribution to the 1920s craze for 'machine music'. In the search for music that reflected the century of the aeroplane, composers constructed noise machines which imitated the sounds of factories and industry. In 1926 Antheil caused a sensation in Paris with his *Ballet mécanique* scored for eight pianos, eight xylophones, pianola, two electric doorbells and an aeroplane propeller.

anthem Until the Reformation this word was synonymous with **antiphon**. The new Anglican Church swept away the antiphon in praise of the Virgin Mary (which traditionally concluded Evensong) and replaced it with a more general choral work, so that now the word is used to denote any non-liturgical choral composition that is suitable for use in the Anglican and other Reformed Churches.

For the earliest composers of anthems in the 16th century there were two opposing stylistic ideals. One was the *short* style, which heeded the church leaders' directive that "for every syllable there should be a note" and which was generally used for everyday, simple anthems. The second was the broad, polyphonic **motet** style, differing from the works of the Continental Catholic composers only in having English rather than Latin words. In fact, most early anthems use aspects of both these forms. Another contemporary division was into full anthems, in which the whole choir sang throughout, and verse anthems, which included passages for soloist(s) accompanied by organ, viols or cornets and sackbuts. Early masters of the anthem include **Byrd**, **Gibbons** and **Tomkins**.

After the Restoration the verse anthem continued its ascendancy and composers for the Chapel Royal responded to King Charles II's predilection for violins by writing for string accompaniment. **Purcell** and **Blow** were among these, and later **Handel**.

By the later 18th and 19th centuries sacred music had lost its former position as the priority of composers, and the quality of anthems suffered correspondingly. Nevertheless, those of **Boyce**, **Stanford**, **Parry** and **Wood** have never lost their popularity.

anticipation Unaccented note sounded before, and then repeated with, the **chord** to which it belongs. It is usually sounded on a weak beat. More than one note of a chord may be anticipated.

antiphon Term with three meanings, the first two in connection with Western liturgy.

First, it denotes a text sung in association with a psalm. In the Roman Catholic Office Hours the proper antiphon precedes and follows each psalm. Antiphons also feature in the current form of the proper of the mass, although down the years the accompanying psalms have been reduced to only one verse, or omited altogether. The Introit and Gradual retain the form antiphon – psalm verse – repeat of antiphon, while the Offertory and Communion retain only the antiphon.

Second, a number of texts in praise of the Virgin Mary are collectively known as Votive or Marian Antiphons, and these have frequently been set to music. The four most common Votive antiphons are *Salve regina*, *Alma redemptoris mater*, *Ave regina coelorum* and *Regina coeli*.

Third, a musical performance is said to be antiphonal if it involves two or more groups playing or singing alternately. This can refer either to the antiphonal performance of a pre-existing work (e.g. a plainsong psalm), or a work expressly composed to include antiphonal effects.

antique cymbal **Cymbals** that are considerably smaller than their modern counterparts, and are shaped differently, having an upward curve. This gives them a tinkling sound which has been used in orchestral works for special effect by composers such as **Ravel** in *Daphnis et Chloé* and **Debussy** in *Prélude à l'après midi d'un Faune*.

anvil Small steel bar, struck with a hard wooden or metal beater, which has sometimes been used as a percussion instrument. The anvil's use is most frequently found in operatic works as stage props whose sound is integrated into the musical content, e.g. as in **Verdi**'s *Il Trovatore* and **Wagner**'s *Das Rheingold*.

appassionata (It.) Impassioned. The term is well known as the title of a piano sonata by **Beethoven** (Op. 57 in F minor, 1804). The name was not used by the composer but added by his publisher to describe the overall mood of the work, which has become one of Beethoven's most celebrated compositions.

appoggiatura (It.) Melodic **ornament**, usually involving a note one step above or below the main note. Sometimes called a leading note, it takes half the time value from the main note. It may appear in small type or in normal notation. It usually

Appoggiatura

creates a **dissonance** with the harmony of which the main note is a member. Its presence was taken for granted in certain contexts, even when not notated, in the Baroque, Classical and early Romantic periods, especially in **recitative**. The French and German equivalents are *appoggiature* and *Vorschlag*.

appoggiature (Fr.) Equivalent of the Italian **appoggiatura**.

Apostel, Hans Erich (1901-1972) German composer who settled in Vienna. His work reflects his allegiance to the Second Viennese School of composers and passes through a period of **expressionism** to a period of strict **serialism**.

arabesque (Fr.) Originally used to describe something in the Arabian style. There are now two specific uses in music.

First, it is a ballet term dating from the 18th century describing the position in which the body is supported on one leg with the other leg extended horizontally backwards.

Second, it is a florid, delicate composition, for example **Debussy**'s *Deux arabesques* for piano.

Arbeau, Thoinot (anagrammatic pen-name of Jehan Taburot, 1520-1595) Canon of Langres, chiefly remembered for having written the most authentic and detailed surviving record of the 15th- and 16th-century social dances, the *Orchésographie* (published 1589). As well as giving descriptions and tunes for some 40 dances, he discusses style and instrumentation and gives sample drum beats. The one harmonized piece in the collection is the vocal pavane *Belle qui tiens ma vie*.

Arbós, Enrique Fernández (1863-1939) Spanish violinist, conductor and composer. He studied with **Vieuxtemps** and **Joachim**, with whom he later performed. For a time he was professor of violin at the Royal College of Music in London and later turned to conducting. His orchestras included the Madrid Symphony and he was guest conductor with several United States orchestras, including the Boston Symphony. A champion of 20th-century music, Arbós gave the premier of **Stravinsky**'s *Rite of Spring* in Spain.

Arcadelt, Jacques (*c*1505-1568) Flemish or northern French composer. In his middle years he lived and worked in Italy, where he applied Franco-Flemish polyphonic techniques to the new genre of the madrigal, of which he published six volumes between 1539-1544. His most often printed madrigal was *Il Bianco e Dolce Cigno*. In 1551 he returned to France and turned to producing large numbers of chansons.

Archer, Violet (1913-) Canadian composer who studied with **Bartók** and **Hindemith**. Her works include several concertos and the *Cantata sacra* for solo voices and chamber orchestra.

arco (It.) Bow. As a musical term (*arco* or *coll'arco*, with the bow) it is a direction to string players indicating that the bow is to be used. It usually follows and counteracts the direction *pizzicato* (plucked).

Arditi, Luigi (1822-1903) Italian violinist, conductor and opera composer who worked extensively in London. His operas were numerous and, though now all but forgotten, were widely known in his day.

Arensky, Anton Stepanovich (1861-1906) Russian pianist, composer and conductor. As a teacher he numbered **Rachmaninov** and **Scriabin** among his pupils. Arensky's music reflects the work of his idols, **Chopin** and **Tchaikovsky**, and it is his variations on the latter's *Legend* that has remained his best-known piece.

Argento, Dominick (1927-) American composer and teacher. He has composed many stage works, both operas and incidental music, as well as orchestral music and songs. A founder of the Minnesota Opera, and a professor at the university there, he was winner of the Pulitzer Prize in 1975.

Argerich, Martha (1941–) Argentinian pianist renowned for her dynamism, technical brilliance and forceful tone. Numbering Gulda, Magaloff and Michelangeli among her teachers, she is best-known for her performances of the Romantic repertory, as well as for her interpretations of **Prokofiev** and **Bartók**.

aria Set piece for solo voice with instrumental accompaniment, mainly associated with opera, but also a feature of oratorio and cantata. In the 16th century, the term described a **strophic** setting of a poem, as opposed to a **madrigal**, which was **through composed**. It did not necessarily imply music for solo voice, but the form was important in the early development of **monody**. The aria around 1600 is well represented in Giulio **Caccini**'s *Le nuove musiche* (1602). All are strophic and set for solo voice with **continuo** accompaniment.

In the first half of the 17th century, composers tended to vary the settings of each strophe, often over an **ostinato** bass. It was not until towards the end of the 17th century that the aria showed more of the emphasis on **melody** that we now expect. Another development in the latter half of the 17th century was the use of the ritornello, a recurring instrumental passage between the strophes.

The **da capo** aria was the dominant form for about 100 years after 1650. The highly accomplished operatic librettos by the poet Pietro Metastasio were so successful that they were used by composers throughout the 18th century, thus perpetuating the poetic form of the aria. In the late 18th century many composers, notably **Gluck** in his 'reform' operas, rejected the *da capo* aria as being essentially non-dramatic.

The rise of comic opera alongside Metastasian **opera seria** gave composers the opportunity to experiment with freer and more varied forms. In the early 19th century, pairs of contrasting arias were commonly used, called **cavatinas** (slow)

Martha Argerich

and **cabalettas** (fast). The old **bel canto** singing gave way to dramatic realism. These developments reached their peak in the music-dramas of Richard **Wagner**, where the music forms a seamless narrative from which set pieces cannot easily be detached. Similarly, **Verdi**'s last two operas, *Otello* (1887) and *Falstaff* (1893), have no detachable arias.

The 20th century has been eclectic in its use of the aria. **Stravinsky**, for example, used the form in his neo-Classical opera *The Rake's Progress*, while other composers have used song-like arias in an openly undramatic way.

The term aria may also refer to a short instrumental piece used as the basis for a set of variations, as in **Bach**'s *Goldberg Variations*. See also **arietta; arioso**.

arietta (It.) Piece in an opera, shorter than a fully developed **aria**, and usually in binary form. The term came into use only after the aria form had attained some degree of sophistication.

ariette (Fr.) Early 18th-century term used in French operas for a piece modelled on the Italian aria da capo, often in a brilliant vocal style and with Italian words. Later in the century it was used to describe a song inserted into spoken dialogue in a type of French comic opera, known as *comédie mêlée d'ariettes.*

arioso (It.) In the style of an **aria**. A style of singing that is halfway between declamation and **melody**; an arioso passage often occurs at the beginning or the end of a **recitative**. It has been used to mean a flowing melodic style, a short aria, or an instrumental piece in a semi-recitative style.

Ariosti, Attilio (1666-*c*1729) Italian musician and composer whose work has attracted considerable scholarly interest but is rarely performed. He played many instruments and held court and church posts throughout Europe. As a composer, Ariosti was prodigious, writing operas, Italian cantatas, oratorios and some instrumental music. He is particularly remembered for his imaginative use of instruments.

arja (Bali) Popular operatic form with plots taken from the 14th-century Javanese *Panji* romance. *Alus* (distinguished or elegant characters) sing and speak in Kawi, an ancient Javanese language, which is then translated into modern Balinese for the benefit of the audience by *penasar* or clowns during comedy interludes. It is commonly performed by youths and young girls, although leading parts in the comedy sections may be taken by older men. There are usually twelve dancer/actors involved.

The performance is accompanied by a small **gamelan** consisting of two small flutes or **suling**, drums, cymbals, a guntang (single-string bamboo tube zither), and a small gong.

Armstrong, Sheila (1942-) English soprano who studied at the Royal Academy of Music, winning the Kathleen Ferrier Memorial Scholarship in 1965. In the same year she made her operatic debut at Sadler's Wells as Despina, singing the role of Belinda (*Dido and Aeneas*) the following year at Glyndebourne. Her Covent Garden debut was as Marzelline in 1973.

Arne, Michael (*c*1740-1786) English composer, son of the more celebrated Thomas **Arne**. He was also famous as a keyboard player, performing works by his father and by **Handel**. As a conductor he introduced the latter's *Messiah* in Germany. Arne's compositions, mainly for the theatre and pleasure gardens are now largely forgotten.

Arne, Thomas Augustine (1710-1778) English composer and violinist. His first stage work, the masque *Dido and Aeneas*, was performed in 1734, and from then until his death he worked almost continuously, producing music for the London stage. He was one of those responsible for bringing the Italian *coloratura* style to London, but was also noted for the tunefulness of his songs, the most famous being *Rule, Britannia* from the masque *Alfred* (1740). This tune was used in works by **Handel**, **Beethoven** and **Wagner**, and is sung each year at the last night of the Henry Wood Promenade Concerts. Also among his 88 stage works are *Comus* (1738), *Artaxerxes* (1762) and *Thomas and Sally* (1760). He also composed secular cantatas, some sacred music, and his instrumental works include *VIII Sonatas or Lessons* for keyboard (1756).

Arnell, Richard (1917-) English composer; a pupil of John **Ireland**, he later became a teacher at Trinity College of Music, London. His reputation is mainly in the United States, and his work reflects his deep affinity with the Romantic repertory. Arnell's most celebrated works are the symphonic poem *Lord Byron* and the ballet *Punch and the Child*.

Arnold, Malcolm (1921-) English composer who studied with Gordon Jacob at the Royal College of Music (1938-1940) and then earned his living as a trumpeter before turning to composition in 1948. He is well known for his film scores, such as that for *Bridge over the River Kwai*, but has also written seven symphonies, numerous concertos and chamber works.

Arnold, Samuel (1740-1802) English composer and keyboard player. In sacred music he was active in the Chapel Royal, for which he wrote oratorios. In the theatre he was for a time chief keyboard player at Covent Garden, but later acquired, with his wife's money, the pleasure gardens at Marylebone. Later he moved on to the Little Theatre in the Haymarket, and in his church affiliations became organist at Westminster Abbey. His output was prolific but of variable quality.

arpa (It.) Harp; thus *quasi arpa* means in the manner of a harp.

arpeggio (It.) From *arpeggiare*, to play the harp, a term with two meanings.

First, it is the notes of a chord played in succession, ascending or descending, either on or before the beat. Many notations have been used to denote an arpeggiated chord, the most common being a wavy vertical line preceding the chord to be arpeggiated. In the keyboard music of the 17th and 18th centuries the word *arpeggiando* was sometimes used to indicate that a whole passage of chords was to be arpeggiated at the will of the player.

Arpeggio

Second, it is also used to describe the method of playing successive notes of a chord over the range of an instrument for practice purposes.

arpeggione Fretted six-stringed instrument similar to a cello, and played with a bow. It was tuned in the same way as the modern guitar. **Schubert**'s *Arpeggione* sonata was composed for this now obsolete instrument, and is its main claim to fame, although the sonata is now played mainly on the cello.

arrangement Term with three meanings.

First, it is an adaptation or transcription of a musical composition for performance by forces other than those it was originally written for.

Second, it is the addition of harmonized accompaniment to an existing melody.

Third, it is a composition that uses as its basis themes and other salient features of another piece of music.

Arrau, Claudio (1903-) Chilean pianist who studied with Martin Krause in Germany. His extensive and successful touring began before he was 20. Although his early reputation was partly based on his **Bach** playing, it is with the Romantic repertory that he has made his most lasting impression, along with his interpretations of the works of **Mozart** and **Beethoven**. Widely recorded, his playing reflects a profound understanding of the music rather than a dazzling virtuosity.

Arriaga (y Balzola), Juan Crisóstomo (Jacobo Antonio) (1806-1826) Spanish composer and violinist. His prodigious talent, especially in instrumental music, was displayed during his teens. Had he lived longer there is no doubt that he would have been a major force. It is now largely in Spain that Arriaga is remembered.

Arroyo, Martina (1937-) American operatic soprano, best known for her interpretation of principal roles in Italian opera. She gave her first Covent Garden performance as Aïda, and has sung at most major opera houses in the world. Her voice is rich but flexible.

ars antiqua (Lat.) Ancient art. This term was used in French theoretical writings of the early 14th century to describe notational systems used before the technical advances of the **ars nova**. The rhythmic notation was much stricter than in the *ars* *nova*, when it became more broken up. Forms used during the *ars antiqua* period include organa, conductus, hockets, motets and cantilenas (only motets and cantilenas being continued into the *ars nova* period). The term is often used to describe all **polyphonic** music of the 12th and 13th centuries, especially that of the Notre Dame School as exemplified by Léonin and Pérotin.

ars nova (Lat.) New art. The term first appeared about 1322 in a treatise by Phillipe de Vitry, which gave an account of the new notational techniques used by the French in the 14th century. *Ars nova* is generally used to describe all French music from the *Roman de Fauvel* manuscript (1320) up to the death of **Machaut** (1337). A new system of notation also grew up in Italy at that time, but not with such a dramatic change, and by the end of the 14th century composers were using a combination of the two systems to achieve a much greater range of expression and rhythmic variety than before.

Art of Fugue, The (*Die Kunst der Fuge*) Collection of 20 fugues and canons by J. S. **Bach**, written at Leipzig in the mid- to late 1740s and published incomplete by his sons after his death. All but the last of the pieces are based on one subject, starting with simple fugues and working through more complex ones, employing the full range of contrapuntal devices: inversion, stretto, augmentation, diminution, canon, double fugues, and finishing with a triple fugue, the third of whose themes is based on the notes B-A-C-H (see **counterpoint**). This, and the fact that Bach does not state what instruments are to be employed (although a keyboard instrument seems most likely) caused *The Art of Fugue* to be regarded primarily as a series of teaching pieces; it was not until the work was revived in performance in Leipzig in 1927 that it was also recognized as a magnificent piece of music.

Chamber and orchestral arrangements have been made of *The Art of Fugue*, and attempts have been made by Donald **Tovey**, among others, to complete the unfinished final fugue.

Asafiev, Boris (1884-1949) Russian composer, teacher and writer on music. After studying with **Rimsky-Korsakov**, Asafiev first worked in Leningrad as a professor of composition and music history. He moved to Moscow in 1943 and is mainly known for his writings on Russian music, although he was also a prolific composer, especially of ballets.

āsāvarī (India) One of the ten parent scales (**that**) in Hindustani music, corresponding to C, D, E♭, F, G, A♭, B♭, C′. An alternative transliteration is asawari.

ASCAP Acronym for (The) American Society of Composers, Authors and Publishers. ASCAP was founded in 1914 as a non-profit-making copyright collection agency. Its function is to establish licensing rates and to distribute fees to its members for any public performances of their works. Any writer or publisher of music with at least one regularly performed work may join ASCAP.

Ashkenazy, Vladimir (1937-) Soviet pianist who has settled in Iceland and also lives in Switzerland. In 1962 he was joint

Vladimir Ashkenazy

winner (with John **Ogdon**) of the first prize in the Tchaikovsky competition. He has recorded widely, playing the Classical and Romantic works, and is considered one of the leading exponents of this repertory. Ashkenazy is also to be seen directing concertos from the keyboard, and more recently has turned to conducting.

Ashley, Robert (1931–) American composer and performer of electronic music. Influenced by John **Cage**, Ashley has spent much of his composing career promoting live electronic music with touring companies such as the American-based Sonic Arts Union. He often collaborates with other musicians and visual artists on large-scale electronic music-theatre works such as *The Trial of Anne Opie Wehrer* and *Unknown Accomplices for Crimes Against Humanity* (1968). In 1969, Ashley became co-director of the Centre for Contemporary Music at Mills College, Oakland, California.

astāī (India) See **sthāyī**.

Aston, Hugh (*c*1485-1558) English composer who graduated from Oxford after eight years study in 1510. His *Hornepype* is the earliest surviving piece in the idiomatic keyboard style of the English virginalists.

Atherton, David (1944-) British conductor who studied at Cambridge University and the Royal Academy of Music. He founded the London Sinfonietta in 1967 and served as its first musical director until 1973. In 1968 he became the youngest conductor ever to appear at a Henry Wood Promenade concert, and in the same year made his debut at the Royal Opera House, Covent Garden. He was principal conductor with the Royal Liverpool Philharmoni Orchestra (1980-1983) and musical director of the San Diego Symphony Orchestra (1980-1987). In 1985 he became principal guest conductor of the BBC Symphony Orchestra. Atherton has edited the complete instrumental music of Arnold **Schoenberg** and Roberto **Gerhard**.

atonal Any piece of music that rejects the traditional **tonal** system, although often used to describe, rather inappropriately, music whose harmonic and melodic structure seems unfamiliar to the listener. The 'breakdown' of tonality is usually seen as occurring towards the end of the 19th century, especially in the works of **Wagner** (such as *Tristan und Isolde*) and **Liszt**. Increasing use of chromaticism and transposition at this time inevitably led to a complete reappraisal of the tonal system that eventually saw a systemization of atonality in the form of **twelve-note** or **serial** music.

attacca (It.) Attack, or attach, an indication to begin the next movement or section immediately without a break.

Attaignant, Pierre (*c*1494-*c*1551) Parisian music publisher. He invented the system of music printing in which each note had its own portion of the stave on the same block, which brought printed music within the price-range of large numbers of people for the first time. His publications date from the mid-1520s, and include some of the most important music of his time, notably the chansons of Claudin de Sermisy and Clément **Jannequin**, and seven volumes of dance music, some of which he may have arranged himself.

Atterberg, Kurt (1887-1974) Swedish composer and writer. An active figure in Swedish musical life, Atterberg held many influential posts in the academic and professional world. Like many Nordic composers, much of his output is descriptive or programmatic in conception, and he has written a great deal of ballet music. His nine symphonies are rarely heard but a few shorter pieces have found a modest place in the repertory.

Attwood, Thomas (1765-1838) English composer and organist. After serving as a chorister in the Chapel Royal, Attwood travelled extensively abroad, receiving lessons from **Mozart** while in Vienna. This experience influenced his musical style profoundly. He held appointments as organist at St Paul's Cathedral and later at the Chapel Royal, and was in addition a founder professor of the Royal Academy of Music. In 1792 he made a successful debut as a theatrical composer with *The Prisoner* and wrote music for about 30 different productions during the next decade. Thereafter he turned increasingly to sacred music, and is particularly remembered for his coronation anthems.

aubade (Fr.) Early morning music (from *aube*, dawn). Aubades were played in 17th- and 18th-century courts in honour of royalty. The Spanish equivalent is **alborada**. Composers have used both terms as titles for instrumental music, for example **Lalo**'s *Aubade* for five wind and five string instruments.

Auber, Daniel-François-Esprit (1782-1871) French composer, influential in the rise of **opéra-comique** during the early 19th century. His early attempts attracted the attention of **Cherubini**, under whom he subsequently studied, and from 1820 onwards he achieved lasting successes in collaboration with the librettist Scribe with such works as *La muette de Portici*, *Fra Diavolo* and *Le domino noir*. With 42 operas to his credit, he is best remembered for his vivacious yet melodious music, somewhat influenced by **Rossini**. During his lifetime he received many public honours and in 1842 was appointed director of the Paris Conservatoire in succession to Cherubini.

Aubert, Louis (1720-after 1783) French violinist and son of Jacques Aubert, therefore often referred to as *le jeune*. As a young child he played in the orchestra of the Paris Opéra, eventually becoming first violinist and one of the Opéra's principal conductors. Aubert was also a composer of dance music and of *simphonies*.

auditorium Area in a theatre or concert hall in which the audience is seated.

Audran, Edmond (1840-1901) French composer of some 30 operettas, written during the last quarter of the 19th century. His best-known works include *Les noces d'Olivette* and *La mascotte*. *La poupée*, written towards the end of his career in 1896, is regarded as his masterpiece. His popular style made him a successful rival of Lecocq, and he enjoyed widespread fame throughout Europe.

augmentation Lengthening of a musical **theme** by increasing (usually doubling) the note-values. It is a common device in fugues, canons and other contrapuntal works. It was also used frequently by Renaissance composers for the **cantus firmus** in masses and motets.

augmented interval Perfect or major **interval** that has been increased by a semitone. Augmented intervals occurring naturally in the scale are the augmented 4th (between the 4th and 7th degrees of the major or harmonic minor scale, e.g. F-B in the scale of C) and the augmented 2nd (between the 6th and 7th degrees of the harmonic minor scale, e.g. A♭-B♭ in C minor).

augmented sixth **Interval** of a major sixth increased by a semitone or, more usually, a **chord** containing such an interval. The three commonly used forms of the augmented sixth chord are: the French sixth, which contains a major third and an augmented fourth above the root; the Italian sixth, which contains the major third above the root (in four-part writing this is doubled); and the German sixth, which contains the major third and a doubly augmented fourth (resolving upwards) or a perfect fifth (resolving downwards) above the root. The German

German sixth | Italian sixth | French sixth

sixth is useful for **modulation** because it sounds like a dominant seventh chord, and can be resolved as one.

aulos Most important instrument of ancient Greece, a slender pipe with a double reed having a thumb hole and three to five finger holes. It was played in pairs, both reeds in the mouth and a pipe held in each hand. Although we know nothing of the performance practice and how the two pipes functioned together, the instrument is depicted in use at all kinds of social occasions as a solo instrument and in the accompaniment of solo or chorus singing.

Auric, Georges (1899-1983) French composer who was a member of the group of composers known as Les Six, along with Cocteau, **Poulenc** and others. His large output included several ballets, songs, piano pieces and scores for films by René Clair and Jean Cocteau. He was also a music critic and director of the Paris Opéra (1962-1968).

Austin, Larry (Don) (1930-) American composer who studied at North Texas State University under Andrew **Imbrie** and Darius **Milhaud** and held teaching posts in California, Florida and New York. He was editor of the avant-garde music journal, *Source*, from 1966 to 1971. Many of his compositions attempt to contain group improvisation (often by jazz soloists) within a controlling framework. He has also experimented with electronic and theatrical media.

auxiliary note Unaccented note forming part of the prevailing harmony, which it decorates. It lies a step above (upper auxiliary) or below (lower or under auxiliary) the main note, from which it is approached and to which it returns. More than one auxiliary note may be sounded at once. In American usage it is known as a neighbour note.

Ave Maria (Lat.) Hail Mary, used as the opening words of various texts as set to music down the years. Most however, are based on the Roman Catholic **antiphon** *Ave Maria, gratia plena, dominus tacum...* (Hail Mary, mother of God, the Lord is with thee...). Particularly well-known settings include those of Robert Parsons (d1570), **Schubert** and **Gounod**, whose version comprises a vocal line added to J. S. **Bach**'s Prelude No.1 from *The Well-tempered Clavier*.

Avidom, Menahem (1908-) Israeli composer of Russian birth. His compositions span many styles, from a modal **impressionism** using folk music, to purely **serial** works. His symphonies fall somewhere between these two styles, using an eclectic style based on tonal centres rather than on tonality. Avidom has always been active in Israeli musical life.

Avison, Charles (1709-1770) English composer, conductor and writer on music, who lived all his life in Newcastle upon Tyne. His most important compositions are his concerti grossi, trio-sonatas and other chamber music, which shows the influence of **Rameau**. His *Essay on Musical Expression* (1752) caused a stir on its first publication.

Avni, Tzvi (1927-) Israeli composer born in Germany, who studied with **Copland**. Among his better-known works are *Meditations on a drama*, an orchestral work; *Summer strings*, for string quartet; and *Collage*, for voice, percussion, flute and electric guitar.

Avshalomov, Aaron (1894-1965) Russo-American composer, he studied in Zurich and lived for a time in China, where he studied the native idiom which he integrated into his own compositions. Among his works are two operas, *Kuan Yin* and *The Great Wall*; a symphonic sketch, *Peiping Huntings*; and a ballet, four symphonies and two concertos.

ayre When the word is used with this spelling (rather than **air**), it almost invariably refers to a particular type of English song, generally scored for solo voice and lute, which flourished in the 1600s. Other voices and/or viols or other instruments could often be added *ad libitum*. John **Dowland**'s *First book of Ayres* inaugurated the form in 1597; other composers include Thomas **Campion** and John Danyel.

Axman, Emil (1887-1949) Czech composer and a pupil of **Novák**. His work was much influenced by the music of his native Moravia and he is well known for his choral compositions, most of which are for male voice choir.

B

B Name of the note that lies one tone above A and one semitone below C. The scale of B major has five sharps in the key-signature. In German terminology, however, this note is called H, whereas B refers

B B major

to the English B♭. Hence composers have, in German nomenclature, been able to form themes from the name of **Bach** – B-A-C-H.

Baaren, Kees van (1906-1970) Dutch composer who studied in Germany. His works include Variations for orchestra, a piano concerto and a wind quintet.

Babell, William (*c*1690-1723) English musician and composer, particularly renowned as a harpsichord player, and famous for his arrangements of popular operatic arias for the keyboard. In these he often imitated the elaborate ornaments added by singers and his pieces thus give the modern listener some idea of this lost art. Babell left a repertory of chamber music and small concertos along with arias and harpsichord music.

bacchetta (It.) Term with three meanings.

First, it is a **baton**.

Second, it is the stick of the **bow** as used for stringed instruments.

Third, it is a **drumstick**, *bacchetta di legno* being a wooden one and *bacchetta di spugna* a sponge headed stick

Bacewiez, Graznya (1913-1961) Polish violinist and composer. Her works include four symphonies, a cello concerto, four violin concertos and four string quartets.

BACH When interpreted in German, the letters B, A, C and H can be used to form the musical notes B♭, A, C and B♮. The theme was first used by its creator, J.S. Bach, as one of the subjects in the final and unfinished fugue of his famous collection *The Art of Fugue*, and has since often been included in pieces by various composers in homage to its inventor. Among them are **d'Indy, Busoni, Schumann, Honegger, Reger, Liszt, Rimsky-Korsakov** and **Schoenberg**.

Bach, Carl Philipp Emanuel (1714-1788) German composer and harpsichord player, second son of J.S. Bach and his first wife, Maria Barbara. After working in the employment of Frederick the Great he was engaged as music director for five churches in Hamburg (1767). He is best remembered for his keyboard music and his early use of **sonata form**. His works emphasize **homophony** over **counterpoint** and include large-scale choral works (e.g. *Die Israeliten in der Wüste*), keyboard concertos, 19 symphonies, and solo vocal music. C.P.E. Bach also wrote a treatise on keyboard playing, which provides an invaluable guide to contemporary practice.

Bach, Johann Christian (1735-1782) German composer, the youngest son of J.S. **Bach** and his second wife Anna Magdalena. After studying music with his father and his brother Carl Philipp Emanuel, J.C. Bach studied in Italy with Martini before moving to England in 1762. He produced his first opera in London (*Orione*, 1763) and in the same year was appointed music tutor to Queen Charlotte. He befriended the young **Mozart** on his visit to London and has often been said to have provided him with one of his earliest sources of inspiration. With C.F. **Abel** he founded a series of subscription concerts, which were staged annually between 1764 and 1781. Despite visits to Mannheim (1772) and Paris (1778), Johann Christian maintained his strong ties with England, where he died, and this association led to his popular title of the 'London Bach'. Among his works were many operas, concertos, keyboard sonatas, symphonies and chamber works.

Bach, Johann Christoph Friedrich (1732-1795) German organist and composer; penultimate son of J.S. **Bach** and Anna Magdalena. He studied music with his father and law at Leipzig University. He gained employment at the court of Bückeburg in 1750 as a chamber musician to Count Wilhelm of Schaumburg-Lippe. He has gained the informal title of the 'Bückeburger Bach' from his permanent links with the court where he was to remain for the rest of his life. His compositions include oratorios composed on words by Johann Gottfried Herder, 14 symphonies, keyboard concertos, chamber music (including keyboard sonatas) and an opera (now lost).

Johann Sebastian Bach

Bach, Johann Sebastian (1685-1750) German composer and keyboard player. The most significant member of the Bach family, Johann Sebastian was best known during his lifetime as an organist. His immense fame as a composer originates in a posthumous revival of interest in his work during the 19th century.

Bach was born in Eisenach and first studied music within his highly musical family. Among his teachers were (probably) his father Johann Ambrosius (who was employed at court as a string player and in Lüneburg) and his brother Johann Christoph, who gave him his first keyboard tuition.

Several years as a chorister at Lüneburg were followed by appointments in Arnstadt (1704-1707) and Mühlhausen, where he married his first wife, his cousin Maria

Barbara (1684-1720). In 1708 Johann Sebastian was appointed court organist in Weimar, and this is where he composed most of his works for organ. In 1717 he moved as *Kapellmeister* to Cöthen, where he wrote a large part of his orchestral, keyboard and chamber music and, after the death of Maria Barbara, married Anna Magdalena Wilcke (1721).

In 1723 Bach became cantor at St Thomas's Church in Leipzig. It was there that he composed most of his sacred music and was to live until his death. From his two marriages Bach fathered twenty children, many of whom were to become eminent composers and performers in their own right.

His church music includes settings of the Passions, *St John* (1724) and *St Matthew* (1729), his perfectly constructed Mass in B Minor (1733-1738) and more than 200 cantatas. Bach perfected the writing of chorale settings, examples of which can be heard throughout his large-scale choral works and cantatas.

His best-loved instrumental compositions are probably the six *Brandenburg Concertos* (1721), his violin sonatas, concertos and suites for unaccompanied cello.

Bach's organ music includes more than 140 chorale preludes (a form in which he excelled), toccatas and fugues, preludes and fugues, fantasias, sonatas and trios. His other keyboard music includes the collection *The Well-Tempered Clavier* (1722-1742), the *Goldberg Variations* (1742) and *The Art of Fugue*.

His compositions are catalogued by means of the prefix BWV (*Bach Werke-Verzeichnis*), and a numbering system which was created in 1950 by Wolfgang Schmieder.

Bach's intellectual power, so evident throughout his work in the use of fugue and counterpoint, was never to obscure the joy and vitality present in his compositions. His many hundred works contain some of the best-known and well-loved compositions of all time and demonstrate his complete mastery of every genre he employed. He used contrapuntal writing in a natural and unstilted way and exploited fully every possibility this form offered.

The study of Bach's work remains an essential part of every music student's education and his methods and thematic material have been frequently re-assessed, re-interpreted and analyzed over the years. His compositions are a constant source of inspiration to scholar and composer alike.

Bach trumpet Natural **trumpet**, prominent in the 17th and 18th centuries, pitched slightly higher than the modern valved version. Passages for Bach trumpet may be found in the works of composers such as J.S. **Bach** and **Handel**.

Bach Werke-Verzeichnis (BWV) Title taken from the name of the index of the works of J.S. **Bach**, by Schmieder, *Thematisch-Systematisches Verzeichnis der musikalischen Werke Johann Sebastian Bachs: Bach Werke-Verzeichnis* (Leipzig, 1950). The catalogue has provided the standard system of numbering for the works of Johann Sebastian Bach and extends throughout his many hundreds of compositions.

Bach, Wilhelm Friedemann (1710-1784) German organist and composer, the eldest son of Johann Sebastian and his first wife, Maria Barbara.

After studying music with his father (who wrote the *Klavier-Büchlein* for use in his education, 1720) he was engaged as organist of St Sophia in Dresden (1723) and later for St Mary, Halle (1746). In 1764 he resigned in order to pursue a career as a teacher. His various compositions include keyboard works (concertos, fantasias, sonatas, etc.), symphonies and cantatas.

Bäck, Sven-Erik (1919-) Swedish composer who studied in Rome with Patters. His works include a symphony for strings, *Sinfonia Sacra* for chorus and orchestra, a sonata for solo flute and an opera *Crane Feathers*.

Backhaus, Wilhelm (1884-1969) German

pianist, trained in Leipzig and held to be the last great exponent of the Leipzig tradition. He is known for letting the music speak for itself rather than for dazzling virtuosity. Backhaus's recordings of the Classical and Romantic repertory show careful analysis of the works as a whole and give a sense of their architecture.

Badings, Henk (1907-) Dutch composer who was originally trained in geology, which he taught at Delft University from around 1931. He studied composition with Willem **Pijper** from 1930, and composed his Symphony No. 1 in that year. He has held teaching posts at Rotterdam, The Hague, Utrecht and Stuttgart, and lectured in Australia, South Africa and the United States.

Badings's works demonstrate a concern with problems of **tonality**, a fondness for **counterpoint** and attention to formal coherence. From the early 1950s, he developed an interest in electronic music, and produced some operas and ballets for radio and television. His works include 14 symphonies, concertos and double concertos, choral works, songs, chamber music and solo instrumental music.

Badura-Skoda, Paul (1927-) Austrian pianist and musicologist. A pupil of Edwin Fischer, he has concentrated on the works of the Viennese classics, often using his own collection of late 18th- and early 19th-century pianos for recordings. As an editor, his editions of **Beethoven**, **Mozart**, **Schubert** and **Chopin** are models of excellence, and his book on Mozart interpretation (written with his wife Eva) is a classic. His knowledge of Classical performance practices, respect for the authentic text, and feeling for the tone colour of early pianos have ensured that his recordings are excellent.

bagatelle (Fr.) Short instrumental piece, usually for keyboard. François **Couperin** used the title for some of his *Pièces de Clavecin*, and **Beethoven** wrote 26 piano bagatelles, of which *Für Elise* is one.

bagpipe Generic term for a wind instrument which appears throughout Europe and in a variety of guises. Invariable elements are a reed pipe and a bag which acts as a reservoir of air between the air source and the pipe. Typical variations that may occur are: the air may be provided either by a mouth pipe, or by bellows held under the arm and pressed against the body; the reed pipe or chanter, holed to give a variety of pitches, may be complemented by one or more single tone reed pipes or drones tuned to the tonic and sometimes the dominant; the reed in the chanter may be single or double; the chanter and drone pipes may be cylindrical or conical; and the number of drone pipes may vary.

Bagpipe

baguette (Fr.) Equivalent to the Italian **bacchetta**.

Baillot, Pierre (1771-1842) French violinist and composer of violin music. He is the last representative of the Classical Paris school of violinists who favoured a clarity and neatness of style and a pure tone. His instructional textbook on the instrument, *L'art du Violon* (1834), holds its place as a standard work, although his compositions are now almost entirely forgotten.

Baird, Tadeusz (1928-1981) Polish composer who studied in Warsaw with Kazimierz Sikorski. Although his first works were written in a conventional style, he began to use **serial** methods in 1951 and has emerged as one of the leaders of the Polish avant-garde. His works include *Erotics* (six songs for soprano and orchestra), *Variations Without a Theme* for orchestra, a piano concerto and music for film and theatre.

Baker, Dame Janet (1933-) English mezzo-soprano who studied under Hélène Isepp in London and began her career with the Leeds Philharmonic Choir. In 1956 she came second in the Kathleen Ferrier Competition and made her operatic debut as Roza in **Smetana**'s *The Secret* with Oxford University Opera Club. Other operatic appearances have included **Purcell**'s *Dido and Aeneas*, *Tamerlaino* (1962), *Ariodante* (1964) and *Orlando* (1966). More recently, she has sung the role of Kate in **Britten**'s *Owen Wingrave* (1971 televized, 1973 Covent Garden) and Charlotte in **Massenet**'s *Werther* (1977). Baker was awarded the CBE in1970 and the DBE in 1976. She is considered to be one of the most intelligent opera singers alive and is also well-known for her concert and recital work.

Balakirev, Mily Alexeyevich (1836/7-1910) Russian composer and guiding spirit of the group of 'nationalist' composers known as the Five or, as the Russian critic Vladimir Stasov called them, the **'Mighty Handful'** (*moquchaya kuchka*). Born in Nizhny-Novgorod, Balakirev began learning the piano as a child and subsequently came to the notice of Aleksandr Uliybiychev, a wealthy musical amateur who retained his own orchestra and took the boy into his home, allowed him to rehearse the orchestra occasionally and gave him the run of his vast music library, which was later bequeathed to him. With Uliybiychev, Balakirev visited St Petersburg in 1855, where he met and was encouraged by **Glinka**, who was much impressed by his already burgeoning nationalist aspirations.

Balakirev founded the Five in about 1861, drawing into his orbit the four young composers **Borodin, Cui, Mussorgsky** and **Rimsky-Korsakov**, propelling them on their nationalistic course by the force of his often irascible personality. In 1862 he founded a free music school, promoting the Five's music there, plus works by **Lyadov** and **Glazunov**. He assiduously collected folk songs and edited and produced the operas of Glinka. Overworked and slightly unstable, he suffered a nervous breakdown in 1871 and took a job as a railway official, not returning to music until 1876. From 1883 to 1895 he was director of the Russian Imperial Choir, and devoted his last years to composition, completing or revising earlier pieces and producing a number of new ones, including his two symphonies.

Balakirev wrote several overtures, based respectively on Spanish, Russian and Czech themes. He is perhaps best known for his piano music, which includes the brilliant virtuoso piece *Islamey*, and oriental fantasy, and for his songs. Balakirev's own music, however, is overshadowed by his strenuous championship of his country's indigenous talent, as represented by the Five and their friends.

balalaika Plucked stringed instrument prominent in the folk music of Eastern Europe. The instrument normally has three strings and a body in the shape of a triangle.

Balassa, Sandor (1935-) Hungarian composer who studied at Budapest Conservatoire with Szervansky. His style is freely **dodecaphonic**: one chord used as the germ cell for an entire work. **Serial** principles are used very loosely apart from the *Intermezzo* for flute and piano, his only thoroughly serial composition. Other works include an orchestral piece, *Iris*, *Requiem for Lajos Kassak* and a trio for violin, viola and harp.

Balfe, Michael William (1808-1870) Irish composer, singer and violinist. He began learning the violin and composing at an early age and, on the death of his father in 1823, was sent to London to study music. He studied composition and made his professional debut as a singer in a performance of **Weber**'s opera *Der Freischütz* in Norwich. He went to Paris, where, after meeting **Rossini**, he sang Figaro in *The Barber of Seville* (1827). After singing throughout Italy (including performances at La Scala, Milan), he played the role of Papageno in the first English production of **Mozart**'s opera *The Magic Flute* (1838).

In addition to his highly successful career as a singer, he established his reputation as the foremost operatic composer in Britain. His compositions were all received well in London, but it was the production of his opera, *The Bohemian Girl* in 1843 that brought critical recognition. This work, which was to be performed throughout Europe, demonstrates his synthesis of the continental operatic style and the contemporary British Victorian fashion for **ballad**.

Balfe's works include 29 operas, a ballet, choral works, songs, chamber music and three books of studies for singers.

ballabile (It.) Suitable for dancing. Occasionally used by **Verdi**, among others, for sections of operas. The term also appears as the title of a piano piece by **Chabrier**.

ballad Word originating in dance terminology, but which lost its dance connotation as early as the 13th century, coming to mean a stylized form of solo song. It is the most characteristic of English folk song types, consisting of a number of stanzas in which a story is told, the singer being a dispassionate narrator who takes no active part in the tale. Many have a **refrain**, although its presence does not define the ballad form. In non-literate societies the ballad serves to formalize and preserve historical tradition and mythological material, e.g. the *Oceanic Ballads*.

Much of the repertory of ballad singers in England was collected by Francis Child in the latter part of the 18th century and this collection has become the central body of songs used by today's singers.

ballad opera Accessible form of stage entertainment, which rose to popularity in England after the success of John Gay's *The Beggar's Opera* in 1728. Ballad opera consisted of spoken dialogue, songs parodied from familiar operatic airs and music which used material from folk songs and popular tunes.

ballata (It.) Dance-song. Usually refers to an important poetic and musical form of the Italian *trecento*. The standard poetic form consists of a refrain (*ripresa*), two *piedi*, a *volta* and a repeat of the refrain. In music there are two sections: for the refrain and first verse. The remainder of the text, usually aphoristic and concerned with courtly love, is fitted to these. The most celebrated composer of *ballate* is Francesco **Landini**.

ballet Ballet began to develop as an entertainment in the Renaissance courts of Italy. The first important ballet de cour was *Le ballet des Polonais* (1573) to music by **Lassus** and consisting of a number of scenes in mime and dance, explained with spoken or sung verse.

The next stage in ballet's development was at the French court under **Lully**, where the first ballet with no speech or song, *Le Triomphe de l'Amour* (1681), was performed by professional dancers rather than the nobility.

The *Académie Royale de Danse* was established in 1661 by Louis XIV. Over the next hundred years, ballet became popular throughout Europe and in Russia, and by the early 19th century the methods of teaching Classical ballet which are still being used today had become established.

The light, graceful style of dancing associated with Romantic ballet stems for the most part from the ballerina Maria Taglioni (1804-1884), ending the earlier domination by the male. In the mid-19th century, Romantic ballet declined in Europe (being used mainly in opera), and continued its development in Russia, with ballets such as **Tchaikovsky**'s *Swan Lake* (1877) and *The Nutcracker* (1892).

During the 20th century, the traditional

Classical ballet has continued, but there has also been the development of a freer style of dance, not bound by the academic conventions of technique. This new style was influenced mainly by Americans such as Isadora Duncan (1878-1927), who developed a more expressive style of dance, Ruth St Denis (1877-1969), who began to dance to Oriental music, and Martha Graham (1894-), who has created more than 150 works and collaborated with many leading composers.

ballo (It.) Dance, a term used down the centuries and not just confined to Italy, to denote a social dance or ball at any level of society. It has also been used, particularly in the 16th century, to denote a dance tune. In the 15th century the word acquired a more specific, technical meaning, denoting a courtly dance choreographed by a dancing master; Domenico da Piacenzo, Antonio Cornazano and Guilielmo Ebreo da Pesaro each left descriptions of steps with music.

In the late 16th century the *ballo* often formed part of an *intermedio* or play. Fabrito **Caroso** and Cesareo Negri published steps and music for *balli* from this time, and **Monteverdi**'s *Ballo delle ingrate* includes dance.

balungan (Java) Skeleton-melody (*balung* means bone), the principal melody upon which the instruments of the **gamelan** orchestra elaborate, somewhat similar in concept to the Western **cantus firmus**. The *balungan* is the only notated melodic element in Javanese music. It is played in its exact form by the **saron** or **slentem** metallophone instruments, while other melodic instruments of the ensemble provide elaborated versions.

bamboo pipe Indigenous wind instruments of South East Asia are commonly made of bamboo, so the term covers a multitude of instruments.

The most famous wind ensemble of South East Asia consists of a group of **khaen**. Each *khaen* consists of a group of six to sixteen long bamboo pipes joined at the centre or bottom by a single wind chamber. Each pipe contains a single free reed that vibrates when a hole on the side of the pipe is closed, hence it is related to the *sgeng* of ancient China and the *sho* of Japanese court orchestras.

The most famous legend concerning the origin of Chinese music recounts the tale of Ling Lun who was sent to the western mountains to fetch bamboo pipes from which the fundamental pitches of Chinese music could be derived. The length of the imperial pitch pipes was traditionally calculated by court musicians and astrologers so that the tones resonated with the extra-musical forces of the universe. The first pipe produces the yellow bell tone, and from there the system was cyclic, working on overblown fifths. Panpipes are also generally made of bamboo.

Banchieri, Adriano (1568-1634) Italian composer and theorist. He was one of the pioneers of basso **continuo**; his *Concerti Ecclesiastici* (1598) is one of the first publications to include a separate bass part for a continuo player, and his *L'organo Suonarino* (Op.13, 1605) contains valuable instructions on realizing a bass part and provides bass lines for liturgical chants. He published 12 extant masses and much sacred music, twelve volumes of secular music and three of instrumental. He was founder of the Academia dei Floridi.

band Group of musicians who play together regularly. The ensemble may be of various combinations of instruments, but most commonly the word is associated with groups of brass or wind players and with military instruments, although its use has more recently come to be associated with traditional jazz line-ups (clarinet, trumpet, trombone, banjo, double-bass, drums) and pop groups using a standard format of drums, bass, one or two guitars and vocalist.

bandora Large stringed instrument invented in England by John Rose in 1562

Bandora

and used by such composers as **Ferrabosco** and Morley. The bandora was one of the six instruments necessary to form a **consort of viols** and was very important in music circles in England during the 16th and early 17th centuries. It was used as a **continuo** instrument (playing the **bass** line) and had 14 strings tuned in pairs. It is characterized by its scalloped and fluted decorative outline. An alternative spelling is pandora.

bandurría (Sp.) Twelve-stringed fretted instrument of Spanish origin used predominantly in folk music. The strings are tuned in pairs so that each set of two strings plays identical notes. It is a hybrid of the **guitar** and **cittern** families and has a small body, short neck and very large peg-holder.

Banfield, Raffaello de (1922-) Italian composer whose works include an opera, *Lord Byron's Love Letter* with libretto by Tenessee Williams, and a ballet, *The Duel.*

Banister, John (*c*1625-1679) English violinist and composer who is chiefly remembered for his promotion of the first series of concerts in London open to the public on payment of an admission fee (1662-1669). He wrote incidental music for the theatre, played in the King's Musick and later led the Royal Band of 24 violins. His son, John Banister, was also a violinist whose works include *The Compleat Tutor to the Violin* (1698).

banjo Afro-American stringed instrument of European derivation. It consists of a long neck and a body in the form of an open drum, spanned with parchment as a resonator. It usually has five strings, the highest of these is called the thumb string and is shorter than the other four, starting at the fifth fret. It is most commonly used to accompany **blues** singing and in bluegrass and country music.

Banjo

Banks, Donald Oscar (1923-1980) Australian composer who worked in London during the 1950s and 1960s, writing music for film and theatre and promoting concerts of contemporary music. He studied with Mátyás **Seiber** and **Dallapiccola** and was influenced by Milton Babbit. His works include orchestral pieces, concertos for horn (1965) and violin (1968) and various chamber pieces for diverse ensembles.

Banshchikov, Gennady (1943-) Soviet composer whose works, influenced by Richard **Strauss** as well as **Schoenberg**, include cello concertos, a piano concerto and sonata, one symphony and two operas.

Bantock, Sir Granville Ransome (1868-1946) English composer who, after training as a chemical engineer, studied at the Royal Academy of Music in 1889. He began by composing large-scale works, including a complete setting of Fitzgerald's translation of *The Rubaiyat of Omar Khayyam* as a trio of oratorios, and by conducting.

After World War I, he turned to composing works requiring smaller resources. His appointments included musical director of the New Brighton Tower Pleasure Gardens, principal of the Birmingham School of Music and professor of music at Birmingham University (succeeding **Elgar** in 1907).

Barber, Samuel (1910-1981) American composer and musician. Best-known for his *Adagio for Strings*, extracted from his String Quartet of 1936, and for his setting of Mathew Arnold's *Dover Beach* for baritone and string quartet, he is firmly placed within a tradition that is both Romantic and European. A graduate of the Curtis Institute, Philadelphia, he won a Pullitzer scholarship in 1935 and the American Academy's Prix de Rome in 1936. His music early came to the attention of **Toscanini**, and premieres of his orchestral works were given by such conductors as **Koussevitzky**, **Walter** and **Ormandy**. His opera, *Vanessa* was given at the New York Metropolitan in 1958, and another opera, *Anthony and Cleopatra*, opened the new Metropolitan at the Lincoln Center in 1966. Barber's musical conservatism gave rise to a preference for naturally graceful melody, which kept his music popular.

barber shop Form of part singing which was revived in the United States in the early part of the century.

It is a dense and **chromatic** style of melody and close harmony, in part derived from the Elizabethan madrigal, round and glee. Barber shop songs tend to be of a sentimental and simple nature.

Barbieri, Francisco (1823-1894) Spanish composer. After studying at the Madrid Conservatoire he devoted himself to the composition of theatrical music, and although a lover of Italian opera was more successful as a composer of **zarzuela**. He wrote more than 60 pieces in this genre, many of which are still popular in Spain today. Barbieri also had a passionate interest in the history of Spanish music, acquiring a rich musical library during his lifetime and founding the periodical *La España musical*. He was the first musician to be received into the Royal Spanish Academy.

Barbirolli, Sir John (1899-1970) British conductor, born Giovanni Battista Barbirolli to Italian and French parents, he studied cello at the Trinity College of Music and the Royal Academy of Music in London. He made his debut as a concerto soloist at the age of 12 and joined the Queen's Hall orchestra five years later. After brief army service in World War I he took up a career as a freelance cellist and string quartet player. In 1924 he founded his own string orchestra and became its conductor. From 1926 to 1943 he held conducting posts with the British National Opera Company and the Covent Garden English Opera Company, the Scottish Orchestra (in Glagow), and the New York

Sir John Barbirolli

Philharmonic Orchestra. In 1943 he was appointed conductor of the Hallé Orchestra in Manchester, retaining the post until his death. From 1961 to 1967 he was also principal conductor of the Houston Symphony Orchestra and performed with many internationally famous orchestras throughout the world. Barbirolli was particularly noted as an interpreter of **Elgar** and **Vaughan Williams**, **Mahler**, **Sibelius** and **Puccini**. In 1939 he married the oboist Evelyn **Rothwell**, his second wife.

barcarola (It.) Song in 6/8 or 12/8 time, sung by Venetian gondoliers with an accompaniment suggesting the rocking of a boat. *Barcarole* are found in opera, for example **Weber**'s *Oberon*, and also as instrumental pieces, such as in **Mendelssohn**'s *Songs Without Words*. The French name is **barcarolle**.

barcarolle (Fr.) Equivalent of the Italian **barcarola**.

Bardi, Giovanni de, Count of Vernio (1534-1612) Italian amateur composer and patron of the arts. He hosted the Florentine *camerata*, a group of musicians, poets, playwrights, astronomers and noblemen, among whom the first experiments in dramatic monody and recitative took place. He helped in the creation of the Florentine *intermedii* of 1583, 1584 and 1586 and conceived the theme for the most lavish of them all, that of 1589, for which he composed the madrigal *Miseri habitator del Ciec'averno*.

Barenboim, Daniel (1942-) Israeli conductor and pianist who made his debut in Buenos Aires in 1949. He studied at the St Cecilia Academy in Rome and with Edwin Fischer and Nadia **Boulanger**. He made his concert debut as a pianist in Paris in 1955 and has since performed extensively, including several recital series of the complete **Beethoven** piano sonatas. In 1967 he married the English cellist Jacqueline **du Pré** and settled in England. He has worked as a conductor for many major orchestras, his debut in this capacity being with the English Chamber Orchestra in 1966. He has also worked with the Berlin Philharmonic Orchesrta (1969) the New York Philharmonic Orchestra (1970) and L'Orchestre du Paris (from 1975). His opera debut was at the Edinburgh Festival (*Don Giovanni*, 1973), and he continues to be a successful and popular conductor and pianist.

baritone Male voice with a range lying between those of the **bass** and **tenor**. The usual **compass** is from A to F′. The term was used as early as the 15th century, but the baritone voice was not highly regarded until the late 18th century, when **Mozart** made prominent use of it in his operas *Don Giovanni* and *The Marriage of Figaro*.

Barnby, Sir Joseph (1838-1896) English church musician and an important figure in Victorian church music. He held many posts as organist and choirmaster in London and York. Apart from his enthusiastic conducting of oratorios, Barnby gave the English premiere of **Wagner**'s *Parsifal*. His own music reflects the influence of **Gounod**, and several of his hymns and chants are still frequently performed.

barn dance Social gathering which centres on traditional country dances mostly of English or American origin. Most of the dances involve 'a set' of couples either arranged longways or in a square. Accompanied by a band of musicians, invariably including an accordionist and fiddler, the dancers go through steps as instructed by a caller who shouts or sings directions and figures.

Barnett, John (1802-1890) English singer and composer, mainly of theatre music. He received much critical acclaim in his day and learned much from his work at the English Opera House where he directed operas by foreign composers. **Weber** in particular influenced his style, and he mastered the art of supernatural and 'fairy' choral scenes in the style of Weber's *Oberon*. Some of his songs were popular in Victorian times.

Baroque Term borrowed from art and architecture, and applied to music displaying certain characteristics between the approximate dates of 1580 and 1750. In music, as in the other arts, the term refers to a 'style-period' whose features are an increased dramatic and emotional content, and a love of spectacular effects. The term literally means 'bizarre' but there are formal as well as emotional effects in Baroque music.

Early Baroque music began with the experiments of the Florentine **Camerata** in setting poetry in a 'representative' way – making the voice contain, rather than describe, emotion with ejaculatory words such as *Ahi!* or *Ohimè*. **Monteverdi** developed this style into opera, and also used the polychoral effects developed by **Gabrieli** at St Mark's in Venice.

In France, **Lully** developed all manner of ballets and operas, and the French Baroque developed its own more classical style, based on set dance forms and overtures, and an elaborate but prescribed ornamentation, giving no scope for the emotional 'free' embellishments of the Italians.

England and Germany followed these models, adding some of their inherent traditions. The high Baroque, following in the wake of **Corelli**'s development of the **concerto**, fused the various national styles, with J.S. **Bach** and **Handel** leading this tradition by absorbing all the possible forms of what had become a musical 'common market'.

Barraine, Elsa (1910-) French composer who studied with **Dukas**; among her works are two ballets, *La Chanson du mal-aimé* and *Claudine à l'école*, two symphonies and music for film and theatre.

Barraqué, Jean (1928-1973) French composer who studied at the Paris Conservatoire with **Messiaen** and **Langlais**. His compositions include a piano sonata and *Sequence*, both of which are large scale works using advanced **serialism**; *Song after Song* for six percussionists, voice and piano; a concerto for clarinet and vibraphone and six instrumental ensembles. In 1956 he started work on soundscapes on the novel *The Death of Virgil* by Hermann Broch but completed only three parts before his death. He also published articles and a book on **Debussy** (Paris 1962).

Barraud, Henry (1900-) French composer and critic. He studied with **Dukas** and Caussade at the Paris Conservatoire but was expelled from the institution after writing a string quartet (now lost), considered to be outrageously innovative. His works include three symphonies, a piano concerto, and vocal music including *La Testament de François Villon* and *La Divine Comédie*.

barre (Fr.) Term with two meanings.

First, on bowed stringed instruments, it is a wooden strip glued to the inside of the belly which helps it to take the pressure exerted by the strings.

Second, on plucked stringed instruments, it is the projecting wooden bar which stops the strings at the tuning end.

barré (Fr.) In lute and guitar playing, the stopping of all the strings at the same position with the forefinger. See **capo tasto**.

barrel organ Mechanical instrument based upon the principle of the barrel and pin mechanism. The barrel organ achieved popularity in England in the 18th century and was used by street musicians and in churches. It is a small organ connected with an arrangement of interchangeable barrels, each containing a number of popular tunes.

Barrios, Angel (1882-1964) Spanish guitarist who studied with Del Campo in Madrid and Gedela in Paris. In 1900 he founded the *Trio Iberia* (lute, bandurria and guitar), with whom he toured Europe and for whom he wrote a number of arrangements.

Bartholmée, Pierre (1937-) Belgian composer and conductor who embarked on his musical career as a piano virtuoso. He began his conducting activities when he founded the *Groupe Musiques Nouvelles* in Brussels in 1962, a group committed to promoting contemporary music in Belgium and elsewhere. His own compositions show a preoccupation with Baroque instrumentation and break new ground in the harmonic possibilities of Western music. Both of these concerns are explicit in his work *Tombeau de Main Morais* in which the octave is divided into 21 divisions, rather than the usual twelve.

Bartók, Béla (1881-1945) Hungarian composer, pianist and collector of folk music, arguably the greatest composer and musician of his nation. Born in Nagyszentmiklós, western Hungary (now Sinnicolau Mare, Romania), he received his first piano lessons from his mother, then went on to study at Poszony (now Bratislava) and at the Royal Academy of Music, Budapest. Here he cultivated a growing nationalism along with a fondness for the music of Richard **Strauss**, **Wagner**, **Liszt** and even **Brahms**. His first major work, the tone poem *Kossuth* (1903), was a nationalistic piece inspired by the Hungarian hero of the 1848 Revolution, Lajos Kossuth, but written in a Straussian vein. Leaving the Royal Academy, Bartók toured abroad as a concert pianist of great virtuosity. But in 1905 he began a lifelong interest in Hungarian folk music and started a systematic song collection, often collaborating with his friend Zoltán **Kodály**. Over the years, Bartók made many folk song collecting tours in eastern Europe and in Turkey and Arabia.

In 1907, Bartók and Kodály joined the staff of the Royal Academy of Music in Budapest, Bartók as a piano teacher. Despite much opposition and hostility, the two set about revitalizing the musical life of Hungary. Bartók's own music was showing

Béla Bartók

new influences, namely **Debussy** and **Stravinsky**. In 1909 the first of his six string quartets was written, and two years later he completed his opera *Duke Bluebeard's Castle*, a highly symbolic work in which he successfully married his music to the special phonetic needs of the Hungarian language. In 1917 a successful performance of his ballet *The Wooden Prince* (1914-1917) led to the staging of *Duke Bluebeard's Castle* in 1918. It was followed by performances of his pantomime-ballet *The Miraculous Mandarin* (1918, subsequently censored) and his *Dance Suite* (1923). In the 1920s, Bartók resumed his interrupted career as a concert pianist. He reached maturity as a composer with the first two of his three piano concertos and his piano sonata of 1926, his six volumes of graded piano pieces, *Mikrokosmos* (1926; 1932-1939), his sonata for two pianos and percussion (1937; orchestrated 1940), his impressionistic *Music for Strings, Percussion and Celesta* (1936), and his second violin concerto (1937-1938). In 1934 he received an appointment from the Hungarian Academy of Sciences to make his folk music collection ready for publication. His researches into melody variants proved invaluable and even influenced his own music.

In 1940, Bartók emigrated to the United States, where his talents as a composer and pianist went largely unrecognized. He completed only the ever-popular *Concerto for Orchestra* (1942-1943; revised 1945) for the Koussevitzky Foundation and the Bachian sonata for unaccompanied violin, commissioned by Yehudi **Menuhin** (1944). His former pupil, Tibor Sérly (1900-1978) completed the finale of Bartók's third piano concerto and realized his viola concerto (commissioned by the British musician William Primrose) from Bartók's sketches. Bartók died of leukaemia in New York in 1945 and was buried there. In 1988 his body was disinterred and taken back to Hungary for reburial in Budapest.

Bartolozzi, Bruno (1911-1980) Italian composer who studied violin and composition at Florence and was a professional violinist from 1941 to 1965. He pioneered new techniques for woodwind instruments (described in his book *New Sounds for Woodwind*, 1967), and used these in works such as *Concertazioni* (1973). He has written orchestral, chamber, solo and accompanied vocal works, and a work for the stage, *Tutto cio che accade ti riguarda*.

baryton Brass instrument with six bowed strings popular (in varying degrees) in the 17th and 18th centuries. A number of extra strings (up to 20 or more) were placed beneath the fingerboard; some of these were exposed to allow their plucking from beneath by the player's left hand, while the others produced a drone-like effect. Its chief exponent was Joseph **Haydn**, who wrote some 175 works for his patron Prince Nicholas Esterházy, an enthusiastic amateur baryton player.

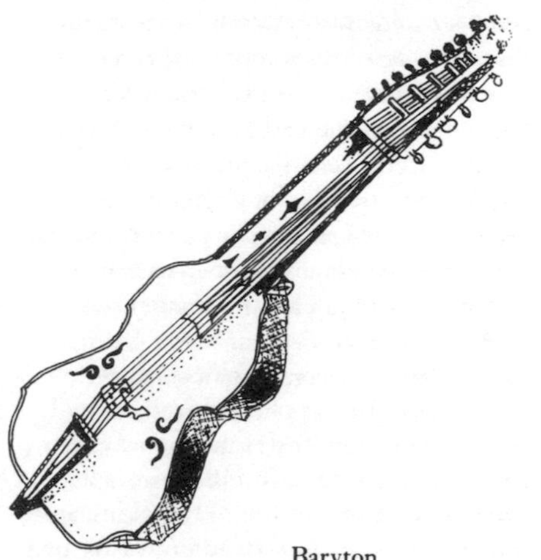

Baryton

basic set Original version of the note-row in a **serial** composition, before it is subjected to inversion, retrograde or retrograde inversion.

bass Term with two meanings.

First, it is the lowest category of the male human voice or instrument within a family.

Second, in harmony, it is the lowest line of music, and the one which forms the basis of the harmonic structure. See also **Alberti bass; double-bass; figured bass**.

basse (Fr.) **Bass**. *Basse de viole* means string bass (see **continuo**); *basse chiffrée* means **figured bass**.

basset-horn Instrument related to the clarinet but with a slightly lower range and wider bore which gives it a richer, less penetrating sound. It first came into vogue around the time of **Mozart**, who remains the only major composer to have made extensive use of it, particularly in his

One form of basset-horn

serenades for wind instruments and the *Requiem*.

bass fiddle Popular name for the string double-bass but sufficiently vague and loosely defined that it could also refer to the cello.

basso continuo See **continuo**

bassoon Large wind instrument with a conical bore, played with a double reed, which originally developed from the 16th-century dulcian. It plays the **tenor** and **bass** lines in the woodwind section of the orchestra. The 8-foot long bore is folded in two, so that the instrument doubles back on itself. At one point there were five different sizes of bassoon in existence, now there are only two: the bassoon and the contrabassoon (which sounds an **octave** lower). Although the bassoon does have a small solo repertory, its main use has been in chamber music and in the orchestra.

Bassoon

Bateson, Thomas (*c*1570-1630) English **madrigal** composer. His two books of madrigals follow in the tradition of **Wilbye** and **Weelkes**.

Bath Festival Annual series of concerts and other events held in the many historical and modern venues in the city of Bath. Founded in 1945, the Festival has had a number of distinguished artistic directors including Yehudi **Menuhin** (whose recordings with the Festival Chamber Orchestra achieved considerable acclaim) and Sir Michael **Tippett**, several of whose works have been premiered in Bath.

baton Short stick, usually made of white plastic, with which a conductor directs an orchestra.

Batten, Adrian (1591-1637) English composer of church music who worked at Westminster Abbey and St Paul's Cathedral as a vicar-choral, and composed services, full and voice anthems. Batten's music reflects the influence of his more famous contemporaries, Orlando **Gibbons** and Thomas **Tomkins**.

battery Term with four meanings, derived from the French *batterie*.

First, it is the **percussion** section of an orchestra.

Second, it is the act of strumming the strings of a guitar rather than plucking them.

Third, it is the 18th-century term for an arpeggiated or **broken chord**.

Fourth, it is a drum roll used as a military signal.

Battishill, Jonathan (1738-1801) English composer, organist and singer. Battishill was renowned for his extemporization and held posts at various London churches including the Chapel Royal. He was also involved in the theatre, and wrote one opera and some incidental music. As a member of the Gentlemen's Catch Club he also wrote glees and catches. His most famous anthem is *Call to Remembrance*.

Bauld, Alison (1944-) Australian composer also experienced in theatrical arts and dance who is rapidly developing new forms and notations for music and dance. Her compositions are mostly theatrical in nature and include *In a Dead Brown Land* for two mime, two speakers, soprano, tenor, chorus and wind instruments, *On the Afternoon of the Pigsty* for female speaker, melodica, flutes and percussion, *One Pearl* and *I loved Miss Watson*.

Bax, Sir Arnold (1883-1953) English composer and novelist. Literary influences, especially the poetry of Yeats, were important in establishing Bax as the leading musical exponent of the so-called Celtic revival. Musical influences included **Liszt**, from whom he learned the art of thematic transformation, as well as the French Impressionist composers and English folk song. Apart from his piano music, his orchestral tone-poems are his best known works, *Tintagel* and *The Garden of Fand* being particularly popular and also representative of his ability to recapture an imagined 'Celtic twilight' in terms of the full palette of the modern symphony orchestra. He also wrote seven symphonies and some fine chamber music for a wide variety of combinations.

bāyān/bhāyān (India) Hemispherical metal drum. It is the larger, left-hand drum of the **tablā** pair.

Bayle, François (1932-) French composer who studied with **Stockhausen** and **Messiaen**. His early works are scored for conventional instruments but later he turned to the medium of tape, producing compositions either exclusively studio orientated or for live musicians with tape. Examples of his work are *Espace Inhabitables*, a juxtaposition of natural and synthesized sounds, *Jeita*, a sequence of short pieces using sound recordings made in a Lebanese cave and *L'expérience accoutique*. The latter is a ten-hour projection intended to be a summary of the composer's ideas about sound and its effect on the listener.

Sir Arnold Bax

Bayreuth Town in northern Germany, known principally for Richard **Wagner**'s Festival Theatre. Wagner chose the site himself for its central situation and peaceful surroundings. His attempts to raise money for the building were disappointing and he had to work on a much lower budget than

Wagner Theatre, Bayreuth

he had anticipated. Nevertheless, the interior of the building was designed to satisfy the composer's theatrical ideals and was based on the Classical Greek amphitheatre. A unique feature is the hood that surrounds the deep orchestra pit, which has the acoustical effect of throwing the sound on to the stage to blend with the vocal sound before being projected past the proscenium.

Regular Wagner festivals have been held at Bayreuth since 1876, when the Ring cycle was first performed in its entirety with the financial aid of Wagner's patron King Ludwig. The annual festivals were staged by Wagner's descendants until 1973, when The Richard Wagner Foundation Bayreuth took over the administrative duties. Tickets are notoriously difficult to obtain and the Bayreuth Festival enjoys an almost cult-like popularity.

Bazzini, Antonio (1818-1897) Italian violinist, composer and teacher. His career as a professional violinist, encouraged by **Paganini**, proved highly successful. He worked in Germany, Denmark, Spain, the Netherlands and France, before finally settling in Breccia in Italy to devote himself to composition and teaching. Despite an attempt at writing an opera, Bazzini was most significant in Italy for the development of non-operatic composition and is chiefly remembered for his chamber music.

While working at the Milan Conservatoire, where he was appointed director in 1882, Bazzini taught the composers **Catalani**, **Mascagni** and **Puccini**, among others.

BBC Abbreviation of British Broadcasting Corporation, originally the British Broadcasting Company.

The BBC began broadcasting in 1922 and grew rapidly, involving itself in English musical life in many ways. In 1924, six symphony concerts were broadcast and in 1927 the BBC took over the Henry Wood Promenade Concerts. In 1930 the BBC Symphony Orchestra was formed, followed four years later by the BBC Northern Orchestra (now renamed the BBC Philharmonic).

During World War II, programmes were combined into a single 'Home Service' but in 1946 this was supplemented by the 'Third Programme', with the forces programmes continuing under the name 'Light Programme'. These have become, respectively, Radios 4, 3 and 2, with a supplementary pop music channel. Televized music began before the war, including attempts at opera productions, but television services were suspended during the war.

Since the war, the concept of the simultaneous broadcast has been at the fore, with productions shared between television and radio. BBC television has since branched out into master-classes and recitals, and it has also commissioned specially-made films about composers (for example by Ken Russell).

The BBC has championed all kinds of music. Contemporary music has had its own programmes, the 'Invitation concerts' proving particularly important during the post-war era. Church music has been fostered through its regular broadcasts of Cathedral services, and concerts from festivals are regularly 'taken' for future broadcasting, or relayed in live transmission. In education, the BBC has put out schools music programmes since the 1930s and this had enormous influence and popularity. In terms of documentaries and magazine programmes, the BBC has also made a useful contribution, and has built up important archives of interviews with musicians and composers.

Beach, Amy Marcy (1867-1944) American pianist and composer who studied the piano with Pedrabo and Baermann. She was largely self-taught in composition and her *Gaelic Symphony* was the first symphony to be composed by an American woman.

Beale, William (1784-1854) English organist and composer who began his musical career as a chorister at Westminster

Abbey and was later the organist at Trinity College, Cambridge. His compositions are mainly madrigals and glees, the best-known of which are *Awake Sweet Muse* and *Come Let us Join the Roundelay*.

beat Term with two meanings.

First, it is the basic pulse in a composition, and thus the temporal unit (see **tempo**). It also refers to the movements of a conductor's hand as he indicates this pulse. In fast tempos (say a fast 2/2 or 3/4) there may be only one beat to a bar; in slow tempos (say a slow 6/8) the beats may be subdivided into smaller units.

Second, it was used in 17th-century English music for a type of **ornament**; either a lower **appoggiatura** or an inverted **trill**.

beating-reed instruments Instruments in which the sound is produced by a fixed reed "beating" (vibrating against) the main body of the instrument. The **clarinet**, **saxophone** and certain types of organ pipe are beating-reed instruments.

beats Acoustical phenomenon produced when two notes almost identical in **pitch** are sounded together. The interference of the sound waves causes the sound to vary slightly in volume at regular intervals. The number of the beats per second is the same as the difference in **frequency** (expressed in hertz) between the two notes. The beats disappear altogether when the notes are in perfect **unison**; they are thus useful for tuning instruments. Slow beats (2-4 per second) are not unpleasant to the ear and are deliberately used in certain organ stops (*voix céleste*, *unda maris*) by using two slightly out-of-tune pipes, to give an undulating effect.

bebung (Ger.) **Vibrato** effect unique to the **clavichord**, obtained by alternately increasing and decreasing the pressure of the finger on the key. This technique was used in the 18th century and is notated by a **slur** and dots written above the note to which it is applied.

Bechstein, Karl (1826-1900) Founder of the firm of piano makers whose pianos are considered to be among the best in the world. After 1870 the firm adopted the Steiner model for their pianos, producing instruments which are iron-framed and overstrung. These are more durable and keep the tuning more constantly than previous models, but are said to have a thinner bass and less brilliant tone. Among current models the model 8 upright, model B grand and concert grand maintain the high reputation of the firm.

Beck, Franz (1723-1809) German violinist and composer. In 1777 he moved to Paris and then to Bordeaux, becoming a concert master there in 1780. Among his works are 24 symphonies, a number of string quartets and piano sonatas, various church music and three operas.

Becker, John Joseph (1886-1961) American composer who was one of a group of avant-garde musicians calling themselves the American Five. The other composers involved were **Ives, Ruggles, Cowell** and Riegger. Becker's compositional style is characterized by clear orchestration and his use of atonal counterpoint and polyrhythmic patterns; while other composers were turning to **neo-classicism** and folk sources, Becker searched for new resources and techniques. Among his works are *Abongo* (1933) for large percussion ensemble; *Soundpieces*, chamber pieces for diverse instrumental ensembles, and a number of stage works in which he attempted to fuse mediums of mime, dance, stage design and music (for example, *A Marriage with Space*, 1935).

Beckwith, John (1927-) Canadian composer whose work explores the possibilities of collage treatment of text, music and theatre, drawing on the folk idioms of his environment (southern Ontario). His compositions include poetic documentaries using spoken and sung words and instrumental sound patterns for example, *Twelve Letters to a Small Town* (1961), *Jonah* a large choral work and *Circle with Tangents* (1967) for harpsichord and solo strings.

Bedford, David (Vickerman) (1937-) British composer and teacher. He studied at the Royal Academy of Music and also took private composition lessons in Venice with the revolutionary Italian composer Luigi **Nono**. A former member of the pop group The Whole World, Bedford makes much use in his work of electric guitar, amplified piano, and other electronic instruments. His compositions range from music theatre for schools, such as his Norse trilogy *Indiof's Saga*, *The Death of Baldur* and *The Ragnarok* (1979-1982) to unaccompanied choruses, such as his setting of Dowson's *The Golden Wine is Drunk*. Many are scored for unusual instrumental combinations with and without voices and carry whimsical titles. Examples include *Star Clusters, Nebulae and Places in Devon* (1971), for chorus and orchestra; *Holy Thursday with Squeekers* (1972), for voice and instruments; *Maple Syrup and Bacon and the TV Weatherman* (1973), for brass quintet; and *SPN/M Birthday Piece* (1983), for string quartet.

Bedford, Herbert (1867-1945) English composer. His music explored the resources of unaccompanied song and of the military band as media for serious musical composition. He wrote a great deal of vocal music, both with and without accompaniment, orchestral works and compositions for **brass band**, examples of his work being *Three Roundels*, *Over the Hill* and *Kit Marlowe* (1897), an opera.

Beecham, Sir Thomas (1879-1961) British conductor who first came to prominence when he founded the New Symphony Orchestra (1905). He staged the British premiere of Strauss's *Elektra* at Covent Gaqrden in 1910 and for the next half century, was at the heart of British music. He founded the London Philharmonic Orchestra (1932) and the Royal Philharmonic Orchestra (1947) and was associated with most of Britain's major

Sir Thomas Beecham

orchestras and many American ones. In the 1930s he was art director of the Royal Opera House. He was probably best known for his interpretations of such coomposers as **Mozart**, **Sibelius** and **Strauss**, and wrote a book about **Delius**. He was knighted in 1915.

Beeson, Jack Hamilton (1921-) American composer whose main preoccupation is with opera, his librettos shaped from United States life and literature. After attending the Eastman School of music he studied composition with **Bartók**. Examples of his operatic works are *Jonah* (1950), *Hello out There* (1957), *New York City Opera* (1965) and *Kansas City* (1975). He also wrote for the orchestra, (*Transformations*), for instrumental ensembles and for voices.

Beethoven, Ludwig van (1770-1827) German composer whose significance in music history was immense. Bridging the gap between Classical and Romantic styles in the early 19th century, he transformed every musical genre in which he worked and, despite deafness in his later years, extended the technical and expressive powers of music beyond measure.

His works are commonly divided into three periods, the first of which, including

Ludwig van Beethoven

Symphonies Nos. 1 and 2 and his early piano sonatas, extended to the turn of the century in a continuation of the style of **Haydn** and **Mozart**. The middle period was marked by an astonishing development in symphonic form, the *Eroica* (No. 3) revolutionary in its scope and dimension, the *Pastoral* (No. 6) unprecedented in its programmatic intent. The first two decades of the 19th century also saw the composition of the majority of Beethoven's concertos and his only opera, *Fidelio*. The last decade of the composer's life gave rise to his greatest achievements: the *Choral Symphony*, his ninth and last, set the precedent for the combination of vocal and instrumental forces in symphonic compositions, and the monumental *Missa Solemnis* gave a new character to religious music, while his later string quartets challenged and greatly extended current harmonic notions. Contemporary response to Beethoven's music was cautious, although his genius was immediately recognized, and his music today is performed more frequently than that of any other composer.

bel canto (It.) Beautiful song. Formal training and vocal requirements of opera in Italy during the 17th and 18th centuries, when an increased size of orchestra and opera house led to the necessity of a more penetrating and powerful tone. This was obtained by more weighty vocal production, which contrasted with the earlier requirement to sing high florid passages in a light and effortless manner.

Bellini, Vincenzo (1801-1835) Italian composer. As the result of a municipal scholarship, he studied at the Naples Conservatoire (1819-1822) where among his teachers was Niccolo **Zingarelli**. Bellini achieved recognition as a significant operatic composer with his third opera, *Il Pirata*, (1827). His next opera *La Straniera* (1829) was even more successful but before the triumph of *I Capuletti ed i Montecchi* (1830), his *Zaira* proved a failure. Bellini's popularity has been unpredictable and irregular; he is remembered chiefly for his highly popular operas, such as *La Sonnambula* and *Norma* (both 1831), but he also composed various instrumental and sacred vocal works.

bémol (Fr.) The flat sign (♭). In the 17th century it was also used to denote the minor key, for example, *mi bémol*, E minor.

Benda, Jiri (Georg) Antonín (1722-1795) Most celebrated composer of a large family of Bohemian musicians. In 1725 he was appointed *Kapellmeister* to Duke Friedrich III of Saxe-Gotha and this period of his life was spent composing cantatas and instrumental music, operas being banned by church edict. This was eventually relinquished and in 1765 Benda's first opera was produced. The same year he visited Italy, becoming acquainted with Italian opera. After this, Benda composed more and more for the stage, while continuing to write sacred and instrumental music.

Benedetti Michelangelli, Arturo See **Michelangelli, Arturo Benedetti**.

Benedict, Sir Julius (1804-1885) English composer and conductor of German birth. Having studied with **Weber** in Dresden, Benedict's musical career started in the theatre conducting opera in many London venues. He also conducted and composed oratorios and was involved in many provincial music festivals. His biography of Weber is an important first-hand source drawn upon by most later writers.

Benevoli, Orazio (1605-1672) Italian composer who received his early musical training in Rome, where he was a chorister between 1617 and 1623. He was engaged as *maestro di cappella* of the Vatican church of Santa Maria in Trastevere, Rome, when he was only 18 and he remained there until 1630. He held similar posts throughout his career and was also a teacher. His compositions, which consist entirely of sacred vocal works, are noted for the use of clearly defined major/minor tonality and his approach to form, in the tradition of **Palestrina**. His works are often polychoral and performed with each self-sufficient choir placed a fair distance from the next; he favoured homophony over complex polyphony and his works contain few solo lines.

Benguerel, Xavier (1931-) Spanish composer who studied in Barcelona with Chrisobal Taltabull. His early works are influenced by **Debussy, Bartók** and **Schoenberg**; later his compositional style was characterized by his use of contrapuntal lines and **serialism**. Among his works are *Music for Three Percussion* and *Musica Riservata*.

Benjamin, Arthur (1893-1960) Australian-English composer and pianist who studied composition with **Stanford** at the Royal Academy of Music. His main influences were **Brahms, Gershwin** and the popular dance idiom of Latin American music. His works are mostly light and accessible, examples of which are *Jamaican Rumba* for two pianos, *The Devil Take Her* (1951), and film music for *An Ideal Husband.*

Bennet, John (*c*1575-*c*1614) English madrigal composer who also wrote songs accompanied by viols, for example, *Eliza, Her Name Gives Honour.* Another of his works, *O God of Gods; To the Almighty Trinity*, a verse anthem for soloists with **viol** accompaniment, weaves contrapuntal lines between the voices and instruments. Most of his madrigals are contained in the volume he published in 1599.

Bennett, Richard Rodney (1936-) British composer and pianist, resident in New York, since 1977. He received his first music lessons from his mother, a former pupil of Gustav **Holst**. Bennett attended the Royal Academy of Music (1953-1956), where his teachers included Lennox **Berkeley**, and then studied with Pierre **Boulez** from 1956 to 1959. He was professor of composition at the Royal Academy of Music from 1963 to 1965. A prolific composer, he shows easy mastery of a variety of styles, embracing jazz, twelve-note music and traditional harmony and forms. His works, in a wide range of genres, include the ballets *Jazz Calendar* (1963-1964) and *Isadora* (1981); the operas *The Mines of Sulphur* (1963-1965) and Victory (1968-1969); a number of orchestral works and concertos; and scores for more than 35 films, including *Far from the Madding Crowd, Murder on the Orient Express* and *Equus.*

Bennett, Robert Russell (1894-1981) American orchestrator, conductor and composer who studied in Kansas, in Paris with Nadia **Boulanger**, and in Berlin and London. He worked in New York, first as a dance-band musician and a copyist and, from 1919, orchestrating theatrical songs. He was the leading orchestrator of Broadway musicals from 1922 until the 1960s, and worked in Hollywood film studios from 1930.

Bennett arranged and orchestrated some 300 musicals, including Jerome **Kern**'s *Showboat* (1957), Richard **Rodgers**'s *The Sound of Music* (1959), and works by Rudolf **Friml**, George **Gershwin**, Cole **Porter**, Irving **Berlin** and Frederick **Loewe**.

He wrote many concert pieces, sometimes based on popular material by other American composers such as Stephen Foster and Jerome Kern. His book on orchestration, *Instrumentally Speaking*, was published in 1975.

Bennett, Sir William Sterndale (1816-1875) English composer who, although his works are now largely forgotten, ranked as one of the most distinguished of the English Romantic School. He began his musical career as a chorister at Kings College, Cambridge, and entered the Royal Academy of Music at the age of ten. Between the ages of 17 and 23 he studied in Leipzig where he made close friends of both **Mendelssohn** and **Schumann**, and it was during this period that most of his works were written. Among his orchestral writings are five symphonies, four piano concertos and a number of concert overtures and fantasias. He also wrote for chamber ensembles and for solo piano.

Benoit, Peter Leopold Leonard (1834-1901) Belgian composer, conductor and teacher who was the initiator of the Flemish music movement which brought the country's music to the attention of the rest of Europe. He was a teacher of great reputation and in 1867 founded the Flemmish School of Music in Antwerp. Benoit's compositional style is firmly rooted in 19th-century Romantic Nationalism, using melodies and rhythmic gestures from traditional Flemish folk styles. Much of his work is vocal, including three operas, three oratorios, a choral symphony *The Mowers*, two masses and a number of songs.

Bentzon, Jørgen (1897-1951) Danish composer and pianist. His first interest was in jazz, and he worked with Leo Mathiesen and then with Jeppesen at the Copenhagen Conservatoire. Among his works are 12 symphonies, a concerto for piano and orchestra, three string quartets, an opera (*Faust*), choral works and solo piano pieces.

Bentzon, Niels Viggo (1919-) Danish composer, teacher, pianist and critic. An early interest in jazz was cultivated by studying with Leo Mathiesen; he later studied piano, organ and theory at the Copenhagen Conservatoire. He is one of Denmark's best-known and most prolific composers since **Nielsen**, his compositional style being dissonant, but tonal in concept with a free, almost improvisatory character. Despite his book on *Twelve Tone Theory* his own work has never fully embraced **serialism**. Many of his works allow room for **improvisation**, some using graphic scores and **aleatory** techniques (*Variable Music*) or the modern jazz milieu (*Third Stream Music*). He has written two operas, many orchestral works including 18 symphonies, chamber music and solo piano pieces.

berceuse (Fr.) Lullaby, or cradle-song, normally in 6/8 time with a rocking accompaniment. *Berceuses* occur as songs and short instrumental pieces, often for piano, such as those by **Schumann** in *Kinderszenen* and **Fauré** in the *Dolly Suite*.

Berezovsky, Nikolai (1900-1953) American composer, violinist and conductor, of Russian birth. After studying music in the Imperial Chapel in St Petersburg and working professionally as a violinist and conductor throughout Russia, he emigrated to the United States (1922).

Berezovsky studied composition at Juilliard, played the violin with the New York Philharmonic Orchestra and the Coolidge quartet, and worked as a conductor. His compositions include an oratorio, four symphonies, a children's opera based on the stories of Babar the Elephant, chamber music, and numerous orchestral compositions for ensembles of various sizes. Berezovsky also played the viola and gave the first performance of his own Viola Concerto in 1941.

Berg, Alban (1885-1935) Austrian composer who, with **Schoenberg** and **Webern**, was a leading figure in the Second Viennese School, which ushered in the use of **atonality** and the **twelve-note system** and profoundly influenced the music of the 20th century.

He was born in Vienna and, untaught in composition, he began writing romantic *Lieder* at the age of 15. After his father's death in 1900, he entered the Austrian civil service. However, Schoenberg took him on as a pupil, and he eventually gave up his civil service job to devote himself to music. Along with his friend and fellow disciple of Schoenberg, Anton Webern, Berg now entered the Viennese avant-garde, which was dominated by the towering figure of Gustav **Mahler**. Berg's early music – some songs and a set of piano variations – received performances in Vienna over the next few years. In 1913 the presentation of two of his five *Altenberglieder* at a concert of contemporary Viennese music led to a riot. After military service in World War I, for which he was medically unfit, Berg began work on his first opera, *Wozzeck*. It received its premiere in Berlin in 1925 to public acclaim and critical condemnation. It was followed by a series of masterpieces that included the *Chamber Concerto* (1925), the *Lyric Suite* for string quartet (1926) and the concert aria *Der Wein*. In 1929 Berg began work on the opera *Lulu*. The full score remained unfinished at his death and was not completed until after 1976. In 1935 he began a violin concerto to a commission from Louis Krasner and this was finished shortly before Berg's death.

Berg's music adheres much less closely to the letter of Schoenberg's twelve-note system and to the principals of atonality

Alban Berg

than that of his colleagues in the Second Viennese School. A meticulous and slow worker (he completed only 22 mature works), he was a master of structure and form but his own passionate personality never allowed form to cloud meaning. His works are much more accessible than those of Schoenberg and Webern, and he did not shrink from returning to traditional harmony if it would serve his emotional purposes. This can best be seen at the end of the violin concerto, in the stunningly beautiful and effective introduction of the Bach chorale *Es ist genug*, set in extraordinary contrast to the composition's twelve-note material.

bergamasca (It.) Originally used to describe peasant dances and songs from the district around Bergamo in northern Italy. By the late-16th century the dance had a fixed harmonic pattern, which was used into the 17th century, particularly for guitar pieces. Bergamo is associated with the *commedia dell'arte*, and the title appeared frequently in the 18th and late-19th centuries in France, whenever there was an interest in the Harlequin figure. **Debussy** wrote a *Suite Bergamasque* for piano, and **Fauré** wrote an orchestral suite entitled *Masques et Bergamasques*. The English and French translations are bergomask and *bergamasque*, respectively.

Berganza, Teresa (1935-) Spanish mezzo-soprano. After training as a pianist at the Madrid Conservatoire she began her vocal studies with a former pupil of Elisabeth **Schumann**, Rodriguez Aragon. She made her stage debut at Aix-en-Provence, France, as Dorabella in **Mozart**'s *Così fan Tutte* and quickly established an international career. Among her early engagements was the role of Neris in **Cherubini**'s opera *Medea*, which she sang alongside Maria **Callas**. Although her reputation is centred on her interpretations of Mozart and **Rossini**, her highly flexible and even-toned voice is equally suited to the performance of **Purcell**, **Monteverdi**, **Cesti** or the songs of her native Spain.

Berger, Arthur (1912-) American composer, teacher, music critic and journalist. He studied under Walter **Piston**, Nadia **Boulanger** and **Milhaud**. After various teaching positions he was appointed professor of music at Brandeis University in 1962. He has written orchestral, vocal and chamber music, and several works for piano, and while his early works are neo-Classical in style, compositions from the late 1950s use serial techniques. His literary works include a book on Aaron **Copland**.

Berger, Jean (1909-) German composer who studied at the Universities of Heidelberg and Vienna. After a long residence in France he moved to the United States and was eventually naturalized. His compositions include the choral work *Vision of Peace* and *The Pied Piper*, a play with music.

Berger, Theodor (1905-) Austrian composer who studied under Franz **Schmidt** at the Vienna Academy. He has written a variety of choral and orchestral works which are Romantic in style, and several scores for films, radio and television.

Bergman, Erik (Valdemar) (1911-) Finnish composer who studied at the Helsinki Conservatoire (now the Sibelius Academy) and Helsinki University from 1931 to 1938, later acquiring a grounding in **twelve-note** techniques from Vladimir Vogel in Switzerland (1949-1950). After World War II, he took up a career as a music critic and choral trainer, while composing music that placed him at the forefront of Finland's musical avant-garde. Appointed professor of composition at the Sibelius Academy in 1963, Bergman continued his musical development beyond serialism into aleatorical methods. His compositions, mainly choral, include a setting of the *Rubayyat of Omar Kayyam* (1953), for male chorus and orchestra, *Aubade* (1958), for orchestra, *Noa* (1976), for baritone, voices and orchestra, and a violin concerto (1983-1984).

Bergonzi, Carlo (1924-) Italian tenor. After studying as a **baritone** with Grandini in Parma he entered the Boito Conservatoire. His early professional career was interrupted by World War II, during which he was imprisoned by the Germans as a result of his anti-Nazi activities. Bergonzi finally made his professional debut in Lecce in 1948 as Figaro in **Rossini**'s opera *The Barber of Seville*. Further studies led to a second debut, this time as a tenor, when he performed in *Andrea Chenier* in Bari (1951). Bergonzi quickly established an international reputation for his interpretation of the tenor roles of **Verdi**'s operas. His musicianship, competent acting skills and fine voice have led to great popularity with opera audiences throughout the world.

Carlo Bergonzi

Bergsma, William (1921-) American composer and teacher, who studied at Stanford University with **Hanson** and **Rogers** and went on to teach composition at the Juilliard School where he instigated curricular reforms, bringing the syllabus up to date. Later he became professor and director of the School of Music at Washington University. His compositional style is essentially tonal, lyrical and conventionally orchestrated although his later works embrace many of the movements of the avant-garde. His works include two ballets, two operas, a number of orchestral pieces, vocal works and four string quartets.

Beringer, Oscar (1844-1922) English pianist, composer and teacher, born in Berlin. Beringer's family moved to London in 1849, where he gave his first public performance in 1859. Later he studied in Leipzig and Berlin. From 1869 to 1871 he taught in Berlin, but then returned to a performing career in England and ran a highly successful Academy for the Higher Development of Pianoforte Playing (1873-1897). He gave the first English performance of **Brahms**'s Piano Concerto No. 2, in 1882. His compositions include songs, pieces for piano and an *Andante and Allegro* for piano and orchestra, but Beringer is probably best remembered for his piano tutors and technical manuals, and for his editions of piano classics.

Berio, Luciano (1925-) Italian composer who studied under **Ghedini** at the Milan

Academy and with **Dallapiccola**. He has taught at several major American music schools, including Harvard University and the Juilliard School of Music. He founded the Milan Electronic Studio in 1955. Berio's music is avant-garde. He has experimented with **serialism**, electronic music and 'collage' techniques (for example, his *Sinfonia* quotes several other composers including Mahler's Symphony No. 2. He is a prolific composer and has written for many instrumental and vocal configurations and for the theatre. His electronic music includes *Mutations* (1954), *Theme* (1958) and *Chants parallèles* (1974). He is often associated in his work with his former wife, the mezzo-soprano Cathy Berberian, for whom he wrote several works, including *Recital I (for Cathy)* (1972).

Beriot, Charles Auguste de (1802-1870) Belgian violinist and composer, whose instrumental technique combined the brilliance and showmanship of **Paganini**'s playing with the elegance and clarity of the Paris style (as exemplified by **Kreutzer**), establishing a more Romantic approach and modernizing the French school of playing. His compositions are technically ingenious and aim rather for effect than depth. He wrote 10 violin concertos, 12 airs and other shorter pieces for solo violin as well as violin duets and chamber music works.

Berkeley, Sir Lennox (1903-) English composer. Berkeley's music has always betrayed a French influence, perhaps because of his partly French ancestry, and because of his studies with Nadia **Boulanger**. The clarity and lightness of **Fauré** and **Ravel**, and the classicism of **Mozart** may be felt in his music, which owes nothing to either **serialism** or the English pastoral composers. His operas and early orchestral music are seldom heard but his chamber music is frequently played. Among his vocal music the *Four Poems of St Teresa of Avila* are perhaps the most celebrated songs, and he also wrote a good deal of piano and sacred music. His style is generally accessible and frequently witty.

Berkeley, Michael (1948-) British composer, son of Sir Lennox **Berkeley**. He attended the Westminster Cathedral Choir School and the Royal Academy of Music, studying also with his father and with Richard Rodney **Bennett**. From 1976 to 1979 he was a full-time BBC Radio 3 continuity announcer and still broadcasts from time to time, chiefly on television. His works cover a wide variety of genres and include the anti-war oratorio *Or Shall We Die?* (1982), a symphony entitled *Uprising* (1980), a chamber symphony (1980), a number of pieces for vocal/instrumental ensembles, chamber music, and organ works.

Berlin, Irving (1888-) Tin Pan Alley composer who wrote popular songs and musicals in the 1920s and 1930s. His first hit was *Alexander's Ragtime Band*, a simplified popular **rag**. His best known song is probably *White Christmas*, made famous by Bing Crosby. His best-known musicals include *Annie Get Your Gun* (1946) and *Call Me Madam* (1950).

Irving Berlin

Berlin Philharmonic Orchestra Celebrated orchestra founded in 1877 and now the major orchestra of West Berlin, as well as being one of the world's finest orchestras. Its lineage of conductors has included **Joachim**, von **Bülow**, **Nikisch**, **Furtwängler** and **Celibidache**. Since World War II, Herbert von **Karajan** has maintained the orchestra's traditional precision and warmth of string tone, matched by players of the highest standards in all other sections. The orchestra has made numerous recordings of most of the Classical and Romantic orchestral repertory. Several smaller ensembles have also been formed from within the orchestra.

Berlioz, Hector (1803-1869) French composer and leading figure of French Romanticism. Berlioz began to compose at the age of 14 and went to Paris at the age of 17 to study medicine. He remained in Paris for the rest of his life, abandoning his medical studies in favour of a career as a composer. He attended the Paris Conservatoire from 1826 to 1830, winning the Prix de Rome on his fifth attempt.

After the public success of the *Symphonie Fantastique* in 1830, Berlioz produced a vast output over the next 10 years, including operas, symphonies and a Requiem. Not all his works were well received, however, and he never obtained a permanent musical post in Paris.

From 1842 to 1862 Berlioz spent much time travelling in Europe, finding audiences outside Paris more receptive to his innovative ideas. He composed less and less until he wrote the opera *Les Troyens* (1856-1858), which he never saw performed in its complete version.

Berlioz's works are nearly all for large-scale ensembles – he wrote no chamber music, preferring to use the orchestra as his instrument. In 1816 he published a treatise on instrumentation called *Grand traité d'instrumentation et d'orchestration moderne*, which contained many new ideas for instrumental sonorities. His use of colour is most noticeable in *Symphonie Fantastique*, although the use of unusual instrumental combinations and timbres is a general characteristic of his music.

Bernac, Pierre (1899-1979) French baritone widely known for his association with Francis **Poulenc** and as a teacher. Many of Poulenc's songs were written for Bernac and his records with Poulenc accompanying are classics. His meticulous diction was the basis of the art he passed on in his celebrated master-classes and his book *The Interpretation of French Song*.

Berners, Lord (Gerald Hugh Tyrwhitt-Wilson) (1883-1950) English composer, writer and painter. He is often considered a mere eccentric, obscuring the fact that in his early years he was judged an important and avant-garde figure, much admired by **Stravinsky**. Berners is perhaps best remembered for his ballet *The Triumph of Neptune* but there is also a corpus of piano music and songs. His novels were also well received and his film scores for *Champagne Charlie* and *Nicholas Nickleby* are considered classics of their kind.

Bernstein, Leonard (1918-) American composer, pianist and conductor, who studied at Harvard University (1935-1939), the Curtis Institute, Philadelphia (1939-1941) and under Koussevitzky at the Tanglewood summer schools (1940-1943).

Bernstein made a highly successful debut in 1943, substituting for Bruno **Walter** at a New York Philharmonic concert. Following

Leonard Bernstein

an international career as a conductor he became music director of the orchestra (1958-1968). As a composer, his greatest success has been the musical *West Side Story*. However, he has also composed many works for the concert platform, including *The Chichester Psalms*, an operetta *Candide* and an opera to his own libretto *Trouble in Tahiti*.

Bertini, Henri Jerome (1798-1876) French pianist and composer. He was considered a disciple of Muzio Clementi whose art Bertini learned from his own brother. Although he was a leading figure in his day, Bertini's compositions for piano and chamber groups are now largely forgotten.

Berwald, Franz (Adolf) (1796-1868) Swedish composer and violinist. His father, brother and uncle were members of the Royal Swedish Orchestra, and Berwald himself sometimes played violin in it during his teens and 20s. His early compositions went unnoticed. In 1828 he won a scholarship to study in Berlin but again met disappointment and supported himself as an orthopedic therapist. In the 1840s he twice visited Vienna and found some encouragement there. In 1846 Jenny Lind sang in his opera *Ein ländisches Verlobungfest in Schweden* (*A Swedish Country Betrothal*, 1847). But generally his music failed to impress. Returnng to Sweden in 1849 he remained as neglected as ever and spent most of the rest of his life running a glass factory, composing in his spare time. Berwald is now acknowledged as Sweden's greatest 19th-century composer. Very much a Romantic in a Berliozian mould, he has left four symphonies, of which only No. 1 (*Sérieuse*) was performed in his lifetime, several operas, including *The Queen of Golconda* (1864), a concerto each for violin and piano, three string quartets, two piano quintets, and a septet in B♭.

Best, William Thomas (1826-1897) English organist. Best was one of the most famous exponents of the 19th-century grand manner of organ playing, which exploited the full orchestral resources of large town-hall organs. He was for a long time organist to the Liverpool Philharmonic Society and it was he who inaugurated the organ at the Royal Albert Hall. Particularly celebrated for his arrangements of orchestral music as well as piano pieces, Best edited and arranged a large amount of music, some of which is still in use today.

Bevin, Elway (1554-1638) English composer, organist and theorist of Welsh extraction. He worked at Wells and Bristol and later at the Chapel Royal. He is mainly known for his Dorian or Short Service, and for an explanatory treatise *A briefe and Short Instruction in the Art of Musicke* (1631).

bhairav (India) One of the ten parent scales (*thāt*) in Hindustani music, corresponding to C, D♭, E, F, G, A♭, B, C′.

bhairavi (India) One of the ten parent scales (*thāt*) in Hindustani music, corresponding to C, D♭, E♭, F, G, A♭, B♭, C′.

bhāyān (India) See **bāyān**.

bian jing Stone chimes, used in the Chou court orchestras of China. The twelve tones (*lu*) of Chinese music are divided into two series of six so that the system is in line with the male-female *yin* and *yang* principles of Chinese metaphysics. The male and female chimes are arranged separately outward from the middle of the instrument rather than in ascending order.

Biber, Heinrich Ignaz Franz von (1644-1704) South German violinist and composer. He was described by many as the greatest violinist of his age, although he rarely travelled outside his native area to play. From the mid-1660s to 1670 he served in the chapel of Prince-Bishop Karl, Count Liechtinstein-Kastelkorn of Olomouc in Kromeríz. His best-known works are those for solo violin, demanding an unprecedented level of virtuosity, and making use of several special effects, notably **scordatura**, especially in his *Mystery* (or *Rosary*) sonatas, and in the *Harmonia artificiosa-ariosa*.

In his other instrumental music and in his sacred vocal music he makes unusually extensive use of wind instruments, such as in his sonata *Sancti polycaroi* and the *Requiem five* for choir, soloists, strings and trombones. His sonata for two violins and trombone demands as much virtuosity from the trombone as from the violins.

bilāval (India) One of the ten parent scales (*thāt*) in Hindustani music, corresponding to the Western major scale C, D, E, F, G, A, B, C.

Billings, William (1746-*c*1800) New England composer whose publication in 1770 of *The New-England Psalm-Singer* was the first American volume to consist entirely of works written by one composer. He wrote choral music, psalms, hymns, patriotic anthems and what he himself called *fuguing tunes*. His patriotic song *Chester* was one of the most popular anthems of the American revolution.

bīn/bīna (India) Northern Indian plucked stringed instrument which comprises two large gourd resonators fixed at each end of a tube zither. It has fixed frets and no sympathetic strings.

Binchois, Gilles (*c*1400-1460) French or Flemish composer, at the forefront of the music of his era. After an episode in the service of William Pole, Earl of Suffolk, Binchois joined the chapel of the court at Burgundy some time in the late 1420s. Burgundy had the most lavish private musical establishment in Europe at the time, and Binchois was a major contributor to the then flourishing 'Burgundian style'. His chief output was secular songs concerned with various aspects of courtly love – 54 *rondeaux* and seven *ballades* survive in this genre. His song *Dueil angoisseus* was used as the basis for a mass by John Bedyngham, and his *Filles à Marier* became adapted as a popular court *Basse danse*. Twenty-eight of his motets survive, as well as six magnificats, and several isolated mass movements. *Deolorations* were composed by Dufay and Ockeghem on his death, and he was hailed by all contemporary music theorists as one of the greatest composers of his age.

Binkerd, Gordon (1916-) American composer and academic. Influenced by Walter **Piston**, his style is essentially tonal, and displays a strong grasp and complex use of harmony and counterpoint. He was for a long time professor of music at the University of Illinois.

Birtwistle, Harrison (1934-) English composer, sometimes referred to as belonging to the Manchester School, having been a pupil of Richard **Hall** alongside Peter Maxwell **Davies** and Alexander **Goehr**. He was important at this time in his interest in the music of the Second Viennese School and also for his allegiance to **Stravinsky**, **Varèse** and English medieval music, of which he has made some arrangements. His music-theatre pieces have also reflected an interest in English folk music, especially the dramatic pastoral *Down by the Greenwood Side*.

There is often a streak of violence in Birtwistle's works (*Punch and Judy* is significant in this context), and his purely instrumental music has arrestingly clear timbres. Several pieces have associations with the Classical world of Ancient Greece, in which the Greek use of chorus and refrain has been influential. His best-known orchestral piece is *The Triumph of Time*. Operas include *Yan Tan Tethera* and *The Mask of Orpheus*.

bis (Lat.) Again. See **encore**.

bisbigliando (It.) Whispering; a virtuoso effect in orchestral harp playing. It consists of rapidly repeated notes or chords played pianissimo in the upper or middle registers of the instrument, resulting in a soft tremolo. It is played on adjacent strings or sets of strings previously set to the same pitch with the pedals.

Bishop, Sir Henry (1786-1855) English composer, most famous for his song *Home, Sweet Home*. He worked at Covent Garden, Drury Lane and Vauxhall Gardens and had enormous success with his many stage works. He also wrote prolifically in other fields and his dance music and songs were favourites in Victorian times. Towards the end of his life his public deserted him, and few of his works are remembered today.

Bishop-Kovacevich, Stephen (1940-) American pianist of Yugoslav extraction, formerly known as Stephen Bishop. He studied with Myra Hess and has recorded and performed widely, mainly the standard repertory. He has shown a particular interest in **Beethoven** and **Schubert**, but has also played some 20th-century music. His performances are always considered and never brashly virtuosic.

bitonality Simultaneous use of two different keys in a musical composition. It has been used almost exclusively in the 20th century, although early examples exist (Hans Neusidler's *Der Juden Tantz*, **Mozart**'s *Ein Musikalischer Spass* K522). One famous example is the use of C against F♯ in the fanfares in **Stravinsky**'s *Petrushka*.

Bitonality was widely used in the first half of the 20th century by the group of French composers known as Les Six, especially by Darius **Milhaud**. It has also been much used in the piano repertory, often in teaching pieces intended for children (**Prokofiev**, *Sarcasmes*, Op. 17 No. 3, **Bartók**, *Mikrokosmos*). See also **polytonality**.

biwa (Japan) Japanese lute, originating from India and China and believed to be a direct descendant of the Chinese **p'ip'a**. Strings of gut or silk are attached to a scroll at the neck and stretched over high frets and secured to a tailpiece. The strings are pressed down either between or onto the frets, and plucked with a large plectrum of wood or bone.

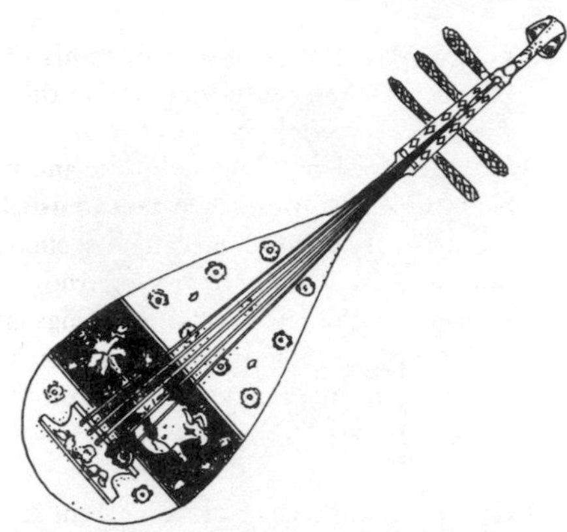

Japanese biwa

The *biwa* may be found in a variety of forms, the most common of which are the *gaku-biwa*, *Heike-biwa* and *Satsuma-biwa*. The *gaku-biwa*, used in the **gagaku** court orchestra, has four frets and four strings which are pressed down only onto the frets, resulting in a limited number of definite pitches. It plays short fixed motifs at regular intervals and its function may therefore be considered **colotomic**. The *Heike-biwa* is the middle-sized of the three main types, with five frets and four strings, and is used as an accompaniment to the narrative tradition associated with the epic concerning the wars of the Heike clan. There were two schools of lute players associated with the blind priest or *moso-biwa* tradition, the *Chikuzen* and *Satsuma*. Of these, the latter flourished and its *biwa* is relatively narrow, but has a larger scroll than other *biwas*, usually having four strings and four frets.

Bizet, Georges (1838-1875) French composer. He was also a prodigious pianist, although Bizet is now best known for his opera *Carmen*. His career as a student was brilliantly successful, and his Symphony in C, written when he was 17 but not performed until 60 years after his death, is often heard. Among his influences, **Weber** and **Gounod** may be listed, but he soon broke free enough to form a highly individual style. His first important opera was *Les*

Georges Bizet

pêcheurs de Perles (The Pearl Fishers). This was followed by *La Jolie Fille de Perth*. Apart from *Carmen*, with its marvellous and influential music in the Mediterranean style, its musical characterization of the *femme fatale* and Don José's hopeless decline, *L'Arlésienne* is perhaps his best-known work, now usually performed as a suite. He also composed many songs, important contributions to the development of the French *mélodie*.

Björling, Jussi (1911-1960) Swedish tenor. He made his name just before World War II, singing Italian tenor roles in Europe and at the Metropolitan Opera in New York where he became a particular favourite. His voice was smooth and ringing at the top, suited to roles by **Gounod** and **Puccini** as well as his particular specialization in **Verdi**. Among his best-known records is his interpretation of the role of Rodolfo in **Beecham**'s recording of *La Bohème*.

Blacher, Boris (1903-1975) German composer and teacher. He worked as a teacher of composition in Berlin and Dresden. Unusual among Germans, he was highly influenced by French composers, Les Six in particular. Many of his works are for the theatre, and they include several adaptions of Shakespeare. Blacher's style is mainly tonal, although late in life he experimented with **serialism**. He often employed short motifs, developing them with great wit and economy of instrumentation. The work that established him on the international scene was his *Variations on a Theme of Paganini*, complementing those by **Brahms**, **Rachmaninov** and **Lutoslawski**.

Blake, David (1936-) English composer. Blake's grounding in music mainly came through his contact with Hans Eisler, from whom he learned the techniques of the Second Viennese School. An interest in Far-Eastern culture has also influenced the subject matter of his work, which includes operas and song cycles as well as chamber music. Among his many commissions for major festivals is the choral piece *Lumina*, based on texts by Ezra Pound, written for the Leeds Festival. He has also written a striking violin concerto and an opera, *Toussaint*.

Blavet, Michel (1700-1768) French composer and one of the leading flautists of his age. He was one of the first composers of flute sonatas, successfully adapting the French violin sonata style. His *Receuils de Pièces* achieved great popularity, containing many arrangements for flutes at all levels of difficulty, including duets for pupil and teacher. He wrote four stage works for the Count of Clermont's chateau at Berny, where he served from 1731 up to his death.

Blech, Harry (1910-) English violinist and conductor. For many years he led the Blech Quartet but later turned to conducting. His most celebrated ensemble is The London Mozart Players which he founded in 1949, and of which Jane **Glover** is now conductor. He also founded the Haydn-Mozart Society but these obvious affinities with the Viennese Classical tradition have not prevented him exploring a more contemporary repertory.

Bliss, Sir Arthur (1891-1975) English composer. He studied with E.J. Dent and Charles **Wood**, and he knew **Elgar**, who made a deep impression on his early style. Later he was much taken with the music of **Stravinsky** and with that of Les Six. He was also a conductor and directed his own *Colour Symphony* at the Three Choirs Festival. Also continuing the Elgar tradition is his *Music for Strings*, a natural successor to Elgar's *Introduction and Allegro*. He wrote film scores, incidental music and works for brass band and military band, in addition to works for various chamber ensembles. Among his ballets, *Checkmate* is the most frequently performed. He was appointed Master of the Queen's Music in 1953, and his fanfares have adorned many royal occasions. His music is tonal and accessible.

Blitheman, John (*c*1525-1591) English composer, 12 of whose works survive: four settings of the plainsong *Eterne rerum conditor* and six of *Gloria tibi trinitas* (i.e. *In Nomine*) for organ, and two vocal works, one of them the extremely effective *In Pace*.

Blitzstein, Marc (1905-1964) American composer who wrote mainly for theatre, films and broadcasting. Consciously 'proletarian' in his approach he orientated his work towards the creation of a 'music of the people'. *The Cradle Will Rock* (1936), a stage work which was a political piece concerning the struggle to establish a steelworker's union in a company-dominated town, is his best-known work. His translation of *The Threepenny Opera* by Kurt **Weill** and Bertold **Brecht** is the version now most often heard.

Bloch, Ernest (1880-1959) Swiss-born composer who studied with Knorr in Frankfurt. He emigrated to the United States in 1916, but returned to Switzerland from 1930 to 1938. Much of his work up to that time has Jewish associations, of which the *Hebraic Rhapsody Schelomo* for cello and orchestra (1915-1916) is best known. Other works from this period include his early opera *Macbeth* (1904-1909), the Jewish sacred service setting *Avodeth Hakodesh* (1930-1933) and *Baal Shem* for violin and piano (1937-1938). Bloch returned to the United States in 1939, where he remained until his death. In this final period he concentrated on larger abstract works such as the second and third quartets (1945 and 1952), and the *Concerto Symphonique* for piano and orchestra (1947-1948).

block Hollow wooden percussion instrument which, when struck with a stick produces a dry, knocking sound. Blocks are used for their unusual timbre and colouristic effect in many post-Romantic orchestral pieces, such as Constant **Lambert**'s cantata *The Rio Grande*. Blocks are also often to be found (chiefly for their novelty value) in dance bands and popular groups. Also known as a Chinese block, Korean temple block or temple block.

Blockx, Jan (1851-1912) Belgian composer. Influenced by **Grieg** and **Sinding** among others, Blockx is best remembered for his operas, which infuse a somewhat eclectic style with Belgian nationalism, partly attained through his studies of Flemish folk songs which he married to a Wagnerian **leitmotiv** technique. Most of his works are settings in the Flemish language.

Blomdahl, Karl-Birger (1916-1968) Swedish composer and teacher, remembered particularly for his dissemination of the theories of **Hindemith** in Sweden. During the war years he held meetings for young composers known as The Monday Group, influential in moving Swedish music away from Romantic Impressionism. He wrote in many genres, and his music was performed in his own country and abroad, but is little heard today. His style, though varied, frequently shows the influence of Hindemith's structural styles.

Blow, John (1649-1708) English composer and organist, teacher of **Purcell**, who succeeded him as organist at Westminster

Abbey, London. He wrote a masque, *Venus and Adonis*, more than 100 anthems, church services and many secular songs.

blues Afro-American song form of a plaintive nature in which usually three-line stanzas are sung over four musical lines in **common time**. In its more developed accompanied form, it employs a standard chordal progression over a twelve-bar period (the twelve-bar blues), and has influenced a wide variety of dance and popular song styles such as **boogie**, **rock 'n' roll** and **rhythm and blues**. Melodically, unstable flattened third and seventh tones are prominent, commonly known as 'blue notes'. The blues possibly originates from field **hollers**.

Blüthner, Julius (1824-1910) Founder of a Leipzig firm of piano makers which has become one of the most important in the 20th century. He patented a 'repetition action' in 1854 and is also celebrated for his Aliquot stringing, a system in which a sympathetic string is added to the normal trichord stringing, giving added resonance. Blüthner pianos are usually of mellow tone, and some fine large upright pianos are among his most successful.

Boccherini, Luigi (1743-1805) Italian cellist and the most mature Italian composer of chamber music of the Classical period. Born in Lucca, he travelled to Paris where, in 1767, his first works were published. His next, and final, move was to Madrid where in 1770 he was appointed to the service of Don Luis, the Spanish Infante. From 1786 he received patronage from Freidrich Wilhelm, Prince (later King) of Prussia. Most of his output is chamber music, including more than 100 string quintets, nearly 100 string quartets and more than 100 other chamber works. He also wrote some 29 symphonies; one opera (*La Clementina*) and orchestral and sacred works. His music is highly individual although its pervading charm, gentleness and even effeminacy led contemporary violinist Giuseppe Puppo to term him "Haydn's Wife".

bodhran (Ireland) Frame drum about 60 cm (23 in) in diameter and 12 cm (4 in) deep, with a goatskin or deerskin head fixed to the ash rim with brass rivets. It is struck with a short, double-ended stick swivelled in the hand. Generally used as accompaniment to social dances.

Boehm, Theobald (1794-1881) German flautist and instrument maker, inventor of the system of keywork used on the modern flute. It was devised in two stages, the 1832 Boehm keywork and the 1847 Boehm System. The system combines a large bore with large soundholes, covered not by the player's fingers, but by pads operated by keys. It made the instrument louder, with a larger range and fully chromatic, but compromised the flexibility and softness of tone of earlier flutes.

Boëllmann, Léon (1862-1897) French organist and composer. A pupil of **Gigout**, Boëllmann worked mainly in Paris and enjoyed a modest success. He is most remembered for his *Suite Gothique*, which ends with a celebrated toccata.

Boethius, Anicius Manlius Severinus, (*c*480-*c*524) Greek mathematician and philosopher. His book on music theory, *De Institutione Musica*, was the only Greek musical work known in the Middle Ages, and as such was the one on which medieval theorists based their system of modes and the Renaissance theorists their philosophy of the classification and function of music. In fact the book is an annotated translation of Nichomachus' lost *De musica* and Ptolomy's *Harmonica*.

Böhm, Karl (1894-1981) Austrian conductor. He studied at Vienna and Graf Conservatoires and made his conducting debut in 1917. He was chief conductor of the Munich Opera from 1921 to 1927, and from 1933 was associated with the Vienna Philharmonic Orchestra. He was Director of the Vienna State Opera in 1943-1945 and

1954-1956 and achieved the honour of Austrian *Generalmusikdirektor*. He is most closely associated with the works of **Mozart**, **Wagner** and Richard **Strauss**, of whose *Die Schweigsame Frau* (1935) and *Daphne* (1938) he conducted the first performances. He has made recordings of the complete Mozart symphonies, and three versions of *Così fan Tutte*.

Boieldieu, (François-) Adrien (1775-1834) French composer who contributed greatly to the development of the **opéra-comique** during the first quarter of the 19th century. His first opera, *La Fille Coupable*, was performed in 1793 and over the next decade he wrote 12 further works for the Parisian stage, including *Le Calife de Bagdad* and *Ma Tante Aurore*. In 1803 he was appointed director of the Imperial Opera at St Petersburg and remained in Russia for eight years. On returning to Paris he enjoyed further successes – most notably with *La dame blanche* – upholding the tradition of French comic opera amid the vogue for **Rossini**'s music. Known as 'the French Mozart', he wrote works that have great melodic appeal; his harmony is not always profound but his instrumentation is colourful and exciting.

Boismortier, Joseph Bodin de (1689-1755) French composer with a prolific output of chamber music geared towards the wealthy amateur. He was one of the first composers to become rich on sales of his music alone (that is, without relying on patronage). He had more than 100 sets of works published. He wrote much for flutes, including a set for five flutes with basso continuo. Sixteen of his sets are marked suitable for *musettes de court* (court bagpipes) and/or *vielles* (hurdy-gurdies). He was the first French writer of solo concerti. He wrote four stage works and a set of very entertaining *Recueil d'airs à boire et sérieux* for voices.

Boito, Arrigo (1842-1918) Italian composer and poet chiefly remembered for his collaboration with **Verdi**. On completing his studies in Milan he travelled to Paris where he met Victor Hugo, **Berlioz**, **Rossini** and Verdi. In 1880-1881 he revised the libretto to Verdi's *Simon Boccanegra* and subsequently provided the composer with the texts for his two last and greatest operas, *Otello* and *Falstaff*. Boito was an accomplished operatic composer in his own right, creating both libretto and music for *Mefistofele* and leaving unfinished *Nerone*, which was performed posthumously in 1924.

bol (India) Syllables of the mnemonic system or **theka** learned by drummers for rhythmic patterns of the **tabla** or **pakhavaj** drums. Each *bol* indicates the exact manner in which the drum head should be struck.

Bolcom, William (1938-) American composer and pianist who has held many posts in academic institutions, as critic as well as composer-in-residence. His music is unusually direct and striking, strongly rooted in music-theatre and showing the influence of jazz and ragtime.

bolero (Sp.) Dance and song in moderate tempo and usually triple time, popular at the end of the 18th century and throughout the 19th. It is still danced in Andalusia, Castile and Mallorca. The dance is normally performed by a couple, and is in three sections, with the music being in A-A-B form.

There is a Cuban version of the bolero which is in duple time, and out of which developed the conga.

The title *Bolero* has been used by several major composers, such as in **Beethoven**'s *Bolero a Solo*, and there are many examples in the opera repertory. **Ravel** wrote a *Bolero* which is widely known today.

Bolshoi Moscow theatre, first built in 1825 and used for all types of concerts as well as opera and ballet. A seminal force in Russian musical life, its productions of new national works have been numerous. Despite this, it has always been international in outlook as far as performers are concerned, and many of the world's best-known singers and conductors have performed there. The Bolshoi Ballet has become particularly celebrated.

bombarde Term with three meanings.

First, in the 14th and 15th centuries it was the French and English word for an alto-pitched **shawm**.

Second, in Germany from the 1820s the word was taken up as *bombardon(e)* to refer to various bass cup-mouthpiece instruments, such as the bass horn or **ophicleide**. In England the *bombardon* at that time was the equivalent of the **tuba**, and in Italy *bombardino* is the **euphonium**.

Third, in France, bombarde today refers to a double-reed instrument which accompanies the **bagpipe** in Brittany.

bonang (Java) Set of bronze knobbed gongs, forming part of the **gamelan** ensemble. They are suspended horizontally in two rows, on ropes fixed across a wooden frame and struck with two long, padded sticks. There are three different sizes of *bonang* in a gamelan, each providing its own octave groupings.

bongo drum Small single headed drum of Afro-Cuban origin which produces a high clear sound. The bongos are generally played in pairs, tuned about a fourth apart, and may be seen in an increasing variety of types of music including Latin American dance bands and Western **jazz** fusion styles. The drums are played with the hands, subtle tone and pitch control are attained using varying pressure from the finger tips and palm of the hand.

Bongo drums

Bonnet, Joseph (1884-1944) French organist who studied with Alexandre **Guilmant** at the Paris Conservatoire and was appointed organist of St Eustace in 1906. He travelled widely as a recitalist. As well as composing many works for the organ, he edited unknown early organ music, including **Frescobaldi**'s *Fiori Musicali*.

Bononcini, Giovanni (1670-1747) Italian composer and cellist, son of Giovanni Maria **Bononcini** and prolific producer of operas in London in the 1720s and 1730s. His first instrumental works – three instrumental collections – were published when he was 15. It was in Rome in 1692 that he achieved his first international success with the opera *Il Trionfo di Camilla*, which was produced throughout Europe and may well have contributed to the spread of the *galant* style.

He composed some 60 operas and other dramatic works, and 270 cantatas. They were popular for their tunefulness and conciseness, although some contemporary Londoners derided his ability to lull listeners to sleep and his music was condemned by "some very fine Gentlemen for its too great simplicity".

Bononcini, Giovanni Maria (1642-1678) Italian composer and music theorist, father of Giovanni **Bononcini**. He studied with Marco Ucellini in the tradition of the Modenese violinist-composers. His first nine *opere* are instrumental, including *sonate da chiesa* and *da camera*, which are perhaps the last dance suites actually intended for social dancing. He composed the first *cantata per camera*. His one treatise, *Musico Prattico* (Venice, 1678), was an important step in the changeover from modal to tonal thinking.

Bonporti, Francesco Antonio (1672-1749) Italian composer. Four of his *inventions* were mistakenly attributed to J.S. **Bach** in the *Bach-Gesellschaft* edition and it is now thought that Bach's inventions were modelled on those of Bonporti.

He published 12 volumes of chamber sonatas and was ordained a priest in 1697.

Bonynge, Richard (1930-) Australian conductor. Through his association with Joan **Sutherland** (his wife), Bonynge is mainly known as a conductor of opera. Most concerned with the revival of performance practices of the 18th century, his recordings of **Mozart** have been important in re-establishing the lost art of **ornamentation**. He has conducted at many major opera houses and has recorded ballet music as well as opera.

boogie-woogie Jazz piano style developed in the early part of this century and based on a 12-bar **blues**. The style is characterized by an **ostinato** figure in the bass in 4/4 time, using quavers or dotted quavers. The right hand introduces syncopated elements above.

Borodin, Aleksandr Porfiryevich (1833-1887) Russian composer. Born at St Petersburg, the illegitimate son of a Russian prince, he was brought up by his mother and showed an early aptitude for music and chemistry. He studied medicine at St Petersburg, Heidelberg and elsewhere, and carried on an active career as a research chemist and government inspector of scientific facilities throughout Russia. In 1862 he became associate professor at the St Petersburg Academy of Medicine. In 1872 he founded a medical academy for women and remained its director until his death.

Borodin studied music in whatever spare time was left to him after discharging his official duties. In 1862 **Balakirev** persuaded him to take up music seriously and he became a member of the group known as The Five, or the **Mighty Handful**. Less prolific as a composer than other members of the group, such as **Rimsky-Korsakov** or **Mussorgsky**, he nevertheless won great popularity, especially outside Russia, thanks to the interest of **Liszt**. His music often strikes a lyrical vein, rich in original melodies, Slavic-influenced, founded upon inventive harmonies that owe something to **Mendelssohn** yet bespeak great artistry in composition. His works include three symphonies (the last unfinished, but completed and orchestrated by **Glazunov**); the opera *Prince Igor*, which occupied him for 18 years, but had to be completed by Rimsky-Korsakov and Glazunov; the tone poem *In the Steppes of Central Asia*; two string quartets and a handful of piano pieces.

Bortnyansky, Dmitri (1751-1825) Ukrainian composer. His two major contributions are to the repertory of opera and church music. His anthems in particular, stemming from his time as composer to the Imperial Chapel Choir, are skilful and lyrical in effect.

Bösendorfer, Ignaz (1796-1859) Founder of a Viennese firm of piano makers, still trading today, and the most highly regarded manufacturer of Austrian pianos. The resilience of his pianos impressed **Liszt**; while other instruments collapsed under the strain of his playing, those of Bösendorfer survived. He employed both Viennese and English actions in his pianos and his modern concert grands are second only to **Steinway** in popularity. They are particularly renowned for their resonant bass register.

Boston Symphony Orchestra Main orchestra of Boston, Massachusetts. Founded in 1881, it began with mainly German players and its links with Europe have always been strong. The orchestra quickly established a high reputation and employed the best conductors available. From 1924 to 1949 its chief conductor was **Koussevitzky**, who commissioned many major works. More recently, **Münch**, **Leinsdorf** and **Ozawa** have been among its chief conductors. An offshoot of the orchestra is the Boston 'Pops', specializing in arrangements and the light Classical repertory.

Boucourechliev, André (1925-) French

composer and writer on music. He was involved with the Domaine Musical concerts in the 1950s and attracted attention with his pieces involving tape-recordings. He worked in studios in Milan and Paris, and contributed further tape pieces. His *Archipels* are memorable for their use of sound events mapped out on navigational charts which are followed by the performers. Despite these avant-garde activities, he has also published books on Classical and Romantic composers.

Boughton, Rutland (1878-1960) English composer and writer. Boughton was as much known for his socialist views and plans for artistic communes as for his music. He planned an Arthurian cycle of operas to be performed in a festival at Glastonbury. His most famous opera, *The Immortal Hour*, was performed at Glastonbury in 1914, and subsequent operas were performed there and at Covent Garden. He gradually moved from a Wagnerian style towards a simpler, folk-like opera. As a writer, his Marxist views are striking and he has contributed stimulating books on **Bach** as well as on *The Music Drama of the Future*.

Boulanger, Lili (1893-1918) French composer and sister of Nadia **Boulanger**. Ill-health dogged her career and she died young, but she was a composer of great promise and the first woman to win the coveted Prix de Rome. Her winning entry, the cantata *Faust et Hélène* shows allegiance to **Fauré**'s late style but also a striking individuality. She composed several psalm settings and left an unfinished opera based on Maeterlinck's *La Princesse Maleine*.

Boulanger, Nadia (1887-1979) French composer, conductor and reknowned teacher. Sister of Lili **Boulanger**. She studied at the Paris Conservatoire (composition under **Fauré**), where she won many prizes. She was awarded the second Prix de Rome for her cantata *La Sirène* (1908). She taught at several schools of music, including the Juilliard in the United States, the Paris Conservatoire, and the Ecole Normale de Musique, Paris. In 1937 she became the first woman to conduct an entire concert of the Royal Philharmonic Society, London.

Nadia Boulanger

Boulanger taught and influenced many outstanding composers and conductors, including **Berkeley**, **Carter**, **Copland**, **Piston** and **Thomson**.

Boulez, Pierre (1925-) French composer and conductor. He entered the Paris Conservatoire in 1942, studying composition with Olivier **Messiaen**. He also studied counterpoint with Andrée Vaurabourg (wife of the composer Arthur **Honegger**) and **twelve-note technique** with René **Leibowitz**, a pupil of **Schoenberg** and **Webern**. Under Leibowitz's influence, Boulez evolved a rigorous form of **serialism** in which not only pitches but also rhythms followed a strictly controlled sequence. From 1946 to 1956 he was music director of the Barrault-Renaud theatre company, based in Paris. His first two piano sonatas, his *Livre pour Quattuor* (1948-1949) for string quartet, and his composition *Le Mateau sans maître* (1952-1954; revised 1957) attracted much attention, and he became the centre of a circle of contemporary composers including **Stockhausen** and **Berio**. In 1953 he founded a series of Sunday concerts of contemporary music, including his own works among those of Schoenberg, **Berg**, Webern and **Stravinsky**. Boulez conducted an increasing number of these concerts, which became known as the Domaine Musical. In 1966 he conducted **Wagner**'s *Parsifal* at Bayreuth. He broke off his connections with Paris on political grounds, giving up the Domaine Musical concerts in 1967. He was principal guest conductor of the Cleveland Symphony Orchestra (1969-1970) and chief conductor of the BBC Symphony Orchestra (1971-1975) and the New York Philharmonic Orchestra (1971-1977). In 1976 he returned to Bayreuth to conduct Patrice Chereau's notorious centenary production of Wagner's *Ring*, and three years later directed the first complete performance of Berg's *Lulu* at the Paris Opéra. In 1976, Boulez became director of the Institut de Recherche et de Coordination Acoustique/ Musique (IRCAM), a Paris-based institute dedicated to research into modern composition techniques and funded by the French government.

As a composer, Boulez has been an uncompromising adherent of strict serialism, a characteristic best seen in *Structures: Book I* (1952), for two pianos. But he has also been an original experimenter. *Le Visage nuptial*, in its revised version for female soloists, women's chorus and orchestra (1951), uses choral speech, spoken *portamenti*, whispering and crying. *Pli selon pli*, a five-movement 'portrait of Mallarmé' for soprano and orchestra, was first composed in 1957-1962 but, like many of his works, has been subject to continuous revision, in line with Boulez's view that a composition is never finished. Its five movements can be played in any order, except for the third, which must be placed centrally in the work.

Boult, Sir Adrian (1889-1983) English conductor who studied at Oxford and the

Sir Adrian Boult

Leipzig Conservatoire (1912-1913), and joined Covent Garden in 1914. During his career he held conducting posts with the Bach Choir (1928-1931), the City of Birmingham Symphony Orchestra (1923-1930), the BBC Symphony Orchestra (1930-1950) and the London Philharmonic Orchestra (1950-1957). He championed British composers, and introduced much new music to London, such as **Berg**'s *Wozzeck* (1934) and important works by **Bartók**, **Stravinsky** and US composers.

bourdon (Fr.) Sustained low note, such as a **drone** or pedal point. It is used to describe the lowest drone on the hurdy-gurdy, the free vibrating strings of the larger lutes, and for the large pipes on an organ.

Bourgeois, Derek (1941-) English composer who studied at Cambridge and with Herbert **Howells** at the Royal College of Music. Bourgeois has written symphonies and chamber and organ music, but is best known for his choral works written for schools and amateur performers. From 1971 he taught at Bristol University.

Bourgeois, Louis (*c*1510-*c*1560) French composer and theorist, chiefly remembered as one of the music editors of the Calvinist Psalter, in which monophonic popular and church tunes were adapted to the new French translation of the Psalms for the Reformed Church.

Bourgeois was one of the many composers who used these tunes as the basis for polyphonic composition. His theoretical work *Le Droict Chemin de Musique* (1550) displays his keeness for teaching practical music to children, and provides some very early evidence for *notes inégales*.

Bourguignon, Francis de (1890-1961) Belgian composer and pianist who studied at the Brussels Conservatoire and then worked as a concert pianist and as Dame Nellie **Melba**'s accompanist in Australia. Thereafter he devoted himself to composition, teaching at the Brussels Conservatoire until 1955. His works, neo-Classical in style, include chamber and choral pieces, orchestral works, piano music and songs.

bouzouki/buzuq (Greece/Turkey) Long-necked lute (larger than the **saz**), traditionally having three double courses of strings tuned E-B′-E′ and moveable frets. Before the 20th century it was used for solo improvisations on Turkish *maqamat* (see **maqam**), with the lower strings providing a drone, but the modern Greek *bouzouki* is designed for the more Western-style music which has been popular since the 1930s. It now has fixed metal frets and four double courses of strings tuned D-G-B′-E′, making chords easier to play.

Bouzouki

bow Arched piece of wood strung with horsehair. In its original form it had the shape of a bow as used in archery, and in many cultures the bow has retained this shape. It is used to play some form of string instrument by drawing the bow across the strings, producing a unique and sustained sound. The most widespread of these is now the violin family of Western music, using a bow developed gradually from the mid-18th century and standardized by the work of François Tourte (1747-1835). The Tourte bow is made from Brazil-wood, which is lighter than snakewood from which earlier bows were fashioned, curved inwards toward the hair and diminishing in thickness from the heel to the tip. This style of bow allows subtle dynamic variation and accentuation not afforded by earlier versions.

With the surge of interest in authentic performance practice of early and **Baroque** music, 'outcurve bows' are often used for the undifferentiated singing sound which results from their particular technical limitations.

Bowen, York (1884-1961) English composer and pianist. After studying at the Royal Academy of Music he established a reputation as a pianist of prodigious talent, as well as being a respected composer. He was one of the first English pianists to correctly interpret the music of **Debussy** and **Ravel**, as is testified by his important book *On Pedalling the Modern Pianoforte* (1936). His compositions include three piano concertos, as well as genre pieces and a fine oboe sonata.

Bowles, Paul (1910-) American composer, a pupil of Aaron **Copland**, Virgil **Thomson** and Nadia **Boulanger**. His work is mainly operatic and is influenced by jazz and the music of South America.

Bowman, James (1941-) English countertenor who studied at Oxford and made his stage debut in 1967 as Oberon in **Britten**'s *A Midsummer Night's Dream*. His wide repertory includes much 17th-century music and many of **Handel**'s castrato roles as well as roles created for him by 20th-century composers: Priest Confessor in Maxwell **Davies**'s *Taverner* and Voice of Apollo in **Britten**'s *Death in Venice*, 1973. Bowman has a powerful voice and a remarkable stage presence.

Boyce, William (1711-1779) English composer. He was a Chorister of St Paul's Cathedral and studied with Maurice Greene. In 1734 he became organist of the Earl of Oxford's chapel, and in 1736 became both organist at St Michael's, Cornhill, and Composer to the Chapel Royal. He also composed much music for the Society of Apollo and for the Three Choirs Festival. His most serious and forward-looking opera, *Peleus and Thetis*, was produced in 1740, and 1747 saw the publication of his very popular *Twelve Sonatas for two Violins and Bass*. In 1755 he was made Master of the King's Musick, and composed a *Birthday Ode* and a *New Year Ode* practically every year thereafter. Among his 14 stage works *The Secular Masque* (*c*1746) is particularly fine, while his 65 anthems include *O be Joyful in God* and *O where shall wisdom be found* (*c*1769). His eight *Symphonies in eight parts* are overtures to odes.

Bozay, Attila (1939-) Hungarian composer. His early work is almost entirely **serial**, but more recent pieces have relaxed his rigorous adherence to this method of composition.

Braga, Gaetano (1829-1907) Italian cellist and composer. Apart from several successful tours as a cellist, Braga was a composer of operas and later in life much in demand as a coach. His salon piece *An Angel's Serenade* has become a popular classic.

Braham, John (1774-1856) English singer and composer. Highly successful abroad as a singing partner to Nancy Storace, several composers (including **Cimarosa**) wrote roles for Braham when he was still a boy soprano. After his voice broke, he returned to the stage and again found great success. He was known for his ability to pander to the audience and sing in any style that was demanded. His compositions never equalled his fame as a singer.

Brahms, Johannes (1833-1897) German composer. He was one of the greatest 19th-century symphonists after **Beethoven**, and contributed masterpieces to almost every genre, particularly orchestral and chamber music, piano music and song.

He came from a poor family, having to play in taverns at an early age to support himself. In his early 20s he met **Liszt**, who was impressed by him, and **Schumann**, who hailed him as a genius and brought him into the public eye. Brahms lived in Hamburg, conducting and teaching to earn his living, and moved to Vienna in 1863. With the success of his *German Requiem* (1868), he found a good publisher and was able to give up teaching. Most of his large orchestral works, including four symphonies, two piano concertos, one violin concerto and a double concerto for violin and cello, were written between 1873 and 1887. In his later life he turned his attention to chamber music and songs, and in all, wrote 200 of the latter. Highly prolific, Brahms' music was always composed in the Classical style, although in temper he yielded to the Romantic style.

Brain, Dennis (1921-1957) British horn player, son of Aubrey Brain. His tragic death in a car accident robbed the world of a horn player who was perhaps England's finest. He recorded widely, and his legacy includes chamber music as well as concertos. Probably best-known is Brain's recording with Peter **Pears** of the *Serenade for tenor, horn and strings* by Benjamin **Britten**.

branle (Fr.) Family of dances, originating in France in the Middle Ages, and remaining popular up to the present day.

The many different types of branle – simple, double, de Champagne, d'Ecosse etc. – are all characterized by the dancers holding hands in a line or in a circle, and by a swinging, side-stepping motion.

During the 16th and 17th centuries many publications of dance music contained branles, beginning with the *Eighteen Basses Dances...*(1530) for lute published by **Attaignant** and continuing through Michael Praetorius's *Terpsichore* (1612) for instrumental ensemble to Robert Ballard's *Deuxième livre* (1614) for lute. **Arbeau**'s *Orchésographie* contains the largest surviving collection of descriptions of the steps of branles, including several 'mimed' branles in which dancers imitate horses, washerwomen, etc. The branle has survived (or resurfaced) in many parts of France.

The English and Italian equivalents are brawl and *brando* respectively.

Brant, Henry (1913-) American composer. Brant is in some ways an artistic descendant of Charles **Ives**. His experimental attitude to composition was established early in his career, and many of his pieces demand the spatial separation of instruments or groups of players. His compositions have been innovative in other ways too, using 'found objects' as well as conventional instruments. He has taught at several universities in the United States, and has composed in many genres. Perhaps his most celebrated piece is *The Grand Universal Circus* (1956).

brass band Although any large ensemble of **brass instruments** may be called a brass band, the term is used specifically to refer to the British 'competition' band, which has the standard line-up of 1 Eb cornet, several B♭ cornets, 1 flugelhorn, 3 E♭ horns, 2 baritones, 2 euphoniums, 2 tenor trombones, 1 bass trombone, 2 E♭ basses and 2 B♭ basses. The National Brass Band Festival was established in 1860.

Many brass bands were originally founded to provide musical recreation for employees of mines and factories, especially in the north of England (where the movement has always been strong) and from where come the most distinguished bands such as the Grimethorpe Colliery Band and the Brighouse and Rastrick Brass Band.

Many established composers have written music for brass band, including **Elgar** (*Severn Suite*, 1930), **Holst** (*A Moorside Suite*, 1929), Herbert **Howells** (*Three Figures*, 1960) and Harrison **Birtwistle** (*Grimethorpe Aria*).

brass instruments Family of musical instruments in which the sound is produced by the vibration of the player's lips against each other. The name derives from the fact that most modern representatives of the family are made of brass or similar metal, although certain instruments made of other materials (wood, clay and horn) could also be included in the definition.

The brass section of a modern orchestra generally includes French horns, trumpets, trombones and a tuba. For the instruments used in a British brass band see **brass band**. Other brass instruments in current use include the valve trombone, bugle and sousaphone.

The origin of brass instruments is ancient; simple horns can be easily constructed from an animal horn or a conch shell. The Roman army used large brass instruments called *tuba* and *buccina*. Brass instruments were used extensively in the Renaissance, namely the cornett, slide trumpet, sackbut and (natural) trumpet. Brass instruments have always had particular associations with the military (trumpets and bugles) and with the hunt (horns).

All brass instruments have the same method of sound production, the 'buzzing' or vibration of the player's lips is transferred via the mouthpiece to the air inside the instrument. The only notes that may properly be obtained from a **natural** instrument (that is one with an air column of fixed length) are those of the **harmonic series**, and in a natural trumpet, horn or bugle, only these notes are used. In order to fill in the gaps between the natural harmonics, various methods are employed to enable the player to shorten or lengthen the resonating length of the tube, such as valves (trumpet, tuba) a slide (trombone, slide trumpet), holes closed by fingers (cornett, serpent) or keys (keyed bugle, ophicleide).

The tonal characteristics of all brass instruments are loud, majestic and stirring, and it is for these properties that they have been used down the ages.

bravura (It.) Brilliance or virtuosity in vocal or instrumental music. Particularly in common use during the 18th century.

break Jazz term used to describe a brief solo by one or more of the instrumentalists. Usually the players improvise unaccompanied by the rhythm section. The word is also used to describe the unison playing of a planned riff which temporarily suspends the time of the piece.

Traditionally the break is used at the end of the **bridge** section or in the last bar and a half of a four bar phrase.

breaking of the voice Process which occurs in adolescent men and, less dramatically, in women, whereby the voice becomes deeper and more mature. The term is particularly used of a boy's treble voice changing to a male alto, tenor or bass. The name has the connotation of a sudden, almost overnight change, which while true for a few people, is somewhat misleading because most people experience a gradual change.

Bream, Julian (1933-) English guitarist and lutenist. His first guitar teacher was his father and he later studied at the Royal College of Music. Since making his London debut in 1950 he has travelled extensively and has given a number of first performances of important guitar pieces, such as the concerto by **Villa-Lobos**. His interest in the lute also dates from this period and both his solo performances of **Dowland** and his accompaniments to lute

Julian Bream

songs (recorded with Peter **Pears**) were revelatory in their day. Bream's expert and exciting playing has inspired many composers to write works for him, including Richard Rodney **Bennett**, **Walton** and **Britten**.

Brecht, Bertholt (1898-1956) German writer. Much of his work has been set to music, either in direct collaboration with a composer (such as **Weill**, **Hindemith**, Eisler and **Dessau**) or as a source of texts for other composers. Some of the collaborations are through-composed works, for example *Aufstieg und Fall der Stadt Mahagonny* (1927-1929, with Weill), and others are plays with music, such as *Happy End* (1929, also with Weill).

In his early collaborations with Weill and Hindemith he performed the role of librettist, but in his later collaboration with Hanns Eisler, following his conversion to Marxism, the works they produced showed the music to be subordinate to the text, for example *Die Massnahme* (1930). During the time of his collaboration with Eisler he was in exile and relative obscurity in the United States. He returned to East Berlin in 1949, where he formed the theatre company *The Berliner Ensemble* which was acclaimed as one of the world's greatest and Brecht came to be recognized as one of the major figures in 20th-century theatre.

Brendel, Alfred (1931-) Austrian pianist now resident in Britain. Brendel is especially esteemed for his recordings of the Viennese classics although his repertory extends to **Schoenberg** and embraces the major Romantic composers. He is a pianist whose playing has been supplemented by musicological studies and he is a great believer in faithfulness to the urtext, as is testified in his highly regarded writings on music as well as his master-classes both for television and for the major festivals of Europe, where he is much in demand. His playing demonstrates a respect for the composer's intentions and a deep feeling for style, as well as a sound palette rich in extremes and subtleties.

breve Note half the value of a long and twice that of a **semibreve**. In the 13th century it was the shortest note in use, hence its name (from the Latin *brevis*, short). It is only occasionally used in modern music. The US term is double whole note.

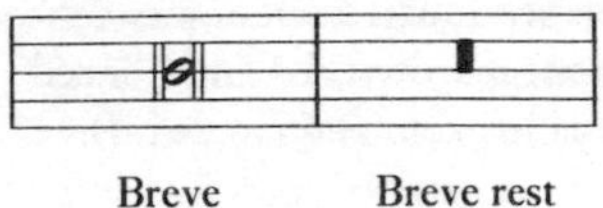

Breve Breve rest

Brian, Havergal (1876-1972) English composer, music critic and editor. Many of his compositions are scored for large choral and orchestral forces – the Symphony in E minor, for example, involving 16 horns – sometimes reminiscent of Richard **Strauss** in their complex textures and expansive, grandiose themes. In all, he wrote 32 symphonies and five operas in addition to several cantatas and part-songs, but the extravagant nature of his larger works meant that they received only occasional performances. In the 1950s, however, the BBC broadcast several of Brian's compositions, and this served to focus attention on many previously little-heard pieces.

bridge Term with two meanings.

First, in string instruments, it is a wooden wedge raising the strings above the soundboard and allowing them to communicate their vibrations to the main body of the instrument.

Second, in composition, a bridge (passage) is a short section joining together two larger sections in a full-scale work, often by means of a key change.

Bridge, Frank (1879-1941) English composer, conductor and accomplished violist. He studied under **Stanford** at the Royal College of Music, initially writing chamber music and songs, then turning to more substantial orchestral works. Among these, the three *Idylls* for string quartet and the symphonic poem *Summer* reflect the influence of his contemporary, **Delius**.

After World War I Bridge's style underwent considerable change in terms of harmonic language, rhythm and texture, and works from this period (for example the third and fourth string quartets) have been placed on a par with compositions by **Schoenberg**. Bridge played with several string quartets, conducted opera (Savoy Theatre, Covent Garden), and numbered **Britten** among his composition pupils.

Bridge, Sir John Frederick (1844-1924) English organist and composer. From 1869 he served at Manchester Cathedral, and at Westminster Abbey as deputy organist (1875-1882) and organist (1882-1918). While at the Abbey he saw to the modernization of the organ and arranged the music for Queen Victoria's Jubilees in 1887 and 1897, and for the coronations of Edward VII and George V. From 1905 he was professor of music at London University. His compositions were mainly for the church (oratorios) and for music festivals.

Bridgewater, Ernest Leslie (1893-1975) English pianist and conductor who held various musical posts in theatres and from 1935 to 1942 was based at the BBC light music section. He composed incidental music for films and stage.

brindisi (It.) Popular song involving the drinking of a toast. A well-known operatic example is the chorus *Libiamo* from *La Traviata*.

brio (It.) Spirit, vivacity; hence *con brio*, an expression mark directing the performer to play with brilliance and spirit. Also, *allegro con brio*.

Britten, Benjamin (1913-1976) English composer, pianist, accompanist and conductor. He studied composition with **Bridge** and **Ireland** and became one of the most distinguished and prolific of 20th-century British composers.

Primarily a composer of vocal music, his

Sir Benjamin Britten

lifelong friendship with the tenor Peter **Pears** was a great influence on his music – many of his operas (for example *Peter Grimes*, *Billy Budd*) and song cycles were written for Pears – but he also enjoyed writing for amateurs and children (*Let's Make an Opera*, *St Nicholas* and *Noye's Fludde*). In 1948 he founded the **Aldeburgh Festival**.

Britten's style, while essentially **diatonic**, uses **modal** and **chromatic** idioms and at times incorporates **serialism**.

Brixi, Frantisek (1732-1771) Most celebrated member of an extensive Czech family of musicians. The son of Simon Brixi, he was best known as a choirmaster and composer. His music draws heavily on the contemporary music of Italy and Vienna, and Alessandro **Scarlatti** and **Fux** may be cited as particularly important. Apart from writing more than 400 sacred works, he produced some school dramas, both serious and comic, as well as symphonies. Brixi was instrumental in bringing **Mozart** to Prague in the 1780s.

broken chord Type of melodic or accompanying figuration produced by playing the notes of a chord successively in any order rather, than simultaneously; the Alberti bass is a particular example of broken chord figuration.

Broken chord

broken consort Small 16th- and 17th-century instrumental group made up of a mixture of string and wind instruments.

Brott, Boris (1944-) Canadian violinist and conductor, son of the composer and conductor Alexander Brott. Apart from studying with his father, he also took lessons with **Monteux, Bernstein** and **Markevich**. He founded the Philharmonic Youth Orchestra of Montreal in 1959 and has since conducted in many countries. He has been principal conductor of the Northern Sinfonia. He has conducted the Royal Ballet and gave the premiere at Covent Garden of **Stravinsky**'s *The Soldier's Tale*. He is also widely known as a guest conductor as well as in the role of television presenter of programmes on music.

Brouwer, Leo (1939-) Cuban composer, guitarist and conductor. He has written many film scores, music for the guitar and *Hexahedrons* (music for any six instrumentalists or multiples of six).

Brown, Earle (1926-) American composer, closely associated with the Avant-Garde New York School established in the early 1950s by John **Cage** and Morton Feldman.

After participating in the famous Darmstadt Summer Courses, Brown worked as a recording engineer for Capitol Records before becoming composer-in-residence at institutes in Baltimore and West Berlin.

During the early 1950s, as one of the leaders of the American avant-garde, Brown developed the technique of graphic notation in pieces such as *November 1952* and *December 1952* and of open form in *Twenty Five Pages* (1953) and *Available Forms I* (1961).

Browne, John (*c*1490-?) English composer and one-time clerk at Windsor. Little is known about his life but a number of his compositions are preserved, some of them in *The Eton Choirbook*. These works are rich and complex, and ahead of their time in an expressive use of dissonance. A few carols also survive.

Brubeck, Dave (1920-) American composer and jazz pianist with leanings towards Classical music. He numbers both

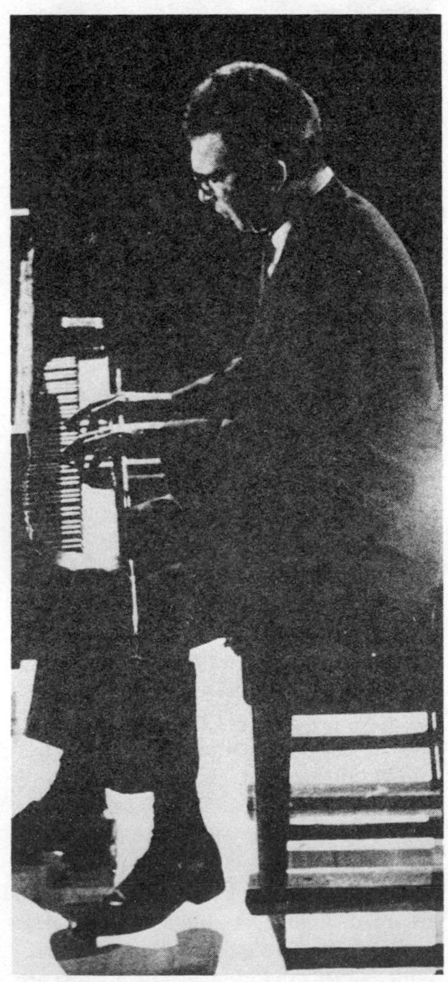

Dave Brubeck

Schoenberg and **Milhaud** among his composition teachers. Brubeck has formed several ensembles, the most famous of which is his quartet, formed with the saxophonist Paul Desmond. Brubeck's compositions include the popular number *Take Five*, a piece in 5/4 time.

Bruch, Max (1838-1920) German composer who was born in Cologne and studied there and in Bonn. His opera *Loreley*, first performed in 1863, reflects his roots in the Rhineland. He held various posts in Mannheim, Berlin and Koblenz, and was for some years conductor of the Liverpool Philharmonic Society. He wrote one other opera, *Hermione*, and some church music, but it is for his pieces for violin and orchestra that he is best remembered. They include several concertos and the *Scottish Fantasy*, based on melodies he collected while in Britain.

Bruckner, Anton (1824-1896) Austrian composer, best known for his nine symphonies. In his early years Bruckner's musical training centred on the church and he was much impressed by 18th-century sacred music. He was for many years a schoolteacher in the provinces and was too timid to apply for more prestigious musical posts despite his talents. He also studied rigorously until he was nearly 40, taking courses in strict counterpoint and in orchestration.

In the 1860s his encounter with the music of **Wagner** was to prove a major turning point and the major output of symphonies began in the 1870s. During his lifetime his works had a stormy reception, the critic Hanslick in particular attacking him for his slavish allegiance to Wagner.

The 20th century has reassessed Bruckner's music, with its exciting use of brass and its capacity to absorb lyrical melody into large-scale symphonic forms, and his works are frequently performed and recorded. Among his church music, a *Mass in F minor* and a *Te Deum* are particularly remembered, and his *a cappella* motets are frequently performed by church choirs. It is often forgotten that he was also highly esteemed as an organist: his recitals at Crystal Palace and the Albert Hall in the 1870s received standing ovations.

Brüggen, Frans (1934-) Dutch player of recorder and Baroque flute, and one of the great modern popularizers of these instruments. He studied at the Musieklyceum, Amsterdam, and has taught at the Royal Conservatoire, The Hague. In 1972-1973 he was Erasmus professor of late Baroque music at Harvard University. Recordings include many with the harpsichordist Gustav Leonhardt. In 1986 he founded the Orchestra of the Eighteenth Century, and he is their principal conductor.

Brüll, Ignaz (1846-1907) Austrian pianist and composer. He was respected in his day as a concert pianist and was known to **Brahms**. His opera *Das Goldene Kreuz* was his best-known work, performed in Berlin and London.

Brumel, Antoine (*c*1460-*c*1515) French composer. He became a cleric at Notre Dame de Chartres in 1483, master of the Innocents at St Peter, Geneva in 1486 and thereafter was ordained. As a priest he worked at Laon Cathedral and Notre Dame in Paris, and in 1505 was appointed *maestro di cappella* to Alfonso I d'Este at Ferrara.

His 15 masses form a major part of his output, and all are of high quality and craftsmanship. His *Missa et ecce terrae motus* is the earliest surviving mass in twelve voice parts. His other masses are scored for four voices, and of these the *Missa de dringhs* displays his economical style and sense of humour. Among his secular songs his arrangement of Ockeghem's *Fors Seulement* is remarkable for its low ranges and rich sonorities.

Bruneau, Alfred (1857-1934) French composer and critic. A pupil of **Massenet**, Bruneau shared this composer's taste for Zola and for that author's realist doctrines. His music translates many features of Italian *verismo* into the French operatic medium. In Bruneau's day, *Messidor* (1897) and *L'Ouragan* (1901) were well-known, but in the early years of the century his work went out of favour as Zolaesque naturalism was replaced by more subtle aesthetics. As a writer, he produced many books and articles, including books on **Fauré** and **Massenet**.

Brunswick, Mark (1902-1971) American composer. His training was in France with Nadia **Boulanger** and in Vienna, where he came into contact with **Webern**. Among particular interests that have affected his music, 16th-century polyphony has been important and much of his work displays great contrapuntal facility. He also wrote verse and set many of his poems to music. Between 1946 and 1967 he was chairman of the music department at the City College of New York.

Brymer, Jack (1915-) English clarinettist. Although originally trained as a schoolteacher, his career changed direction when **Beecham** appointed him to play in the Royal Philharmonic Orchestra in 1947. He has worked with many other orchestras and is much admired for his concerto and chamber playing. His tone is warm and vibrant, and his sense of style exemplary. He also gives entertaining lectures on the clarinet and on his experiences as a player.

Bucchi, Valentino (1916-1976) Italian composer who studied at the conservatoire in Florence before beginning a teaching career. His compositional activities have been accompanied throughout his career by work as a music critic and teacher. He employs an easily absorbed compositional style; his music is essentially **diatonic**, with easily followed contrapuntal movement. His numerous compositions include many operas, ballets, songs, film scores and orchestral pieces.

buffo, buffa (It.) Gust or puff, now used to mean comic. Thus *opera buffa* is comic opera, *basso buffo* a comic bass singer and *stile buffo* means in a comic style.

bugaku (Japan) Traditional court dance, and a term applied to **gagaku** when the music is used as an accompaniment to the dance. Movement in *bugaku* is extremely slow and is performed on a raised square stage in front of the orchestra. The dances correspond to the division of **gagaku** into 'music of the left' (*Tāgaku*) and 'music of the right' (*Komagaku*), and are accompanied by the music and ensemble, excluding stringed instruments, of the appropriate side. The dancers are dressed in elaborate costume, the dominant colour for left being red and for right being green. Generally the order of dances in a performance is fixed, the dance of the right following the dance of the left to form a pair.

bugle Military brass instrument traditionally used for signalling. Like the **post horn** it is an instrument based on the notes of the harmonic series, forming a perfect fifth and octave from the bell note and then a major triad, using **harmonics** from the second to the sixth. Bugles are usually tuned in G or B♭ but occasionally in F.

The word is also used as a generic term for the family of brass instruments constructed after the principles of the **flugelhorn**.

Bugle

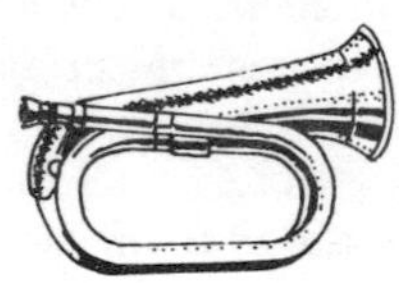

buka (Java) Short, often unmeasured, introduction to a performance of a **gamelan** composition.

Bull, John (*c*1562-1628) Welsh or English virginalist, organist and composer of keyboard and vocal music. His earliest teacher was William Blithemann. In 1573 he became one of the Children of the Chapel Royal, where he was taught by the Master, William Hunnis. In 1587 he became organist of Hereford Cathedral, and in 1586 a Gentleman of the Chapel Royal. In 1613 he left England never to return, going first to Brussels and in 1615 becoming organist of Antwerp Cathedral. His keyboard music is preserved largely in two sources, the *Fitzwilliam Virginal Manuscript* and the publication *Parthenia* (1612-13), and falls into four broad types: arrangements of popular songs, arrangements of plainsong and sacred models, fantasias on pre-existing polyphonic compositions, and dances, of which one of the galliards strongly resembles the British National Anthem and may have been the origin of the tune. He also wrote 16 sacred choral works and 200 canons, displaying his mastery of polyphony.

Bull, Ole (1810-1880) Norwegian violinist and composer, highly influential in the development of 19th-century Norwegian music. As a player he was influenced by the *hardanger* style of folk-fiddling of his native Norway, and he adopted the characteristic flatter bridge and longer bow of this style even when he performed Classical music. This was much admired on his extensive European tours, where he was influenced also by **Paganini**. He embarked upon prodigiously busy concert tours in England, Germany and Russia and on his return to Norway was welcomed as a national hero. Bull's compositions are inseparable from his own personality as a violinist.

bullroarer Australian aboriginal instrument consisting of an oblong wooden board, one of the two sides of which is carved in relief, making the surface uneven. The board is whirled around above the head on a string, producing a thunderous whirring, used in rituals to personify the sound of the supernatural itself.

Bülow, Hans Guido Freiherr von (1830-1894) German conductor, pianist and composer. Bülow studied piano with Friedrich Wieck and **Liszt** and then toured extensively, giving first performances of many important works (including **Tchaikovsky**'s Piano Concerto No. 1 in Boston, 1875). He worked throughout Europe as a conductor, in Germany presenting many influential operatic premieres – *Tristan und Isolde* (1865) and *Die Meistersinger von Nürnberg* (1868). He composed several piano pieces and various orchestral works.

Bumbry, Grace (1937-) American mezzo-soprano who studied under Lotte **Lehmann**. She made her debut at the Paris Opéra in 1960 in *Aïda*, and was the first black singer to appear at Bayreuth (1961). Since 1970, she has also sung soprano roles. Bumbry is probably best known in the roles of Carmen and Salomé and is considered to be a fine operatic singer with considerable stage presence.

bunraku (Japan) Puppet theatre with a **shamisen** lute accompanying the narrator-singer. The narrator portrays all the characters in the play, both male and female, old and young, and his intense singing style is generally known as **Gidayū-bushi**, after its most famous exponent. *Bunraku*, whose plots tend to be tragic, is characterized by extravagant gestures and heightened representation of all emotions. The puppets are animated by on-stage puppeteers. The performance is split into five main parts or *dan* and consists of *uta* (songs) and *odori* (dances). Its music has stereotyped melodic and rhythmic patterns.

Bürger, Gottfried August (1747-1794) German poet, important in the establishment of the early Romantic movement. He published old German folk ballads in a collection which was much in favour in the early 19th century. **Schubert** was one of several composers to set Bürger's work.

Burgmüller, Johann Friedrich (1806-1874) German composer, best known for his music for children, piano studies and light salon pieces.

Burkhard, Paul (1911-1977) Swiss composer and conductor, whose professional conducting career included posts as resident conductor in theatres in Berne and Zurich. He conducted his own works, mainly light operettas, throughout Europe and also wrote liturgical plays for school use. In addition he wrote film and television music, and incidental music for several plays. He is best remembered for the song *O Mein Papa*.

Burkhard, Willy (1900-1955) Swiss composer. He studied in Switzerland and under Karg-Elert in Leipzig and later became a teacher of composition at the Zurich Conservatoire. Although his work shows allegiances to several other composers' styles, including those of **Bartók** and **Hindemith**, he retained an individual style, largely through his own enthusiasms for the Baroque, and for church modes. He blended these influences with a highly developed **chromaticism** in works such as the oratorio *Das Jahr*. His later music embraced **serialism**.

Burleigh, Henry Thacker (1866-1949) Black American composer and singer. In the latter capacity he showed talent at an early age, and sang spirituals to **Dvorák** when he visited the United States. In 1911 he was employed as an editor at the Ricordi publishing house, and he published many arrangements of spirituals as well as original compositions.

burletta (It.) Musical farce. The term was originally used in England for Italian comic operas and then came to be applied to English imitations. The first English *burletta* was *Midas* by Kane O'Hara, first performed in Dublin in 1762. At first, *burlettas* were popular entertainments featuring songs and comic dialogue, but by the beginning of the 19th century the term was applied to comedies of all sorts that featured music.

Burt, Francis (1926-) English composer. After studying with Howard **Ferguson** and Boris **Blacher**, Burt presented pieces at the Darmstadt festivals of the 1950s. He was appointed professor of composition at the Vienna Hochschule für Musik in 1977 and has produced many works for the stage, mainly performed in Germany.

Busch, Fritz (1890-1951) German conductor and pianist. He trained at the Cologne Conservatoire and then worked in opera houses throughout Germany (Aachen, Stuttgart, Dresden), conducting first performances of operas by **Hindemith**, Richard **Strauss**, **Busoni** and **Weill**. He was dismissed during the Nazi regime and subsequently worked in Scandinavia, Buenos Aires, New York and England, where he was the first conductor of the Glyndebourne Opera (1939-1945).

Bush, Alan (1900-) English composer, pianist and teacher. Four years training at the Royal Academy of Music were followed by private study under John **Ireland** (composition), and under **Schnabel** and **Moiseiwitsch** (piano) in Berlin (1929-1931). Since 1925 he has been professor of composition at the Royal Academy of Music. His first success as a composer came in 1923 with the String Quartet in A minor, and this was followed by further chamber works, a variety of orchestral pieces and several operas including *Wat Tyler* and *Men of Blackmoor*. In 1936 Bush founded the Workers' Music Association.

Busnois, Antoine (*c*1430-1492) French composer, working for most of his life at the court of Burgundy. In 1467 he entered the private chapel of Charles the Bold, Duke of Burgundy, and on the Duke's death served his heir, Mary of Burgundy until her death in 1482. Contemporary observers hailed him as one of the greatest composers of his age. His works include two complete mass cycles, one on the *L'homme Armé* theme and some eleven motets, including *In Hydraulis*, which pays homage to Ockeghem. His major output, however, was secular songs, more than 60 of which survive. The contemporary popularity of two of them is evident, for his *Je ne Demande Lialté* served as a basis for several instrumental versions, including those by Obrecht and Agricola, and his *Fortuna Desperata* was used as a *cantus firmus* by **Josquin** and **Senfl**.

Busoni, Ferruccio (1866-1924) Italian pianist and composer, who settled in Berlin. He was an infant prodigy and was passionately interested in the music of **Bach**. He is best known as an editor and transcriber of Bach's works, such as the famous piano arrangement of the *D minor Chaconne* for violin. Most of his piano music requires a Lisztian technique. Busoni held several teaching posts and was director of the Bologna Conservatoire.

Busser, Paul Henri (1872-1973) French composer and conductor. He studied the organ with **Franck** and **Widor**, and composition with Ernest **Guiraud**. In the early years of the century he established a reputation as a conductor. **Debussy** admired his conducting, and Busser orchestrated several of his works, including *Printemps* and the *Petite Suite*. Several of his stage works were well received and he composed chamber and orchestral music as well as songs. His style is indebted to early Debussy, among others.

Bussotti, Sylvano (1931-) Italian composer who was also a writer, painter, and film and theatre director. Musically, he was initiated as a **serialist** but rapidly moved on to become more interested in the ideas of John **Cage**. His scores became highly graphic, with distorted staves and visual images sometimes replacing any semblance of conventional notation. The *Rara Requiem* (1969-1970) is considered an important work, summing up Bussotti's career. His many music-theatre pieces (which include a *Passion According to Sade*) are equally thought-provoking and include all kinds of unconventional effects. Bussotti has also written extensively on contemporary music.

Butt, Dame Clara (1872-1936) English contralto. After studying in Bristol and at the Royal College of Music in London she made her debut as Ursula in **Sullivan**'s *Golden Legend* (1892). Her immense popular acclaim was centred on her performances on the concert platform and she is perhaps best remembered for her interpretation of Elgar's *Sea Pictures* and the arrangement for contralto soloist and orchestra of *Land of Hope and Glory*. Her exceptionally powerful and resonant voice has made her a unique and unforgettable concert performer.

Butterley, Nigel (1935-) Australian composer, active also as a conductor and pianist. His many interests are reflected in the lively variety of his compositions. His earlier style reflected the current vogue for the formalism of the music of **Hindemith**, but plainsong, serialism and impressionism have all in their own way influenced his style. Visits to Europe inspired *Laudes*, four impressions of cathedrals, and religious mysticism is a recurrent preoccupation. Among lighter pieces is a collaboration with Barry Humphries entitled *First Day Covers*, but his more serious music includes works in most mediums.

Butterworth, Arthur (1923-) English composer and teacher, a pupil of Richard **Hall**. Although he experimented with **twelve-note composition**, most of his work is tonal, and is associated with the landscapes of his native north of England.

Butterworth, George (1885-1916) English composer and collector of folk-songs. After meeting Cecil **Sharp** and **Vaughan Williams** he became interested in the movement to revive English folk music and incorporate folk-songs into compositions. His best-remembered orchestral compositions that demonstrate this are the rhapsody *A Shropshire Lad* and *The Banks of Green Willow*. His setting of six poems from Housman's *A Shropshire Lad* use no direct folk-song quotations, although they are among the finest cycles of the English pastoral tradition.

Buxtehude, Dietrich (1637-1707) Danish composer and organist. Also known as Diderik Buxtehude, he was born at Oldesloe, Holstein, the son of a church organist. After holding posts as organist in Hälsingborg and Helsinger, in 1668 he succeeded Franz **Tunder** as organist at the Marienkirche in the north German town of Lübeck, retaining the post until his death. In 1673 Buxtehude revived Tunder's annual series of *Abendmusiken*, musical performances given in conjunction with church services on the five Sundays leading up to Christmas. Buxtehude's playing won such a following throughout Germany and the rest of Europe that the youthful **Handel** and Matheson went to Lübeck to hear him perform, and J.S. **Bach** is supposed to have walked the 300 km from Arnstadt to Lübeck for the same purpose in 1706. Bach was one of many young composers of the time who were greatly influenced by Buxtehude's organ compositions and trio sonatas. Buxtehude also composed more than 100 cantatas, arias and other vocal works, and several suites and sets of variations for harpsichord. His music is personal and subjective and he never mastered the more technical aspects of structure and counterpoint; yet he passed on to the succeeding generation a tradition of deeply felt music dating back to **Monteverdi**.

buzuq (Turkey/Greece) Alternative spelling for **bouzouki**.

BWV Abbreviation of **Bach Werke-Verzeichnis**.

Byrd (or Byrde), William (*c*1543-1623) English organist and composer who studied under **Tallis** and held posts as organist at Lincoln Cathedral and at the Chapel Royal. Byrd wrote secular and church choral music (both Protestant and Catholic), music for viols and keyboards. These include 17 *Cantiones Sacrae*, 200 Latin motets and masses for three, four and five voices. He was one of the founders of the English Madrigal School and as such profoundly influenced the development of English music. With Tallis, Byrd also held the monopoly on music printing.

William Byrd

C

C Name of the note that lies one tone below D and one semitone above B. The scale of C major has no sharps or flats in the key-signature. Because it is the keynote of the major scale on the white keys of the piano (and therefore without key-signature), it is often the first note to be learned. Middle C is the starting point for keyboard players because it is the centre of the keyboard. Before A became the standard tuning note, C was often used by tuners and is more correct than A as the centre of many historical **temperaments** such as **mean tone**.

C　　C major has a blank key-signature

Caballé, Montserrat (1933-) Spanish soprano who studied at the Barcelona Conservatoire and made her operatic debut with Basle Opera in 1956. Over the next decade she established her reputation in opera houses across Europe (Covent Garden, 1972, as Violette) specializing in 19th-century Italian opera. She records extensively and appears often in recitals, most notably of Spanish songs.

cabaletta (It.) At one time used to refer to a short, rhythmic **aria** in which the player was allowed to improvise ornamentation during the repeat. Later it came to be applied to the last section of the extended aria, generally in rapid tempo; an example of this kind is to be found in the first act of **Verdi**'s *La Traviata*. The term was revived by **Stravinsky** in *The Rake's Progress* (1951).

Cabezon, Antonio de (1510-1566) Spanish organist and composer who was blind from early childhood. He studied in Valencia and entered the Royal Chapel in 1525, serving Queen Isabella until her death in 1539 and later Prince Philip (Philip II). His keyboard works can be divided into four main categories: settings of plainsong hymns and other chants for use in services; elaborate arrangements (*glosas*) of vocal chansons, madrigals and motets; arrangements of popular dances; and newly composed polyphonic works, many of them called *tientos*. These last were often marked as equally suitable for harp, **vihuela** or an ensemble of instruments.

caccia (It.) Musical and poetic genre that flourished in 14th-century Italy. The word, literally meaning chase, is similar to the English catch or round because the top two of the three voices, or sometimes all three voices, sing the same tune but enter one after the other. The text almost always tells of the hunt, with the intentional *double entendre* of the chase of love.

Caccini, Giulio (*c*1545-1618) Italian singer and composer who pioneered the *stile recitativo* opera and the use of *basso continuo*. In the 1570s and 1580s he was closely involved with the Florentine Academy. It was there that the *stile* *recitativo* evolved, although Caccini's claim to have invented it himself was challenged by **Cavalieri**. For the most lavish of all the Florentine *intermedii* – that of 1589 – he composed the **madrigal** *Lo che dal ciel cader farel la luna*, for the accompaniment of which it was said the **chittarone** was invented. He composed some of the music for the first opera ever performed, **Peri's** *Euridice* (1600). His own setting of the same drama was the first published opera (published 1600). His collection of songs, *Le nuove musiche* (1601) contains a valuable introduction in which he explains his new monodic style and discusses the types of ornaments used by himself and other singers of the day. Of the songs in the collection the most famous is the first, *Amarilli mia bella*, which was adapted and arranged numerous times in the 17th century and has never left the singer's repertory.

cachucha (Sp.) Andalusian dance which originated in Cadiz in the early 19th century. It is a graceful dance in triple time, similar to the **bolero**. A famous but somewhat bastardized example occurs in Gilbert and Sullivan's *The Gondoliers*.

cadence Progression of two chords marking the end of a phrase, a section or an entire piece. There are four main types in tonal music.

First is the perfect cadence (authentic, final or full cadence; full close), consisting of a tonic chord approached from a dominant chord (e.g. V-I, or V7-I). If one or both of the chords is an inversion, the cadence may be referred to as 'inverted'.

Second is the plagal cadence, consisting of a tonic chord approached from a subdominant chord (IV-I). This type is also known as an 'Amen cadence', because it is commonly used to harmonize the Amen at the end of hymns.

Third is the imperfect cadence (half cadence, half close), consisting of a dominant chord approached from any other chord (commonly I, II or IV). In American usage, 'imperfect' sometimes refers to

Perfect cadence Imperfect cadence

Plagal cadence Interrupted cadence

cadences whose chords are not in root position (inverted cadences).

Fourth is the interrupted cadence (deceptive cadence, false close), consisting of a dominant chord resolving to some chord other then I, usually VI.

Of the cadences described here, the first two are suitable for use at the end of a piece (the perfect cadence is far more common in this context), and the second two serve as intermediate cadences.

Another important type is the Phrygian cadence, which originated in medieval music but continued to be used well into the Baroque era. Characterized by a falling semitone in the bass, it sounds like an imperfect cadence in a minor key.

In pre-tonal music, cadences depended not on harmonic progressions but on linear movement, and were characterized by melodic formulae. Many 20th-century composers have treated cadences in this way, or have avoided the tonal implications of traditional cadences by using modal progressions or dissonant chords.

cadenza Improvisatory passage, intended to show a solo performer's inventiveness and technical skill. It is mainly associated with the **concerto** and the operatic **aria**, and frequently occurrs shortly before the final **cadence**. Classical composers expected the soloist to provide his or her own cadenza, usually improvised around the thematic material of the movement, although **Beethoven** and **Mozart** both provided them for many of their concertos. Later composers, including **Schumann** and **Brahms**, usually wrote cadenzas as an integral part of a work and this has continued to be common practice in instrumental music. Composers of vocal music tended to leave the cadenzas unwritten or simply to sketch them in, although **Verdi** composed his own for his later operas. By the end of the 19th century, performers were rarely required to improvise. Modern performers of concertos often use original cadenzas, or those written by later composers and performers (such as Busoni's for Mozart's piano concertos and Joachim's for Beethoven's and Brahms's violin concertos).

Cadman, Charles Wakefield (1881-1946) American composer, pianist and teacher. His arrangements of American Indian music, set into a conservative 19th-century harmony, were very popular in their time; examples are his songs *At Dawning* and *Sky Blue Water*. He wrote one opera, *Shanemis or the Robin Woman*, produced by the Metropolitan Opera in 1918.

Cage, John (1912-) American composer and writer, father-figure to the avant-garde, not only in the United States. He studied with **Schoenberg** and with Henry **Cowell**. He was involved as a composer for dance at an early age, and this involvement has resulted in important collaborations with the Merce Cunningham Dance Company.

After a period of **serialism**, Cage moved towards experimentation with percussion and with prepared piano, of which the *Sonatas and Interludes* are perhaps the most lasting result. His next phase, catalyzed by his involvement with Eastern philosophies, was to explore **aleatoric** techniques, introducing an element of chance into composition.

His writings – notably the book *Silence* – complemented his work by challenging accepted aesthetics and proposing further possibilities for musical exploration. *Music of Changes* involved stop-watches and long silences, *4' 33"* a more extreme use of silence performable by any instrument or instruments – all that happens is that the performers enter, remain silent for the stipulated time, and then leave.

To many, these experiments were mere nonsense, but Cage built up a circle of followers, such as Morton **Feldman**, David **Tudor**, Christian **Wolff** and Earle **Brown**. Today his experiments seem less shocking, particularly when compared to those in the neighbouring arts, in which Cage was always deeply involved. Other composers have been keen to collaborate; he was invited to Darmstadt in the late 1950s and to Italy by **Berio**. Cage has taught at many universities throughout the world and has given master-classes.

Caimo, Giuseppe (*c*1545-*c*1584) Italian composer and organist based in Milan, where he is known to have acted as cathedral organist. Many of his compositions are now lost, but his extant works include madrigals and canzonettes.

Caix d'Hervelois, Louis de (*c*1680-1760) One of the thriving late 17th-18th century school of French viol players/composers. From 1710 to 1750 he published six collections of music for viols and two for flutes. He is noted for the virtuosity and sensitivity of his pieces within a miniature framework. He appears to have eschewed membership of the Royal Bands and to have supported himself on private patronage.

cake-walk Term with two meanings.

First, it is a dance that originated among Black slaves in the United States in the mid-19th century, of the same musical genre as **ragtime**. The strutting dance, mocking the mannerisms of white plantation owners, became very popular towards the end of the century; between 1889 and 1903 it became an international dance craze.

Second, during the period that the cake-walk dance became popular, the musical elements evolved into a multithematic instrumental **march** featuring syncopated melodic rhythms. **Debussy** used this form in *Golliwog's Cake-walk* from his *Children's Corner*.

calando (It.) Dropping or lowering. Instruction to a performer to decrease the volume, and sometimes the tempo, of the music.

Caldara, Antonio (*c*1670-1736) Italian composer. He was immensely prolific with more than 90 operas and other stage works and 43 oratorios. He was born in Venice, probably a pupil of Legrenzi, and sang in the choir of San Marco until 1699 when he moved to Mantua as *maestro di cappella* to Ferdinand Carlo, last Gonzaga Duke of Mantua. Other posts include appointments at the court of Prince Ruspoli in Rome, and *Vicekapellmeister* to the Emperor in Vienna.

In 1708 his oratorio *Il maritro di S. Caterine* was performed at the Chancellery Cardinal Pietro Ottoboni in Rome, on which occasion he probably met **Handel**, **Scarlatti** and **Corelli**.

He wrote dramatic works each year for the Austrian Emperor's nameday and bi-annually for the Empress's birthday, as well as occasional smaller-scale works. An evolution can be detected in his operas and oratorios, perhaps becoming weaker, less dramatic and more easily assimilated. He also composed two volumes of instrumental works and some sacred music (including several masses and more than 500 canons).

Calinda, La Dance found in South America and the United States. It was considered indecent by white colonists, but it remained popular among blacks and Indians. Literary references to it, under slightly varying names, go back to the 17th century.

Callas, Maria (1923-1977) Greek soprano. She was brought up in the United States, but moved to Greece in 1937, where she studied at the Athens Conservatoire. She made her debut at the Athens Opera in 1941 as Tosca. Her career took off after Zentaello engaged her for *La Gioconda* under Serafin in the Arena at Verona (1947). With her penetrating, individual voice and dramatic powers, she was then in demand in Italian theatres for roles such as Aïda, Turandot, Isolde and Brunnhilde. In addition to these 'heavy' roles, her amazing

Maria Callas

vocal versatility meant that she was much in demand for revivals of earlier operas such as **Haydn**'s *Orfeo ed Euridice* and **Gluck**'s *Alceste*. She had a spectacular career, spanning the major opera houses of the world until she was forced to withdraw because of increasing vocal problems. Her last operatic appearance was at Covent Garden as Tosca in 1965.

Callcott, John Wall (1766-1821) English composer and theorist. Entering music as a self-taught amateur, he became a popular composer of **glees** and a respected authority on musical theory, publishing a book, *Musical Grammar*, in 1806. He had a mastery in composition for the unaccompanied voice, but wrote little instrumental music. His most popular glees were *Forgive Blest Shade*, *The New Mariners* and *The Red Cross Knight*. He also composed solo songs and anthems.

calypso (Caribbean) Song-dance form which developed through the Trinidad carnival tradition during the 19th and 20th centuries, combining elements of African, French, Hispanic and British musical traditions.

The song form is thought to have its origins in the canboulay (stick burning/combat processions) of the early carnivals and the bawdy kalinda songs performed by chantuelles which accompanied them. Bands from different neighbourhoods would compete for prowess on these occasions. Calypso lyrics generally contain elements of boasting and 'robber talk' (outrageous lies) stemming directly from these confrontations, and may also concern political, social and personal issues. Calypsonians commonly take heroic stage names, prefixed by Mighty, Lord, etc.

Pan calypso is the popular, instrumental, dance form developed during the 1940s. See also **steel band**.

camera, da (It.) For the chamber, term that came into use during the Baroque period, applied to music considered suitable for performing in a room or chamber (as opposed to the church or the theatre). Since the late 18th century *musica da camera*, or chamber music, has come to imply music for one player to each part.

Camerata (It.) Name given to a group of intellectuals, musicians and literary men who frequented the palace of Count Giovanni de' **Bardi** in Florence in the 1570s and 1580s. The Camerata made music together and discussed poetry, philosophy, astrology and science. Musicians associated with the group included Giulio **Caccini**, Vincenzo **Galilei** and Pietro Strozzi. Galilei, with Bardi's encouragement, was particularly concerned with developing a style of music similar to that of ancient Greek drama.

The name Camerata was also used for a group under Jacopo Corsi whose experiments with musical drama in the 1590s led to the production of **Peri**'s *Daphne* (1597, now lost) and *Euridice* (1600).

Camidge, Michael (1764-1844) English organist, composer and arranger of hymns and other sacred music. He was a chorister of the Chapel Royal, and in 1799 succeeded his father as organist of York Minster and in 1801 he became organist at St Michael-le-Belfry, where he remained until his retirement in 1842.

His *Musical companion to the Psalms used in the Church of St Michael-le-Belfry* became widely known, and pioneered the use of Anglican chant. His first volume of *Cathedral Music* contains services and anthems, including *Lift up your heads* and *O save thy people*.

campana (It.) Bell. Campanella means little bell and has also been used as an alternative word for the glockenspiel. It is also the name of a study by **Liszt** (a piano adaption of the piece of the same title for violin by **Paganini**), in which the sound of small bells is imitated.

campanology Art of bell-ringing.

Campion, Thomas (1567-1620) English

poet, lawyer, composer and physician. His contribution to English song is unique among the Lutenist school in that he wrote the texts for all of his songs.

His earliest published compositions appeared in **Rosseter**'s *Ayres* of 1601, but his best-known songs occur in the four books of airs which he composed (*c*1513-*c*1517). The songs are elegant and poised, with a balance between music and text which is unequalled in the work of his contemporaries. In addition to his output of independent secular solo song, he produced songs for five masques. His lyrics were set by many other composers of the time, including **Pilkington** and **Ferrabosco**. Campion also wrote an important treatise on quantative metre (1602) and a smaller theoretical work concerning the nature of **counterpoint** (1613). An alternative spelling of his name is Campian.

can-can High-kicking dance, popular in French music halls in the late 19th century, which was a development of the **quadrille**. Initially it was infamous for its vulgarity, but became respectable as it was used by composers of operetta (for example, **Offenbach** in *Orpheus in the Underworld*).

cancrizans (Lat.) Crab-like, a term indicating that a musical line is to be heard or played backwards, a technique also defined by the term 'retrograde'. Most often applied to the **cantus firmus** in medieval music and to one of the basic operations in **serial** music.

Cannabich, Johann Christian (1731-1798) German violinist, conductor and composer. A pupil of **Stamitz**, and later of **Jommelli**, he became leader (1759) and then director (1775) of the Mannheim orchestra, where he secured a fine reputation as a conductor. His compositions include many operas and ballets, several symphonies and a variety of chamber music.

Cannon, Philip (1929-) English composer and conductor who studied under Imogen **Holst** at Dartington and then at the Royal College of Music with **Vaughan Williams** and Gordon **Jacob**. He became professor of composition at the Royal College of Music in 1960. Cannon has written various orchestral and choral pieces, three operas and several songs.

canon Principle of composition whereby an entire piece is based on a single melody imitated exactly by one or more voices in unison or at different intervals.

There are many types, distinguished first of all by the temporal distance of the voices (imitation at a minim, a bar, two bars, etc.) and by the interval of imitation (unison, fifth, fourth, etc.).

Another important distinction is between the 'closed' and 'perpetual' types; the latter is represented by the famous Reading rota *Sumer is icumen in*.

In a two-part canon, the terms *dux* and *comes* are used for the leading and the following voices respectively. The *comes* may be an augmentation or a diminution of the *dux*; it may be an inversion of the *dux*; or imitate it in retrograde motion (i.e. working through the melody backwards – the earliest known example of this is Guillaume de Machaut's rondeau *Ma fin est mon commencement*). The combination of inversion and retrograde motion produces what is known as a 'mirror canon', in which the melody sung or played by the *comes* is produced by reading the printed music upside-down. Canons for many voices are known as group canons, and those for two parts against two are known as double canons.

Canon was a very important compositional technique in the works of the 15th-century Flemish masters, who made complex and sophisticated use of it in polyphonic sacred music. It was also used by **Josquin** in many canonic chansons, and by **Palestrina**, who habitually set the last *Agnus Dei* of his masses in canon. By the 17th century, canon had come to be regarded less as a creative than a didactic means; it was the subject of much theoretical study, and formed an important part of a composer's training. Canon was used in popular music, however, in the English catches. In art music, the canon was restored to its former importance by J.S. **Bach** in his *Goldberg Variations* (which contain a series of canons at all intervals from unison to the ninth), the *Musical Offering* and *The Art of Fugue*. **Haydn, Mozart** and **Beethoven** all made use of the full range of canonic technique. Of the composers of the Romantic era, **Brahms** made the most notable use of canon, his interest in which was stimulated by his studies of Baroque and Renaissance music; his 13 canons, Op. 113, show his mastery of the technique.

The 20th century has seen a resurgence of interest in canon, as augmentation, diminution and retrograde motion again became the basic technique in serial composition. **Stravinsky, Schoenberg, Berg** and **Webern** have all made extensive use of canon, and **Messiaen** and **Boulez** have used 'rhythmic canon' in which the voices imitate rhythmic rather than melodic patterns, sometimes in retrograde.

cantabile (It.) Direction to indicate that a piece or line of music should be performed in a singing style, optimally expressive of its melodic qualities.

cantata Vocal work with instrumental accompaniment, usually in several movements and based on a continuous narrative text which may be sacred or secular.

It originated in Italy in the early 17th century as a secular genre; it was usually for solo voice and could contain **strophic arias** or a mixture of **arioso** and **recitative** sections with instrumental ritornellos.

In the early 18th century the form became standardized, consisting of two or three arias connected by recitative – Alessandro **Scarlatti** wrote more than 600 cantatas of this type. By the time of J.S. **Bach**, most Lutheran cantatas were settings of the poetic texts of Pastor E. Neumeister, based on scriptural passages. Bach's cantatas usually open with a fugal chorus, followed by arias and recitatives, and close with a **chorale** setting; they generally use an orchestra.

The cantata became much less important after about 1750, and the term came to be applied to a variety of works. Cantatas for special occasions were written by **Haydn** (*Birthday Cantata* for Prince Nikolaus Esterházy, 1763), **Mozart** (*Die Maurerfreude*, 1785), and **Beethoven** (*Der glorreiche Augenblick*, 1814) and by many later composers, but there was no consistent development of the form. It was one of the prescribed forms for the Prix de Rome, however; both **Berlioz** and **Debussy** wrote cantatas for this prestigious award (Berlioz succeeded in 1830 with *Sardanapale*; Debussy in 1884 with *L'enfant prodigue*). In the 20th century cantatas have been written by various composers including **Boulanger, Hindemith, Bartók, Webern, Stravinsky** and **Britten**.

cantatrice (Fr., It.) Female singer.

Cantelli, Guido (1920-1956) Italian conductor who studied at the Milan Conservatoire and held various conducting appointments in Italy, quickly establishing an international reputation with debuts in New York (1949) and Edinburgh (1950). During the early 1950s he worked with the Philharmonia Orchestra. Shortly after his appointment as musical director of La Scala, Milan, he was killed in an air crash.

Canteloube, Marie-Joseph (1879-1957) French composer who studied under **d'Indy** and subsequently wrote his teacher's biography. His works include two operas and several vocal and instrumental pieces, but he is best known for his *Chants d'Auvergne*, collections of folk songs in the local dialect for voice and piano (or orchestra) which describe his native countryside.

canticle From Latin *canticulum* or *canticum*, song. Song or lyrical passage from the Bible other than a psalm, used in the liturgies of both the Eastern and Western Christian Churches. Canticles taken from the New

Testament are called *cantica majora* (greater canticles). Three of these are used daily: the Benedicite is sung at morning prayer, and the Magnificat and Nunc Dimittis in the evening. Canticles taken from the Old Testament are called *cantica minora* (lesser canticles). In the Roman Catholic rite, these are sung at lauds, one for each day of the week.

The earliest form of music for the canticles was plainchant, and this is still used, mainly in Roman Catholic churches with a strong musical tradition. In the Anglican Church the canticles are sung either to Anglican chants or to specially composed settings, of which there are many, both unaccompanied and accompanied by elaborate organ parts. See also **plainsong**.

cantilena (Lat.) Term applied at different periods to various types of vocal music. It was used as a term for plainchant and, from the 9th century onwards, for secular **monophony**. From the end of the 13th century it was applied to **polyphonic** songs, such as those by Adam de **la Halle** and, in the 14th century, to settings of poetry by English musicians. *Cantilena* was used by 19th-century musicians to describe a sustained lyrical melody, either vocal or instrumental.

cantillation Musical chanting of religious texts or prayers by a solo singer; the term is used particularly for such chanting in the Jewish Church, but is used also in connection with various Christian traditions.

Cantiones Sacrae (Lat.) Sacred Songs. It is most often found as the generic title of collections of Latin **motets** in the 16th and 17th centuries. Among the composers to use this title for their works were **Schütz**, **Byrd** and **Tallis**.

canto (It.) Song. The term's use may be interpreted as an indication of a melody or prominent line in a vocal or instrumental composition. The term *col canto* is interchangeable with the more usual *colla voce* to note that the accompaniment must follow carefully the tempo, dynamics, etc. of the solo line during a particular section.

cantometrics Formal analytical procedure for the cross-cultural study of folk song styles, devised principally by Alan Lomax in an attempt to show how worldwide variations in song style depend upon cultural context. In the published findings, songs of 233 cultures were rated by 37 musical parameters and statistically correlated with ethnographic data, so that universal relations between musical style and social organization were established.

cantor (Lat.) Singer. The term is used in sacred music, where it refers to the leader of singing in Jewish or Christian churches. In the Lutheran church, cantor refers to the director of music in a church (not merely the singing), of whom the most famous was probably J.S. **Bach**.

In modern Anglican churches the cantor is more commonly known as the precentor and leads the singing of psalms, the creed, responses, etc.

cantoris In an **antiphonal** choir (i.e. a choir divided into identically-formed parts), the cantoris refers to the half of the choir that is seated in the stalls on the north side of the chancel, near the stall of the **cantor** or precentor. The second part of such a choir, which sits in the choir stalls facing the cantoris, is known as **decani**.

cantrach (Scotland) Ancient mnemonic aid for acquiring the repertory of **pibroch**, the Highland bagpipe music, in which standard melodic motifs and their embellishments are represented by single syllables. The term is derived from the Gaelic, *canntaireachd*.

cantus (Lat.) Song. In 12th-century usage, the original voice part in a **polyphonic** composition (the added one was called *discantus*, descant).

In the 16th century it came to replace the term *superius* for the top voice of a polyphonic composition. It was also used to describe any vocal composition as, for example, Canti A, Canti B and Canti C, the three volumes of the *Odhecaton* (1501).

Cantus figuratus and *cantus fractus* were used for melodies in measured notation; *cantus compositus* was an alternative term for polyphony.

cantus firmus (Lat.) Fixed melody. Melody in long notes used as the basis for a contrapuntal composition. It refers particularly to the use of such melodies in **polyphonic** compositions of the 14th, 15th and 16th centuries, when it was the most important method of composition.

The *cantus firmus* usually appeared in the tenor voice; it was often derived from plainchant, but could be taken from other polyphonic compositions or even popular song.

From the 17th century *cantus firmus* declined as a method of composition but remained important as a compositional technique in German Protestant church music. A *cantus firmus* taken from a chorale melody formed the basis of chorale preludes for organ and cantata movements by **Buxtehude, Bach** and **Brahms**, among others.

canzona (It.) Song or ballad. The term can refer to either a vocal or an instrumental composition. Sometimes also written *canzone*. There are three main uses of the word.

First, the vocal *canzona* was a 16th-century Italian part song, which involved the **polyphonic** setting of a particular Italian verse form. This poetic form is an important component of the early literature of the **madrigal** and proved popular with composers largely as a result of its flexibility of metre and structure.

Second, the instrumental canzona evolved from its vocal predecessor. The Italian genre *canzon alla francese* originated in the French **chanson**, the rhythms of which were felt to be apt for instrumental transcription. By the end of the 16th century and the beginning of the 17th century, the genre had moved far away from its vocal origins.

Third, it was also used in the 18th century to refer to a light style of solo song.

canzonet Light song form popular in England and Italy from the end of the 16th century and the beginning of the 17th century. The canzonet was polyphonic and tuneful, and written either for several voices (with or without instruments) or for a solo voice and lute accompaniment. The term was loosely applied (some canzonets should be more properly classified as **madrigals**) and by the time of **Haydn**, the term was used for any song written in the English language.

canzonetta Tuneful song of the late 16th century, whose classification is often interchangeable with that of the **canzonet**. Later, canzonetta often referred to a short and simple song (which was not an **aria**) occurring in an opera.

cappella (It.) Chapel. Term with two meanings.

First, in the 14th century, it was a group of clerical singers; after 1600 it came to mean any large group of musicians.

Second, it was originally used for music suitable for performance in church, (*a cappella*) and came to mean any unaccompanied vocal music, whether sacred or secular.

Caplet, André (1878-1925) French composer and conductor who studied at the Paris Conservatoire, where he was awarded the Prix de Rome in 1901. In 1899 he became director at the Odéon and was later appointed conductor at the Boston Opera (1910-1914). A close friend of **Debussy**, he orchestrated *Children's Corner* and *The Martyrdom of St Sebastian*, conducting the work's first performance. He wrote many songs, choral works and other pieces, most of which show some influence of Debussy.

capo, da (It.) From the beginning. Frequently found in all genres of music to indicate that the player should return to the beginning of the composition and perform it once more until the word *fine* appears; this is an instruction to end the performance. The term *da capo* is also often to be found in connection with the vocal **aria**. Its usual abbreviation is D.C.

capo tasto (It.) Device used to shorten the string length on fretted instruments such as the guitar to facilitate transposition without having to alter the fingering. The device consists simply of a bar, covered with either felt or leather, which clips on by various means to the neck of the instrument.

caprice (Fr.) Equivalent of the Italian **capriccio**.

capriccio (It.) Whim or fancy. Used as a title for compositions since the 16th century. *Capriccios* are by definition miscellaneous in character, their one common feature being a disregard for established forms and procedures. There are distinct groups, however: the keyboard *capriccios* of the early 17th century, including those of **Frescobaldi**, which were important in the development of the **fugue**; dances and dance collections of the 17th and 18th centuries; and collections of **cadenza**-like virtuoso pieces or studies written in the 18th and early 19th centuries. A good example of such a collection would be **Paganini**'s Op. 1 (*c*1810).

Carafa, Michele (1787-1872) Italian composer, born in Naples. He was mainly concerned with **opera**, becoming a lifelong friend of **Rossini**. His work had a mixed reception, but was acclaimed in France and, accordingly, Carafa settled there. Although he composed prolifically, his work has not survived. "He made the mistake," claimed Rossini, "of having been born my contemporary."

Cardew, Cornelius (1936-1981) Musician who formed the Scratch Orchestra in London in 1968, a group of mostly unskilled musicians who gathered to improvise, to play collective compositions and pieces by its members. He was a pioneer of the movement within art music which suggested that everyone might be a creative musician. His scores ask that inner reflection and considered sonic action should be integrated as musical composition. Later in his career, Cardew repudiated his early music and devoted himself to the projection of his political views (Marxist) through his music.

Carey, Henry (1689-1743) English dramatist, poet and composer who took composition lessons in order to set his own poems to music. He had a burlesque and witty style, sometimes misunderstood. He wrote a number of stage works, most of them in a popularized operatic form. Many of his works gained great popularity, including, *Britannia*, an opera which replaced the aria with **ballads**, and *Cephalus and Procris* which was further lightened by a pantomime interlude. *Nancy*, written in 1739, was the most original of his works. It was a sequence of interval songs inspired by Italian **intermezzos** and remained popular until the end of the century.

carillon Set of tuned bells, usually mounted in a tower, which work mechanically. The skill of tuning them has taken many years to perfect. The bells may be operated by a baton keyboard, or by perforated paper rolls or cassettes, and the music ranges from simple hymn tunes to specially composed pieces.

Carissimi, Giacomo (1605-1674) Italian composer. From 1625 he was organist at Tivoli Cathedral and from 1627 *maestro di cappella* at the Cathedral of St Rufino, Tivoli. In 1629 he was appointed *maestro di cappella* of the Collegio Germanica, Rome, with responsibility for music at the church of St. Apollinaure.

Carissimi was one of the first writers of oratorios, and developed the form from its origin as a long motet into a lengthy, multi-sectioned work. Of his 14 oratorios, the most renowned was *Jephte*, the central lament of which was more famous in its day than any of **Monteverdi**'s, and which influenced many succeeding composers such as **Charpentier, Handel** and **Purcell**.

His works are striking, simple but effective. He was one of the composers responsible for the triumph of tonal over modal composition. He wrote more than 100 motets, some for large forces in the style of **Palestrina**, some for small forces with *basso continuo* after Viadana. His *Missa l'homme armé* was the last of its type. He wrote over 200 secular cantatas.

carmen (Lat.) Often translated as song or poem. Carmen is probably best known in this usage as the result of its appearance in the title of the cantata *Carmina Burana* (Songs from Beuren) by Carl **Orff**. It is sometimes used in early music manuscripts to denote the vocal line of a composition, or the highest voice part.

carol The modern popular meaning of the word – a festive Christian song associated with Christmas – is only one of a number of meanings the term has had over the centuries; the Christmas association in particular is quite recent. Several types of carols can be distinguished.

The term itself derives from the medieval French *carole*, a round dance accompanied by a song, one of the most well-known of which is the anonymous tune to which Raimbault de Vaqueiras set the words *Kalenda Haya*.

The 15th-century English courtly carol has been described as the only indigenous English musical form. Several of these lively polyphonic works survive with words and music intact – still more with words only. The form is characterized by a refrain or burden, which is sung at the beginning and at the end, and repeated between the several verses. The text may celebrate a person or event, such as the well-known Agincourt song *Deo Gratias Anglia*, but many of them are for Christmas, such as *There is no rose of such vertu*.

Most European countries have a tradition of folk carols (French *Noëls*), some of very ancient origin, combining Christian with pre-Christian symbolism, such as in the English carols *The Holly and the Ivy* and *I saw Three ships*. Other 'traditional' carols may be of more recent origin, such as *God Rest ye Merry Gentlemen* and *Past Three O'clock*.

The present interest in 'Christmas carols' dates from the end of the 19th century, with the revival of interest in folk carols, many of which were being collected and popularized at the time. New seasonal words were set to old tunes, such as J.M. Neale's *Good King Wenceslas* (to the tune of *Tempus Adeste Floribus* from *Piae Cantiones*) and G.R. Woodward's *Ding Dong Merrily on High* (to the tune of *Bransle de l'officiel* from Arbeau's *Orchésographie*). Many of the older composed 'carols' such as *Hark the Herald Angels Sing* and *While Shepherds Watched their Flocks by Night* are more properly Christmas hymns.

In the 20th century, carols have formed a very good opportunity for composers to handle a small-scale popular style which has a good chance of being performed in Christmas carol services and concerts which are extremely popular in Britain. Among the most enduring modern carols are Benjamin Britten's *A ceremony of Carols*, Boris Ord's *Adam lay y-bounden*, Holst's *In the Deep Mid-winter* and David Wilcocks's and John Rutter's contributions to the series *Carols for Choirs*.

Carpenter, John Alden (1876-1951) American composer who studied composition at Harvard. On graduating in 1897 he became a businessman but continued to compose, studying with **Elgar** in 1906 and later with Bernard Ziehn. His compositions are largely influenced by American popular music and include a jazz pantomime *Krazy Kat* (1921); a ballet based on Oscar Wilde's *The Birthday of the Infanta* (1919); two symphonies; and several song cycles. His most important work is the ballet *Skyscrapers*; a depiction of modern life in the United States, it includes three saxophones and traffic lights operated by a keyboard.

José Carreras

Carreras, José (1946-) Spanish tenor who, after studying in Barcelona, made his debut in **Verdi**'s *Nabucco* and later won the Verdi Competition. He has since performed worldwide and is considered as ranking among the best operatic tenors in the world.

Carrillo, Julian (1875-1965) Mexican musician of Indian origin who studied the violin, composition and acoustics at the conservatoire in Mexico City. As a violinist he led the Leipzig Gewandhaus Orchestra under **Nikisch**. At the same time he developed the theory and practice of microtones and incorporated them in orchestral pieces which were performed and recorded, attracting considerable attention. **Stokowski** commissioned a *Concerto for 1/3 tone piano*, and this is complemented by symphonies and concertos, as well as instrumental pieces, both with and without microtones.

Carse, Adam (1878-1958) English composer and historian of instruments, Carse was educated at the Royal Academy of Music and later became professor of harmony there. His music is lightweight and it is more for his studies of instruments and their use that he is remembered. He wrote two important books tracing the history of the orchestra.

Carter, Elliott (1908-) American composer who studied with Walter **Piston** at Harvard University and with Nadia **Boulanger** in Paris (1932-1935). In his early works he was a neo-Classicist, showing the influence of **Stravinsky** in the ballet score *Pocahontas* (1938-1939) and the *Holiday Overture* (1944). However, he moved away from neo-Classicism with his piano sonata (1945-1946) and the sonata for cello and piano (1948). In both of these works he concentrated on exploiting the character of the instrument itself, its tone colour and resonances. Since then, Carter has produced many works in different genres, including string quartets, *Variations for Orchestra* (1965), the Double Concerto for harpsichord, piano and two chamber orchestras (1961), and the Piano Concerto (1964-1965). In more recent works, Carter has experimented with metre and rhythmic relationships.

In addition to his composition Carter has written widely, and a volume of his *Collected Writings* was published in New York in 1977.

Carulli, Fernando (1770-1841) Italian guitarist and composer of more than 400 works. Carulli was probably the first great guitar virtuoso, in an age when the guitar was not an accepted 'serious' instrument. He was originally a cellist, but gave this up in order to teach himself the guitar. After several foreign tours he settled in Paris in 1808 and began teaching. He also wrote a treatise on the art of accompanying on the guitar, as well as publishing many study pieces.

Caruso, Enrico (1873-1921) Italian tenor, considered to be the greatest of this century. Caruso made his operatic debut in 1894 in Naples but achieved his first real triumph in 1901 in *L'elisir d'amore* at La Scala, Milan. Subsequently he sang in Britain, Spain, Germany, Austria and

Enrico Caruso

France, but performed most often for the Metropolitan Opera, New York (1902-1920).

Caruso's voice was characterized by its baritone-like timbre, coupled with a smooth tenor range. His high notes impeccable, intonation exact and breath control superb, Caruso excelled in lyric opera such as **Puccini**'s *Tosca* as well as in lighter 19th-century opera. He was also a notable interpreter of **Verdi**. Caruso made many recordings during his lifetime.

Cary, Tristam (1925-) English composer whose main interest lies with electronic music and who has done much to make the genre more widely known and accessible through his writing, teaching and composition. He founded the electronic studio at the Royal College of Music, first of its kind in Britain. After a conventional music education at Trinity College of Music he became known in the 1950s through his music for film, television and theatre. He has also written chamber music, electronic music for performance in most accepted genres and has published two books on electronic music.

Casadesus, Robert (1899-1972) French pianist and composer. As a student at the Paris Conservatoire he was awarded a first prize for piano. Casadesus travelled widely as a concert pianist and his many recordings include the complete works of **Ravel**. As a composer he wrote a number of works for the piano including *24 Preludes* (1924) and *Six Pieces* (1938), a work for two pianos intended for performance with his wife Gaby, with whom he formed a piano duo.

Casals, Pablo (or Pau) (1876-1973) Catalan cellist, conductor, pianist and composer. Casals' mastery of the cello led to a new public appreciation of the instrument in the first half of the 20th century. Casals' technique combined a beautiful tone with technical surety, already apparent in recordings of the 1920s of trios by **Beethoven**, **Brahms** and **Haydn** made with **Thibaud** and **Cortot**. In 1919 Casals founded the Orguestra Pau Casals in Barcelona, launching his career as a conductor, which was only halted by World War II, when Casals moved to Prades. He gave many concerts in aid of the French Red Cross, but always refused to play in any country that recongized the Franco regime. In the 1950s, Casals began a new series of recordings, directed music festivals in Puerto Rico and Perpignan, and gave

Pablo Casals

master classes in many musical centres. In 1962 he launched a peace campaign with his own oratorio *El Pessebre*, which was performed worldwide. Casals was generally acknowledged in his lifetime as one of the greatest cellists in the world.

Casanova, André (1919-) French composer who originally studied law as well as music. His compositions include a piano concertino, first performed by Yvonne **Loriod** in 1959, as well as symphonies and operas.

Casella, Alfredo (1883-1947) Italian composer and pianist who came from Turin and, after showing early talent as a pianist, began to study composition. He was more drawn to French and Russian music than German, and he studied for a time with **Fauré**. Later influences included **Debussy**, **Ravel**, **Bartók** and **Stravinsky**.

In 1915 he returned to Italy where he was to have a decisive influence on Italian musical taste, partly by introducing French music to Italian audiences and partly by attracting students, (both of piano and composition), such as **Malipiero**, **Pizzetti** and **Respighi**, who were to be influential. Together they formed the *Società Italiana de Musica Moderna* which promoted many concerts and in which Casella was a driving force. His own music changed in style many times and is uneven in impact. His *Scarlattiana*, based on themes from sonatas by Domenico **Scarlatti** is still performed, as are some of his piano pieces.

Cassadó, Gaspar (1897-1966) Catalan cellist and composer. He attended the Barcelona Conservatoire and in 1910 moved to Paris to study with **Casals**. Cassadó began his concert career in 1918, giving recitals with such celebrated pianists as Harold Bauer and **Rubinstein**. His compositions show the influence of **Falla** and **Ravel** and include string quartets, a piano trio and *Rapsodia Catalana* for orchestra.

cassation Informal 18th-century instrumental form, most common in Austria and neighbouring regions. Usually of a light nature, cassations were not limited to 'serious' evening concerts, and they were often performed in the open air, as a sort of street entertainment. Cassations could be scored for full orchestra or smaller groups of instruments, and would have an indeterminate number of movements in divertimento style. The movements were often shorter, more numerous and of a lighter nature than in symphonic compositions. There are examples of writing in this genre by **Mozart** and **Haydn**.

Cassuto, Alvaro Leon (1938-) Portuguese composer and conductor. He studied composition in Lisbon, Hamburg and Darmstadt, and conducting at the Vienna Conservatoire. He has worked as assistant conductor of the Lisbon Gulbenkian Chamber Orchestra and the American Symphony Orchestra, and in 1970 became permanent conductor of the Radio Orchestra of Lisbon. Cassuto was the first Portuguese composer to write a serial work for orchestra, *Sinfonia Breve No. 1* (1958). In 1969 he won the Koussevitzky prize for composition.

castanets (Sp.) Small hand-held percussion instrument usually used by dancers to provide their own musical accompaniment in the **bolero**, **fandango** and related dance forms. They consist of two shell-shaped pieces of wood hinged together by a piece of string which the player passes between his thumb and first finger, tapping out a rhythm and producing a clapping sound. Orchestral castanets may be mounted on a short handle.

Castelnuovo-Tedesco, Mario (1895-1968) American composer and pianist of Italian birth. After studying piano and composition at the Florence Conservatoire, he worked as a freelance throughout the inter-war period. His Jewish origins forced him to move to the United States in 1939, where he was to settle permanently. He was a prolific composer and an active teacher.

His works are still largely unpublished and include eight operas (e.g. *The Importance of Being Earnest*, 1962), many film scores, ballets, oratorios, overtures, songs and chamber music.

castrato (It.) Male singer castrated before puberty in order to preserve his alto or soprano voice into adulthood (also called *evirato*). The enlarged chest and small larynx of the *castrato* combined to enable superior breath control and powerful vocal production in these ranges. This practice was common in Italy from the 16th to the early 19th centuries, becoming more popular in the 17th century with the rise of opera. Composers of this period, such as **Handel**, often included prominent parts for *castrati*, ensuring the elevation of some such singers to international stardom. Italian churches often employed *castrati*; the Sistine Chapel used them from the late 16th century until 1903. The last famous *castrato* was probably Alessandro Moreschi (1858-1922).

Castro, Juan José (1895-1968) Argentinian composer and conductor who studied in Buenos Aires and, on winning the Europa prize, moved to Paris to study with Vincent **d'Indy** at the Schola Cantorum. As a conductor he held many posts including director of the Teatro Colón. His works include *Sinfonia Argentina*, operas and ballet music. His opera *Proserpina y el extranjero*, first performed in Milan in 1952, was awarded the Verdi prize in 1951.

Catalani, Alfredo (1854-1893) Italian opera composer, important for his influence on the **verismo** school. He wrote many operas, the most successful of which was *La Wally*, first performed at La Scala in 1892. His music is often considered loose in construction, although moments of inspiration shine through.

catch 17th- and 18th-century English **round** or **canon**, generally written for men's voices. Many, including some of **Purcell**'s finest, were written to bawdy texts, and have only recently been considered suitable for revival. The first published collection of catches was Thomas **Ravenscroft**'s *Pammelia* (1609).

Causton, Thomas (*c*1520-1569) English composer whose anthems and sacred services are in John Day's *Certain notes set forth in foure and three parts*: the first published collection of English cathedral music (1565). His psalm settings are included in Day's *The whole psalmes in foure parts* of 1563. His style is simple and chordal with some interesting harmonic effects.

Cavalieri, Emilio de' (*c*1550-1602) Italian composer and choreographer. He was stage manager of the Florentine *Intermedii* of 1589, the most lavish of such series ever conceived. He wrote several pieces for it, including the final chorus *O che nuovo miraculo* which became one of the greatest 'hits' of the Renaissance. Many contemporary arrangements were made, with titles *Aria del grand Duca*, *Aria di Fiorenza*, *Ballo di Palazzo* etc. He was composer of the earliest surviving play set entirely to music, the *Rappresentatione di Anima et di Corpo...per recitar cantando* (1600). The printed score was the first to use a **figured bass**. He also claimed to be the inventor of the *stile recitativo*, although in this he was in competition with **Caccini**. His sacred compositions include some fine Lamentations and Responsories for Holy Week.

Cavalli, (Pietro) Francesco (1602-1676) Italian composer. His main works are his operas, of which he composed nearly 30 for the Venetian opera houses. He was the successor in this respect to Claudio **Monteverdi**. He entered the *Capella* of St Marco in 1616, under Monteverdi's direction; in 1639 he became second organist and in 1665, first organist. It was, however, his operas to which he directed most of his energy. His first success was *Le nozze di Teti e di Peleo*. His greatest contemporary success came with *Gascione* (1649). His *Egisto, Callisto* and *Ormindo* have achieved popularity in recent years because of their revival by Raymond **Leppard**.

cavatina Term used in 18th-century opera for a short solo piece, simpler in structure than an **aria** and without repetition, e.g. *Porgi amor* in **Mozart**'s *The Marriage of Figaro*, 1786. In 19th-century Italian opera cavatinas were used for elaborate arias requiring some virtuosity, such as *Una voce poco fà* in **Rossini**'s *The Barber of Seville*, 1816; these were often paired with a **cabaletta**. *Cavatina* is also used occasionally as a title for song-like instrumental pieces.

Cavendish, Michael (*c*1565-1628) English composer of lute-songs and madrigals, published in a single volume in 1598. One of his madrigals, *Come gentle swains*, makes use of a refrain, "Long live fair Oriana", an idea borrowed from Giovanni Croce and later included in countless English madrigals from Morley's anthology, *The Triumphs of Oriana* (1601).

cebell Musical genre, popular in England between 1690 and 1710, of pieces based on the *Descente de Cybelle*, a chorus with orchestral accompaniment from the last act of Lully's *Atys* (1676). Among the 21 surviving cebells are an open arrangement by John Bannister (1695), the anonymous contrafactum *Lord, how men can claret drink*, and Purcell's *Trumpet Tune, called the cebell*. A cebell is characterized by its duple metre starting at the half bar and often having episodes with a running bass moving in crotchets or quavers. Alternative spellings are cibell and sebell.

Ceccata, Aldo (1934-) Italian conductor, mainly of opera, who studied for a time with de **Sabata**. He has conducted at most of the major opera houses of the world and was also principal conductor of the Detroit Symphony Orchestra during the 1970s.

Cecilia, St Christian saint thought to have been murdered in Sicily by the Romans in the 2nd or 3rd century AD. She became associated with music in Italy in the 16th century after a misreading of a Latin text; she was soon being depicted in contemporary paintings with musical instruments, and the legend of her musical prowess grew. Music festivals commemorating St Cecilia began to appear annually in many European cities, the first on record being at Evreux, Normandy in 1570. The Feast of St Cecilia is celebrated annually on 22 November.

Saint Cecilia

cédez (Fr.) Instruction to a performer to slacken the pace of the music; it is equivalent to the Italian term *ritenuto*.

ceilidh (Scotland, Ireland) Gaelic, night-long, informal gathering for the performance of songs, instrumental music and dance.

celempung (Java) Plucked zither with 13 pairs of strings passing over a single bridge. The tapered box resonator stands on four legs.

celesta Percussion instrument with keyboard invented by Auguste Mustel in 1886. A piano-like action causes steel plates to be struck by hammers, producing a light, ethereal sound. **Tchaikovsky** used a celesta for *The Dance of the Sugar-plum Fairy* in his ballet *The Nutcracker*, 1892, as did **Bartók** in his *Music for Strings, Percussion and Celesta*, 1936. Its range extends five octaves upwards from C; music for celesta is written on two staves (as for piano), and an octave lower than it sounds.

Celibidache, Sergiu (1912-) Romanian conductor who studied in Berlin and in 1945 was appointed principal conductor of the Berlin Philharmonic Orchestra, a post he held until 1952. He has attracted much attention for his curious but effective baton technique and has been guest conductor in many countries including North and Latin America.

cello Common term for the violoncello, a bowed four-stringed instrument. The bass member of the violin family, it is pitched one octave below the **viola**, with strings tuned to C-G-D-A. It has a compass of more than three octaves. The instrument is large and is therefore held between the knees of the player, supported on a spike known as a peg. Cellos are to be found in every orchestra and string quartet. Concertos for cello have been written by such composers as **Elgar** and **Dvorák** and probably the most notable cello player of the 20th century was Pablo **Casals**.

Cellier, Alfred (1844-1891) English conductor and composer. He began his career as organist of St Alban's, Holborn, and later became conductor in several theatres in London and Manchester. As a composer, he is often compared to **Sullivan**; his best-known works are operettas – *Dorothy* (1886) and *The Mountebanks* (1892) to a libretto by W.S. Gilbert.

Celtic harp Instrument of the harp family, considerably smaller than the classical harp, having between 24 and 34 strings. It has a flat soundboard, rounded back and a hand-operated mechanism of blades or levers for tuning the strings. The tradition of harp playing had almost died out in Ireland until the early 19th century, when there was a revival of interest. Now it again holds a central position in the traditional music of Ireland in the accompaniment of song and as a solo instrument. The Celtic harp is sometimes also known as the Irish harp.

cembalo (It.) Term with two meanings.

First, it is an abbreviation of *clavicembalo* (harpsichord).

Second, in Italian popular music, it denotes the tambourine.

cent Exact measure of a musical interval by which 100 cents equal one tempered semitone, and consequently an octave comprises 1200 cents.

ceòl beag/ceòl meadhonach/ceòl mor (Scotland) Little, middle and big music, with reference to Highland bagpipe repertory. *Ceòl beag* includes marches, strathspeys and reels; *ceòl meadhonach* includes Highland folk songs, lullabies and slower marches; *ceòl mor* includes salutes to individuals, laments, special tunes in honour of important historical events and the **pibroch** repertory.

Certon, Pierre (?-1572) French composer influenced by **Josquin des Prez**. He held a number of appointments, including that of clerk at Notre Dame and the Sainte-Chapelle. He was at the latter from 1532 until his death. He composed parody masses, motets and some chansons in the style of **Jannequin**.

Cesti, Antonio (1623-1669) Italian composer and singer. In 1637 he was ordained a priest, but conflict between his musical and priestly duties, particularly with the success of his operas, caused him to renounce his vows in 1659. With *Orontea* (1649), *Alessandro vincitor di se stresso* (1651) and *Il Cesare Amanti* (1651) performed in Venice, his success was assured. From 1652 to 1657 and 1659 to 1665 he was at the court of Innsbruck, where many of his stage works were produced, including his largest, *Il pomo d'oro*. In 1668 he went to Florence as *maestro di cappella* to the Tuscan court.

His 15 stage works were written mainly for private theatres, and so their scale is grand, incorporating dance and often elaborate stage machinery. He also composed some 74 secular cantatas and five sacred choral works.

Chabrier, Emmanuel (1841-1894) French composer, largely self-taught but influential on subsequent generations of French composers including **Debussy, Ravel** and **Poulenc**. Although he came under the spell of **Wagner**, his lasting achievement was to re-orientate French music away from Germanic influences and to return to French ideals of conciseness and clarity, as well as encouraging musical **impressionism**. *España* (1883) is perhaps his best-known piece. He also wrote cantatas, songs and vocal music, and several operas and operettas.

chaconne Dance in triple time of Latin American origin, which became popular in Spain and Italy in the early 17th century, soon spreading to northern Europe. The dance typically features a basic progression of chords (I-V-IV-V) acting as melodic or harmonic ostinatos; some composers used this chord sequence to generate a series of melodic themes in the bass, which were repeated over and over again (i.e. ground **bass**). Other composers used a repeated theme but moved it through the instruments, or used a series of different melodies. J.S. **Bach** wrote a chaconne for solo violin which has been arranged for several instruments, notably for the piano in the celebrated transcription by **Busoni**. See also **passacaglia**.

chacony Old English term for **chaconne**. **Purcell** wrote several pieces with this title.

Chadwick, George Whitefield (1854-1931) American composer and teacher who studied in Boston, Leipzig and Munich. In 1897 he became director of the New England Conservatoire. As a composer he played an important part in trying to create a distinct American style, breaking with the German Romantic tradition.

Chagrin, Francis (1905-1972) British composer of Romanian birth. He studied in Bucharest, with Nadia **Boulanger** and **Dukas** in Paris, and with Mátyás **Seiber** in London. He earned his living from composing film music, produced a small output of compositions showing a variety of modernist influences and conducted his own ensemble. He was instrumental in founding the Committee (later Society) for the Promotion of New Music (1943), set up to encourage young British composers.

Chailly, Luciano (1920-) Italian composer who first studied the violin in Ferrara and later composition in Milan. He has worked as artistic director at both La Scala, Milan, and at the Teatro Regio in Turin, and has taught at the Milan Conservatoire. His compositions include operas, ballets and chamber works and show something of the influence of **Hindemith**, with whom he studied in 1948.

Chaliapin, Fyodor Alternative transliteration of **Shaliapin**, Fyodor.

chalumeau (Fr.) Term with three meanings.

First, it is a reedpipe, or the chanter of a bagpipe.

Second, it is the single-reed orchestral wind instrument from which the clarinet developed. The instrument was called for in the scores of **Fux** and others in Vienna from 1704, and it was also used in two concertos by **Vivaldi**.

Third, it is also commonly used for the lowest register of the clarinet.

chamber sonata Late 17th and early 18th century sonata intended to be played in a secular rather than sacred setting. The movements were generally dance types, typically following a prelude there would be, say, an allemande, corrente, sarabande, gigue and gavotte. The chamber sonatas of **Corelli** (Op. 2, 1685 and Op. 4, 1692) are typical early examples. The Italian equivalent is *sonata da camera*. See also **church sonata**.

chamber orchestra Small orchestra of about 25 players which, until about 1800, was the normal orchestra size. Since then the symphony orchestra – which is twice the size or more – has been more commonly written for, although several 20th-century composers have produced works specifically for the chamber orchestra.

Chaminade, Cécile (1857-1944) French pianist and composer. She is best known for her songs and piano music (more than 200 works). Her other works include chamber music, a *symphonie dramatique*, *Les Amazones* (for chorus and orchestra) as well as an opera.

Champagne, Claude (1891-1965) Canadian composer, best known as the leader of a nationalist tradition in Canadian music, who incorporated the folk music of his country into many types of composition Fiddle music was a major influence, but he also had a rigorous academic training, mainly in France. He was one-time professor of music at McGill University and founded the Montreal Conservatoire. His music is influenced by the so-called Impressionist composers; several of his pieces for orchestra reflect the Canadian landscape.

change-ringing Ringing of a set of bells in an order determined by mathematical permutations rather than melody. Each bell is assigned a number (the bell with the highest pitch being number one), and the bells are then rung in various sequences. The basic principle is that bells that become adjacent in one sequence then change places in the next. The methods of mathematical permutation by which sequences avoid repetition have traditional names, e.g. 'Plain hunt', 'Plain bob', 'Grandsire' and 'Stedman'. Change-ringing originated in England in the 17th century. It enjoyed a revival in the second half of the 19th century and now flourishes throughout Britain.

changgo/changko (Korea) Double-headed, hourglass-shaped drum with lashed skin heads. The head to the right of the player is played with a stick, while that to the left is played with the palm of the hand or a small, round-headed mallet. It is the main percussion instrument in traditional Korean music, featuring in **sijo** and in **p'ansori**.

Chanler, Theodore (1902-1961) American composer and critic who studied piano and composition at the New York Institute of Musical Art and with **Bloch** at the Cleveland Institute. After studying for three years with Nadia **Boulanger** in Paris, he returned to the United States to work as a music critic and teacher. His compositions include ballets, choral music and songs, displaying polytonality alongside more lyrical writing.

chanson (Fr.) Song, broadly any song with French text. It is most commonly used to refer to French **polyphonic** art-songs of the Middle Ages and Renaissance, but may describe the secular songs of the **troubadours** and **trouvères** of the 12th and 13th centuries; the *airs de cour* of the late 16th and 17th centuries; and popular songs of the 17th, 18th and 19th centuries, usually short **strophic** songs on amorous subjects, sung and sold in the streets. In the 19th and 20th centuries it came again to be applied to art music, and also to folk-song.

In the 14th century, *chansons* were usually in three parts, two of which were probably intended for instruments, and written in one of the poetic *formes fixes* (*ballade*, *rondeau*, *virelai*); these are typified in the work of **Machaut**. Towards the end of the 14th century there arose the Mannerist school (including Johannes **Ciconia** and Matteo da Perugia), the adherents of which wrote chansons of great rhythmic and contrapuntal complexity. The intricacies of Mannerist writing were replaced by a simpler style which culminated in the work of two Burgundians, Guillaume **Dufay** and Gilles **Binchois**, the finest *chanson* composers of the first half of the 15th century. These were in turn succeeded in the second half of the century by Antoine **Busnois** and Johannes **Ockeghem**, in both of whose works the treble-dominated style gave way to a more equal-voiced polyphonic style. This eventually led to the use of imitative counterpoint based on melodic motifs, which is found in the chansons of **Josquin des Prez** in the 16th century.

The 16th century also saw the gradual abandonment of the *formes fixes*, and the wide distribution of *chansons* through the publication of printed music. The Paris-based printer Pierre Attaignant printed 70 *chanson* collections between 1528 and 1549, most of them written in a new, simple homophonic style by French composers such as Claudin Sermisy and Clement **Jannequin**. Later in the century the French firm Le Roy & Ballard succeeded Attaignant as the most important publisher of *chansons*; composers included Jacques **Arcadelt**, Claude **Goudimel** and Roland de **Lassus**. This period also saw the rise of the *chansons spirituelles*, with moralistic or sacred texts.

chant Term with two meanings.

First, it is a harmonized melody used in the Anglican rite for singing psalms and canticles. The melody is traditionally written in four time, but is often made metrically irregular to accommodate differing word and phrase lengths. The Roman Catholic Church uses **Gregorian chant**, which evolved from plainsong or plainchant. This traditionally features an unaccompanied monophonic melody line, is rhythmically free, and has its own notation system.

Second, it is the French term for song, or singing.

chanty Alternative spelling of **shanty**.

chapel-master Term used on the continent of Europe (but rarely in England) to describe a person in charge of music in a chapel, be it a private chapel at court, a collegiate chapel or a cathedral. A great many of the composers of the 16th and 17th centuries earned their livings as chapel-masters. The duties varied from chapel to chapel, but they invariably included conducting the choir and organizing music for the chapel services, and often playing the organ. The composition of music for the chapel was not necessarily part of the contract, but the job invariably left time for the incumbent to compose, and indeed, he was most often expected to, because it was considered a mark of great prestige to have a well-respected composer as one's chapel-master. The European equivalents are: (Ger.) *Kapellmeister*; (Fr.) *maître de chapelle*; (It.) *maestro di cappella*; (Sp.) *maestro de capilla*.

Chapel Royal Choir retained by successive monarchs in England to perform services for the Royal Family. At first it was largely a peripatetic body, travelling with the royal household, but in 1702 it was established permanently in St. James's, where it remains today.

The members of the choir were members of the royal household and their conditions were so good that the choir attracted singers of the highest standard. The size of the Chapel Royal has fluctuated throughout history, depending on the interest of the monarch of the time, but there would sometimes be as many as 32 men and 16 children. The size and ability of the choir encouraged many English composers to write works specifically for it, and these include John **Dunstable**, William **Byrd**, John **Bull**, Orlando **Gibbons** and Thomas **Tomkins**.

The Chapel Royal has suffered a decline since the largely unmusical Hanoverian Dynasty in 1714, and although it is still maintained today there are only six men and ten children (drawn from the City of London Boys' School).

Chapí, (y Lorente) Ruperto (1851-1909) Spanish composer who studied with Arrieta at the Madrid Conservatoire where, in 1869, he was awarded first prize in harmony. On leaving, he worked for a time as cornet player in a theatre orchestra, and most of his compositions are for the stage. His one-act opera, *Les Naves de Cortés* (1874), was awarded a three-year government grant, which enabled him to study in Rome, Milan and Paris. He wrote more than 100 other one-act operas (**zarzuelas**), including *La Hija de Jefté* (1876) and *Musica Classica* (1880).

character piece Short, 19th-century composition which embodies a specific programmatic idea or expresses a particular mood. Most character pieces are for piano solo and have titles that indicate their brevity and intention (bagatelle, impromptu, etc.)

Schubert's *Impromptus*, **Mendelssohn**'s *Lieder ohne Wörte* and many of **Chopin**'s piano pieces are character pieces. **Schumann** developed the idea further by choosing separate names for individual pieces, highlighting their mood, and by grouping them together in cycles representing a unified whole. Thus we have his *Novelletten*, *Nocturnes* and *Albumblätter* and the cycles *Papillons* and *Carnaval*. **Debussy**, with his carefully titled *Préludes*, is the direct inheritor of these ideas.

These characteristic pieces are most often in ternary (ABA) form, with A and B representing two contrasting moods within the general programmatic idea. Their precursors are to be found in the harpsichord suites of François **Couperin**, in which one basic motif can be heard to dominate a whole movement.

charleston Dance particularly associated with the 1920s. The charleston had its origins in African dance and was adapted by black Americans at the turn of the century. It was popularized through its inclusion in shows and musicals, (for example, *Runnin Wild*, 1923) and by the mid-1920s had become an international craze. Its complicated footwork and side kicks were eventually incorporated and simplified in the quick-step.

Charleston

Charpentier, Gustave (1860-1956) French composer whose style was influenced by **Wagner** and **Berlioz**. He studied at the Paris Conservatoire under **Massenet** and was awarded the Prix de Rome for his cantata *Didon* in 1887. Most of his works were composed in the 1880s-1890s, including *Impressions d'Italie* and *La vie du poète*. He is best known for his opera *Louise*, which was first performed in 1900, and was made into a film in 1936 under Charpentier's supervision.

Charpentier, Marc Antoine (1645-1704) French composer who studied in Rome with **Carissimi**, where he learned the Italian style. On returning to France he found himself opposed by **Lully** and at odds with the French nationalist style. In spite of Lully's jealousy (which kept him from a position in the royal household) he was employed by Molière to write incidental music for the troupe, which was to become the *Comédie Française*. Charpentier was also favoured by the royal household and the Jesuits, who appointed him music master at their most important church, St Louis. He was honoured with the post of *maître de musique* at the Sainte-Chappelle in 1693. He composed a number of small-scale sacred dramas, oratorios, grand motets and one full-scale opera, *Médée*.

chasse (Fr.) Hunt. Term with two musical meanings.

First, it is used to describe instruments originally used for hunting, e.g. *cor de chasse* – hunting horn.

Second, it is a medieval piece whose text concerning hunting is reflected in the canonic nature of its composition. See also **caccia**.

Chausson, Ernest (1855-1899) French composer who, while influenced musically by César **Franck** and **Wagner** was also deeply involved in contemporary literary movements and in painting. His reaction to fashionable trends in literature is shown in his memorable setting of Bouchor's *Poème de l'amour et de la mer* for soprano and orchestra, which is a landmark in the setting of symbolist poetry. His assimilation of the wandering harmonies of Franck and Wagner is not always successful but there are many passages of striking originality in his works. Among the most successful are the concerto for piano, violin and string quartet and the *Poème* for violin and orchestra.

Chávez, Carlos (1899-1978) Mexican composer. He was essentially self-taught, but met **Varèse** and others in New York in the 1920s. He was conductor of the Mexico Symphony Orchestra (1928-48) and director of the Mexican National Conservatoire (1928-1935). He was instrumental both in stimulating music in his own country and in taking Mexican music abroad. He used the influences of pre-Colombian South America in several of his works, for example the *Sinfonia India* and the ballet *Xochipili-Macuilxochitl*, which was written for an ensemble of native instruments.

chef d'attaque (Fr.) Leader of the first violins in an orchestra.

chef d'orchestre (Fr.) Conductor of an orchestra.

Cheltenham International Festival Founded in 1945, the Cheltenham Festival takes place during the summer, originally announced as a festival of British contemporary music, and even though this has now become diluted with other events, it still retains this original intention. It has been directed since 1969 by John Manduell and since the opening year, when **Britten** conducted the first concert performance of the *Sea Interludes* from *Peter Grimes*, hundreds of first performances of works by British composers have been given.

cheng (China) 16-stringed, plucked zither. The strings are traditionally of silk, but more recently copper or steel strings have been used; they are stretched over moveable bridges and are tuned to an anhemitonic pentatonic scale.

chengcheng (Indonesia) Pair of cymbals, a group of cymbals or a single large cymbal used mainly in the **gamelan** gong orchestra of Bali.

Cherkassky, Shura (1911-) Russian-born American pianist who studied with his mother and with Josef **Hofmann** at the Curtis Institute in Philadelphia. Cherkassky made his debut and soon embarked on a series of world-wide concert tours. He is best known for his performances of the Romantic repertory and for his recordings of Soviet music.

Cherubini, Luigi (1760-1842) Italian composer who worked mainly in France. During his 20s he left Italy for London, where he had some success with his operas. In Paris, his entry into influential circles was aided by Viotti and he introduced many Italian operas there. His opera *Médée* used bold Romantic techniques to capture the psychological conflict of its heroine, and its strength has ensured it a place in the repertory. His church music, of which he wrote a large amount, has considerable power, in particular his *Requiem*. Cherubini's music (in particular *Faniska*) had a profound influence on **Beethoven**, whom he met in Paris.

chest of viols Set of instruments, usually stored in a cupboard or chest. In the 16th century this was a usual household item among the wealthy. The complete set (consort) of viols corresponded to the range of the bass to soprano voices, and consisted of two of each of three sizes, these being the treble, tenor and bass (also known as the viola da gamba).

chest voice Lower register of the voice, produced from the chest, as opposed to the higher register – **head voice**.

Chevreuille, Raymond (1901-1976) Belgian composer. Besides composing he worked as an acoustical engineer for Belgian Radio, where he was also controller of French music broadcasts. Not surprisingly, his compositions include a number of scores for radio, such as *D'un diable de briquet* for which he was awarded the Italia Prize in 1950.

Chicago Symphony Orchestra American symphony orchestra, founded in 1891 by Theodore Thomas and originally named the Chicago Orchestra. Between 1906 and 1912, it was named the Theodore Thomas Orchestra and after that time took its present name. It is the third oldest orchestra in the United States. Its conductors have included **Kubelik** (1950-1953) and **Solti** (from 1969). The orchestra has toured and recorded widely.

chiesa, da (It.) In Baroque music, sonatas or cantatas designated for use in church, as opposed to those marked *da camera* which were for secular use. Sonatas marked *da chiesa* included more serious abstract movements than those marked *da camera*, which had more movements based on stylized dance forms.

Chilcot, Thomas (*c*1700-1766) English organist and composer whose life centred on his position as organist at Bath Abbey, which he held from 1728 until his death. Although his compositions were well known in his lifetime, very little of his music was published and no manuscripts survive. His works include six suites for harpsichord and 12 harpsichord concertos.

Child, William (1606-1697) English organist and composer, predominantly of church music. His works include many anthems, services and psalm settings, as well as some secular instrumental pieces and catches. From the Restoration until his death, Child was a court musician to King Charles II.

Childs, Barney (1926-) American composer and teacher. Childs was largely self-taught, although in the 1950s he studied at Tanglewood with **Chavez** and

Copland, and privately with Elliot **Carter**. His academic background was literary rather than musical and his compositions explore improvisatory and aleatoric techniques. They include *Interbalances* (1960-1963), works for wind ensemble, two symphonies and choral works.

ch'in/qin (China) Seven-stringed fretless zither, plucked with the finger tips and nails. The body of the instrument is made of wood painted with many layers of protective lacquer. The open strings are tuned to an anhemitonic pentatonic scale and are pressed by the left hand, guided by 13 embedded studs to change pitch. It is the oldest of the indigenous Chinese instruments and is used extensively as a solo instrument.

ching (Thailand) Small pair of teacup-shaped, hand-held cymbals used as time-markers, named after the sound they emit when hit together. They are employed in virtually all forms of traditional Thai music and especially in the **pi'phat** ensemble.

Chisholm, Erik (1904-1965) Scottish composer and conductor. He began his career as conductor of the Glasgow Grand Opera Society in 1930, where he introduced audiences to works outside the usual repertory, giving first performances of *The Trojans* and *Beatrice and Benedict* by **Berlioz**. In 1946 he moved to South Africa, becoming professor of music at the University of Capetown. He has composed operas, two symphonies and concertos for violin and for piano.

chitarra (It.) Guitar. See also **chitarrone**.

chittarone Member of the **lute** family. It was larger than other lutes and was developed to play **continuo** parts. It had a double neck to carry a second set of strings of the bass notes. Historians disagree as to whether the chittarone was synonymous with the **theorbo**, another double-necked or arch lute which appears in the music of that period. By 1600, the chittarone was the favourite instrument for accompanying the human voice and there was also a certain amount of solo music written for it.

chiuso (It.) Term with two meanings.
First, it is used in horn music to mean stopped, indicating that notes should be stopped with the hand.
Second, it is a medieval term meaning the second-time ending in music, the first being called *aperto*.

choir Term with four meanings.
First, it is a group of singers.
Second, it is a position in a church reserved for the choir in the above sense.
Third, it is a group of similar instruments, sometimes forming part of a larger ensemble (e.g. brass choir).
Fourth, it is an abbreviation for **choir organ**.

choir organ In England, the lowest manual of the organ, traditionally operating a set of pipes placed behind the player if the organ was in a gallery, but also used in other organs.
In the 19th century, sweet-toned solo stops, rather than a balanced chorisis, rendered the manual less suitable for its original purpose of providing a foil to the other manuals.

chöömij (Mongolia) See **xoomij**.

Chopin, Frédéric (1810-1849) Polish composer, mainly of piano music. He began his musical career as a pianist, renowned for his soft tone and subtle nuances, and this early love for the piano was carried through to his compositions. He became one of the major forces in 19th-century piano music and influenced many composers in the 20th century. He, in turn, was influenced by several other composers, but **Hummel** may be singled out, who showed Chopin new aspects of keyboard virtuosity; and **Bellini**, from whose operatic arias Chopin transferred the highly ornamented **bel canto** lines to the piano keyboard.

Frédéric Chopin

These come out particularly in the *Nocturnes* and in the slow movements of the two piano concertos.

The dances of Chopin's native Poland (such as the **mazurka** and **polonaise**) were also a major influence and his work had much appeal among his audiences, particularly during the many years he spent in Paris.

Chopin composed largely at the keyboard, and much of his music derives from pianistic ideas rather than abstract concepts. His reliance on the sustaining pedal was as much a part of his compositional technique as it was a part of his piano playing. Among his best-known compositions are the 24 Preludes (1839), two sonatas (one containing the celebrated *Funeral March*), two sets of studies (including many known by names, such as *The Revolutionary*, the *Black Key* study and the *Winter Wind*), scherzos and waltzes. There is also a small amount of music for other instruments, including a cello sonata and some songs.

choragus Official post at the University of Oxford dating from 1626. The choragus was appointed to conduct music practices twice a week.

choral Term with three meanings.

First, it is something of or belonging to a choir.

Second, it is a hymn tune or sacred melody, more commonly spelled **chorale**. A choral cantata is thus a cantata written for choir, whereas a chorale cantata is a cantata based on a sacred melody.

Third, in German, it refers to the hymn tunes of the German Protestant Church, and is thus equivalent to the English word chorale.

chorale Hymn of the German Protestant Church. Luther was very influential in building up the repertory of chorales and favoured vernacular texts and simple, tuneful melodies. Many were adaptations of **Gregorian** hymns and medieval German religious songs.

Written for congregational use, chorales have simple tunes, many based on secular songs, but often have complex contrapuntal harmonizations. One of the first important collections was that published by Lukas Osiander in 1586. It was different from many previous collections in that Osiander placed the melody at the top of the texture, rather than in the tenor line. Many chorale melodies are familiar today, such as *Nun danket alle Gott* and *Jesu meine Freude*. J.S. **Bach** made a great many chorale harmonizations and also used chorales as a basis for many other types of composition, such as chorale **fantasias**, chorale **fugues** and chorale **motets**.

chord Group of two or more notes sounded together; the basic element in harmony. Chords are named according to the **intervals** of which they are formed (e.g. six-four chord, containing a fourth and a sixth above the lowest note) and, in a harmonic context, according to the degree of the scale on which they are built (e.g. dominant seventh, a chord built on the dominant and containing the seventh above it).

The common chords of traditional harmony are **triads**, consisting of a third and a fifth above the bass. These may be used in **inversion**, giving a six-three chord (first inversion) or a six-four chord (second inversion). Other notes, such as the seventh or ninth above the root, may be added. In modern music, chords may be formed by any combination of intervals, including some highly dissonant ones.

Triads in: root position, first inversion and second inversion

chording Term with two meanings.

First, it is the spacing of **chords** in a piece of music, or the **intonation** of a chord.

Second, in performance, it is the degree of unanimity with which the notes are sounded.

chordophone Generic term for instruments in which the sound is produced by means of stretched strings fixed at both ends. It includes all classes of zithers, lutes, guitars, violins, viols and harps.

chord symbol Term with two meanings.

First, it is the symbol written below a stave or system of notation which identifies the **chord**. Roman numerals are usually assigned to each chord, indicating which degree of the scale the chord is built on. Major chords are conventionally assigned upper-case symbols; minor chords, lower-case. Lower-case letters a, b, and c denote root position, first and second inversion respectively, whereas superior numbers indicate intervals other than those of the basic **triad** occurring in the chord.

Second, in music for guitars and guitar-like instruments, it refers to the grids that represent the strings and frets, with dots to indicate where the fingers should be placed for each different chord; or just the names of the chords. These may be written underneath text alone, or underneath text and a piano part.

choreographic poem Extended piece of music composed in the form and spirit of a dance, e.g. **Ravel**'s *La Valse*.

choreometrics Analytical method for the cross-cultural study of dance, developed by Alan **Lomax** and Irmgard Bartenieff from a similar system devised for song styles (**cantometrics**). It attempts to show how various types of dance movement are related to the dynamic qualities of everyday life in different cultures.

choro (Port.) Term loosely used to describe many kinds of ensemble music in which one instrument dominates the others in a virtuoso manner. Originally a Brazilian term for a group of serenaders, and then for their music (*musicas de choro*), the *choro* is often used by **Villa-Lobos** and other Brazilian composers.

chorus Group of singers who perform together either in unison or in parts, often accompanying soloists or as an adjunct to a group of instruments. By extension, this term also refers to a work written for several voices, such as the *Hallelujah chorus* in **Handel**'s *Messiah*.

Chorzempa, Daniel (1944-) American organist who studied at the University of Minnesota and at Cologne. He has received much critical acclaim for his recitals on the piano and harpsichord in addition to his organ playing. His repertory is wide and his playing notable for its colour and energy. His performances of the works of **Liszt** are especially admired.

Chou, Wen-Chung (1923-) Chinese-born American composer and teacher. He moved to the United States in 1946 and originally studied architecture before going on to study music at the New England Conservatoire, Columbia University and privately with **Varèse**. His music combines Chinese melodic patterns with Western orchestration and he is influenced by Chinese philosophy, painting and poetry. This is most obvious in *The Willows are New*, and *Yü Ko* and in *Metaphors* for wind ensemble, based on the *I Ching*.

Christoff, Boris (1918-) Bulgarian bass who studied in Sofia, Rome and Salzburg and made his debut in **Mussorgsky**'s *Boris Godunov*, a work with which he has been associated ever since. His extraordinary acting ability is matched by an excellent diction and depth of tone. His performance of **Verdi** is highly esteemed.

chromaticism In its broadest sense, a term that refers to the use of notes not belonging to the key in which a piece or passage is written. Melodically, it applies to **motifs** based on sequences of adjacent semitones; in this sense it was a feature of ancient Greek music.

From the late Middle Ages, chromaticism was regarded mainly as an expressive means within an essentially diatonic framework, as used by the Italian madrigalists.

In the Baroque period, composers often used chromatic motifs, and chromatic chords such as the diminished seventh. In the works of the Romantic composers, particularly **Wagner**, chromaticism came into its own. Further developments were the whole-tone language of **Debussy** and, ultimately, the **twelve-note** technique of **Schoenberg**.

chromatic scale Sequence of twelve consecutive semitones. An instrument on which the chromatic scale is available is said to be chromatic and can play in any key.

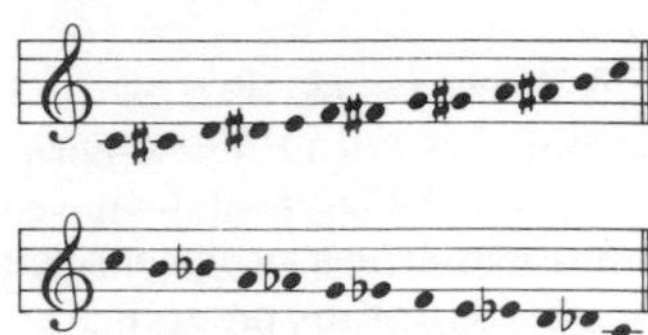

Chromatic scale

Chung, Kyung-Wha (1948-) Korean violinist who studied at the Juilliard School in New York and in 1968 made her debut there with the New York Philharmonic Orchestra. She has frequently performed as a soloist and in chamber ensembles in Europe and is much admired for her vibrant and warm tone. Her recordings include many concertos and the solo violin music of **Bach**.

church cantata English equivalent of the Italian **cantata da chiesa**.

church modes Eight modes (referring both to scale and to melodic type) under which **Gregorian chant** was classified.

The authentic modes were those that can now be obtained by playing D-D′, E-E′, F-F′ and G-G′ on the white notes of a keyboard instrument; D, E, F and G were the *finals* of the modes.

The plagal modes were obtained by beginning a fourth below the final of the authentic modes. In the 16th century the notes A and C′ were added, giving four more modes (two authentic, two plagal).

Although their meaning was different, the names most commonly given to these modes today are borrowed from ancient Greek modes: Dorian (D-D′), Phrygian (E-E′), Lydian (F-F′), Mixolydian (G-G′), Aeolian (A-A′) and Ionian (C-C′); the plagal modes take the prefix 'hypo-'.

church sonata (Italian: *sonata da chiesa*) Sonata that was considered suitable for church use (as opposed to a **chamber sonata**). The term came into use in the second half of the 17th century. Generally the form consisted of four movements in two pairs – slow, fast, slow, fast – the slow movements acting as introductions to the fast ones. There is some evidence that as plainsong declined, church sonatas were played in its place at services.

ciaccona (It.) Equivalent of the French **chaconne**.

cibell Alternative spelling of **cebell**.

Ciccolini, Aldo (1925-) Italian-born pianist. When only nine he enrolled at the Naples Conservatoire and at the age of 22 became professor of piano there. In 1942 he made his debut with **Chopin**'s F minor concerto and subsequently went on to win many prizes, including the St Cecilia prize in 1948. He moved to France in 1949 and is much admired for his performances of the French repertory, especially **Ravel** and **Debussy**. His recordings include the complete works of Erik **Satie** and the **Saint-Saëns** piano concertos.

Ciconia, Johannes (*c*1335-1411) French composer who, working in both France and Italy, fused the French *ars nova* with the Italian 14th-century style. The 'Ciconia style' continued to be apparent in music for some 20 years after his death. By 1350 he was in the service of Alienore de Commynges, and by 1358 of Cardinal Albonnoz, in whose retinue he travelled to Italy. In 1372 he returned to his home town of Liège. His surviving works include eight Glorias and four Credos for the mass, 12 motets, three French songs (including *Le ray du soleil*), 15 Italian songs (including *La flamma del to amor*) and four songs in the 14th-century madrigal style. He also wrote three musical treatises. One is lost, but his *Nova Musica* and its later reworking, *De proportionibus*, survive. They contain distilled teachings of Pythagorus, **Boethius**, Jehan de Murs and Marchetto di Padova.

Ciléa, Francesco (1866-1950) Italian composer and teacher who studied at the Naples Conservatoire from 1881 to 1889. After two rather unsuccessful attempts at composing opera (*Gina*, 1889, and *La Tilda*, 1892), he supported himself by teaching, first at the Naples Conservatoire and then at the Reale Istituto Musicale in Florence. He went on to compose three more operas, *L'Arlesiana* (1897), *Adriana Lecouvreur* (1902) and *Gloria* (1907). *Adriana Lecouvreur* achieved a certain amount of success and is still performed.

Cimarosa, Domenico (1749-1801) Italian opera composer, educated at the Conservatorio di St. Maria di Loreto, where he developed as a gifted singer and composer. His first opera, *Le stravaganze del conte*, was heard in Naples in 1772. By the mid-1780s, Cimarosa had established himself as one of the most popular **opera buffa** composers of his day. He was *maestro di cappella* at the court of Catherine II in St Petersburg from 1787 to 1791, and spent a year in Vienna where he composed his most famous opera *The Secret Marriage* (*Il matrimonio segreto*), before returning to Naples in 1793. In addition to his vast output of nearly 70 operas, Cimarosa also composed sacred works, concertos and keyboard sonatas.

cimbalon Hungarian **dulcimer**. The smaller and older variety is similar to the English instrument. A larger and recently invented version allows chromatic notes to be obtained and is fitted with a damper pedal. The cimbalon has been adopted by dance bands and is used occasionally in symphonic works.

Cimbalon

cinema organ Type of organ used in cinemas between 1925 and 1950 to accompany silent films and for entertainment during intermissions. The instrument often featured some unusual **stops** producing novelty sounds (e.g. motor horn). The demise of this instrument rapidly followed the invention of motion pictures with soundtracks. It is also known as a theatre organ.

cipher Name given to the continued sounding of an organ pipe caused by a mechanical fault.

cipher notation System of notation in which numbers are used as a substitute for staff notation, advocated, among others by Rousseau in the 18th century.

cither Alternative spelling of **cittern**.

cithern Alternative spelling of **cittern**.

cittern Small-bodied stringed instrument of the same family of instruments as the lute and guitar, differing from these in that it had metal rather than gut strings. It was plucked with a quill or plectrum rather than the fingers, and was used widely throughout Renaissance Europe for music of all kinds.

The cittern was developed in Italy in the late 15th century from the citole, and passed out of use in the mid-18th century with the development of new metal-strung instruments. It is now being made and played again because of a revival of interest in medieval and Renaissance music. Alternative spellings are cither and cithern.

City of Birmingham Symphony Orchestra (CBSO) Orchestra that started life as the City of Birmingham Orchestra in 1920, when **Elgar** conducted its first concert with a programme of his own works. The orchestra was renamed in 1948 and gave its first London concert that year. Supported by the Birmingham City Council, the CBSO gave a regular Thursday evening and Sunday afternoon series as well as touring the Midlands area. The Sunday series has now been dropped, but there is still a Thursday evening concert series in Birmingham Town Hall.

The orchestra rose to prominence under Louis Frémaux (1969-1978). It developed unusual programmes and made a large number of recordings. The CBSO's reputation became even greater after the appointment of Simon **Rattle** as its conductor in 1980.

claribel Sweet-sounding 8-foot wooden organ stop known also as clarabella or claribel-flute.

clarinet Woodwind instrument with a cylindrical tube and single-reed mouthpiece. It was devised by J.C. Denner in Germany in the early 18th century, developing out of the **chalumeau** or 'mock-trumpet', but did not become established in the orchestra until the time of **Beethoven**.

In addition to its orchestral use, the clarinet has always been very popular as a chamber music instrument, in military bands, dance orchestras and folk music. It is a **transposing instrument** and appears in several sizes, the most popular being in B♭ (that is, sounding a tone lower than notes as written) and A. Other members of the clarinet family are the basset horn (sounding a fourth below the B♭ clarinet), the bass clarinet (sounding an octave below the B♭ clarinet) and the contrabass clarinet (in two sizes, sounding either a fifth or an octave below the bass clarinet).

Clarinet

clarino Term with two meanings.
First, it is the high register of the **clarinet**.
Second, it is a virtuoso method of trumpet playing practised by trumpeters in the 17th and 18th centuries, trained specially and exclusively in the art of producing the highest harmonics, where they form a continuous scale. Such players were able to play the very difficult trumpet parts in, for example, **Bach**'s cantatas on the Baroque natural trumpet. Today these passages are normally played on the Bach trumpet, a short, straight, three-valve instrument introduced by J. Kosleck in 1884, designed to play *clarino* parts in Bach's works.

Clarke, Jeremiah (1674-1707) English composer and organist. He began his career as chorister of the Chapel Royal and was appointed organist of Winchester College in 1692. At various times he was also vicar-choral at St Paul's Cathedral and organist at the Chapel Royal. His compositions include anthems, odes, harpsichord pieces and incidental music for the stage. His best-known work is the *Trumpet Voluntary*.

Clarke-Whitfield, John (1770-1836) English composer and organist who held a number of appointments as church organist before becoming Professor of Music at Cambridge in 1841. His compositions are conservative in style and show the influence of **Handel**. His two **oratorios**, *The Crucifixion* and *The Resurrection*, were well known in their day. He also edited the music of Handel and **Purcell**.

clarsach Small Celtic harp used for the accompaniment of folk song. The Gaelic name is *clairseach*.

claves Cylindrical hardwood blocks originating in Cuba and the Antilles. They are struck together, with the cupped palm of the hand providing resonance. They were introduced into concert works by **Varèse** and used since by **Copland** and **Berio** (in *Circles*), among others.

clavichord Stringed keyboard instrument in which the strings are activated from below by brass blades or 'tangents', which are fixed upright on the key levers. The clavichord first appeared in the 15th century and in some countries was in use until the early 19th century. It is a quiet but expressive instrument which many people used in preference even to the early piano. J.S. **Bach** is said to have preferred the clavichord to any other keyboard instrument, apart from the organ.

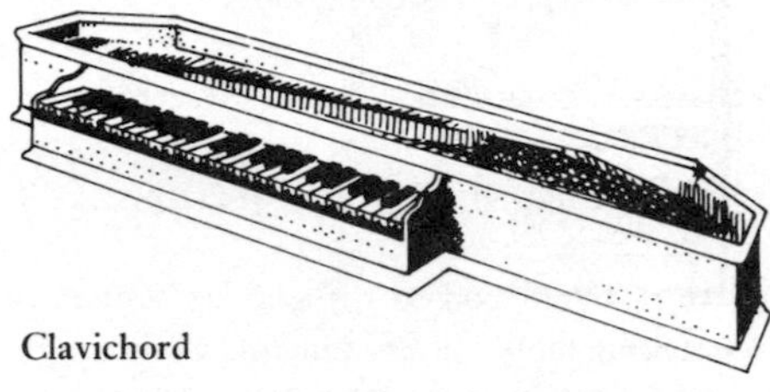

Clavichord

There are two kinds of clavichord: 'fretted' and 'unfretted'. In the unfretted variety, each note has its own string (or pair of strings). However, on the earlier fretted clavichord, two or more notes shared the same string, with the tangent striking it a little nearer or further away from the bridge. This made the earlier instrument very compact.

clavier (Fr.) Keyboard of an instrument. In the Baroque period, as *Klavier*, it was a generic term in German for keyboard instruments (clavichord, harpsichord, spinet, organ), as in **Bach**'s *Das Wohltemperierte Clavier*; sometimes it was used to denote the clavichord in particular. In modern German, *Klavier* means piano.

clavicembalo (It.) Alternative term for **harpsichord**.

clavicytherium Upright harpsichord. The first recorded use of the term is *c*1460. The world's oldest surviving keyboard instrument is a clavicytherium from the late 15th century, now in the Royal College of Music, London. The advantages of the upright soundboard are that the instrument takes up less space and the sound is pro-

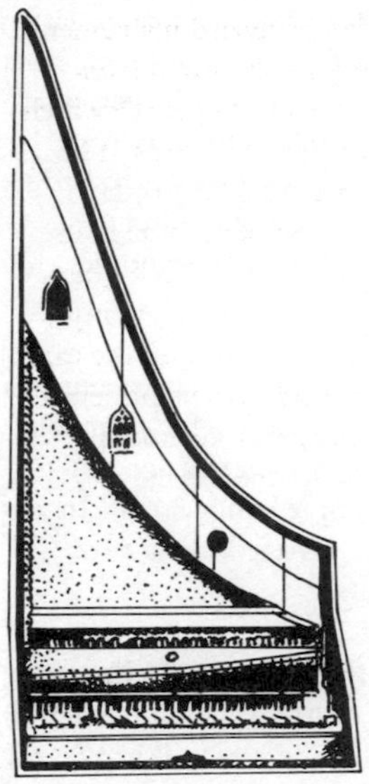
Clavicytherium

jected better into the room, but the fact that the jacks cannot return to their resting place under their own weight tends to give a heavy, uneven action, so the instrument has never proved as popular as the horizontal harpsichord. Clavicytheria nevertheless continued to be made until the 18th century.

clef Symbol placed at the beginning of a stave which sets the pitch represented by the lines in relation to itself. Three types are generally used today; the G (or treble) clef, the F (or bass) clef, and the C clef; their position on the stave indicates the note after which they are named. The clefs originally consisted of the letters G, F and C; the signs now in use are stylizations of these. In music after 1750, the G and F clefs are invariably used in the same positions. The C clef is commonly used in either of two positions: on the middle line of the stave it is referred to as the alto clef, and on the fourth line it is referred to as the tenor clef.

G clef F clef C clef

Clementi, Muzio (1752-1832) Italian composer, keyboard player and teacher who travelled to London in 1766, where he made his debut in 1770. He is most important as a composer of piano sonatas. **Beethoven** thought highly of him in this capacity, and he is now considered to be the first composer to write successfully for the piano, with its specific qualities (as opposed to the harpsichord). His Gradus ad Parnassum (a series of 100 piano études, published in 1817) is particularly well-remembered.

Cleveland Orchestra American orchestra founded in 1918 and resident at Severance Hall since 1931. Conductors have included Sokolov (1918-1933), Szell (1946-1970) and **Maazel** (from 1972). The Cleveland Orchestra has recorded widely and is generally considered to be of world standard.

Cliburn van, Lavan Harvey Jr (1934-) American pianist who studied with Rosina Lhévinne at the Juilliard School in New York after having made his debut at the age of four. He went on to win a great number of prestigious awards, including first prize at the Tchaikovsky Competition in Moscow. He is best known for his performances of the Romantic repertory and for the competition he founded in 1962 in Texas.

close Alternative term for **cadence**.

close harmony Use of chords that are spaced so that the parts lie as close together as possible: in four-part harmony there is no more than a twelfth between the outer parts. See also **Barber shop**.

cluster Group of notes, adjacent or close together, and usually strongly dissonant, forming a **chord**; also known as a tone-cluster. Clusters are most often used in keyboard music, where they may easily be played with the fist or forearm. They were used first by Henry **Cowell**, and later by **Bartók**, **Ives**, **Stockhausen** and **Ligeti**.

Coates, Albert (1882-1953) English conductor and composer who studied conducting with **Nikisch** at the Leipzig Conservatoire. After being conductor of Elberfield Opera (1906-1908) he held appointments at Dresden and St Petersburg. On his return to England, Coates worked regularly with the London Symphony Orchestra, with whom he conducted the first performance of *The Planets* by Gustav **Holst** as well as that of the First Symphony by **Bax**. His compositions include the operas *Samuel Pepys* and *Pickwick*.

Coates, Eric (1886-1957) English composer and viola player. After studying at the Royal Academy of Music, Coates joined the Queen's Hall Orchestra as principal viola (1912). From 1919 he concentrated solely on composition, and his works, although light in mood, are generally admired for their craftsmanship. They include more than 100 songs, several orchestral suites and marches. The best-known of his works is undoubtedly the *Dambusters March*.

cobza (Romania) Plucked lute found in parts of Moldavia. It has a pear-shaped, wooden resonator with a very short neck terminating in a large rectangular peg-box, bent back from the fingerboard. Its eight to twelve strings are tuned in fourths or fifths and are set in four courses of two or three strings each. It usually accompanies the violin.

coda (It.) Section at the end of a composition which is not an integral part of the structure but serves to round off the piece. In a polyphonic work, it may involve some of the voices continuing against held notes in one or more of the others, particularly against a pedal point.

In a fugue, the coda is anything that is played after the last complete statement of the subject. In sonata form, the coda is anything that occurs after the recapitulation (assuming that the recapitulation is an exact repeat of the exposition). **Beethoven** often wrote very lengthy codas which used thematic material in such a way as to be like second development sections. After Beethoven the coda became a standard feature of sonata form.

codetta (It.) Short **coda**. It usually refers to material added to a section of a movement (particularly the exposition of a sonata) rather than to a complete movement. In a fugue it refers to a passage linking two entries of the theme.

Cohen, Harriet (1895-1967) English pianist who studied with Matthay and at the Royal Academy of Music. She was well known for her performances of **Bach**, and also gave several first performances of contemporary works, including the piano concerto by **Vaughan Williams** and many piano solos by **Bax**. In 1948 a hand injury cut short her concert career, although she continued to play left-handed until 1961. Her recordings include **Elgar**'s Piano Quintet and piano music by Bax. In 1961 the Harriet Cohen International Prizes were founded.

Cohn, Arthur (1910-) American composer who studied at the University of Pennsylvania and the Juilliard. He has held a number of appointments, including director of the Fleisher Music Collection at Philadelphia, and has worked as conductor and editor. Cohn's compositions include four string quartets and a Percussion Concerto (1970).

col (It.) With the, an abbreviation of *con il*. This is also written as *coll'* and *colla*, for example *colla destra, sinistra* (with the right, left hand).

Coleman, Edward (?-1669) English composer and counter-tenor. He sang in *The Siege of Rhodes*, the first English opera (1656), and was employed at the court of Charles II. His compositions include songs published in the volumes entitled *Select*

Musicall Ayres and Dialogues (1653-1669).

Colgrass, Michael (1932-) American percussionist and composer. He studied at the University of Illinois, and after graduating won a number of prestigious awards. His compositions include works for percussion, music theatre and songs. They display acquaintance with a wide variety of styles, including atonality and jazz.

col legno (It.) In string instrument playing, striking the strings with the bow-stick instead of playing with the hair of the bow.

colophony Rosin for the bow of a stringed instrument.

coloratura (It.) Colouring, a term common in 18th- and 19th-century writing and applying to elaborate decoration, notated or improvised, of a vocal part. It also applies to a singer with a high range and fluid style capable of performing virtuosic arias, such as those for the role of the Queen of the Night in **Mozart**'s *The Magic Flute*.

colotomic Originally used by the ethnomusicologist Jaap Kunst to describe the timing structure of Javanese **gamelan**, in which particular gongs mark off sections or subdivisions of a complete time or metrical cycle. Many instruments in Far-Eastern cultures (e.g. Tibet, Korea, Japan and Indonesia) are said to have a colotomic function when, by virtue of a particular rhythmic event, they punctuate phrases or cycles.

colour organ Organ in which the projection of visible colours is in some way connected with various sound colours. A. Wallace Rimington (1854-1918) invented a colour organ which projected colours to music played on another instrument, intensifying the colour in higher octaves. Since then several other variants have been produced, some giving a visual representation of rhythm. None has been really successful, probably because of the fallacious nature of direct parallels between colour and sound.

combination tones Acoustical phenomena, consisting of a third tone heard when two loud tones are sounded together. They are produced not by external factors but by the workings of the inner ear, and are thus sometimes described as subjective tones.

come (It.) As; used in music in phrases such as *come prima*: as before.

comma of Pythagoras Minute difference in pitch between twelve perfect fifths and seven octaves if the intervals are pure. On a well-tempered instrument there should be no difference.

commodo (It.) Comfortable. The term describes a tempo and is used as a qualification to other tempo marks, as in *allegro commodo*. An alternative spelling is *comodo*.

common chords Major and minor **triads**. In American usage, major triads only.

common metre Standard poetic metre in hymns corresponding to a quatrain in which the first and third lines are of eight syllables, and the second and fourth lines are of six, all in iambic rhythm.

common time 4/4 time, indicated in the time signature by a letter C. This is derived from the half-circle used in medieval music to denote duple division of breve and semibreve; it is not C for common.

Common time

community singing Massed singing of popular songs or chants by the public at a meeting or sporting event. It has existed for many centuries in one form or another. Psalms were at one time sung by crowds outside churches, and even today hymns are sometimes sung at football matches.

Community singing is also an important activity in school music in many countries.

compass Range of an instrument or voice, or the range of notes used in an instrumental or vocal part.

composer's counterpoint Alternative term for **free counterpoint**.

composition Act of writing a piece of music. Originally composers were anonymous; no idea of self-expression was connected with their work. In the Western world, composition began as the addition of new music and words to the **alleluia** of the anonymous **plainsong** rite and composers often remained unknown. Later composers began to acknowledge their art, taking control of the various parameters of a piece of music. In the Renaissance, **instrumentation** was often not the concern of the composer; pieces were described as 'apt for voices or viols'. In the **Baroque** era, embellishment was often considered the job of the performer, and composers wrote 'skeleton' movements over which **ornamentation** was presumed. Later the trend was for more and more precision on the part of the composer – tampering with their notated intentions was discouraged rather then expected.

In the 20th century, composers have again involved the performer, introducing **aleatoric** techniques and elements of improvisation with a greater or lesser degree of control.

composition pedal Foot-operated lever of an organ that activates a pre-selected combination of stops.

composition piston Thumb-button or toe-stud on an organ which the player can use to activate a pre-selected combination of stops.

compound interval **Interval** that is larger than an octave. For example, the interval between C in one octave and F in the next octave above is a compound interval, and can be described as an eleventh or as a compound fourth.

compound time Time signatures that divide each main beat into three, such as 6/8 (two beats of three quavers each), 6/4 (two beats of three crotchets each), or 12/8 (four beats of three quavers each), as opposed to **simple time**, in which the beat divides into two.

comprimario (It.) Operatic role of secondary importance, or the singer performing this part.

con (It.) With. Used to link a qualifying term to a principal instruction, e.g. *allegro con brio*, quickly with spirit. Depending on the subsequent word, it may be written *cogli*, *coi*, *col*, *coll'*, *colla* or *colle*.

concert Musical performance, usually by a large group of musicians playing to an audience. A solo or duo performance is normally termed a **recital**, except in pop and rock music, where even solo performers give concerts. Public concerts, with admission by ticket, became established during the late 17th century, and the demand for this type of performance led to the building of many purpose-built concert halls throughout Europe from the 18th century onwards.

concertante (It.) To act together. It signifies music with a **concerto**-like element. *Sinfonia concertante* indicates music in symphonic style, but with soloists, in the manner of a **concerto grosso**. In keyboard **sonatas**, the term implies an essential, or **obbligato**, string part, rather than an optional one.

concert band Band consisting of woodwind, brass and percussion (but without strings), which is popular in the United States. It is similar to the British **military band**. **Schoenberg** and **Hindemith**, as well as many American composers, have written works for this instrumentation. See also **wind band**.

Concertgebouw Amsterdam's foremost concert hall, opened in 1888. Its resident orchestra, also founded in that year, bears the same name. Principal conductors there have included Bernard **Haitink** and Eugen Jochum.

concertina Portable, bellows-operated, free-reed instrument. The English concertina, developed by Charles Wheatstone in 1829, has two hexagonal heads connected by an expandable bellows, each casing containing a keyboard of buttons, which correspond to individual notes.

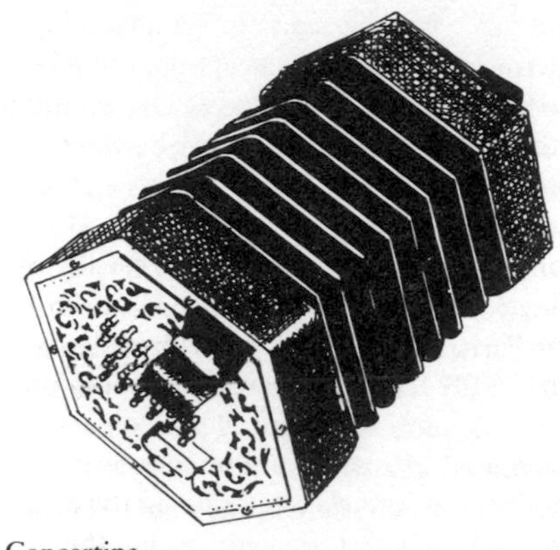

Concertina

The German concertina, constructed by Carl Friedrich Uhlig in 1834, has rectangular ends and five buttons on each side, which control different pitches depending on whether the bellows are moving in or out.

Although the extensive Victorian repertory for the concertina, by composers such as Giulio Regondi, is not often heard nowadays, the instrument has remained popular among folk musicians. Charles **Ives** and Percy **Grainger** have composed for it.

concertino In a **concerto grosso**, the small group of soloists, as opposed to the **ripieno**, or full body of strings. In the 19th and 20th centuries, it has also been used to indicate a small-scale (and usually rather light) **concerto**.

concertize American musicians' and promoters' term for arranging a **concert** or concert tour.

concertmaster Derived from the German *Konzertmeister*, the American term for the **leader** of an orchestra, who is responsible for deciding on bowing for the strings, for performing solo passages, and for communication between conductor and players.

concerto (It.) Derived from the verb concertare, to compete. Its earliest use was in the late 16th century when concerto pieces employed opposed groups of singers or players. Giovanni **Gabrieli**, organist of St Mark's, Venice, was famous for his ecclesiastical concerti which used different groups of musicians in the various galleries of the church. At about the same time, **Monteverdi** wrote concerto madrigals: secular pieces similarly involving various groups.

In its late Baroque and Classical form a concerto is a work for solo instrument(s) and orchestra, usually in three movements, fast-slow-fast. The soloist(s) is given virtuoso material, contrasting with the simpler orchestral parts, and an unaccompanied **cadenza** (originally improvised, but from the mid-19th century onwards, usually notated by the composer) at the end of the first movement may give further opportunity for virtuosity.

concerto grosso Type of orchestral work pioneered by **Corelli** (and others) during the 1680s and 1690s, contrasting a small group of string players (**concertino**) with the full string section (**ripieno**). The concerto grosso was developed from the **trio sonata** (two violins with continuo) by reinforcing sections of the music with full strings, and the form became very popular during the first part of the 18th century, particularly in England, where **Handel** composed many pieces based on the Corelli model. The concerto grosso subsequently fell into disuse, although 20th-century composers such as **Bloch** and **Martinu** have resurrected the form.

concert overture One-movement orchestral work composed specifically for the concert hall, rather than as an introduction to an opera or oratorio. The practice began in the early 19th century, when **Mozart**'s opera overtures and **Beethoven**'s stage overtures were played as separate items in concerts. Later, **Mendelssohn**'s *Hebrides* overture, with its evocative depiction of the sea, set the trend for this type of composition, the titles of which tend towards descriptive, historical, or literary reference.

concert pitch Following the (almost) universally accepted international agreement on a pitch standard in 1939, this has been set at A′ = 440 hertz (cycles per second). This is a semitone higher than the A′ = 415 Hz, used nowadays by most players in 'authentic' performances of **Baroque** music, but is on the whole lower than the standard pitch used in the 19th century.

concord Interval or chord that is considered to be harmonious and musically stable, unlike a **discord**, which demands resolution by moving to a concord. In medieval music theory, concordance was restricted to perfect intervals (fourths, fifths and octaves), but for many centuries major and minor thirds and sixths have also been included.

conducting Direction of an **ensemble** of musicians by hand (or foot) indications, which have varied somewhat through the centuries.

In ancient Greece the practice of giving an audible beat was known, and existed in performances well into the 18th century; it is still sometimes used for training amateur ensembles or choirs. Pitch has also been indicated by hand movements, singers being given hand signs to indicate the rise and fall of the melody – a practice which survives in the teaching methods of **Kodály**, based on the methods of John Curwen (1816-1880).

Renaissance woodcuts commonly show directors of music using a long staff to indicate the time, and in the Baroque era the tendency was for shorter sticks (although **Lully** was celebrated for the long stick with which he injured his foot and subsequently died). When the **continuo** section of the orchestra finally disappeared, the baton became popular and this has lasted until today, although some conductors merely use their hands. Since the 19th century conductors have also indicated phrasing and encouraged particular moods. Although the conductor's art in its final form is seen on the concert platform, his or her rehearsal technique, rather than baton technique, is of paramount importance.

conductus (Lat.) Medieval song. The earliest pieces called *conductus* are found in a mid-12th-century manuscript from Norman Sicily. The songs appear to have been used for processional and recessional purposes. Some *conducti* are set for two to four voices, and this form was developed by the Parisian composers of the late 12th and early 13th centuries (the Notre Dame School), such as Pérotin. These works were composed in a wide variety of styles, from pieces in which there is one note per syllable of text, to other pieces containing long **melismas** to certain syllables. The form dropped out of use from the mid-13th century, when the **motet** became the most popular form of composition.

conjunct motion Melody in which the movement is from one note of a diatonic scale to an adjacent one (a step). If the melody proceeds by larger intervals, it moves by **disjunct motion** (a leap). See also **contrary motion**.

Connolly, Justin (1933-) English composer, who studied and now teaches at the Royal College of Music. His style was influenced by Elliott **Carter**, particularly his use of small intervallic units to construct large, dense structures. Among his most important works are *Cinquepaces* (1965-1966), *Tetramorph* (1972) and *Anima* (1974).

consecutive intervals In harmony, any interval that occurs in the same two parts in two adjacent chords. In conventional harmony, consecutive perfect fifths and octaves are considered to give a poor effect, although composers from **Debussy** onwards have used them to advantage. The medieval practice of **organum**, or harmonizing of a plainchant, consisted almost entirely of adding parts consecutive to the original.

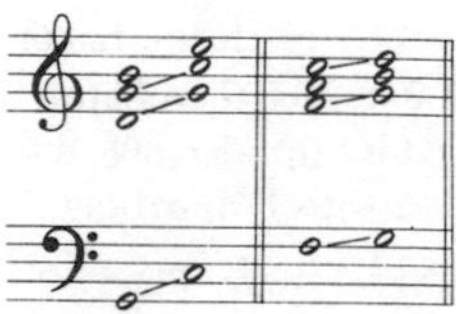

Consecutive octaves and fifths

conservatoire (Fr.) Place of musical training, originally an orphanage. During the 18th century those in Venice and Naples were renowned for their excellent standards of performance. In more recent times, the word has come to mean a place of higher education, where performers are trained for orchestral or concert careers, such as the Paris Conservatoire de Musique, equivalent to the Royal College or Royal Academy of Music in London. The Italian equivalent is *conservatorio.*

console Control desk of an organ, including keyboard, pedals, pistons and organ stops. There is no standard arrangement of a console, either with regard to keyboard size or the arrangement of stop-knobs, and therefore an organist has to master each new organ individually. If the console is separated from the organ, and operated by electric action, it is known as a detached console.

consonance Similar to **concord**. In acoustical physics, a consonance consists of any two (or more) frequencies which relate to each other as small whole numbers, such as the perfect fifth (3:2) or fourth (4:3). Perceived consonance is, however, largely a social, psychological judgement, and can be used about any group of sounds that are heard as stable and harmonious, i.e. that do not demand resolution.

consort Small ensemble of voices or instruments before about 1700. The whole consort was a group composed entirely of one type of instrument, e.g. a consort of viols. The broken consort signified various different types of instrument in combination. A common Elizabethan broken consort consisted of treble viol, recorder, bass viol, lute, cittern and bandora.

Constant, Marius (1925-) Romanian-born French composer and conductor, who studied at the Paris Conservatoire after World War II with **Messiaen, Boulanger** and **Honegger**. As a conductor, he became the musical director for dance at the Paris Opéra in 1971. His most important compositions include the ballets *Cyrano de Bergerac* (1959) and *Nana* (1976). He is also known as an arranger and orchestrator, as well as a conductor.

continental fingering In piano-playing, the standard system of indicating fingering, in which the thumb is represented by 1, and the fingers as 2-5. The English system, where the thumb was + and the fingers 1-4, is now obsolete.

composer's counterpoint Alternative term for **free counterpoint**.

continuo Abbreviation of *basso continuo* (continuous bass). In the scores of Baroque composers (e.g. **Bach** and **Handel**), the bass part was performed by the harpsichord or organ and often with additional instruments such as a viola da gamba and/or lute. Players read from a single line of music, providing harmony which was indicated with figures written above the notes (the **figured bass**).

The use of continuo began around 1600 when organs were used to accompany sacred choral pieces. The organist was provided merely with a figured bass line which he would then fill out to provide any missing harmonies and support the inner voices. This organ line was, in effect, an abbreviated score. Continuo also became important with the growth of **recitative** in the first operas and **monodies**. A much greater emphasis was given to the expression of words by the solo human voice, and the continuo provided the harmonic support. It was also vital in the Baroque **trio sonatas** and **concerti grossi** for providing the harmony beneath one or more solo melodic instruments. The use of continuo carried on throughout the Baroque and into the early Classical period, when a harpsichord or fortepiano played with an orchestra as in **Haydn**'s and **Mozart**'s choral works, concertos and symphonies. However, the continuo line was largely redundant by that period because the inner harmonies were taken by other instruments in the orchestra.

The practice of playing continuo in Classical works has ceased, except for performances by groups aiming to achieve 'authentic' performances.

contrabasso (It.) Double-bass, the largest and lowest of bowed, stringed instruments. It is usually tuned E′ A′ D G although lower notes can be achieved by using an E′ string extension, or a five-stringed instrument. The double-bass is not a member of the violin, but of the viol family.

contrafagotto (It.) Double-bassoon, which sounds an octave lower than the standard **bassoon**, reaching down to B′ (below the double-bass). The modern form was developed by Wilhelm Heckel in 1877-1879. The distinctive buzzing quality of its lowest register has been used to great effect by **Mahler** and **Strauss**.

contralto Lowest type of female voice, ranging from G–G′, and with a sombre, rich tone. In choirs, the male voice of this range is termed alto.

contrary motion In harmony, two parts that move in opposite directions, as opposed to **similar motion**, in which the parts move up or down together.

contredanse (Fr.) Originated in England as a country dance, and became the most popular French dance of the 18th century. In its final form, it consisted of a binary form melody, in duple time, and a set pattern of steps which was danced nine times. Many tunes were used, including *Greensleeves*, which became *Les manches Vertes* in France. **Beethoven** composed a set of 12 *contredanses* for orchestra in 1802.

Converse, Frederick Shepherd (1871-1940) Boston-based American teacher and composer, who studied with **Rheinberger** in Munich. From 1903 to 1907, he taught at Harvard College, devoting himself to composition and to the administration of the Boston Opera Company. He composed six symphonies, and his operas *The Pipe of Desire* (1905) and *The Sacrifice* (1910) enjoyed great success. After World War I he became head of the theory department at New England Conservatoire.

Conversi, Girolamo (*fl*1571-1584) Italian composer, known principally for his six-part madrigals (settings of Petrarch, Castiglione and others, Venice, 1571-1575) and his **canzoni** (Venice, 1572), which combine the popular **villanella** form with the more sophisticated madrigal.

Cooke, Arnold (1906-) English composer, born in Yorkshire, and a pupil of **Hindemith**. His work is characterized by fluent instrumental writing, and the use of contrapuntal technique in a diatonic idiom. His major works include the Symphony No. 1 (1949), and the Cello Concerto (1972-1973).

Cooke, Benjamin (*c*1695-1743) English music publisher, active in London between 1726 and 1743. His most notable publication was the complete works of **Corelli** (1732), printed unusually in full score, rather than in parts. Cooke also played a vital role in the re-establishment of music at the Chapel Royal after the Restoration, in his capacity as Master of the Children.

Cooke, Benjamin (1734-1793) English organist and composer, son of the above, and a pupil of **Pepusch**. From 1752 he was conductor at the Academy of Ancient Music in London. His output included church music, glees and many works for organ.

Cooke, Henry (*c*1615-1672) English composer and singer, who introduced into the Chapel Royal Italian influences, such as a more improvised and highly ornamented style than was then prevalent in England. His singing was favourably remarked upon by Pepys and Playford, the latter calling him "that Orpheus of our time". His compositions are of lesser interest.

Cooper, John (*c*1575-1626) English composer, better known by his Italianized names, Giovanni Coperario and John Coprario. His instrumental works, particularly his fantasias for viols, make striking use of advanced Italian dissonant harmony and **chromaticism**. Charles I appointed him Composer-In-Ordinary in 1625.

coperto (It.) On the snare drum, instruction to the player to cover the upper (or batter) head with a cloth, giving a muffled sound. More generally, it is used to indicate that any drum should be covered with a cloth, e.g. for funeral music.

Copland, Aaron (1900-) American composer, a pupil of Nadia **Boulanger**, with whom he studied in Paris. Many of his most successful works are strongly influenced by American jazz, popular and folk song idioms (e.g. *Appalachian Spring* and *Rodeo*), and by Latin American music (*El Salón Mexico*). However, some works, notably the early piano variations, are strongly dissonant. Other popular compositions include *Quiet City* and *A Lincoln Portrait*. He has published several books.

cor (Fr.) Horn. Specifically the large orchestral valve horn in F, known in England as the French horn and in France as the *cor d'harmonie*. Before 1850, this instrument was without valves, there being a series of interchangeable **crooks** to alter the length of the tubing. It produced only notes of the harmonic series, semitone adjustments being possible by skilful use of the hand inside the bell of the instrument (see **chiuso**). In earlier times, cor referred to any blown horn, such as an ox horn or one made from ivory, with or without finger-holes. See also **cor anglais**.

cor anglais (Fr.) Not a horn, but a tenor double-reeded woodwind instrument of the **oboe** family, with a large bulb-shaped bell.

Cor anglais

It is a transposing instrument, sounding a perfect fifth lower than written, with a lowest note of E and a range of about two-and-a-half octaves. Although tenor oboes have existed from the late 17th century, the modern instrument was developed by Brod in Paris in 1839.

Aaron Copland

corda (It.) String. On bowed instruments, the instruction *corda vuota* means an open string, and *corda soprano*, the highest string. On the piano, *una corda* instructs the player to use the soft pedal, so that in instruments whose mechanism works in this way, the hammer strikes only one string. *Tre corde* cancels this, causing the hammer to strike all three strings.

Corelli, Arcangelo (1653-1713) Italian performer and composer. He spent most of his life in Rome, where he was in great demand as a violinist. He composed only instrumental music, publishing four sets of **trio sonatas**, a set of solo violin sonatas and his best-known set of 12 concerti grossi (which include the famous *Christmas Concerto*). Although his music never had the incisive rhythmic quality of that of **Vivaldi** or **Bach**, he was a popular and widely influential composer who died a very wealthy man.

Corelli, Franco (1923-) Italian tenor, born in Ancona who, after studying in Milan, Florence and Spoleto, made his operatic debut as Don José in *Carmen*, Spoleto, 1951. He sings regularly at La Scala, Milan, and has established himself as one of the world's leading Italian heroic tenors, his dark-timbred voice being suited as much to **spinto** as to **verismo** roles.

Franco Corelli

Corigliano, John (1938-) American composer whose output includes various chamber and orchestral works, notably *The Naked Carmen*, an arrangement of **Bizet**'s *Carmen* for rock groups and **Moog** synthesizer.

Cornelius, (Carl August) Peter (1824-1874) German composer, author and friend of **Liszt** and **Wagner**. Cornelius was a firm disciple of the New German School. His comic opera *Der Barbier von Bagdad* was produced by Liszt at Weimar in 1858, but because of organized opposition it was withdrawn, with the result that Liszt resigned as court conductor. Cornelius wrote two other operas, *Der Cid* and *Gunlöd*, and many other vocal works, including a Christmas hymn for baritone and chorus, known in England as *Three Kings from Persian Lands Afar*.

cornamuse In English the name refers to a now obsolete reed instrument common in the 16th century. In its French (*cornemuse*) and Italian (*cornamuse*) forms it refers simply to the **bagpipes**. **Verdi** wrote for it in *Otello*, but suggested that the part might equally be taken by two **oboes**.

cornet Term with two meanings.

First, it is a soprano brass instrument, also known as *cornet-à-pistons* (Fr.), similar to the modern trumpet but with a slightly more conical bore and mellower tone. The

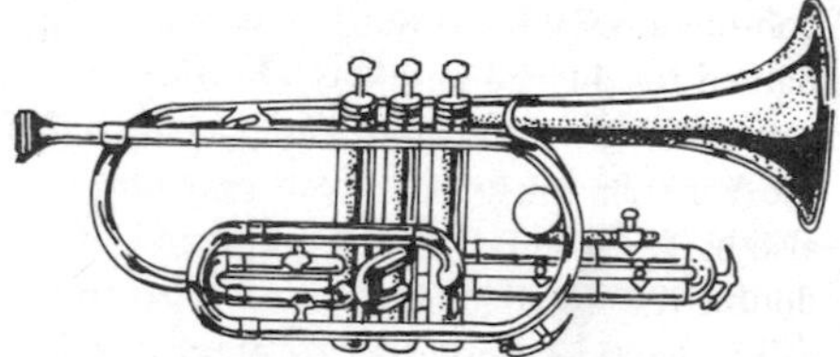

Cornet

cornet first appeared about 1828 and its orchestral debut was probably in **Rossini**'s *William Tell* the following year. Its agility and flexibility were exploited in brilliant popular solos during the latter part of the 19th century, and for a time its popularity was such that it threatened to oust the trumpet from the orchestra. Nowadays, however, it is generally found only in military and brass bands.

Second, it is an important organ stop, invariably a mutation rather than a reed. In England the stop was mounted at the top of the organ (hence, mounted cornet) and was extensively used by 18th-century composers such as John **Stanley** and Maurice **Greene**.

cornet-à-pistons (Fr.) Equivalent of the English **cornet**.

Cornet, Pierre (*c*1575-1633) Flemish composer and court organist at Brussels from 1603 to 1626. He wrote organ pieces in the Venetian style, and was influenced by **Sweelinck** and **Scheidt**.

cornett Wind instrument that appeared as early as the 13th century but rose to prominence in the late 16th and early 17th centuries. The cornett is approximately two feet long, slightly curved, and made from wood covered with leather. It has seven fingerholes and is played with a cup mouthpiece similar to a brass instrument. The sound produced is something like a gently-played trumpet or horn, but it has a facility in articulation and expression that makes it sound at times like a wordless soprano voice. Cornetts were used in the 16th century in church music to support the choir, often alongside **sackbuts**. This combination of instruments was specifically named for the opening toccata of **Monteverdi**'s *Orfeo*, and was frequently used in the Venetian music of the two **Gabrielis**; also by J.S. **Bach** in certain cantatas to double the treble line.

The less common mute cornett is a straight instrument, turned in wood with no leather covering. There is no separate mouthpiece but merely a conical recess cut into the narrow end of the tube. The sound is less bright than that of the curved cornett. This instrument was very popular in chamber ensembles in 16th-century Italy.

Cornish, William Alternative spelling of **Cornyshe, William**.

corno (It.) Horn. See also **cor**; **cor anglais**.

corno di bassetto (It.) Term with two meanings.

First, it is a **basset-horn**. George Bernard Shaw adopted the Italian form as a pseudonym for his music criticisms in *The Star* in the 1880s and 1890s.

Second, it is an organ stop.

cornopean Early type of **cornet**, but more usually the name of an organ stop, often found on the swell organ of English organs.

Cornyshe, William (*c*1465-1523) English composer, actor and playwright who became a member of the Chapel Royal in 1496 and Master of the Children of the Chapel Royal in 1509. As pageant-master at the court of Henry VIII he was responsible for organizing the many masques, pageants and banquets. His compositions include some particularly cheerful part-songs. Some of his church music was included in *The Eton Choirbook*.

Coronation Anthem Anthem written for a coronation, often for chorus and orchestra. One of the first was *My Heart is Inditing* composed by **Purcell** for the coronation of James II in 1685.

The title often refers to the four anthems for chorus and orchestra by **Handel**, written for the coronation of George II in 1727: *Zadok the Priest*, *The King Shall Rejoice*, *My Heart is Inditing* and *Let Thy Hand Be Strengthened*.

Correa de Arauxo, Francisco (1576-1654) Spanish composer and organist whose life centred on Seville, where he was organist at St Salvador. All his work survives in one collection, which also includes an important theoretical treatise on the change from the Renaissance **modes** to baroque tonality. His work, with its complex rhythms and extravagant embellishments, marks the beginning of the Spanish Baroque. His name is alternatively spelled Araujo or Azavedo.

Corrette, Michel (1709-1795) French composer and organist whose works include concertos for harpsichord, flute, organ and hurdy-gurdy, as well as sacred music and organ solos. He also wrote treatises instructing in the art of playing various instruments.

Cortot, Alfred (1877-1962) Swiss-born pianist and conductor who spent most of his life in France. He trained at the Paris Conservatoire and made his debut as a pianist in 1896, followed by a period as an assistant at **Bayreuth**. He was an active **Wagner** propagandist and in 1902 conducted the first performance in France of *Götterdämmerung*. From 1905 Cortot toured widely as a solo recitalist and with **Thibaut** and **Casals** as a trio. His editions of **Schumann**, **Chopin** and **Liszt** are widely used today. He made many recordings which have become classics in their field, particularly of the works of Chopin. His playing was free and romantic, always imaginative and with frequent moments of inspiration.

Costa, Sir Michael Andrew Agnus (1806-1884) Conductor and composer born in Naples who went to England at the age of 21 and remained to achieve prominence as a conductor of opera, oratorio and orchestral works. As a composer his best-received works were the oratorios *Naaman* and *Eli* and a number of operas. He was knighted in 1869.

Cotrubas, Ileana (1939-) Romanian soprano who studied in Bucharest. Her vibrant, Slavic timbre first came to wider notice when she won first prize in the highly esteemed Dutch s'Hertogenbosch Competition. She made her Glyndebourne debut in 1969 as Mélisande and her Covent Garden debut came in *Eugene Onegin* in 1971. However, it was at La Scala in 1975 that she rose to stardom almost overnight when she understudied Mirella Freni as Mimi in *La Bohème*.

couched harp Alternative term for **spinet**.

counterpoint Derived from the Latin *punctus contra punctum*, note against note, or, by extension, melody against melody. It denotes music of two or more lines that sound simultaneously. Counterpoint is the horizontal element of texture in music, the vertical element being **harmony**. In counterpoint, the individual melodies are treated more or less equally (as opposed to those styles in which the treble or bass lines are prominent).

After counterpoint first began to be used, in the 13th century, it evolved a complex system of rules governing the **intervals** and **dissonances** that could appear between the parts. **Palestrina**'s masses are good examples of late 16th-century counterpoint, and J.S. **Bach**'s fugues show how far it had developed by the 18th century. Counterpoint continued to be used throughout the 18th and 19th centuries, but has found a new importance in the 20th century with the development of the serial or **twelve-tone** system by **Schoenberg**, in which the emphasis on the individual lines, has led to the virtual disappearance of any traditional harmonic element.

counter-subject One of the **melodies** in a **fugue**, heard against the main subject and normally contrasting with it.

counter-tenor Alternative term for the male **alto** or adult male voice with the range of a female **contralto**. This is usually produced by developing the falsetto register.

country dance Generic term that covers a whole series of figure dances originating on the English village green. The music for such dances included folk tunes and was typically constructed in eight-bar phrases. Country dances were popular among all classes during the reign of Elizabeth I, and both dance steps and music were described in detail by John Playford in his *English*

Dancing Master, published in various editions from 1651 to 1728. Around 1700 many of these dances became popular in France as **contredanses**. In the early 19th century, however, the **waltz** and **quadrille** superseded the country dance in the English ballroom, but it has seen a revival in the 20th century, largely because of the efforts of folklorists such as Cecil **Sharp**.

coup d'archet (Fr.) Bow stroke.

Couperin, François (1668-1733) French composer and keyboard player. The most famous member of a family of musicians, and known as *le grand*. He was organist at St Gervais in Paris, a post that was promised to him when he was only 10 years of age. His compositions include several vocal works for the church in which his style was unusual because he used a combination of Italian **recitative** and **aria** with French ornamentation and instrumentation. He is, however, best known for his four books of harpsichord suites or *ordres* (1713-1720) and his treatise, *L'art de toucher le claveçin* (1717).

Couperin, Louis (1626-1661) French composer, violist and keyboard player. In about 1650 he and his two brothers were heard by Chambonnières and taken to Paris. Louis became the organist of St Gervais, a post held by the Couperin family for the next 175 years. He was an uncle of the better-known François **Couperin**. His keyboard music shows the influence of Chambonnières and **Froberger**.

coupler Mechanical device in organs and harpsichords for connecting one keyboard to another so that their notes sound together. An octave coupler couples notes an octave above on the same keyboard.

couplet (Fr.) Term with three meanings.

First, it denotes a **strophic** song, often in a light or humorous vein, in which the same music recurs for each verse.

Second, it is the forerunner of the **episode** in **rondo** form (or the French *rondeau* as cultivated by **Couperin** and others), referring to the sections between recurrences of the main theme.

Third, it is an alternative term for **duplet**.

courante (Fr.) Baroque dance movement in triple time which by about 1630 had become a regular part of the solo **suite**, following the **allemande**. Two versions, considered French and Italian, co-existed, although most composers used the titles *courante* and *corrente* (It.) interchangeably. The true Italian type is in a fast 3/4 or 3/8 time, whereas the French *courante* was a slower 3/2, its pulse nearer to that of the **sarabande**, and with many cross-rhythms between two groups of three and three groups of two. Both types are usually binary in form, beginning on the upbeat and ending on the strong beat of the bar.

cow-bell Everyday cow-bell of mountainous central Europe, sometimes specified in orchestral works. With the clapper removed and played with a drumstick, it often appears in the popular music of Latin America.

Cow-bells

Cowell, Henry (Dixon) (1897-1965) American pianist, theorist and composer who was highly individual, experimenting with original instrumental effects and trying to find the common ground between the Eastern and Western musical arts. He was co-inventor of the Rhythmicon.

Cowen, Sir Frederick (Hymen) (1852-1935) Jamaican-born conductor and composer who went to England as a baby; at the age of six he published a waltz, and at eight an operetta. After making a name for himself as a young pianist, he went on to conduct the Hallé Orchestra in Manchester. His compositions ranged widely from popular Victorian ballads to more serious art songs, operas and oratorios, of which *Ruth* (1887) is best known. He was knighted in 1911.

cow-horn Lip-vibrated wind instrument traditionally made from the horn of a cow and played by herdsmen. Where **Wagner** calls for such instruments in *Der Ring des Nibelungen* and in *Die Meistersinger von Nürnberg*, they are usually played on specially-made straight brass instruments with a perfectly conical bore.

Cowie, Edward (1943-) English composer and painter. After studying at the University of Southampton and with Alexander **Goehr**, Cowie was appointed as composer-in-residence and lecturer at the University of Lancaster. His composition, although using no strikingly avant-garde techniques, has a highly original language and is deeply influenced by his interest in ornithology and landscape. The Lancashire coast inspired many pieces, including *Leighton Moss* and *Stimmungsbild: Hest Bank*. His large orchestral piece *Leciathian* was given its first performance at a Henry Wood Promenade Concert and his opera *Commedia* was also premiered in London. He has for some years been Professor of Music in the Department of Performing Arts at Wollongong, Australia, and his more recent pieces (and paintings) reflect his experience of the Australian landscape.

Craft, Robert Lawson (1923-) American conductor best known for his long association with Igor **Stravinsky**, as pupil and interpreter of both his music and thoughts. His books on Stravinsky have become classics.

Cramer, Johann Baptist (1771-1858) Son of the violinist Wilhelm **Cramer** and piano pupil of **Clementi**, he became a celebrated pianist, touring Europe widely. Of his prolific output as a composer (100 sonatas and numerous concertos), only the piano studies are in use today. In 1824 Cramer founded the piano makers and music publishing company Cramer & Co., which is still in business.

Cramer, Wilhelm (1745-1799) Violinist born in Mannheim who went to London at the age of 27 and soon attained celebrity as a soloist and as leader of all the chief orchestras.

Crawford, Robert (1925-) Scottish composer and critic who won the Festival of Britain Arts Council prize in 1951 with his string quartet. His works include much incidental music for the BBC.

Crawford, Ruth Porter (1901-1953) American composer who studied at the American Conservatoire in Chicago and went on to teach there. She later studied composition in New York with Charles Seeger, whom she married. An interest in American folk song led her to transcribe several thousand of them from recordings and to write piano accompaniments to some 300 more. Her compositions include a string quartet (1931) and a violin sonata (1927).

crescendo (It.) Increasing in loudness, a direction often indicated on a score by a graphic marking consisting of a pair of diverging horizontal lines.

Crespin, Régine (1927-) French **soprano** who studied at the Paris Conservatoire and made her debut in Mulhouse in 1950 as Elsa in *Lohengrin*. In recent years, Crespin has been taking mezzo-soprano roles.

Creston, Paul (1906-) American composer and organist of Italian origin (he changed his name from Giuseppe Guttoveggio), self-taught in harmony and composition. He was organist at St Malachy's, New York 1934-1967. Compositions include five symphonies and concertos for many instruments, including saxophone and accordion.

Creighton (Creyghton), Robert (*c*1636-1734) Canon and precentor of Wells cathedral from 1674, who wrote anthems and settings of the liturgy. He lent his name to the 'Creiyghtonian seventh' after his practice of preceding a final perfect **cadence** by a subdominant chord with an added **seventh**.

Cristofori, Bartolomeo (1655-1731) Italian harpsichord-maker who, in Florence in about 1700, invented the *gravicembalo col piano e forte*, the forerunner of the modern piano. Instead of the strings being plucked, they were hit by a series of hammers. By 1720 he had improved the design by graduating the force of the fall of the hammers and putting a damper above instead of under the strings. Today only three Cristofori pianos survive.

croche (Fr.) French name for a **quaver**. *Monsieur Croche* was the pseudonym under which **Debussy** wrote some of his music criticism.

Croft, William (1678-1727) English organist and composer who collaborated with **Blow** and others in *Ayres for the Harpsichord or Spinet*. He composed many fine anthems and a burial service, and also wrote the hymn tune *St Anne*, to which is usually sung *O God our Help in Ages Past*.

crook Detachable accessory section of tubing applied to the mouthpiece of a brass instrument to lengthen the instrument's tube and thus give it a different (lower) key and range of notes.

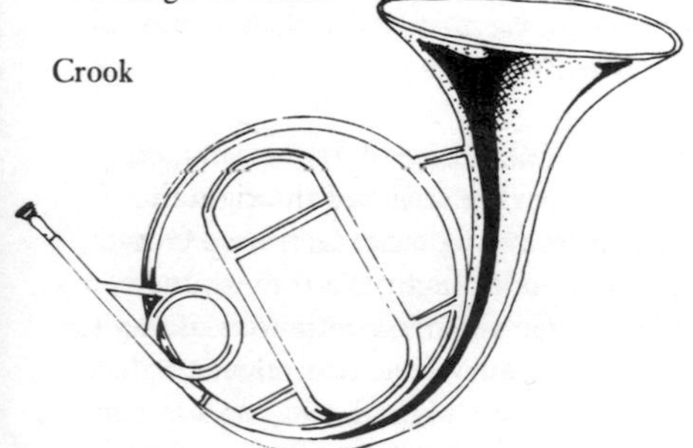

Crook

croon Originally, a term meaning to sing softly, e.g. to a baby. But since the 1930s it has been used to refer to a particular style of soft, mostly sentimental, singing, usually by a man and often with dance band accompaniment. The most famous crooner was Bing Crosby.

Cross, Joan (1900-) English soprano. She studied with Gustav **Holst** and Dawson Freer at Trinity School of Music. After singing in various opera choruses she became principal soprano at Sadler's Wells, where she was also director. She remains best known for the roles she created in the operas of Benjamin **Britten**, which included Ellen Orford in *Peter Grimes*, Lady Billows in *Albert Herring* and Mrs Gross in *The Turn of the Screw*. A tireless champion of English opera, Cross was a founder member of the English Opera Group in 1946, and of the Opera School in London, which later became the National School of Opera.

Crosse, Gordon (1937-) English composer who studied composition with **Wellesz** at Oxford University in 1961. Crosse's output includes several works for children, four operas and two symphonies. His music is both declamatory and lyrical, following more in the style of **Britten** than the European avant-garde. His earliest works, however, were written in serial form and influenced by **Webern**. Crosse was composer-in-residence at King's College, Cambridge, in 1973.

cross fingering Referring to wind instruments with side-holes, a cross fingering is one in which open and closed holes alternate. This is in contrast to 'normal' fingering in which all open holes are at the lower end of the instrument and all closed at the upper end. Whereas normal fingerings produce most of the **diatonic** tones of the octave, cross fingering is necessary to produce semitones and tones of the higher octave. Its effectiveness is reduced in relation to the remoteness of the key from the basic key in which the instrument is pitched.

Cross fingerings are largely avoided on modern-day instruments, such as the flute, oboe and clarinet, through the use of elaborate systems of keys, which have overcome the difficulties of playing in more remote keys.

cross relation Alternative term for **false relation**.

crotchet Note that is half the value of a **minim** and twice that of a **quaver**. In American usage it is called a quarter-note. As the denominator in a time signature, the crotchet is represented by the number 4.

Crotchet Crotchet rest

Cruft, Adrian (1921-1987) English composer who studied at the Royal College of Music under Sir Adrian **Boult**, Gordon **Jacob** and Edmund **Rubbra**. He had a varied career as double-bass player, teacher, conductor and composer, and became chairman of the Composers' Guild in 1967. His music is **diatonic** and straightforward in idiom, often written specifically for children and amateurs. His output includes settings of the canticles, cantatas, orchestral works and chamber music.

Cruft, Eugene (1887-1976) English double-bass player and father of Adrian **Cruft**. He played in most of the leading London orchestras and was the orchestral organizing secretary for the coronations of George VI and Elizabeth II.

Crumb, George (1929-) American composer who studied at the Universities of Illinois and Michigan. His musical output includes many settings of verse by Lorca, such as the four books of *Madrigals* (1965-1969) and *Ancient Voices of Children* (1970). His music is characterized by an imaginative use of vocal and instrumental colour, and by the inclusion of theatrical elements such as dance and the use of masks. He has also taught at the Universities of Colorado and Pennsylvania.

crumhorn Woodwind instrument that has a double reed enclosed in a cap and a curved or crook-shaped bottom. The crumhorn flourished during the 16th century as a **consort** instrument. Its tone was soft, albeit buzzing, and blended with most other instruments of the time. There were at least five regular sizes of crumhorn, ranging from the small treble to the great bass, although all had the limited pitch range of a ninth and an equally limited dynamic range.

Little is known of the instrumentation of the music of the period, and it is assumed that the crumhorn played as important a role as any other instrument of the day in both sacred and secular polyphonic compositions. It is almost certain, however, that by the 17th century it was used less and less because of its limitations, and was soon replaced by the more versatile recorder and oboe.

Crusell, Bernhard Henrik (1775-1838) Finnish clarinettist and composer who studied with Tausch and Lefèvre before becoming a court musician in Stockholm in 1793. His many compositions for clarinet, originally intended for an eleven-keyed instrument, are still performed today. Crusell was also an accomplished linguist, and in 1837 was awarded the Swedish Academy's Gold Medal for his translations of French, German and Italian operas for the Swedish stage.

crwth (Welsh) Bowed lyre. Usually, the bowed lyre that was used throughout Britain from Anglo-Saxon times but had retreated to Wales by the 16th century, where it remained in continuous use up to the 19th century. The equivalent English word is *crowd* and the Latin, *chorus*. The crwth in medieval illustrations has only three strings, whereas the later Welsh instrument usually had six strings in three courses.

csárdás 19th-century Hungarian dance. It is in duple time and has slow sections alternating with fast ones. Johann **Strauss** incorporated a *csárdás* into his operetta, *Die Fledermaus*.

cuckoo Small one-holed wind instrument designed to imitate the call of the cuckoo. Leopold **Mozart** used it in his *Toy Symphony*.

Cuénod, Hugues (1902-) Swiss tenor who studied at the Basle Conservatoire and in Vienna. He was well known as an interpreter of humorous character roles and appeared in the main European opera houses. He had a high, light tenor voice and made fine recordings of lute-songs, **Couperin**, and of the Evangelist role in J.S. **Bach**'s *St Matthew Passion*.

Cui, Cesar Antonovich (1835-1918) Russian composer and critic who studied at St Petersburg, where he became a professor at the Academy of Military Engineering. He started composing after meeting **Balakirev** in 1856, and subsequently became a member of the group of composers known as The Five. Balakirev himself helped with the orchestration of Cui's first pieces. Cui composed a large number of works, including 15 operas. He was most at ease composing miniatures, both songs and short piano pieces, in which he showed the influence of **Chopin** who had fascinated him since childhood. He is now best remembered for his critical writings.

cuivre (Fr.) Ringing, indicating a brassy sound. The term is most often used with regard to the French horn.

curtal Name used in England from the late 16th century to the early 18th century for both the dulcian and the **bassoon**.

Curzon, Sir Clifford (1907-1982) English pianist who entered the Royal Academy of Music in 1919 to study with Charles Reddie. Later teachers included **Schnabel** and **Boulanger**. In his youth, Curzon was associated with a wide-ranging repertory, giving world premieres of English works including **Berkeley**'s *Sonata* and **Rawsthorne**'s Concerto No. 2. He later concentrated on performing classical works, especially those of **Mozart**. After World War II he played in every important European and American musical centre, and earned himself the accolade of being the greatest living Mozartian. He was made a CBE in 1958 and knighted in 1977.

Cutting, Francis (*fl*1583-*c*1603) English lutenist and composer, known to have worked in London and thought to have come from East Anglia. Eleven of his typically light-hearted pieces for the six-course lute are to be found in Barley's *A New Booke of Tabliture* (London, 1596). Cutting's last work was written no later than 1603.

cyclic form Composition in which thematic material heard at the beginning of a work is reintroduced in the last movement. **Haydn**'s Symphony No. 32 in D and **Brahms**'s Symphony No. 3 both have finales that close with the works' opening material following the principle of strict cyclic form.

The term can also be used where thematic material is more loosely linked or repeated across more than one movement. **Mendelssohn**, **Schumann** and **Liszt** in particular were greatly concerned with the cross-reference of thematic material between movements, in an attempt to create more cohesion and continuity in multi-movement form, as was **Berlioz** in his *Symphonie Fantastique*. Among others, **Franck**, **d'Indy**, **Saint-Saëns** and **Fauré** were also fond of using cyclic form.

cymbals Percussion instrument consisting of two thin circular metal plates; they are slightly convex with a deep depression in the centre to which handles are attached. When struck together, only the edges of the plates touch, and this is usually in a

Two types of cymbal

brushing motion, producing a sound of indefinite pitch. A single cymbal, suspended on a stand, can be struck with a hard or soft drum stick to produce a harsher sound, or with two sticks in rapid succession to produce a roll. Cymbals are also a component in a drum kit, in which one cymbal is fastened to the top of the bass drum and the other is clashed against it (called a high-hat). Small cymbals are known to have been used in ancient Egypt, Greece and Rome.

Czerny, Karl (1791-1857) Austrian pianist, composer and piano teacher who is best known for his hundreds of piano studies and exercises, especially his *Complete Theoretical and Practical Pianoforte School*, Op. 500. Czerny could play the piano by the age of three, and became a much-admired pianist in his day. At ten he became a pupil of **Beethoven** and was subsequently renowned for his interpretations of Beethoven's piano works, all of which he could play from memory. After 1805 Czerny gave up the life of a travelling virtuoso to spend his time in Vienna as a composer and piano teacher, who counted the young Franz **Liszt** among his numerous pupils.

D

D Term with two meanings.

First, it is the name of the note that lies one tone above C and one tone below E. The scale of D major has two sharps in the key-signature.

Second, the works of **Schubert** are given D-numbers, being categorized by the chronology established by Otto Deutsch. For example, Piano Quintet D.667 (*The Trout*).

D.C. Abbreviation of **da capo**.

da capo From the beginning, an indication that the performer should start again from the beginning of a piece. *Da capo al fine*, indicates that the performer should continue up to the word *fine* (end), or the sign in the score.

Dalayrac, Nicholas-Marie (1753-1809) French composer of songs, string quartets and more than 50 operas, including *Nina* (1786) and *La Maison à vendre* (1800).

d'Albert, Eugen (Francis Charles) (1864-1932) German pianist and composer, born in Glasgow, but of French descent. He won the Mendelssohn Scholarship (1861) to study in Vienna under **Liszt**. After a career as a concert pianist he became director of the Berlin Hochschule (1907). He composed numerous instrumental works and 20 operas, including *Der Tiefland* (1903).

Dalcroze, Emile Jacques- See **Jacques-Dalcroze, Emile**

Dale, Benjamin James (1855-1943) British composer of sonatas for piano, violin and viola, songs, and choral and orchestral works. In later years he was involved with educational work for the Royal Academy of Music and Associated Board.

Dallapiccola, Luigi (1904-1975) Italian pianist and composer, who was the earliest Italian exponent of the **twelve-note technique**. He later experimented with **serialism**, notably in his choral work *Canti di prigionia* (1938-41). His later compositions reflect a polyphonic style, which came to the fore in his *Piccola musica notturna* (1954). Dallapiccola studied composition at the Cherubini Conservatoire, Florence, and was influenced in his work by **Schoenberg**, **Debussy** and **Monteverdi**. After 1945, he spent much of his time teaching and composing in the United States.

Damase, Jean-Michel (1928-) French composer and pianist who studied at the Paris Conservatoire. His works include the ballet *La Croqueuse de Diamants* (1950) and compositions for piano, violin and harp.

Dampfer (Ger.) Mute. Applies to the muting of bowed and wind instruments, and to the use of the soft pedal of a piano.

damper pedal Alternative term for the soft pedal of a piano.

Damrosch, Leopold (1832-1885) German composer and conductor who did much to enhance the reputation of New York's Metropolitan Opera House. He was a violinist in the Weimar court orchestra, and became a close friend of its conductor, **Liszt**. Damrosch moved to the United States in 1871 and became co-founder and first conductor of the New York Oratorio Society. At the Metropolitan Opera House, he organized and conducted a season of German opera, which included the first American performance of **Wagner**'s *Die Walküre*.

Damrosch, Walter (1862-1950) Born in Germany, the younger son of Leopold, he followed his father to the United States and introduced many important works there. He succeeded his father as conductor at the New York Oratorio in 1885, and became an assistant conductor at the Metropolitan Opera House. He conducted the first US performance of **Wagner**'s *Parsifal* there in 1896, and in 1900 formed a touring opera company which performed Wagner's operas, some for the first time. As conductor of the New York Symphony Orchestra (1903-1927) he directed the first US performances of works by such composers as **Bruckner** and **Mahler**. Among his compositions are five operas, including *The Scarlet Letter* (1896) and *Cyrano de Bergerac* (1913).

dance band Instrumental group consisting of three different sections: saxophones, brass and rhythm. This form of band became popular in the 1930s, originally in the United States, but was almost entirely replaced in the popular idiom by groups using electric instruments from the 1950s onwards. Probably the most famous dance band was the Glenn Miller Band.

dance poem Description sometimes given by composers to a major orchestral work intended for ballet and having a narrative interest. See also **choreographic poem**; **symphonic poem**.

Dancla, Jean Baptiste (1817-1907) French violinist and composer who became a tutor at the Paris Conservatoire in 1857. Among his compositions are four symphonies, six violin concertos and works for string quartet.

Dandrieu, Jean-François (1682-1738) French priest and composer who wrote mainly for the keyboard. He became a member of the Chapel Royal in 1724. He wrote a set of symphonies *Les charactères de la guerre* and three volumes of harpsichord pieces.

danmono (Japan) Compositions for **koto** which comprise several *dan* or sections. Each *dan* contains 104 beats, except for the first which has an extra four beats. Pieces are known by the number of *dan* they contain, e.g. *Rokudan* (*roku* means six), *Hachidan* (*hachi* means eight), etc. *Danmono* begin slowly with a gradual acceleration through all the *dan* until the last few bars; they begin and end quietly, rising to a climax towards the end of the last section. The two most common tunings are *hirajoshi* and *kumoijoshi*, derived from the popular **in** and **yō** scales. See **Japanese scales**.

dan tranh (Vietnam) Horizontal plucked zither which has sixteen steel strings stretched over moveable bridges. Similar to the Japanese **koto**, the Chinese **cheng** and the Korean **kayagŭm**.

Daquin, Louis Claude (1694-1772) French composer famous for his *Le Coucou* for harpsichord. A child prodigy, Daquin played for Louis XIV at the age of only six years old. He succeeded **Dandrieu** as organist at the Sainte-Chapelle in 1739. His name is sometimes spelled D'Acquin.

Dargason English folk tune used from the 16th century onwards as a country dance, and as such was incorporated into **Holst**'s *St Paul's Suite*.

Dargomizhsky, Alexander Sergeyvich (1813-1869) Russian pianist and composer who studied with **Glinka** and became associated with The Five. His works include the operas *Rusalka* (1856) and *The Stone Guest* (1872) which was completed after his death by **Cui** and orchestrated by **Rimsky-Korsakov**.

dastgah (Persia) Classical form consisting of a modal system which acts as a basis for solo instrumental improvisation. A performance of a *dastgah* entails the exposition of several tunes chosen from a set repertory of about 10 to 30 melodies, or *gusheh*, in any given mode or **maqam**, of which there are 12. The tunes chosen embrace the characteristics of a single mode, selected to convey the particular sentiment of the *dastgah* performance.

David, Félicien César (1810-1876) French composer whose passion for eastern music coloured his own work and influenced **Gounod**, **Bizet** and **Delibes**. His symphonic ode *Le désert* (1844) for chorus and orchestra was admired for its oriental coloration. He also composed operas, including *La perle du Brésil* (1851) and *Lalla Roukh* (1862), and works for string quintet.

David, Ferdinand (1810-1873) German violinist and composer who also taught at Leipzig conservatory. His friendship with **Mendelssohn** led to his giving the first performance of the latter's violin concerto (1845). Among his many works were an opera, and concertos for violin and chamber music.

Davies, Sir (Henry) Walford (1869-1941) Welsh composer and organist who wrote the famous *March of the Royal Air Force* in 1918. He encouraged musical festivals, composing his oratorio *Everyman* for the Leeds Festival in 1904, and his *Solemn Melody* for organ and strings for the tercentenary of Milton's death in 1908. He was made Master of the King's Music in 1934. His main compositions were sacred choral works, although other works included violin sonatas, orchestral overtures and music for children. Davies was also a pioneer of music broadcasting for schools.

Davies, Hugh Seymour (1943-) English composer associated with avant-garde electronic music. He studied at Oxford University and became an assistant to **Stockhausen** in 1964. In 1967 he was appointed director of London University's electronic music workshops. His compositions include a quintet for five performers using five microphones, sine-/square-wave generators, a 4-channel switching unit, potentiometers and six loudspeakers.

Davies, Sir Peter Maxwell (1934-) British composer of highly individual music, often characterized by angular melodies and complex rhythms. He attended Manchester University and the Royal Manchester College of Music. His fellow students included Harrison **Birtwistle** and Alexander **Goehr**, later (like Davies himself) to become prominent members of Britain's avant-garde. After studying in Italy with **Petrassi** and at Princeton with Roger **Sessions**, Davies spent a year in Australia as resident composer at Adelaide University. In 1967 he became director of the Pierrot Players, a chamber ensemble performing contemporary music. Re-formed by him into the Fires of London in 1971, this group served as a major vehicle for his gifts as a composer until it was disbanded in 1987. From his days with the Pierrot Players comes one of his most notable theatre pieces, *Eight Songs for a Mad King* (1969), a work in eight movements for actor-singer and chamber ensemble including a train whistle, chains and a dijeridoo. Other theatre pieces include *Miss Donnithorne's Maggot* (1974), *Le Jongleur de Notre Dame* (1978), which features a children's band, and *The Number 11 Bus* (1983-1984). The dramatic potential of his music was fully realized in his opera *Taverner* (1962-1970). Davies has had a rewarding association with the poet George Mackay Brown, whose poetry was set in such works as *Solstice of Light* (1979), for choir and organ, and whose work inspired Davies's own libretto for his chamber opera *The Martyrdom of St Magnus* (1976-1977). From 1979 to 1984 Davies was director of Dartington Hall music summer school. In 1985 he became associate conductor/composer with the Scottish Chamber Orchestra, for which some of his most recent works, such as his oboe concerto (1987), have been written. His many other works include three symphonies, *St Thomas' Wake* (a foxtrot for orchestra, 1969), choral pieces, chamber music, piano works, and film scores (for Ken Russell's *The Devils* and *The Boy Friend*, both 1971). He has also made transcriptions and realizations of Renaissance and Baroque pieces. He was knighted in 1987.

Davis, Sir Colin (1927-) British conductor and former clarinettist. He conducted the BBC Symphony Orchestra (1967-1974), and in 1971 became musical director of the Royal Opera at Covent Garden. As a performer, he has become closely associated with the works of **Berlioz, Mozart, Britten** and **Tippett**.

Sir Colin Davis

Davy, John (1763-1824) British composer, violinist and organist. He wrote music for light opera and theatre, including the song *The Bay of Biscay*, and songs for Shakespeare's *The Tempest*.

Davy, Richard (1467-1507) English composer and priest who was appointed choirmaster of Magdalen College, Oxford in 1491. There he composed a respected *St Matthew Passion* and six antiphons. He also wrote several motets, and began a Magnificat in 1500, which was never completed.

Dawson, Peter (1882-1961) Australian bass-baritone who studied under Charles Santley (1834-1922) in London. He made his Covent Garden debut in 1909, but went on to pursue a career in more popular song. He made many recordings (starting in 1904, the early days of the gramophone), including the well-known *The Road to Mandalay*, and sold something in the region of 13 million records. Dawson remained an extremely popular singer for more than half a century.

dbyangs (Tibet) General term for singing, melody, etc., especially religious song. More specifically, it refers to a sustained style of singing in Buddhist ritual in which the vowel sounds of each syllable in certain sacred texts are modified according to the neumatic score (*dbyangs-yig*). Each sound is extended for some length of time, so that one's sense of ordinary time is lost, and is subject to a variety of tonal inflections, glides and tremolo. In some traditions, special techniques including voice constriction and multiphonics are used.

dead march Slow, ceremonial march (often for funerals), such as those in **Handel's** oratorios *Saul* and *Samson*.

debayashi (Japan) On-stage ensemble in the **kabuki** theatre and largely responsible for performing its **nagauta** music. The ensemble is generally placed at the back of the stage on tiers, with **shamisen** (lute) and singers above, and with the drum and flute (**hayashi**) ensemble at floor level. The number of players on the stage varies according to the plot. A subsection of the *debayashi*, the *chobo*, may be found in plays deriving from the **bunraku** puppet theatre, and consists of **Gidayū** singers and **shamisen** players behind a bamboo curtain.

Debussy, (Achille-) Claude (1862-1918) French composer whose ability to paint musical pictures with great delicacy and detail led to his being described as an impressionist, despite the fact that he laid great stress on the demands of form. A brilliant exponent of orchestral and pianistic colouring, he pioneered many technical innovations of composition, such as the use of modal harmonies and shimmering mystical whole-tone and oriental scales. His exploring spirit blazed a trail that many others followed, including **Bartók, Messiaen** and **Boulez**, making him arguably the most influential compoer of the 20th century.

Born in Paris, Debussy received little formal education. From 1872 he attended the Paris Conservatoire, where he proved a wayward pianist and a rebellious student, impatient with prevailing academic theories. In the summers of 1880 and 1881 he went to Russia serving as pianist to Nadiezhda von Meck, **Tchaikovsky**'s patron. In 1884 he won the Prix de Rome with his cantata *L'Enfant Prodigue*. Required to study in Rome, he took the opportunity of meeting **Liszt** and **Verdi** and heard **Wagner**'s opera *Lohengrin*, which much impressed him. In 1887-1888 he wrote his second choral work, *La damoiselle élue*, for soprano, mezzo-soprano, female chorus and orchestra.

He attended the **Bayreuth** festivals of 1888 and 1889, but other influences eventually ousted Wagner. At the Paris Exposition of 1889 he heard a Balinese **gamelan** orchestra for the first time and was startled by its impact and the harmonic avenues that it opened up to him. His friendship with poets such as Mallarmé and the Symbolists and his meeting with Erik **Satie** in 1890 went hand in hand with a feeling that he was a "*musicien français*". In 1893 he wrote a string quartet in F, his only essay in the genre. His first major success, *Prelude á l'après-midi d'un faune*, an orchestral evocation of the atmosphere conjured up in a poem by Mallarmé, carne in 1894. Its apparent formlessness caused a great stir among critics. In 1902 *Pelléas et Melisande*, an opera based on a Symbolist play by Maeterlinck, was staged at the Opéra-Comique, a decade after Debussy had begun it. In 1905 his three symphonic sketches comprising *La Mer* received their premiere. They were followed by three orchestral *Images* (1905-1912) and the ballet *Jeux* (1913), written for the Ballets Russes.

Besides the works already cited, Debussy produced a wealth of piano music of the highest quality. It includes the *Suite bergamasque* (1890, revised 1905); the three movements *Pour le piano* (1896-1901); *Estampes* (1903); *L'Ile joyeuse* (1904), two books each of *Images*, *Préludes*, and *Etudes*; and the ever-popular *Children's Corner* suite (1906-1908). He also wrote songs and chamber pieces.

decani (Lat.) Of the dean. Section of the choir that is positioned on the south side (that is, the dean's side) of the chancel in a cathedral. See also **cantoris**.

decrescendo (It.) Instruction indicating that the music is to become quieter, represented graphically by a pair of converging lines.

Defesch, William (1687-1761) Flemish composer who moved to London in 1733. He studied the organ, violin and cello, and became choirmaster at Antwerp cathedral in 1731. Among his compositions are the oratorios *Judith* and *Joseph*, performed in London (1732), and several masses, songs and instrumental sonatas.

degree Note of the **diatonic** scale relative to other notes. Alternative names for the 1st-7th degrees (major or minor scales) are tonic, supertonic, mediant, subdominant,

dominant, submediant and leading note.

dehors (Fr.) Outside. Indication that a melody or instrument should stand out.

Delage, Maurice Charles (1879-1961) French composer, a pupil of **Ravel** at the Paris Conservatoire. Delage blended elements of an impressionistic style with themes from Indian music, of which he made a study. He introduced an exotic flavour to his works, particularly in his ballet *Les batisseurs de ponts*, the symphonic poem *Conte par la mer* and *Quatre poèmes hindous* for violin and orchestra. In 1926 he completed an orchestral version of **Debussy**'s *Chansons de Bilitis*.

Delalande, Michel Richard (1657-1726) French composer who was well known at Versailles for the grand Baroque style of his ecclesiastical compositions. He became Musician at Court to Louis XIV, taught the king's daughters, and composed music for the Sainte-Chappelle. He wrote 42 motets and other devotional pieces, as well as several ballets for performance at the court in Versailles.

Delannoy, Marcel François Georges (1898-1962) French composer who abandoned a career as an architect to take up music. He was largely self-taught, but was influenced by **Honegger**, adopting some of his neo-Romantic styles. Among his compositions are the operas *Le pourier de misère* (1927) and *Puck* (1949). He also wrote a ballet-cantata, *Le fou de la dame*.

Delden, Lex van (1919-) Dutch composer of chamber and choral music, children's ballets and seven symphonies. Delden's *In Memoriam* for orchestra was written for the Dutch flood victims of 1953.

Délibes, (Clément Philibert) Léo (1836-1891) French composer and organist whose works were almost entirely for the stage. He is especially known for his ballets *Coppélia* (1870) and *Sylvia* (1876). Other works include operas, such as *Lakmé* (1883), choruses and songs.

Delius, Frederick (1862-1934) English composer of Prussian parentage, who left his native Bradford in 1882 to manage an orange plantation in Florida. However, he neglected his duties in favour of studying music with Thomas Ward, an organist. While in Florida, Delius was profoundly influenced by Negro melodies.

On returning to Europe, Delius studied composition in Leipzig, meeting **Greig** and other Scandinavian musicians. He then moved to Paris, where he completed the *Florida Suite* and *Appalachia*. He finally settled in France, where his tonal works were composed. In the 1920s, he became incapacitated by paralysis and blindness, but continued to work with the aid of his amenuensis, Eric Fenby. He completed several works with Fenby, including his Violin Sonata No. 3 and *Idyll* (1932).

Delius's compositions clearly reflect the natural landscapes that were his inspiration. His tonal impressions for full orchestra *Brigg Fair* (1907), *In a Summer Garden* (1908) and *North Country Sketches* (1914) all share a romantic, rhapsodic and chroma-

Frederick Delius

tic use of harmony. He also wrote several operas, including *Fennimore and Gerda* (1908-1910) and *The Magic Fountain* (1893). His short orchestral work, *On hearing the first cuckoo in spring* (1912) is probably one of his most well-known.

Della Casa, Lisa (1919-) Swiss soprano who studied under Margarete Haeser in Zurich. She made her debut in Solothurn-Biel in 1941 in *Madama Butterfly*. Della Casa has sung worldwide and is best known for her performances of **Strauss** and **Mozart**.

Deller, Alfred (1912-1979) British counter-tenor who founded the Deller Consort (1950) to revive English lute songs and madrigals. Composers such as **Britten, Fricker, Mellers, Ridout** and **Rubbra** wrote pieces for him.

Dello Joio, Norman (1913-) American composer and organist noted for his command of melody. He has written for the stage and has composed some respected operatic works, including *The Ruby* (1953) and *The Lamentation of Saul* (1954). His work shows the influence of **Gregorian chant** and Italian opera. He became organist at St Ann's, New York in 1934. Later he studied with **Hindemith** and Wagenaar in New York (1940-1941) and was appointed musical director of the Loring Dance Players in 1941.

Del Mar, Norman (1919-) British conductor associated with 20th-century British music. He founded the Chelsea Symphony Orchestra (1944) and was conductor of the Yorkshire Symphony Orchestra (1954-1955) and the BBC Scottish Symphony Orchestra (1960-1965). He conducted the first performance of Benjamin **Britten**'s *Let's Make An Opera!* and has published a three-volume study of the works of Richard **Strauss**.

Del Monaco, Mario (1915-1982) Italian tenor who studied at Pesaro Conservatoire. He joined New York Metroplitan Opera (1951-1959) where he became very popular in the **Verdi** repertory.

Delvincourt, Claude (1888-1954) French composer who became director of the conservatoires in Versailles (1932) and Paris (1941). Among his works are piano solos and duets, songs and operas.

demisemiquaver Note with half the time value of a **semiquaver**, and a thirty-second that of a **semibreve**. In American usage, it is known as a thirty-second note.

Demisemiquaver and its rest

Demus, Jorg (1928-) Austrian pianist and recitalist who often appears as accompanist to artists such as **Suk**. He is also celebrated for his recitals and recordings of music played on early pianos.

Denisov, Edison Vasilievich (1929-) Soviet composer who was persuaded by **Shostakovich** to abandon mathematics and study at the Moscow Conservatoire (1951-1956). He became a tutor there in 1959 and composed at the Experimental Studio of Electronic Music in Moscow from 1958. He combined elements of Russian folk music with modern styles in compositions that range from *Peinture* for orchestra to *Crescendo e Diminuendo* for the harpsichord.

Denza, Luigi (1846-1922) Italian composer of the opera *Wallenstein* (1876) and of more than 600 songs, including the famous Neapolitan *Funiculì, funiculà*, composed to celebrate the opening of a funicular railway. This song was borrowed by Richard **Strauss** for his *Aus Italien* (1887). He studied at the Naples Conservatoire under **Mercadante**, and in 1898 became professor of singing at the Royal Academy of Music, London.

Dering (or Deering), Richard (*c*1580-1630) British composer and organist who worked as an organist in the court of Charles I. He is said to have been one of the first organists to use the basso continuo method. His compositions include *Cantiones sacrae* for several voices, church music, motets, fancies and other pieces for viols.

Dernesch, Helga (1939-) Austrian soprano who studied at the Vienna Conservatoire (1957-1961). She was notable as a performer in operas by **Wagner**, and also **Strauss**. In 1979 she began to appear in mezzo roles.

descant Originally (from about the 12th century) referred to a second part composed in counterpoint to a piece of plainsong. In this sense musicologists favour the spelling discant.

In the 13th century the term was extended to become a virtual synonym for polyphony in general, most of which was in two parts. As polyphony became more complex, the word discant came to describe an additional accompanying part written above the other two.

The modern uses of the word, now more usually spelled descant, denote firstly a high part freely composed or extemporized above a composed melody, such as a hymn or carol, and secondly the highest-pitched member of a family of instruments that is in normal use, for example a descant recorder.

Dessau, Paul (1894-1979) German composer and conductor associated with Berthold **Brecht**. He studied in Berlin and became an opera tutor at Hamburg, 1913. In 1918 he became conductor of the Cologne Opera, and in 1926 he conducted at the Berlin State Opera. He left Germany when the Nazis came to power, and lived in the United States (1939-1945). He wrote music for Brecht's *Mutter Courage* (1926), *Der Gute Mensch von Sezuan* (1947) and *Mann ist Mann* (1951), while Brecht provided librettos for his operas *Die Verurteilung des Lukullus* (1951, revised) and *Puntila* (1957). His choral work *Deutsches Miserere* was also to a text by Brecht.

detaché (Fr.) Detached or separated. A bowing style in string playing that produces detached notes, but without the sound being perceptively interrupted as in **staccato**.

deutsche tanze (Ger.) Country dance in the form of a slow waltz, cultivated by **Beethoven, Mozart, Schubert** and others.

development Section of a movement in **sonata form** in which the thematic material is developed and expanded, before its restatement in the original form.

dhrupad (India) Solemn vocal style which originated in the northern Indian courts of the 15th century, using Hindu texts on noble themes. Although less florid than the currently popular **khyāl**, it is the most demanding Indian genre, particularly when a greatly extended **ālāp** or introduction is included. The song consists of two or four long sections, the first of which (**sthāyī**) is repeated as a refrain between subsequent improvisations. It is accompanied by the **pakhāvaj** drum.

Diabelli, Anton (1781-1858) Austrian composer who became a partner in Peter Cappi's publishing business. Cappi withdrew in 1824, and Diabelli & Co. was formed, publishing works by such composers as **Beethoven, Schubert, Czerny** and **Liszt**.

Diabelli studied singing with Michael **Haydn** at Salzburg before moving to Munich to become a priest. But he abandoned the priesthood in 1803 and settled in Vienna. His first independent publication was the *Vaterländische Künstlerverein*, a collection of variations by 50 composers on one of his own waltz compositions, including 33 variations by **Beethoven**: the *Diabelli Variations*, Op. 120.

diabolus in musica (Lat.) The devil in music. One of the names given to the interval of an augumented fourth. It is also known as a tritone.

Diaghilev, Sergei (1872-1929) Russian impresario who studied law and music at St Petersburg. In Paris (1909) he organized the highly successful Ballets Russes company. Among the many talented artists associated with the company were Nijinsky, the dancer, Fokine, the choreographer, and Picasso. He encouraged many composers to write for him, including **Stravinsky**, **Ravel**, **Debussy** and **Prokofiev**.

Diamond, David Leo (1915-) American composer who was noted in the 1940s for his new lyricism and his combination of romantic colours and a neo-Classical discipline.

He studied at the Cleveland Institute, the Dalcroze Institute in New York, and at the Paris Conservatoire with the influential tutor Nadia **Boulanger**. He wrote eight symphonies, some concertos, and a series of *Rounds* for string orchestra. He also wrote six string quartets and other pieces of chamber music. His later symphonies – the Sixth (1954) and *Sinfonia Concertante* (1955) – reflect a difficult and violent style which is seen by some critics to herald a transitional phase in his work.

diapason (Greek) Through all. Foundation stops (open and stopped) of an organ, which give the instrument its distinctive tone.

diapason normal Former standard of pitch in which the note A has a frequency of 435 hertz.

diaphonic song (Yugoslavia) Part-song type, from the western region of Croatia and the Istrian peninsula, characterized by its narrow interval style which is thought to be of ancient origin. In rural areas these songs usually occur as duets. The voice parts are of equal importance and are closely intertwined, with intervals of major and minor seconds (not considered dissonant) predominating. However, the voices may occasionally be less interdependent, as in instances of parallel part movement, counterpoint and drone singing. Unique to this region is an unusual scale, known as the Istrian, approximating to E, F, G, A♭, B♭ and C♭.

Sergei Diaghilev

diaphony Simple **organum**, usually with only two voices.

diatonic To do with any given **major** or **minor** scale.

A diatonic scale is any of the major or minor scales, as opposed to the **chromatic scales**.

A diatonic harmony is one in which the prevailing major or minor scales are used without significant recourse to notes outside those scales.

A diatonic **interval** is one between two notes of the same scale.

Diaz, Alirio (1923-) Venezuelan guitarist. He is prominent as a soloist throughout

Europe and the United States. Since 1954, Diaz has taught at the Accademia Chigiana in Siena, Italy.

Dibdin, Charles (1745-1814) British composer, singer and author. In 1798 he began his series of 'table entertainments' at which he recited, sang and accompanied. One of the most successful, *The Oddities*, contained the song *Tom Bowling*. Many other songs, including sea-songs, and works for harpsichord formed part of his repertory.

Dichtung (Ger.) Poem. For example, *symphonische Dichtung*, **symphonic poem**.

Dickinson, Peter (1934-) English composer and pianist who has written many songs and a series of impressionistic pieces for strings, orchestra and piano. Many of his pieces represent experimental combinations of instruments, in particular his *Winter Afternoons* (1971) for six solo voices and double bass, *Solo* (1976) for baritone, tape and viola da gamba, and *The Unicorns* (1982) for soprano and brass band. He studied the organ at Queen's College, Cambridge, and was elected to Juilliard School in 1958. He was a pianist with the New York City Ballet and lectured at London and Birmingham Universities. From 1974 he was professor of music at Keele University.

diction Enunciation in singing.

diddling Practice of singing dance tunes to nonsense syllables in the absence (or prohibition) of instrumental resources. Also known as mouth music.

didjeridoo Alternative spelling of **didjeridu**.

didjeridu (Australia) Wind instrument of the North Australian Aboriginees, consisting of a straight end-blown tube at least a metre long. It is generally played with 'circular breathing' techniques (i.e. blowing out through the mouth while breathing in through the nose), using the cheeks as a bagpipe-like air reservoir to maintain a continuous sound. The didjeridu is capable of producing sounds approximating to bird calls, trills, croaks, etc. Also spelled didjeridoo.

Didjeridu

Diepenbrock, Alphons (1862-1921) Dutch composer and friend of **Mahler** who became an important teacher. His sacred works, including two settings of the *Te Deum* and a *Stabat Mater*, reflect the influences of Wagner and Palestrina. He also wrote music for the theatre (notably for Sophocles's *Electra*) and a number of songs.

Dieren, Bernard van (1884-1936) Dutch composer of complex polyphonic and impressionistic work, who was much admired by British intellectuals including Gray, Gerald Cooper and the Sitwells. Born in Rotterdam, he trained in the sciences, but in 1909 moved to London as a correspondent of the *Nieuwe Rotterdamsche Courant*. He became interested in musical composition and wrote music criticism for this and for other periodicals. His compositions include a *Chinese Symphony* (1914) for soloists, chorus and orchestra; a comic opera *The Tailor* (1917); and a volume of critical essays, *Down Among the Dead Men*

(1935). He also wrote five quartets, a solo violin sonata, piano pieces and some songs.

Dies Irae (Lat.) Day of Wrath, the sacred piece that forms the second section of the Requiem Mass. It appeared in 19th-century symphonic works, such as **Berlioz**'s *Symphonie Fantastique* and **Saint-Saëns'** *Danse Macabre*.

difference tone **Combination tone** that is created by the sounding together of two loud notes. The difference tone is that which is heard to be below the two notes in pitch. Its companion, the **summation tone**, is heard at a higher pitch than the original two.

dim Abbreviation of **diminuendo**.

diminished Perfect or minor **intervals** that have been reduced by a semitone. Triads are diminished if the 5th is reduced by a semitone.

diminuendo (It.) Getting quieter. See also **decrescendo**.

diminution Shortening of a melody or phrase by its reduction to smaller note-values, often by half.

d'Indy, (Paul Marie Théodore) Vincent (1851-1931) French composer who founded the Schola Cantorum in Paris with Charles Bordes and **Guilmant** (1894). He was an influential admirer of **Debussy** and of **Wagner**'s *Nibelungenlied*, and he did much to assist **Lamoureux** (who introduced Wagner's works in Paris).

As a boy he studied piano with Diemer and harmony with Lavignac. He became a pupil of **Franck** at the Paris Conservatoire in 1872. In 1875 he became choirmaster of the Concerts Collone. **Duparc** had first introduced him to Wagner's work and in 1876 he attended the first Bayreuth Festival. In 1900 the Schola Cantorum became a general music school and d'Indy immersed himself in his tutorial work. He wrote a treatise on teaching method, the *Cours de composition* (1906), and taught **Auric, Roussel** and **Satie**. In 1911 he became sole director of his school.

His richly-orchestrated compositions include the operas *Le chant de la cloche* (1879), *Fervaal* (1897), *L'Etranger* (1903) and *La légende de S. Christophe* (1920). He also wrote two symphonies and a number of tone-poems for orchestra, *Wallenstein* (1882), *Symphonie sur un chant montagnard* (1886) and *Jour d'été à la montagne* (1905).

dirge Funeral composition, usually vocal, performed at a burial.

discant Alternative spelling of **descant**.

discord Feeling of 'restlessness' or 'dissatisfaction' created either by a chord in itself (the seventh, ninth, eleventh and thirteenth are chords that create this effect alone, known as fundamental discords), or by a suspended note in a chord progression that needs to be resolved. See **resolution**; **suspension**.

disjunct motion In harmony, the progress of a single part by leap, as opposed to by step (called conjunct motion). See also **contrary motion**; **parallel moton**; **similar motion**.

dissonance Sounding together of notes to produce **discord**.

Distler, Hugo (1908-1942) German composer who studied the organ in Leipzig and became organist at the Jakobkirchc, Leipzig (1931). In 1921 he became an organist in Lübeck and was appointed professor of composition at the Stuttgart Conservatoire in 1937. His compositions are devotional and include more than 50 motets, a setting of the *Passion*, and *Nativity*, and an oratorio. He also wrote a string quartet and a harpsichord concerto.

Dittersdorf, Carl Ditters von (1739-1799) Austrian composer of operas and symphonies, he is known to have played in Vienna in a string quartet with **Vanhal**,

Haydn and **Mozart**. He travelled to Italy with **Gluck** (1763), achieving great success as a violinist, and also became *Kapellmeister* to the Bishops of Grosowardein (1765) and Breslau (1769). His major works include the opera *Doktor und Apotheker*, and 12 symphonies based on Ovid's *Metamorphoses*. He also wrote 115 other symphonies, 40 operas, 35 concertos and a great deal of other music.

divertimento (It.) Diversion. Work for an instrumental ensemble in several movements which is predominantly light-hearted in character.

divertissement Term that is used mainly in connection with ballet, in which it means a group of dances. In a musical sense it can either refer to music played between acts, or pieces based on familiar tunes performed as light entertainment.

divisi (It.) Divided. Indication that a string section of an orchestra is to be split into two or more groups playing different parts.

divisions Term with two meanings, both now obsolete.

First, during the 17th and 18th centuries, it was the equivalent of variations, in which the melody of a theme is broken up into notes of smaller value.

Second, during the 18th century, it was applied in vocal music to the long florid runs associated with composers such as **Handel**.

Dixieland Style of jazz playing which was originated in the United States by a group of white southerners, based on the music played by black musicians in the **New Orleans Style**.

dodecaphonic Alternative term for **twelve-note** composition.

Dodgson, Stephen (1924-) English composer and musical broadcaster, who studied under R.O. Morris. Among his compositions are symphonic works, including a *Symphony for wind* (1947), a guitar concerto, *Epigrams from a garden* (1977) for contralto and clarinets, and various songs and piano pieces.

doh Name for the tonic note in any key in **tonic sol-fa**, represented by the symbol d.

Dohnányi, Ernst von (1877-1960) Hungarian pianist with a Viennese repertory, who abandoned a successful career in order to compose. He is now known outside his home country only for his *Variations on a Nursery Song*, completed in 1916. Dohnányi was widely respected in Hungary, and became an influential tutor at the Budapest Academy and eventually the conductor of the Budapest Philharmonic Orchstra in 1927. Later, he was appointed director of the Hungarian Broadcasting Services.

Ernst von Dohnányi

doina (Romania) Lyrical song form, in free rhythm, which incorporates improvisation of a highly ornamental and recitative-like nature on the skeleton of a tune using traditional formulaic patterns. Increasingly popular outside Romania are instrumental *doinas*, particularly those that feature the **nai** panpipes.

Dolmetsch, Arnold (1858-1940) British antique instrument maker and performer of early music, of Swiss descent. He settled in England (1914) and set up his own workshop for harpsichords, viols, lutes and recorders, and also arranged annual festivals of ancient music and was the writer of the first important book on the interpretation of early music. His son, Carl Dolmetsch (1911-), continues with his father's work.

dominant Fifth note of the major or minor scale above the **tonic**, or the fourth below it. In harmony, the dominant may be said to be the second most important note of the scale after the tonic. See also **secondary dominant**.

Domingo, Placido (1941-) Spanish tenor who, after studying in Mexico, made his debut at the Metropolitan Opera House, New York in 1968. He has toured the world extensively and has appeared in more than 40 roles. He is now probably one of the best-known and popular tenors in the world, taking as his main repertory the heroic Italian roles.

Placido Domingo

dompe Alternative spelling of **dump**.

Donatoni, Franco (1927-) Italian composer noted for his experimentation with a number of varying styles, and for the composition *Black and White* for two pianos, in which the performers are given no actual notes to play or tempos to follow, just advice about which fingers to use. He studied at the Verdi Conservatoire, Milan (1946) and the Martini Conservatoire, Bologna (1948). He entered the Accademia Sta Cecilia in Rome with **Pizzetti** (1952) and has taught in many conservatoires since 1954. Among his compositions are *Per Orchestra*, *Strophes* and *Sezioni* for orchestra, three *Improvisations* for piano, and works for strings, brass and percussion.

Donizetti, (Domenico) Gaetano (1797-1848) Italian composer of more than 60 operas, most of which characterized Italian Romanticism, although one in particular (*La Fille du Regiment*, 1840) was in French. His first major success was *Anna Bolena* (1830), followed by others such as *L'Elisir d'Amore* (1832), *Lucrezia Borgia* (1833), *Lucia di Lammermoor* (1835) and *Don Pasquale* (1843). Donizetti was born in Bergamo and studied locally under Johann Simon **Mayr**. In 1843, following the success in Paris of his *Don Pasquale*, he was appointed *Kapellmeister* to the Emperor of Austria.

doppel (Ger.) Double.

doppelshlag (Ger.) Double stroke, the German equivalent of **turn**.

doppio (It.) Double, for example, *doppio movimento*, at double the preceding speed.

Dorati, Antal (1906-1988) Hungarian composer and conductor who recorded an important collection of **Haydn**'s symphonies with the Philharmonia Hungarica. He studied in Budapest at the Academy (where he was a pupil of **Kodály** and **Bartók**) and at the university. Later he continued his research at Vienna Univer-

Antal Dorati

sity. He followed an early career as a conductor in Budapest, Dresden and Munster. He has conducted for several major ballet companies, including the Ballet Theatre (1941). In 1948 he became an American citizen and continued to conduct, with the Minneapolis Symphony Orchestra (1949), the BBC Symphony Orchestra (1962), the Stockholm Symphony Orchestra (1966), the National Symphony of Washington (1970), the Royal Philharmonic (1976) and the Detroit Symphony Orchestra (1977). His compositions include symphonies, a violin concerto, ballets, cantatas and music for strings.

Dorian mode First of the Ambrosian modes, which are also known as the authentic modes. On the keyboard it can be played as a white-note scale starting on the note D. See also **modes**.

dot Indication that the time-value of a note is to be altered. A dot above or under a note normally indicates that the notes are to be played **staccato**. If a dot is placed after a note it means that the time-value of the note should be extended by half. In 1769, Leopold **Mozart** introduced the double dot to indicate that the time-value of the note was to be extended by half and half again.

Dots indicate different things, depending on their position

In French Baroque music, dots have a special significance as denoting *notes égales*.

In jazz jargon, 'dots' refer to written music.

double Term with three meanings.

First, it is the practice of being able and equipped to play two instruments alternately in the same piece. In jazz music, for instance, some clarinettists double on saxophone, and orchestral flautists often double on piccolo.

Second, it is the duplication of a melody or voice by more than one instrument.

Third, it is used to indicate an instrument of low pitch, such as the double bassoon, double harp, double-bass, etc. See also **doublé**.

doublé (Fr.) Doubled. Form of variation in which the strain of a dance is repeated in a more ornamented version.

double bar Pair of bar lines placed close together to indicate that a piece of music, or a section of it, has come to an end. It may be followed or preceeded by a repeat sign.

double-bass Largest string instrument, originally of the viol family. The double-bass formerly had three strings, but now usually has four, and a compass from E just over an octave below the bass stave, upwards for nearly three octaves. It is tuned in fourths: E-A-D-G.

double counterpoint **Invertible counterpoint** in two parts.

Double-bass

double flat Accidental (♭♭) that lowers the pitch of a note by two semitones.

double sharp Accidental (♯♯ or X) that raises the pitch of a note by two semitones.

double stopping Production of two notes simultaneously on a bowed stringed instrument.

double suspension In harmony, the suspension of two parts to act as a temporary discord against the following chord.

double tonguing Technique whereby a brass or woodwind player articulates very quickly with the tongue against the embouchure, making the sounds T-K or alternatively D-G.

double-whole-note American alternative for **breve**.

doux (Fr.) Gentle in volume or sweet in tone, or both.

Dowland, John (1563-1626) English composer, probably born in Westminster. Little is known of his early life, except that he visited Paris in 1580 as the servant of the Ambassador, Sir Henry Cobham, and was converted to Catholicism. This prompted Elizabeth I to reject him as a putative court musician in 1554. Instead, he visited Venice and Florence under the patronage of the Duke of Brunswick and, in 1597, completed his *First Booke of Songs.* In 1598 he was appointed lutenist to Christian IV of Denmark, composing his *Second* (1600) and *Third and Last Booke of Songs* (1603) while holding this position. He was dismissed in 1606, returning to England to be made one of the King's musicians in 1612.

Dowland's songs and his compositions for solo lute are enriched by continental influences as well as by traditional melodies. He is widely regarded today as an important figure in the development of lutine harmonies.

downbeat Alludes to the downward motion of a conductor's baton or hand and refers to the first or stressed beats of a bar. See also **upbeat**.

down bow Motion of the bow in the playing of stringed instruments in which the player pulls the bow from the heel towards the point. The sign indicating a downbow is derived from the N for *Nobilis*.

Downes, Edward Thomas (1924-) British conductor and horn player who studied with Scherchen. He was associate conductor at the Royal Opera (1952-1969) and of the Australian Opera (1971-1977), and has been guest conductor for many leading symphony orchestras. He is noted as the first to conduct **Wagner**'s *Der Ring des Nibelung* after the end of World War II (1945).

Downes, Ralph (1904-) British organist who has appeared as a recilatist on many occasions. As a noted organ designer, he was responsible for the organ at the Royal Festival Hall, London.

Draghi, Giovanni Battista (1640-1710) Italian composer and harpsichordist who moved to England and became organist to Queen Catherine of Braganza at the court of Charles II, and taught music to the future Queen Anne. His compositions include a setting of Dryden's ode *From Harmony, From Heavenly Harmony*, his *Song for St Cecilia's Day* (1687), and a number of pieces for harpsichord and organ.

Dragonetti, Domenico (1763-1846) Italian double-bass player and composer. At the age of 13 he was admitted to the opera orchestra at Venice. His works include several concertos for double-bass. From 1794 he settled in London, where he formed a partnership with the cellist Lindley.

dramma per musica (It.) Play through music. 17th-century term for **opera**.

Drdla, Frantisek (1868-1944) Czech composer and violinist who became a member of the Vienna Court Opera orchestra. He composed two operettas, songs, piano pieces and works for the violin and piano such as *Serenade* and *Souvenir*, which are still popular today.

Dresden Amen Threefold version of the sung Amen, associated with the Royal Chapel of Dresden. Using a traditional melody, this particular setting was composed (*c*1764) by J.G. **Naumann**.

Drigo, Riccardo (1846-1930) Italian composer and conductor who is best known for the *Serenade* from his ballet *Les millions d'Arlequin* (1900). He was conductor at the St Petersburg Court Opera from 1876 and became the principal conductor at the Maryinsky Theatre in 1886. He composed operatic works as well as ballets and chamber pieces.

drone Three lower pipes of the **bagpipe** that provide a continuous, fixed chord above which the melody is played on the chanter. A drone is also evident in many forms of Eastern music. The term is also used to indicate a similar effect in other music.

Druckman, Jacob Raphael (1928-) American composer who was awarded a Pulitzer Prize (1972) for his orchestral composition *Windows*. He studied at the Juilliard School (1949-1956) with **Copland**, Mennin and Wagenaar. In 1957 he studied in Paris and finally moved to the Columbia-Princeton Electric Music Center, 1965. He has also been associated with electronic music studios at other universities. Among his compositions are impressionistic orchestral pieces including *Chiaroscuro* (1976) and *Lamia* (1974) for soprano and orchestra. He also worked extensively with tape, notably in his *Animus* in three parts (1966, 1968, 1969).

drum Popular term for the family of membranophones which includes in Western music the following instruments: kettledrums (timpani), bass drum, bongos, snare drum, tabor, tambourine, tenor drum, etc. Some drums have a specific pitch (e.g. the kettledrums are tuneable either by taps which are positioned at points around the side of the instrument to change the tension of the membrane and thus the pitch of the note produced, or by pedals, which perform the same function). Other drums are of indefinite pitch.

drumstick Wooden stick used to strike a drum, thus creating a sound. Drumsticks come in many shapes and sizes, and the head of the stick may be hard or soft.

Drysdale, Learmont (1866-1909) Scottish composer of operas, orchestral works, concert overtures and songs. Among his operas are *Hippolytus* (Euripides translation) and *The Plague*.

Dubensky, Arkady (1890-1966) Russian composer and violinist who was notable for the unusual combinations of instruments demanded by his compositions. He studied at the Moscow Conservatoire and became leader of the Moscow Imperial Opera Orchestra. In 1921 he moved to the United States and joined the New York Symphony Orchestra. His compositions include a fugue for 18 violins, *Fantasy on Negro Themes* for tuba and orchestra, an overture for 18 toy trumpets, and a concerto for three trombones, tuba and orchestra.

Dubois, (François Clément) Théodore (1837-1924) French composer and organist who composed a number of operas, ballets, cantatas and orchestral pieces, and was an influential teacher. He studied at the Paris Conservatoire and became professor of harmony there in 1871. In 1877 he became organist at La Madeleine, returning to the Conservatoire as director in 1896. He resigned this post in 1905 in support of **Ravel**, who had been refused the chance to compete for the Prix de Rome by a prejudiced jury. He is best known for his sacred music and writings on harmony and counterpoint.

due corde (It.) Two strings. In violin music, indicates that a section is to be played on two strings rather than one, to give an undulating effect. In piano music, the term indicates that the **una corda** pedal is to be raised, causing both strings for each note to be sounded.

duet Composition for two performers (vocal or instrumental), with or without accompaniment. For example, a piano duet is a work for two pianists at one keyboard (as opposed to a duet for two pianos).

Dufay, Guillaume (*c*1400-1474) French composer, regarded by both his contemporaries and modern experts as probably the greatest of the 15th century. After singing in the choir at Cambrai Cathedral, he spent his 20s and 30s in Italy, singing in the Papal chapel and discharging the duties of curate in Savoy. In 1434 he met the Franco-Flemish composer **Binchois**. Back in Cambrai on a fairly regular basis from 1439, Dufay served as a cleric at the cathedral. Nearly 200 works by him survive, including eight complete masses and more than 80 songs. He may have been the first to use a secular folk tune such as *L'Homme armé* as the *cantus firmus* (core melody) of a mass. His warm harmonies and expressive melodies prefigure the music of the Renaissance. He is also said to have composed the earliest Requiem, now lost.

Dukas, Paul (1865-1935) French composer and widely respected critic, who wrote the first piano sonata by a major French composer (the piano sonata in E♭ minor, 1901), and who developed some of **Debussy**'s techniques in his work.

He studied at the Paris Conservatoire (1882-1889) and became a professor of composition there in 1909, and devoted his time to musical criticism. In the 1920s his confidence failed him and he destroyed much of his work. He passed his later years assisting **Saint-Saëns** in the completion of Guiraud's opera *Frédegonde* and editing some operas by **Rameau**. His most famous composition is the orchestral scherzo *The Sorcerer's Apprentice* (1897). He also composed operas – including the acclaimed *Ariane et Barbe-bleue* (1907) – and the ballet *La péri* (1912).

Duke, Vernon (1903-1969) Russian-born composer whose original name was Vladimir Dukelsky. He became an American citizen (1922) and, under his new name, composed for the cinema, sometimes working with Harberg. His song *April in Paris* for the 1952 film of the same name has become a classic. He studied music at the Kiev Conservatoire with **Glière**. His ballet *Zephyr et Flore* was produced by Diaghilev's *Ballets Russes* in 1925. He wrote other ballets, and concertos for the piano, violin and cello, and a harpsichord sonata.

dulcimer Instrument with a set of strings stretched over a sound-board which are

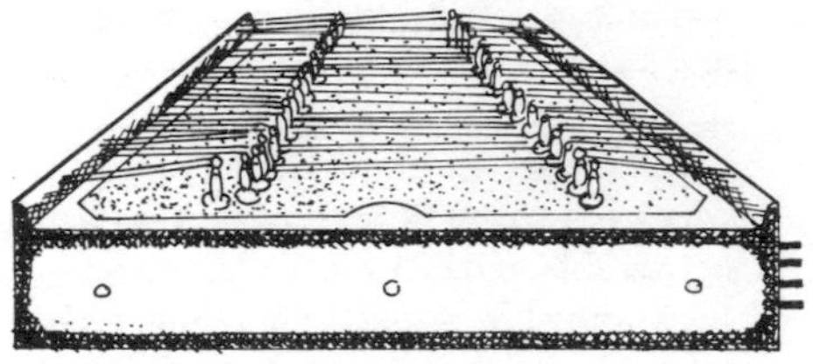

Dulcimer

struck by hammers. The Hungarian **cimbalon** is the only type of dulcimer still in use.

dumka Lament of Slavonic folk-origin which takes the form of a slow piece alternating with more animated sections. The form was used by **Dvorák** in his piano trio *Dumky* (1891).

dump Name used in the 16th and 17th centuries for a doleful piece of English music. An alternative spelling is dompe.

dung-chen (Tibet) Large, straight trumpet which is typically two to three metres (six to nine feet) long and constructed with telescopic sections of copper or brass, and mouthpiece. Although it probably has military origins, it is now used in pairs in Buddhist ritual to provide drones and occasional two- or three-note patterns.

Dunhill, Thomas Frederick (1877-1946) British composer, teacher and writer who was a pupil of **Stanford**. Dunhill is best remembered for his didactic compositions, mostly for the piano. Other works include a symphonic operetta *Tantivy Towers* (1931), and *Elegaic Voices* (1933), a symphony, chamber music and songs.

Duni, Egidio Romualdo (1708-1775) Italian-born composer who settled in Paris in 1757. He became a leading composer of *opèra-comique*, such as *Le Caprice Amoureux*, *Le Milicien* and *Les Sabots*.

Dunstable, John (*c*1385-1453) English composer and mathematician who was known throughout Europe. His work has been discovered in early French and Italian manuscript collections. He was one of the first composers to use an instrumental accompaniment for devotional music. He was in the service of the Duke of Bedford, who was a regent of France (1422-35), and he was able to travel widely. His compositions – notably his setting of *O rosa bella* – reflect the influences of **Dufay** and **Binchois**. He wrote a number of masses, as well as other choral pieces, and was an authoritative author of astronomical texts.

duo Term with two meanings.

First, it is a composition for two voices or instruments.

Second, it is the name given to the players who perform such a composition. See also **duet**.

Duparc, Henri Fouques (1848-1933) French pianist and composer whose settings of Baudelaire's poems, particularly the *L'invitation au Voyage*, attached new importance to the text of songs. Educated under **Franck** at the Jesuit College of Vaugirard, he joined Franck's collective of composers and travelled to Weimar to study Teutonic styles. He was strongly influenced by **Wagner**, whom he met at **Liszt**'s house in 1869. His interest in literature dictated his choice of texts for his songs, and he was driven by a passion for emotionalism in music.

duplet Group of two notes that occupy a time of three. Also known as a couplet, marked with a figure 2.

Duplet

duple time Time signature that indicates two beats in the bar, such as 2/4 or 6/8.

Duplex-coupler piano Piano with two keyboards tuned an octave apart. Designed in 1921 by Emanuel Moor (1863-1931).

du Pré, Jacqueline (1945-1987) British cellist who studied with **Tortelier** and **Rostropovich**. She gained a world-wide reputation as a soloist but was stricken in 1972 with multiple sclerosis, which brought about her untimely death. In 1967 she married Daniel **Barenboim**, the pianist and conductor. She recorded widely, and is especially associated with **Elgar**'s Cello Concerto.

Dupré, Marcel (1886-1971) French composer and organist. He studied at the Paris Conservatoire and gained the Prix de Rome (1914) as a pupil of **Widor**. He became the first organist to present the complete cycle of **Bach**'s organ music. As director of the Paris Conservatoire (1954-1956) he edited the organ works of **Liszt, Schumann, Bach** and **Handel**. His compositions include many organ works, including two organ symphonies, other symphonic pieces, and a violin sonata.

dur (Ger.) Equivalent of the English major, referring to the major key.

Durante, Francesco (1684-1755) Italian composer associated with the Neapolitan School. He studied with **Scarlatti** and became *maestro di cappella* at the Conservatorio de Santa Maria di Loreto in 1742. His compositions include devotional music and pieces for the harpsichord and strings. He was an influential tutor, numbering Piccini, **Pergolesi** and **Jommelli** among his pupils.

durchfuhrung (Ger.) Equivalent of the English **development**.

durchkomponiert (Ger.) Through-composed. Term used for a work, especially a song in a continuous form, that does not repeat itself in successive stanzas.

Durey, Louis (1888-1979) French composer who attended the Schola Cantorum, Paris, and joined Les Six (1920), abandoning them a year later. His works include three string quartets and other chamber compositions, songs, choral music and an opera (*L'occasion*).

Durko, Zsolt (1934-) Hungarian composer, and pupil of **Petrassi** and Farkas. Among his works are *Hungarian Rhapsody* for two clarinets and orchestra (1964), *Altamira* (1968) and the music drama *Mozes* (1977).

Duruflé, Maurice (1902-1986) French organist and composer who was a pupil of **Vierne**, and later became a professor at the Paris Conservatoire (1943). His compositions include *Prelude et fugue sur le nom Alain* (1942) for the organ, *Cum Jubilo* (1967) and *Requiem* (1947) for organ, orchestra and choir, as well as some fine unaccompanied motets.

Dussek, Johann Ladislav (1760-1812) Czech pianist and composer, a pupil of C.P.E. **Bach** and friend of **Haydn**. He was a prolific composer, writing 28 piano sonatas and 15 concertos, 38 violin and 16 flute sonatas, as well as pieces for two pianos, a ballad opera and a mass. An alternative spelling of his name is Jan Dusik.

Dutilleux, Henri (1916-) French composer noted for his technical skills and use of dissonant styles as well as his development of styles created by **Ravel** and **Roussel**. He studied at the Paris Conservatoire and was awarded the Prix de Rome in 1938. He became a broadcaster in 1944, and in 1961 was appointed professor of composition at the Ecole Normale de Musique. His compositions include two symphonies (1950, 1958), a ballet *Le Loup* (1953), sonatas for the piano and oboe, string quartets and music for film, and more recently a violin concerto.

Dvorák, Antonin (1841-1904) Czech composer sometimes named as the greatest of his nationality. Dvorák displayed an affinity with nature in his compositions. His work is characterized by a grand sensuality and a freshness that **Brahms**, among others, found captivating.

Born near Prague, Dvorák took up the violin and became a pupil at the city's organ school in 1857. He was influenced by **Wagner**, paticularly in his opera *Alfred* and his third (1873) and fourth (1874) symphonies, also by **Smetana**, who

Antonin Dvorák

directed the Opera Orchestra in which Dvorák played. In 1873 he became organist at St Aldabert's Church and embarked upon his most creative period, receiving the Austrian State Prize for four years in succession. His *Slavonic Dances* and *Moravian Duets* (1878) extended his fame and he was commissioned by the Vienna Philharmonic Orchestra to produce a new symphony in 1880. The Symphony in D Major was a triumph. In 1885 he presented his Symphony in D Minor in London, and continued a close relationship with Britain throughout his life. He became professor of composition at Prague, 1885. In 1891 he visited the United States to head the New York Conservatoire, and composed the Symphony in E minor, *From the New World* and the cello concerto (1893). These last two remain among Dvorak's best-known works.

Dykes, John Bacchus (1823-1876) British composer and Anglican clergyman who composed many hymn tunes, along with other church music. He assisted in compiling *Hymns Ancient & Modern* and composed some hymns himself, including *Nearer my God to thee* and *Jesu, lover of my soul.*

dynamics Graduations of volume in music.

Dyson, Sir George (1883-1964) English composer and organist, best known for his composition *The Canterbury Pilgrims* (1931) which is a cantata setting of Chaucer's text (modernized), first performed in Winchester in 1941. He studied at the Royal College of Music before travelling to Italy and Germany on a scholarship (1904-1908). He taught music at English public schools, including Rugby and Winchester, and became director of the Royal College of Music in 1937. He was knighted in 1941. Among his other compositions are the orchestral works *St Paul's Voyage to Melita* (1933) and *Quo Vadis* (1939).

Dzerzhinsky, Ivan Ivanovich (1909-1978) Russian operatic composer whose work is considered to be technically naive and dependent for its form and melodic character upon Russian folk songs. But when **Shostakovich** fell from favour with the Soviet government in 1936 for producing works in which Pravda detected "petty-bourgeois sensationalism", Dzerzhinsky's work was used as a model of correctness, perhaps because of the closeness of its ties with traditional music. He studied at the Leningrad Conservatoire and produced a number of operas, including *Quiet Flows the Don* (1935), *Virgin Soil Upturned* (1937), *Blood of the People* (1941) and *Grigory Melekhov* (1967). He also composed for the piano and orchestra.

E

E Name of the note that lies one tone above D and one semitone below F. The scale of E major has four sharps in the key-signature.

Edinburgh International Festival Annual international festival of the arts held in three weeks in August and September in Edinburgh. Main festival activities include concert performances, recitals and operas, although there is also a very active 'fringe' festival involving many less formal performances, especially of plays and revues. The festival was founded in 1947 under Rudolf Bing, and his successors have included Ian Hunter (1949-1961), Peter Diamand (1966-1978) and John Drumond (from 1979). Almost all the major world orchestras have appeared at Edinburgh.

einleitung (Ger.) Introduction; prelude.

eisteddfod Competitive festival of music and literature that originated in Wales. One form of Eisteddfod is an annual international festival held in Llangollen, Wales, where choirs and dancers from throughout the world compete. The present festival was started in 1947.

A second type is the National Eisteddfod, founded in 1880, which is held in a different Welsh town every year, to assess the accomplishments of the bards (poets). Festivals of this kind date back to the Middle Ages, although the term eisteddfod was not used until the 18th century.

Elder, Mark (1947-) English conductor and bassoonist who studied at Cambridge University. In 1970 he acted as assistant to Raymond **Leppard** at **Glyndebourne**. Conducting posts have included Covent Garden and Australia Opera (1972-1974) and he was appointed principal conductor of the English National Opera in 1979. Elder is mainly known as a conductor of opera and especially noted for his interpretations of **Strauss**.

electronic music Music which is produced or changed by electrophonic instruments. Often the musical elements are assembled on magnetic tape, using electronic sound mixing equipment, synthesizers and computerized instruments (such as drum machines). Sometimes, electronic instruments and computers are used in live performance in conjunction with more conventional musicians. One form of popular electronically-produced music that has come to the fore recently is known as house music, in which motifs, tunes and rhythms previously recorded (and often the copyright of someone else) are 'sampled' electronically and then put together to form a coherent composition.

electric organ Organ in which signals created by electronic oscillators are amplified and converted into sound by a loud-

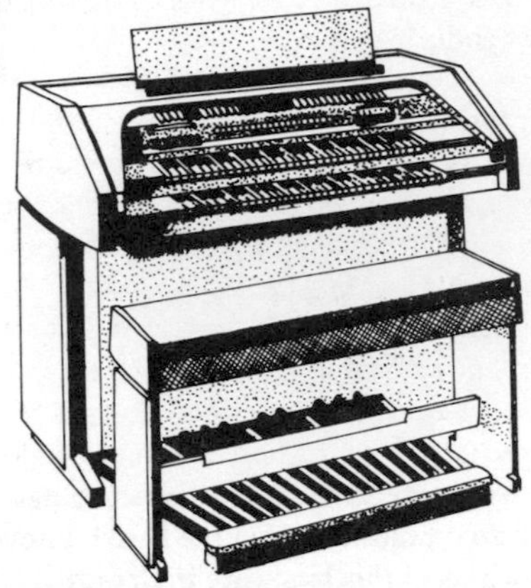
Electric organ

speaker. A modern electronic organ usually has two or three manuals and an electronic rhythm section, and can produce a wide variety of sounds.

electrophonic Describing musical instruments in which the notes are transmitted through electric circuits to amplifiers. Instruments such as electric guitars, violins and pianos are electrophonic instruments.

elegy Vocal or instrumental piece of reflective or mournful quality, named after the poetic form of the same nature. **Berlioz**'s *Elégie en prose* from *Neuf melodies Irlandaises* (1830), which he dedicated to Harriet Smithson, is an example of this type of composition.

Elgar, Sir Edward (1857-1934) English composer, born near Worcester. He was self-taught and began to write pieces for local performance, notably for his local church choir. He was engaged in 1888 to one of his piano pupils, Caroline Roberts, and composed *Salut d'Amour* in celebration. He continued to write choral pieces, and in 1900 *The Dream of Gerontius* was presented at the Birmingham Festival. 1899 saw the completion of the *Variations on an Original Theme* (the 'Enigma' variations) and *Pomp and Circumstance*. These works, together with the overture *Cockaigne* (1901) and the *Introduction and Allegro for Strings* (1905) were preludes for symphonic composition.

Elgar's first symphony (1908), with its subtle variations of theme, was a master-

Sir Edward Elgar

piece. His difficult Violin Concerto (Op. 61, 1910) was equally successful. The coming of war in 1914 induced Elgar to compose patriotic pieces, including *Carillon* and *The Spirit of England*, but after the death of his wife (1920) he seemed to lose his previous inspiration, although his Cello Concerto (Op. 85) is a bold and moving work. He died before work on his third symphony could be completed.

Elgar was capable of expressing dominant and patriotic themes in his music. His *Pomp and Circumstance March No. 1* became an anthem for the nation, and its popularity was increased by the advent of the gramophone. However, Elgar also voiced a deep and personal introspection and a more subtle and brilliant modelling of musical ideas.

Elizalde, Frederico (1907-1979) Spanish composer and pianist. After a number of successes on the jazz scene in England during the 1920s, he became conductor of the Manila Symphony Orhestra in 1930 and President of the Manila Broadcasting Company in 1948. His best-known work is the opera *Paul Gaugin*, which reflects the influences of his tutor, **Bloch**.

Ellington, Duke (Edward Kennedy E.) (1899-1974) American jazz conductor, composer and orchestrator who came to have a seminal influence on the development of jazz music.

Ellington was born in Washington D.C., but achieved his first successes at New York's Cotton Club. He wrote hundreds of pieces during his career, for his own band, and also for stage and screen, providing film scores for *Anatomy of a Murder, Paris Blues* and *Assault on a Queen*. He developed many styles of composition, extending pieces such as *Black, Brown and Beige* (1943) beyond the usual 32-bar format, to allow his themes to develop unhindered. He also experimented with vocal works, adapting songs from Shakespeare's plays in *Such Sweet Thunder*, and using the voice of Adelaide Hall as an instrument in *Creole Love Call*. Among his other works, *Take the 'A'-Train* and *Mood Indigo* are possibly the most enduring.

Ellis, Osian (1928-) Welsh harpist and singer. Born in Ffynnongroyw, now in Clwyd, he attended the Royal Academy of Music. He has gained a great reputation both inside and outside Wales as an exponent of Welsh folk song, especially the form known as **penhillion**, in which the words of a poem are sung as a composed or improvised **descant** to a traditional melody or *alaw*, played on a harp. Ellis's reputation has also spread to the field of better-known music. He is a member of the British chamber group, the Melos Ensemble, and was a close friend of **Britten**, who wrote his *Harp Suite* Op. 83, for him.

Eloy, Jean-Claude (1938-) French composer who studied under **Milhaud** at the Paris Conservatoire and **Boulez** at the Basle Academy of Music. Much of his orchestral work, particularly his *Polychromes I & II* (1964) and *Faisceaux-Diffractions* (1970), display the influence of his tutors in their polychromatic style. His work became popular in the United States during his visit there in 1967.

Elsner, Joseph Xavier (1769-1854) Polish composer, who acted as *Kappelmeister* to the Archbishop of Lemberg in 1792. He was self-taught, but his pedagogic skill led him to become director of the Warsaw Conservatoire in 1821. While in Warsaw, Elsner became one of **Chopin**'s tutors. His compositions include a ballet, three symphonies and more than 20 operas.

embouchure (Fr.) Mouthpiece, meaning the position and application of the lips to the mouthpiece of a wind instrument.

enchainez (Fr.) To link together. Indication that the next movement or a section of a piece should follow its predecessor without a break.

Encina, Juan del (1468-*c*1530) Spanish poet and composer of romances and villancios. Most of these were reprinted in Barbieri's *Cancionero* (1890). Encina is known to have entered the service of the Duke of Alba from 1492. He then moved to Rome as a cleric and became the Archdeacon of Malaga in 1509, and finally the Prior of Leon in 1519.

encore (Fr.) Again. Used in English as a call to a performer to repeat all or part of a work just played in a concert. On some occasions an encore is not a repetition of a piece just played, but a different piece. The word is not used in French for such an occasion. Instead the Latin, *bis* is used.

Enescu, George (1881-1955) Hailed as the 'father of Romanian national music', Enescu blended themes from folk songs with powerful romantic colours in his work, particularly in his two *Romanian Rhapsodies* (1901 and 1902). Born in Liveni-Virnav, Enescu became an accomplished violinist and recitalist, studying in Vienna and entering the Paris Conservatoire in 1897. While there, he conducted his own work and became one of **Menuhin**'s tutors.

English Chamber Orchestra British chamber orchestra, founded by Arnold Goldsbrough and Lawrence Leonard in 1948 (when it was known as the Goldsbrough Orchestra). It changed its name in 1960 when the repertory progressed beyond 18th-century music.

Although primarily known for its classical music, the English Chamber Orchestra has been associated with Benjamin **Britten** and the **Aldeburgh Festival**, and has performed many premieres of the works of British composers. It has no permanent conductor, but regular conductors have included Colin **Davis**, Daniel **Barenboim**, Raymond **Leppard** and Pinchas **Zukerman**.

English horn Alternative term for **cor anglais**.

English Music Theatre Company Founded in 1947 by Benjamin **Britten**, John Piper and Eric Crozier, when it was called the English Opera Group. Its main objectives were devoted to the creation and performance of new operas and to encourage poets and playwrights to write librettos in collaboration with composers. Since its foundation it has been responsible for establishing and directing the **Aldeburgh Festival** (1948). Among the new works it has produced are Britten's *Albert Herring* (1947), *The Turn of the Screw* (1954) and *Death in Venice* (1973); Lennox **Berkeley**'s *A Dinner Engagement* (1954) and *Ruth* (1956), and Harrison **Birtwistle**'s *Punch and Judy* (1968).

In 1964 the group became the first British opera company to tour the Soviet Union. The management of the company was taken over in 1961 by Covent Garden, and in 1975 it was reorganized as the English Music Theatre Company.

English National Opera British opera company based in London, which before 1974 was known as Sadler's Wells Opera. The original Sadler's Wells Theatre was built in 1765 where musical performances were held, and in the 19th century the occasional opera was also produced. At one stage the theatre operated as a music hall until it fell into disuse. In 1931 it became the northern branch of the Old Vic Theatre for the alternate production of classical drama and opera. From 1935 plays were confined to the Old Vic and opera to Sadler's Wells. In 1948 Norman Tucker began his long association with the company. Sadler's Wells expanded and many new operas and existing operas were produced, and all performed in English.

The company moved to the Coliseum Theatre in 1968 under the direction of Stephen Arlen. At its new home, there were several adventurous productions such as **Berlioz**'s *Damnation de Faust*, **Prokofiev**'s *War and Peace*, and the Ring Cycle conducted by Reginald Goodall. The company's musical directors have included Alexander Gibson, Colin **Davis**, Charles Makerras, Sir Charles Groves and Mark **Elder**.

enharmonic interval Note that has changed its name but not its pitch. For example, when F♯ becomes G♭ or B♯ becomes C.

ensemble (Fr.) Together, term with three meanings.
First, it is a group of performers, either vocalists or instrumentalists, of no fixed number.
Second, it is used to describe a group's ability to play together – they are either good ensemble or bad ensemble.
Third, it is an item in an opera in which two or more soloists sing together, such as a duet, trio or quartet.

entr'acte (Fr.) Music played between the acts of plays and operas. See also **intermezzo**.

entrée (Fr.) Dance or group of dances unified by subject in French 17th-century *ballet de coeur*. The term thus often signified a scene. In later *tragedie lyrique* and opera-ballet it was used for the instrumental march or air at the start of a **divertissement** of songs and dances found in most acts.

epicedium Mournful funeral ode such as **Blow**'s *The Queen's Epicedium* (1695) on the death of Queen Mary II, based on a poem by George Herbert.

episode Incidental passage in a composition which is a digression from the main theme or themes. For example, in a **rondo** it is a contrasting section between recurrences of the main theme, whereas in a **fugue** it is a passage that does not contain a complete entry of the subject. It may, however, be derived from the main thematic material.

éponge (Fr.) Sponge. For example, *baguettes d'éponge* refers to drumsticks with sponge heads.

equale (Fr.) Equal. Voices or instruments of equal pitch. The term was used specifically for formal funeral music such as **Beethoven's** three *Equali* (1812) for trombone quartet.

equal voices Term with two meanings.
First, it is a vocal composition written for voices of equal or comparable range, such as two sopranos or three tenors.
Second, it has come to mean more loosely music for only female or only male voices.

Erb, Donald James (1927-) American composer, born in Youngstown, Ohio, who studied at Ohio State University, the Cleveland Institute, and at the Paris Conservatoire with **Boulanger**. He created a style of composition that used tape recorders and electronic sound mixers in conjunction with traditional instruments.

Erbse, Heimo (1924-) German composer who was influenced by the tonal and variable rhythm techniques of his tutor Boris **Blacher**. He studied in Weimar from 1945 and entered the Berlin Hochschule in 1950. He became a producer of opera and a singing tutor in 1947. His compositions include the operas *Julietta* and *Der Herr in Grau*, as well as pieces for chorus, orchestra and wind instruments.

erh-hu (China) Two-stringed fiddle with a hexagonal sound box. Both the neck and body are made of wood, and one side of the hexagon is covered with snakeskin. The strings are attached to the top of the neck and to the sound box, forming an angle with the neck, there being no bridge. It is bowed held vertically and used in the orchestra of the traditional Chinese opera, as well as being a popular solo instrument.

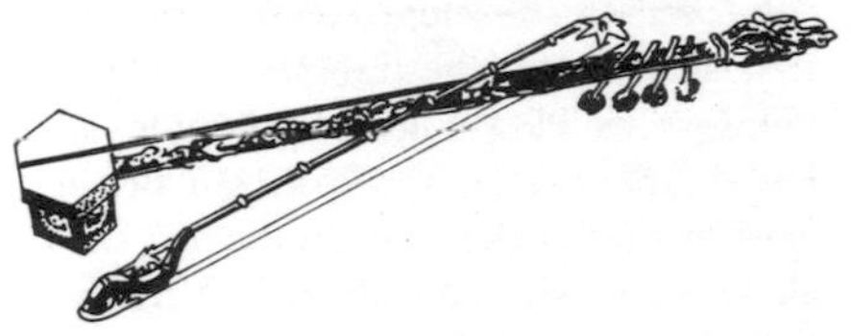

Erh-hu

Erickson, Robert (1917-) Avant-garde American composer, influenced by **dode-**

caphonic forms and by the patterns of *musique concrète*. Erickson studied and taught at the San Francisco Conservatoire (1957) and San Diego University (1967). He was influenced by Krenek's theories of free **atonality** and abandoned the **twelve-note** form in 1957 to concentrate on freer techniques. This new freedom is shown in his *Chamber Concerto* (1960) and in *High Flyer* (1969).

Erkel, Ferenc (1810-1893) Hungarian conductor and nationalist composer who enjoyed as much adulation from Hungarians as **Smetana** from his Czech compatriots. He became conductor of the Budapest National Theatre (1838) and founded the Budapest Philharmonic Orchestra (1840). As a professor at the Hungarian National Academy of Music he encouraged composers in the use of ethnic idioms, and always strove to preserve a national musical identity among his pupils. His opera *Hunyady László* (1844) was a great success, as was his *Bánk Bán* (1844-1852) which is still played on the national holiday. He also composed the music for the Hungarian national anthem.

Ernst, Heinrich Wilhelm (1814-1865) Moravian composer and violinist who modelled his style on the legendary **Paganini**. He studied at the Vienna Conservatoire before moving to Paris in 1832. He toured Europe as a performer before settling in London in 1855. He composed a number of concertos and other pieces for violin.

Escher, Rudolph (1912-1980) Dutch composer who developed an interesting arrangement of orchestral players in some of his pieces. He studied composition in Rotterdam (1931) with **Pijper** and began work in 1961 at the Delft studio for electronic music and later at the Utrecht State University. He was a respected critic and published books on the French Impressionist composers, including **Debussy** and **Ravel**. His compositions include two symphonies, a tone poem *Le Tombeau de Ravel* (1952) and the spectacular *Summer Rites at Noon* (1973) for two orchestras arranged as the **cantoris** and **decani** halves of a choir.

Esplá, Oscar (1886-1976) Spanish composer who trained as an engineer but left the profession to devote his time to composition. His works include operas, symphonic pieces, choral works and chamber music, and reflect the patterns and rhythms of Spanish folk music. Esplá did not receive any formal musical training, and a measure of his independence can be seen in his creation of a new scale, the 'Levantine', equivalent to the scale C-D♭-E♭-E-F-G♭-A♭-B♭.

Esposito, Michele (1855-1929) Italian composer and pianist who founded and conducted for the Dublin Orchestra Society (1899). He studied at the Naples Conservatoire and then moved to Paris (1878). In 1882 he moved again to Dublin, and was appointed professor of piano at the Royal Irish Academy of Music. Among his compositions are the operetta *The Postbag* (1902), the *Irish Symphony* (1902) and music for strings and orchestra. He returned to Italy shortly before his death.

estampie (Fr.) Instrumental piece or dance of the 13th and 14th centuries, related to **troubador** forms. The *estampie* consisted of between four and seven sections (known as *puncta*), each of which is stated twice, with a different ending the second time.

estinto (It.) Extinct, indication that a passage is to be performed extremely softly, in an almost toneless manner.

estudiantina (Sp.) Piece of music played in a light-hearted manner, generally performed by wandering students to a street audience.

etherophone Alternative term for **thérémin**.

ethnomusicology Study of the music of

world cultures, especially primitive and non-Western systems of music, in relation to their anthropological and historical development. In the 1880s it was known as comparative musicology, but in the 1930s Jaap Kunst, a specialist in Indonesian music, renamed this type of research ethnomusicology.

Etler, Alvin Derald (1913-1973) American composer and oboist who wrote pieces for electronic performance as well as for conventional orchestral settings. He studied at the Cleveland Institute of Music (1931) and at Yale University (1942) with **Hindemith**. He became oboist for the Indianapolis Symphony Orchestra (1938) and followed a career as a lecturer in several academic institutions. Among his compositions are many works for wind instruments, concertos for orchestra, for violin and wind quintet, for orchestra and brass quintet and for orchestra and strings.

étouffez (Fr.) Direction to deaden or dampen the tone on instruments that are liable to vibrate after being sounded, such as the harp, kettledrum or cymbals.

étude (Fr.) **Study** or exercise. For example, Chopin Op. 25 for piano.

euphonium Also known as a saxhorn or

Euphonium

tenor tuba, a four-valved brass instrument of the tuba family, with a wide, conical bore, sounding in B♭. It was invented by Sommer of Weimar, Germany in 1843 and is now used mainly in brass and military bands.

eurthythmics System of teaching music, especially rhythmic music, by bodily movement. It was invented by Emil **Jacques-Dalcroze**, who set up an institute for it in Dresden (1910). Apart from being helpful to performers of ballet and modern dancing, it has proved valuable to general physical and mental education.

Evans, Sir Geraint (Llewellyn) (1922-) Welsh baritone who studied at the Guildhall School of Music and in Hamburg (with Theo Hermann) and Geneva (with Fernando Carpi). He made his debut at Covent Garden in 1948 in *Die Meistersinger von Nürnberg* (**Wagner**). He has since sung all the major roles for his voice, including Figaro, Papageno, Masetto and Leporello. He has created several roles, including Mr Flint in *Billy Budd* and Antenor in *Troilus and Cressida*. His voice is warm and he has a wide range. Evans was awarded the CBE in 1959 and was knighted in 1969. He is considered to be one of the greatest baritones of his day.

exercise Term with three meanings.

First, it is a vocal or instrumental piece of little or no artistic value, which is intended to develop technique, such as a five-finger exercise for piano. The French equivalent is **étude**.

Second, it is a form of 18th-century keyboard suite. As an example, some of D. **Scarlatti**'s early sonatas were published under the Italian equivalent of the term.

Third, it is a composition which candidates are expected to write for a music degree.

exposition Part of a fugue or **sonata** movement in which the original theme or themes are stated before the middle or development section begins.

Expressionism Term borrowed from the visual arts and applied to a movement in music that originated in Germany and Austria in the 1910–1930 period. It was partly a reaction to French Impressionist painting. Although there is a technical meaning to Expressionism in art, it is difficult to see how its tenets may be applied to music. However, the style can be characterized as being harshly dissonant and atonal.

Two composers most closely associated with expressionism are Arnold **Schoenberg** and Alban **Berg**.

extemporization Alternative term for **improvisation**.

extension organ Alternative term for **unit organ**.

F

F Term with two meanings.

First, it is the name of the note that lies one semitone above E and one tone below G. The scale of F major has one flat in the key-signature.

F F major

Second it is an abbreviation of Fanna. It was used as a prefix to indicate the numbers of **Vivaldi**'s works catalogued by Antonio Fanna (1968). A later catalogue by Peter Ryom superceded Fanna's catalogue in 1973.

fa In **tonic sol-fa**, name given to the subdominant note in any key, represented by the symbol f.

faburden Term with two meanings.

First, in the late 14th and early 15th centuries it was a method of improvising three-voice parallel harmony to **plainsong**, with the melody at the top of the texture.

In modern usage, it is a part added to a hymn and sung by a choir's sopranos and tenors. The congregation sings the tune itself, and the remaining voices of the choir sing their parts much as usual. This is also known as **descant**.

facile (Fr., It.) Easy. It is applied, for example, to a solo passage written for a virtuoso performer so that he or she performs fluently without any signs of labouring.

fado Popular Portugese song performed in streets and cafés, accompanied by the guitar and enlivened by dancing. Following its popularity in Lisbon during the 1850s it spread to the provinces.

fagott (Ger.) **Bassoon**. Also refers to a 16-foot reed organ stop that produces a bassoon tone.

fah Alternative spelling of **fa**.

Fall, Leo (1873-1925) Austrian composer who enjoyed some success in France, Germany and England with his light operettas. He studied at the Vienna Conservatoire and then in Berlin, Hamburg and Cologne. Among his works are two serious operas and the operettas *Der Rebell* (1905), *Die Dollarprinzessin* (1907), *The Eternal Waltz* (first performed in London, 1912) and *Madame Pompadour* (1922).

Falla, Manuel de (1876-1946) Spanish composer and pianist who reflected the themes from Andalusian folk music in his earlier works and adopted neo-classical styles in his later compositions.

Falla first received musical instruction from his family and relatives. He studied the piano at the Madrid Academy with Trago (1898-1899) and composition under Pedrell (1902), and composed his first pieces, two zarzuelas, at this time. In 1905 he completed his opera *La Vida Breve* and won the Madrid Academy of Fine Arts

Prize. His four *Pièces Espagnoles* were first performed in Paris (1909) and then in London (1911). In 1916 he completed his most important work, *Noches en los Jardines de España*, an atmospheric piece which reflected the influences of **Debussy** and **Ravel**. His most famous work, the opera *The Three-Cornered Hat*, was completed in 1919 and produced in London by **Diaghilev**. Other works include *Fantasia Bética* (1919), *El Retablo de Maese Pedro* (1923) and *L'Atlántida*.

false relation Special effect of harmony in which two different versions of the same note (for instance, E♯ and E♭) occur simultaneously or in immediate succession in different parts. 16th- and early 17th-century composers accepted simultaneous false relations, and they were still being used by English composers in the latter half of the 17th century, mainly as a result of tradition and as a means of expression. Also known as cross relation.

fancy 16th- and early 17th-century English term for a composition for lute, keyboard or instrumental ensemble. The fancy had no distinct form, but always made considerable use of **counterpoint**, and was generally divided into a number of sections, played without a break and not connected thematically. In the latter part of the 17th century, the sections became more distinct, and in the works of Henry **Purcell**, John Jenkins and Matthew **Locke** they were often interspersed with dance movements. See also **fantasia**.

fandango (Sp.) Spanish dance in triple time which probably originated in South America. The guitar and castanets are prominent in the accompaniment. A slower form also exists, and was used by **Gluck** in his ballet *Don Juan* and later by **Mozart** in the finale of Act III in *The Marriage of Figaro*.

fanfare Flourish for trumpets or other brass instruments, usually by way of an introduction or at the head of a procession. Fanfares have been used in operas such as **Beethoven**'s *Fidelio*, **Bizet**'s *Carmen* and **Verdi**'s *Otello*.

fantasia Composition in which the composer's imagination is given free rein without being subject to the rules of structure or form. The term was first used by 16th-century lutenists such as Luis de **Milan** (1535) and Francesco da Milano (1536). It may also be a composition based on a selected theme from another composer's work, such as a folksong, popular tune or operatic air. See also **fancy**.

farandole (Fr.) Dance form which originated in Provence, performed by groups of people in the streets and accompanied by pipe and tabor. The music is in 6/8 time. A farandole appears in **Bizet**'s *L'Arlésienne* (1872), but its form is not traditionally correct, although it is based on an authentic Provence tune.

Farmer, John (late 16th century) English composer who became the organist of Christ Church, Dublin. Little is known about his life, other than that he moved to London in 1599. He wrote a series of canons in 1591 and composed a collection of madrigals in 1599, including *Fair Phyllis I Saw Sitting All Alone*. He also wrote pieces for Thomas East's *Whole Booke of Psalmes*.

Farnaby, Giles (1566-1640) English composer of keyboard music, madrigals, psalms and canzonets.

In 1594 he moved from London, his birthplace, to Lincolnshire, and is known to have taught the children of Sir Nicholas Saunderson. While there, he composed his *Canzonets to Foure Voices* (1598). In 1614 he returned to London and continued to write. He contributed more than 60 pieces to the *Fitzwilliam Virginal Book*, including *A Dreame*, *a Toye*, and *His Humour*.

Farrant, Richard (*c*1530-1580) English composer who became organist and master of the choristers at St George's Chapel, Windsor, and a member of the Chapel

Royal. He composed anthems, including *Hide Not Thou Thy face*, *Call to Remembrance* and songs for the court.

farruca (Sp.) Lively and energetic Andalusian dance of gypsy origins. It is used by **Falla** for the miller's dance in *The Three-Cornered Hat* (1919).

Fasch, Johann Friedrich (1688-1758) German composer who founded Leipzig's Gewandhaus concerts. He studied in Leipzig at the Thomas-schule (1701-1707) and became *Kapellmeister* to the court of Zerbst in 1722. Among his compositions include three operas, concertos, chamber and church music.

fasola (US) Notation and style of hymnodic singing, which originated in the New England region. Fasola Folk are those people who practise this form. The name originates from the combination of names given to the different notes of the scale fa-sol-la, deriving from Guidonian solmization via the Elizabethan diatonic major scale fa-sol-la-fa-sol-la-mi. Spiritual hymnody in this style reached its heyday with the foundation of the Singing Schools in the late 18th century and may be split into four categories: those deriving from European folk tunes; those with psalm tunes for the melody; revivalist hymns; and fuguing tunes. Songs are learned by heart, each singer learning all parts, at first to the syllables fa-sol-la, etc. Singers may exchange parts at will during a performance. In some rural southern states of America, songs in this style are still sung and often known, after the title of published collections, as *Sacred Harp* songs. See also **shape note**.

Fauré, Gabriel (Urbain) (1845-1924) French composer and organist who blended Germanic idioms with a French style in compositions that were striking in their originality and harmonic sensitivity. His *Requiem Mass* (1887) grew in popularity in the 1950s and is now his most famous work.

Gabriel Fauré

Fauré studied at Louis Niedermeyer's school from 1854, and while there worked under **Saint-Saëns**. In 1866 he became organist at Rennes and remained there until the outbreak of the Franco-Prussian War (1870), in which he fought. In 1871 he became an organist at St Sulpice, Paris, and started his teaching career at the Niedermeyer School. He became assistant (1877) and then chief (1896) organist and choirmaster at La Madeleine, and became a professor of composition at the Paris Conservatoire (1896). His pupils included **Boulanger**, **Ravel** and **Enescu**. In 1905 he became director of the Conservatoire.

Apart from his Requeim are the operas *Prométhée* (1900) and the masterpiece *Pénélope* (1913), both of which reflect the influence of **Wagner**. He also wrote several widely acclaimed song cycles, including *La Bonne Chanson* (1891) and *Le Jardin Clos* (1915). His orchestral pieces *Pavane* (1887), *Masques et bergamasques* (1920), *Ballade* (1881) and *Fantasie* for piano and orchestra (1919) were sometimes scored by other composers.

fauxbourdon Technique for improvising on a chant. See also **faburden**.

Fayrfax, Robert (1464-1521) English composer who was a member of the Chapel

Royal by 1509. He was much admired, and was still in Henry VIII's service at the Field of the Cloth of Gold in 1520. He composed masses, motets and other devotional pieces.

feierlich (Ger.) Festive or solemn.

Feldman, Morton (1926-) American composer whose work was influenced by **Cage**, **Brown** and **Tudor**. He attempted to reflect the physical canvasses of art in musical paintings, and his love of Jackson Pollock's work is a clue to the temperament of his compositions. Feldman studied composition with Reigger and was appointed Edgar Varèse Professor at the State University and a director of the Center for Creative and Performing Arts in New York.

Among his compositions is *Projection* (1951), which contains an element of flexibility in its form that needs to be interpreted by the performers. Feldman also composed *The Swallows of Salangan* (1962) for chorus and 16 instruments, *Durations* I, II, III and IV (1960-1962) for various combinations of players, and a number of works for smaller ensembles.

feminine cadence **Cadence** in which the concluding chord is reached on a weak instead of a strong beat.

Ferguson, Howard (1908- Northern Irish composer who studied the piano with Samuel in 1922, and entered the Royal College of Music in 1923 to study composition with Morris. He later became a professor at the Royal Academy of Music. Among his compositions are the ballet *Chauntecleer*, four *Diversions on Ulster Airs* for orchestra, a sonata and concerto for piano, two violin sonatas, and *Amore Langueo* for soloist, choir and orchestra.

fermata (It.) Pause, indicated by a sign prolonging a note or a rest beyond its normal length.

Fernandez, Oscar Lorenzo (1897-1948) Brazilian composer and teacher who wrote in the Brazilian tradition, drawing upon folk styles and emphasizing a nationalist theme. He wrote chamber pieces, ballets and orchestral works, and is best known for his opera *Malazarte* and his symphonic suite *Trio brasiliero*.

Ferneyhough, Brian (1943-) English composer of complex works who has experimented with electronic instruments. He studied at the Birmingham School of Music from 1960, and at the Royal Academy of Music. He moved to the Netherlands and studied with Ton de **Leeuw** (1968). He emigrated to Switzerland in 1969 and studied at the Basle Conservatoire with Klaus **Huber**, teaching in Germany from 1973. Among his compositions are a sonata for clarinet and bass clarinet, and pieces for wind instruments and sonatas for string quartet.

Ferrabosco, Alfonso I (1543-1588) Italian composer who lived in Italy and England and composed much devotional music. In 1546 he was appointed *maestro di cappella* at the Basilica Vaticana in Rome. In the 1560s he moved to England, entering the service of Elizabeth I. He left England in 1578 to serve the Duke of Savoy.

He published two volumes of Italian madrigals in 1587, but composed many more madrigals, motets and pieces for instrumental consort. Some of these are known to have influenced William **Byrd**, who competed with Ferrabosco in a setting of the plainsong *Miserere* for instruments.

Ferrier, Kathleen (1912-1953) English contralto who studied with such teachers as J.E. Hutchinson and Roy Henderson. Ferrier began her musical career as a concert singer. Her concert repertory included *Messiah* (**Handel**) and *The Dream of Gerontius* (**Elgar**). She made her opera debut in 1946 (Glyndebourne, premiere of **Britten**'s *The Rape of Lucretia*). She also performed under such conductors as Bruno **Walter** and Sir John **Barbirolli**. Ferrier made many recordings and became one of the most popular and well-loved singers of her time.

Festa, Constanzo (*c*1490-1545) Italian composer who became a singer in the choir of Pope Leo X in 1517. He composed numerous madrigals, masses and other sacred polyphonic pieces. His *Te Deum* is still performed at the election of a new pope.

Festing, Michael Christian (*c*1680-1752) English composer and violinist who studied under **Geminiani**. He joined the King's Musicians in 1735 and became director of the Italian Opera in 1737. He composed symphonic pieces, concertos and sonatas for the violin, songs, odes and a cantata.

Fibich, Zdenek (1850-1900) Czech composer and conductor, best known for his serenade *At Twilight* and for his spoken orchestral melodrama *Hippodamia*. He was a pupil of **Moscheles** and Jadassohn at the Leipzig Conservatoire from 1865 and became a tutor at Wilno in 1870, returning to Prague in 1874 to become an assistant conductor at the National Theatre. Most of his compositions were written after 1881 and include more than 500 pieces, which range from the operas *Sarka* (1897), *The Tempest* and *Hedy* (based on Byron's *Don Juan*), to symphonies, symphonic poems and chamber pieces.

fiddle Colloquial term for members of the violin family and their medieval predecessors, the vielle and **rebec**. The instruments have a variety of shapes and sizes, and the family includes the single-stringed folk instruments of Ethiopia, the square-bodied *morinchur* of Mongolia and the *sarangi* of India.

Field, John (1782-1837) Irish composer and pianist who was admired by **Liszt** and who developed the **nocturne**, a short piece for the piano, further explored by **Chopin**. He studied in Dublin with **Giordani** and was apprenticed to Clementi in London, who took him to France, Germany and Russia in order to demonstrate his pianos. He settled in Russia in 1803, appearing in Moscow as a performer and becoming a teacher. Field composed more than 20 nocturnes and seven piano concertos, as well as numerous other works for the piano.

fife Simple and obsolete form of high-pitched flute, with finger holes and no keys, normally used in military bands. The name now applies to a military flute with six finger holes and several keys which is used in drum and fife bands, although it is not identical to the orchestral flute or piccolo.

fifteenth Diapason organ stop in which 2-foot pipes produce notes two octaves (15 steps of the diatonic scale) above those played on a manual keyboard.

fifth **Interval** of five notes (counting the first and last notes). For example, a perfect fifth is C-G or D-A; a semitone less gives a diminished fifth (D♯-A or D-A♭), and an augumented fifth has one semitone more (D♭-A, or D-A♯).

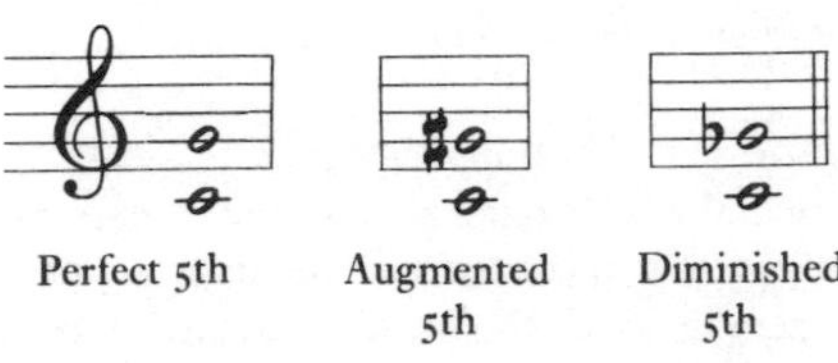

Perfect 5th | Augmented 5th | Diminished 5th

figured bass System of shorthand notation for keyboard instruments indicating the harmony above a written-out bass part by means of figures. The original system, which was practised in the 17th and 18th centuries, was to help players of keyboard and plucked instruments (lute, chitarrone) to play **continuo** parts without a score.

The basic principle of this method is that notes forming the harmony are indicated by the interval they make with the bass and are written as numbers. For example, if the key is C major, and the bass note C, the figure 5 would indicate G, and 5♯ would indicate G♯. However, the choice of the octave in which this G or G♯ is to be placed is left to the performer. In addition, some conventional abbreviations are used to assist the composer or copyist, and also to make reading easier for the player.

film music In the early days of the cinema at the beginning of the 20th century, silent films were shown to the accompaniment of a piano, organ or small orchestra. The music chosen for the films corresponded to the various scenes depicted on the screen. With the introduction of talking films came the integrated sound-track, which demanded the commissioning of new scores or an adaptation of existing works. Some early scores for the cinema included works by **Bliss** (*Things to Come*, 1933), **Shostakovich** (*New Babylon*, 1929) and **Auric** (*A Poet's Blood*, 1930). **Vaughan Williams** made a valuable contribution to film music, culminating in the music for *Scott of the Antarctic* (1948), and so did William **Walton** who wrote the music for *Henry V* (1944), *Hamlet* (1948) and *Richard III* (1956).

fin (Fr.) End.

final Tonic note on which the scales of authentic **modes** end.

finale (Fr.) Final movement of any instrumental work having several movements. It also refers to the last number in an act of an opera in which the music is divided into more or less distinctly separate pieces. This assumes that the number is on a large scale. For example, the great ensemble piece at the end of Act II in **Mozart**'s *The Marriage of Figaro* is a finale, whereas the aria at the end of Act I is not.

fine (It.) End. Used occasionally by composers at the end of a score to show that a composition is complete. It is also used before the end of a score where an earlier portion is to be repeated to form the closing section. See also **da capo**.

Fine, Irving (1914-1962) American composer and critic whose work reflects an evolution of style from **neo-Classical** methods to use of the **twelve-note** technique. He studied at Harvard from 1933. He moved to Cambridge, England, then to Paris as a pupil of **Boulanger**. In 1946 he returned to Harvard to become a professor of music, and six years later became chairman of the School of Creative Arts at Brandeis University.

Among his compositions are the *Music for the Modern Dance* (1941), three choruses from *Alice in Wonderland* (1942), *The Hourglass* (1949) for chorus and orchestra, the orchestral 'diversion' *Blue Towers* (1959), and other pieces for strings and orchestra.

fingerboard Part of the neck of a stringed instrument on to which the fingers press the strings in order to change their length and thereby produce different notes.

finger holes Holes in the tube of a wind instrument that are opened and closed with the fingers. Finger holes are used (sometimes with keys) on a variety of instruments, such as flutes, clarinets, oboes, recorders, bagpipes and some horns. Opening finger holes provide a method of shortening the tube of the instrument, which in turn reduces the length of the column of vibrating air within it, thus raising the pitch.

fingering Use of fingers on musical instruments to produce notes in various ways. It is also an indication on paper to show which fingers to use to produce a particular note or sequence of notes. For instance, in piano-playing, the thumb is indicated as 1 and the other fingers are 2-5. This is sometimes called continental fingering, as opposed to English fingering in which the thumb is marked with a + and the other fingers as 1-4.

When playing instruments of the violin family, the thumb is not used, and the fingers are numbered 1-4. Exceptions to this are the cello and double-bass, which require the use of the thumb in the higher positions.

Finney, Ross Lee (1906-) American composer who used **tonal** and **serial** techniques in his work but also borrowed from ealier traditions of American music.

He studied at the University of Minnesota and moved to Paris in 1927 as a pupil of **Boulanger**. In 1931 he studied with **Berg** in Vienna. He became a tutor at Smith College in 1929 and established the electric music studio at the University of Michigan in 1947.

Finney adopted themes from the *Ainsworth Psalter* in his cantata *Pilgrim Psalms* (1945) and developed folk-melodies in his piano concerto and in his *Barber-shop Ballad* (1937). He also composed six string quartets, *Communiqué* for orchestra (1943) and a number of sonatas.

Finnessey, Michael (1946-) English composer who studied composition at the Royal College of Music and later moved to Italy to continue his research. He formed a music department at the London School of Contemporary Dance, and taught there from 1969. He is a frequent lecturer and has taught at the Chelsea School of Art and at Dartington's Summer School. Among his compositions are many works for musical theatre, *Medea* (1973) and *Circle, Chorus, and Formal Act* (1973), and for voice and ensemble, *Horrorzone* (1966). He also composed for orchestra, *Transformations of the Vampire* (1971), and for the piano.

Finzi, Gerald (1901-1956) English composer with a gentle, pastoral, melodic style, noted particularly for his songs. He studied at York with Bairstow (1918-1922) and later with Morris in London. In 1930 he became a tutor at the Royal Academy of Music, but left during World War II to work in the Ministry of War Transport (1941-1945). Finzi was inspired by English literature; his compositions include settings of poems by Thomas Hardy, Christina Rossetti, John Milton and songs by Shakespeare. Other works have a depth and sensitivity that stem from literary associations, particularly in his *Intimations of Immortality* for tenor, chorus and orchestra (1950), the cantata *Dies Natalis* (1940) and the song-cycle *To a Poet*. He also composed concertos for the cello and clarinet, as well as works for voices and orchestra.

fioritura (It.) Decoration of a plain melodic passage with ornaments, either according to the composer's notation or improvised by the performer.

fipple Piece of wood that diverts the air blown through a mouthpiece of an instrument of the fipple flute family, of which the chief member is a **recorder**.

Fischer, Annie (1914-) Hungarian pianist who studied at the Franz Liszt Conservatoire and under such teachers as Székeley and **Dohnányi**. She made her debut in Budapest in 1922 and has toured worldwide.

Fischer-Dieskau, Dietrich (1925-) German baritone and conductor who studied at the Berlin Hochschule für Musik. By the 1950s he was acknowledged to be one of the greatest living exponents of *Lieder*. Operatic roles have included Posa (*La Forza del Destina*), Falstaff, Don Giovanni, and Wozzeck. He took up conducting in 1975.

Fischer, Johann Kaspar Ferdinand (*c*1670-1746) German composer and organist who became *Kapellmeister* to the court of the Markgraf in Baden. His works include *Ariadne Musica Neo-organoedum* (1702), a collection of 20 preludes and fugues in different keys for the organ, as well as other pieces for the keyboard.

Fitelberg, Jerzy (1903-1951) Polish composer, son of Gregorz Fitelberg who founded the Young Poland collective of composers in Berlin (1905). Jerzy studied in Berlin but moved to Paris in 1933 and to the United States in 1940. His compositions include string quartets, concertos for the violin and cello, wind quintet pieces, and other works for the chamber orchestra.

flageolet Type of **recorder** used in the 17th, 18th and 19th centuries. The English version had six finger holes and the French

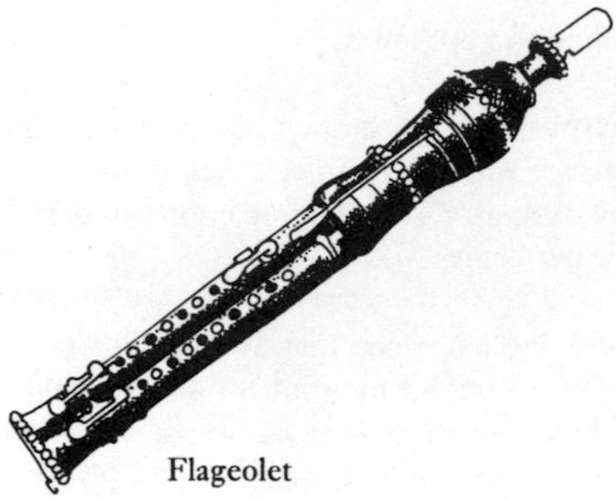
Flageolet

had four finger holes and two thumb holes. An example of the use of the instrument may be found in **Handel**'s opera *Rinaldo*, first performed in London, 1711.

In modern usage, flageolet is an alternative name for the **tin whistle**.

flam Double stroke, as distinct from a **roll**, played on a side drum.

flamenco (Sp.) Andalusian song and dance of gypsy origin, often with the accompaniment of guitars. The song is often a ballad, and the dance is a highly rhythmic style, punctuated by the tapping of the toes and heels of the shoes of the dancers. The accompanying guitarists (often improvising) display an unusual technique in that they use the body of the instrument to produce percussive effects.

Flanagan, William (1923-1969) American composer and music and theatre critic for the *New York Herald Tribune*. He studied at the Eastman School of Music under **Honegger** and worked with **Diamond** and **Copland**. He also collaborated with Ned **Rorem** as a promoter of American songs, and with Edward Albee, writing music for four of his plays, including *The Sandbox* and *The Death of Bessie Smith*.

Flannagan's compositions include the opera *Bartelby* (1957), a setting of A.E. Housman's poetry in the song cycle *The Weeping Pleiades* and choral works. His compositions for orchestra include the charming and lyrical *A Concert Ode* (1951), *Notations* (1960) and *Narrative for Orchestra* (1964).

flat Term with two meanings.

First, it is a sign (♭) placed before a note or in a key-signature to reduce the pitch of that note by one semitone.

Second, it is used when a singer or instrumentalist is singing or playing flat, that is, slightly lower than the written note, often producing a discord.

flat keys Keys that have flats in their key-signatures. Such keys are: B♭ with two flats, E♭ with three flats, A♭ with four flats, D♭ with five flats, and G♭ with six flats. The relative minor keys have, in each case, the same signatures as the major keys given.

Flatterzunge (Ger.) Flutter-tonguing. Technique of playing the flute or clarinet that produces a fluttering, bird-like sound. See also **double tonguing**.

flautando (It.) Flute-like tone produced on a violin when drawing the bow lightly over the strings near the end of the fingerboard.

flautist Player of the **flute**. In the United States, the word is usually spelled flutist.

flauto (It.) **Flute**.

flebile (It.) Plaintive, mournful.

flexatone Instrument that is similar to the musical saw. It consists of a steel blade against which two knobs vibrate when the instrument is shaken (but not bowed) to make it vibrate. Thumb pressure on the blade is used to alter the pitch.

flicorno (It.) Brass instrument used in military bands which is similar to the saxhorn and **flugelhorn**. It is found in various sizes: soprano (flugelhorn), basso, basso grave and contrabasso.

florid Any musical passage that is highly ornamented, especially one in which a theme or melody is elaborated.

Flothius, Marius Hendrikus (1914-) Dutch composer and musicologist who studied in Amsterdam and became the assistant manager of the Concertgebouw Orchestra in 1937. In 1945 he became music critic of the Amsterdam newspaper *Het Vrije Volk* and he has written a number of books on English composers, **Monteverdi** and **Mozart**. Among his compositions are concertos for piano, violin, flute and horn, *Hymnus* for soprano and orchestra, a sinfonietta concertante for clarinet, saxophone and chamber orchestra, a cello sonata and some songs.

Flotow, Friedrich von (1812-1883) German composer whose initial success in the world of opera with works that combined gaiety with some sentimentality was not sustained. He studied at the Paris Conservatoire under Reiche and produced operas for grand occasions with **Offenbach**. He wrote ballets, chamber music and 18 operas, including *Le Naufrage de la Meduse*, successful in Paris when it first appeared in 1839, *Alessandro Stradella* (1845), popular in Hamburg for a time, and *Martha* (1847), the only one of his works still performed.

flourish Fanfare of trumpets, although in modern musical terminology it is a florid passage used as an embellishment rather than as a theme.

Floyd, Carlisle (1926-) American composer noted for his ambitious attempts to translate powerful literary stories into opera. He studied at Spartanburg and Syracuse Universities and took piano tuition from Firkusny. He now teaches at the University of Tallahassee. Floyd's operas were composed to his own libretti and include *Susannah* (1955), a skilful combination of the biblical tale and the plot of Somerset Maugham's novel *Rain*, *Wuthering Heights* (1958), *Of Mice and Men* (1970) and *Bilby's Doll* (1976).

flue-pipe Organ pipe into which air is made to enter directly to produce sound in a similar manner to a whistle or recorder. The pipe has an open mouthpiece, as opposed to reed stops which have vibrating metal tongues. An alternative term is flue-stop.

flugelhorn Brass instrument similar to the keyed bugle and alto saxhorn. It has a trumpet-like mouthpiece and a horn-like conical bore, and is used in British brass bands as an alto in B♭, being played with the cornets, with which it has an identical range. It is also made in two other pitches, soprano and tenor.

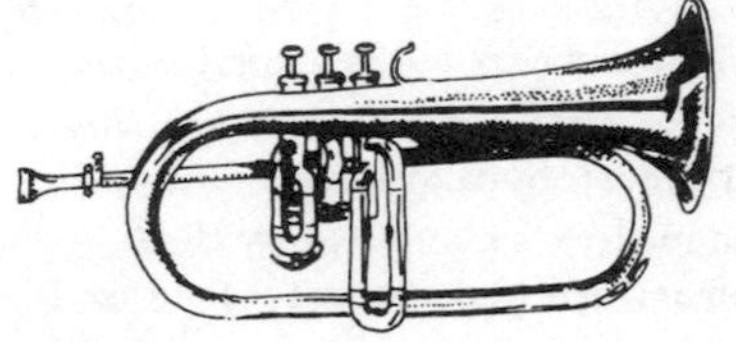

Flugelhorn

flute General name for various types of woodwind instrument. Some of the oldest flutes were made of bone and date back to 10,000 BC, when successful attempts were made to reproduce the sounds of nature, such as the call of an owl.

The modern flute is made either of wood or of metal (silver in colour), and is held horizontally (hence the name transverse

Flute

flute). Air is blown into the tube through the mouth-hole (called the embouchure). The pitch of the resulting sound is altered by covering or uncovering a combination of finger-holes.

Other varieties of flute include the nose-blown flute in which the player plugs one nostril and blows with the other; the piccolo, a smaller version of the flute, sounding an octave higher; the alto flute, pitched a fourth or fifth lower than the standard instrument and the bass flute, an octave lower.

Apart from its use in an orchestra and a military band, the flute is also used as a solo instrument. Sonatas for the flute and keyboard were composed by **Bach**, **Mozart** wrote concertos for flute, and **Hindemith** a sonata for flute and piano.

flute-à-bec (Fr.) Beak-flute, equivalent of the English **recorder**.

flutist US alternative for flautist.

Foldes, Andor (1913-) Hungarian composer and pianist who is considered the finest performer of the work of **Bartók**. He studied at the Budapest Academy with **Dohnányi** and in 1933 was awarded the International Liszt Prize. He toured Europe as a virtuoso pianist and in 1948 settled in the United States, writing books on piano technique and composing a certain amount for the piano.

folk music Body of songs, tunes and dances that have been handed down from generation to generation and accepted in several different versions or corruptions as part of the oral tradition of a region, nation or people.

Interest in folk music arose towards the end of the 19th century, when the phrase was coined. Many composers and academics transcribed the folk music of many areas. In England these include Cecil **Sharp** and **Vaughan Williams**. Many composers have since used folk tunes as material – **Dvorák** and **Bartók** are only two.

Recently, in popular music, the term has been used (outside its strict meaning) for music based on folk tunes and forms, often used as protest songs. The songs of Woody Guthrie and Bob Dylan are examples.

foot Unit of length used to measure the pitch of an organ stop, based on the length of the lowest pipe. For example, an 8-foot pipe refers to the approximate pitch length of the pipe sounding C below the bass clef on the keyboard. Therefore, a pipe 4-feet long produces C an octave higher, and a 16-foot pipe, C an octave lower and so on.

Foote, Arthur William (1853-1937) American composer and organist who was one of the Boston or New England group of composers which strove to bring to the United States some of the methods of composition that they had been taught in European conservatoires. Foote studied music at Harvard and became organist at the First Unitarian Church, Boston (1878). He was one of the founders of the American Guild of Organists and became its president in 1909.

Among his compositions are orchestral works as well as organ pieces, choral pieces and songs. He also wrote cantatas on Longfellow's *The Farewell of Hiawatha* (1885) and *The Wreck of the Hesperus* (1887).

Ford, Thomas (*c*1580-1648) English composer and lutenist who wrote one of the best-known English lute songs, *Since first I saw your face*. He entered the service of the Prince of Wales and eventually became a musician to Charles I in 1626. Many of his compositions – airs, madrigals and anthems – were published in a collection entitled *Musicke of Sundry Kindes* in 1607.

forlana (It.) Dance-form in 6/8 or 6/4 time. A typical example of its use is in **Bach**'s *Overture* (Suite) in C (undated), and **Ravel**'s *Le Tombeau de Couperin* (1917) for piano.

form Structural principles involved in

composition from the beginning to the end in such a way that a piece unfolds logically. Various views have been expressed on the subject of form, ranging from Aristotle who maintained that the main properties were wholeness, unity, logic and cohesion to the contemporary view expressed by Roger Smalley: a composer is no longer in the position of beginning from a fixed point in time and moving forwards from it; rather he is moving in all directions within a materially circumscribed world". See also **concerto**; **fugue**; **minuet**; **overture**; **rondo**; **sonata form**; **suite**; **symphony**; **ternary form**; **variations**.

formalism School of thought based in the Soviet Union during the early part of the 20th century, embracing literature, language studies and philosophy. The movement maintained that art (music, literature, etc.) is best understood by an intellectual examination of its form rather than its content, its 'message'. Composers such as **Prokofiev** and **Shostakovich** were criticized by Soviet authorities for their preoccupation with form, rather than following the tenets of socialist realism.

forte, fortissimo (It.) Loud, very loud. Instruction to players to play loud, or very loud. Abbreviated to f or ff.

fortepiano (It.) Early Italian alternative term for pianoforte.

Foss, Lukas (1922-) German composer and conductor (original name Fuchs), widely respected for his romantic lyricism and combination of American and European styles.

He studied in Berlin, then at the Paris Conservatoire, and later at the Curtis Institute, where he worked with Scalero and **Hindemith**. He became professor of music at the University of California in 1953. In 1963, he became conductor of the Buffalo Symphony Orchestra. Foss's compositions reflect a movement of style that leads from the influences of the German Romantic tradition and a Mahlerian temperament in his earlier works to a later 'New World poetic' that is more often associated with **Copland**. *The Prairie* for orchestra, chorus and soloists (1944) is a powerful indication of his earlier influences, while the opera *The Jumping Frog of Calaveras County* (1950) displays the vivacity of his later style. His other compositions include the oratorio *A Parable of Death* (1952) and the orchestral piece *Recordare* (1948).

Foster, Stephen Collins (1826-1864) American composer of more than 200 songs which have entered the fabric of American culture and are regarded as authentic 'folk songs'. Songs such as *Oh! Susanna* (1845), *Camptown Races* (1850), *My Old Kentucky Home* (1853), *Jeanie with the Light Brown Hair* (1854) and *Beautiful Dreamer* (1864) serve as an eloquent voice for United States sentimentality. Self-taught, Foster began writing at an early age and fell prey to unscrupulous publishers. *Oh! Susanna* grossed $15, 000 but Foster received nothing. With the minstrel craze at its height in the 1850s, Foster began to receive commissions and his income increased. He formed a potentially fruitful partnership with George Cooper, a lyricist, but this did not last long.

fourth Interval of four notes (counting both the first and the last note) or five semitones. A perfect fourth is C-F or D-G, and an augumented fourth has one semitone more, D♭-G or D-G♯. The diminished fourth (C-F♭ or D-G♭)is one semitone less than the perfect.

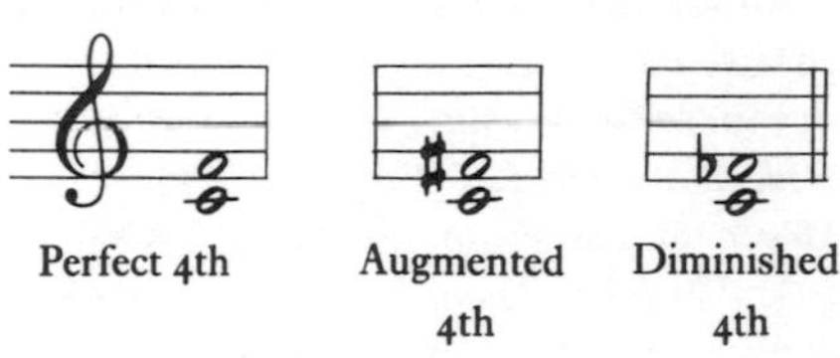

foxtrot American ballroom dance dating from about 1912, and cultivated mainly by jazz bands. It developed into two forms, one quicker than the other, and its popularity spread throughout the United States and Europe during the 1930s and 1940s.

Françaix, Jean (1912-) French composer and pianist noted for his concise style and skills as a performer. He studied composition with **Boulanger** at the Paris Conservatoire. He became a respected pianist and completed several successful tours of Europe. Among Françaix's compositions are the oratorio *Apocalypse de St Jean* (1933), a comic opera *Le diable boiteux* (1937) and a full-scale opera *La main de gloire* (1945). He also wrote ballets, a concertino for orchestra and piano, and a piano concerto (1936).

Franck, César (1822-1890) Belgian composer, pianist and organist who was never officially recognized for his compositions in his lifetime. Franck's orchestral works reveal the powerful and precise temperament of the organ as well as more romantic and sentimental elements contained within a cyclic form.

He studied at the Liège Conservatoire and in 1837 at the Paris Conservatoire with Reicha. His first orchestral work, the oratorio *Ruth*, was performed at the Paris Conservatoire in 1846. In 1858 he became organist at the church of Sainte-Clotilde and caught the attention of **Liszt** with his brilliant technique. In 1872 he became professor of the organ at the Conservatoire, where his pupils included **d'Indy**, Bréville, **Chausson** and Bordes. His pupils organized the first performance of his Symphony in D major (1888) in Paris and encouraged his efforts at composition.

Most of his finest compositions were completed in the 1870s and included devotional works such as the oratorios *Rédemption* and *Les Béatitudes* (1873-1875), the symphonic pieces *Les Eolides* (1877) and *Variations Symphoniques* (1885, considered to be his finest work), a piano quintet and the powerful *Prélude, choral et fugue* and *Prélude, aria et finale* for piano.

Franck, Melchior (*c*1579-1639) German composer who became *Kapellmeister* to the Duke of Coburg. He composed German songs, church music and instrumental pieces. A modern edition of some of his instrumental works is in *Denkmaler Deutscher Tonkunst XVI* (1904).

Francoeur, François (1698-1787) French composer and violinist. He became music director of the Paris Opéra (1739) and in 1772 music director at the Court of Louis XV. He composed violin sonatas, operas and ballets.

Frankel, Benjamin (1906-1973) English composer and conductor who wrote incidental music for more than 100 films. He studied in Germany and at the Guildhall, London. He worked as a café musician during World War II and as a jazz violinist. He cut his compositional teeth arranging popular scores and in 1946 became a tutor at the Guildhall. Apart from film music, Frankel wrote a violin concerto (1951), five string quartets, eight symphonies and sonatas for the violin and viola.

Franz, Robert (1815-1892) German composer of choral music and a series of highly-regarded songs. He studied in Dessau (1835) and was appointed organist at Ulrichskirche in Halle. In 1859 he became the musical director of Halle University. In 1868 illness forced him into semi-retirement, but he managed to edit works by **Bach** and **Handel**.

He composed more than 200 songs of a quality that was noted by **Liszt** and **Schumann**. He also wrote additional accompaniments to **Bach**'s *St Matthew's Passion* and *Magnificat* and **Handel**'s *Messiah*.

free counterpoint Counterpoint that is built up without reference to specific rules (species) of such composition. Free counterpoint is also known as composer's counterpoint and is often defined by contrast with student's (or **strict counterpoint**).

free fantasia In **sonata form**, an alternative term for **development**.

French horn Brass instrument with tube bent into a circular form. In its early form it could produce only the natural harmonics and was used mainly for playing hunting fanfares. In the early 18th century, when composers began to write for the instrument, they were still restricted to the natural harmonics. However, with the invention of a series of **crooks** (tubes) which could be inserted into the main part of the instrument's tubing, the length of the tube could be altered and the instrument played in a variety of keys.

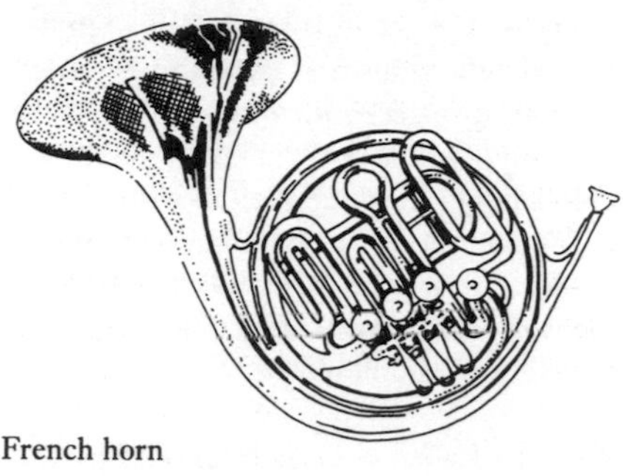

French horn

In the middle of the 19th century the horn evolved into its modern form, with a series of valves replacing the detachable crooks. Most of this development occurred in France, hence the name French horn, an instrument to be found in most modern orchestras. Concertos for horn have been written by **Mozart, Haydn** and Richard **Strauss**, and apart from orchestral music, they are also used by military bands. See also **flugelhorn** and **saxhorn**.

French sixth Augmented sixth chord, consisting of a major third, augumented fourth and an augumented sixth above the bass (for example, A♭-C-D-F♯).

frequency Measure of the pitch of a note in terms of the number of vibrations per second of the vibrating body producing it. The higher the frequency of sound, the higher is its pitch, the lower the frequency, the lower its pitch. Frequency is measured in hertz (cycles per second).

Frescobaldi, Girolamo (1583-1643) Italian composer and respected virtuoso organist. He studied with Luzzaschi in Ferrara and was appointed organist at St Peter's, Rome, in 1608 after a year in Antwerp. He also served the Grand Duke of Tuscany in Florence (1628-1633). While in Rome, he taught the German organist **Froberger** and influenced both his playing and his composition.

Frescobaldi composed a series of madrigals and motets and some brilliant toccatas, notably those in the second book (1627), and fugues. His collection of organ works, *Fiori musicale* (1635), including ricercari, canzoni and variations, is still widely performed.

fret Small strip of wood, gut or metal fixed onto the fingerboard of certain stringed instruments (e.g. the lute, viol, guitar, mandoline, banjo and ukelele, but not the violin family). The performer presses his or her finger against a fret to shorten the length of the vibrating string, and thus raise its pitch.

Fricker, Peter Racine (1920-) English composer who reflects the influences of **Stravinsky** and **Bartók** in his richly-patterned and personal work. He studied at the Royal College of Music and with **Seiber**. In 1953, he became director of music at Morley College, succeeding **Tippett**, and a professor of composition at the Royal College in 1956. In 1964 he was appointed visiting professor of music and composer in residence at the University of California. In 1947 his wind quintet won the Alfred Clements Prize and he was awarded the Koussevitsky Prize for his Symphony No.1, 1950. Among his other compositions are three symphonies, a violin concerto, *Fanfare for Europe* (1972) for trumpet, a large number of choral works that range from his *A Cappella Madrigals* (1947) to the oratorio *The Vision of Judge-*

Peter Fricker

ment (1957) for soloists, choir and orchestra and other pieces for full and chamber orchestra, organ and piano.

Frid, Geza (1904-) Hungarian composer and pianist who studied at the Budapest Academy (1912) with **Kodály** and **Bartók**. He moved to Amsterdam in 1929 and became a Dutch citizen in 1948. His compositions include a symphony, a concerto and sonata for the piano and string quartets.

Friml, Rudolph (1879-1972) Czech composer who studied at the Prague Conservatoire. He visited the United States as a pianist with the virtuoso violinist and composer Jan **Kubelík** in 1901. He settled in the United States and performed his first piano concerto with the New York Symphony Orchestra in 1906. Friml composed a series of piano works and some chamber music, as well as a number of popular operettas including *Katinka* (1916), *Rose Marie* (1923) and *The Vagabond King* (1925).

Froberger, Johann Jacob (1616-1667) German composer and organist who was appointed organist at the court of Vienna in 1637 and studied with **Frescobaldi** in Italy (1638-1642). He travelled extensively, visiting Paris, Brussels, Rome and London. He composed a number of organ and harpsichord pieces.

frottola (It.) Late 15th- and early 16th-century Italian song originating in Mantua, for a group of several voices or a solo voice and instruments. It was set to poems and varying metres, and successive stanzas were sung to repetitions of the same music. The frottola was an important predecessor to the **madrigal**.

Fry, William Henry (1813-1864) American composer and critic notable for his opera *Leonora* (1845), which is considered to be the first important American operatic composition.

Fry was largely self-taught. In 1846 he moved to London and Paris and became the music correspondent to the New York Tribune. On his return to the United States (1852) he continued to write, advancing the work and reinforcing the confidence of other American composers. He composed some symphonic pieces and a selection of choral music.

fuga (It.) Italian equivalent of the Engish **fugue**.

fugato (It.) Composition in the style of a **fugue**, but not considered to be in the same form.

fughetta (It.) Little fugue. Unlike the **fugato**, it is formally a proper **fugue**, although greatly condensed.

fugue Contrapuntal composition founded on a short theme (known as the subject), and written for two or more voices (so-called, whether the work is vocal or instrumental) or parts.

Common to all fugues is the exposition, in which the parts enter in turn with the subject, in tonic key, and then with its transposed form (known as the answer) in the dominant. The answer may reply literally, imitating exactly the shape of the subject.

In the course of the fugue, there are often

several complete entries of all voices (with the order of entry changing). The complete entries are separated by episodes. When each subject has been announced, the subject or answer passes to another thematic element called the counter-subject. Once all voices have entered, the fugal exposition is complete.

After all the initial entries of the subject and answer, there is generally an episode derived from the material already heard or completely independent, leading to a further entry of the subject. The remainder of the fugue is made alternately of episodes and entries, which may include treatment of the subject in **canon**. Towards the end of the fugue, overlapping entries (known as stretto) may occur when the answer enters before the subject is completed. A **codetta** is a linking passage between the subject and the answer.

The most famous exposition of fugue structure is Bach's *The Art of Fugue*.

Fuleihan, Anis (1901-1970) American composer and pianist who wrote an early concerto for the Thérémin flute, an electronic instrument that is played by movements of the hand that do not touch the instrument. Fuleihan was born in Cyprus and moved to the United States in 1915. His first appearance as a pianist was with the New York Symphony Orchestra in 1919. During the 1920s he composed ballets for two companies. In 1947 he became professor of music at Indiana University and he returned to the Middle East to become the director of the National Conservatoire in Beirut (1953). Fuleihan conducted the Tunis Orchestra (1963-1965) and then returned to Illinois University to teach. Among his other compositions were two symphonies, concertos for the violin, piano, cello and bassoon and *Cyprus Serenades* for orchestra.

full anthem **Anthem** that is written for full chorus throughout, as opposed to the **verse anthem**, which includes sections which feature smaller groups (solo, duet, quartet, etc.).

full orchestra Orchestra that consists of the four usual sections (strings, woodwind, brass and percussion) and of normal concert-hall strength. See **orchestra**.

full organ The terms *organo pleno* (It.) and *plein jeu* (Fr.) have the same meaning and indicate that an organ passage should be played using the full extent of the instrument's power.

full score **Score** that shows all the parts at once. See also **vocal score**.

fundamental First partial of a harmonic series. It is the note produced by touching a bowed string at suitable (nodal) points, or similarly by making a hole in an organ pipe.

fuoco (It.) Fire. *Con fuoco* indicates that the playing of a particular passage should be vigorous and powerful.

furiant Lively Czech dance with changing rhythms, often used by **Dvorák** in place of a **scherzo**.

Furtwängler, Wilhelm (1886-1954) German composer and conductor who was noted for his interpretations of **Beethoven**, **Bruckner** and **Wagner**. He studied in Munich under **Rheinberger** and conducted in Zurich and Lübeck, before succeeding **Nikisch** as conductor of both the Leipzig Gewandhaus Orchestra and the Berlin Philharmonic in 1922. He was a frequent conductor at **Bayreuth** during the 1930s and 1940s, and also conducted at the Salzburg Festival. In 1936 he was withdrawn from the New York Philharmonic Orchestra in protest at his pro-Nazi activities, but in 1946 his career recovered and he again toured widely as a conductor. Furtwängler composed three symphonies, a *Te Deum*, a piano concerto and some chamber music.

futurism Attempt by the Italian poet Marinetti and the painter-musician Luigi Russolo to combine traditional sounds of music with sounds of explosions, shrieks, screams and groans. The Futurist movement began in Rome in 1909, at which time it received the support of Mussolini, and it continued until the late 1930s. Marinetti (*Futrismo e fascismo*, 1924) and Russolo (*L'arte dei rumori*, 1916) both wrote books on the subject. The composer, Francesco Pratella (1880-1955), was a strong advocate of musical futurism.

Fux, Johann Joseph (1660-1741) Austrian composer and organist who rose to prominence in Vienna, where he commanded the respect of both court and clergy. Fux entered the Jesuit University in Graz in 1680 and was employed as an organist by the Primate of Hungary, resident in Vienna. Emperor Leopold I was impressed with his compositions and sent Fux to study in Rome in 1698. On his return to Vienna (1700), Leopold's successor, Joseph I, appointed him court composer. He became choirmaster at the church of St Stephen (1705) and *Kapellmeister* (1715).

He was a prolific composer, completing 19 operas including *Constanza e fortezza*, written to celebrate the coronation of the Emperor Charles VI as King of Bohemia (1723), 50 masses, oratorios, partitas and other instrumental works. He also wrote a seminal treatise on counterpoint, *Gradus ad Parnassum* (1725).

G

G Name of the note that lies one tone above F and one tone below A. The scale of G major has one sharp in the key-signature.

Gabrieli, Andrea (1510-1586) Italian composer and organist associated with the most magnificent era of the Venetian school. He developed the *cori spezzati* style, which positioned instruments and singers at various points within the chapel to create separate centres of sound.

Gabrieli studied with **Willaert**. He toured Germany in 1562 and was greatly influenced by Lassus. He succeeded **Merulo** as organist at St Mark's in 1566. His pupils included his nephew Giovanni **Gabrieli**, **Hassler** and **Sweelinck**.

He composed a series of motets, psalms and madrigals as well as masses and instrumental pieces, including the motets *Cantiones Ecclesiasticae* (1576) and *Cantiones Sacrae* (1565). Also of interest are his madrigals *Jiustinianae* (1571), musical caricatures of various Venetian figures. Perhaps his greatest work, however, was published after his death, notably the *Canzoni alla Francese* (1605) and Ricerari (1589-1596).

Gabrieli, Giovanni (1557-1612) Italian organist and one of the great composers of ceremonial music and of *Sacrae symphoniae* – motets with instrumental accompaniment. Some critics believe his *Sonata Pian e Forte* (1587) to be one of the earliest instances of music to contain expression marks.

He studied with his uncle Andrea and followed him to Germany, becoming a musician with Lassus at the Bavarian court before returning to Venice in 1584. He succeeded Andrea as organist of St Mark's, Venice, in 1585, composing and teaching such figures as **Schütz**.

Gabrieli's compositions include various *canzone*, toccatas and motets, including *Angelus ad Pastores* (1587), *O Magnum Mysterium* (1587), *Hodie Christus Natus Est* (1597) and *Jubilate Deo* (four versions, 1597-1615).

Gade, Niels (Wilhelm) (1817-1890) Danish composer, organist and violinist with the Royal Orchestra whose work reflects the influences of **Mendelssohn** and **Schumann**, as well as national characteristics. Gade visited Italy and Germany, becoming the assistant conductor of the Gewandhaus Orchestra in Leipzig (1844) and befriending Mendelssohn. He returned to Copenhagen in 1848 and was appointed *Kapellmeister* to the court there in 1861. He visited England in 1876 and conducted at the Birmingham Festival. He received a Doctorate in 1879 and was eventually made a Commander of the Order of Daneborg. Among Gade's compositions are eight symphonies, six overtures, including *In the Highlands* (1844) and *Michelangelo* (1861), cantatas, the opera-ballet *The Fairy Spell*, music for the piano and for strings, and a series of songs.

gagaku (Japan) Refined music, a general term for imperial court orchestral music of Japan. It may be purely orchestral (**kangen**), or used to accompany dance (**bugaku**). The repertory is divided into two main categories, Old Music (kogaku) and New Music (Shingaku). These categories are divided into a further two classes according to their origin: **Togaku**, (music of the left), denotes the repertory imported from China, while **Komagaku** is (music of the right), is imported from Korea and Manchuria. There is a slight difference in the instrumentation of *Togaku* and *Komagaku*, although they both share oboes (**hichiriki**), mouth-organs (**shō**), flutes and drums. The *Togaku* orchestra, when performing *kangen*, adds the lute (**biwa**) and a form of zither. *Komagaku* is generally used only for *bugaku* accompaniment and not as an independent orchestral form.

gaida General name for various bagpipes in Southern and Eastern Europe (also oboes in Iberia and North Africa – see **zurna**). In Bulgaria, where it is particularly common, the sheepskin or goatskin windbag is filled by a mouthpiece (not by bellows, as in parts of Yugoslavia, Czechoslovakia and Poland) and has one or two chanters in addition to a drone pipe. It occurs in three sizes, the largest being used to accompany the male voice. In ensembles including a frame drum, it accompanies dances on festive occasions. An alternative transliteration is *gaita*.

gaillarde Alternative spelling of **galliard**.

gaita Alternative transliteration of **gaida**.

gaku-biwa (Japan) Type of **biwa** or lute.

galanteries Extra dances or other musical pieces added to those in the standard Baroque suite. The most frequently used were *bourrées*, **minuets** and gavottes.

galant style (Fr. *style galant*, It. *stile galante*) Term used in the 18th century to decribe music with regular melodic phrases and light accompaniment, with delicate feeling and graceful formality. Used in the titles of opera-ballets by Campra (1697) and **Rameau** (1735) and of paintings by Watteau, the description has been applied to the works of F. **Couperin**, **Telemann**, D. **Scarlatti**, **Galuppi**, **Soler** and J.C. **Bach**.

Galilei, Vincenzo (*c*1520-1591) Italian composer, lutenist and father of the astronomer Galileo Galilei, who wrote some important theoretical texts and was a member of a group of poets and musicians whose discussions influenced the early development of opera.

This group, the Camerata, met at **Bardi**'s Florentine villa and included the composers **Peri**, **Caccini** and **Cavalieri**. They debated the revival of Greek drama and assisted the development of early forms of declamatory song for the solo voice, important in the evolution of opera.

Galilei wrote a treatise on style and tuning, *Dialogo della musica antica e della moderna* (1581), and a book on lute playing, *Il fronimo* (1568). Among his compositions are a number of madrigals and lute pieces.

galliard Lively 16th-century dance in triple time, often linked thematically with the **pavane** (England), or *passamezzo* (Italy). It is now obsolete, but was revived by **Vaughan Williams** in *Job, A Masque for Dancing* (1930).

galop Quick ballroom dance in duple time with a leap or hop at the end of each phrase. The dance first appeared under this name in Paris (1829), but it originated in Germany, where it was known as a *galopp*.

Galuppi, Baldassare (1706-1785) Venetian composer who found success in Italy and England with comic operas which influenced the development of that genre. He studied with **Lotti** and became choirmaster of St Mark's, Venice and director of the

Conservatorio degli Incurabili in 1762. He visited London in 1741 and St Petersburg in 1765-1767.

Galuppi composed oratorios, devotional music and sonatas for harpsichord as well as more than 100 operas, including *Adriano in Siria* (1740), *Scipione in Cartagine* (1742), *Il filosofo di campagna* (1754) and *Il Re Pastore* (1762).

gamaka (India) Standard embellishments used to characterize individual notes. It is the primary means by which subtlety of expression is achieved in all melodic styles, and includes all varieties of glides, bends and vibrati.

gamba Shorthand term for viola da gamba. Also, an open metal organ stop imitating the tone of the *viola da gamba*, ranging over 4, 8 and 16-foot pipes.

gambang (Java) Type of xylophone and the only instrument in the **gamelan** ensemble with keys made of wood. The keys, spanning two to four octaves, are laid over a wooden box frame and are hit with two sticks made of buffalo horn tipped with small, padded, round discs.

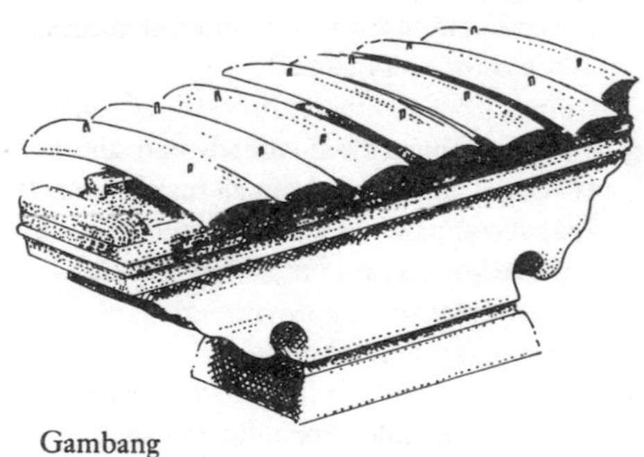

Gambang

gambuh (Bali) Archaic theatrical form, with plots taken from the literature of 14th-century court life in East Java. The ensemble is unusual because it includes the large, wailing **suling** flutes. Otherwise, it is a small ensemble consisting of **rebab**, a pair of drums, gongs, cymbals and bells. Although *gambuh* is not frequently performed, it has provided the foundation for all Balinese dance and drama, and many of the more popular, small **gamelans** are derived from the *gambuh* ensemble.

gamelan (Indonesia) Generic name for a musical ensemble or orchestra, derived from the Javanese word *gamel* meaning 'hammer' and therefore suggesting the percussive method of playing. A *gamelan* may vary in size from just a few instruments to as many as 80. The fundamental instruments common to both Balinese and Javanese *gamelans* are keyed metallophones, which elaborate with intricate interlocking patterns a fixed, repeated melody of equal note length; and knobbed gongs, whose function being **colotomic** subdivide binarily the temporal cycle of the melody.

In Java there are two kinds of *gamelan* playing, the 'loud style' which makes use of the louder bronze instruments and is led by a drummer, and the 'soft style' which, led by a two-string bowed lute (**rebab**), may additionally feature a flute (**suling**), a wooden-keyed xylophone (**gambang**), a female singer and a male chorus.

In contrast to the generally sedate character of the Javanese *gamelan*, the Balinese *gamelan* is more brilliant and more rhythmically dynamic, making greater use of melodic interplay between pairs or quartets of keyed metallophones and often adding sets of small cymbals.

gamut Term with three meanings.

First, it is the entire range of musical pitches, from the highest to the lowest.

Second, it was the name for one particular note, the G on the bottom line of the bass stave (from *gamma*, the lowest note of the **hexachord**, plus *ut*, the first note of the scale).

Third, it also came to be used to mean the scale.

gangsa (Bali) Single octave metallophone of the **gamelan** orchestra, with bronze keys suspended over a sound box, the ends of each resting on cushions. The instrument is struck with a single mallet. Built in pairs or quartets, *gangsas* play complex interlocking parts which, together, elaborate the melodic line of the composition. Half of the number of *gangsas* are 'female' and tuned slightly lower than their 'male' counterparts, so that when played together they produce the distinctive shimmering effect of the **gamelan**. Equivalent to the Javanese **saron**.

Ganze-note (or Ganze Taktnote) (Ger.) Equivalent of the English **semibreve**.

gapped scale Any scale having fewer than seven notes. For example, the **pentatonic** scale, which has five notes.

Gardelli, Lamberto (1915-) Italian conductor and composer of four operatic works. He studied in Pesaro and Rome and became a singing tutor and rehearsal director at the Rome Opera in 1940. He conducted in Rome, his debut being there in 1945, in Stockholm (1946), Budapest (1961) and at Glyndebourne (1964). Gardelli has also conducted at Covent Garden and in New York.

Gardiner, Henry Balfour (1877-1950) English composer who strove to bring recognition to the work of Gustav **Holst**. He studied at Oxford and in Frankfurt with Ivan Knorr and was appointed music master at Winchester College. He promoted performances of contemporary English music (1910-1920) and became its most enthusiastic and influential champion.

Among Gardiner's compositions are the *Shepherd Fennel's Dance* for orchestra (1911), pieces for choir and orchestra such as *News from Whydah* (1912), a symphony and chamber works.

Gasparini, Francesco (1668-1727) Italian composer who contributed to the practice of **figured bass** accompaniment with a treatise on the harpsichord, *L'Armonico Practico al Cimbalo* (1708). He studied with **Corelli** and **Pasquini** and became choirmaster at the Ospedale della Pietà in Venice, 1701. In 1725 he was appointed *maestro di cappella* at St John Lateran in Rome. Gasparini composed oratorios and other devotional pieces, cantatas and a number of operatic works, including *Amleto* (1705).

Gassmann, Florian Leopold (1729-1774) German composer who studied with Padre **Martini** in Bologna and was employed as a court musician to Count Leonardo Veneri in Venice. In 1763 he moved to Vienna to succeed **Gluck** as a composer of ballets. In 1772 he founded the *Tonkünstler Sozietät*, a benevolent trust for the dependents of musicians.

Gassmann composed 20 operas, including *La Contessina* (1770) and *L'Amore Artigiano* (1779), 54 symphonies, as well as works for the chamber and chapel. His music was admired by his pupil **Salieri** and by **Mozart**.

Gastoldi, Giovanni Giacomo (*c*1552-1622) Italian composer whose *Balletti a cinque voci con li suoi versi per cantare, sonare, e ballare* (1591) heavily influenced **Hassler** and **Morley**, who imitated its style in his *First Booke of Balletts to Five Voices* (1595). Gastoldi was appointed a singer at the ducal palace in Mantua in 1581 and composed a number of madrigals, Latin psalms and masses.

gat (India) Short, fixed composition set in any tempo and any **tala** in an instrumental **rāga**, accompanied by **tablā**. It follows the **ālāp** and **jor** sections and is used as the basis for extensive improvisation, its theme recurring as a kind of refrain.

gatra (Java) Smallest melodic unit in Javanese compositional theory. It consists of a set of four sonic events, including silences if they occur, and recognizable as set patterns with a specific melodic contour.

Gaultier, Denis (1603-1672) French composer and lutenist who composed elaborate conceits for the lute in collections of dances, notably *La Rhétorique des Dieux* (*c*1652). His style of composition influenced later harpsichordists, who like **Froberger** and Chambonniéres imitated his use of **broken chords** and **arpeggios**.

Gauntlett, Henry John (1805-1876) English composer and organist who composed hundreds of hymn tunes, including *Once in Royal David's City*. He became organist at Southwark Cathedral in 1827 and lectured at the London Institute (1837-1843) on aspects of the organ's construction.

Gaveaux, Pierre (1761-1825) French composer and singer who left a career as a tenor at the Opéra-Comique to compose for the same theatre. About 30 of his operas were performed there in the 1790s, including *Leonore* (1798), to a libretto by Bouilly from which **Beethoven** constructed *Fidelio*.

Geminiani, Francesco (Xaviero) (1687-1762) Italian composer and violinist who published *The Art of Playing on the Violin* (1751). He also wrote *A Treatise of Good Taste* (1749), *The Art of Playing the Guitar*, and *The Art of Accompaniment*. He studied with A. **Scarlatti** and **Corelli** and became a member of the Naples opera orchestra in 1711. He toured England in 1714 as a soloist and won wide acclaim. He lived in Dublin (1733-1740) and spent the intervening years living and working in Paris and London.

Geminiani's compositions include 18 concerti grossi, 24 violin sonatas, and pieces for the cello and harpsichord. He also composed the ballet *La Foresta Incantanta* (1754).

gendèr (Indonesia) Family of metallophones with a range of two or more octaves, made of thin bronze keys suspended over individual tubular resonators. The instrument is struck with two mallets or padded discs on short sticks, and produces a mellow, non-percussive sound. There are two or more *genders* in each **gamelan**, which together play interlocking parts, elaborating the melodic line. The shadow puppet play **wayang kulit** is accompanied by its own quartet of *gendèrs*.

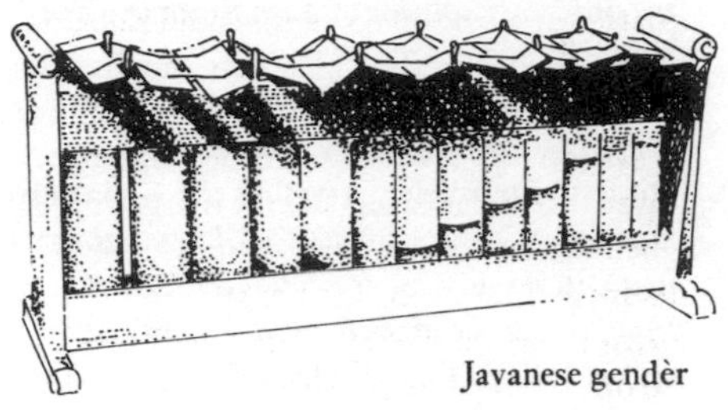

Javanese gendèr

gending/ghending (Indonesia) Generic term for composition.

Genée, (Franz Friedrich) Richard (1823-1895) German composer and conductor, notable for his libretto *Die Fledermaus* (1872), for which Johann **Strauss** composed the music.

He conducted for many orchestras, including the *Theater an der Wien* orchestra in Vienna (1868-1878). He also composed several successful operettas.

Genzmer, Harold (1909-) German composer who studied at the Berlin Conservatoire with **Hindemith** and became a professor of composition at the *Hochschule für Musik*, Freiburg, in 1946. He studied and composed for electronic instruments, including the trautonium. Among Genzmer's compositions are the *Bremer Symphony* (1942), concertos for orchestra, strings, piano, cello, flute, oboe and trautonium, and a number of choral pieces and sonatas.

Gerhard, Roberto (1896-1970) Spanish composer of Franco-Swiss descent who became identified with the Spanish idiom and later with the methods of **Britten** and **Tippett**. He studied with **Granados** and Pedrell at Barcelona and with **Schoenberg** in Vienna and at the Berlin Conservatoire (1924). He was appointed a tutor and music librarian at the Catalan Library in Barcelona in 1929, but when Spain suffered its Civil War, he moved to England and settled in Cambridge in 1940. He was later to become an important figure in innovative English music.

Gerhard's compositions reveal an Impressionist influence, gleaned from a study of **Debussy**, as well as the **serialism** associated with Schoenberg. They nonetheless still retain a Spanish flavour and preserve an air of stylistic independence and subtlety. The serialism displayed in his second symphony (1959), for example, is very individual and conventionally harmonic. His ballet suites, *Alegrias* (1944) and *Don Quixote* (1941) and the opera *The Duenna* (1947) also betray a similar independence. Gerhard completed four symphonies in total as well as several concertos and other chamber pieces.

German, Sir Edward [G. E. Jones] (1862-1936) Welsh composer who had great success with his incidental pieces for Shakespeare's plays, including *Richard III* (1889), *Henry VIII* (1892), *Romeo and Juliet* (1895) and *As You Like It* (1897). He studied at the Royal Academy of Music and began playing in theatre orchestras as a violinist. In 1888 he became conductor and musical director at the Globe Theatre and began composing for the stage. He was made a Fellow of the Royal Academy of Music in 1895 and was knighted in 1928.

German composed several light operettas, including the popular *Merrie England* (1902), *The Princess of Kensington* (1903) and *Fallen Fairies* (1909). He also produced some orchestral pieces, including two symphonies and the *Welsh Rhapsody* (1904) as well as pieces for the theatre.

Germani, Fernando (1906-) Italian composer and organist who is widely respected for his bold recitals and for his edition of the works of **Frescobaldi**. He studied at the Rome Conservatoire and at the Papal School of Church Music. In 1936 he travelled to the United States to become an organ tutor at the Curtis Institute, Philadelphia. He became an organist at St Peter's, Rome, in 1948.

German sixth Form of **augmented sixth**.

George Gershwin

Gershwin, George (1898-1937) American composer and pianist who combined jazz idioms with conventional orchestrations to produce an archetypal musical expression of 20th-century American culture. Gershwin's parents emigrated from Russia in 1893 to settle in Brooklyn, New York.

He composed songs, stage and film musical scores, and pieces for the concert orchestra. Among the hundreds of songs he completed, with his brother Ira as lyricist, are *Embraceable You*, *The Way You Look Tonight*, *I Got Rhythm*, *A Foggy Day*, *Fascinating Rhythm*, *Let's Call the Whole Thing Off* and *Swanee* (1916), an early success that boosted the career of Al Jolson.

In 1919, he wrote his first stage musical *La La Lucille*, with which he captured the public imagination. For the next 40 years Broadway persistently demanded more Gershwin compositions. Among his most enduring stage shows were *Primrose* and *Lady Be Good* (1924), *Tell Me More* (1925), *Oh, Kay* (1926), *Strike Up The Band* (1927), *Funny Face* (1927) and *Girl Crazy* (1930). Some shows, like *Funny Face*, have been made into film musicals including *Shall We Dance* and *The Goldwyn Follies* (1938) and many other musicals benefitted from Gershwin songs. The film *An American in Paris* featured five Gershwin songs and introduced film audiences to two of his concert pieces, *An American in Paris* (1928), an ingenious rhapsodic instrumental piece that caused scandal with its powerful evocation of a blues melody, and the Concerto in F Major for piano and orchestra (1925), commissioned by Walter **Damrosch**. *Rhapsody in Blue* (1924) for piano and orchestra was orchestrated by Ferde **Grofe**, but Gershwin himself scored later pieces. His opera *Porgy and Bess* (1935), written for a black cast, is still the only American operatic work to enjoy an established place in the repertory.

Gesualdo, Carlo, Prince of Venosa (1560-1613) Italian nobleman who composed devotional works and six books of madrigals which are considered to be of a very advanced chromatic complexity and sensitivity to text. He played at the court of the Estensi at Ferrara from 1594 to 1596 and composed four books of madrigals in this time. He returned to Naples in 1597. His fifth and sixth books of madrigals were published in 1611.

Gevaert, François-Auguste (1828-1908) Belgian composer and historian who published several important works on instrumentation and contributed greatly to modern understanding of ancient music. He studied at the Ghent Conservatoire and won the Prix de Rome in 1847. He travelled throughout Europe finding success in Paris with his operas before becoming musical director of the Paris Opéra in 1867. In 1871 he was appointed director of the Brussels Conservatoire. Gevaert composed a number of operas and operettas and wrote a treatise on orchestration, *Nouveau traité général d'instrumentation* (1885). He also published collections of earlier music, including *Gloire d'Italie* (1868) and *Chansons du XVe siècle* (1875).

geza (Japan) Lower place, refers to the off-stage ensemble in the **kabuki** theatre, found behind a slatted screen, down-stage right. The ensemble provides music, sound effects, noise and signals not covered by the on-stage **debayashi** ensemble, often underlining and punctuating dialogue and action. The *geza* ensemble comprises melody instruments including **shamisen**, **koto**, **shakuhachi**, a **noh** flute, and a large selection of percussion instruments, including drums (*taiko*, *ō-tsuzumi*), gongs, chimes, bells and xylophones.

ghazal (India) Light classical genre of 19th-century origin, now very popular among Muslims of northern India and Pakistan. It consists of an Urdu text on a romantic theme, set to a short, simple melody.

Ghedini, Giorgio Federico (1892-1965) Italian composer who produced several transcriptions of works by **Bach**, **Monteverdi** and **Frescobaldi**. He studied at the Turin and Bologna conservatoires and became assistant conductor at the Teatro Regio, Turin. In 1937 he was appointed professor of harmony and composition at the Turin Conservatoire but moved to Parma (1938) and then to Milan Conservatoire (1942) where he became director in 1951.

Among his compositions are eight operas, including *Billy Budd* (1949), which was produced at least a year before **Britten**'s opera of the same name. He also wrote a symphony, concertos for the piano, violin and viola, as well as chamber music, choral works, songs and film scores.

ghending (India) See **gending**.

Giannini, Vittorio (1903-1966) American composer who combined the influences of **Verdi**, **Puccini** and the vigour and fullness of Richard **Strauss** in his operatic work. He studied at the Milan Conservatoire and at the Juilliard School, New York. His compositions include the symphony *In Memoriam Theodore Roosevelt* (1935), concertos for the piano and organ, a *Stabat Mater* and nine operas, including *Lucidia* (1934), *The Scarlet Letter* (1938) and *The Servant of Two Masters* (performed in 1967).

Giardini, Felice de (1716-1796) Italian composer and violinist who produced a number of operas and a large amount of music for strings. He was a member of the Milan Cathedral Choir and played in opera orchestras in Rome and Naples. He toured Germany (1748) and England (1751) as a virtuoso performer, settling in England as the leader of the orchestra at the Italian opera in 1756. He contributed to three choral festivals in the 1770s and in 1790 he founded a comic opera company at the Haymarket Theatre.

Gibbons, Orlando (1583-1625) English composer and organist whose works form an important contribution to sacred music in English. His style reflects an exchange of ideas between the solo voice and other voices or instruments which verges on the **polyphonic** form. In 1596 Gibbons became a chorister at King's College, Cambridge. He was appointed organist at the Chapel Royal in 1604. While in the service of James I, he performed as a chamber musician and later became organist at Westminster Abbey (1623).

Among his compositions are the anthems *O Lord in Thy Wrath* in six parts, much admired for its intensity, and *This is the Record of John* which has an accompaniment for viols rather than the usual organ. His madrigals (such as *The Silver Swan*) were published in a collection entitled *Madrigals and Motets of Five Parts* (1612). He also composed many keyboard works and a number of fantasies, pavans and galliards for instrumental consort (viols).

Gidayu-bushi (Japan) Narrative vocal form, named after its most celebrated exponent and used in the **bunraku** puppet theatre. It was later adopted by the **kabuki** theatre. Accompanied by the **shamisen** lute, it consists of heightened speech and intense extremes of vocal expression. *Gidayu kyogen* are plays written for the puppet theatre, recited in the *Gidayu-bushi* style. There are regular *Gidayu-bushi* competitions in Japan.

Gielen, Michael Andreas (1927-) Austrian composer, conductor and pianist who was born in Germany and has travelled widely as a conductor. He studied at Buenos Aires and became a tutor at the Teatro Colon in 1947. In 1951 he moved to Vienna to join the staff of the Vienna State Opera and was appointed resident conductor in 1954. He became chief conductor of the Royal Swedish Opera in 1960 and a conductor for the West German Radio Orchestra at Cologne in 1965. In 1969 he was appointed Director of the National Orchestra of Belgium. He has also conducted in New York and with the BBC and Cincinnati Symphony Orchestras. Among his compositions are choral pieces and works for the chamber orchestra.

Gigout, Eugène (1844-1925) French composer and organist who enjoyed considerable acclaim as a virtuoso performer. He studied at the Ecole Niedermeyer with **Saint-Saëns** from 1855, and was appointed a professor there after graduation. He became organist at St Augustin in 1863 and held the post until his death. In 1885 he founded an organ school and in 1911 became a professor of the organ at the Paris Conservatoire. Gigout's compositions include many works for the organ, including toccatas, fugues, anthems and concertos, noted both for their power and technical brilliance, and liturgical pieces based on Gregorian chant.

Gilbert, Henry Franklin Belknap (1868-1928) American composer who studied in Boston with MacDowell and became heavily influenced by folk music and by the traditional melodies of the Black population. His work reveals a romanticism inherited from MacDowell and a melodic structure gleaned from Negro spirituals.

Gilbert's compositions include a *Comedy Overture for Negro Themes* (1905), *Three American Dances* (1911) and *Negro Rhapsody* (1913). He also wrote a number of symphonic pieces and prologues as well as a ballet, *Dance in Place Congo* (1918).

Giles, Nathaniel (1558-1633) English composer of anthems and services. He was choirmaster at Worcester Cathedral and from 1585 at St George's Chapel, Windsor where he was also one of the organists. In 1597 he was appointed Gentleman and Master of the Children of the Chapel Royal.

Gillis, Don (1912-1978) American composer who wrote comic and serious pieces and never forgot the popular idiom to which he was introduced as a brass player at college. He studied at the Texas Christian University and joined Fort Worth Radio in 1932 as a composer and arranger. In 1944 he was appointed programme director and producer of the National Broadcasting Company in New York, where he worked with **Toscanini**. He was chairman of the Southern Methodist University music department from 1967 and chairman of fine arts at Dallas Baptist College from 1968.

Among his compositions are ten symphonies, including the *Symphony No. 5+*, subtitled *Symphony for Fun* (1946), *No. 8 The Man Who Invented Music* (1950) and *A Short Short Symphony* (1975), some comic operas and an oratorio, *The Crucifixion*.

Gilson, Paul (1865-1942) Belgian composer and critic who sensed a lack of direction in Belgian music at the turn of the century and attempted to inspire young composers. He studied at the Brussels Conservatoire with **Gevaert** in 1887 and became music critic for *Le Soir* in 1906. He helped to produce *La Revue Musicale Belge*, 1924, with which he attempted to encourage his musical contemporaries. He became an inspector of music in Belgian schools in 1908. Gilson's compositions include operas, cantatas, overtures and organ works.

gimel Alternative spelling of **gymel**.

Ginastera, Alberto (1916-1983) Argentinian composer whose style developed from naive nationalistic influences to a mature grasp of serialist techniques. He is still widely regarded for his operatic works.

Ginastera studied at the Williams Conservatoire in Buenos Aires (1928) and at the National Conservatoire from 1936 with Athos Palma. He moved to New York in 1942, returning to Argentina in 1948. He founded the Centre for Advanced Musical Studies in Buenos Aires and became its director in 1963. Among his compositions are the operas *Don Rodrigo* (1964) and *Bomarzo* (1967), the ballets *Estancia* (1941) and *Variaciones Concertantes* (1953), an *Argentine Concerto* (1961) for piano and orchestra, and other choral and chamber pieces.

giocoso (It.) Jocose. Indication that the music is to be played in a merry or playful style.

Giordaniello Nickname of the Italian composer Giuseppe **Giordani**.

Giordani, Giuseppe (*c*1753-1798) Italian composer commonly known as Giordaniello. After his studies at the Conservatoire in Naples he wrote many operas for Mantua (including, *Ritorno d'Ulisse*, 1782 and *La Vestale*, 1786) Florence, Pisa and Rome, (including, *Ifigenia in Aulide*, 1786). He also wrote oratorios, beginning with *La fuga in Egitto* (*c*1775) and in 1791became choirmaster at Fermo Cathedral.

Giordani, Tommaso (1730-1806) Italian composer and conductor. After leaving his native Naples (*c*1745) to perform Italian operas with his family, he spent some years in London (1753-1756 and 1768-1783) composing for the King's Theatre in the Haymarket and for the Vauxhall Pleasure Gardens, and Dublin (1764-1768 and 1783-1806), where he worked as an impresario (1783-1784) and music director of the Theatre Royal in Crow Street (1788). He composed more than 50 operatic pieces in Italian and English, including the comic operas *Il acio* (1782) and *The Cottage Festival* (1796), as well as many songs (including some for the first performance of Sheridan's *The Critic*, 1799) and many solo chamber and orchestral pieces, including the very successful keyboard *Six Concertos* (Op. 14, 1775), in the **galant** style. The popular song *Caro mio bien* often ascribed to Tommaso was probably written by Guiseppe **Giordani**.

Giordano, Umberto (1867-1948) Italian composer of opera with a bold, expressive style who had some early success which he was unable to sustain. He studied at the Naples Conservatoire from 1880 and achieved his first success with the opera *Mala Vita* in Rome in 1892. This work exploited a *verismo* style which captured the demands of the audience for realism in opera, a style which he abandoned in his later pieces. Subsequent operas were far more romantic, notably *Regina Diaz* (which failed on its appearance in Naples in 1894) and the more enduring *Andrea Chenier* (Milan, 1896).

Giovannelli, Ruggiero (1560-1625) Italian composer who was appointed *maestro di cappella* at St Peter's, Rome, succeeding **Palestrina** in 1594. In 1599 he became a member of the Sistine Choir. He composed several madrigals, four of which were translated by **Morley** in his *Madrigalls to Five Voices* (1598), a 12-part mass and other masses and motets.

Giovanni da Cascia (1560-1625) Florentine composer active in Verona (and possibly Milan) in the mid-14th century. His works include 16 two-voice madrigals and three three-voice *cacce* in florid style. He was also known as Johannes de Florentia or da Firenze.

Gipps, Ruth (1921-) English composer, pianist, oboist and conductor who studied at the Royal College of Music with **Vaughan Williams** and Morris. She became an oboist with various orchestras and a concert pianist. In 1948 she became choirmaster with the City of Birmingham Choir and conducted the London Repertory Orchestra from 1955. In 1961 she founded the Chanticleer Orchestra and became a professor of composition at the Royal College of Music in 1967. Gipps composed five symphonies, concertos for the oboe, piano, violin and viola, the cantata *Goblin Market*, a tone poem for wind instruments and other choral works.

giraffe piano Form of upright piano made in Germany in the 19th-century, but now obsolete. It is fundamentally a grand piano, the body of which stands on end. The bass strings on the left are encased in an elongated box not unlike the neck of a giraffe in appearance.

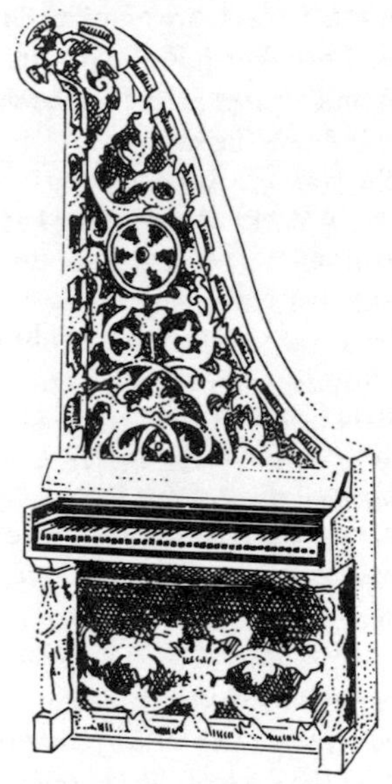

Giraffe piano

Gis (Ger.) Equivalent of the English G♯.

gittern Medieval form of guitar with four strings, played with a **plectrum**. The body and neck of the gittern were carved from the same block of wood, with a hole beneath the fingerboard for the performer's thumb. It survived in England until the late 17th century.

Giuliani, Mauro (Giuseppe Sergio Pantaleo) (1781-1828) Italian composer and guitarist who was largely self-taught, but who toured widely as a virtuoso performer. In 1806 he settled in Vienna and while there befriended **Beethoven**. In 1814 he was made *virtuoso onorario di camera* for Napoleon's second wife. He settled in Naples after accumulating crippling debts in the Austrian capital.

Giuliani composed more than 200 pieces for guitar, including three concertos, chamber pieces and numerous songs.

Giulini, Carlo Maria (1914-) Legendary Italian orchestral and operatic conductor, noted for his impassioned yet disciplined style of conducting and his association with the works of Verdi. Having studied at the Accademia de Santa Cecilia in Rome, he made his reputation after the end of World War II, serving as musical director of Italian Radio (1946-1951). He made his opera conducting debut at Bergamo in 1951 in a performance of Verdi's *La Traviata* and for the next five years held the post of music director at La Scala, Milan. Following his British debut, conducting the **Glyndebourne** Company in a performance of Verdi's *Falstaff* at the 1955 Edinburgh Festival, he began a long association with the Philharmonia Orchestra, conducting many concerts, including gripping performances of the Verdi *Requiem*. He also appeared with the Hallé orchestra and from 1958 to 1967 was a guest conductor at Covent Garden, where in 1958 he conducted a memorable performance of Verdi's *Don Carlos*. He returned to Covent Garden in 1982 to give a much-talked-about performance of *Falstaff*. From 1969 to 1972 he shared with Sir Georg **Solti** the conductorship of the Chicago Symphony Orchestra, and from 1978 to 1984 he was conductor of the Los Angeles Philharmonic Orchestra.

giusto (It.) Just, or proper. Used to indicate moderation or exactness of tempo.

Glanville-Hicks, Peggy (1912-) Australian composer who worked in the United States between 1922 and 1959 to encourage concert performances of contemporary pieces. She studied with Fritz Hart at the Melborne Conservatoire (1929-1931). In 1932 she moved to Europe and studied at the Royal College of Music, London, with **Vaughan Williams**, with **Wellesz** at the Vienna Conservatoire and with **Boulanger** at the Paris Conservatoire. In 1942 she settled in New York, composing and later working as music critic for the *New York Herald Tribune* (1948-1958) and organizing concerts of contemporary music.

Glanville-Hicks's compositions reflect a combination of **serialist** techniques with ancient and oriental idioms. They include the opera *Nausicaa* (1961), the ballets *Tragic Celebration* (1964) and *Saul and the Witch of Endor* (1964), two symphoniettas, the *Etruscan Concerto* for piano and orchestra, and a number of songs and chamber pieces.

glass harmonica Instrument consisting of glass vessels, partly filled with liquid, and tuned to produce musical notes when rubbed round the rim with dampened fingers. In 1763 Benjamin Franklin invented a machine, which he called musical glasses. It consisted of graded sizes of glass half-globes that were attached to a spindle in a trough of water. A pedal was used to revolve the spindle, and then by touching the half-globes with the fingers, notes were produced.

Glass, Philip (1937-) American composer who studied at the University of Chicago and at the Juilliard School. Later he worked under **Boulanger** at the Paris Conservatoire (1964-1966). In 1966 he met the Indian **sitar** virtuoso and composer Ravi **Shankar** and abandoned the styles of composition that he had developed to embrace Indian idioms. He later adopted the 'minimalist' style – short repetitive melodies with steady driving rhythmic and static harmonies. His works include the operas *Einstein on the Beach* (1975), *Akhnaten* (1985), the ballet *Glass Pieces* (1982), instrumental works such as *Music in 5ths*, *Music in Similar Motion* (1969) and *Music with Changing Parts* (1970), as well as incidental music and film scores, including music for John Irvin's *Hamburger Hill*.

Glazunov, Alexander Konstantinovich (1865–1936) Russian composer whose work reveals the dominant influences of **Liszt** and **Wagner** and is characterized by its technical brilliance and wit. In his earlier years, he was associated with the group of Russian nationalist composers, The **Mighty Handful**.

The son of a wealthy publisher, he studied privately with **Rimsky-Korsakov** from 1880 and became a tutor at the St Petersburg Conservatoire in 1899. His first symphony, in E♭ major, was performed in 1882 conducted by **Balakirev**, and was a great success. A series of Russian concerts at the Paris Exhibition of 1899 included two of Glazunov's symphonies and his tone poem *Stenka Razin* (1885). In 1906 he was appointed director of the St Petersburg Conservatoire. His ballet *The Seasons* (1899) was adopted by Pavlova.

Glazunov completed eight symphonies, all of which reflect the temperament of the Russian school, concertos for the piano, violin, cello, saxophone and strings, six orchestral suites, chamber music and a number of choral works including the *Hymn to Pushkin* (1899).

glee Light-hearted choral composition for unaccompanied male voices that was especially popular in England in the 17th, 18th and early 19th centuries. The glee is written in sections, which vary according to the mood of the line of poetry set. The Glee Club of London, founded in 1783 and lasting until 1857, gave performances of glees, madrigals, motets, cannons and catches. In the United States, glee clubs exist in universities today, but these are merely groups singing many forms of music, and not just glees.

Glière, Reinhold Moritzovich (1875–1956) Soviet composer and conductor, best known for his ballet *The Red Poppy* (1926), based on the events of the Russian Revolution. It exhibits a powerful social realism that stresses the connection between music and the imagery of life. Glière studied at Kiev (1891) and at the Moscow Conservatoire (1894) with **Arensky**. In 1905 he entered the Berlin Conservatoire. He was appointed director of the Kiev Conservatoire in 1913 and a tutor of composition in Moscow in 1920. In 1939 he became chairman of the Organizing Committee of Soviet Composers.

Among his powerful, nationalistic compositions are three symphonies, the *March of the Red Army* (1924) and the *Victory Overture*. His later pieces sometimes reflect the influences of Eastern Soviet folk music, particularly in his opera *Shah Senem* (1934) and the symphonic poems *Cossacks of Zaporozhy* (1921) and *Trizna* (1915). He also wrote chamber music, including 175 works for the piano, and songs.

Glinka, Mikhail Ivanovich (1804–1857) Russian composer regarded by **Tchaikovsky** as "the acorn from which the oak of Russian music sprang" and revered by successive schools of Soviet composers.

While at school in St Petersburg he took piano tuition from John **Field**. He worked in the Ministry of Communications from 1824 but gave recitals as a singer. In 1828 he studied composition with Zamboni and went to Milan, Vienna and Berlin, where he studied with Siegfried Dehn in 1833. On his return to St Petersburg in 1836 he was appointed *Kapellmeister* to the Imperial Chapel. In 1844 he visited Paris and met **Berlioz**, and travelled in Spain and other countries before returning to Russia in 1847.

Glinka's compositions developed a strong Russian temperament. His first opera *Ivan Sussanin (A Life for the Tsar*, 1836) was a reaction against the prevailing supremacy of Italian opera with its clarity and simplicity. His second, *Russlan and Ludmilla* (1842), was powerfully Russian, betraying oriental colours and folk melodies from the Eastern steppes. A similar atmosphere invades his instrumental fantasy *Kamarinskaya* (1848). His *Jota Aragonesa* (1845) is based upon Spanish rhythms, but most of his works, including many song-cycles and piano pieces, are steeped in Russian idioms.

glissando Sliding scale played on a piano or harp, not by fingering, but by sliding over the keys or strings. On a piano or similar keyboard instrument, a glissando can be played only in C major, by sliding the fingers over adjacent keys.

On bowed instruments a glissando is played on one string by sliding the finger up or down while bowing. Glissando passages can also be played on a trombone by not interrupting the breath while the slide is moved to another position.

Globokar, Vinko (1934-) Yugoslav composer and virtuoso trombonist whose incredible command of this instrument enabled him to perform the avant-garde pieces that his tutor **Berio** composed for him. He was born in France and studied at the Ljubljana Conservatoire from 1949 and at the Paris Conservatoire with Liebowitz, Lafosse and **Berio** (1959-1963). He became a trombone tutor at Cologne's Musikhochschule in 1968. Among his compositions are *Plan* (1965), *Fluide* (1967), *Etude Pour Folklora I & II* (1968) and *La Ronde* (1970) for various combinations of instruments, as well as choral and chamber pieces.

glockenspiel Percussion instrument, consisting of a set of tuned steel plates played either with two hammers, one held in each hand, or with a mechanism operated by a piano keyboard. It has a range of two and a half octaves and produces a bell-like sound.

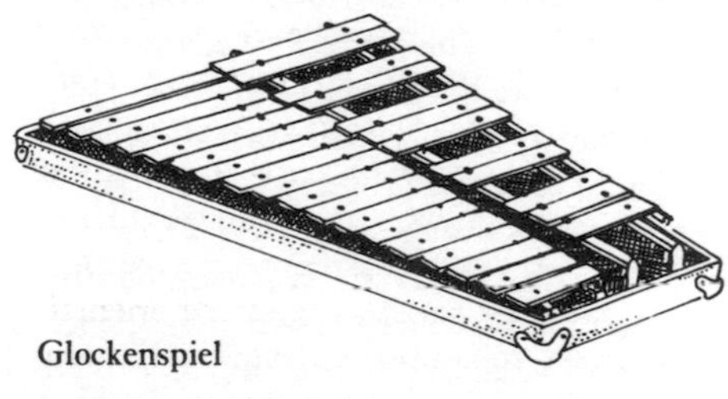

Glockenspiel

Glover, Jane (Alison) (1949-) British conductor, musicologist and broadcaster. She was educated at Oxford University and became a research fellow at Wolfson College, Oxford, in 1975. She made her debut as a professional conductor at the Wexford Festival in 1975. In 1980 she became chorus-master at Glyndebourne and has conducted performances with Glyndebourne Touring Opera and at Glyndebourne itself. In 1983 she was appointed musical direcor of the London Choral Society and in 1984 she became artistic director of the London Mozart Players. She has performed and broadcast with major British orchestras and in 1988 became the second woman to conduct an opera performance at the Royal Opera House, Covent Garden. She has edited operas by **Monteverdi** and Cavalli and has made BBC television series on a history of the orchestra and the life of **Mozart**.

Gluck, Christoph Willibald von (1714-1787) German composer of opera who wrote to satisfy varied tastes and eventually developed a new and dramatic style in his work.

Gluck entered a Jesuit School in 1726 and Prague University in 1732. He earned a living performing on the violin and piano and by teaching until he was appointed to the court of Prince Lobkowitz at Vienna in 1736. In 1737 he moved to Milan with Prince Melzi to continue his study with **Sammartini**, and wrote his first opera *Artaserse* (1741). He travelled to London in 1745 at the height of his success and met **Handel** and gave two recitals on the **glass harmonica**. He visited other countries before being appointed director of the court musicians to Joseph, Prince of Saxe-Hildburghausen) in Vienna in 1754. His compositions during this period reflect the levity and humour demanded by his audiences. In 1773 he moved to Paris in order to perform *Iphigenie en Aulide* for the Opéra. He returned to Vienna in 1779.

His early operas *Artaserse* (1741), *Demofoonte* (1742), *Demetrio* (1742), *Il Tigrane* (1743), *La Sophonisba* (1744) and *Ipermestra* (1745) reflect Italian styles, whereas later ones, including *La Cythere Assiegée* (1759), *L'Ivrogne Corrigé* (1760), *Orfeo ed Eurydice* (1762), *Alceste* (1767) and

Echo et Narcisse (1779), are in the French manner. *Orfeo*, *Alceste* and *Paride ed Elena* (1770) reflect a new style which subordinates virtuosity to dramatic truth and seeks to use the music of opera to express the poetry of its libretto. Their narratives are direct and continuity is maintained through the abandonment of traditional **secco** recitatives in favour of the sustained dramatic tempo of classical Greek drama.

Glyndebourne Name of the house and estate of John Christie (1882-1962) where the Glyndebourne Festival Opera was founded in 1934. The first performances were *The Marriage of Figaro* and *Così fan Tutte*.

Up to the beginning of World War II the repertoire was mostly devoted to the works of **Mozart**. The conductor was Fritz **Busch**, the producer Carl Ebert and the manager Rudolf Bing, who between them set high standards, attracting internationally acclaimed singers. During the post-war years several premieres were given, including **Britten**'s *Rape of Lucretia* (1946) and *Albert Herring* (1947), and at the same time its repertory extended to the works of other composers. The Royal Philharmonic and London Philharmonic Orchestras have appeared for the opera company, whose conductors included Vittorio **Gui**, who was responsible for the inclusion of several of **Rossini**'s operas, John **Pritchard** and Bernard **Haitink**.

Gnecchi, Vittorio (1876-1954) Italian composer memorable for his quarrel with Richard **Strauss** whom he accused of plagiarism, Strauss's *Elektra* (1909) resembling his own *Cassandra* (1905). He studied at the Milan Conservatoire and produced several successful operatic works, including *Cassandra* and *La Rosiera* (1927).

Gobbi, Tito (1913-1984) Italian baritone who studied in Rome and made his debut in 1935 as Rodolf (*La Somnambula*, **Bellini**). Gobbi sang at Covent Garden, San Francisco and Chicago, as well as at all the Italian opera houses and in Vienna. His repertory covered nearly 100 operas and he has made many films. Gobbi was best known for his interpretations of **Verdi** and **Puccini** and was also a fine actor. In 1965 he turned to opera production and published his autobiography in 1979.

Godard, Benjamin (Louis Paul) (1849-1895) French composer and violinist who studied at the Paris Conservatoire from 1836 and in 1885 founded and conducted the *Concerts Modernes* in Paris. Among his compositions are two concertos for violin, a symphony and works for the piano. He also wrote eight operas which are now forgotten, chamber pieces and more than 100 songs.

Godowsky, Leopold (1870-1938) Polish composer and pianist who became an American citizen in 1891. He studied at the Berlin *Hochschule* with **Saint-Saëns** in 1887 and toured the United States as a performer. He became a piano tutor in Philadelphia in 1890, and in 1894 was appointed director of the piano school at the Chicago Conservatoire. He toured in Europe as a tutor and recitalist, returning to America in 1912. Godowsky's compositions include *53 Studies on Chopin*, *Etudes* and *Triakontameron* (all for the piano) and three symphonic pieces.

Goehr, Alexander (1932-) English composer who employs serial techniques and is a member of the Manchester School of composers, which includes Peter Maxwell **Davies**, Harrison **Birtwistle** and John **Ogdon**. The son of the German conductor Walter Goehr, he studied composition with Richard **Hall** at the Royal Manchester College of Music. In 1957 he began studies at the Paris Conservatoire with **Messiaen**. He joined the BBC in 1960 and became composer in residence at the New England Conservatoire in 1968. He held academic posts in the music departments of Yale, Leeds and Cambridge Universities and has brought his conservative musical principles to bear on many contemporary composers. Among his compositions are the opera *Arden muss* *sterben* (1966), orchestral works, including a *Little Symphony* (1963), *Pastorals* (1965), a *Symphony in One Movement* (1970) and various romances for strings, as well as choral and vocal works (notably *Five Poems and an Epigram of William Blake*, 1964) and chamber pieces.

Goetz, Hermann (Gustav) (1840-1876) German composer who studied at the Stern Conservatoire, Berlin in 1860 and became organist at Winterthur in 1863. He composed the successful opera *The Taming of the Shrew* (1874). He settled in Zurich and started work on a second opera, *Francesca de Rimini*. However, he died before it was finished, Ernest Frank taking up and completing his work. He also composed *Frühlingsoverture* for orchestra, a symphony, and concertos for the piano and the violin as well as chamber pieces and songs.

Goldberg, Johann (1727-1756) German composer, and keyboard player who studied with **Bach** from 1742 and became a chamber musician at the court of Count Bruhl in 1751. He composed two concertos for the keyboard and music for the flute and harpsichord. Bach's 30 variations for harpsichord were dedicated to him and are known as the *Goldberg Variations*.

Goldmark, Karl (Károly) (1830-1915) Hungarian composer and violinist. He studied at the Vienna Conservatoire and remained in Vienna as a tutor, composer and critic. He became a friend of **Brahms** during this time and was undoubtedly influenced by him. In 1848 he joined a theatre orchestra at Gyor in Hungary. Goldmark's compositions include six operas (of which *The Queen of Sheba* 1875, and *Merlin*, 1886, are the best known), the symphonic poem *Rustic Wedding* (1876) and two overtures, *Im Frühling* and *Sakuntala*. He also composed concertos and choral works, pieces for the piano and a number of songs.

Goldmark, Rubin (1872-1936) American composer and nephew of Karl **Goldmark**, who studied at the New York Conservatoire and later at the Vienna Conservatoire. He returned to New York to study at the National Conservatoire with **Dvorák**. In 1895 he became director of the Colorado College Conservatoire and was appointed director of the composition department at the Juilliard School in 1924. While there he taught **Copland** and **Gershwin**. Goldmark's compositions include a *Requiem* for orchestra, a *Negro Rhapsody*, *Hiawatha* and other chamber pieces.

Goldschmidt, Berthold (1903-) German composer and conductor who assisted Deryck Cooke as principal conductor of the definitive performance of **Mahler**'s Symphony No. 10 in 1964. He studied at Hamburg University and at the Berlin *Hochschule* with **Schreker** in 1922. His conducting career began with an assistantship at the Berlin State Opera in 1926 and with the Darmstadt Opera in 1927. He moved to England in 1935 and was appointed choirmaster at **Glyndebourne** in 1947. He has conducted with many British orchestras. His compositions include the opera *Beatrice Cenci* (1951), a symphony, concertos for the violin and clarinet, music for strings and other chamber pieces.

Gombert, Nicholas (*c*1500-*c*1556) Flemish composer and follower of **Josquin des Prez**. He served Emperor Charles V until 1540 and won a high reputation for his motets, masses and chansons. He was admired by *Finck* for his use of the **polyphonic** style, which developed through his 160 motets into a distinctive form in which voices imitate each other in a complex relationship of melodies.

gong Circular percussion instrument made

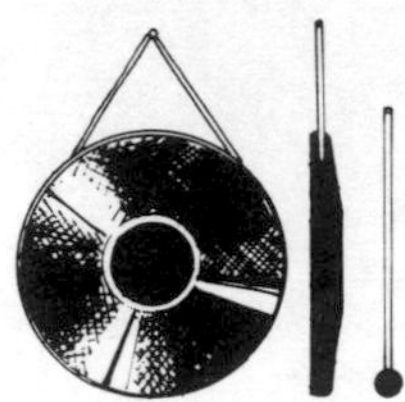

Gong

of bronze with turned-down rims. It is struck with a mallet covered with various materials according to the quality of sound required.

gong-ageng (Indonesia) Largest form of gong which hangs in an imposing frame at the back of the larger **gamelans** and serves as the primary **colotomic** or time-marking instrument in the *gamelan*.

gongan (Indonesia) Complete melodic period or phrase ending with a stroke on the largest gong, usually the **gong-ageng**. It is the fundamental **colotomic** or time-marking event in a **gamelan** composition and usually consists of multiples of eight beats. The *gongan* is subdivided by other time-marking gongs, such as the **kenong, kempul** and **ketuk**.

Goossens, Sir Eugene (1893-1962) English composer and violinist who encouraged the performance of new music and enjoyed a successful career as an international conductor. He studied at the Bruges Conservatoire, the Liverpool College of Music and at the Royal College of Music with **Stanford**. He conducted many orchestras in London, where he was an assistant to **Beecham** (1916-1920), as well as in the United States and Australia. He was knighted in 1955. His compositions include the opera *Judith* (1929), which has a libretto by Arnold Bennett, a symphony and *Symphonietta* (1922) for orchestra, and choral works such as *Silence* (1922) and the oratorio *Apocalypse* (1952). He also wrote chamber music.

Eugene Goossens

gopak Russian folk dance with music of a lively character, in duple time. It originated in the Ukraine. An alternative spelling is hopak.

Gossec, François Joseph (1734-1829) Belgian composer who wrote many pieces that glorified the ideals of the French Revolution. He was a chorister at Antwerp Cathedral and taught himself composition. In 1751 he moved to Paris and befriended **Rameau**, who secured him a post as conductor of concerts organized by La Pouplinière. He was appointed musician to the court of the Louis-Joseph de Bourbon, Prince de Condé in 1762. In 1773 he was made a director of the *Concert Spirituel* and a second conductor at the Paris Opéra. He became a professor of composition at the Paris Conservatoire in 1795.

Gossec composed more than 30 symphonies and 15 operas, as well as ballets and devotional pieces, including the *Messe des Morts*(1780) which experimented with complicated arrangements of instruments and voices.

Gotovac, Jakov (1895-1982) Yugoslav composer and conductor who studied in Split and at the Vienna Academy and became conductor of the Croatian Opera in 1923. His compositions include the opera *Ero the Joker* (1935) which reflects the folk music of his country, and a number of chamber and choral works.

Gottschalk, Louis Moreau (1829-1869) American composer, conductor and pianist who studied with **Hallé** and **Berlioz** in Paris and began a career as a virtuoso pianist. He toured widely as a popular performer and conductor. A scandal involving one of his female students in 1867 forced him to move to South America, and he embarked upon an arduous schedule of tours in order to remain solvent. He wrote two symphonies and works for the chamber and stage which have largely been lost. His compositions for the piano, however, *The Aeolian Harp* and *The Dying Poet*, are still performed.

Goudimel, Claude (*c*1520-1572) French composer who wrote a number of masses and motets before his conversion to Protestantism, when he abandoned the ornate style of his earlier sacred works to compose simple psalms and spiritual songs for the Huguenot community. He was killed at the hands of Catholics at Lyons in the St Bartholomew's Day Massacre of 1572.

Gould, Glenn (1932-1982) Canadian pianist who studied at the Toronto Royal Conservatoire. He made his debut at the age of 14. Gould had an extremely wide repertory and toured all over the world, including the USSR.

Gould, Morton (1913-) American composer, pianist and conductor who is highly regarded for his skills as an orchestrator. His compositions reflect a fusion of the idiom of popular American music with the form and structure of classical works. He has also experimented with jazz as in his *Boogie-Woogie Etudes* for piano (1943). Gould studied at the Institute of Music and Art, New York and followed a career as a broadcaster working for NBC and CBS. He also found time to be a guest conductor with many American orchestras.

His compositions include three symphonies, a concerto for tap dancer and orchestra, *Cowboy Rhapsody* (1944), an orchestration of *The Battle Hymn of the Republic* (1951), *Lincoln Legend* (1941) and *The Fall River Legend* (1947). He has also written several Broadway musicals, including *Delightfully Dangerous* and *Billion Dollar Baby* (1945).

Gounod, Charles François (1818-1893) French composer, organist and conductor whose work is still widely respected today and has retained a place in the international repertoire. After a classical education, during which he received piano instruction from his mother, he entered the Paris Conservatoire, studying with **Halévy** and Lesueur. He was organist at the Eglise des Missions Etrangères, Paris, for a while. His earlier compositions reflect his ecclesiastical background, comprising mainly masses and oratorios. He won the Grand Prix de Rome in 1839 and visited Austria and Germany. In 1870 he moved to England to conduct for the Royal Choral Society. His most famous composition is his opera *Faust* (1859), which is still popular today. Other operas include *Philemon et Baucis* (1860), *La Reine de Saba* (1862), *Mireille* (1864), *Roméo et Juliette* (1867), and *Le Tribut de Zamora* (1881). He also wrote some orchestral pieces, including two symphonies and choral works, many of which reflect the influence of **Palestrina**, whose work he studied while in Rome.

Gow, Nathaniel (1763-1831) Scottish composer, violinist and trumpeter who became leader of the Edinburgh Assembly Orchestra in 1791. He composed many dance pieces, and as a publisher produced several collections of his own work and the works of others. He wrote *Caller Herring* as a harpsichord piece that combined the tones of St Andrew's Cathedral with the melodies of the cries of Edinburgh's fishwives.

Grabu, Louis (?-*c*1694) French composer and violinist who settled in England in 1665. He was then appointed Master of the Musick to Charles II from 1666 to 1674. He composed for the stage, completing music for Dryden's nationalist opera *Albion and Albanus* in 1685.

grace note Ornamental note considered additional to a melody or harmony. It is often printed in small type on a score.

Gradual I Responsorial chant following the reading of the Epistle and before the

Gospel in the mass. It is coupled with the **Alleluia** or Tract, and is also known as the musical equivalent of the Missal.

gradulka Bulgarian fiddle, held vertically and rested on the knee, as opposed to being held horizontally, rested against the chest or shoulder and played like a modern **violin**.

Grainger, Percy Aldridge (1882-1961) Australian-born composer and pianist who became a United States citizen in 1919. He was admired by **Britten** and others, chiefly for his experiments with folk melodies, which he arranged for the orchestra in an original and striking style. His use of English instead of Italian to mark the dynamics of his scores is unusual.

Grainger studied in Melbourne, Frankfurt and later at the Berlin Conservatoire, where he was a pupil of **Busoni**. In 1900 he toured England as a recitalist and settled there, befriending **Grieg** by whom he was invited to Norway to study his Piano Concerto in A Minor. He came to the attention of **Delius** with his arrangement of the folk melody *Brigg Fair*, which Delius himself was later to rhapsodize. In 1915 he performed in the United States and moved there shortly afterwards. He was appointed chairman of the music department of New York University in 1932.

Grainger's best-known compositions include *Country Gardens* (1925), *Handel in the Strand* (1911), *Shepherd's Hey* (1922) and the *Rosenkavalier Ramble* for piano. He also composed *Shallow Brown* for chorus and orchestra (1927), *Over the Hills and Far Away* (1928) and *Molly on the Shore* (1921) for orchestra.

grama (India) Ancient name for basic scale forms used in the Sanskritic tradition of northern Indian music. Each is characterized by a unique set of intervals (**shrutis**) governed by certain rules.

Granados, Enrique (1867-1916) Spanish composer of music in the nationalistic idiom and virtuoso pianist. He studied composition with Pedrell in Barcelona and the piano with de **Beriot** in Paris. He returned to Barcelona to found his own piano school and the Society of Classical Concerts in 1900.

Among his compositions are the operas *Maria del Carmen* (1898), *Gaziel* (1906), *Liliana* (1911) and *Goyescas* (1916; originally two books of seven pieces for the piano) which has a memorable intermezzo and is based upon paintings by Goya, a series of orchestral suites including *Elisenda*, *Suite Arabe* and *La Nit del Mor*, and works for voice and piano. His piano pieces and songs are, perhaps, the most brilliant – the songs *Cancions Amatorias* and his *Allegro de Concierto* reflecting a deeply poetic and elegant character.

gran cassa (It.) Equivalent of the English bass **drum**.

Grandi, Alessandro (?-1637) Italian composer of sacred music in the concerto-style, as well as of solo cantatas, motets and accompanied madrigals. He became choirmaster at Ferrara Cathedral in 1615 and from 1617 singer and later assistant director to **Monteverdi** at St Mark's, Venice. In 1625 he was appointed *maestro di cappella* at Santa Maria Maggiore, Bergamo.

grand jeu (Fr.) Organ stop that brings the whole instrument into play.

grand opera Style of opera established in Paris in the late 1820s, which was built around grandiose plots and made use of large ensemble scenes, expanded orchestral resources and colourful pageantry. It catered for the new and relatively uncultured classes of that time, and after the mid-1800s these characteristics became less pronounced and grand opera merged with comic opera. Among the operas of this genre were **Rossini**'s *William Tell* (1829) and **Meyerbeer**'s *Les Huguenots* (1836).

grand piano **Piano** whose shape was originally derived from the harpsichord. Its

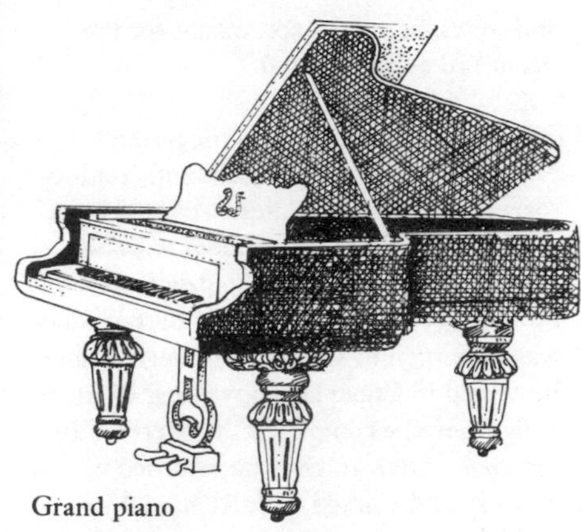
Grand piano

strings are laid out horizontally, and each string corresponds in position to the relevant key on the keyboard. It remains the most popular form of piano for performance purposes, the baby grand superseding the **upright piano** for domestic use.

Granjany, Marcel (1891-1975) French composer and harpist who studied at the Paris Conservatoire and began a career as a recitalist in 1908. He served with the French Army and after World War I taught at the Fontainbleu Summer School. In 1936 he moved to America, becoming director of the harp department at the Juilliard School and the Conservatoire de Musique de Quebec in 1938. In 1956 he was appointed a tutor at the Manhattan School of Music. His compositions for harp are technically demanding but lyrical and passionate. They include *Colorado Trail*, *Divertissement* and a *Rhapsody*. He also composed *Poème* for harp, horn and orchestra, and an *Aria in Classic Style* for harp and strings.

graphic notation Certain newer (post-1950s) types of musical notation in which graphics indicate the action required by a performer, or in which the harmonic sequence is shown by abbreviations for the names of the chords.

Graun, Carl Heinrich (1704-1757) German composer who worked as a tenor at the Brunswick Opera from 1725 and was appointed second *Kapellmeister* there in 1726. He entered the service of Crown Prince Frederick of Prussia in 1735 and was appointed conductor of the Berlin Royal Opera by him on his coronation in 1740.

Graun composed more than 30 operas in the Italian style, including *Rodelinda* (1741), *Montezuma* and *Ezio* (1755) and a passion *Der Tod Jesu* (1755).

grave (Fr.) Indicates a slow, serious tempo.

gravicembalo (It.) Alternative term for harpsichord.

grazia (It.) Grace. Used alone to indicate the character of a piece or passage, or more often in combination with a tempo indication such as *allegro grazioso*, or *andantino grazioso*.

great organ Principal manual keyboard of the organ.

great service Anglican musical service of the late 16th and 17th centuries. Among the composers of this type of work were William **Byrd** (1543-1623), Orlando **Gibbons** (1583-1625) and Thomas **Weelkes** (*c*1576-1623).

Grechaninov, Alexander Tikhonovich (1864-1956) Russian composer, and pianist. He studied at the Moscow Conservatoire with Safonov and at the St Petersburg Conservatoire with **Rimsky-Korsakov**. In 1925 he moved to France and then to the United States in 1939, settling in New York. His compositions include five symphonies, operas, cantatas, sonatas for violin, cello and clarinet, more than 200 songs and a number of choral works, including litanies and masses for both the Russian Orthodox and the Roman Catholic Churches. His *Missa Oecumenica* (1944) was intended to bridge the cultural divide between these two devotional forms.

Greene, Maurice (1695-1755) English composer and organist at St Paul's Cathedral, London, from 1718. He became organist and composer at the Chapel Royal in 1727. In 1735 he was appointed Master of the King's Musick and a professor of music at Cambridge University. He was a friend of **Handel**, a notable collector of English church music and a composer of oratorios, organ works, songs and anthems such as *Lord let me know mine end*, which was published as part of a collection in his *Forty Select Anthems*, 1743.

Gregorian chant Official repertory of **plainsong** traditionally associated with Pope Gregory I (St Gregory, *c*640-*c*604), which became standard in the Roman Catholic Church. The term is often used as an alternative for plainchant. Gregorian chant differs from its predecessor, **Ambrosian chant**, in that it used four more modes and one dominant tone as a reciting note. Gregorian chant was superseded as the major Western musical form in about the 10th century with the rise of harmonized forms based around the **cantus firmus**.

Gregorian tones Chants of the Gregorian psalmody sung in groups corresponding to the eight church **modes** (four authentic and four plagal).

Grétry, André-Ernest-Modeste (1741-1813) Belgian composer of operas who exploited the French style, with its accentuation of the dramatic, and who published several treatises concerning the composition of operatic music. He studied in Rome from 1759 and composed the intermezzo *La Vendemmiatrice* there (1761). In 1767 he moved to Paris and found success with his light comic operas. Napoleon gave him a pension and he was appointed an inspector of the Paris Conservatoire in 1795. His more serious and tragic works, however, were less well received.

Grétry composed more than 50 operas, including *Richard Coeur de Lion* (1784) his masterpiece, *Le tableau Parlant* (1769), *Zemire et Azor* (1771) and *L'Amant Jaloux* (1778). He also wrote a requiem, motets and songs, as well as six sonatas for the piano and a flute concerto.

Grieg, Edvard Hagerup (1843-1907) Norwegian composer, pianist and conductor who developed a unique style within a nationalistic idiom. He studied with his mother, and entered the Leipzig Conservatoire in 1858. His first concert performance was in Bergen in 1863, and following this he settled in Copenhagen, visiting Rome in 1865 where he completed the overture *In Autumn* (1865). In 1867 he returned to Norway and worked with Richard Nordraak, who was attempting to establish a national school of music. On another visit to Rome (1870) he met **Liszt**, who greatly admired his work. The Norwegian Government and Ibsen commissioned him to write incidental music to *Peer Gynt* (1876) and it was this piece that brought him international acclaim. He toured in England with his wife, giving recitals, and met both **Delius** and **Grainger**.

Grieg's compositions for orchestra include two revised suites from *Peer Gynt* (1888, 1891), the Piano Concerto in A Minor (1869) for which he is most widely

Edvard Grieg

known today, a suite for strings and *Symphonic Dances* (1898). He wrote a Sonata in E Minor for piano and a number of ballads and songs, including the popular *I Love Thee* and the choral works *Landjaenning* and *Foran Sydens Kloster* (1871).

Griffes, Charles Tomlinson (1884-1920) American composer who combined an impressionistic style with reflections of American Indian and Japanese themes, and later developed a polytonal approach to composition.

He studied in Berlin at the Stern Conservatoire with **Humperdinck** from 1903 and taught there, as well as working as an accompanist and recitalist, until 1907. He then returned to the United States to teach at the Hockley School, New York. Among his compositions are *Nocturne* (1919), *The White Peacock* (1919), *The Pleasure Dome of Kubla Khan* (1919) for orchestra, a series of dance-dramas including *The Kairn of Koridwen* (1916), *Tone Pictures* (1914) and *Four Roman Sketches* (1916) for piano, and some chamber pieces, including *Two Sketches Based on Indian Themes* (1918).

Grigny, Nicholas de (1672-1703) French composer who was appointed organist at Rheims Cathedral in 1694. He composed liturgical pieces for the organ in his *Livre d'Orgue* (1699) which was later copied by **Bach**.

Grofe, Ferde (Ferdinand Rudolph von G.) (1892-1972) American composer and conductor who was acclaimed as an orchestrator and developed the idiom of symphonic jazz. He studied in New York and was awarded an honorary doctorate from Illinois University. He became a violist with the Los Angeles Symphony Orchestra and often worked with theatre orchestras. Admired for his skills as an arranger, he was employed by the bandleader Paul Whiteman to exploit the increasingly popular idiom of symphonic jazz. He orchestrated **Gershwin**'s *Rhapsody in Blue* in 1924.

All his compositions are symphonic jazz pieces, and include the *Grand Canyon Suite* (1931), *Broadway at Night* (1937) and *Symphony in Steel* (1937), notable for its use of four pairs of shoes, brooms, a locomotive bell and a compressed air tank. Among his other suites for orchestra are *Mississippi Suite*, *Hollywood Suite*, *Death Valley Suite* and *Aviation Suite*.

grosse caisse (Fr.) Equivalent of the English bass **drum**.

grosse orchester (Ger.) Equivalent of the English full orchestra.

grosse Trommel (Ger.) Equivalent of the English bass **drum**.

ground Melodic figure used as a bass in a composition, constantly repeated (although sometimes repeated transposed) while the upper parts proceed in free style. Sometimes also called ground bass.

Groven, Eivind (1901-1977) Norwegian composer and collector of national folk music, noted for his work regarding the tuning of instruments to natural intervals. He has composed two symphonies, several symphonic poems, pieces for the piano and choral works, and has arranged many folk songs for the orchestra.

Gruenberg, Louis (1884-1964) American composer and pianist, born in Russia, who was captivated by the free rhythms and melodies of jazz. He studied in New York, Vienna and at the Berlin Conservatoire with **Busoni** and Koch. From 1912 he toured with the Berlin Philharmonic Orchestra as a pianist, but returned to the United States to become a professor of composition at the Chicago College of Music in 1930. Gruenberg's compositions include four symphonies, the operas *Emperor Jones* (1933) and *Volpone* (1945), a jazz suite for orchestra (1925) and concertos for the piano and violin. He also wrote chamber pieces and works for piano which reflect the influences of jazz music.

gruppetto (It.) Equivalent for the English **turn**.

Guarneri (or Guarnerius) Italian family of violin- and cello-makers of the 17th and 18th centuries. Andrea Guarneri (*c*1626-1698) lived in Cremona, where (along with Antonio **Stradivari**) he was instructed in the art of violin-making by Nicola **Amati**. Of Andrea's sons, Pietro Giovanni Guarneri (1655-1720) broke away from the family business in Cremona and set up as a violin-maker in Mantua, whereas Giuseppe Giovanni Battista Guarneri (1666-1739) developed an individual style of making violins. The most important member of the family was Bartolomeo Giuseppe Guarneri (1698-1744), known as del Gesù. A nephew of Andrea, Bartolomeo worked all his life at Cremona, producing instruments second in quality only to those made by Stradivari. Reviving the tradition of the Breschia School, Bartolomeo made instruments whose tone was rich and strong.

Guarnieri, Camargo Mozart (1907-) Brazilian composer and conductor whose work illustrates the influences of folk music and is rich in colour and variety. He seldom quotes directly from folk songs, preferring to reflect them in melodies of his own devising. He studied in Paris in 1938, becoming a pupil of **Koechlin**. On returning to Brazil, he became a professor at the Sao Paulo Conservatoire and a conductor with the Sao Paulo Philharmonic Society. He was awarded first prize at the Caracas Music Festival (1957) for his *Choros* for piano and orchestra. His compositions include three symphonies, the *Suite Brasiliana* and *Dansa Brasileira* for orchestra, and concertos for the piano and violin. He has also written songs and chamber pieces.

Guglielmi Family of Italian opera composers active between 1750 and 1830. Pietro Alessandro (1728-1804) studied with his father, Jacopo, and later with Durante in Naples, where he worked from 1776-1793, when he became choirmaster at St Peter's in Rome. He wrote more than 100 operas, including *Il re pastore* (1765), several oratorios, cantatas, sonatas and quartets. His son, Pietro Carlo, known as Guglielmini (*c*1763-1817) wrote more than 40 operas, mainly in his native Naples.

Gui, Vittorio (1885-1975) Italian composer and conductor, noted for his revival of a number of operas by **Rossini**. He studied at the Liceo di St Cecilia in Rome. While there, he conducted a performance of *La Gioconda* by **Ponchielli** and came to the notice of **Toscanini**, who appointed him as an assistant in Milan in 1923. He conducted for various Italian opera houses, founded the Stabile Orchestra of Florence in 1928 and participated in the foundation of the Maggio Musicale Fiorentino in 1933. He also conducted at Glyndebourne, and was a guest conductor with several other orchestras. Gui's compositions include symphonic pieces and the opera *La Fata Malerba* (1927).

Guido d'Arezzo (*c*995-*c*1033) Monk, musical theorist and teacher who reformed musical notation by adding a third and fourth line to the staff and devising a system of solmization using the syllables *ut*, *re*, *mi*, *fa*, *sol*, *la* as a means of learning notes in the sequence of a hexachord (six-note scale). These were the first syllables on each line of a hymn to John the Baptist, supposedly written by Guido. Born in Paris and educated at the Benedictine abbey of Pomposa, he was appointed in about 1025 to teach in the cathedral school of Arezzo and commissioned to write down his theories in the *Micrologus de disciplina artis musicae*. In about 1029 he moved to the Camaldolese monastery at Avellana. The Guidonian hand, a diagram of a left hand attributed to him and used as a means of teaching notes, is not in fact mentioned in his writings.

Guillemain, Louis-Gabriel (1705-1770) French composer and violinist who wrote pieces for the harpsichord and for strings, including trio symphonies, solo, trio and quartet sonatas.

Guilmant, Félix Alexandre (1837-1892) French composer and organist who studied in Paris with Lemmens and at the Brussels Conservatoire. He became the organist at La Trinité, Paris in 1871. As a virtuoso performer he toured widely, visiting both England and the United States. He founded the Schola Cantorum with Bordes and **d'Indy** and acted as organ tutor there. In 1896 he was appointed professor of organ studies at the Paris Conservatoire.

He wrote organ symphonies, eight sonatas and other works such as toccatas and fugues. In addition he edited volumes of ancient music for the organ, collecting them in the *Archives des Maîtres de l'Orgue* (1898).

Guiraud, Ernest (1837-1892) French composer who wrote an important treatise on instrumentation (1892), completed the controversial recitatives for **Bizet**'s *Carmen* (1875) and orchestrated *The Tales of Hoffmann* by Offenbach (1881). He studied at the Paris Conservatoire and became a professor of composition there in 1880. He composed several operas including *Piccolino* (1876), and the ballet *Gretna Green* (1873).

guitar Plucked stringed instrument. There are various types of guitar, of which the principal one came to other European countries from Spain, and as a result is often known as the Spanish guitar. This normally has six strings, tuned E, A, D, G, B, E, and has a range of three octaves and a fifth from E below middle C. The guitar has a flat back, a waisted bodyshape, and the sound-hole in the sound-board is often decoratively carved. The fingerboard is fretted.

The 20th-century classical guitar, as it is now called, has gained in popularity as a result of the teaching and playing of the Spanish virtuoso Andres **Segovia**. Among more recent composers who have written music for the guitar are **Villa-Lobos**, **Falla**, **Roussel** and **Britten**. The Spanish composer **Rodrigo** is especially known for his *Concierto de Aranjuez* (1939) for guitar and orchestra. See also **Hawaiian guitar**.

Guitar

Gundry, Inglis (1905-) English composer who studied at Oxford and the Royal College of Music, where he was a pupil of **Vaughan Williams**. His compositions include five operas, symphonic pieces, and chamber music.

Gungl, Joseph (1810-1889) Hungarian composer and bandmaster who founded his own band in Berlin (1843) and toured the United States in 1849. He was appointed *Kapellmeister* to the Emperor of Austria in 1876 and composed more than 300 marches and dances for his band.

Guridi, Jesús (1886-1961) Spanish composer and organist who studied at the Schola Cantorum, Paris, with **d'Indy**, and became a professor of organ and later director of the Madrid Conservatoire. He composed a number of operas, choral works and pieces for the organ, all of which reflect in some measure the flavour of Basque folk music.

Gurlitt, Manfred (1890-1973) German composer and conductor who studied with **Humperdinck** at the Berlin Conservatoire and conducted orchestras in Essen (1911), Augsburg (1912) and Bremen (1914). He left Germany in 1939 after the Nazi authorities banned his compositions, and he settled in Tokyo.

He composed the opera *Wozzeck* (1928), which is an evocative version of Buchner's play and in many ways supercedes **Berg**'s attempt (1922). He also wrote the *Goya Symphony* (1938) and *Shakespeare Symphony* (1954) for orchestra and chorus, and a number of chamber pieces and songs.

Gurney, Ivor (1890-1937) English composer, poet and organist who sang in the choir at Gloucester Cathedral and became organist there in 1906 as a pupil of Brewer. He studied composition under Stanford at the Royal College of Music from 1911.

He spent much time setting his own poetry and that of A.E. Houseman to music, and composed 82 songs and a number of sensitive song-cycles, including *Ludlow and Teme* and *The Western Playland*.

gusla Slavonic one-stringed bowed instrument. The bow is an ordinary stick with a small branch attached to it into which the hair is wound. The instrument is played resting on the knee, and it is used to accompany narrative songs sung by the player. An alternative spelling is gusle.

gusle Alternative term for **gusla**.

gusli Russian **zither** used in folk music as an accompaniment to singers. It was used in **Rimsky-Korsakov**'s ballet-opera *Sadko* (1867).

Guy, Barry (1947-) English composer and double-bass player who studied at the Guildhall School of Music with **Orr** and Buxton and became a leading performer with a number of chamber orchestras. He founded the London Jazz Composers' Orchestra in response to calls from other musicians. His compositions reflect both his interest in jazz and his own technical skill as a performer. They include *Eos* (1977) and *Anna* (1974) for double-bass and orchestra, *Songs for Tomorrow* for orchestra (1975) and *Play* (1976) for chamber ensemble.

Guy, Helen See **Hardelot, Guy d'**

gymel Vocal composition in two parts, both of the same range. A characteristic feature is the use of parallel thirds. The terms first appeared in the 15th century, when it was used to refer to a divided voice-part in a **polyphonic** composition, but examples are found as early as the 13th century. An alternative spelling is gimel.

Gyrowetz, Adalbert (1763-1850) Bohemian composer whose work was admired by **Mozart** and whose compositions were performed in Paris under the name of **Haydn**. He studied law in Prague but abandoned the legal profession to study music in Naples and at the Paris Conservatoire. In 1798 he moved to London, but returned to Vienna in 1804 and became *Kapellmeister* to the two court theatre orchestras. He composed 60 symphonic works, 30 operas and 40 ballets, as well as a large amount of work for chamber orchestras.

H

H German symbol for the note B♮.

Haba, Alois (1893-1973) Czech composer and violinist who was influenced by Oriental and Moravian folk music and by the atonal technique of **Schoenberg**. His own **microtonal** style has influenced many present-day composers. He studied at the Prague Conservatoire with **Novak** and then moved to the conservatoires of Vienna and Berlin.

After 1921 he developed a microtonal technique which he taught as director of music at the Prague Conservatoire (1923). His opera *Matka* (1929) is in quarter tones, and his third operatic piece, *Prijd Kralovtsvi Tve* (1934), uses one-sixth tones. Both place great demands upon performers. The use of these tones in orchestral works such as his *Fantasy for Piano* (1954), in string quartets and pieces for the chamber, necessitate the adaptation of various instruments including the clarinet, trumpet and piano.

habañera Dance and song form, introduced into Spain from Africa via Cuba. It is a moderate 2/4 time and has a basic rhythm of four quavers, the first of which is dotted. Its rhythm is clearly exemplified in the famous habañera of **Bizet**'s opera *Carmen* (1875).

Hadley, Henry Kimball (1871-1937) American composer and conductor who championed US music and helped to found the National Association of American Composers and Conductors. He studied composition at the conservatoires of New England and Vienna and conducted various European orchestras, before returning to the United States. He then conducted for the Seattle (1909) and San Francisco (1911) Symphony Orchestras, and the New York Philharmonic (1920). His compositions include four symphonies, several operas including *Cleopatra's Night* (1920) and *A Night in Old Paris* (1925), the tone poem *Salome*, chamber music and works for chorus.

Hadley, Patrick Arthur Sheldon (1899-1973) English composer of music for voice and orchestra who was inspired mainly by literary themes and influenced by **Delius** and **Vaughan Williams**. He studied at Cambridge and at the Royal College of Music, where he became a tutor in 1925. In 1946 he was appointed a professor of music at Cambridge University. His compositions include *Ephemera* (1929), *Scene from Hardy's The Woodlanders* (1926), *La Belle Dame sans Merci* (1935) and *Lines from Shelley's "The Cenci"* (1951).

haegŭm/haekum (Korea) Popular two-stringed fiddle with a curved neck. It is held vertically and played with a horse-hair bow inserted between the strings, which are made of twisted silk.

haekum See **haegŭm**.

Hageman, Richard (1882-1966) American composer who was born in the Netherlands and studied at the Brussels Conservatoire. He became chief conductor of the Amster-dam Royal Opera in 1900 and emigrated to the United States in 1907, where he conducted at the New York Metropolitan from 1912. His compositions include the opera *Caponsacci* (1932), a series of songs and film music.

Hahn, Reynaldo (1874-1947) French composer and conductor, born in Venezuela, who studied the works of **Mozart** and was influenced by him in his own operatic compositions. He studied composition at the Paris Conservatoire from 1886 with **Massenet** and **Dubois**. In 1945 he became director of the Paris Opéra. He composed ballets, cantatas, operettas and chamber music, as well as the opera *Ciboulette* (1923) and the musical comedy *Mozart* (1925). He also wrote a series of songs (including the famous *Si mes vers avaient des ailes*) and settings of poems by Verlaine.

Haitink, Bernard (1929-) Dutch conductor and violinist who studied at Amsterdam Conservatoire. He began his musical career as a violinist in the Netherlands radio orchestra and from 1967-1979 conducted the Concertgebouw orchestra and the London Philharmonic Orchestra (1967-1977). From 1978 he acted as music director at Glyndebourne. His repertory has included *Don Carlos*, *The Rake's Progress*, *Don Giovanni* and *Lohengrin*. He was appointed director of Covent Garden in 1987. Haitink has made many recordings and was awarded an honorary KBE in 1978.

Bernard Haitink

Halévy, (Jacques François) Fromental (1799-1862) French composer who studied at the Paris Conservatoire with **Cherubini** and in Italy. He won the Prix de Rome in 1819. He returned to Paris in 1926, became a chorus master at the Opéra and taught at the Conservatoire, where he became a professor of composition in 1840. **Bizet** and **Gounod** were among his students. In 1854 he was appointed permanent secretary to the Académie des Beaux-Arts. He composed more than 30 operas, including *La Juive* (1835) which was his greatest success, as well as ballets, cantatas and songs.

half close Alternative term for **interrupted cadence**.

Halffter, Christobal (1930-) Spanish composer and nephew of Ernesto and Rodolpho **Halffter**. He studied with Conrado del Campo and **Tansman**, and was appointed professor of composition at the Madrid Academy in 1960. He has composed a number of orchestral pieces, including *Sequences* (1965), *Requiem por la libertad imaginada* (1971) and *Elegies for the Death of three Spanish Poets* (1974). Choral works and pieces for voice and orchestra, notably the *In exspectatione resurrectionis Domini* (1965) for baritone, male choir and orchestra, are also among his compositions.

Halffter, Ernesto (1905-) Spanish composer and conductor who studied at the Madrid Academy with **Falla** and whose *L'Atlantida* was completed in 1927. He founded a chamber orchestra in Seville and composed the opera *The Death of Carmen* as well as other orchestral pieces.

Halffter, Rodolfo (1900-) Spanish composer who settled in Mexico after the Spanish Civil War. He was privately tutored by **Falla** and studied the works of **Schoenberg**, whose influence can be heard in his compositions, notably in the *Overtura Concertante* (1932) for piano and orchestra. He has also composed ballets and a violin concerto (1940).

Hall, Richard (1903-1982) English composer who became an influential professor of composition at the Royal Manchester College of Music in 1938. Among his students were **Birtwistle**, Maxwell **Davies** and **Goehr.** His compositions include a number of orchestral fantasies, four symphonies, a piano concerto and some chamber pieces. He reveals the influence of twelve-note technique in some of his work.

Hallé English orchestra, choir and concert series founded by Sir Charles Hallé (1819-1895) in 1857-1858, and based in Manchester. The orchestra's conductors have included **Barbirolli** (1943-1968) and James **Loughran** (1971-1983). The Hallé orchestra has an international reputation.

Halleluja Praise Jehovah, used in choruses in Restoration anthems and in oratorios such as **Handel**'s *Messiah* (1741).

halling Lively Norwegian dance, which sometimes involves somersaults, originating from the Hallingdal district. It is usually in 2/4 time at a moderately quick pace. **Grieg** uses the halling in his second volume of *Lyric Pieces* Op. 71 No. 5 (1883).

Hambraeus, Bengt (1928-) Swedish avant-garde composer and organist who is best known for his *Rota* for three orchestras, percussion and tape recorder (1962) and for his early use of electronic techniques. He studied at Upsala University from 1947 and in Darmstadt with **Messiaen** and **Krenek**. In 1957 he began a career in broadcasting with the Swedish Broadcasting Company and became their director of chamber music in 1965. He was appointed professor of composition at McGill University, Montreal (1972), and has composed at the electronic music studios in Cologne, Munich and Milan. He championed the works of **Boulez, Nono** and **Stockhausen** and has written a number of complex *Constellation* pieces for instruments and electronic voices.

Hamerik, Ebbe (1898-1951) Danish composer and conductor, the son of Asger Hamerik who was director of the Baltimore Conservatoire at the Peabody Institute. He studied with his father and became a conductor at the Royal Theatre, Copenhagen, 1919. Among his compositions are several operas, including *The Travelling Companion*, based on Hans Christian Andersen, and *Leonardo da Vinci*, as well as five symphonies and *Variations on an Old Danish Folk Tune* for orchestra. He also wrote chamber music and works for the piano.

Hamilton, Iain (1922-) Scottish composer and pianist who reflects the influences of **Bartók** and **Berg**, as well as later serialist techniques in his work. His search for inspiration from foreign schools of composition has distressed some Scottish audiences, particularly at the Edinburgh Festival which commissioned his *Sinfonia* (1958) to commemorate Robert Burns' bicentenary. Other critics have acclaimed his virtuoso handling of orchestration.

He studied as an engineer, but entered the Royal Academy of Music in 1947, studying composition with **Alwyn**. He was awarded the Prix d'Honneur at the Academy in 1951 and the Koussevitsky Foundation Prize. In 1952 he became a lecturer at Morley College and at London University in 1955. He was appointed a professor of music at Duke University, North Carolina in 1961.

Among his compositions are the operas *The Cataline Conspiracy* (1974), *The Royal Hunt of the Sun* (1967) and *Anna Karenina* (1979); the ballet *Clerk Saunders* (1951) and pieces for the orchestra which include two symphonies, two violin concertos and two piano concertos. He has also composed a large body of work for chorus, various voices and chamber orchestras.

Hammerstein II, Oscar (1895-1960) American librettist and producer who wrote some of the most enduring musicals. His adaptation of **Bizet**'s *Carmen* for the stage was critically acclaimed and other

Oscar Hammerstein

musical productions have found wide audiences in both their stage and screen versions. He and Richard Rodgers commissioned **Copland**'s only operatic work, *The Tender Land* (1954).

His compositions were most successful when he worked in collaboration with other songwriters, notably Romsberg and Friml, Jerome **Kern**, with whom he wrote *Show Boat* (1927), and Richard Rodgers, with whom he wrote *Oklahoma!* (1943), *Carousel* (1945), *South Pacific* (1949), *The King and I* (1951) and *The Sound of Music* (1959).

Handel, George Frideric (1685-1759) German composer who lived in England from 1726 and whose style dominated English music for the next century. His greatest works, the dramatic oratorios and operas, are characteristically noble, and all his compositions reflect a combination of the traditions from which he developed his own style. German ideals of contrapuntal techniques are blended with Italian solo styles and elements of the English choral tradition, to produce a melodically and technically masterful quality. Despite his apparent plagiarism of other composers' work – a common practice during a period in which pasticcios were popular – Handel "took other men's pebbles and turned them into diamonds", as one of his contemporaries remarked.

Although his father was unwilling to allow him a musical education, he did tolerate Handel's study under Zachau, the local organist at St Michael's Church, Halle. He studied law at Halle University and began to study music seriously only when his father died in 1703. He joined the Hamburg Opera Orchestra, conducted by **Keiser**, as second violinist and completed the opera *Almira* which Keiser had started in 1705 and the opera *Nero* (1705). In 1706 Handel visited Italy and was exposed, through meetings with **Corelli** and A. **Scarlatti** in Rome, to Italian styles of composition which he soon mastered, much to the admiration of contemporary Italian musicians. His opera *Agrippina* was produced in Venice in 1709 and at its first performance he met the younger brother of the Elector of Hanover. The following year he was appointed *Kapellmeister* to the court of the Elector of Hanover. It was the success in London of his opera *Rinaldo* (1711) that prompted him to move to England, and to compose the operas *Il Pastor Fido* (1712), *Silla* (1714) and *Amadigi* (1715) in the same style.

When his former patron, the Elector of Hanover, was crowned King George I of England in 1714 he was given a life pension of six hundred pounds and composed the *Water Music Suite* for a royal water party in 1717. In 1718 he became musical director to the Duke of Chandos, as well as director of the Royal Academy of Music at the King's Theatre, Haymarket, which sought to produce Italian **opera seria**. He wrote 14 operas for this venture, until the theatre closed in 1728, as well as 15 solo sonatas, eight suites for the harpsichord, and nine trio sonatas. George II was crowned in 1727 to the sound of four of Handel's anthems including *Zadok the Priest* (1727), which has since been played at every British coronation.

The declining popularity of the Italian operatic style, caused in part by the dramatic success of *The Beggar's Opera* by

John Gay, led Handel to compose dramatic oratorios, including *Esther* (1732), *Deborah* (1733), *Saul* (1733) and *Israel in Egypt* (1739), which reflected the fullness and richness of the *opera seria* style but released him from the restrictions of the genre. He conducted many of these himself, despite seriously deteriorating health. He suffered a stroke in 1737, but still carried on composing and wrote another series of oratorios, including the *Messiah* (1742), *Samson* (1743), *Judas Maccabaeus* (1746) and *Solomon* (1748). In 1751 he succumbed to blindness, but continued conducting performances of his oratorios and revised some of his scores. He was buried in Westminster Abbey.

Among his many other compositions are *St John Passion* (1704), the oratorio *La Resurrezione* (1708), two *Te Deum* works for the Utrecht Peace (1713) and for the Duke of Chandos (1718); six concertos for the oboe (1729), 12 for the organ (1738), *Music for the Royal Fireworks* (1749), 12 concerti grossi (1739) and numerous chamber pieces, songs and cantatas for two or more voices.

Handl, Jacob (1550-1591) Slovenian composer who experimented in the motet form with the Venetian style, blending the voices of three or four choirs at different locations in the chapel. He became *Kapellmeister* to the Bishop of Olmutz in 1579 and later cantor at St Johann's, Prague. He composed 16 masses, numerous motets which appear in the collection *Opus Musicum* (1586-1591), and other devotional pieces. Four books of secular motets entitled *Harmoniae morales* appeared between 1589 and 1596.

Hanslick, Eduard (1825-1904) German composer who criticised **Wagner**'s ideas about the future of music and found himself the subject of bitter satire. He became the prototype of Beckmesser, the pedant in *Die Meistersinger von Nürnberg* (1868). His compositions reflect the influence of **Brahms**, who attempted to retain the symphonic forms of music.

Hanson, Howard (1896-1981) American composer of Swedish origin whose work reflects Nordic images and themes, and is both traditional and eclectic. His compositions have a poetic quality which allies them closely with those of **Sibelius** and **Franck**. He studied composition with Goetschius at the Institute of Musical Art, New York, and won the Prix de Rome in 1921. He also studied at the American Academy, Rome until 1924, when he returned to the United States to become director of the Eastman School of Music, New York. In 1925 he established the Rochester Festivals at which contemporary American composers exhibited their work. He became a director of the Institute of American Music at Rochester University in 1964. Altogether he received more than 30 honorary degrees as well as numerous commissions.

Among his compositions are six symphonies, orchestral suites and symphonic poems such as *Summer Seascape* (1959). His choral work includes the *Lament for Beowulf* (1926) and the *Song of Human Rights* (1963). He also composed the opera *Merry Mount* (1934) and chamber music.

hardänger fiddle (Scandinavia) Short-necked, low-bridged fiddle with sympathetic strings, used for playing dance music. The low bridge makes it ideal for providing its own chordal accompaniment.

Hardelot, Guy d' (1858-1936) Pen-name of Helen Rhodes (née Guy), a French composer who studied at the Paris Conservatoire and toured the United States as a singer. She composed a number of songs which found their way into the repertories of singers such as Dame Nellie **Melba**, Emma Calvé (with whom she toured in 1896) and Victor Maurel.

harmonica Modern term for mouth organ, a small wind instrument with metal reeds (one to each note), enclosed in slots in a narrow box. Air is blown into or sucked out of the box by the player. The notes sounded depend on the position of the box in the mouth and the use of the player's tongue. As a musical instrument, it is sometimes considered a toy, although when played by a virtuoso it can produce very moving music. Larry **Adler** is the most notable exponent of the harmonica, and compositions by **Vaughan Williams** and Darius **Milhaud** have been written for him.

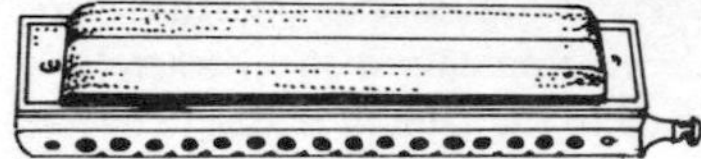

Harmonica

harmonic series Every sound consists of one fundamental note and a cloud of harmonics which are generated above it. The fundamental note is heard, but it is the number and relative strength of the harmonics that give the note its distinctive timbre (tone colour). The harmonic series consist of ascending notes which become more closely spaced and less distinct the higher they are. A note whose fundamental is strongly heard while the higher harmonics are relatively weak, has a dull, flat timbre. If the fundamental is weak and the upper harmonics relatively strong, the timbre is sharp and brilliant. By lightly touching the string of an instrument such as the violin at certain places, it is possible to eliminate the fundamental completely, and produce only one of the harmonics.

In the playing of brass wind instruments, valves or slides are used to obtain different fundamentals by shortening the tubing. By means of lip and wind pressure, either the fundamental is blown or one of its attendant harmonics is selected and sounded. Harmonics are also known as overtones and upper partials. See also **acoustics**.

Harmoniemusik (Ger.) Music for woodwind, brass and percussion.

harmonium Small, portable keyboard instrument, the sound of which is produced by reeds, played by wind coming from pedal-operated bellows worked by the player's feet. In later models the bellows are operated by an electric motor. The harmonium was invented in the early 19th century, and in some instances has been used as a substitute for an organ, especially for hymn singing.

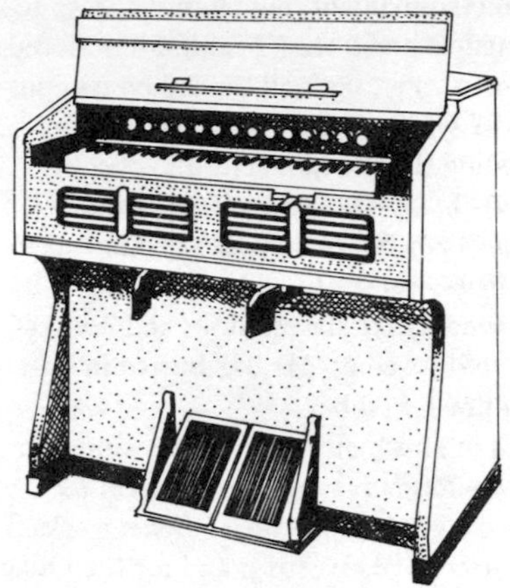

Harmonium

harmony Whereas **counterpoint** is concerned with a horizontal approach to music (interweaving melodies), harmony is the vertical aspect, concerned with **chords** and chord progressions. There is evidence that harmony was used before the 9th century AD, but it is generally agreed that the real beginning of harmonic music occurred with the first written appearance of parallel fourths and fifths, in about the 9th century.

The study of harmony concerns the structure of individual chords, the relationship of one chord to another and the construction of music with particular regard to the succession of chords which support or surround the melodic line.

harp Stringed instrument with a series of strings of different lengths stretched parallel across a frame. The strings produce notes of fixed pitch: the longer the string, the lower the note produced. The strings are vibrated by plucking with the fingers.

The harp was among the earliest stringed instruments. It is referred to in the Old Testament, and is shown in Egyptian tomb paintings and appears on a *bas-relief* found in Nineveh dating from the 7th century BC.

The modern concert harp has a range of six and a half octaves and the strings represent the diatonic scale of C♭ major. However, each note can be raised or lowered individually throughout all the octaves at once by a semitone or by a whole tone by means of a set of pedals at the base of the instrument. This means the harp can be tuned in a moment to any diatonic scale. The **chromatic** scale is available only on the chromatic harp.

Many composers included harp parts in their orchestral music, including **Bizet**, **Ravel** and **Tchaikovsky**.

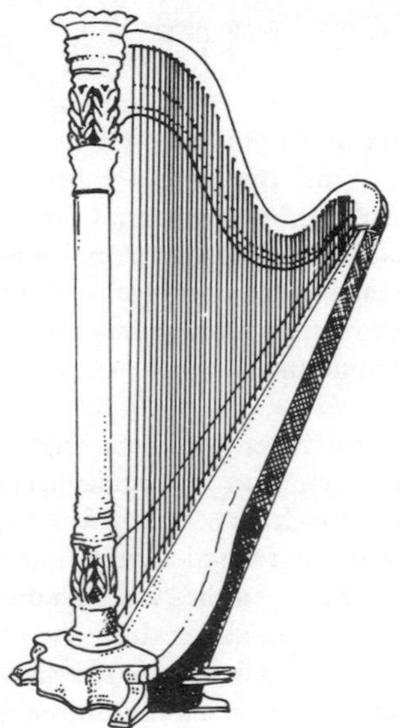

Harp

harpsichord Keyboard instrument usually shaped like a grand piano. A note is sounded by plucking the strings with a quill plectrum (as opposed to a piano, in which the strings are struck by hammers). The square-shaped **virginal** and **spinet** are instruments of the same type but smaller in size.

Harpsichords often have two keyboards, each controlling a set of quills, one harder than the other. There are frequently stops by which yet other ranges of quills can be set into action. However, the tone cannot be controlled by the player's fingers.

At the beginning of the 19th century the harpsichord was replaced in popular use by the piano, although it has been revived in the 20th century for playing Baroque music.

Composers such as **Scarlatti, Bach** and **Handel** wrote pieces for the harpsichord, but much of this music is now played on the piano.

Harpsichord

harp stop Device on a harpsichord that dampens the strings so that the sound produced resembles that of a harp.

Harris, Roy (1898-1979) American composer who is considered to be the United States' leading symphonist of the 1930s. His style is bold, angular and irregular and reflects the influences of folk music and hymn melodies. Some critics find points of comparison between his work and that of **Janáček**, but it is essentially American in its buoyancy and momentum.

He studied at the Paris Conservatoire with **Boulanger** (1926) and returned to the United States to teach at the Westminster Choir School, Princeton. He became a tutor at the Juilliard School and Cornell University, and in 1940 was appointed composer in residence at the University of California.

His compositions include 16 symphonies, the overture *When Johnny Comes Marching Home* (1935), the *Farewell to Pioneers* (1936) and a concerto for amplified piano (1968), as well as chamber pieces. He also wrote choral works, including *Songs for Occupations* (1934), *Symphony for Voices* (1936), a *Mass* for male choir and a number of works for various voices and orchestra.

Harris, William Henry (1883-1973) English composer and organist who is best known for his composition *The Hound of Heaven* (1919) for baritone, choir and orchestra. He studied at the Royal College of Music with Parratt and **Stanford**, and became an organist at New College and later at Christ Church, Oxford (1919-1928). In 1921 he became a professor of the organ and harmony at the Royal College of Music, and was appointed organist at St George's Chapel, Windsor in 1933. He was knighted in 1934.

Harrison, Julius (Allen Greenway) (1885-1963) English conductor and composer who studied at the Birmingham and Midland Institute with Bantock and conducted his first performance at Covent Garden in 1913. He went on to conduct various orchestras before becoming a professor of composition at the Royal Academy of Music. Among his compositions are the cantata *Cleopatra*, *Cornish Sketches* and *Bredon Hill*, as well as a mass and a *Requiem* and works for violin, orchestra and voice.

Harrison, Lou (1917-) American composer who has experimented with various musical forms, as well as with **atonal** techniques and **serial** procedures. He studied at the San Francisco State College and organized concerts with John **Cage**. He became a tutor at Mills College in 1936, but left in 1939 to study with **Schoenberg**. In 1943 he moved to New York, where he enjoyed success as a ballet composer and critic. He also edited some of the works of Charles **Ives** and conducted the first performance of his Symphony No. 3 in 1947.

His compositions include the atonal and serialist opera *Rapunzel* (1954), the puppet opera *Young Caesar* (1971), several ballets (including *Johnny Appleseed*, 1940), a series of harpsichord sonatas and works for percussion instruments, the sextet *Schoenbergiana*, a violin concerto and *Four Strict Songs* for eight baritones and orchestra in pure **intonation**.

Harsányi, Tibor (1898-1954) Hungarian composer who studied at the Budapest Academy of music with **Kodály** and settled in Paris in 1924. He composed operas, ballets, symphonic pieces and chamber music.

Hartmann, Johan Peter Emilius (1805-1900) Danish composer who became a director of the Copenhagen Conservatoire in 1840. He composed several operas, including *The Raven* (1832) with a text by Hans Christian Andersen, as well as symphonic and chamber pieces.

Hartmann, Karl Amadeus (1905-1963) German composer who studied at the Munich Academy of Music with Haas and **Webern**, but refused to perform publicly or to compose for the Nazi authorities. In 1945 he organized the Music Viva concerts in Munich, which became showcases for new composers. His own compositions reflected the influences of **Berg** and **Stravinsky** and include eight symphonies, the opera *Des Simplicius Simplicissimus Jugend* (1949), and concertos for the piano, viola and violin.

Harty, Sir (Herbert) Hamilton (1879-1941) Irish composer, organist and conductor who became an important figure in the history of the Hallé Orchestra. He was given organ tuition by **Esposito** who heard him play in Belfast and Dublin. In 1900 he moved to London, where he continued to find success as an accompanist and later as a composer. He conducted for both the Covent Garden and the London Symphony Orchestras, and was eventually appointed conductor of the Hallé Orchestra in 1920. He was knighted in 1925 and received the Gold Medal of the Royal Philharmonic Society in 1934.

His compositions include the questionable modern arrangements of **Handel**'s *Water Music Suite* and *Music for the Royal Fireworks*, the lyrical *Irish Symphony* (1924), *Ode to a Nightingale* (1907) for soprano and orchestra, a violin concerto and symphonic poems, notably *With the Wild Geese* (1910).

Harvey, Jonathan (Dean) (1939-) English composer who has incorporated the use of tape recordings into his work. He studied at the Universities of Glasgow and Cambridge. **Stockhausen** heard his work in Darmstadt in 1966 and suggested a further period of study with Babbett in 1969. In 1970 he was appointed senior lecturer in music at Southampton University.

Among his compositions are *Benedictus* (1970), *Inner Light III* (1975), a symphony for orchestra (1966), several cantatas for voice and instruments or orchestra, and a number of pieces for the chamber orchestra including *Inner Light I* (1973) for instruments and tape.

Haskil, Clara (1895-1960) Romanian pianist who studied at the Paris Conservatoire under **Fauré** and **Cortot** and in Berlin with **Busoni**. She made her debut in 1902 and was best known for her performances of Classical and Romantic music.

Hasse, Johann Adolph (1699-1783) German composer of Neapolitan opera who enjoyed considerable success in his day with his elegant and graceful style. When only 19 he sang as a tenor at the Hamburg Opera and he composed his first opera, *Antioco* (1721), at the age of 22. In 1724 he studied with A. **Scarlatti** in Naples and completed several popular operas in the Italian style. He spent some time in Venice before returning to Germany to become director of the Dresden Opera (1731). He moved to Vienna, 1763 and continued to compose in the Italian manner, despite some controversy. In 1775 he left permanently for Italy, living in Venice until his death.

He composed more than 100 operatic pieces, as well as masses and oratorios, but most of his manuscripts were destroyed.

Hassler, Hans Leo (1564-1612) German composer and organist who studied in Venice with A. **Gabrieli** and became organist to Octavian Fugger at Augsburg in 1585, moving on to take up similar posts at Nuremberg (1600) and Dresden (1608). He wrote in the Venetian polychoral manner and composed a number of polyphonic *Lieder*, as well as madrigals and motets.

Haubenstock-Ramati, Roman (1919-) Polish composer who studied at Cracow University and became musical director of Cracow Radio in 1947. He was appointed director of the music library and a professor of music at the Tel Aviv Academy in 1950.

He was influenced by *musique concrète* and worked for some time in France on his electronic pieces. In order to write music for electronic instruments he experimented with new methods of notation and developed an early form of graphic score. His compositions include an opera (*America*), a symphony entitled *K* and the symphonic poems *Les Symphonies de Timbres* and *Petite musique de nuit*. He has also written chamber music and some choral pieces.

Hauer, Joseph Mattiaus (1883-1959) Austrian composer who was largely self-taught. His stylistic independence is reflected in his invention of a twelve-note system, developed quite separately from that of **Schoenberg**. He wrote the opera *Salammbo* and concertos for the piano and violin, as well as a series of songs. All his work illustrates his **dodecaphonic** technique.

Haussmann, Valentin (*c*1570-*c*1614) German composer and organist at

Gerbstedt, near Merseburg. He wrote secular songs, madrigals and dances as well as devotional motets and instrumental pieces. He also published works by **Vecchi** and **Gastoldi** with German texts and undoubtedly assisted in the development of early music by this cross-fertilization of national influences.

hautbois (Fr.) Alternative term for **oboe**.

hautboy Obsolete English name for **oboe**.

Hawaiian guitar Type of guitar differing from the normal instrument in the tuning of the strings, and in the fact that the strings are stopped not with the fingers, but with a small metal bar (the steel). This forms a moveable nut passing across the strings. By sliding the steel, tuning can be reproduced at any pitch, and this makes possible the sliding thirds which are a feature of music for this instrument. The Hawaiian-style of dance music played on the Hawaiian guitar was popular before World War II.

Hawaiian guitar

hayashi (Japan) Generic term for drum and flute ensemble. When used in festivals to play folk music, it consists of three drums - **ō-daiko** and two *taiko* – with a six- or seven-holed flute, and is often accompanied by a small, suspended brass gong. In **noh** drama, there are again three drums – *ō-tsuzumi*, *ko-tsuzumi* (see **tsuzumi**) and *taiko* – with a seven-holed flute, the *nohkan* or *noh* flute. In both **kabuki** and **nagauta**, the *hayashi* is borrowed from the *noh* ensemble, but more drums often are added.

Haydn, (Franz) Joseph (1732-1809) Austrian composer whose work displays a masterful balance between contrapuntal and harmonic elements and an energy that does not break the pattern and texture of his music. He was an important figure in the development of both the symphony and the string quartet.

As a boy, Haydn showed early musical promise and at the age of eight he was sent by his father to Vienna as a chorister in St Stephen's Cathedral. When his voice broke he became a servant and accompanist to the composer Porpora in order to earn a living. He wrote his first *Quartets* (1755) at this time. In 1757 he became musical director to Count Morzin and composed his first symphony in that year. His symphonies *Le Matin*, *Le Midi* and *Le Soir* were composed in 1761. Also in 1761 he was appointed *Vice-Kapellmeister* by Prince Paul Eszterházy at Eisenstadt, where he remained until 1790.

During his years at the Eszterháza palace Haydn's work was internationally recognized. He published a great deal of work and received commissions from Cadiz for the oratorio *The Seven Words of the Saviour on the Cross* (1784) and from the Concert de la Loge Olympique for six symphonies. He also befriended **Mozart** and each composer reflects the influence of the other during this period. Haydn was later to recall these years as being among his most fruitful.

In 1791 Haydn visited England and was hailed as a genius. He wrote four symphonies, and heard **Handel**'s *Messiah* at Westminster Abbey and was deeply impressed. He returned to Vienna in 1792 and became **Beethoven**'s tutor for a while before returning to England to compose six more symphonies. In 1796 he again went back to Vienna and wrote six settings of the mass (1796-1797), the oratorio *Die Schopfung* (The Creation) (1798) and *Die Jahreszeiten* (The Seasons) (1801). Both of these works reveal the influence of Handel. The 1790s also saw the composition of the 12 'London' symphonies by which he is best remembered, including No. 94 *The Surprise*, No. 96 *The Miracle* (1791), No. 101 *The Clock* (1794) and No. 104 *The London*. At this time his health deteriorated and he appeared less and less in public. He died during the French occupation of Vienna.

Haydn composed 104 symphonies, 13 keyboard concertos and at least 17 concertos for other instruments. He also completed 18 operas, eight oratorios, 12 masses, 84 string quartets, 31 piano trios, 52 keyboard sonatas, 125 songs and a further 377 arrangements of airs.

Haydn, (Johann) Michael (1737-1806) Austrian born composer who was somewhat overshadowed by his brother, Franz Joseph **Haydn**, but who revealed in his religious compositions a masterful dignity and structural complexity. He was a chorister and deputy organist at St Stephen's Cathedral, Vienna, from 1745, and in 1757 became choirmaster to the Bishop of Grosswardein in Hungary. He taught himself composition using **Fux'** *Gradus ad Parnassum* as a guide. In 1762 he was appointed *Konzertmeister* to the Archbishop of Salzburg and organist at his cathedral. He composed more than 50 symphonies, concertos for violin, horn trumpet, harpsichord, flute and viola. In addition he wrote a large amount of devotional music, including over 30 masses, oratorios and shorter works for the chapel.

Head, Michael (1900-1976) English composer and pianist who became a professor of piano at the Royal Academy of Music in 1927. He wrote a number of light operas, cantatas and song cycles.

head voice The highest register of any voice, produced by using the head cavities as resonators. The other two registers are known as the medium voice and the **chest voice**.

heckelclarina Instrument, similar to a clarinet, but with a conical bore, invented by the German firm of Heckel. It was used for the playing of the shepherd's pipe in Act III of **Wagner**'s *Tristan and Isolde* (1865).

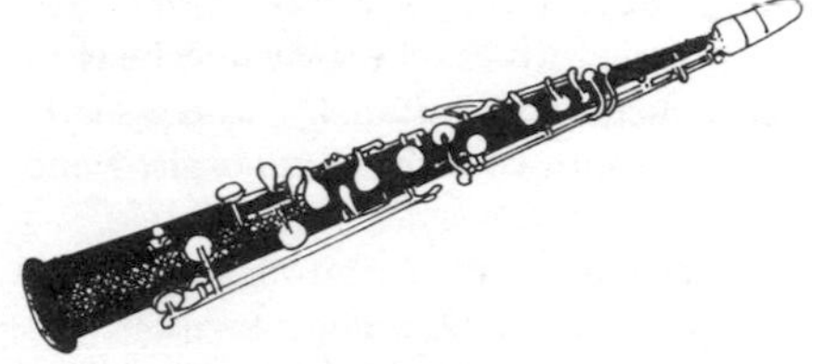

Heckelclarina

heckelphone Double-reed instrument invented by the German firm of Heckel. It is similar to an **oboe**, but sounds an octave lower in pitch.

Heifetz, Jascha (1901-1987) Lithuanian-born American violinist widely regarded as the 20th century's most dazzlingly brilliant exponent of the instrument. He was admired more as a virtuoso with a faultless technique than as a musician of passion. He began playing the violin at the age of five and studied at the Imperial Conservatoire, St Petersburg (now Leningrad), Russia. He emigrated to the United States in 1917, around the outbreak of the Soviet Revolution, becoming an American citizen in 1925. As a performer, he played the classics as well as many showpieces by such composers as Pablo de Sarasate and Fritz Kreisler. He also commissioned many new works, including the **Walton** and **Schoenberg** violin concertos. He retired from the concert platform in 1972.

Heike-biwa (Japan) Type of **biwa** or lute.

helicon Brass instrument and a member of

Helicon

the **tuba** family, which is similar to the **bombardon** but made in a circular form so that it may be carried over the shoulder when marching in a military band.

Heller, Stephen (1813-1888) Hungarian composer and pianist who studied at the Vienna Academy and settled in Paris in 1838. He toured Europe as a virtuoso performer and met both **Chopin** and **Liszt**. He visited England in 1850 and 1862, and wrote more than 100 short pieces for the piano and chamber ensemble.

Hely-Hutchinson, Victor (1901-1947) South African composer, pianist and conductor who spent most of his time in England. He studied at Eton, Oxford and the Royal College of Music and became a lecturer in music at Cape Town University in 1922. He returned to England in 1926 to join the BBC. Until 1934, when he was appointed a professor of music at Birmingham University, he was head of music for the Midland Region. He became director of Music for the BBC in 1947. His compositions include *A Carol Symphony* and settings of Edward Lear's *Nonsense Songs*, as well as chamber works.

hemidemisemiquaver Note having half the time value of a **demisemiquaver** and a sixty-fourth that of a **semibreve**.

Hemidemisemiquaver and its rest

hemiola Change of rhythm effected by the substitution of three beats where two would be normal. For example, when three minins replace two dotted minins.

Henry, Pierre (1927-) French composer noted for the fluency of his compositions in an electronic medium and for his pioneering experiments with Henri Barraud. Henry studied at the Paris Conservatoire with **Boulanger** and **Messiaen** and became a director of the *Groupe de Recherches de Musique Concrète* at the French Radio Studios in 1950. he worked with Paul Schaeffer on electronic composition and founded the first private electronic studio in France at Aponse in 1958. His compositions, all electronic, include *Le Voile d'Orphée* (1953), La *Messe de Liverpool* (1967) and *Gymkhana* (1970).

Henschel, Sir George (1850-1934) German-born composer, pianist, conductor and singer, who became a British citizen in 1890. His debut as a pianist was in 1862, and he studied at the Liepzig Conservatoire in 1867 and later at the Berlin Conservatoire. He also had a well-developed baritone voice and in 1868 played the part of Hans Sachs in a production of **Wagner**'s *Die Meistersinger*. He conducted various orchestras including the Boston (1881) and London (1886) Symphony Orchestras and the Scottish Orchestra (1893) in Glasgow. As a singer he accompanied himself and recorded a number of works for radio. His compositions include three operas, choral works, songs and chamber music.

Henze, Hans Werner (1926-) German composer who deserted from the German army in 1944 and went into hiding in Denmark as the inconspicuous organist of Esbjerg church. He studied at the Brunswick State Music School (1942) and at Heidelberg University (1946). He worked in Darmstadt with **Leibowitz**, studying **Schoenberg**'s twelve-note system and again with Leibowitz in Paris. In 1950 he became musical director of the Hessian State Opera Ballet company but moved to Italy in 1953.

His earlier works reflect the influences of Schoenberg and **Stravinsky**, whereas later pieces are infused with the atmosphere and richness of Italian styles. Among his compositions are the lyrical drama *Boulevard Solitude* (1951), the opera *König Hirsch* (1952) with its Mediterranean gloss, the opera *Der Prinz von Homberg* (1960) and *Der Junge Lord* (1965) which satirized German society. His opera *The Bassarids* (1966) was produced for the Salzburg festival.

After 1945, Henze declared his affiliation to the extreme left and his later compositions are coloured by revolutionary fervour, including *The Raft of the Medusa* which ends with the percussive chant of "Ho! Ho! Ho-Chi-Minh!" Although preoccupied with choral and operatic composition, Henze wrote a large amount of orchestral music including six symphonies.

Herbert, Victor (August) (1859-1924) Irish composer, cellist and conductor who studied at the Stuttgart Conservatoire and became a principal cellist with the Stuttgart Court Orchestra in 1883. In 1886 he moved to the United States and became principal cellist at the New York Metropolitan in 1877. He conducted the Pittsburgh Symphony Orchestra, 1898.

His compositions include more than 30 operettas, including *Naughty Marietta* (1910) and *Babes in Toyland* (1903), two more serious operas, *Madeleine* (1914) and *Natoma* (1911), the *Irish Rhapsody* (1892) for orchestra and other chamber pieces.

heroic tenor Tenor voice of power best suited to heroic rather than lyrical or comic parts. In German, such a voice (*heldentenor*) is classed as a character type as well as a voice. **Wagner**ian roles such as those in *Tannhäuser*, *Lohengrin*, *Tristan*, *Die Walküre* and *Siegfried*, demand a voice of this description.

Herold, (Louis Joseph) Ferdinand (1791-1833) French composer who studied piano with his father, C.P.E **Bach** and later with Louis Adam at the Paris Conservatoire (1806-1810). In 1812 he won the Prix de Rome and was appointed pianist to Queen Caroline in Naples (1820). He was accompanist at the Théâtre des Italiens until 1827, when he became a choirmaster at the Opéra in Paris.

He composed more than 20 *opéras-comiques*, including *La Clochette* (1817) and *Marie* (1826), as well as ballets and cantatas.

Herrmann, Bernard (1911-1975) American composer and conductor who wrote the memorable score for Alfred Hitchcock's film *Psycho*. He studied at the Juilliard School with Wagenaar, and founded the New Chamber Orchestra in 1931. He became musical director of CBS (1934) and conductor of the CBS Symphony Orchestra (1940). Both Hitchcock and Orson Welles commissioned him to compose music for films, among them *Citizen Kane*, *The Magnificent Andersons*, *Marnie*, *Psycho* and *Farenheit 451*. He also composed the opera *Wuthering Heights* (1950), two symphonies, the orchestral suite *For the Fallen* (1943), choral works (including the cantata *Moby Dick*, 1937) and some chamber music.

Hertel, Johann Wilhelm (1727-1789) German composer and violinist who studied with **Benda** and became *Kapellmeister* to the court of Schwerin in 1775. He composed many symphonies, concertos and sonatas, as well as several volumes of chamber music.

Hervé (1825-1892) Pen-name of Florimond Roger, a French composer, organist and singer who studied under **Auber** at the Paris Conservatoire and became a conductor with several opera orchestras. He composed more than 100 operettas, including *L'Oeil Crevé* (1867), *Chilpéric* (1868) and *Le Petit Faust* (1869), and sometimes appeared in them himself. In 1870 he moved to London to conduct at the Empire Theatre. He also composed for the orchestra and wrote his own librettos.

Heseltine, Philip English composer who worked under the pen-name of Peter **Warlock**.

heterophony Single melody existing in different simultaneous forms. Although heterophony occurs in Western classical compositions, the term is often used in non-Western or folk music contexts – for example, when an instrument embellishes a vocal melody – or when variations, intentional or accidental, occur between individual participants in a **monodic** chorus.

hexachord Scale of six notes which Guido d'Arezzo (in the 11th century) named Ut, Re, Mi, Fa, Sol, La. There are three hexachords beginning on the notes G, C and F, and the same names were used for the notes of each. The G hexachord was called hard (*durum*), the C natural (*naturale*) and the F soft (*molle*). The German names for major (*dur*) and minor (*moll*) are derived from the Latin names for two of these hexachords.

hichiriki (Japan) Short, double-reed woodwind instrument of Chinese origin, traditionally considered to be imbued with supernatural properties. It is made of bamboo wrapped in strands of cherry bark, lacquered inside, with seven finger-holes on top and two thumb-holes behind, and is found in Shinto ceremonial music and in the **gagaku** court orchestra.

high fidelity Often abbreviated to hi-fi, a method of electronic sound reproduction of high quality without distortion.

Hill, Alfred (1870-1960) Australian composer and conductor who studied at the Leipzig Conservatoire and played in the Gewandhaus Orchestra as a violinist before settling in New Zealand. He became fascinated by Maori music and collected some of their traditional pieces. In 1915 he was appointed professor of composition and harmony at the New South Wales Conservatoire. His compositions reflect the influence of Maori culture, particularly in his *Maori Symphony* (1900) and *Maori Rhapsody* and the cantata *Hinemoa* (1895). He also wrote several operas, symphonies and string quartets.

Hiller, Ferdinand (1811-1885) German composer, pianist and conductor who became an exponent of **Beethoven**'s piano works and who had some success in Paris with his operas, written mainly in the French style. He studied with **Hummel** and visited Beethoven with him in 1827. In 1828 he moved to Paris as a virtuoso pianist and performed Beethoven's Piano Concerto No. 5 at his debut. He conducted in Frankfurt, Dusseldorf and Cologne and founded the Cologne Conservatoire in 1850. In 1852 he was appointed director of Italian opera in Paris.

His compositions include six operas, three symphonies, two oratorios, concertos for the piano and violin and pieces for the chamber ensemble.

Hiller, Johann Adam (1728-1804) German composer and conductor who was one of the inventors of the *Singspiel*, an opera-form with spoken dialogue and the *Lied* developed for stage purposes. He studied at the conservatoires of Dresden and Leipzig and moved to Leipzig in 1758 to become the conductor of the Gewandhaus Concerts, which he founded in 1781. He conducted for various other orchestras until 1789, when he became a cantor at the Thomasschule. Among his compositions are a number of *singspiel* operas, including *Der Teufel ist los* (1766), and some church music.

Hilton, John (*c*1560-1608) English composer, lay-clerk at Lincoln Cathedral (1584) and organist at Trinity College, Cambridge, from 1594. He composed anthems and motets, as well as the madrigal *Fair Oriana, Beauty's Queen* which was included in **Morley**'s collection *The Triumphs of Oriana*, presented to Elizabeth I in 1601.

Hilton, John (1599-1657) English composer and organist, son of John Hilton (*c*1560-1608), a composer of anthems and a contributor to the *Triumphs of Oriana*. Born perhaps at Cambridge, Hilton became organist of the church of St Margaret's, Westminster in 1628. He published a set of balletts under the title *Ayres, or Fa La's* and an extremely popular collection of rounds and canons known as *Catch as Catch Can*.

Himmel, Fredrich Heinrich (1765-1814) German composer who studied at the Dresden Conservatoire and in Italy. In 1795 he became *Kapellmeister* to the court at Berlin. He visited England, Austria and Russia, producing operas successfully in several cities. Among his compositions are a number of operas and operettas in Italian and German, the *Liederspiel Frohsinn und Schwarmerei* (1801) and the opera *Fanchon, das Leiermädchen* (1804). He also wrote works for piano, orchestra, as well as songs, oratorios and masses.

Hindemith, Paul (1895-1963) German composer, violinist and conductor who began by shocking the world and ended by being regarded by the avant-garde as a conservative. His earlier works reveal the influences of Richard **Strauss**, while later works reflect the styles of **Bartók** and **Stravinsky**. His compositions were tonal, and held dissonance and consonance in constant tension despite a rhythmic energy.

He studied composition at the Hoch Conservatoire in Frankfurt from 1913 with Sekles and Arnold Mendelssohn, as well as studying the violin. In 1915 he became leader of the Frankfurt Opera Orchestra. He served in the German Army (1917-1919) but continued to compose, and eventually returned to the Opera orchestra. His second string quartet was performed by a group led by Licco Amar at Donaueschingen in 1921, and so the Amar Quartet was formed strictly for the performance of modern works, with Hindemith performing and providing material for it. These years were very productive and his opera *Cardillac* (1926), with its echoes of **Handel**'s style, was a success.

In 1927 he was appointed a professor of composition at the Berlin Hochschule and taught **Leigh, Cooke** and **Reizenstein** among others. He also sent compositions to the conductors **Furtwängler** and **Klemperer**, including his opera *Neues vom Tage* (1929), which featured a soprano singing in a bathtub. In 1933 he began work on his opera *Mathis der Maler* only to fall foul of the Nazi authorities, who viewed him as a musical degenerate. Despite the protestation of Furtwängler, the opera was banned by Goebbels.

Paul Hindemith

Hindemith resigned from the Berlin Hochschule in 1937 and moved to New York where he was appointed visiting professor at Yale University in 1940. He also taught at the Tanglewood Festivals where his pupils included Leonard **Bernstein** and Lukas **Foss**. After the war he returned to Europe and toured extensively, revising some of his scores and lecturing in Berlin at the Hochschule. He conducted for various orchestras, taught at the Universities of Yale and Zurich, and composed his later, introspective compositions, among them the opera *Die Harmonie der Welt* (1957).

His compositions completed in the 1920s (including the song-cycle *Das Marienleben* (1923), the operas *Morder* (1921), *Hoffnung der Frauen* (1922), *Sancta Suzanna* (1921) and *Das Nusch-nuschi* (1920), six chamber sonatas, four quartets, many sonatas for various instruments and pieces for the chamber ensemble), are individual in style, but still based upon traditional influences. One of these influences is found in the linear counterpoint of **Bach** and is described by Hindemith in his important treatise, *The Craft of Composition* (1937). Later pieces reflect his notion of *gebrauchmusik* (music for use), and have a degree of technical simplicity. Other works, including the ballets *Nobilissima Visione* (1938) and *The Four Temperaments* (1940), are more clearly tonal.

Hob. Abbreviation of Hoboken, after Anthony van Hoboken (1887-1983), the Dutch musicologist, who compiled the definitive catalogue of **Haydn**'s works. References to this cataloguing system are given as Hob., followed by a roman and an arabic numeral.

hocket Device used in medieval vocal and instrumental music consisting of phrases broken up by rests, in such a way that when one part is silent, another fills the gap. The term is derived from the Latin *hoketus* (hiccup). **Machaut**'s *Hoquetus David* is a piece in which this technique is pre-dominant.

Hoddinott, Alun (1929-) Welsh composer whose work reflects the influence of **serialism** in a casual manner and is both richly romantic and carefully patterned. He studied at the University College of South Wales and became a lecturer at Cardiff College of Music and Drama in 1951. He returned to University College as a lecturer, becoming a professor of music in 1976. He won the Arnold Bax Medal for composers in 1957.

His compositions include four operas, five symphonies, other pieces for orchestra such as *Fugal Overture* (1953) and *Fioriture* (1968), concertos, choral and chamber works and a series of song-cycles.

hoe down American get-together for folk dancing, originating in the 19th century, which includes such dances as jigs and reels. A hoe down is featured in Aaron **Copland**'s ballet *Rodeo* (1942).

Hoffding, Finn (1899-) Danish composer who studied in Copenhagen and at the Vienna Conservatoire with Joseph **Marx**, and became a professor of composition at the Royal Danish Conservatoire in 1931. He founded the Copenhagen Folk Music School (1935) with Jorgen **Bentzon**. His compositions include the opera *The Emperor's New Clothes* and chamber pieces which reveal the influences of folk music.

Hoffmann, Ernst Theodor Amadeus (1776-1822) German composer, conductor and critic who was the hero of **Offenbach**'s *Les Contes d'Hoffmann* (1881) and was most successful as an author of intriguing tales and essays. His character Kreisker the *Kapellmeister*, who appears in his *Fantasiestucke in Callot's Manier* (1814), was the inspiration behind **Schumann**'s *Kreiskeriana*.

He studied law but continued his musical education and became conductor of the Bamberg Theatre Orchestra in 1808, after some time in the civil service. He also conducted with many other orchestras, notably in Leipzig and Dresden. Among his compositions are ten operas, a symphony, ballet scores, piano sonatas and chamber music.

Hoffmeister, Franz Anton (1754-1812) German composer and choirmaster who founded the Bureau de Musique with Kuhnel at Leipzig, 1800. He returned to Vienna in 1805 to compose. He wrote a large number of works for clarinet, flute and strings, as well as songs and devotional music.

Hofhaimer, Paul (1459-1537) Austrian composer and organist who became organist at the Imperial Chapel, Innsbruck in 1480. He moved to Augsburg in 1507 to take up a similar post there. In 1526, with word of his virtuoso playing becoming more widespread, he was appointed organist at Salzberg Cathedral. He composed for the organ, but most of his compositions have been lost.

Hofmann, Joseph (1876-1957) Polish composer and pianist who became an American citizen in 1926. As a performer he was a masterful exponent of **Chopin**'s works. He was a child progidy and made his first solo appearance with the Berlin Philharmonic Orchestra when only nine years old. He toured Europe and the United States until the Society for the Prevention of Cruelty to Children stopped him until he was 18. He studied with **Rubinstein** for a while before returning to the United States in 1898 to conduct another series of tours. In 1925 he became director of the Curtis Institute, Philadelphia.

His compositions include five piano concertos that reflect his sensitivity to romantic themes, equally manifest in his playing. He also wrote a symphony, sonatas and other pieces for the piano.

Holborne, Anthony (?-1602) English composer of whose life little is known. He worked with the cittern and composed an exquisite series of pieces for it. In 1597 he published *The Cittharn Schoole*, with 57 pieces for cittern and bass viol. His other compositions were published in the collection *Pavans, Galliards, Almans and other Short Ayres* (1599). Compositions by Holborne also appear in John **Dowland**'s *Variety of Lute Lessons* (1610).

Holbrooke, Joseph (1878-1958) English composer and pianist who challenged the musical establishment both by his background and with his views. From an early age he worked as a music hall pianist. He was admitted to the Royal Academy of Music in 1893. He studied there with Corder until he returned to the stage with a travelling pantomime for which he conducted and performed. He composed a number of serious pieces, including the symphonic poem *Byron and the Raven* (1900), which became popular at music festivals. He also wrote three Celtic operas – *The Children of Don* (1912), *Dylan* (1913) and *Bronwen* (1929) – as well as orchestral variations on the themes *Auld Lang Syne* and *Three Blind Mice*. Little is heard of Holbrooke's work today.

holler Long, wavering one- or two-line call used by black agricultural workers in the United States and the Caribbean. It may have been used as a calling and signalling device, and was often sung in African dialect. Features such as falsetto breaks and falling motifs at the end of lines are characteristic of the **blues** style of singing, and suggest the field holler may have been a contributory precursor of the blues.

Holler, Karl (1907-) German composer who became a teacher at the Hoch Conservatoire in Frankfurt in 1937. He was appointed a professor at the Munich Conservatoire in 1947, and composed *Variations on a theme of Sweelinck* for orchestra as well as a symphony, concertos for the violin, cello and organ, and chamber pieces.

Holliger, Heinz (1939-) Swiss composer and organist who has experimented with unusual combinations of instruments, and more latterly with electronic techniques. He studied at the conservatoires in Berne, Basel and Paris (1952-1963) and became first oboist with the Basel Orchestra in 1959. His compositions include many works for the oboe with other instruments, such as *Trio* (1966) for oboe, viola and harp, and *Siebengesang* for oboe, voices and orchestra (1967), a work which exhibits the tones of the oboe magnified and distorted by electronic means. He has also composed *Dona Nobis Pacem* (1968) for 12 unaccompanied voices, *Pneuma* (1970) for 34 wind instruments, percussion, voices and radio and *Der Magische Tanzer* (1965) for two singers, two actors, two dancers, choir, orchestra and tape.

Holloway, Robin (1943-) English composer of romantic and occasionally introspective works which reflect the influence of Richard **Strauss** as well as an individual understanding of harmony and melody. He studied at St Paul's Cathedral Choir School and then at Cambridge and Oxford. He returned to Cambridge as a research student at Gonville and Caius College, and became a Fellow there in 1969. In 1974 he was appointed a lecturer in music at Cambridge.

Among his compositions are the opera

Clarissa (1975), *Souvenirs de Schumann* (1969) for orchestra, the symphonic poem *Domination of Black* (1973), *Romanza* (1978) for small orchestra, and choral music, including *The Consolation of Music* (1979) for unaccompanied choir and *Five Madrigals* (1973). He has also written extensively for the chamber orchestra and for voice and piano, his most sensitive songs being *Songs for Eliot's Sweeney Agonistes* (1965), *The Leaves Cry* (1974) and *A Poor Soul Sat Sighing* (1977).

Holmboe, Vagn (1909-) Danish composer who was influenced by the folk melodies he collected. His style is expansive and essentially rugged, although his grasp of melody tends to smooth an otherwise primitive tendency. He studied at the Royal Conservatoire, Copenhagen, with **Hoffding** (1927) and at the Berlin Hochschule with **Toch**. He collected Danish folk melodies and became a critic for the periodical *Politiken* in 1947. In 1950 he was appointed a professor of composition at the Danish Conservatoire. His compositions include ten symphonies, two operas and a *Requiem for Nietzsche*. He also wrote a number of chamber pieces and 14 motets.

Holst, Gustav (1874-1934) English composer of Swedish origin who freed himself from Teutonic traditions and wrote colourful, exotic music that is both demonstrative and impressionistic and which developed from classical to polytonal forms.

He studied the piano with his father and became organist and choirmaster at Wyck Rissington in 1892. In 1893 he was admitted to the Royal College of Music after the first performance of his opera *Lansdowne Castle* (1893). He studied composition with **Stanford** and befriended **Vaughan Williams**. In 1898 he joined the Carl Rosa Opera and the Scottish Orchestra as a trombonist. At this time some of his early works were performed, including the *Cotswold Symphony* (1902) and *Mystic Trumpeter* (1903).

He went on to become a music teacher, first at Dulwich girls school (1903) and then

Gustav Holst

at St Paul's School for Girls (1905), composing his *St Paul's Suite* for strings in that year. He also began collecting English folk melodies and cultivating an interest in both Sanskrit literature and Hindu scales. *Somerset Rhapsody* (1907) was to reflect the influence of folk music, while his Eastern preoccupations produced the *Choral Hymns from the Rig Veda* in 1911. In 1907 he became director of music at Morley College and continued to compose. He completed the chamber opera *Savitri* (1909) and began to work on *The Planets Suite*, a task that was to occupy him until 1916.

After World War I Holst began to experiment with larger orchestras and choirs. In 1917 he began his choral work *The Hymn of Jesus*, and two years later the first performance of *The Planets* met with success. He joined the teaching staff at the University of Reading and the Royal College of Music shortly afterwards. His compositions at this time include the *Choral Symphony* (1925), based on poems by Keats, *At the Boar's Head* (1925) and *Egdon Heath* (1927), a masterful orchestral setting of a picturesque theme. In 1923 he visited the United States, conducting his own works at Michigan University.

His health began to fail in the early 1930s (he had never recovered from a fall from a podium in 1923), and he died at the height of his powers. His later works reveal a deeper lyricism which is particularly notable in *Twelve songs by Humbert Wolfe* (1929) and *Choral Fantasia* (1931).

Holst's compositions include a large body of choral work, chamber music, hymns and songs. His orchestral pieces number over 20 suites, a form which he exploited with ease, in addition to concertos, sonatas and smaller ensemble works.

Holst, Imogen (1907-1984) English conductor and editor, the daughter of Gustav **Holst**. She studied at the Royal College of Music. She edited and conducted for recordings of several of her father's works and wrote books on **Britten** (for whom she acted as musical assistant), **Byrd** and Holst. She was also for a time director of the **Aldeburgh** Festival.

homage Composition dedicated to a composer and written in his or her style. For example, **Falla's** *Homenaje*, for guitar, is inscribed for the grave of **Debussy**.

homophonic Music in which the individual lines making up the harmony have no independent significance.

Honegger, Arthur (1892-1955) Swiss composer of neo-romantic and tonal works with a deep sense of power and passion. He studied at the conservatoires in Zurich (1909) and Paris (1911) and joined Les Six, a group of French composers formed in 1920. The successful oratorio *Le Roi David* was composed in 1921 and the masterful *Pacific 231*, a portrait of a steam engine, in 1924. He composed prolifically, completing five symphonies, including the fifth, *di tre re* (1951) which has three movements each ending on the note D, the symphonic movement *Rugby* (1928), *Jeanne d'Arc au bucher* (1938), the operas *Antigone* (1927) and *L'Aiglon* (1937), which he wrote in collaboration with **Ibert**, and film and chamber music as well as songs.

Arthur Honegger

Hopkins, Anthony (1921-) English composer and pianist who became a respected broadcaster with his educational radio series *Talking About Music*. He studied at the Royal College of Music and became director of the Intimate Opera Company in 1952. He has composed several chamber operas, including *Three's Company*, and music for radio, theatre and film.

Hopkinson, Francis (1737-1791) American composer, harpsichordist and statesman who was one of the signatories of the Declaration of Independence in 1776. He wrote the first piece of art music by an American, *My Days Have Been So Wondrous Free* (1759). He also dedicated a series of harpsichord pieces to George Washington and composed the oratorial entertainment *The Temple of Minerva*, none of which survives today.

horn Alternative term for **French horn**.

Horn, Charles Edward (1786-1894) English composer who acted and sang on the London stage from 1809. He moved to the United States in 1833 and had some success with his operatic productions in New York. In 1843 he returned briefly to England, but settled for the rest of his life in Boston after 1847. He wrote a number of choral and operatic works, including the song *Cherry Ripe*, which are still popular among choral societies today.

Horn, Karl Friedrich (1762-1830) German composer and organist, and father of Charles **Horn**. He settled in London (1782) and was appointed music master to Queen Charlotte and the Royal Household in 1811. He became the organist at St George's Chapel, Windsor in 1823. His compositions include a number of piano sonatas and an edition of **Bach**'s *Well-tempered Klavier*, which he produced with Samuel **Wesley**.

hornpipe Lively English dance, so-called because it was first accompanied on a pipe of the same name which was made from an animal's horn. Originally it was in 3/2 time, although the later form is in 2/4. It was known as the sailor's hornpipe, and an example appeared in the operatta *Ruddigore* by **Sullivan** (1887). The occasional hornpipe also appears in works by **Purcell** and **Handel**.

Horovitz, Joseph (1926-) Austrian composer, conductor and teacher who studied at Oxford and the Royal College of Music. He became an assistant director of the Intimate Opera Company in 1952, and a professor of composition at the Royal College in 1961. He has composed two operatic works, 11 ballets, concertos for various instruments and a series of popular parodies for the music festivals organized by Gerard Hoffnung in London.

Horowitz, Vladimir (1904-) Russian pianist who studied at the Kiev Conservatoire and made his debut in Kharkov in 1921. He emigrated to the United States in 1928 and made many recordings, gaining an international reputation as a virtuoso pianist. His concert career was halted by illness in 1936-1938 and after this time he appeared, with very few exceptions, only to make recordings.

hot Lively and exciting, especially associated with jazz music.

Hotteterre, Jacques Martin (?-1760) French composer and flautist who came from a large family of woodwind instrument makers and performers. He studied in Rome and is believed to be the first musician to play a transverse flute, at the Paris Opéra in 1697. He composed a number of flute pieces, suites for two flutes and pieces for the musette.

Hovhaness, Alan (1911-) American composer and organist who was deeply influenced by Eastern music. His works reflect a combination of Western elements with a modal, oriental harmony and the tones of oriental instruments. This is clearly heard in his *Fantasy on Japanese Footprints* (1965).

He studied at the New England Conservatoire and at the Tanglewood Studios with **Martinu**. In 1948 he became a tutor at the Boston Conservatoire, and settled in New York in 1952. His compositions include more than 20 symphonies, operatic works, the suite *Mysterious Mountain* for orchestra and the now well-known *And God Created Great Whales*, which features the recorded call of the humpbacked whale.

Howells, Herbert Norman (1892-1983) English composer and organist who worked

Vladimir Horowitz

with music academically and more popularly in music festivals. His compositions reveal the influences of **Vaughan Williams** and **Elgar**, although not to the detriment of his individual creativity.

He studied at Gloucester with Brewer before entering the Royal College of Music in 1912, where he studied composition with **Stanford**. In 1917 he became an assistant organist at Salisbury Cathedral, and succeeded **Holst** as music director at St Paul's School for Girls in 1936. He became an organist at St John's College, Cambridge in 1941 and was appointed a professor of music at London University in 1954. He composed both devotional and secular music, including the picturesque *Pastoral Rhapsody* (1923) for orchestra and *Pageantry Suite* (1943) for brass band. His choral works suggest the boisterous nature of country pursuits as in the *Kent Yeoman's Wooing Song* (1933), and a more sublime eloquence in sacred works such as *Hymnus Paradisi* (1950) and *Missa Sabrinensis* (1953). He also composed works for voice and accompaniment, and for the chamber ensemble as well as for the organ.

hsaing-waing (Burma) Largest and most common Burmese percussion ensemble, taking its name from the 21-piece drum-chime which leads the group. The instrumentation depends upon the function of the music – whether for monastic rituals, dramas, festivals or state visits. A full professional ensemble may include two types of gong chime, an oboe, barrel drums, slit drum, clappers, large cymbals and hand cymbals.

hsiao/xiao (China) Set of well-tempered pipes, blown across the open end, similar to panpipes. There are usually 16 pipes mounted in a row, ascending from left to right by the interval of a semitone. They are set into a bottomless wooden case which is painted red and ornamented with a dragon or a phoenix.

Huber, Klaus (1852-1921) Swiss composer and violinist who studied at the Leipzig Conservatoire and with **Blacher**. He became a tutor at the Zurich Conservatoire in 1950 and a professor of harmony at the Basel Conservatoire in 1961. His compositions include *Tenebrae* for orchestra and a number of chamber pieces.

Hughes, Arwel (1909-) Welsh composer and conductor who studied at the Royal College of Music with **Vaughan Williams** and was appointed conductor of the BBC Welsh Orchestra in 1950. His compositions include the opera *Menna* (1951) and other works for orchestra and chamber ensembles.

Hughes, Herbert (1882-1937) Irish composer who studied at the Royal College of Music and became the music critic for the *Daily Telegraph* in 1911. He was an important collector of Irish folk music and a competent arranger of these works in orchestral settings.

Hullah, John Pyke (1812-1884) English composer and organist who visited Paris in 1839 to study G.L. Wilhelm's method of teaching singing from sight. He introduced this method into English schools in 1841. From 1844 he was a professor of vocal music at Queen's College and Bedford College, London University, and in 1872 became a schools inspector. He composed a number of devotional pieces and several song cycles, as well as the opera *The Village Coquette* (which had a libretto by Charles Dickens).

Hume, Tobias (?-1645) English composer and master of the viola da gamba. He wrote a series of works for the lyre viola, *The First Part of Ayres* (1605) which includes the first recorded instruction – *con legno* (with the back of the bow). His only other collection of pieces *Captain Hume's Poeticall Musicke* followed in 1607.

Humfrey (or Humphrey), Pelham (1647-1674) English composer who became a chorister at the Chapel Royal and studied with **Lully** in Paris by order of Charles II.

He returned to London in 1666 and was appointed a Gentleman of the Chapel Royal and a Master of the Children in 1672. He composed a series of secular and devotional songs, anthems and motets, and provided a score for Shakespeare's *The Tempest*.

Hummel, Johann Nepomuk (1778-1837) Austrian composer and pianist of great ability whose improvisational skills were considered to be greater than **Beethoven**'s. His compositions are noted for their elegance and polish, and influenced **Chopin** with their lightness and decoration. He studied with **Mozart** while still a boy and toured Germany, Holland and England as a virtuoso performer. He also received tuition from Clementi and **Salieri**, whom he met in Vienna in 1793. In 1804 he was appointed *Kapellmeister* to the court of Esterházy and then at Stuttgart (1816). He conducted the German Opera in London from 1833.

Among his compositions are some now forgotten operatic pieces and more than 100 instrumental works, including concertos and sonatas. He also wrote the influential tutorial book *Piano School* (1828).

humoresque Instrumental composition of capricious or fantastic rather than humorous character. It was a term used particularly by **Dvorák** and **Schumann**.

Humperdinck, Engelbert (1854-1921) German composer whose operatic work reveals the influence of **Wagner** in its orchestration and moral sensibilities. He studied at the Cologne Conservatoire with **Hiller** and moved to Munich to compose. On a visit to Italy in 1879 he met **Wagner** and assisted him in the production of *Parsifal* at Bayreuth. He became a professor of harmony at the Barcelona Conservatoire in 1885, and returned to take up a similar post at the Hoch Conservatoire in 1890. He also became a music critic for the *Frankfurter Zeitung* in that year. In 1893 his opera *Hansel and Gretel* was produced in Weimar and was an immediate success. It is still widely performed today.

Humperdink's principal compositions include other operas such as *Dornroschen* (1902) and *Konigskinder* (1910), but none of them matched the success of his first. He also wrote some incidental pieces for the theatre, including *The Merchant of Venice* (1905), *The Winter's Tale* (1906) and *As You Like It* (1907).

hurdy-gurdy Mechanical violin consisting of six strings vibrated by a wheel turned with a handle. The tune is played on the top string by means of a keyboard, the lower strings remaining unchanged in pitch and therefore acting as a drone. Both **Mozart** and **Haydn** wrote compositions for the instrument. It is also known as a barrel organ or street piano, because like them it is operated by a handle. An alternative term for the hurdy-gurdy is organistrum.

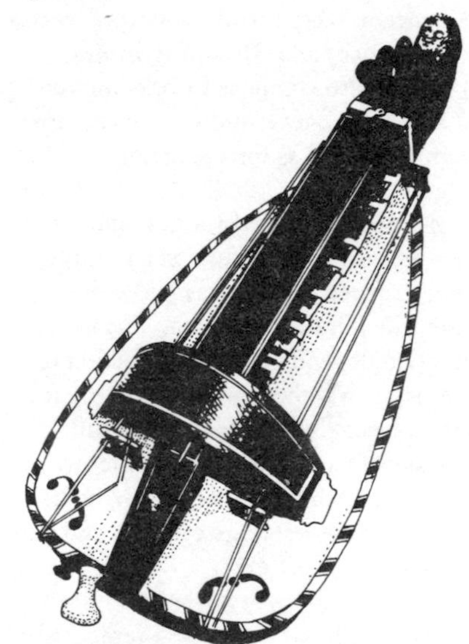

Hurdy-gurdy

Hurlstone, William Yeates (1876-1906) English composer and pianist who studied with **Stanford** at the Royal College of Music and became a tutor of counterpoint there in 1905. His compositions include *Fantasy-Variations on a Swedish Air* (1903) for orchestra, the ballad *Alfred the Great* and works for the piano, songs, and chamber pieces.

Husa, Karel (1921-) Czech composer and conductor who studied at the conservatoires in Prague and Paris with **Boulanger**, **Honneger** and Fournet. He became a conductor with various orchestras in Paris and was appointed a professor of composition at Cornell University in 1954. His compositions include orchestral and chamber works.

hyangak (Korea) Native court music and music originating from China before the T'ang dynasty. The main instruments of the orchestra include a *p'iri* (oboe), a *taegŭm* (flute), a *haegŭm* (bowed fiddle), a *changgo* (drum) and often an *ajaeng* (bowed zither). See also **aak**; **tangak**.

hydraulis Ancient type of organ invented in Egypt by Ctesibius in the 3rd century BC, and used by the Greeks and Romans. The pipes were played by wind forced through them by the pressure of water, and for this reason it is also sometimes known as a water-organ.

hymn Song of praise to a god or saint, set in the Christian church, either to a **plainsong** or more usually now as a four-part harmonization of a simple melody intended for congregational singing.

The hymn formed part of the earliest devotional music, formally established in the 4th century by St Ambrose of Milan. Between the 16th and 17th centuries the English hymn emerged and many fine tunes were composed, most of which are still used today. Charles Wesley (1757-1834), the English composer, wrote more than 6,000 hymns.

I

Ibert, Jacques (1890-1962) French composer noted for his lightness of touch and wit, as well as his sensitivity to melody and harmony. From 1909 he studied at the Paris Conservatoire, and was appointed director of the French Academy in Rome in 1937. He returned to France in 1955 to become an assistant director at the Paris Opéra and the Opéra-Comique.

He composed a number of light operas including *Angélique* (1927) and *Gonzague* (1930), and collaborated with **Honegger** on the opera *L'Aiglon* (1937). He wrote two orchestral pieces which reflect the influences of the New World, the *Louisville Concerto* (1953) and the *Bostoniana* symphony (1955), as well as *The Italian Straw Hat* (1903) and *Escales* (1922), a descriptive piece which journeys between the ports of Valencia, Tunis and Palermo. Ballet scores, chamber pieces, works for voice and piano, including *The Little White Donkey* (1940), are also among his compositions.

idée fixe (Fr.) Term used by **Berlioz** for a theme (as in the *Symphonie Fantastique*, 1830-1831), which recurs obsessively in varying forms in the course of a composition as an allusion to some idea. See also **leitmotif**.

idiophone Any musical instrument that is self-sounding, such as cymbals, xylophones, bells, gongs, rattles and tambourines. In other words, when an idiophone is hit, rattled or stroked, it produces its own sound. Drums, however, are not in this category because they are **membranophones**.

idyll Composition that describes a peaceful, pastoral picture, such as **Wagner**'s *Siegfried Idyll* (1857).

illustrative music Piece that describes or refers to non-musical sources such as a poem, play, picture, landscape or a particular emotional experience. Examples of this type of music are **Beethoven's** Symphony No. 6, *Pastoral* (1807-1808), and the tone poem *Till Eulenspiegel* (1896) by Richard **Strauss**. See also **programme music**.

Imbrie, Andrew Welsh (1921-) American composer and pianist whose works display a lucid, neo-Classical style. He studied composition with **Sessions** and piano with Ormstein, and lectured at the University of California from 1948. He spent several years (1947-1949 and 1968-1969) composing in Rome and was appointed a professor of music at the University of California in 1960.

His compositions include the opera *Three Against Christmas* (1962), symphonies, *Shaggy Dog* (1947) for wind quintet and piano, and *Divertimento for Six Instruments* (1948) for flute, bassoon, trumpet, violin, cello and piano. He has also written concertos and sonatas for the piano and violin, chamber pieces, and works for voice and orchestra, notably *Drum Taps* for chorus and orchestra.

imitation Device in a composition in which a voice or instrument repeats a theme or motif previously stated by another. An imitation may be either deferred until the first statement has been completed or made to overlap it (stretto). **Canon** and **fugue** employ imitation according to strict and regular patterns.

imperfect cadence **Cadence** made up of the chord progression I-V, giving the impression that the phrase is unresolved and is therefore to continue.

Impressionism Term borrowed from the visual arts, in which it was applied to such painters as Monet and Renoir of the late 19th and early 20th centuries. Although disapproved of by **Debussy**, he was identified as the leader of musical Impressionism after his composition *Prelude à l'apres-midi d'un faune* was performed (1894). Its influence can also be seen in the works of **Ravel, Dukas,** Delius and **Falla**.

impromptu Music, usually for piano, written in such a way as to suggest that it is an **improvisation**. **Schubert** composed eight (D899 and D935) for piano in 1827 and **Chopin** composed several, including Op. 29 (1837) and Op. 36 (1840).

improvisation (extemporization) Art of playing or singing music not written down by a composer, but following directly from the player's imagination. Improvised cadenzas were expected of singers and instrumental soloists in the 17th and 18th centuries, and to a certain extent survived into the 19th century. Improvisation is a technique particularly important to the training of an organist.

in (Japan) One of the two principal scales of folk origin. See **Japanese scales**.

incipit (Lat.) It begins, indication of the first few bars of a musical work as quoted in an index or catalogue.

indeterminacy In the 1950s, a type of music emerged in which some modern composers left certain elements to the choice of the performer. Karlheinz **Stockhausen** was active in this particular form of music, best exemplified in two of his works: *Gruppen* (1955-1957), for three orchestras, and *Zyklus* (1959), for one percussion player who may begin on any page of the score. See also **aleatory**.

Ingegneri, Marc'Antonio (1547-1592) Italian composer singer and instrumentalist who was one of **Monteverdi**'s tutors. He studied with Ruffo and became choirmaster at Cremona Cathedral by 1572. He composed several books of masses and motets, at least eight books of madrigals, and a set of 27 *Responsories for Holy Week* (which were attributed to **Palestrina** until 1897).

Inghelbrecht, Désiré-Emile (1880-1965) French composer, conductor and author of the books *The Conductor's World* (1953) and *The Composer's World* (1954). He conducted the Swedish Ballet Orchestra in Paris and became an assistant conductor at the Pasdeloup concerts. In 1924 he conducted at the Opéra-Comique, and in 1945 at the Paris Opéra and with the French National Radio Orchestra. His compositions include the ballet *El Greco*, choral and orchestral works, as well as chamber pieces.

in modo di (It.) In the manner of.

In nomine Instrumental composition of the late 16th or 17th century for viols or keyboard based on a plainsong melody used as a *cantus firmus*. The melody is that of the chant *Gloria tibi Trinitas*, as used in a mass by **Taverner**. Part of the Benedictus of the mass begins with the words 'In nomine Domini'.

instrumentation Art of writing music for instruments in a manner suited to the nature of each instrument. See also **orchestration**.

instrument Any device used for the production of musical sound. The usual practical classification is into percussion, wind and stringed instruments. However, this type of classification can be imprecise because the piano, for instance, uses strings but is percussive in mechanism. To avoid such ambiguity, Eric von Hornbostel and Curt Sachs published in 1914 a classification, according to what it is that actually makes the sound, into aerophones, **chordophones, idiophones** and **membranophones.**

Intendant (Ger.) Superintendent or administrative director of a German opera house or theatre.

interlude Piece of music inserted between longer pieces or between the acts of plays. In 16th- and 17th-century France such entr'actes were called *intermède* – in Italy *intermedio.*

intermezzo Term with three meanings.

First, it is an instrumental piece in the middle of an opera, performed when the stage is empty, as in *Cavalleria Rusticana* by **Mascagni** (1890).

Second, it is a short instrumental piece for piano, such as *Three Intermezzos for Piano* (1892) by **Brahms.**

Third, it is a comic operatic piece played as an interlude between acts of a serious opera in the 18th century. The most notable example is **Pergolesi**'s *La Serva Padrona* (1732).

interrupted cadence **Cadence** in which the dominant chord is followed by an unexpected chord – usually the submediant.

interval Distance in pitch between two notes, whether sounded simultaneously or in succession. There are two main divisions: simple intervals, in which the distance is an octave or less, and compound intervals, in which the distance exceeds an octave.

In the major scale (say, the scale of C major), the following simple intervals exist: second (C-D), third (C-E), fourth (C-F), fifth (C-G), sixth (C-A), seventh (C-B) and octave (C-C′). Of these the fourth, fifth and octave are spoken of as perfect intervals, and the second, third, sixth and seventh as major intervals. If a major interval is decreased by one semitone, it becomes a minor interval (e.g. C-A♭). The perfect intervals may be increased or decreased to the extent of a semitone, and then are termed augumented or diminshed (e.g. C-G♯ and C-G♭, respectively).

When the two notes of an interval belong to the same scale, it is known as a diatonic interval.

intonation Term with two meanings.

First, it is the act of intoning, the singing of the opening phrase of a piece (for example, in church service responses) by a singer in authority so as to ensure that the right melody will be sung by the group and at the proper pitch.

Second, it is the degree of accuracy that a singer or instrumentalist is able to achieve as regards pitch. Thus, a singer with good intonation is able to pitch a note very accurately indeed.

intrada Used in the 16th and 17th centuries for the opening number of a suite of dances, with a festive and martial style. **Beethoven** applied the term to the short overture *Wellington's Victory* (1813).

introit Opening item of the Proper of the Mass, accompanying the entrance of the ministers and choir. It was introduced by Pope Celestine I in the early 5th century.

inventions Title given to **Bach**'s two sets of short keyboard pieces composed strictly in two and three parts respectively, and possibly designed as technical studies. He called the three-part set 'symphonies', but there is no distinct difference between these and the two-part inventions.

inversion Term with three meanings.

First, it is the process of changing the position of the notes in a chord. For instance, the chord of C major is said to be in the root position in the form of C-E-G. Its first inversion is in the form E-G-C, its second inversion is in the form G-C-E.

Second, it is the act of writing a melody 'upside-down', which means that the intervals remain the same but the movement in the opposite direction.

Third, it is the process of changing over the upper and lower melodies in invertible **counterpoint**.

Root position

First inversion

Second Inversion

inverted mordent **Ornament** that indicates that three notes are to be played in the time-value of the principal note, consisting of the principal note, plus the note below it and the principal note repeated. An alternative term is lower mordent. See also **upper mordent**.

invertible counterpoint Two melodies in **counterpoint** may be inverted by the upper becoming the lower and vice versa.

Ionian mode In the 16th century, Henricus Glareanus, a Swiss theorist, recognized two authentic **modes**, one being Aeolian and the other Ionian. The Ionian mode is represented by the white keys of the piano beginning from C, and corresponds exactly to the modern C major scale.

Ippolitov-Ivanov, Mikhail Mikhailovich (1859-1935) Russian composer and conductor who studied at the St Petersburg Conservatoire with **Rimsky-Korsakov** and became head of the Tbilisi Conservatoire in 1883. His *Caucasian Sketches* for orchestra were published in 1895, and his reputation spread to the capital. After the revolution in 1917, he was appointed director of the Moscow Conservatoire and in 1925 a conductor of the Moscow Opera.

His compositions reflect his Soviet patriotism, notably in his *Song of Stalin* and other marches and songs. He also composed operas, including *Ruth* (1887), *Treachery* (1909) and *The Last Barricade* (1934), symphonic pieces, sonatas, cantatas, *An Evening in Georgia* for harp and wind instruments, and chamber music. In 1931 he completed **Mussorgsky**'s opera *The Marriage*.

Ireland, John (1879-1962) English composer and pianist who used his understanding of the piano to compose descriptive works that were inspired by the landscape, nature and a meditative temperament. He studied at the Royal College of Music with **Stanford** in 1893, and mixed with such contemporaries as Gustav **Holst** and **Vaughan Williams**. He also taught composition at the college, and was organist as St Luke's, Chelsea, until 1926. After destroying all of his early work (pre-1908), he concentrated on the composition of picturesque orchestral pieces such as *The Forgotten Rite* (1913), *Mai-Dun* (1921), *A London Overture* (1936) and a *Concertino Pastorale* for strings (1939).

He wrote many piano pieces, including the acclaimed piano concerto (1930), as well as deeply poetic and sensitive songs which released English song composition from the grip of Teutonic styles.

John Ireland

Irish harp Alternative term for **Celtic harp**.

isometric Describing rhythmic structures that are measured in units of equal length. This includes all Western compositions that use the same time signature throughout.

isorhythmic One of the most important structural devices of the 14th and 15th centuries used by composers of **polyphonic** music. It consisted of a reiterated rhythmic pattern imposed on a melody or phrase, which might be repeated several times. The pitch of the notes may, however, differ.

istesso tempo (It.) At the same tempo, a direction given where a change in time-signature is indicated, but the composer wishes the music to continue at the same pace or beat in the new rhythm.

Italian sixth Form of **augmented sixth** chord with a major third (for example, A♭-C-F♯).

Ives, Charles Edward (1874-1954) American composer of exceptional inventiveness, who borrowed many themes from other composers but who created in such an individual way that he is acknowledged as a great innovator. Idioms developed by him long before can be identified in the subsequent works of **Stravinsky** and **Hindemith**. He is also credited as an influence by many American composers writing today.

Ives' first pieces, such as *Variations on America* (1891), were composed before he began to study music at Yale University, where his well-developed and individual sense of composition put great strain on his relationship with his tutor, Horatio Parker. He played the organ while at Yale and later in New York. His most productive period of composition began at this time, starting with his second symphony in 1897 and his third in 1904, until eventually his health suffered from the strain. He composed very little after 1917, but revised many of his manuscripts so chaotically that performers faced grave difficulties later. Some of his work was published in 1919, but his fourth symphony met with failure.

His compositions include the *Concord Sonata* (1915) for piano, *Three Places in New England* (1914) and *The Holidays Symphony* (1913). These are sometimes filled with deliberate chaos and sometimes with a more structured power. He also wrote shorter pieces, 11 volumes of chamber music, and more than 200 songs including *Evening* and *Soliloquy*, which reflect a more lyrical style. In the 1920s he planned a *Universe Symphony* for several different orchestras and huge choirs positioned in valleys and on mountain peaks.

J

jack Mechanism in the **virginal, harpsichord** and similar instruments by which the strings are plucked.

Jacob, Gordon (1895-1984) English composer, conductor and teacher who wrote much instrumental music that is highly polished and traditional in style. He studied at the Royal College of Music with **Stanford** and **Boult** and became a professor of theory, composition and orchestration. He transcribed **Vaughan Williams'** *English Folk Songs* for full orchestra in 1927.

His compositions include two symphonies, a symphonietta (1942), concertos for various instruments, ballets, as well as numerous arrangements of pieces by other composers and from popular songs and rhymes, among them the *Passacaglia on a Well-Known Theme* (the theme being *Oranges and Lemons*).

Jacobi, Frederick (1891-1952) American composer, conductor and pianist who made a study of American Indian music and the music of the Jewish litany, and incorporated both these styles into his work. He studied composition with **Goldmark** in New York and later at the Berlin Hochschule. In 1913 he became assistant conductor at the New York Metropolitan and from 1936 taught at the Juilliard School. His compositions include *Sabbath Evening Service* (1952), *Indian Dances* for orchestra, the opera *The Prodigal Son* (1943), concertos for the violin, piano and cello, chamber music and songs.

Jacques-Dalcroze, Emile (1865-1950) Swiss composer, notable for his development of eurhythmics, a new connection between musical rhythm and physical movement. Dalcroze studied at Geneva, Vienna (where he worked with **Bruckner**) and Paris. He composed operatic works including the popular *Sancho Panza* (1897) and experimented with music for strings. In 1915 he founded the *Institut Jacques-Dalcroze* in Geneva to promote eurythmics as an influence in ballet and gymnastics.

jam session Improvised performance by jazz musicians.

Janáček, Leos (1854-1928) Czech composer, organist and conductor whose 19th-century work reflects the styles of **Smetena** and **Dvorák** but whose later

Leos Janáček

works display a shattered and fragmented structure in which the natural rhythms of sound are explored.

He studied at the Augustinian monastery in Brno as a chorister and entered the Prague Organ School in 1874. His early attempts to find fame in Europe failed, and after a short visit to Leipzig and Vienna he returned to Brno to teach. He began to study and collect Moravian folk music at this time and compiled collections and arranged some of the melodies. In 1881 he founded an organ school in Brno and directed it until 1919.

His first success came with the opera *Jenufa* (1904) in Brno, but because of a disagreement with the director of the Prague Opera, Kovarovic, it was not released in Prague until 1916. During the 1920s he completed his most exciting pieces, including the rhapsody *Taras Bulba* (1918), *Mladi* (1924), *The Diary of One Who Disappeared* (1919), the *Glagolitic Mass* for solo voices (1927) and the operas *The Makropulos Affair* (1924), *Kata Kabanova* (1919) and *From the House of the Dead* (1927).

Janequin, Clément (1475-1560) French composer who worked as a singer and choirmaster in Bordeaux (1505) and Angers (1534) before enrolling at the University in Paris (1549) and eventually receiving a court appointment. Ordained a priest before 1526, he published only two masses and onebook of motets (now lost), but is more famous for his 250 plus *chansons* – mostly in four parts – including *La Guerre* and *Le Chant des Oiseaux*. He also composed *chansons spirituelles* (1556) and French metrical psalms, notably the 82 *Pseaumes de David* (1559) – which may indicate Huguenot sympathies in his later years. The alternative spelling Jannequin is also found.

janissaries Turkish infantry who acted as bodyguards to a sultan from the 14th to the early 19th century. Their music made use of special percussion instruments, including the **jingling johnny**. As a result, the term janissary music evolved, which **Brahms** playfully applied to the 3rd movement of his Symphony No. 4 in E minor, Op. 98 (1884-1885).

Järnefelt, Armas (1869-1958) Finnish composer and conductor who became a Swedish citizen in 1910. He studied in Helsinki, Berlin and at the Paris Conservatoire and became the conductor of the Viipuri Orchestra in 1898. In 1907 he conducted the Stockholm Royal Opera Orchestra and in 1940 was appointed a professor at Helsinki University. He composed the popular *Praeludium* for orchestra and *Berceuse* for piano, as well as songs and choral work.

Jannequin, Clément Alternative spelling of Clément **Janequin**.

Japanese scales **In** and **yō** are the two principal scales of folk origin. *In* is essentially a hemitonic **pentatonic**, with two auxiliary tones, corresponding to E, F, (G), A, B, C, (D), and produces what is recognized as the distinctive character of much Japanese music. This scale is used extensively in **shakuhachi**, **shamisen** and **koto** music, the latter's open strings being tuned to two forms of the scale.

Yō is an anhemitonic pentatonic scale, again with two auxiliary tones, corresponding to A, (B), C, D, E, (F), G.

Ryo and **ritsu** are the two basic pentatonic scales in Buddhist music theory and **gagaku** court music. *Ryo*, including four chromatic auxiliary or 'passing' tones, corresponds to D, E, F♯, (G/G♯), A, B, (C/C♯), and *ritsu*, with a pair of auxiliary tones, corresponds to E, F♯, (G), A, B, C♯, (D).

jazz Form of popular music that originated in New Orleans in the latter part of the 19th century among the black population. It developed out of ragtime and blues, which emerged from negro spirituals and work songs in the 1860s.

Jazz relies for its effects mainly on syncopated rhythm and improvisation on a melodic theme. Jazz uses a special combination of instruments, including plucked stringed instruments, saxophones, double and muted brass. The distinctive style of black New Orleans jazz (later known as 'traditional' jazz) was followed by the Dixieland style of the white southerners. In the 1930s this was replaced by big-band swing, and in the 1940s came beebop, followed by the cool jazz of the 1950s. Jazz has influenced many composers, including **Stravinsky** (*Scherzo à la Russe*, for jazz ensemble, 1944), **Gershwin** (*Rhapsody in Blue*, 1924), **Copland** (*Billy the Kid*, 1938), and **Lambert** (*The Rio Grande*, 1929). Many jazz musicians have become household names, and some have starred in films and made careers in radio and television. Jazz has also contributed to many styles of popular music.

Jelinek, Hanns (1901-1969) Austrian composer who was largely self-taught but met and studied with **Schoenberg** and **Schmidt**. His compositions, all of which are in the twelve-note form, include *Prometheus* (1936) for voice and orchestra, and the *Symphonia brevis* (1938) for orchestra.

Jensen, Adolph (1837-1879) German composer and pianist who studied with Ehlhert and **Liszt** and who performed and taught in Berlin and Copenhagen. He composed a large number of songs, cantatas, choruses and other choral works, as well as the opera *Turandot*, which he never completed.

jhala (India) Section following the **jor** in an instrumental **raga**. It is a stylistic treatment of the *jor* in which the drone strings are rapidly strummed between the main melody notes. Its driving rhythms can also make it an exciting way of concluding a **gat**.

jig Popular 16th-century English dance in binary form, usually in 6/8 or 12/8 time. It was the fourth of the dances regularly found in the Classical suite. The jig's popularity spread to France and Italy, where it was called *gigue* and *giga*, respectively.

jingling johnny Obsolete percussion instrument, formerly used in military bands, shaped in the form of a tree, pavilion roof, or Turkish crescent hung with bells. It is sometimes called a Chinese pavilion.

Jirák, Karel Boleslav (1891-1972) Czech composer and conductor who studied in Prague and at the Vienna Conservatoire with Foerster. In 1915 he was appointed conductor of the Hamburg Opera, and in 1920 he became a professor of composition at the Prague Conservatoire. He moved to the United States in 1948 and became a tutor at the Chicago Music College. He composed five symphonies, an opera and various chamber works, including six string quartets.

jiuta (Japan) Important ensemble form which originally referred to the **shamisen** music of Kyoto, but became well known as an ensemble form with *koto* and *shamisen* in combination. It includes a third instrument, at one time a bowed fiddle, but later replaced by the **shakuhachi** flute. See also **tegotomono**.

Joachim, Joseph (1831-1907) Hungarian composer and violinist whose playing was admired by **Mendelssohn** and **Brahms**, who dedicated his violin concerto to him. He was a child prodigy, performing from the age of seven, and studied in Vienna with **Boehm** before entering the Leipzig Conservatoire in 1843. He performed at the Gewandhaus Concerts and in 1849 became the leader of **Liszt**'s Weimar Court Orchestra. In 1869 he was appointed a director of the Berlin Hochschule. Joachim toured widely as a soloist, visiting England in 1887, and achieved great success as an interpreter of **Beethoven** and **Brahms**.

His compositions include an orchestration of **Schubert**'s *Grand Duo* (1855), the *Hungarian Concerto* for violin and orchestra, five overtures and a number of songs.

jod See **jor**.

jo-ha-kyū (Japan) Important structural concept in Japanese music, concerned with tripartite division. For example, in **gagaku**, *jo* is the introduction, *ha* is the 'breaking apart' or exposition, and *kyu* is the 'rushing to finish'. This can apply to both the whole composition and individual sections. In **noh** drama, a composition consists of five main units or *dan*. These are divided into *jo* (first dan), *ha* (second to fourth dan), and *kyū* (fifth, concluding dan).

Johnson, Robert Sherlaw (1932-) English composer, lecturer and pianist who became an authority on the works of **Messiaen**. He studied at Durham University and entered the Royal Academy of Music in 1953. In 1957 he studied with **Boulanger** at the Paris Conservatoire. He has lectured at the Universities of Leeds (1961), York (1965) and Oxford (1970). Among his compositions are the opera *The Lambton Worm* (1978), works for soprano, piano and tape, including *Praises of Heaven and Earth* (1969), *Green Whispers of Gold* (1971) and *Where the Wild Things Are* (1974), originally intended for soprano and tape but later adapted for operatic performance. He has also written a number of religious pieces, including *The Festival Mass of the Resurrection* (1974) for chorus and orchestra.

Jolivet, André (1905-1974) French composer who, with **Messiaen**, Lesur and Baudrier, founded the *Jeune France* group of composers which set out to re-establish a more humanized style of composition. He studied at the University of Paris with **Varèse** from 1928, and became a musical director of the Comédie Française in 1942. He was appointed a professor of composition at the Paris Conservatoire in 1965. His compositions reflect his interest in the sonorities of instruments and are transparent and dissonant. They display the influence of **Schoenberg** as well as of polytonal and oriental idioms.

Among his compositions are three symphonies and a number of concertos, including the *Concerto for Ondes Martenot* (1947) and the *Suite Française* (1957), as well as the opera *Dolores* (1942) and works for the chamber orchestra. His devotional compositions include *Le Coeur de la Matière* (1965) and other works for voice and orchestra.

Jommelli, Niccolò (1714-1784) Italian composer who studied at Naples and Rome, and who subsequently went to Bologna and Venice to compose. He visited Vienna in 1748 and became *Kapellmeister* to the court at Stuttgart in 1753. In 1769 he moved back to Naples but found little success there. While in Vienna he befriended Metastasio and used a number of his texts in his operatic compositions. He developed, from the Neapolitan tradition, a style that accentuated the dramatic elements of opera and which avoided the digressions of arias as much as possible. He composed more than 60 operas, including *L'errore amoroso* (1737) and *Ifigenia in Aulide* (1751) and *Ifigenia in Tauride* (1771), as well as a large body of devotional music.

Jones, (James) Sydney (1861-1946) English composer who concentrated on light opera and operetta. His *Geisha* (1896) was successful in London and transferred to the New York Metropolitan in the same year.

Jongen, Joseph (1873-1953) Belgian composer, organist and pianist who studied at the Liège Conservatoire and became a tutor there in 1903. He was appointed a professor of counterpoint and a director at the Brussels Conservatoire in 1920. He composed the ballet *S'Arka*, a number of concertos for the piano, violin, cello and harp, as well as a symphony and chamber music.

jongleur Medieval minstrel, whose accomplisments could include juggling, but who was also a story-teller, singer and instrumentalist. Jongleurs were often called upon to assist **troubadours** (who were generally more creative artists), although on occasions they did reverse roles.

Joplin, Scott (1868-1917) American composer and **ragtime** pianist whose work has received new interest due to the efforts of the American pianist Joshua **Rifkin** and because of the film *The Sting*, which used his composition *The Entertainer* and several popular arrangements of some of his other rags. His early jazz style is notable for its use of complete compositions which do not allow a performer to improvise.

Joplin worked as a pianist in a number of brothels in Chicago and St Louis before moving to New York, where he composed many of his best known pieces, including *Maple Leaf Rag* and *The Entertainer*. He also composed the first ragtime operas, *A Guest of Honour* (1903) and *Treemonisha* (1911), but the massive failure of these projects destroyed his confidence.

jor/jod (India) Transitional section in a **rāga** following the **ālāp**, in which the melodic outline of the *alap* is played in strict time and without embellishment. In this way the soloist sets the tempo before the entry of the **tablā** or **pakhāvaj**.

jōruri (Japan) Musical narrative style, derived from Japanese epic poetry, which was sung originally with **biwa** accompaniment by blind priests. Now, it is generally sung with **shamisen** accompaniement, particularly in the *bunraku* puppet theatre.

Josephs, Wilfred (1927-) English composer who first studied dentistry at Newcastle University and then music at the Guildhall School, London. He entered the Paris Conservatoire in 1958 and studied with Deutsch. His compositions include a large number of works for film and television, as well as nine symphonies and other orchestral pieces. Among them are *Monkchester Dances* (1961), *Variations on a Theme of Beethoven* (1969), *The Four Horsemen of the Apocalypse* (1974) and *The Ants* (1955). He has also composed the television opera *The Appointment* (1968), a number of choral and vocal works, and music for chamber orchestra.

Josquin des Prés (1440-1521) Most renowned of the Flemish composers, Josquin's style is considered to represent a bridge between the later Middle Ages and the Renaissance, with its use of expressive phrasing and division of the choir into contrasting groups. He was a prolific composer, writing more than a 100 motets and chansons; his *Princeps Musicorum* was admired by Martin Luther for its technical brilliance.

He was a pupil of the influential **Ockeghem** and became a singer at Milan cathedral in 1459. He travelled to Rome to join the Papal Chapel in 1486, but then returned to France to join the Chapel of Louis XII. His last post was a provost to the church at Condé.

Joubert, John (1927-) South African composer who studied at the South African College of Music and at the Royal Academy of Music in London. He became a lecturer and musicologist at the universities of Hull and Birmingham, and a composer of evocative and sometimes picturesque music in the English tradition. His works include *Herefordshire Canticles* (1979) and the opera *Silas Marner* (1961), as well as various symphonic works and concertos, choral pieces and sacred music.

Jubilate Canticle from the Anglican service of Matins which includes the text of Psalm 100 (*O be joyful to the Lord*). Occasionally it is set for concert and ceremonial purposes, as an expression of rejoicing. In addition, its setting for soloists, chorus and orchestra include **Purcell**'s *Te Deum and Jubilate* for St Cecilia's Day (1694) and **Handel**'s *Utrecht Te Deum and Jubilate* (1713).

Juilliard School Leading American teaching institute for the performing arts located in New York was originally established in 1905 as the Institute of

Musical Art. In 1919 the wealthy New York businesman Augustus D. Juilliard died leaving some 20 million dollars to a foundation for the advancement of musical education in America. In 1926 the Institute of Musical Art and the Juilliard Foundation came under the same board of directors and the IMA became known as the Juilliard School of Music. The school and the foundation formally merged under that name in 1946. In 1952 dance was added to the music syllabus, with a drama department opening there in 1968. The name was changed in 1968 to the Juilliard School in order to reflect the broader base of the teaching offered. The Juilliard School moved into its present buildings within the Lincoln Center arts complex in 1969.

just intonation Playing or singing which distinguishes between **enharmonic intervals**.

K

K When followed by a number, an abbreviation of **Köchel**.

Kabalevsky, Dmitri (1904-) Russian composer, conductor and pianist who studied in Moscow with **Miaskovsky**. In 1939 he was appointed professor of composition at Moscow Conservatoire. He was greatly involved with the Soviet war effort, his compositions encompassing Soviet Realism and hymns of patriotism. In 1948 he conducted in Moscow with Vladimir **Ashkenazy** as soloist. He has since travelled throughout Europe and the United States. In 1972 he was awarded an honorary degree by the International Society of Musical Education. Kabalevsky is prolific in all fields of composition. Although best known in his own country for his songs and hymns, his chamber music and operas such as *Colas Breugnon* (1936-1938) have received much wider acclaim.

Kabelác, Miloslav (1908-1979) Czech composer, involved for many years in the development of Czech radio as conductor and director of musical productions. Kabelác's compositions combined an interest in traditional Czech themes with contemporary electronic composition. An example of his work is *Euphemias Mysterion* (1965), for soprano and chamber orchestra.

kabuki (Japan) Popular theatre which involves narrative, songs and dance sequences. Traditionally *kabuki* is an all-male domain, although originally it was performed by women. It incorporates both musical and theatrical elements of various Japanese entertainment forms, such as **noh** drama and the **bunraku** puppet theatre. Most *kabuki* plays fall into one of two categories: *jidaimono*, historical plays, based on 11th- to 16th-century heroic characters; and *sewamono*, domestic, middle-class dramas. See also **debayashi**; **geza**.

Kadosa, Pál (1903-1983) Hungarian pianist and composer who studied in Budapest with **Kodály** and taught at the Fodor Music School. By the early 1930s he achieved international acclaim with his Piano Concerto No. 1. He was appointed head of piano at the Budapest Academy in 1945. Although he owes much of his style to **Bartók**, there are undeniable elements of traditional Hungarian rhythms and melody. This combination of old and new is in evidence in the seven *Attila Jozsef* songs (1964). Kadosa was made an honorary member of the British Royal Academy of Music in 1967.

kāfī (India) One of the ten parent scales (**thāt**) in Hindustani music, corresponding to C, D, E♭, F, G, A, B♭, C' (the same notes as the Western **dorian** mode.

Kagel, Mauricio (1931-) Argentinian-born multi-media artist and self-taught composer. He settled in Cologne in 1957 to pursue interests in film, drama and art, as well as composition. *Musica para la torre* (1952) is one of the last purely musical works he composed, and he has taken references from Dada and other modernist movements for his more recent compositions. His iconoclasm has aroused much critical debate. While pieces such as *Pas de cinq* combine music and theatre, even more recent works such as *Der Schall* (1968) show a heterogeneous use of household objects and car horns in a characteristically detailed score.

kagok (Korea) Long lyric song form, consisting of a cycle of courtly songs with instrumental preludes, interludes and postludes. The present repertory of 20 or so suites dates from the 17th and 18th centuries. Each five-line stanza is sung in a highly melismatic style, with syllables drawn out in virtuosic sequences, making it one of the most difficult vocal genres in Korean music. It is usually accompanied by a small instrumental ensemble, including **kŏmun'go, taegŭm, p'iri, haegŭm** and **changgo**.

Kajanus, Robert (1856-1933) Finnish conductor and composer who studied in Paris with Svendsen (1879-1880) and was chosen by the French government to present a concert of Finnish music in Paris. Although he founded an orchestral school and the first permanent orchestra in Helsinki, he is best known for his pioneering work on behalf of **Sibelius** and Finnish music in general, bringing them to a wider audience in Europe. Kajanus has left some fine interpretations of Sibelius's work in his early 1930s recordings with the London Symphony Orchestra.

kakegoe (Japan) Calls made by the drummers in **noh** drama to mark the subdivision of a musical line or rhythmic phrase – an integral part of the *noh* ensemble sound. It also refers to the audience calls in **kabuki** theatre, in which set cries are used to mark the appreciation of certain theatrical devices, complex dance routines, etc.

kakko (Japan) Small, horizontal drum with two lashed heads of deerskin. Both heads are struck with two light drumsticks. The *kakko* is used in the **gagaku** court orchestra and assists in leading the ensemble by marking time with three basic set patterns, of which two are rolls and one a single tap with the right-hand stick.

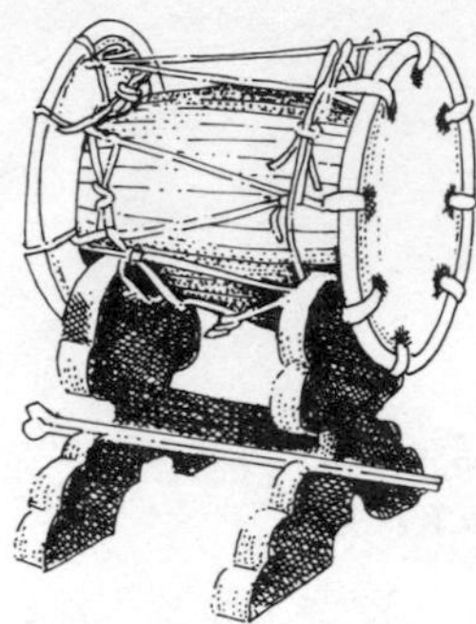

Kakko

Kalabis, Viktor (1923-) Czech composer and radio programmer, whose compositions show an affinity with those of **Brahms**. Although he has never been prolific, works such as his second quartet show him to be a masterful – if under acknowledged – composer.

Kalevala Group of Finnish epic songs from the Kaleva region of Finland. For centuries they were passed down by word of mouth, but in the mid-19th century they were published. **Sibelius** was much influenced by the Kalevala, exemplified in such works as *Kullervo* (1893), *Pohjola's Daughter* (1906) and *The Swan of Tuonela* (1893).

Kálmán, Emmerich (1882-1953) Hungarian composer and critic who studied in Budapest with **Bartók** and **Kodály**. It is for his light operas, such as *The Gay Hussar* (1908), rather than for his more serious compositions that he is best remembered. Living in Vienna until the *Anschluss*, he combined the best elements of Viennese operetta with contemporary Hungarian themes and achieved great acclaim throughout Europe and the United States. He became an American citizen.

kalyan (India) One of the ten parent scales (**thāt**) in Hindustani music, corresponding to C, D, E, F♯, G, A, B, C′, and similar to the Western **Lydian** mode.

Herbert von Karajan

Kammer (Ger.) Chamber. Hence *Kammermusik*, chamber music.

Kanawa, Dame Kiri Te (1944-) New Zealand soprano who studied under Vera Rosza and in San Francisco and at **Glyndebourne** in the early 1970s. She has gone on to establish herself as a major recording and performing artist. Perhaps her greatest role is that of Elvira in **Mozart**'s *Don Giovanni*. Te Kanawa's voice is vibrant and mellow and she tends towards a style of fresh simplicity.

kangen (Japan) **Gagaku** court music that is performed in a purely orchestral context without dance or song. It refers only to music of Chinese origin (**Tōgaku**) and employs three sets of instruments: *sankan* (wind instruments), including *ryūteki* (flute), *hichiriki* (oboe) and *shō* (mouth organ); *nigen* (stringed instruments) – a zither and a *biwa* (lute); *sanko* (percussion) – *taiko*, *kakko* (drums) and *shōko* (gong).

Kapelle (Ger.) Originally a term for the musical establishment of a king's or prince's chapel. Later it became known as any orchestra or other musical body.

Kapellmeister (Ger.) Originally a choirmaster, or a musician in charge of a court chapel. By the 19th century, it was used to refer to the musical director of an orchestra.

Karajan, Herbert von (1908-) Austrian conductor and pianist. His career was temporarily halted after World War II because of his involvement with Nazism. This hiatus was broken by his appointment to La Scala, Milan, as producer and conductor for the 1948-1949 season. From 1950 he made many recordings with the London Philharmonic Orchestra. From 1954 onwards he was conductor of the Berlin Philharmonic Orchestra, and acted as director of the Vienna State Opera from 1957 to 1964. Closely involved with the Salzburg Festivals, von Karajan has been awarded many posts throughout Europe. His flamboyant style and perfectionism is well known, and he has recorded widely.

katarimono (Japan) Generic name for a narrative song accompanied by the **shamisen** lute. Of the wide variety of *katarimono* styles that exist, often named after their founder, the most celebrated is *Gidayū-bushi* used principally in the **bunraku** puppet theatre.

Katin, Peter (1930-) British pianist who studied at the Royal Academy of Music at the age of 12 with Harold Craxton. His debut was at the Wigmore Hall in 1948. In addition to touring extensively, Katin has done much to help young musicians. He is credited with a masterly understanding of **Mozart** and of the Romanticism of such composers as **Chopin**.

Kay, Ulysses (1917-) American musician and composer who studied piano, saxophone and violin on the advice of his uncle, Joseph 'King' Oliver, the New Orleans jazz band leader. He studied with **Hindemith** at Yale, and during World War II he played in a United States Navy band and jazz orchestra. After the war he was granted a fellowship at Columbia University and, following a period of travel around Europe with various grants and scholarships, he was made professor at City University, New York. Acclaimed even in his 20s, Kay wrote the music for the film of *The Quiet One* (1948) and many other film and television scores. In 1958 he was one of the American musicians selected for a cultural exchange with Moscow.

kayakeum See **kayagŭm**.

kayagŭm/kayakeum (Korea) Indigenous zither with 12 moveable bridges and a relatively thin body. Strings are plucked with the right hand while the left hand twists and presses them down beyond the bridges, giving a wide variety of sound effects. It is used in both court and social music, especially the solo instrumental form sanjo.

Kb. (Ger.) Abbreviation of *Kontrabass* **(double-bass)**.

kecak (Bali) See **ketjak**.

Keiser, Reinhard (1674-1739) German composer who studied in Leipzig with Schelle and in Hamburg with Kusser. He was a highly prolific composer of operas (he produced more than 100, the first of which, *Basilius*, was first performed in 1693). His importance to German opera is widely recognized, and his immediate influence extended especially to the young **Handel** and helped to make Hamburg a centre for opera. He is believed to have brought the Italian **aria** style to German opera, most notably in his *Die Verdammte Staat-Sucht* (1703). *Der Carnival Von Venedig* (1707-1708) was one of his most successful operas, using the Hamburg dialect (as opposed to Italian) in its comic scenes and arias. Keiser also wrote sacred music. Much of Keiser's work is now lost.

Kelemen, Milko (1924-) Yugoslav composer who studied with Sulek in Yugoslavia, and with **Messiaen** and Aubin in Paris. His work has been mostly in the field of electronic music (following a scholarship to the Siemens Electronic Studio, 1966-1968). In 1961, he founded the Zagreb Biennial Festival of New Music, thereby bringing avant-garde composition and music to Yugoslavia virtually single-handed. His compositions include the opera *The Plague*, and a bassoon concerto.

Kell, Reginald (1906-1981) English clarinettist who studied at the Royal Academy of Music with Haydn Draper. From 1935 to 1948 he taught clarinet at the Royal Academy, and took Draper's post on his retirement. Kell pioneered an unusual vibrato technique which has since proved very influential. He has been principal clarinettist in many orchestras, including the London Symphony Orchestra (1936-1939). In 1948 he emigrated to the United States, and in 1968 published *The Kell Method*.

Kelly, Michael (1762-1826) Irish tenor, who sang in the first performance of **Mozart**'s *The Marriage of Figaro*. Kelly's studies and work took him throughout Europe, especially to Naples, Venice and Vienna (where he met Mozart). Returning to England in 1787, Kelly sang leading tenor at Drury Lane and then throughout the country. Although he aspired to be a composer in later life, it is for his voice that he is chiefly remembered.

Kempe, Rudolf (1910-1976) German conductor and oboist whose conducting debut was with the Leipzig opera in 1935. After World War II he received a series of appointments, beginning as general music director of Dresden Andlater Bavaria Staatsoper (1952-1954). His conducting debut in Britain was at Covent Garden in 1953 with *Arabella*, after which he made numerous visits until 1960. Greatly admired for his masterful conducting of **Wagner**'s *Ring*, he was much loved by performers. Although Covent Garden offered him the post of resident conductor, his activities in Europe precluded his acceptance. However after Sir Thomas **Beecham**'s death in 1961 he became principal conductor of the Royal Philharmonic Orchesra. In 1970 he was honoured with the title of 'Conductor for life' with the RPO, but resigned to become principal conductor with the BBC Symphony

Orchestra in 1976, but died before he was able to take up the post.

Kempff, Wilhelm (1895-) German pianist who entered the Berlin Hochschule at the age of nine, after a thorough musical education from his father. He studied composition with Robert Kahn and piano with Heinrich Barth. His concert career began in 1916 and he toured extensively with the Berlin Cathedral Choir. Although he played in South America (1918–1921), it was not until 1964 that he toured the United States. His debut in Britain was in 1951.

Kempff has gained a reputation as a distinguished teacher, taking master classes from as early as 1924. In 1957 Kempff began the first of an annual series of master classes teaching **Beethoven** at Positano, demonstrating his gift for interpreting this composer above all others. Kempff composed opera, ballet and two symphonies as well as orchestral work and songs, much of which has been recorded.

kempul (Java) Set of fairly large, hanging, knobbed gongs. Along with the *kenong* and *ketuk* gongs, it performs a **colotomic** function in the **gamelan** ensemble, subdividing the musical phrase into shorter periods.

kendang (Indonesia) Pair of barrel drums with two lashed heads, of which the *kendang lanang* is the higher-pitched or 'male' and the *kendang wadon* is the lower-pitched or 'female'. In many **gamelan** ensembles the *kendang* players may lead, or conduct the performance.

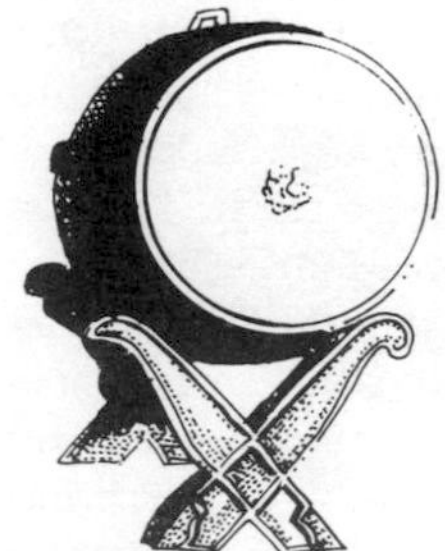

Kendang

kenong (Java) Large knobbed gong which hangs in a wooden frame. Along with the **kempul** and **ketuk** gongs, it performs a **colotomic** function in the **gamelan** ensemble, subdividing the musical phrase into shorter periods.

Kenong

Kent bugle Brass instrument with valves, roughly the size and pitch of a bugle. It was related to the **ophicleide** and has now been superseded by the **cornet**. It is also known as a key bugle or keyed bugle.

Kentner, Louis (1905-) British pianist of Hungarian birth who studied under **Kodály** and Szekely. Following an official debut at the age of 15, he toured extensively in Europe and the United States. Kentner premiered **Bartók**'s Piano Concerto No. 3 in Europe, (London, 1946), and he is considered one of the major exponents of Bartók's compositions. He settled in London, 1935, where he performed extensively a repertory of **Beethoven** and **Schubert**. Once in England he began to favour contemporary English composers and **Walton**'s violin sonata was composed specially for Kentner and his brother-in-law, Yehudi **Menuhin**. Kentner has himself composed several works including the *Serenade for orchestra* and many songs. He was awarded the CBE in 1978.

Kern, Jerome (1885–1945) American pianist and composer, believed to have been the most prolific song writer for the stage ever to emerge from the United States. He wrote more than 1,000 songs for more than 100 shows. Following a brief stay in Europe in the early 1900s, where Kern studied composition in Germany, he returned to the United States where his first song was published (1903). His first success was the musical comedy *The Red Petticoat* (1911). This followed a spell as a rehearsal pianist on Broadway. *The Red Petticoat* was followed by a series of hit musicals on Broadway, and his style was already becoming influential to composers of the era such as George **Gershwin**. During World War I Kern wrote four musicals of which *Oh Boy* (1917) proved the most successful.

His success is largely attributable to the popularity of his brand of musical comedy, which effectively superseded European light opera. Kern is best remembered for the musical *Showboat* (1927) with words written by Oscar **Hammerstein** II and including the song *Ol' man river*.

Kertesz, István (1929-1973) German conductor who was Hungarian by birth. He studied at the Franz Liszt Academy, Budapest with **Kodály** and **Weiner**. In 1953 Kertesz became resident conductor at Györ and went on to become conductor and *répétiteur* with the Budapest Opera, 1955. Following the Hungarian Uprising (1956), Kertesz moved to Germany. From 1964 he acted as general music director at Cologne. In 1965 he was invited on a world tour with the London Symphony Orchestra and became principal conductor until 1968. Kertesz had a great love of the works of **Bartók**, **Stravinsky** and **Britten**, and conducted the German premiere of the last composer's *Billy Budd* in that country.

Ketèlbey, Albert William (1875-1959) British composer who produced his first piano concerto at the age of 11. By the age of 16 Ketèlbey had been appointed organist of St John, Wimbledon. He was appointed to the Vaudeville Theatre at the age of 22. He composed songs, anthems, and pieces for many different instruments. He wrote many popular narrative pieces, such as *In a Monastery Garden* (1915) and *In a Persian market*. He also composed music for the silent films of the time, including *Wonder Worker* (1915).

kethuk See **ketuk**.

ketjak/kecak (Bali) Popular choral and theatrical form, performed by concentric circles of seated men who can number as many as 200. It is a night-time form, derived from the choral accompaniment to trance dances, but which developed as an independent form at the beginning of the 20th century, based on the legends of the monkey armies from the *Ramayana* epic. It is essentially a vocal **gamelan**, each circle of men energetically chanting onomatopoeic sounds (the most common being 'cak', giving the form its name), in interlocking rhythmic parts, with coincidental arm gestures. At the climax of the performance, the men are supposedly transformed into screeching monkey armies. *Ketjak* is performed nowadays almost exclusively for the benefit of tourists.

kettledrum Drum with a single head of calf-skin stretched over a cauldron-shaped receptacle. The kettledrum is of ancient Egyptian origin and produces notes of a definite pitch which can be altered by turning the screws at the rim of the cauldron to change the tension of the skin or by a pedal which indirectly performs the same function. The sound is produced by striking the head of the drum with a pair of sticks which are covered with various materials to provide a harder or softer timbre.

Kettledrum

The modern orchestra has at least three kettledrums of different sizes, depending on the type of composition being performed. The introduction of drums that can be tuned mechanically by way of pedals has allowed rapid changes of pitch in the middle of a movement, and also the use of **glissando**. These drums are referred to as pedal drums or chromatic timpani.

An alternative term for kettledrums is timpani.

ketuk/kethuk (Java) Small horizontal gong hung by rope in a wooden frame. Often referred to as the 'kettle', it is struck with a padded stick which produces a rather dead sound in comparison to other Javanese gongs. Along with the **kenong** and **kempul** gongs, it performs a **colotomic** function in the **gamelan** ensemble, subdividing the musical phrase into shorter periods.

key Term with two meanings.

First, it refers to the levers on a keyboard instrument such as piano, harpsichord or organ or woodwind instrument which when depressed by a finger or foot produce a note of a certain pitch.

Second, it is the prevailing tonality of a composition, based on the notes of a scale. The first note of the scale is known as the keynote and defines the key, which may be either major or minor (e.g. if the keynote is C, the key may be either C major or C minor, the difference between the two being identified by the use of certain **accidentals**). The key is identified by the **key-signature** at the start of a piece and may be altered by **modulation**. See also **major scale**; **minor scale**; **modes**.

keyboard Framework of finger-operated levers or switches that conventionally consists of a row of long, broad keys surmounted by another row of shorter, narrow keys in a contrasting colour. By convention on modern instruments, the long, broad keys are white, whereas the shorter keys are black, although on some older instruments, such as an authentic harpsichord or a copy of one, the colours may be reversed. The long keys play a diatonic scale of C major on modern instruments; the short keys, grouped alternately in twos and threes, give all the sharps and flats in any given key.

The need for a keyboard arises in instruments in which a large number of strings or pipes need to be controlled by one player, and up to a point the complexity of the keyboard has increased with the complexity of musical composition and style. Sharp-and-flat keys have been added as and when they became essential for the proper rendering of such effects as *musica ficta* or scale chromatic passages. It would be possible to devise a keyboard that provided the microtonal variations required to show the difference between, say, D♯ and E♭, but in view of the natural restrictions on a player's ability to manipulate, it is easier and far less costly in terms of extra pipes and strings to allow these notes to be controlled by the same key and compensate for the lack of discernible pitch difference by adopting a specific tuning method or avoiding certain musical keys. See **temperament**.

On an organ a keyboard is often referred to as a manual to distinguish it from a pedal keyboard, which is played with the feet. On electronic instruments the keys of a keyboard activate switches which send an electric current through circuits called oscillators to produce a sound.

The description of a work as being for keyboard means that it can be played on any keyboard instrument (piano, organ, harpsichord, etc.).

keyboard instrument Any musical

Keyboard

instrument operated by striking keys (and, where applicable, pedals). They include the organ, virginals, clavichord, harpsichord, piano and the 20th-century electronic instruments such as the electronic organ and the synthesizer. See also **keyboard**.

key bugle Alternative term for **Kent bugle**.

keyed bugle Alternative term for **Kent bugle**.

key-signature In written music, an indication placed at the start of a composition, after the **clef**, but before the **time signature** (and at key changes during a composition) which indicates the prevailing **key**. It takes the form of a series of sharps

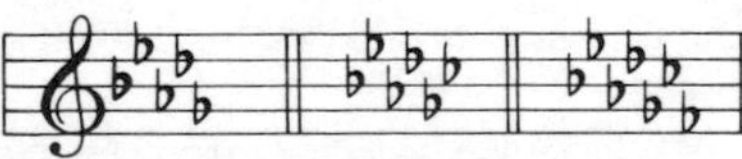

Sharp keys (above), Flat keys (below)

(♯) or flats (♭), in a given order (for sharp keys, the order is F, C, G, D, A, E, B; for flat keys the order is the reverse: B, E, A, D, G, C, F). Each note indicated in this way shows that each time this note appears in the music, it should be played sharp or flat. If there are no sharps or flats shown, the key is taken to be C major or A minor. Deviations from the prevailing key and the sharpened or flattened notes in the minor keys are marked by **accidentals**.

Khachaturian, Aram (1903-1978) Soviet composer who first studied at the Moscow Conservatoire under such teachers as Shebalin and Myaskovsky. He later became senior lecturer in instrumentation at the Academy. Although he did not turn to composition until later in his career, he has been prolific, writing symphonies, music for ballet (e.g. *Spartacus*, 1956) orchestra and chorus (e.g. *Mig Istorii*, 1971, a choral work dedicated to the memory of Lenin), chamber, piano and incidental music and music for films (e.g. *Lenin*, 1948-1949). His work draws heavily on the traditional music of the Caucasus. Later in life he came to conduct his own works, and in 1968 he toured the United States as conductor of the National Symphony Orchestra.

khaen/khene (Thailand/Laos) Bamboo mouth organ of north-east Thailand, consisting of two rows of six to 16 bamboo pipes, reaching lengths of 1m (3ft) or more, each with a metal reed. They are fixed in order of size into a central windchest, held cupped in the player's hands, with finger holes above. There are four sizes but the 16-pipe version, with a two-octave range, is the most common. In Laos there is a system of modes (*lai*) used for improvisations, while melodies are often played in parallel fourths, fifths or octaves. The instrument is capable of playing both chords and a melody simultaneously, and often produces a drone. It is essentially a folk instrument, and although not as widely used in Thailand as in Laos, it may still be found there in ensembles playing classical songs.

Khaen

khamāj (India) One of the ten parent scales (**thāt**) in Hindustani music, corresponding to C, D, E, F, G, A, B♭, C′. It is, therefore the same as the Western **Mixolydian** mode.

khene (Thailand/Laos) See **khaen**.

Khrennikov, Tikhon (1913-) Soviet composer who studied at the Gnesin Music School, Moscow, and with Shebalin at the Moscow Conservatoire. His debut as composer/pianist of the Piano Concerto Op. 1 in 1933 brought him much acclaim. He began a long association with the Vakhtangov Theatre, composing scores such as that for *Much Ado about Nothing* (1936). Moving from theatre to opera in the 1930s, Khrennikov wrote *V Buryu* (1939). He received many state awards for his film scores and became an outspoken advocate of Soviet trends of socialist realism in music and the arts. Khrennikov was made head of the Soviet Composers Union during the late 1940s in the purge which accused **Prokofiev** among others of anti-Soviet beliefs and practices. In 1963 he was appointed to the Moscow Conservatoire to teach composition, and on his 60th birthday was made a Hero of the Soviet Union to commemorate his work.

khyāl (India) Principal classical vocal genre in northern Indian music, which developed from **dhrupad** during the 18th and 19th centuries. The genre is more ornate than **dhrupad**, with musical virtuosity tending to supersede textual enunciation. Its two sections (**sthāyī** and **antarā**) form the basis of extensive melodic and rhythmic improvisations, including **sargams**. Having virtually replaced the *dhrupad*, many *khyāl* singers now include a slow **ālāp** in the *dhrupad* style.

Kienzl, Wilhelm (1857-1941) Austrian composer who studied under **Rheinberger**. In 1876 he travelled to Bayreuth to attend the first performances of **Wagner**'s *Ring*. This served to confirm Kienzl's growing admiration of Wagner. Following a brief period of study with **Liszt**, Kienzl moved to Bayreuth (1880), where he encountered the social circle that Wagner moved in. It was there that Kienzl was able to lecture on Wagner's work and attend many of Bayreuth's Festivals. Until 1883 he travelled extensively throughout Europe, but his travels were curtailed by his appointment as head of German Opera in Amsterdam. His first opera, *Urvasi*, was completed in 1884. Five years later, Kienzl was conducting in both Munich and Hamburg. His most famous and successful opera, *Der Evangelmann*, was completed in 1894. Having moved to Vienna in 1917, Kienzl was given the task of composing the anthem of the first German Republic in 1918 to words presented to him by the Austrian Chancellor. After a cycle of three operas with texts written by his second wife, he turned to the composition of choral works and songs. From the 1920s, Kienzl violently opposed the growing atonality of modern composition and in the 1930s watched the popularity of his operas fall into decline.

Kilpinen, Yrjö (1892-1959) Finnish song writer who studied sporadically at the Finnish Music Institute between 1908 and 1917. He moved to Europe and completed his studies in Vienna and Berlin. In 1948 he was elected to the Finnish Academy. Kilpinen's lyric songs evoked the Finnish landscape, and many of them became closely linked to the *lied* tradition. His popularity spread to Germany in the 1930s. Kilpinen has left more than 300 songs (including *Songs of the Fells*, 1929) in published form, and it is believed that he composed at least 500 more.

kinnor Biblical form of lyre, supposedly played by King David. Knowledge about the instrument is limited, although it would

Kinnor

appear that the kinnor was played by hand and is similar to the Greek **kithara**.

Kipnis, Alexander (1896-1978) American bass of Ukranian birth who studied music at the Warsaw Conservatoire and in Berlin. In 1919 Kipnis joined the Charlottenburg Opera where he was leading bass for over a decade. Between 1930 and 1934 (when he became an American citizen), Kipnis sang with the Berlin Staatsoper. He also appeared in many Bayreuth and Salzburg music festivals and was admired for his performances of **Mozart** and **Wagner**. Kipnis' reputation grew and he was to appear in Opera Houses throughout the world, including a season at **Glyndebourne** (1936), where he appeared in *The Magic Flute* as Sarastro. His citizenship followed from his many appearances in the United States, particularly in Chicago where he regularly appeared between 1923 and 1932. After his debut at the Metropolitan Opera House in New York in 1940 as Gurnemanz in *Parsifal*, he settled in the city.

Kipnis retired in 1943 leaving many fine operatic recordings, one of the most critically acclaimed being *Simon Boccanegra* recorded in Berlin in the early 1930s.

Kirchner, Leon (1919-) American composer, conductor and pianist who studied at Los Angeles City College and later at the University of California with **Schoenberg**. Before World War II he spent some time working with Roger **Sessions**, and after 1945 he took up various teaching posts.

As a conductor Kirchner is well known for his interpretations of **Mozart** and **Schubert**. As a composer, he has received many awards, including the Pulitzer Prize for his *Third Quartet with Electronic Tape* (1966). Although influenced by Schoenberg, there are seen to be strong Classical strains in his compositions.

Kirkpatrick, Ralph (1911-1984) American harpsichord player, scholar and editor who studied piano from the age of six, turning to the harpsichord in 1930 while studying at Harvard. He also studied in Paris with **Boulanger** and **Landowska**. His debut as a harpsichord player was at Cambridge, Massachusetts. After his European debut, performing **Bach**'s *Goldberg Variations* to great acclaim in Berlin, he toured Europe and the United States. He is well known for his repertory of 18th-century keyboard music, including all of Bach's keyboard works and **Scarlatti**'s sonatas. His love of **Mozart**'s works brought him to a teaching post in the Salzburg Mozarteum in 1933.

kithara Ancient Greek instrument similar to the **lyre**. It had between three and twelve strings that were plucked, a large square resonator at the base and an upper crossbar.

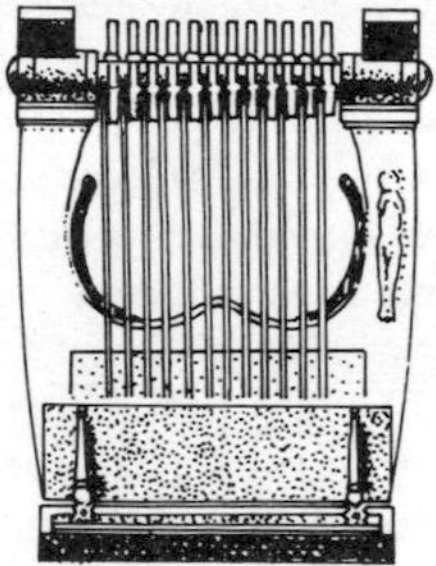

Kithara

Kjerulf, Halfdan (1815-1868) Norwegian composer and pianist who did not formally study music until 1849 (with Carl Arnold at Christiania, Oslo), long after his first compositions (*Six Songs, Op. 1*) were published. He then travelled to Copenhagen and Leipzig and studied with Richter at the Leipzig Conservatoire. On his return to Norway (1851) he settled down to earn a living as a piano teacher. Kjerulf was a prolific composer, particularly after his period of study in Leipzig and Copenhagen. His songs show varied influences, including that of **Schumann** and **Schubert**, but it is his links with folk music that have made Kjerulf so crucial to the development of Norwegian music. Pieces such as *Ingrids Vise Op. 6 No. 4* (1859) are modelled on traditional Norwegian dance rhythms. He is also remembered for his settings of many texts to music, including poems by King Carl XV. His piano works bring to bear Romantic and typically Norwegian themes, works such as *Brureslatt* (1861) clearly paving the way for later Norwegian composers, particularly **Grieg**.

Klavier (Ger.) Originally used to describe any keyboard instrument, but in modern usage it generally refers to the piano. In French, the word is spelled *clavier*.

Klavierauszug (Ger.) Score of a work arranged for piano; a piano score.

Klebe, Giselher (1925-) German composer who studied with Kurt von Wolfurt, and with Rufer and Boris **Blacher**. From 1946 to 1949 he worked for Berlin Radio as a programmer. However, it was his orchestral compositions, such as *Die Zwitschermaschine* (1950), that brought him acclaim. In 1957 Klebe was elected to the Royal Academy of the Arts, Berlin.

Wilfully experimental, Klebe has sought to widen the expressive possibilities of composition at the expense of more traditional themes and elements. He has composed operas as well as modern instrumental pieces. Klebe's diversity is shown by his ten operas, which are more approachable than his avant-garde leanings would suggest.

Klecki Alternative spelling of the name of Paul **Kletzki**.

Kleftic/Klephtic song (Greece) Songs which relate to the heroic deeds of the Klefts in battles against the Turks. They are unmeasured (although some have instrumental interludes in 7/8), highly ornate and melismatic, with an imitative accompaniment usually played by a trio of clarinet, violin and lute.

Kleiber, Erich (1890-1956) Austrian conductor who was taught violin in Vienna, and who attended the court opera, then directed by **Mahler**. In 1908 he attended Prague University and Conservatoire, and in 1911 was appointed to the post of chorus-master to the German Theatre, Prague. He made his conducting debut at the Berlin Staatsoper, and he was appointed general music director, succeeding Leo Bloch. In 1924 he conducted Janáček's *Jenufa*, the performance of which established him firmly as one of the leading conductors of the day. He also premiered **Berg**'s *Wozzeck* (1925). He left Germany in 1935 and toured the world. Kleiber was considered at his best conducting the works of **Mozart** and **Beethoven**, and for his minute attention to the score. In particular he has left critically-acclaimed recordings of Beethoven's symphonies.

Klemperer, Otto (1885-1973) Jewish-born German conductor and composer who attended the Frankfurt Conservatoire, studying piano with James Kwast and theory with Ivan Knorr. In 1905 he met **Mahler** while conducting that composer's Symphony No. 2. On the strength of this

Otto Klemperer

performance, Mahler recommended Klemperer for the post of chorus master and later conductor to the Deutsches Landestheater, Prague, in 1907. It was in these posts, particularly after World War I, that Klemperer firmly established himself as a major German conductor, famous for his wide repertory.

In the 1920s he visited the United States, conducting the New York Symphony Orchestra. In 1925 he was appointed director to the Berlin Staatsoper, where he was to conduct many contemporary works. This became known as the Kroll Opera, and was to lay the foundations for much of this century's modern opera. Political problems with the Weimar Republic in 1931 closed down the theatre which had given premieres of such works as **Stravinsky**'s *Oedipus Rex*, as well as works by **Hindemith**, **Schoenberg**, **Weill** and **Janáček**. This experimental approach was reflected in the choice of contemporary set designers, including Moholy-Nagy. Returning to the Staatsoper in 1933, he conducted *Tannhäuser* to commemorate the 50th anniversary of **Wagner**'s death. The rise of Nazism caused Klemperer to emigrate to the United States, where he was appointed conductor to the New York Philharmonic Orchestra and was able to study with Schoenberg in Los Angeles. A brain tumour operation in 1939 left Klemperer unable to perform until 1947, when he was appointed to the Budapest Opera, a post he held until 1950. He became principal conductor of the Philharmonia Orchestra in 1959 and conductor for life in 1964. He retired in 1972 having been made an honorary member of the British Royal Academy of Music, 1971.

Critics are curiously divided over his interpretations of such composers as **Mozart** and **Brahms**, but the directness of his approach has given him undisputed authority over the works of Mahler.

As well as being a conductor, Klemperer composed more than 100 *Lieder*, six symphonies and an opera, *Das Ziel* (1915).

Klephtic song See **Kleftic**.

Kletzki, Paul (1900-1973) Polish conductor, composer and violinist who studied at the Warsaw Conservatoire and the Berlin Academy. During World War I he joined the Lotz Philharmonic Orchestra and in 1923 made his conducting debut in Berlin, conducting his own compositions. Kletzki left Berlin (1933) for Italy, where he taught composition and orchestration in Milan. In 1937 he was appointed musical director of the Kharkov Philharmonic Orchestra. Settling in Switzerland in 1947, he was offered many conducting posts around the world.

He wrote about 50 compositions, including four symphonies, string quartets and chamber music. Although many compositions were destroyed during World War II, recordings of many of his concerts remain. An alternative spelling of his name is Klecki.

Klien, Walter (1928-) Austrian pianist who studied piano, composition and conducting in Frankfurt, Graz, and finally at the Vienna Academy with Josef Dichler and **Hindemith** (1950-1953). After winning several prizes in the early 1950s he toured Europe, Africa and the Americas, making his debut in the United States in 1969. He has played concertos with many prominent orchestras and conductors. Klien has made many recordings which have justly earned him much critical acclaim, including all of **Schubert**'s piano sonatas and the first complete catalogue of **Brahms**'s compositions for solo piano.

Knight, Joseph Philip (1812-1887) English clergyman and composer. Born in Wiltshire, Knight studied organ with Corfe in Bristol and composed songs from the early 1830s. Visiting the United States for two years (1839-1840), he published his most successful song *Rocked in the Cradle of the Deep*, which displays a strong melody typical of Knight's composition. He returned to live in the Isles of Scilly and in England.

Knussen, Oliver (1952-) English composer, the son of Stuart Knussen, the celebrated double-bass player. Composing from the age of six, Knussen studied with John **Lambert** until 1968 and later with Gunther **Schuller**. At the age of 15 he received much publicity when he conducted his own Symphony No. 1. More recent works such as *Océan de Terre* (1972-1973) have been well received.

Kochanski, Pau (1887-1934) Polish violinist who studied with Emil Mynarski as early as 1894. At the age of 14 he was appointed first violin with the Warsaw Philharmonia. In 1903 he went to Brussels, where he studied with César Thomson at the Brussels Conservatoire. In 1913 Kochanski was appointed professor at the Imperial Conservatoire, St Petersburg, and it was there that he first met and promoted the violin concertos of **Szymanowski**. He also collaborated with Szymanowski on works such as *Mity* (1915) and the Concerto No. 1 (1916). A spell on the staff of the Kiev Conservatoire was curtailed by the Russian Revolution. Leaving Russia he emigrated to the United States in 1921, where he was invited to appear with the New York Symphony Orchestra. In 1924, while still making concert appearances, Kochanski joined the staff of the Juilliard School.

Köchel, Ludwig von (1800-1877) Austrian music bibliographer, best known for his **Mozart** catalogue. Born in Vienna, Köchel studied at the University of Vienna and by 1827 was tutor to the four sons of Archduke Carl. Devoted to the works of Mozart, Köchel was prompted to order the previously uncatalogued compositions into a chronological list. The catalogue that Köchel subsequently produced featured the first few bars of each work, which for the first time were given a catalogue number, any manuscript source and finally a reference to the contemporary biography by Kahn. Mozart himself began cataloguing his works after 1784, but Köchel had to contend with 450 compositions to order, many undated. The catalogue, *Chronologisch-Thematisches Verzeichnis Sämtlicher Tonwerke Wolfgang Amadeus Mozart* was first published in 1862. It had no antecedents and despite subsequent revision remains a standard text on the subject.

Kodály, Zoltán (1882-1967) Hungarian composer and educationist who studied at Budapest University. The period of his life spent in rural Hungary (until the age of 18) was significant for the volume of folk music that he must have encountered and which provided the basis for a lifetime's work. Coming from a musical background, Kodály studied Hungarian and German, and while in Budapest he enrolled at the Academy of Music. It was there that he was to study composition with Koessler. During this period he began a series of many journeys around Hungary collecting folk tunes and met **Bartók**, who shared his passion for the music. In 1906, before Kodály travelled in Europe, they collaborated on the text *Hungarian Folksongs*. With the scholarship that had been awarded to Kodály he travelled to Berlin and Paris where he studied with **Widor**. On his return Kodály was appointed professor of music theory at the Academy. It was not until 1910 that Kodály's compositions Opp. 2, 3 and 4, were publicly performed by Bartók and a quartet. The following year Kodály and Bartók together founded the New Hungarian Music Society, with the

Zoltán Kodály

intention of bringing to the fore contemporary Hungarian music. Throughout World War I, Kodály continued to collect and classify Hungarian folk music and by the time the war ended, he was working as a critic writing primarily on the work of Bartók. In 1921 the much-acclaimed work *Psalmus Hungaricus* was published. This composition, based on a 16th-century religious work, received its first performance, 1923. Following this success Kodály wrote the opera *Háry János* (1926). As well as composing, Kodály travelled extensively in the late 1920s as guest composer, appearing in Cambridge and London in 1927. At home in Hungary, Kodály turned his attention to musical education and in a decade radically revised the teaching of music in schools.

In 1934 Bartók emigrated, leaving Kodály with the task of compiling a major summary of Hungarian folk music. During World War II, Kodály was to compose several heroic songs, including *Miracle of God*. The end of conflict saw Kodály showered with accolades both for his compositions and for his teaching methods. This recognition continued throughout the 1940s–1960s, and he was made president of the Hungarian Art Council as well as receiving many honorary doctorates from all over the world. Throughout his life he pursued two main fields: that of music education and the study of Hungarian folk music. Before his death his major text *Corpus Musicae Popularis Hungaricae* had begun publication, and thorough musical education had been introduced into most of Hungary's schools.

Koechlin, Charles (1867-1950) French composer and teacher who studied at the Paris Conservatoire from 1890. It was there that he studied composition with **Fauré** from 1896. With other pupils including **Ravel**, the Société Musicale Independante was founded with the intention of promoting new music. By the end of World War I, Koechlin was prominent in Parisian music circles and was acquainted with major figures such as **Satie**. By the 1930s Koechlin had made two lecture tours of the United States and had become a notable critic and theorist, which overshadowed his compositional work. However, a cycle based on Rudyard Kipling's *Jungle Book* occupied him until World War II. Koechlin's wide-ranging influences are shown by the many pieces written in homage to female film stars of the 1930s, works such as *Five dances for Ginger* (1937).

Kogan, Leonid (1924-1982) Soviet violinist who studied at the Central Music School at the age of ten and later at the Moscow Conservatoire, where he became a tutor. His reputation as a violinist spread while he was still a student, and he made his performing debut in Moscow at the age of 17. Travelling widely throughout Europe and the Americas in the 1950s, he was awarded the Lenin Prize in 1965. His repertory includes all of **Bach**'s solo works as well as **Paganini**'s caprices and many classical concertos.

Kokkonen, Joonas (1921-) Finnish composer who studied at the Sibelius Academy and read musicology at Helsinki University. He returned to the Sibelius Academy as a lecturer and in 1959 as professor of composition. Kokkonen has composed for the stage and orchestra, as well as chamber music and choral works. The opera *The Last Temptations* (1975) proved to be a major break from his earlier works, influenced as they were by strongly Finnish elements, and **Bartók**.

komagaku (Japan) Music of the right, in **gagaku** court music. Influenced by Korean and Manchurian forms it is associated with the colour green. It is differentiated from **Togaku**, or 'music of the left', that of Chinese origin, by its instrumentation and absence of stringed instruments. *Komagaku* is used to accompany **bugaku** dance and never as a separate orchestral form or **kangen**.

kŏmun'go (Korea) Ancient, native, plucked **zither** with six strings of twisted silk.

Three strings, tuned by adjusting pegs, pass over fixed bridges whereas the remaining three pass over moveable bridges.

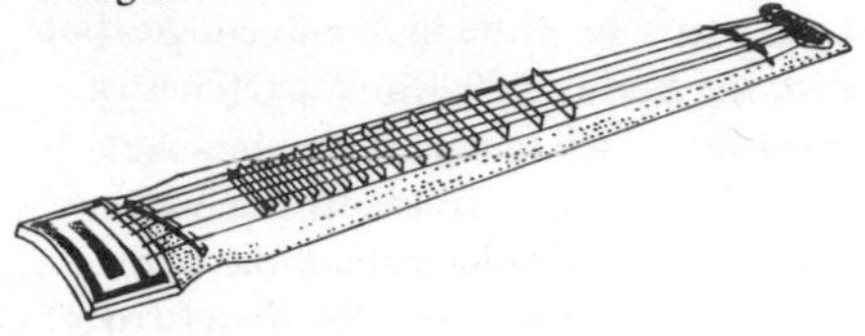

Kŏmun'go

Kontarsky, Aloys (1931-) German pianist who studied at the Cologne Musikhochschule with F. Maurits Frank (1952-1957). In 1955 he and his brother Alfons won acclaim by winning the prize for piano duo in Munich's Radio Festival. Following this, the brothers toured extensively together. While their repertory includes work by **Mozart** and **Debussy**, it is Kontarsky's abiding interest in modern music that has brought him much respect with performances, many of them premieres, of the works of **Stockhausen**, **Zimmerman** and **Kagel**, among others. In 1960 he joined the staff of the Darmstadt New Music Festivals.

Kontrabass (Ger.) German equivalent of **double-bass**.

Kontrafagott (Ger.) German equivalent of **double bassoon**.

Konzertmeister (Ger.) The **leader** of an orchestra.

kora (Africa) Stringed instrument with a sound box, large bridge and 21 strings. The sound box is a large, half-calabash with skin stretched over it and a sound hole. Strictly, it should be referred to as a harp-lute, because the size of the bridge combined with the placing of the strings, ten on one side and eleven on the other, bring it as much into line with the harp family as the lute. Strings are tuned differently according to the geographical area in which the instrument is found.

Korngold, Eric Wolfgang (1897-1957) Austrian composer who later assumed American citizenship and proved to be exceptionally talented from an early age. At the age of ten, he was introduced to **Mahler**, on whose recommendation he was sent to Vienna, where he studied with Fuchs and **Zemlinsky**. His pantomime *Der Schneemann* was performed at the Vienna Court Opera in 1910, and following its resounding success he composed the Piano Concerto in E, which gained attention throughout Europe. His opera *Violanta* (1916) was lauded by many, including **Puccini**, and the opera *Die Tote Stadt*, composed at the age of 20, is considered a masterpiece. In the late 1920s Korngold was appointed a professor at the Vienna Staatsakademie at a time when public acclaim placed him on a par with **Schoenberg**. Korngold travelled to Hollywood and turned his attention to film music; two of his scores, including *Robin Hood*, won Oscars. After World War II, he composed many pieces, including a Violin Concerto (1945), and spent an increasing amount of time in Europe and Vienna.

Kósa, György (1897-1984) Hungarian pianist and composer who studied piano with **Bartók** at the age of ten and later at the Budapest Academy under **Kodály** until 1912. During World War I he was appointed co-répétiteur at the Budapest Royal Opera House and performed in the premiere of Bartók's *Wooden Prince*. Until the 1920s he travelled through Europe, returning to Budapest where he was appointed professor of piano at the Budapest Academy in 1927; he was to hold this post until 1960. With other prominent Hungarian musicians including **Kadosa**, he was a founder member of the Society of Modern Hungarian Musicians wherein he expressed an interest in both contemporary music and traditional composition. After World War II, he returned to concert performances as well as composing pieces such as *Fantasy on Three Folksongs* (1948). In 1972 he was made an Honoured Artist of the Hungarian People's Republic.

Kostelanetz, André (1901-1980) American conductor, Russian by birth. After studying at the St Petersburg Conservatoire, he left for the United States (1922), where he was appointed as a rehearsal accompanist at the Metropolitan Opera, New York, and conductor of the CBS Radio Network (1930). As well as becoming involved with American cinema and radio broadcasting, he organized concerts for the American forces in World War II. He is chiefly remembered for his popular concerts of classical music, conducted in a typically vivacious style, and for his arrangements of light music.

koto (Japan) Horizontal plucked zither, about 2m (6ft) long, with 13 silk strings and moveable bridges. The body is constructed from two pieces of paulownia wood of which one is hollowed out to form a sound box. The inside of the instrument is carved with special patterns to improve the tone. The strings are plucked with ivory picks, *tsume*, which are fitted on to the middle three fingers of the right hand. Strings may be played open or may be pressed down, or twisted with fingers of the left hand to produce variations in pitch of up to a whole tone. See also **danmono**.

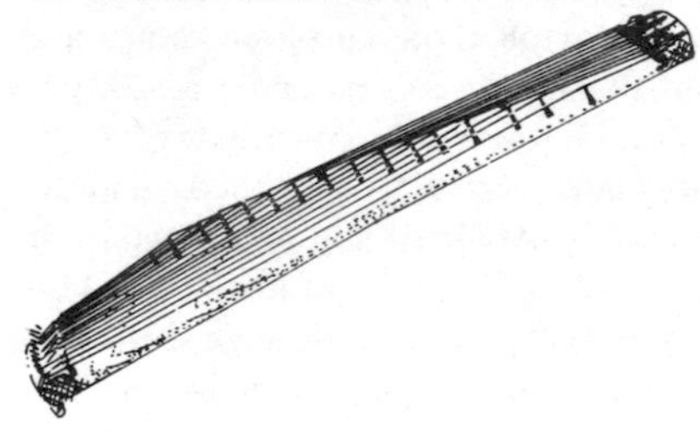

Koto

Koussevitsky, Serge (1874-1951) American conductor, Russian by birth who became a pupil at the Moscow Philharmonic Music School (1898), studying double-bass with Rambousek. From 1894 he toured Europe with the Bolshoi Theatre Orchestra, and received much acclaim in Berlin with a double-bass recital in 1903. The repertory for the double-bass being somewhat limited, Koussevitsky adapted and composed several pieces, giving the premiere of a double-bass concerto in 1905. In that year he resigned from the Bolshoi Orchestra and travelled to Germany in 1908 where he made his conducting debut with the Berlin Philharmonic Orchestra. His abilities led to a guest conducting post with the London Symphony Orchestra. In 1909 he established a publishing house which was to print works by **Stravinsky**, **Rachmaninov**, **Prokofiev** and others. He founded an orchestra in order to give greater exposure to composers he favoured, as well as playing traditional pieces. Throughout his life in Europe and after 1924 in the United States, Koussevitsky championed the cause of modern music, commissioning or premiering such pieces as Stravinsky's *Symphony of Psalms* and **Ravel**'s Piano Concerto. Koussevitsky established the Berkshire Music Center in the United States and began to teach conducting; Leonard **Bernstein** was his pupil and successor. He received many honorary degrees and in memory of his wife established the Koussevitsky Music Foundation to commission new work from around the world, the first opera commissioned being **Britten**'s *Peter Grimes*. He has left many recordings, those of **Tchaikovsky**'s symphonies being particularly highly regarded.

Koutzen, Boris (1901-1966) Russian composer and violinist who emigrated to the United States at the age of 21. While at the Moscow Conservatoire, he studied composition with **Glière** and violin with Leo Zetlin. On his arrival in the United States, Koutzen joined the Philadelphia Orchestra and was appointed to the staff of the Philadelphia Conservatoire as violin teacher. His works such as the Violin Concerto (1952) retain a distinctly Russian flavour.

Kovacevich, Stephen See **Bishop-Kovacevich, Stephen**

krakowiak Polish dance in quick 2/4 time originating in the region of Kracow, sometimes introduced into ballrooms and ballets in the 19th century under the name *Cracovienne*. Originally it was danced by assembled groups of dancers with improvised singing. **Chopin** composed *Krakowiak* (1828), a concerto rondo for orchestra.

Krauss, Clemens (1893-1954) Austrian conductor who studied at the Vienna Conservatoire with Reinhold. At the age of 19 Krauss was appointed director of the Brno State Theatre Choir. A succession of appointments throughout the years of World War I led to a post as conductor of the Vienna State Opera and an appointment as teacher of conducting at the Vienna Academy (1922). In 1929 Krauss travelled to the United States and on the strength of this tour was appointed musical director of the Munich Opera (1937) until the outbreak of World War II. A close friend of Richard **Strauss**, Krauss wrote the libretto of Strauss's opera *Capriccio*.

Krebs, Johann Ludwig (1713-1780) German composer and organist who entered the Thomasschule, Leipzig in 1726, where he studied the lute, violin and organ. He remained there for nine years and was for some of this time a pupil of **Bach**. Throughout his life he only held three posts. The first was as organist to the Marienkirche, Zwickau (starting 1737). He acted as organist at Zeitz Castle for 12 years, followed by a spell at the castle of Prince Friedrich of Altenberg, where he composed the Concerto in A minor for two harpsichords. Krebs left a large canon of work, highly regarded even during his own lifetime. Despite difficulties in attributing some of the early work, many of his organ pieces including a fugue based on the name B-A-C-H are undoubtedly his own, and others are based on Bach's work. Many of his organ compositions were posthumously published, whereas other pieces for clavier and lute were circulated widely during his own lifetime.

Kreisler, Fritz (1875-1962) Austrian-born composer and violinist who as a child

Fritz Kreisler

studied violin under Jacques **Auber**, and then at Vienna and the Paris Conservatoire, graduating in 1887 with a gold medal. He then toured the United States for two years. Kreisler abandoned the violin to study medicine and to enter the army. After a period of military service he returned with a debut with the Berlin Philharmonic Orchestra led by **Nikisch**. This performance brought him much acclaim and he returned to the United States, this time touring as a soloist. In 1910 Kreisler appeared in Britain with the premiere of **Elgar**'s Violin Concerto, a piece specially composed for him. He took American citizenship during World War II.

Kreisler has been much admired for his effortless performance as well as a characteristic vibrato technique. He was also a composer of some note, composing an operetta *Apple Blossoms* (1919) as well as numerous imitative works which, until he admitted the forgery in 1935, were believed to be works by 18th-century composers.

Krenek, Ernst (1900-) Austrian composer, mainly of avant-garde operas, who studied in Vienna and Berlin. Throughout the

1920s Krenek composed many works and travelled to and Paris where he was much influenced by the French music of the time. He married the daughter of **Mahler** and was influenced for a time by that composer's work. From 1925 to 1927 he worked at the opera houses in Kassel and Wiesbaden, and while in Kassel wrote the memorable *Jonny Spielt Auf*, a 'jazz opera' which has been translated into many languages and performed throughout the world. This success was followed by several one-act operas for which he wrote both music and libretti. Despite a public denouncement of **Schoenberg**'s **twelve-note** system, Krenek turned increasingly to this form in the 1930s, in such works as the opera *Karl V* (1930-1933). This was to bring him into increasing disfavour with the Nazis in the late 1930s, and in 1938 he emigrated to the United States. After World War II Krenek wrote several operas including the successful *Der Goldene Bock* (1963), amalgamating classical issues and contemporary popular culture in the United States. Krenek also interested himself in electronic music in the 1960s.

Kreutzer, Conradin (1780-1849) German composer and conductor who is known to have met **Haydn** in Vienna (1894) and who, it is believed, studied under **Albrechtsberger**. While in Stuttgart in 1812, his opera *Konradin von Schwaben* was staged and he was appointed court conductor on the strength of this. Although employed as *Kapellmeister* to Prince Carl Egon, he became conductor in Vienna following the success of another opera *Libussa* (1822). The period spent in Vienna marked the height of Kreutzer's success with operas such as *Der Verschwender*. Although he became musical director to Hamburg and his operas reached a large audience throughout Germany, the rise of **Wagner** in the mid-1800s inevitably overshadowed this success.

Kreutzer, Rodolphe (1766-1831) French violinist, composer and teacher who was himself taught violin and composition from 1778 by Anton **Stamitz**. At the age of 14 he played a concerto in Paris composed by his tutor. This early performance won him much acclaim. On the strength of his growing reputation, he was appointed first violin with the Chapelle de Roi. In the mid-1780s he became known to Marie Antoinette and the French nobility. During this period he was composing sacred music and performing his own violin concertos. Moving to Paris in 1789, he wrote his first opera *Jeanne D'Arc*, performed in 1790. This was the first of more than 40 operas many of which were to establish him as a foremost composer. He also wrote studies and violin sonatas.

Krieger, Johann Philipp (1649-1725) German composer and organist whose biographical details vary between sources. He is known to have studied with Johann Dretzel and Gabriel Schütz in Nuremburg. He is believed to have been extraordinarily precocious, composing arias and performing to much acclaim at the age of nine. In his mid-teens Krieger travelled to Copenhagen, where he became pupil and assistant of Royal Danish organist Johannes Schroder. In 1670 he was appointed chamber composer to the Bayreuth court and in this capacity travelled to Italy where he studied the clavier and composition. In 1677 he became court organist in Halle, and *Kapellmeister* to the court of Weissenfels in 1680, where he performed both secular and religious works. Krieger is considered by many to have been one of the foremost composers of his day, with a canon of more than 2,000 sacred cantatas alone; many of the texts after 1704 were written by Erdmann Neumeister. Considering Krieger's reputation for virtuosity as a keyboardist, very few keyboard compositions are known to exist.

Krips, Josef (1902-1974) Austrian conductor and violinist who became violinist, and later chorus master and *répétiteur* at the Volkoper while still studying at the Vienna Academy. Krips went on to study opera at the city theatres of Aussig (1924) and

Dortmund (1925). In 1933, following a lengthy period as musical director in Karlsruhe, he became conductor of the Vienna Staatsoper and was then made professor at the Academy in 1935. Following World War II, Krips was able to resume his post with the Vienna Staatsoper and relaunched the famous Salzburg Festival in 1946 with a memorable production of **Mozart**'s *Don Giovanni.* A tour of Europe in the 1940s was followed by a series of posts, including conductor of the London Symphony Orchestra (1950-1954) and the San Francisco Symphony Orchestra (1963-1970). Krips also made many fine recordings.

Kubelík, Rafael (1914-) Czech composer and conductor who later took Swiss nationality. After a period of study at the Prague Conservatoire, Kubelík made his conducting debut in 1934 with the Czech Philharmonic Orchestra. In 1950 he was appointed musical director of the Chicago Symphony Orchestra and introduced many modern works into the repertory of mostly classical pieces. He premiered **Bloch**'s *Suite Hebraique* in 1953. From 1955 to 1958 Kubelík was appointed musical director at Covent Garden, where he performed the original version of **Mussorgsky**'s *Boris Godunov* as well as giving the British premiere of **Janáček**'s *Jenufa.* The appointment of Kubelík to the post of chief conductor of the Bavarian Radio Symphony Orchestra gave him the opportunity to record many pieces, including works by Janáček and **Schoenberg**. As well as performing all of **Mahler**'s symphonies, he toured extensively to Japan and the United States and accepted numerous conducting posts. Although chiefly known as a conductor, Kubelík has composed several operas, perhaps the most famous being *Veronika* (1947), several concertos and a requiem.

Rafael Kubelík

Kuhlau, Daniel Friedrich Rudolph (1786-1832) German-born composer and pianist, later to assume Danish citizenship. Kuhlau studied theory and composition in Hamburg with Schwenke. It was in Hamburg that his first compositions for flute and piano are known to have been composed and published. Kuhlau was forced to flee Napoleon's invasion and travelled to Copenhagen, where he was to lead the most successful part of his life. In 1811 he performed his own Piano Concerto Op. 7 to great acclaim, and in 1813 became court musician. A year later his stage work *The Robbers' Castle* proved successful and in 1817 his first opera was performed. As a result of his piano recitals throughout Scandinavia, he travelled to Vienna and met **Beethoven** in 1825. Modern audiences are perhaps most familiar with the oft-revived play *The Fairy's Mound*, for which Kuhlau wrote the incidental music.

Kuhnau, Johann (1660-1722) German composer, keyboard player and theorist who studied at the Kreuzschule in Dresden with Soloman Krüger. He became cantor and organist of the Johanneskirche and studied law at the University of Leipzig, as well as becoming well known for his performances while a student. In 1701 Kuhnau was appointed cantor to the Thomaskirche and taught several subjects, including singing at the Thomasschule. Throughout the early 1700s he directed music at Leipzig's various churches. Kuhnau's successor to the post of cantor at the Thomasschule was to be **Bach**. As a composer, Kuhnau is chiefly remembered for his many keyboard sonatas, such as the biblical narratives *Biblische Historien* (1700). He is also thought to have composed more than 100 secular songs, now lost.

Kullak, Theodor (1818-1882) German pianist and teacher. His first piano recital was in Berlin at the age of 11, performed in front of the King. While reading medicine in Berlin in 1837 he studied music with Siegfried Dehn. He was later to study with **Czerny** in Vienna and in 1843 became Prussian court pianist after a period as teacher to Vienna's nobility. In 1850 with Stern and Marx he founded the Berlin Conservatoire, and in 1855 established the Neue Akademie.

kumiuta (Japan) Suite of songs, consisting of a fixed sequence of short and often unrelated poems, accompanied by either the **koto** zither or the **shamisen** lute. These suites often consisted of *kouta* (short songs) with wistful or romantic sentiments and which lent themselves very well to use in geisha parties.

Kurtág, György (1926-) Hungarian composer, born in Romania. He studied in Hungary with **Kadosa**, **Weiner** and **Veress**, and in Paris with **Messiaen**. From 1958 Kurtág was coach and tutor to the **Bartók** Secondary Music School and to the National Philharmonia. In 1967 he was appointed professor of piano and chamber music to the Budapest Academy. Kurtág's output has been far from prolific, and works such as String Quartet Op. 1 (1959) owe a debt to the modernism of his education as well as more traditional Renaissance and Baroque elements. Kurtág's most highly regarded work is almost certainly *The Sayings of Peter Bornemisza* (1963-1968), a concerto for soprano and piano, based on an old Hungarian sermon.

Kurz, Selma (1874-1933) Austrian soprano who made her debut in Hamburg in 1895 in the role of Mignon. In 1899 she played the role at the Vienna Court Opera at the invitation of **Mahler**. It was in Vienna that she was most successful, performing such roles as Tosca before moving to such **coloratura** roles as Violetta in *La Traviata*, in which her clear voice came to the fore. She appeared to rapt audiences at Covent Garden for three successive seasons from 1904 as Gilda and in *Rigoletto*.

Kuula, Toivo (1883-1918) Finnish composer and conductor who studied in Helsinki and Europe, before being appointed conductor of the Oulu Orchestra in 1910. From 1911 to 1916 he became assistant conductor of the Helsinki Philharmonia and later conductor of the Viipuri Orchestra. Critics are divided as to his prowess as a composer, some calling him the foremost Finnish composer of his age. Works such as *Morning Song* (1905) show a link with Finnish Romanticism, prevalent at the time and obviously influenced by **Sibelius**.

kyemyŏnjo (Korea) One of the most commonly used **pentatonic** modes, corresponding to the notes A, C, D, E, G.

L

L Abbreviation of Longo, used to number the works of Domenico **Scarlatti**. Longo refers to Alessandro Longo, the compiler of the catalogue of Scarlatti's works (1906-1908). See also **Kirkpatrick, Ralph**.

la Sixth note of the scale as named in **tonic sol-fa**.

la Halle (or Hale), Adam de (*c*1237-1287) French **trouvère** poet and composer. Very little biographical information survives, but he is believed to have been born in Arras and to have studied in Paris. These studies are mentioned in his song *Le Jeu d'Adam* (1276-1277). Soon after this time he travelled to Italy, where he served the court of Artois and it is believed that he was involved with Italy's war with the Sicilians. While serving his uncle in Italy, he composed the pastoral *Le Jeu de Robin et de Marion* (1285). La Halle wrote in many of the styles of the day, composing monographic *chansons* and the famous *jeux partis*, an early comic 'opera' form, as well as many polyphonic works and motets.

Lalande, Michel Richard de Alternative, but incorrect spelling of **Delalande**, Michel Richard.

Lalo, Victor Antoine Edouard (1823-1892) French composer who studied violin with Habeneck at the Paris Conservatoire, as well as taking composition privately. During the 1830s, Lalo spent time teaching, but he also played violin in concerts given by **Berlioz**. In 1848, after composing symphonies and some songs, the best of these along with some violin pieces reached publication in *Six Romances Populaires*. Lalo also composed chamber music, a neglected medium in the 1850s, and in 1855 founded the Armingaud-Jacquard Quartet to play classical quartets. His own String Quartet was published in 1859. In 1865 he married Bernier de Maligny, a contralto who sang many of his songs to much popular acclaim. In 1866 Lalo wrote his first opera *Fiesque*. Although it was never performed, he was to draw upon it extensively for later works such as the Symphony in G Minor and the *Divertissement* (1872). It was not until the mid-1870s that Lalo was to achieve widespread acclaim with several orchestral compositions, such as the flamboyant *Symphonie Espagnole* (1875). Throughout the 1870s he devoted himself almost entirely to orchestral works, except for music written to accompany a libretto by Edouard Blau called *Le Roi d'Ys*. This was not to be performed as a complete opera until 1888, when it was eventually hailed as a masterpiece by French audiences.

Lambert, Constant (1905-1951) English conductor, composer and musicologist. He won a scholarship to the Royal College of Music at the age of 17 and was taught by Morris and **Vaughan Williams** and it was at this time that he showed an early love for French and Russian music. In 1926 he performed (with Edith Sitwell) in Walton's *Façade*, a work dedicated to Lambert. At this time he also met Diaghilev, who commissioned the ballet *Romeo and Juliet*. It was also in the mid-1920s that he was to

Constant Lambert

become greatly influenced by jazz, the orchestral work *Elegiac Blues* (1927) being dedicated to the film star Florence Mills. *Rio Grande*, based on a poem by Sacheverell Sitwell, was broadcast by the BBC and premiered in performance by the Hallé Orchestra (1929), bringing a great deal of attention to the young composer. In 1931 Lambert was appointed musical director of the Sadler's Wells Ballet (later the Royal Ballet) until after World War II, receiving praise for his conducting ability. Ill-health prevented him completing many compositions in the years immediately preceding the war and yet many of the works of the time, including *Horoscope* (1937), were highly regarded. His last ballet, *Tiresias*, received an indifferent public response on its Covent Garden premiere in 1951. It has never been published.

Unconcerned by popular tastes, Lambert drew his influences from many sources. In the 1930s and 1940s he made several guest appearances with the Hallé and other orchestras and made more than 50 broadcasts, including the premiere broadcast of Satie's *Socrates*. He also wrote a provocative and influential book, *Music Ho! A Study of Music in Decline* (1934).

lament Scottish or Irish music played on the **bagpipes**, normally on the occasion of a funeral or some other sorrowful event. It is also a composition written to commemorate the death of a distinguished person. Early laments were those composed on the deaths of Charlemagne (814) and Richard I (1199). More recent examples include **Ravel**'s *Le Tombeau de Couperin* (1917) and **Stravinsky**'s *Elegy for J.F. Kennedy* (1964).

Lamoureux, Charles (1834-1899) French conductor and violinist who studied at the Paris Conservatoire with Girard, taking first prize for violin (1852 and 1854). From the age of 16 he played with the Théâtre du Gymnase Orchestra and the Opéra. Having heard compositions for large choirs in his European travels, he financed a performance of **Handel**'s *Messiah* (1873) as well as **Bach's** *St Matthew Passion* (1874). The subsequent popularity of these enabled him to start the Société Française de L'Harmonie Sacrée in the same year. He conducted performances of works by Handel, **Massenet** and others. He was appointed conductor of the Paris Opéra (1877-1879), whereupon he became conductor to the Nouveaux Concerts (1881) and became a champion of the music of **Wagner** in Paris. With Wagner's permission he produced *Lohengrin* in 1887. Strong anti-German feeling in France eventually jeopardized many of these performances. He visited London each season from 1896, performing with Sir Henry **Wood** in 1899.

Landi, Steffano (*c*1587-1639) Italian composer, singer and teacher. In 1610 he was appointed organist to one church and in 1611 singer to another. In 1618 Landi was appointed *maestro di cappella* by the Bishop of Padua, who became dedicatee of Landi's published book of madrigals. In the following year Landi completed his first opera, *La Morte d'Orfeo*. In 1620, on his return to Rome, Landi's first book of arias was published. In Rome, it is believed that Landi held a variety of posts, as teacher, clerical composer and again as *maestro di cappella*. In 1629 he was honoured with an appointment to the Papal choir. Following this, in the early 1630s, Landi's best-remembered opera *Il Sant' Alessio* was performed. Although suffering from ill-health in the latter part of his life, Landi composed many more arias.

Landini (or Landino), Francesco (*c*1325-1397) Italian instrumentalist and composer. Few details of his early life in Florence are recorded. However, he is known to have lost his sight at an early age. He composed and wrote poetry as well as building organs. He is believed to have been organist at the monastery of Santa Trinita (1361) and as a virtuoso became known as *Francesco degli organi*. He is also thought to have been organist at San Lorenzo for many years. In the 1370s he is known to have built organs both in Santa Annunziata and Florence Cathedral. Landini wrote in many styles prevalent in 14th-century Italy. Many of his works, both secular and sacred, survive, those from the late 14th century displaying popular French influences. In Florence he was considered the most famous exponent of **Ars nova**.

Landowska, Wanda (1879-1959) Polish keyboard player who studied at the Warsaw Conservatoire. In 1896 she studied composition with Urban in Berlin. Her admiration for **Bach** and her prowess as a pianist by the early 1900s earned her a great deal of attention. She researched extensively into 17th- and 18th-century composition and its performance, and became convinced of the value of the harpsichord – at that time an underestimated instrument. She made her harpsichord debut in 1903. Landowska travelled extensively, giving masterclasses in harpsichord. In 1923 she toured the United States with a harpsichord built to her own specification. It was on this occasion that she made her first recordings. In the mid-1920s she was performing her own compositions for the instrument. In 1940 she travelled to Switzerland and later to the United States, where she toured and continued her recordings until her 70s. She was highly regarded for her sense of purpose in her interpretations as well as her understanding of Baroque music and modern techniques.

Langlais, Jean (1907-) French composer and organist who studied in Paris with **Dupré** and went on to win the Paris Conservatoire's Premier Prix in 1930. It was there that he was to study composition with **Dukas**, alongside **Messiaen**. In the early 1930s he became organist of St Pierre de Montrouge, and after World War II became organist of St Clothilde. Most of Langlais's compositions have been religious organ works, loosely based on **plainsong**.

Lanner, Joseph Franz Karl (1801-1843) Austrian dance composer and violinist. Lanner was self-taught and in 1813 joined Pamer's dance orchestra in Vienna, playing alongside Johann **Strauss**. In 1818 he formed a trio, joined later by Johann Strauss as violinist. By 1820 the group had grown to a quintet playing at the heart of Vienna's cultural centre, becoming a full and unwieldy orchestra within the decade. It was therefore disbanded into two smaller orchestras led by Lanner and Strauss, each with its own fervent followers. Lanner's orchestra toured extensively, playing at the Coronation of Frederick II in Milan. Lanner and Strauss composed an enormous volume of popular waltzes and dances. Lanner alone composed 207 popular works, thereby helping to establish the waltz as the most popular dance of 19th-century Vienna.

largamente (It.) Indication that a movement or phrase is to be played in a broad manner. See also **largo**.

larghetto (It.) Indication that the music should be played at a tempo not quite so slow as **largo**.

largo (It.) Indication that the music should be played slowly, in a broad manner.

Larrocha (y de la Calle), Alicia de (1923-) Spanish pianist who gave her first performances at the age of five, going on to study with Marshall at Barcelona, where she was to return as director in 1959. Her concerto debut was at the age of 12 with the Madrid Symphony Orchestra. After World War II she toured extensively in Europe and, in 1955, the United States. In the 1950s and 1960s she was to make several recordings, chiefly of Spanish works by composers such as **Albéniz**, which have earned her much critical acclaim.

Larsson, Lars-Erik (1908-) Swedish composer. He entered the Stockholm Conservatoire in 1925, where he studied composition with Ellberg and conducting with Morales. His Symphony No. 1 was published while he was still a student in Sweden (1927-1928). In 1929 he travelled to Vienna to study with **Berg**. On his return to Sweden he was appointed choirmaster to the Royal Opera in Stockholm as well as teaching in Malmö and Lund. His Sinfonietta (1932) was much acclaimed, and in the late 1930s he was appointed to the Swedish Radio Orchestra as conductor. In 1947 he was appointed professor of composition at the Stockholm Conservatoire and later became director at Uppsala University. Although his early compositions hark back to the prevalent Scandinavian romanticism and classicism, his period of study with Berg changed this, and works of Larsson's dating from 1932 feature the tentative use of the twelve-note technique. Larsson's pre-war period with Swedish Radio saw him concentrating exclusively on film scores and compositions for broadcasting. By the 1960s he had begun to experiment with works such as *Adagio for Strings* (1960), with his own **twelve-note** scale.

La Rue, Pierre de (*c*1460-1518) Flemish tenor and composer. In 1483 he joined Siena Cathedral choir, and in the 1490s he entered the chapel of Maximilian of Austria, remaining there under Maximilian's successor. He held various posts (both ecclesiastical and courtly) in Europe until his return to Holland in 1508. He became singer to the court at Mechlin and attended the court of Archduke Karl. Although La Rue is known to have been an important composer in his day, few of his compositions date from his period spent in Italy. The majority of his works are masses dating from the 1500s. He also composed *chansons*, 30 of which can be attributed, with near certainty, to La Rue.

Lassus, Roland de (Orlando di Lasso) (1532-1594) Franco-Flemish composer who is believed to have been a chorister at St Nicholas Church, Mons. Legend has it that he was kidnapped from there three times to sing in other choirs eager to use his talents. He is known to have travelled widely in Europe, in the service of various European households and courts. Lassus' first compositions are believed to date from a period spent at the Accademia de'Sereni in Naples. In the mid-1500s he is known to have travelled to Antwerp, where his first collection of madrigals and motets was printed. In 1555 a volume of five-part madrigals was published. More madrigals, five- and six-part motets and, it is believed, a mass, were all printed before 1556. Throughout the 1550s and 1560s, with visits to Italy and Paris, his reputation grew, and many of his compositions were put into print. Throughout the 1570s he received many accolades, including an order of nobility from Maximilian II. In 1575 his motet *Cantantibus Organis* won the Evreux prize. His five-volume work *Patrocinium Musices* was published during this time, and in the 1580s he had masses, motets, psalms, *chansons*, drinking songs and even German *Lieder* published, all of which showed the influence of his travels. At his death Lassus left a staggering 2,000 works, both sacred and secular, with more than 100 settings of the Magnificat alone. Posthumous reprinting of many of his works ensured that his reputation did not fade.

lauda, laude (It.) Song of praise, widely used in Italy between the 13th and 19th centuries. It is a religious work for several voices, with its own distinctive poetry and sung by a religious confraternity called *laudisti*. It is said that this type of work contributed to the emergence of the **oratorio** in the 17th century.

Lawes, Henry (1596-1662) English composer and singer, elder brother of William **Lawes**. He was employed by the Earl of Bridgewater to teach his daughters, and in 1631 was appointed musician to Charles I. It was at this time that he first met Milton and composed the songs for his *Arcades*. He also met and composed for many of the famous courtly poets of the day, including Herrick, Suckling, Lovelace and Waller. He was employed in many courtly masques, collaborating with his brother in *The Triumph of the Prince d'Amour* (1636). In the 1650s Lawes was also involved in composing for the operas *First Dayes Entertainment at Rutland House* and *The Siege of Rhodes*. He also wrote many ecclesiastical pieces but it is for his songs (more than 400 in total) that he is best remembered. These are collected in surviving editions of *Ayres and Dialogues*, published in the 1650s. Lawes also composed the anthem *Zadok the Priest* for the coronation of Charles II.

Lawes, William (1602-1645) English composer who was taught by his father, and the Earl of Hertford's music tutor, John Coperario. It seems likely that he performed with the young Charles I who was also taught by Coperario. He was appointed musician to Prince, and later King, Charles I. From the early 1630s he composed many songs and instrumental music for the court. Unlike those of his brother, Henry, none of his works were published in his own lifetime. *Choice Psalmes* (1648) contains 40 of his works. Lawes's chamber music was written for the violin. His success as a composer was dominant over his ability to set the poems of the day to appropriate music. Today, even Lawes's stage music is better remembered than his vocal settings, and he is believed to have been the first English composer to feature continuity passages in dramatic works. Many of his compositions show none of the aversion to Italian Baroque music that his brother's displayed. Lawes may be considered a direct precursor to later English composers such as **Purcell**, whose success overshadowed his own.

leader Principal first violinist in an orchestra, string quartet or other chamber music ensemble. The orchestral leader plays any required solo passages, collaborates with the conductor and has certain administrative responsibilites. He or she also determines the bowing to be used by the string section. In the United States, the term is used as an alternative for conductor.

leading-motif English equivalent of **Leitmotiv**.

leading note Seventh note of a major or ascending minor scale, leading to the tonic a semitone above.

Leclair, Jean-Marie (1697-1764) French composer and violinist, who was a capable violinist while still a teenager. An early manuscript from 1721 contains ten sonatas written by Leclair. He is believed to have been ballet master in Turin and to have studied violin under Somis. In the early 1720s Leclair came under the patronage of Joseph Bonnier and his Op. 1 reached publication, earning him an early reputation as a first-rate composer. After that time many of his works for violin were published and he travelled extensively, duetting with Locatelli (whose Italian influence can be clearly heard in Leclair's Op. 5) in Kassel, and holding several posts in various courts. In his 50th year Leclair wrote his first opera, *Scylla et Glaucus*, first performed at the Royal Academy, Paris. Leclair's surviving work shows him to be one of the most important violin composers of the 18th century, popularizing the instrument in France through his compositions and by his performance. He is known to have played in the Italian manner, using the Tartini bow.

Lees, Benjamin (1924-) American composer of Chinese birth, who studied at the University of California with Halsey Stevens. After a lengthy period of study with George **Antheil** he was awarded a Guggenheim fellowship and travelled to Helsinki, Vienna and Longpont, France, composing away from his American peers and other influences. In 1956 he returned to the United States to establish himself as a teacher and composer. Lees has toured in the Soviet Union and been commissioned to write many works for various groups. Although his early composition shows the influence of such composers as **Prokofiev** and **Bartók**, more recent works such as *Medea of Corinth* (1970) show his wilful individuality.

Leeuw, Ton de (1926-) Dutch teacher and composer. After studying with Toebosch and **Badings**, he travelled to Paris, where he studied with **Messiaen** and **Hartmann**. On his return to Amsterdam in 1950 he studied ethnomusicology with Jaap Kunst. In 1954 he was offered an appointment by Dutch Radio as a music producer, and he became teacher of composition and later director at the Amsterdam Conservatoire. He has studied music in India and Iran, and has taught ethnomusicology and music at Amsterdam University. Leeuw's first published compositions drew considerable acclaim after World War II – works such as *Treurmuziek in memoriam Willem Pijper* (1946), showing the influence of **Bartók** – whereas later compositions, such as *Sonata for two pianos* (1950) show the influence of **Pijper**, whose work Leeuw regards highly. As well as a radio oratorio, *Job* (1956), Leeuw has composed an opera, *The Dream* (1956), based on Haiku. A commissioned work *Symphonies of Wind* (1963) was based on Stravinsky's work of the same name. By the late 1960s Leeuw's works were heavily concerned with physical notions of space, with performers being spread out or changing position in mid-performance.

Lefanu, Nicola (1947-) English composer who studied at Oxford University and the Royal College of Music. Following her graduation she studied with Maxwell **Davies** at Dartington and in Siena. She was later appointed lecturer at King's College, London. She has won many awards for her modern composition, works such as *Antiworld* (1972) and *Dawnpath* (1977).

legato (It.) Bound, or tied, indication that the music is to be played smoothly, one note leading gently to the next. It is the opposite of **staccato**.

leger line Short line written below or above the stave to indicate those notes that fall outside its compass.

legno (It.) Indication (*col legno*) that a passage for a stringed instrument is to be played by striking the strings with the stick (back) of the bow.

legong (Indonesia) Dance-theatre form, traditionally accompanied by the **gamelan** *pelegongan* in Bali. *Legong* is danced by three girls, one of whom is the principal dancer. They are trained from an early age and are dressed in magnificently elaborate costumes. The gamelan ensemble provides sudden rapid *ostinati* contrasting with long melodic periods.

Legrand, Michel (1932-) French composer and conductor who studied at the Paris Conservatoire with Henri Chaland and Nadia **Boulanger** from the age of 11. His compositions were drawn towards jazz and popular music from an early age, earning him a living from arranging music and writing scores for television and the cinema. He travelled to New York, where he conducted Maurice Chevalier's shows in the mid-1950s. His work has won him many awards, including Oscars for the scores of films such as *Summer of '42*.

Lehár, Franz (1870-1948) Austrian composer and conductor. Hungarian by birth, he is known as this century's

Franz Lehár (seated)

foremost composer of operettas. He was taught by his father before joining Prague Conservatoire at the age of 12. In 1885 he obtained private lessons from **Fibich**, and it was at this time that he met **Dvorák**, whose work was to influence him greatly. His works include the march *Jetzt Gehts Los!*, the two operettas *Wiener Frauen* and *Der Restelbinder* and his most famous *The Merry Widow*. The last has been translated into many languages and has been performed throughout the world. The success of *The Merry Widow* ensured Lehár's popularity, and brought the Viennese operetta genre into the 20th century.

Lehmann, Liza (1862-1918) English soprano and composer. She studied singing with Jenny **Lind** in London and composition in Rome and Wiesbaden. Her debut was in the Monday Popular Concerts in 1885, and she appeared in many concerts around Britain in the next nine years. She was remarkable for her exceptionally wide vocal range, more suited to song than opera. At the time of her retirement (1894) she had published various songs, but from this point she was to concentrate on her composition. She is best remembered for her exotic work *In a Persian Garden* (1896).

Lehmann, Lotte (1888-1976) German soprano who studied in Berlin with Mathilde Mallinger. She first appeared with the Hamburg Opera, later progressing to **Wagner**'s Opera. By 1914 she had been engaged by the Vienna Opera and invited to London by Sir Thomas **Beecham** for the 1914 season of *Der Rosenkavalier*. Returning to Vienna in 1916 she performed in *Ariadne auf Naxos*, only leaving Vienna at the time of the *Anschluss* in 1938. In the inter-war years, Lehmann established a wide operatic repertory, and particularly impressed **Strauss**. It is for her performances of *Der Rosenkavalier* as the Feldmarschallin that she became best known. She was to appear almost annually at Covent Garden from 1924-1938 and her debut in the United States came in 1930. By the end of World War II she had settled in the United States, where she gained much attention for her performance of *Lieder* as well as operatic roles. Critics have given her voice and performances the highest praise. There are many recordings available.

Leibowitz, René (1913-1972) Polish-French composer, teacher and conductor. For three formative years from 1930, Leibowitz studied in Berlin with **Webern** and **Schoenberg**, and travelled to Paris to study with **Ravel**, where he was to remain throughout the war years. His debut came in 1937 and from this point he was to travel extensively as a conductor. In 1947 he organized the International Festival of Chamber Music in Paris which was to premiere music by his old teachers, Schoenberg and Webern, as well as pieces by **Berg**. Although these composers were disregarded in Paris until the 1940s, credit must be given to Leibowitz for championing and publicizing their **twelve-note technique** and compositions. His own compositions often allude to the influence of the teachers of his youth, although the opera *Les Espagnols à Venise* of 1970 has lyrical qualities on the whole absent from earlier works.

Leigh, Walter (1905-1942) English composer who studied under Dent. After graduating (1926) he studied with **Hinde-**

mith at the Berlin Hochschule. During this period he had his first works published. In the early 1930s Leigh became director of the Musical Theatre, Cambridge. He was killed during World War II, leaving several works for the stage, including two musical comedies, *The Pride of the Regiment* (1931) and *The Jolly Roger* (1933).

Leighton, Kenneth (1929-) English composer who studied classics and then composition at Oxford. Later he studied in Rome with Goffredo **Petrassi**. He won many awards, including one in 1956 for his *Fantasia Contrapuntistica*. From 1956 to 1968 he was appointed to the faculty of Edinburgh University as lecturer in composition, moving to Oxford in 1968. Leighton has written vocal, orchestral and chamber music, all typified by the use of a characteristic lyrical romanticism.

Leinsdorf, Erich (1912-) Austrian conductor who studied with Paul Emerich at the Vienna Academy. In 1932 he made his debut as a pianist in **Stravinsky**'s *Les Noces*. In 1934 he played in a performance of *Psalmus Hungaricus* by **Kodály** for **Toscanini** in Vienna, following which he travelled to Salzburg to serve as assistant to Bruno **Walter**. He remained in Salzburg until 1937, associated with both Toscanini and Walter, his reputation spreading throughout Europe. He conducted in France and Italy, before accepting the post of assistant conductor to the Metropolitan Opera, New York, where he made his debut with *Die Walküre* in 1938. The success of this initial performance resulted in his giving many other performances of **Wagner**. He has become known as an expert interpreter of Wagner. After many other performances throughout the United States, both during and after World War II, he returned to the Metropolitan Opera as conductor and consultant. In 1962 he was appointed to the Boston Symphony Orchestra as director and conductor, increasing its repertory and reputation. From 1969 he travelled widely, receiving many accolades.

Leitmotiv (Ger.) Leading-motif. Theme associated with an object or idea, or an aspect of a character in an opera, quoted at appropriate moments or worked up symphonically. The chief exponent of the *Leitmotiv* was **Wagner**.

lent, lento (It.) Slow.

Leoncavallo, Ruggiero (1857-1919) Italian composer who entered Naples Conservatoire in 1866. He graduated a decade later having been taught by Rossi. While at Bologna University in the late 1870s he became interested in the Renaissance, and wrote the opera *Tomaso Chatterton*. He travelled throughout Europe and Egypt as a pianist, before settling in Paris where he met other musicians and wrote the opera *A Midsummer Night's Dream*, as well as starting a trilogy, *Crepusculum*. Returning to Italy his next opera, *Pagliacci*, was performed in 1892, directed by **Toscanini**. He wrote several other operas, including *La Bohème* (1897, unfortunately overshadowed by **Puccini**'s version, staged a short time earlier), *Roman von Berlin* (1904), *Maia* (1910) and *Malbruck* (1910). He also wrote songs, including Mattinata (which was recorded by **Caruso**). Condemned to work in a period of operatic change, Leoncavallo's work was less successful than it might have been, but it is for the opera *Pagliacci* and the recorded song Mattinata that he is best remembered.

Leonhardt, Gustav (1928-) Dutch keyboard player and conductor. He studied organ and harpsichord with Müller in Basle after World War II. His debut was in Vienna in 1950. Studying in Vienna, he became professor of harpsichord at the Vienna Academy from 1952 to 1955, as well as at the Amsterdam Conservatoire. In 1955 he founded the Leonhardt Consort dedicated to playing chamber music on authentic instruments. In the mid-1950s he toured extensively in Europe and the United States both as harpsichordist and lecturer. Leonhardt's repertory includes keyboard compositions from the 16th to the

18th centuries, performed on original instruments in a quest for authenticity.

Leppard, Raymond (1927-) English harpsichordist and conductor. He studied at Cambridge with Middleton and **Ord** until 1952. It was in that year that he made his conducting debut at the Wigmore Hall, London, and earned a reputation for his performances of 17th- and 18th-century music. In the late 1950s he was appointed lecturer at Cambridge University. Throughout this period he toured in Britain, appearing in the bicentennial performances of **Handel**'s *Samson* at Covent Garden in 1959. In 1962 at Glyndebourne he performed what was to become the first of a series of Italian opera revivals, including **Monteverdi**'s *L'Orfeo*. In the following year he began his involvement with the English Chamber Orchestra, travelling to Japan in 1970. From 1973 he became principal conductor to the BBC Northern Symphony Orchestra. As a harpsichordist, Leppard is considered a specialist in Baroque music by composers such as **Rameau**.

Lerner, Alan Jay (1918-) American lyricist who has collaborated with such composers as **Weill**, André **Previn** and Leonard **Bernstein**, as well as Frederick **Loewe** with whom he wrote *My Fair Lady* (1956), probably his most famous work.

Leroux, Xavier Henry Napoléon (1863-1919) French composer who studied with **Massenet** and **Dubois** at the Paris Conservatoire, winning the Grand Prix de Rome in 1885 with his cantata *Endymion*. After a period spent in Rome he travelled again to Paris, gaining fame with the opera *La Reine Fiammette* (1903) and later *Le Chemineau* (1907). These were performed widely in Europe and at the Metropolitan Opera, New York. In 1896, Leroux was appointed to the faculty of the Paris Conservatoire as professor of harmony.

Levine, James (1943-) American pianist and conductor who appeared as a soloist in **Mendelssohn**'s Piano Concerto No. 2 at the age of ten. He was tutored by Walter Levin, followed by a period at the Juilliard School where he studied conducting with Jean Morel. In 1956 he took piano lessons with Rudolf **Serkin** in Vermont. At the age of 21 he was offered the post of assistant conductor of the Cleveland Orchestra, and it was at this time that he conducted **Bizet**'s *The Pearl Fishers* to great acclaim. While with the Cleveland Orchestra he taught at the Aspen Music School, at Oakland University and elsewhere. His debut at the Metropolitan Opera, New York, came in 1971 when he conducted *Tosca* and he was appointed principal conductor to the Metropolitan in 1973, making many notable recordings. It was in this year that he made his debut with the London Symphony Orchestra. In 1976 he was appointed musical director to the Metropolitan. Levine's conducting repertory ranges from 18th-century to modern avant-garde composers, as well as performing on, and directing from, the piano.

Lewis, Sir Anthony (1915-1983) English composer, conductor and musicologist who studied at the Royal College of Music, at Cambridge, and later under Nadia **Boulanger** in Paris. After graduating, he was appointed to the BBC as a musicologist, organizing chamber music broadcasts in the pre-war period. After World War II he rejoined the BBC as a key person behind what would become Radio 3. In 1947 he was appointed professor at Birmingham University, producing many rarely heard works, including **Handel**'s Italian operas translated into English by Lewis's colleagues. In the 1940s, Lewis made many recordings, including recording premieres of works by **Lully**, **Monteverdi** and **Purcell**'s *The Fairy Queen*. In 1950 Lewis was appointed secretary and, later, chairman of the Purcell Society. In the same year he organized the publication of *Musica Britannica*, overseeing the first 30 volumes. In 1968 Lewis was appointed to the post of principal of the Royal Academy of Music and received a knighthood in 1972. His published compositions have included an *Elegy* (1947) and a Horn Concerto (1959).

Lewis, Richard (1914-) English tenor. After studying at the Manchester College of Music and the Royal College, Lewis travelled to Scandinavia after World War II, making his British debut in **Britten**'s *Serenade* (1947). A performance of *The Rape of Lucretia* at Glyndebourne, also in 1947, marked his operatic debut. In the same year he appeared at Covent Garden in Britten's *Peter Grimes*. However, it is for his performance of Ferrando in *Così Fan Tutte* that he became best known, performing this role regularly at Glyndebourne in the 1950s, where his repertory widened to include many other performances. He also made regular appearances at Covent Garden, including the role of Aaron in the British debut of **Schoenberg**'s *Moses und Aaron*. In this role he travelled to Europe and the United States. His American debut was in San Francisco in 1953. Since World War II, Lewis has appeared in both opera and concert performances and he has gained critical admiration for his repertory, covering both established and previously unperformed roles.

Lewkovitch, Bernhard (1927-) Danish organist and composer who studied organ at the Royal Danish Conservatoire from 1946 to 1950, graduating in both theory and organ. In 1950 he studied composition with Schierbeck and Jersild, and from 1947 until the early 1960s held the post of organist at St Ansgar. In 1953 he founded the choral society Schola Gregoriana, based in Copenhagen, which performed Lewkovitch's compositions as well as medieval and Renaissance religious music. In 1963 Lewkovitch was awarded the Carl Nielsen Prize. His own compositions are primarily choral, *Mariavise for Chorus* Op. 1 (1947) displaying Lewkovitch's interest in **Gregorian chant**. This interest is evident up to the 1950s, after which the influence of **Stravinsky** is apparent in such religious works as *Cantata Sacra* (1959). It was in the late 1950s that Lewkovitch's work gained in popularity, performances of his compositions meeting with public acclaim at festivals throughout Europe. The avant-garde *Il cantico delle creature* (1962-1963) marked the breaking of Lewkovitch's ecclesiastical links for several years.

Ley, Henry George (1887-1962) English organist and composer. While a chorister at St George's, Windsor, and at the Royal College of Music he studied organ with Walter Parrat. As a student at Oxford he was appointed as organist of Christ Church in 1909. In 1926 he became musical director of Eton, encouraging musical pupils to perform. This post was followed by an appointment to the Royal College of Music as organ teacher. Ley's own compositions include chamber music as well as the orchestral piece *Variations on a theme by Handel*.

Leygraf, Hans (1920-) Swedish pianist. With a precocious ability, Leygraf first appeared with the Stockholm Symphony Orchestra at the age of ten. He went on to study at the Stockholm Conservatoire, in Munich and in Vienna. While still a student, his reputation spread as a first-rate pianist and performer of **Mozart**. In the mid-1950s he was appointed to the faculty of the Salzburg Mozarteum.

Liadov Alternative spelling of **Lyadov**.

libretto (It.) Written text of an opera, oratorio or cantata, originally contained in a small booklet for the benefit of the audience. The role of a librettist was to adapt or translate an existing play, poem, novel or folk tale in conjunction with the composer, who would provide the music. In the past there have been several successful partnerships between librettists and composers, including those of Da Ponte and **Mozart**, Boito and **Verdi**, Gilbert and **Sullivan**, Hofmannsthal and Richard **Strauss**.

licenza (It.) Licence, freedom. *Con alcuna licenza* indicates that the performer has some freedom in such matters as speed and rhythm.

Lidholm, Ingvar (1921-) Swedish composer. At the outbreak of World War II, Lidholm studied violin and theory at Stockholm's Royal College of Music under Barkel, Brandel, Mann and **Rosenberg**. While studying with Rosenberg he joined the Monday Group and became conductor to the Orebro Orchestra until 1956. He travelled throughout Europe, attending the Darmstadt Courses in 1949, and visiting England where he studied with Mátyás **Seiber** in 1954. In 1956 Lidholm was appointed to the post of director of chamber music for Swedish Radio until 1965, when he joined the faculty of the Stockholm Royal College of Music. Publications from the 1970s such as the *Three Aspects of New Music* firmly link Lidholm to the canon of new music appearing in Scandinavia, and his own compositional work features constructivist methods. From the late 1940s Lidholm concerned himself with European compositional advances, as in the **twelve-note** serialism of works such as *A Cappella Bok* (1956). Lidholm is probably best known for his vocal compositions; pieces such as *Skaldansnatt* have deviated from the norm in using words purely as sound structures.

Liebermann, Rolf (1910-) Swiss composer and opera director. While at Zurich University, Liebermann took music lessons at the José Berr Conservatoire (1937-1938), later becoming music assistant to his composition teacher Scherchen in Budapest and Vienna. On his return to Switzerland, he studied composition with Vladimir Vogel. It was from him that he learned about dodecaphonic compositional developments. After World War II, Liebermann was appointed to Swiss Radio as producer and manager. In 1957 he became musical director of North German Radio, Hamburg, and later manager of the Hamburg State Opera. He was appointed artistic director in 1962. This post enabled him to commission work from many contemporary composers, including **Krenek**. The Hamburg State Opera under Liebermann gained a reputation for its critically acclaimed premiere performances of commissioned modern works. On the strength of this he was appointed to the Paris Opera from 1973 to 1980. Liebermann has received many accolades from throughout the world. As a composer he is known for several operas, including *Die Schule der Frauen* (1955) and *A Concerto for Jazzband and Orchestra* (1954). One of his most radical works to date is the *Concert des Echanges*, first performed in 1964, utilizing 52 recordings of industrial equipment.

Lied German song consisting of settings of poetic forms with a piano accompaniment. The most important characteristic of the *Lied* is that its piano part is not merely a decorative support to the song, but an integral and equal part to it. It is in this respect that **Schubert** was able to achieve such creative artistry, because he was able to interpret the full meaning of a poetical text and express it through voices and instruments. Other composers who have written *Lieder* include **Schumann**, **Brahms**, **Wolf** and **Pfitzner**.

ligature Term with two meanings.

First, it is a notational sign indicating that a group of notes are sung to the same syllable. The mark is also used in plainsong to bind several notes together.

Second, it is a metal band that secures the reed to the mouthpiece in instruments of the clarinet family.

Ligeti, György (1923-) Hungarian composer who studied composition at the Kolozsvár Conservatoire with Farkas during World War II, followed by a period of private study with **Kadosa** in Budapest. In 1949 he resumed his studies with Farkas as well as **Veress** at Budapest. He published folksong arrangements in the early 1950s and travelled to Vienna in 1956 because of the Hungarian uprising. It was there that he met many leading avant-garde composers, including **Stockhausen** and Eimert, who invited him to study at the Cologne Electronic Music Studio in 1957 on the strength of his experimental compositions. One of his compositions, *Artikulation*, was broadcast in 1958. It was during this period that he composed one of his major works, *Visions* (which later became *Apparitions*), first performed at the 1960 Cologne ISCM Festival. In the late 1950s Ligeti was much in demand as a lecturer, participating annually at Darmstadt from 1959 and travelling widely in Europe and the United States. His compositional development is most marked by his move to the West, with the subsequent destruction of formal rhythm and pitch structures in a move towards greater expression in his work. *Atmosphères* (1961), with its wide variety of used noises, effects and timbres lay the foundations for later works. His *Poème Symphonique*, using 100 metronomes set at different tempi, was widely acclaimed on its first performance at the Buffalo Arts Festival in 1960.

Lilburn, Douglas (1915-) New Zealand composer who studied at Canterbury University College, New Zealand, and won the Grainger Prize for his overture *In the Forest* (1936). He travelled to London where he studied with **Vaughan Williams** (1937-1940). On his return to New Zealand, he was appointed to the faculty of Victoria University, Wellington, becoming professor in 1963. In 1970 he was made professor of the University Electronic Music Studio, after he had established Australasia's first ever such studio in the 1960s. Lilburn's early compositions evoked the landscapes of New Zealand and were influenced by, but not immersed in, Vaughan Williams's pastoralism. The influences of Vaughan Williams are unmistakable in Lilburn's early Symphony No. 2 (1951), and in the same year, Lilburn composed his *Elegy* in response to the poets of the Central Otago region. Lilburn's work is considered central to the development of post-war music in New Zealand.

Lind, Jenny (Johanna Maria) (1820-1887) Swedish soprano, nicknamed the Swedish Nightingale. In 1830 she became a pupil at Stockholm's Royal Opera School. She studied with **Berg** and made her operatic debut in 1838 in the role of Agatha in *Der Freischütz* and took the title role in Weber's *Euryanthe* in the same year. She appeared regularly for the next three years in a variety of major roles. She studied under Manuel Garcia in Paris in 1841. She returned in 1842 to Stockholm, where she took the role of *Norma*. It was during this period in Paris that **Meyerbeer** heard her sing and wrote for her the part of Vielka in *Ein Feldlager in Schlesien*. In the mid-1840s Lind sang throughout Europe and appeared in a performance of *Norma* for her Viennese debut in 1846. In the same year she appeared with **Mendelssohn** at the Aachen Festival, which further enhanced her reputation in Europe. Her British debut was in a performance of *Robert le Diable* before Queen Victoria in 1847. Lind's subsequent popularity with the British was matched by her reception in the United States, where she toured in 1850-1852. In 1852 she married Otto Goldschmidt, her accompanist, and returned to Dresden, moving to England in 1858. In 1883 Lind was appointed to the Royal College of Music as professor of singing. She is best remembered for her performances in *Norma*, as Amina in *La Sonnambula* and in Spontini's *Robert le Diable*. Most of her career was spent as a recitalist and oratorio singer, and yet her repertory of opera was also wide.

lining out Practice in sacred music whereby the priest or precentor recites a line of text before it is sung by the congregation. The precentor may speak, chant or sing each line.

Linley, Thomas (1733-1795) English composer and teacher. He studied with Thomas Chilcot, organist at Bath Abbey, and later with William **Boyce** in London and, it is believed, Paradisi. From the mid-1750s Linley was director of many of Bath's concerts until the 1770s, when his success led to an appointment with London's Drury Lane Theatre as joint director and later manager. Linley's first notable success in London was the staging of his opera *The Royal Merchant* at Covent Garden in 1767. Linley is best remembered for *The Duenna* (1775), although he also wrote songs for many other comic operas, pantomimes and dramatic performances.

Linley, Thomas (1756-1778) English composer and violinist, son of Thomas Linley (1733-1795). Of precocious ability, Linley performed a violin concerto at the age of seven at Bristol. From the age of seven until he was 12, he studied with his father and Boyce, then with Nardini in Florence, where he became a great friend of **Mozart**. On his return to England he performed extensively in Bath and London, becoming leader at Drury Lane from 1773 to 1778. In these years he is known to have composed extensively, although little of his music has survived.

Lipatti, Dinu (1917-1950) Romanian pianist and composer who studied piano with Florica Musicescu at the Budapest Conservatoire from 1928 to 1932. Winning the second prize at the 1934 Vienna International Competition amid great critical debate, he travelled to Paris to study piano with **Cortot**, conducting with Münch, and composition with Nadia **Boulanger** with whom he made his initial recordings of **Brahms**. Critically acclaimed recitals in Germany and Italy were curtailed by World War II, and he returned to Romania and then travelled to Geneva, where he taught at the conservatoire.

Lipkin, Malcolm (1932-) English composer who studied under Bernard Stevens at the Royal College of Music (1949-1953) and with **Seiber**. His Piano Concerto (1957), first performed at the Cheltenham Festival, brought him much acclaim and in 1967 he was appointed to the music faculty of Oxford University as tutor for external studies. He has written choral as well as orchestral pieces, notably a setting of Psalm 96 (1969).

lira Generic name given to various old bowed stringed instruments, such as the **rebec** and **crwth**.

lira da braccio (It.) Bowed stringed instrument, current in the late 16th and early 17th centuries, which evolved from the fiddle. It had seven strings, five stopped on the fingerboard, and two unstopped drones tuned an octave apart. As the name implies, it was played on the arm.

Lira da braccio

Lira da gamba

lira da gamba (It.) Larger version of the **lira da braccio** that was held between the knees. The number of strings, including drones, varied from 11 to 15.

Liszt, Franz (Ferencz) (1811-1886) Hungarian pianist and composer who laid the foundation for much of the 20th century's composition and invented the **symphonic poem**. He was also a piano virtuoso and highly influential teacher and conductor. Showing an early interest in his father's music, Liszt began to compose at the age of eight and is believed to have given his first public performance at this age. Gaining much praise for his abilities, Liszt's musical education was sponsored for six years. In 1821 he moved to Vienna where he studied piano with **Czerny** and performed in 1822, meeting **Beethoven** the following year. After a series of concerts in Germany, he moved to Paris where he found himself refused entry into the Conservatoire because of his nationality. He composed the operetta *Don Sanche* at the age of 13 and began to move in Paris's literary and fashionable circles of the day. In 1830 he composed *The Revolutionary Symphony* and in the same year met **Berlioz** and later **Paganini**, whose virtuosity inspired Liszt to explore the expressive possibilities of the piano. In the early 1830s Liszt met **Chopin**, another formative influence. The *Fantasias* of the 1830s were contrasted sharply by the poeticism of the *Apparitions*, and the piano work *Lyons* based on a revolutionary theme was also written at this time. In 1835 he travelled to Geneva to teach piano at the Conservatoire and toured extensively through Europe, performing in a Berlioz concert, in a famous 'duel' with his contemporary **Thalberg** and in performances of Beethoven's piano sonatas. In the late 1830s Liszt began the first of his transciptions of **Schubert** and helped to finance a monument to Beethoven in Bonn. Also at this time he returned to Hungary where he heard gypsy and folk music, some of which he transcribed for the piano. It was in Budapest that he gave his conducting debut in 1840, later conducting in Weimar and elsewhere in Germany. In 1848 he was appointed Court *Kapellmeister* in Weimar and abandoned his performing career. It was in this period that he was best able to compose and it was from 1848 until the 1860s that he wrote his most highly regarded works. During this period he also directed and conducted performances, including the first performance of *Lohengrin* in 1850. Gathering pupils around him and supporting **Wagner** in political exile, he became mistrusted in Weimar; in 1859 he wrote *Les Morts* on the death of his son. Public denouncements, including one from **Brahms**, caused him to leave Weimar for Rome, where he composed many religious works including *Missa Solemnis*. From 1869 he held master-classes in both Weimar and Budapest, joining Wagner in the forward-looking *Zukunftsmusik* (*Art Music of the Future*), which reinforced Liszt's symphonic poem format, eschewing more traditional compositional techniques for a close marriage of text or idea and music. Throughout the 1870s and 1880s he was visited by pupils and composers alike, including **Albéniz**, **Borodin**, **Debussy**, and **Fauré**. In the late 1880s there were many performances of Liszt's work throughout Europe, the composer himself failing to attend many through ill health.

Liszt was a man of many facets, worldly but with spiritual leanings, a great supporter of fellow musicians including Berlioz and Wagner, modest and yet flamboyant. He is considered one of the world's greatest pianists, leaving piano compositions of extraordinary complexity. His repertory was extensive and included his own compositions, largely for the piano, and transcriptions of others' works. Liszt's *Faust Symphony* (1857) is considered to be his masterpiece. Critics of the time denigrated Liszt's modernistic sonority, but he remains a composer and pianist unparallelled in his own time.

litany Supplicatory chant consisting of a series of petitions with an infrequently changing response to each. Among the best-known litanies are those of the Roman Catholic Church, and include the Litany of Saints, sung on Holy Saturday and during Rogationtide, and the litany sung in honour of the Virgin Mary. Cranmer's litany of the mid-16th century is still used in Anglican churches, but excludes references to the saints.

Lloyd, Charles Harford (1849-1919) English organist and composer who studied at Oxford and founded Oxford's Musical Club, becoming its president in 1872. In 1876 he was appointed organist of Gloucester Cathedral and conductor of Gloucester's Choral and Philharmonic Societies. In 1882 he was appointed organist of Christ Church, Oxford, and from 1887 taught organ at the Royal College of Music until 1892, when he was appointed to the post of music instructor at Eton. From 1914 he was organist at the Chapel Royal, St James's. Lloyd has left many compositions both religious and secular, including orchestral works such as *Hero and Leander* (1884).

Lloyd, George (1913-) English composer who studied composition with Harry Farjeon. His first opera *Iernin* (1934) was performed in his native Cornwall and *The Serf* was performed in Covent Garden in 1938. His third opera, *John Socman*, was featured at the Festival of Britain in 1951. The libretti of all three operas were written by his father. Lloyd has written other orchestral and choral works, and was awarded an OBE in 1970.

Lloyd Webber, Andrew (1948-) English composer who studied briefly at the Royal College of Music before teaming up with Tim Rice to write popular songs. Their first successful musical was *Joseph and the Amazing Technicolour Dreamcoat* (1968) based on a biblical story, first staged in its full length at the Edinburgh Festival. His second successful work with Tim Rice was *Jesus Christ Superstar* (1970) which became a best-selling recording, and has been staged widely around the world and made into a film. Throughout the 1970s Lloyd Webber wrote film scores and has since had other stage hits, including *Cats* and *Phantom of the Opera* (1987).

Lloyd Webber, Julian (1951-) English cellist, and brother of Andrew Lloyd Webber, who studied with Pierre Fournier in Geneva in 1973. His debut in Britain was at the Wigmore Hall in 1971. Lloyd Webber has travelled extensively as a solo cellist as well as making recordings of **Delius**'s cello compositions and modern British works.

Julian Lloyd Webber

Locatelli, Pietro Antonio (1695-1764) Italian violinist and composer, who studied in Italy, possibly with **Corelli** in Rome. He performed extensively in Italy and was appointed *virtuoso da camera* to the Governor of Mantua from 1725 to 1735. It is believed that Locatelli was a well-known violinist throughout Italy by the 1720s, performing in Venice in 1725 and for the King of Prussia in Berlin in 1728. In the following year, Locatelli is known to have settled in Amsterdam, revising his Concerti Grossi Op. 1 (1721), teaching and partaking in regular concert appearances. In Amsterdam he published many of his own works. His playing was known for its virtuosity, using a short bow and earning his later reputation as the "Paganini of the 18th century" for his technique, famous for the deft use of double stopping. His composition owes much to his formative years spent in Venice, influenced largely by **Vivaldi** and Valentini. There are many compositions attributed to Locatelli.

Locke (or Lock), Matthew (*c*1622-1677) English composer who studied at Exeter Cathedral as a chorister with Edward Gibbons and William Wake. Very little is known of his early life. He was commissioned to write music for Shirley's masque *Cupid and Death* (1653) and in 1656 wrote some of the music for what is arguably the first English opera, *The Siege of Rhodes*, now lost, and for other plays of the 1650s and 1660s. At this time Locke moved among Britain's musical elite, including Henry and Thomas **Purcell**, and was known to writers of the time including Pepys and Aubrey. The 1660 Restoration benefitted Locke because he was given three composing posts in the new royal music establishment and was invited to write music for the 1661 coronation. He is known to have been an outspoken supporter of English music and believed himself to be the foremost composer of his day. Problems ensued both from his Roman Catholicism and from musical disputes with Thomas Salmon and the music faculty of Oxford University over contemporary compositional techniques. Locke has left an extraordinary canon of music both courtly and dramatic. A near contemporary of Purcell and Christopher Gibbons, Locke is remembered primarily for his chamber and dramatic music, his chamber music owing much to the traditional consort music of Lawes and Simpson. *The Broken Consort*, for instance, dates from 1661 and was intended for his eight chamber musicians. His dramatic music is best remembered for the vocal music to accompany Shadwell's *Psyche* and *Cupid and Death*, the only complete surviving scores to the masques so popular at the time. There are also secular songs which can be either definitely or possibly attributed to Locke.

Lockhart, James (1930-) Scottish pianist and conductor who studied at the Royal College of Music. His first appointment was as apprentice conductor to the Yorkshire Symphony Orchestra. He then held the post of *répétiteur* for the operas at Glyndebourne and Covent Garden as well as in Germany. After a period spent at Sadler's Wells, he was reappointed to Covent Garden, this time as resident conductor, and gave the premiere of **Walton**'s *The Bear* (1967). From 1962 to 1972 Lockhart was also professor of conducting at the Royal College of Music and with the Welsh National Opera gave the British premiere of **Berg**'s *Lulu* (1971). In 1972 Lockhart became the first ever British musical director of a German opera house, when he was given the post at Kassel and conducted **Wagner**'s *Ring* cycle in full. As a performer he has appeared as pianist as well as conductor to soprano Margaret **Price**.

loco (It.) Indication that a passage is to be played in the register indicated by written notes, rather than an octave higher or lower as in a preceeding passage.

Loeillet, Jean Baptiste (1680-1730) Dutch-born harpsichordist and flautist. He is known to have settled in London in 1705 after studying in Ghent and Paris. From 1705 to 1710 he played oboe and flute at the Queen's Theatre, Haymarket, and Drury Lane. Performing regularly at his house in Covent Garden, he premiered **Corelli**'s Concerti Grossi Op. 6 in England and became much in demand as a teacher of harpsichord. He is believed to have introduced and certainly popularized the German transverse flute in England and was a major collector of flutes and violins. He has left several lessons and sonatas in the Italian tradition of Corelli and **Vivaldi**.

Loewe, Frederick (1904-) American composer of popular songs, Austrian by birth. He studied piano with **Busoni** and **d'Albert** in Berlin, and performed his first solo with the Berlin Philharmonic Orchestra at the age of 13. In 1924 he emigrated to the United States, where he unsuccessfully pursued a career as a concert pianist. It was in New York that he found a new direction as a composer of popular songs albeit referring heavily to now unfashionable Italian light opera. His career only really

Frederick Loewe

took off when he collaborated with librettist Alan Jay **Lerner**, writing some of the world's most famous musicals including *Brigadoon* (1947), *Paint Your Wagon* (1951), the Pulitzer Prize winning *My Fair Lady* (1956) and *Camelot* (1960).

Löhr, Hermann (1871-1943) English composer who studied at the Royal College of Music, where he was awarded the Charles Lucas Medal. He is best known for his ballads, which include *Little Grey Home in the West* (1911) and *Rose of My Heart* (1911). Löhr also composed music for the theatre including *Our Little Cinderella* (1911). His working life was spent with the English firm of music publishers, Chappell.

Lomax, Alan (1915-) American ethnomusicologist who studied music and anthropology at the universities of Harvard, Texas and Colombia. After working at the Archive of American Folksong (1937), he became director of Folk Music at Decca Records (1946-1949). Since then he has carried out research in the United States, Great Britain, Haiti, Italy and Spain, and has promoted folk song through festivals, radio and lecturing. In 1963, he was appointed director of the **Cantometrics** Project at Colombia University, the results of which he published in *Folk Song Style and Culture* (1968). Other publications include a biography of Ferdinand 'Jelly Roll' Morton (*Mister Jelly Roll*, 1950) and numerous anthologies and bibliographies of folk song and poetry.

Lombardy rhythm Alternative term for the **Scotch snap**.

London Philharmonc Orchestra British orchestra founded in 1932 by Sir Thomas **Beecham** and based in London. Its conductors have included Bernard **Haitink** (1967-1979), Sir Adrian **Boult** (1950-1957) and Sir Georg **Solti** (from 1979). The orchestra's repertoire is extensive and it has appeared regularly at Glyndebourne since 1964.

London Symphony Orchestra British orchestra founded in 1904 by members of Henry **Wood**'s orchestra, who left after a dispute. Its conductors have included André **Previn** (1968-1979), Claudio **Abbado** (from 1979) and Michael Tilson Thomas. The orchestra was also at one time associated with **Elgar**.

Loraine, Alain Original name of conductor Gerard **Victory**.

Lorengar, Pilar (1928-) Spanish soprano who studied at Madrid, and made her concert debut in 1952, appearing in leading roles in the Aix-en-Provence Festival, in New York as *Rosario*, at Covent Garden for several seasons as *Violetta*, and from 1956 for four seasons as *Pamina* at Glyndebourne. Carl Ebert appointed her on the strength of these appearances to play in many different roles at the Deutsche Oper in Berlin. Her Metropolitan debut in 1963 as *Donna Elvira* enhanced her reputation, and she appeared regularly at Covent Garden.

Loriod, Yvonne (1924-) French pianist who studied at the Paris Conservatoire during World War II with Levy, and took composition with **Messiaen** and **Milhaud**. The Conservatoire awarded her seven first prizes. After appearing in the premier performance of Messiaen's *Visions de L'Amen*, she toured extensively giving piano recitals in Germany and Austria. Loriod is Messiaen's second wife and has appeared in all of Messiaen's first performances of new works, many of which have been recorded. Loriod's American debut was in the premier performance of *Turangalila* in 1949. Loriod is known for her recordings and performances of piano compositions by her husband as well as composers such as **Boulez** and Barraqué. She has taught many of France's eminent young pianists.

Los Angeles, Victoria de (1923-) Spanish soprano who studied at the Barcelona Conservatoire. She made her operatic debut in 1945 at the *Teatro Liceo* and in 1947 won the prestigious International Singing Competition in Geneva. On her return to Spain, her repertory included *La Bohème*, *Tannhäuser*, *Lohengrin* and *Der Freischütz*. In the immediate post-war years, her reputation spread, particularly after the BBC chose her to appear in a broadcast of *La Vida Breve* in 1948. She made her Covent Garden debut in 1950, and appeared there for over a decade in a variety of roles, including Madam Butterfly. At this time she also appeared to much acclaim at the Metropolitan Opera House, New York, and in the mid-1960s appeared in Buenos Aires by which time her repertory was most extensive. She retired from operatic appearances in 1969.

Lotti, Antonio (*c*1667-1740) Italian composer and organist who studied in his teens with Legrenzi in Venice, producing the opera *Giustino* at the age of 16. By the end of the 1680s, Lotti was an established alto at San Marco, becoming first organist there in 1704, a post he held until 1736 when he became music master. During his time at San Marco, Lotti composed many ecclesiastical works for the choir as well as writing secular choral works, motets and music for the theatres of Venice. His opera *Il Trionfo Dell'Innocenza* appeared in 1692. In the early 1700s he wrote 16 operas and revised more. Pupils such as **Gasparini** and Alberti studied with him in Venice, and in 1717 Lotti travelled to Dresden. During a two-year period in Dresden he wrote three operas. Lotti returned to Venice in 1719, again to San Marco where his *Miserere* of 1733 was to be performed well into the 19th century. Critics have considered Lotti to be the greatest composer of his day, comparable with A. **Scarlatti**.

Loughran, James (1931-) Scottish conductor. He gained experience with the Bonn Opera where he served as a *répétiteur*, and appeared in the Netherlands and Italy. Winning a British conducting competition, Loughran joined the Bournemouth Symphony Orchestra. In 1963 he appeared at Sadler's Wells and in 1964 at Covent Garden, where he conducted *Aïda*. In 1965 Loughran was appointed first conductor of the Scottish Symphony Orchestra. In 1969 he recorded with the London Symphony Orchestra and in 1970 joined the Hallé Orchestra, making his New York debut two years later. In 1979 Loughran was made principal conductor of

James Loughran

the Bamberg Symphony Orchestra. Loughran has in more recent years conducted first performances of a number of British works.

Lourié, Arthur Vincent (1892-1966) Russian composer who studied at the St Petersburg Conservatoire, where he was influenced by modernism to the exclusion of his formal studies. His *Formes En L'Air* (1915) was dedicated to Picasso. He composed the sacred work *Carona Carmina Sacrorum* and following the 1917 Revolution was made music commissar to the Conservatoire. In 1921 Lourié travelled to Germany and Paris, meeting many of the avant-garde composers of the day including **Busoni** and **Stravinsky**. Lourié travelled to the United States in 1941, taking citizenship after World War II. Initial experiments in atonality, in which his compositions dispensed with staves, were succeeded by modal works such as the *Sonata Liturgica* (1928) harking back to more classical idioms.

lower mordent Alternative term for **inverted mordent**.

lü/lülü (China) Chinese theoretical scale-modal system of twelve pitches within an octave, whose frequencies are related to one another by specific ratios.

Lucas, Leighton (1903-1982) English conductor and composer. A dancer with Diaghilev's *Ballets Russes* from 1918 to 1921, he became conductor to other companies in the early 1920s, arranging classical scores as well as writing his own, the most notable being *The Wolf's Ride* (1935). In the same year Lucas became musical director of the Markova-Dolin Ballet Company until 1937. During World War II, Lucas wrote film scores and in the years following the war he established his own orchestra, which concentrated primarily upon the performance of new works. In the 1950s Lucas's compositions tended towards orchestral works such as his Clarinet Concerto (1956).

Lucier, Alvin (1931-) American composer who studied theory at Yale with **Porter** and later at Brandeis University with **Shapero** and **Berger**. Winning a scholarship to study in Rome in 1960, Lucier returned to Brandeis as a tutor, resigning in 1970 to join Wesleyan University. Lucier's work has been influenced by the electronic experiments of the Cologne Studio and contemporary European composers of the 1960s. Lucier's works from this period, such as *Shelter 999*, rely heavily on arbitrary environmental sounds. In 1970 Lucier was commissioned to write a piece for the Osaka Expo which utilized hundreds of tape recorders to give a collage of sound.

Ludwig, Christa (1928-) German mezzo-soprano. Her parents sang at the Vienna Staatsoper and she studied both with her mother and with Huni-Mihacek. Ludwig's career began with her debut at Frankfurt in *Die Fledermaus*, appearing at Darmstadt for the 1952-1954 seasons, and in 1954 as *Cherubino* at Salzburg. In the following year she sang at Hanover. On the strength of these performances, Ludwig was appointed to the Vienna Staatsoper where she has since made many appearances. Ludwig's New York debut came in 1959 and she appeared a decade later in *Aïda* at Covent Garden. Ludwig is known for a variety of roles from **Verdi** and **Wagner**, and is also highly regarded in **Mahler**'s operatic roles. She has made numerous recordings, each reasonably representative of her mezzo-soprano voice.

Lully, (or Lulli) Jean-Baptiste (1632-1687) Italian-born composer, known as a leading 17th-century exponent of the French style. Lully was appointed to the French court in 1646, where his dancing as well as guitar and violin performances were notable. His attendance at court gave him a good grounding in operatic, concert and popular music performances. Through these concerts he probably became aware of contemporary Italian music and developed a passion for the theatre. In the late 1640s it is believed that Lully studied with the Italian violinist Lazzarini. In 1652 he travelled to Paris to attend the court of Louis XIV, and again was exposed to many court performances and rose through the ranks to compose instrumental music to court ballets and himself danced for the King. At this time, Lully's reputation spread through Louis XIV's court and by 1661 he was appointed composer to the King. Lully subsequently composed music for many ballets until 1671, collaborating with 17th-century France's chief dramatists and writing *Le Bourgeois Gentilhomme* with Molière in 1670. In 1672, facing much competition, Lully helped to establish what was to become Grand Opera, his musical dramas preceding the later comic opera format. Having established a theatre with full royal backing, Lully gathered many of France's best musicians, and himself acted as director, manager and conductor, collaborating with librettist Philippe Quinault. Lully's overtures became sufficiently famous to be named 'Lully Overtures' by many, a typical example being that featured in the ballet *Alcidiane* (1658).

Throughout this period, Lully was placed under increasing pressure to dispense with Quinault, who was out of favour with Louis XIV's court. Operas such as *Psyche* (1671) were written with Thomas Corneille. *Bellérophon* (1679) proved to be a great success and for more than a decade Lully wrote one opera a year.

Lully composed *ballets de coeur*, pastorals and stage tragedies, his early vocal songs being influenced by Italian trends. His comic works were based largely on Italian burlesque and although Lully was not offered ecclesiastical posts at the court, he wrote many motets for the court chapel.

Lumbye, Hans Christian (1810-1874) Danish composer who served in military bands in his youth as well as receiving a musical education. In 1839 he formed his own orchestra after hearing **Lanner** and **Strauss** perform in Copenhagen. Throughout the 1840s Lumbye gained fame both as a composer of waltzes, polkas and other dances of the day as well as in the role of conductor. He collaborated extensively in Copenhagen with Bournonville, writing dances for the latter's ballets and in 1843 became director of the Tivoli Gardens. It was here that he became known as the 'Johann Strauss of the North', composing more than 400 pieces of light music.

Lumsdaine, David (1931-) Australian-born British composer who studied at the Royal College of Music as well as taking private lessons with **Seiber**. Lumsdaine has taught widely in London and in 1961 was appointed to the Royal College of Music as seminar organizer, specializing in recent compositions. In 1970 he was appointed to the faculty of Durham University where he established an electronic music workshop. In 1980, he took up a lectureship at King's College, London. Lumsdaine's work is rooted in serial composition and in the sounds of his environment. Works from the mid-1960s, such as *Annotations on Auschwitz* (1964), showed his increasing preoccupation with contemporary historical issues. The influence of his newly-established electronic studio is evident in pieces from the early 1970s, such as *Kaliban Impromptu* (1972).

Lupu, Radu (1945-) Romanian pianist who made his debut in 1957, and in 1963 studied at the Moscow Conservatoire on a scholarship. He has won many international competitions, appearing in London in 1969 to much acclaim. Lupu's forte is considered to be 19th-century Romantic piano works, and he has also made highly praised recordings of **Mozart**'s sonatas.

lute Plucked stringed instrument with a pear-shaped body and a round vaulted back. One of the earliest known lutes was the Mesopotamian lute dating back to 2000 BC. The lute was introduced into Europe during the Crusades, and continued to be a popular instrument until the 18th century, when the **harpsichord** superseded it in popular use. The early instruments usually

A member of the lute family

had four courses of strings and were plucked with a quill.

By the 16th century the instrument had gained an extra course of strings, thus having five in all, two to each note, and one single string. The tuning of the average sized 16th-century lute was G, C, F, A, D, G (the lowest string sounding G below middle C). Other tunings were adopted in the 17th century. Music for the lute is played from a **tablature** of letters or figures.

The lute has been used for various compositions, such as dance movements, variations and contrapuntal *ricercari* and fantasias. The most notable English lutenists were Francis **Cutting** (*c*1583-*c*1603) and John **Dowland** (1591-1641). J. S. **Bach**'s repertory for lute included four suites and other pieces. Today, Julian **Bream** (1933-), the leading modern exponent of the lute, has revived popular interest in the instrument.

Lutoslawski, Witold (1913-) Polish composer who played the piano and violin as a child and studied at the Warsaw Conservatoire from 1932 to 1937, learning the piano with Lefeld and composition with Maliszewski. During this period Lutoslawsi performed as a pianist, transferring his attention in the post-war period to teaching and composing. He has lectured extensively throughout Europe and the United States, as well as conducting performances and recordings of his own work.

Lutoslawski's compositions from the late 1930s display a great understanding of Classical form, often pursuing folk themes, whereas later works from the 1940s and 1950s – such as *Funeral Music* (1958) – display his post-war leanings towards a system of his own, in many ways parallel to other composers' **dodecaphonic** compositions. The colourful tonality of Lutoslawski's post-war works owes something to **Bartók**. *Funeral Music* is dedicated to this composer.

Lutyens, (Agnes) Elizabeth (1906-1983) English composer who studied initially in Paris and from 1926 to 1930 at the Royal College of Music, where she studied viola, and composition with Darke. The romanticism of her early works, pieces such as *The Birthday of the Infanta*, a ballet first performed in 1932, was replaced in later years by the twelve-note serialism of works such as Chamber Concerto No. 1 showing the early hints of her later notable rhythmic style. Lutyens' modernistic compositions of the 1930s are today considered remarkable in the light of Britain's isolation from European musical development in the inter-war years. The British musical establishment's inability to embrace the ideas of **Schoenberg** and **Webern** made it very hard for Lutyens to become accepted, even though pieces such as *O Saisons, O Chateaux* of 1946 showed her newly crystallized dodecaphonic system to the full.

Works throughout the 1940s and 1950s, such as the String Quartet No. 6, showed the growth in confidence of Lutyens' compositional techniques. Nevertheless it was not until the 1960s that she was fully understood and accepted by the musical establishment in Britain. Lutyens' work of the 1960s, pieces such as *The Valley of Hatsu-Se* (1965), show a confident marriage of text and atmosphere. By the mid 1960s she had begun to pare down the body of her compositions to an insistent and near hollow simplicity. Lutyens' evocation of textual atmosphere is best illustrated by her increasing corpus of works commissioned for cinema and radio. In 1965 she wrote her first opera, *The Numbered*, and in 1969 was awarded a CBE.

Luxon, Benjamin (1937-) English baritone who, after studying at the Guildhall School of Music in London, made appearances in English Opera Group performances, most notably as Owen Wingrave in Britten's television opera of 1970. After a 1972 appearance at Glyndebourne as *Ulysses* he appeared at Covent Garden in *The Taverner* and again in 1974 as *Eugène Onegin*. Also in 1974 Luxon made his debut with the English National Opera and in 1977 appeared as *Don Giovanni* at Glyndebourne. His recordings include many *Lieder* besides the operatic performances for which he is famous.

Lyadov (Liadov), Anatol Konstantinovich (1855-1914) Russian teacher, conductor and composer. In 1870 he joined the Conservatoire of St Petersburg, where he excelled at the piano. It was there that he studied counterpoint with Johannsen and composition with **Rimsky-Korsakov**. By the mid-1870s Lyadov's *Four Songs* Op. 1 had become known to **Mussorgsky**. In 1878, he was appointed to the Conservatoire as a teacher of theory and in 1901 as teacher of counterpoint. Famous pupils included **Prokofiev**, **Stravinsky** and Myaskovsky. Throughout this period Lyadov collaborated with Rimsky-Korsakov on teaching projects. During the 1890s he made many concert appearances as conductor and in 1897 published the first of several folk song collections, after years of travelling and study to compile them. Lyadov's compositions in many cases owe much to traditional folk songs, including works such as his *Eight Russian Folk Songs* (1906). Critics put down his frequent compositional derivation to his famed indolence, and it was his inability to produce a commissioned score for Diaghilev that brought Stravinsky to acclaim for his own composition.

Lyapunov (or Liapunov), Sergey Mikhaylovich (1859-1924) Russian pianist and composer who studied at the Moscow Conservatoire (1878-1883), where he was taught piano by Klindworth and studied composition with **Tchaikovsky** and **Taneyev**. In 1884 Lyapunov went to St Petersberg where he studied with **Balakirev**. Both of them were commissioned to collect traditional folk songs. Lyapunov's compositions of the 1890s and 1900s owe much to his familiarity with these traditional songs. In 1894 Lyapunov replaced **Rimsky-Korsakov** as assistant director of the Imperial Chapel and in 1910 was appointed piano and theory tutor at St Petersburg Conservatoire. In 1919 he emigrated to Paris after touring extensively as a conductor and concert pianist.

Lyapunov's work is essentially derivative, his piano writings referring primarily to **Chopin** and **Mendelssohn**.

Lydian mode One of the ecclesiastical **modes**, represented by the scale beginning on F on the white notes of the piano keyboard.

lyre Most important instrument of ancient Greece and Egypt, the lyre was depicted in Sumerian art around 3000 BC and also in Ur of the Chaldees. The number of strings to the instrument varied. They were stretched on a framework with a hollow sound-box at the bottom and plucked, like those of a **harp**, with both hands, but only the left used the finger tips, while the right played with a **plectrum**. See also **crwth**; **kithara**; **lira da braccio**.

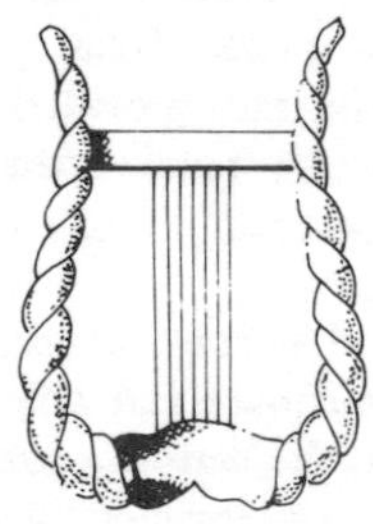

Lyre

M

Maazel, Lorin (1930-) American conductor and violinist. A child prodigy, he conducted at the New York World Fair and the Hollywood Bowl at the age of only nine. He has held many important conducting posts around the world, including the Berlin Radio Orchestra (1965-1975) and at Bayreuth. In 1972 he became the musical director of the Cleveland Orchestra. In 1982 he became the first American to direct the Vienna Operas.

McCabe, John (1939-) British composer and pianist who trained at Manchester University before attending the Royal Manchester College of Music, studying composition under Pitfield. He also studied in Germany under **Genzmer**. His works include three symphonies, three piano concertos, a clarinet concerto, two violin concertos, *Notturni ed Alba* (1970) and *Time Remembered* (1973), two ballets, chamber music, and piano and organ music.

McCormack, John (Count) (1884-1945) Irish tenor who studied under Sabbatino. He made his debut at Covent Garden in 1907 as Turiddu in *Cavalleria rusticana* and confirmed his success later in the same season as Don Ottavio and as the Duke in *Rigoletto*. He spent some time in the United States, where he sang with the Boston Opera Company (1910-1911) and with the Chicago Opera Company (1912-1913). He returned to England in 1924, and spent most of the rest of his career singing a more popular repertoire. His title of 'Count' was a papal award.

MacDowell, Edward (Alexander) (1861-1908) American composer, pianist and teacher, who studied at the Paris Conservatoire, then at Wiesbaden, and finally under Raff at the Hoch Conservatoire, Frankfurt. After spending a year (1881-1882) as the chief piano teacher at the conservatoire at Darmstadt, he was given the opportunity to perform his first piano concerto before **Liszt**, who was highly impressed. Subsequently he was invited to take part in the *Allgemeiner Deutscher Musikverein* in Zurich. In 1887 he returned to the United States and settled in Boston, making his first American appearance in 1888. Between 1896 and 1904 he was professor of music at Columbia University. He continued to teach while giving concerts and producing his two piano concertos. His other piano works include the *First Modern Suite* (1880-1881), *Forest Idyls* (1884) and *Woodland Sketches* (1896).

McEwen, Sir John Blackwood (1868-1948) Scottish composer and educationist. From 1893 he studied in London at the Royal Academy of Music. He became a teacher at the Athenaeum School of Music in Glasgow but returned to the Royal Academy in 1898. In 1924, after the retirement of Sir Alexander **Mackenzie**, McEwen became the principal of the Academy, a position which he held until his own retirement in 1936.

His compositions include *Grey Galloway* (1908), one of three 'border' ballads for orchestra, and a symphony, *Solway* (1911).

Macfarren, Sir George Alexander (1813-

1887) Composer and teacher who entered the Royal Academy in 1829. Composition was his principal study, and in 1837 he was appointed a professor at the Academy, where he taught for 10 years. In 1875 he became professor of music at Cambridge, and principal of the Royal Academy of Music. He was a prolific composer, producing many sacred works, operas, nine symphonies and a piano concerto.

Machaut, Guillaume de (1300-1377) French poet and composer. At an early age Machaut took holy orders and studied theology, probably in Paris. He served as secretary to John of Luxembourg, King of Bohemia (1323-1346) and later King Charles V of France and John, Duke of Berry. Musically, Machaut is most famous for his ballades, rondeaux for two, three or four voices, his *lais* and *virelais* (mostly for one voice), his motets and his Notre Dame mass. His use of syncopation and treatment of chords and discords combined to create a unique style.

machine head Mechanism used for securing and adjusting the tension of strings for instruments such as the double-bass, guitar and mandolin. The strings are attached to spindles that pass through the pegbox parallel to the frets on the fingerboard. Worm gears are attached to the ends of the spindles, and these are rotated by matching worm gears at the end of the pegs. By turning the pegs, the strings can be tensioned.

Mackenzie, Sir Alexander (1847-1935) Scottish composer and violinist who at the age of ten was sent to study music in Germany. He returned to England in 1862 and won the King's Scholarship for a place at the Royal Academy of Music. In 1885-1886 Mackenzie acted as conductor of Novello's Oratorio concerts. In 1888 he succeeded Sir George **Macfarren** as principal of the Academy. His works include operas, concertos for piano and violin, chamber music and songs.

Mackerras, Sir Charles (1925-) Australian conductor and oboist who studied at the New South Wales Conservatoire. He held the position of principal oboist for the Sydney Symphony Orchestra (1943-1946). For four years he conducted the Hamburg State Opera, and from 1970 to 1977 he was principal conductor of Sadler's Wells Opera. He joined the Welsh National Opera in 1987. He received a CBE in 1974 and was knighted in 1979.

Maconchy, Elizabeth (1907-) English composer of Irish parentage, who studied at the Royal Academy of Music. Although a talented piano soloist, she is better known as a composer. Her 11 string quartets are seen as the central strength of her work. She has also written several stage works and a symphony and has composed works for chorus, orchestra, and solo instruments.

McPhee, Colin (1901-1964) American composer whose best-known work is the symphony *Tabuh-Tabuhan* (1936), strongly influenced by the **gamelan** percussion orchestras of Bali, where McPhee lived during the 1930s. His other well-known composition is *Sea Shanty Suite* (1929), for a chorus of male voices. Apart from being a composer and pianist, McPhee also wrote on a variety of subjects, including modern music, jazz and various aspects of Indonesian life.

Maderna, Bruno (1920-1973) Italian composer, conductor and co-director of the Milan Radio Electronic Studio. In 1952 his composition *Musica su due dimensioni* was the first to combine live instruments with tape recordings.

Madetoja, Leevi Antti (1881-1947) Finnish composer and conductor who studied in Helsinki with **Sibelius**, in Paris with **d'Indy** and in Vienna. He conducted the Helsinki Philharmonic Orchestra, and in 1926 was made professor of music at the Helsinki Conservatoire. His works include an opera, three symphonies, symphonic poems and cantatas.

madrigal Form of poetry and music which originated in Italy during the 14th century. It was sung by unaccompanied voices. The texts were strophic and amorous in subject. During the 16th century the use of the term broadened, largely because of the impact of Franco-Flemish **polyphony** and also because of composers such as Jacob Arcadelt (*c*1505-1568), Costanzo **Festa** (*c*1490-1545) and Philippe **Verdelot**.

In 1588, a collection of Italian madrigals was published with translated texts in London, and this paved the way for the English form of madrigal. It usually employed a five-voice texture set to texts on pastoral and amorous subjects and, like French **chansons**, was light in style. The most notable composers of English madrigals were Thomas **Morley**, Thomas **Weelkes** (*c*1575-1623) and John **Wilbye** (*c*1574-1638).

There are three major forms of madrigal: the madrigal proper, the canzonet and the ballett. The true madrigal is **through-composed** and contrapuntal in texture. It differs from the ayre in that the latter repeats the tune for each verse and is less contrapuntal, with more emphasis on the soprano part (the other voices giving accompaniment). The ballett is also in strophic form, but has a refrain, and may have been used as an accompaniment to dancing. The canzonet is sectional and includes repeats.

An important collection of madrigals – *The Triumphs of Oriana* (1601) – was edited by Thomas Morley, and includes 29 English madrigals by various composers addressed to Queen Elizabeth I.

The composition of madrigals has continued into the 20th century with works by such composers as E.J. **Moeran** (1894-1950) and Peter **Warlock** (1894-1930).

Maelzel, Johann Nepomuk (1772-1838) German inventor who is best known for constructing an automatic instrument that manipulated trumpets, flutes, drums, cymbals, strings and a triangle. At one time a close associate of **Beethoven**, they later disagreed over the rights of a battle-piece composed by Beethoven for Maelzel's panharmonicon, an instrument similar to the one previously mentioned, but with clarinets, violins and cellos added. He also patented the **metronome**.

maestoso (It.) Majestically. Indication that the music is to be played in a stately manner.

maestro (It.) Master. Title given by Italians to a distinguished musician, whether a composer, performer or teacher. It is now sometimes used, especially in the United States by musicians addressing a conductor.

maggiore (It.) In a major key. The word is sometimes stated at a point in a composition where the major key returns after a prolonged section in a minor key, especially in **variations**, to prevent the performer overlooking the change of key.

Magnificat The hymn of the Virgin Mary, regularly sung as a Vesper canticle in the Roman Catholic Church and as part of the evening service in the Anglican Church. The title is from the Latin version of the opening words: *Magnificat anima mea Dominum* (My soul doth magnify the Lord).

A concert setting of the words, together with additional text, was composed by **Vaughan Williams** (*Magnificat*, 1922). Other choral settings have been produced by such composers as **Purcell**, J.S. **Bach**, **Stanford**, **Howells** and **Tippett**.

Mahler, Gustav (1860-1911) Austrian conductor and composer who studied at the conservatoire in Vienna from 1875 to 1878. Much of his musical career was spent as an opera conductor. In 1888 he became director of the Royal Opera in Budapest, and from 1891 to 1897 he was *Kapellmeister* at the Municipal Theatre in Hamburg, where he was able to compose while remaining in charge of operatic production. After Hamburg he went to the Court Opera in Vienna, where from his original post of

Kapellmeister he was promoted to artistic director (1897-1907). He spent the last years of his life conducting in Europe and the United States. In 1907 he conducted the New York Philharmonic Society, and later a variety of operas for the Metropolitan Opera House.

During his lifetime, Mahler's standing as a conductor was never questioned, but his compositions received little acclaim. It was not until the 1950s that his work became popular. It is now seen to cross the divide between older, Romantic styles of music and the newer avant-garde, with his extensive use of chromaticism in certain pieces, and the use of less than conventional forms for his symphonies.

Mahler was a prolific composer, producing nine symphonies, songs, song cycles, chamber music and cantatas (including *Das Klagende Lied*, 1880). His work has been extensively recorded and has a place in repertories around the world.

Gustav Mahler

major interval **Interval** of a second, third, sixth, or seventh.

major scale One of the two predominant **scales** (the other being **minor**) of the tonal system. The major scale is made up of two **tetrachords**, with a semitone (rather than a tone) between the third and fourth notes of each. The scale of C major, for example may be played on all the white keys on a piano from C-C′. The other major scales require an accidental sharp or flat to preserve the correct order of tones and semitones. Each major scale has a related minor scale which shares the same key-signature, built on the last three notes of the minor scale. Thus, for example, the scale of C major is related to A minor. See also **minor scale**.

Scale of C major

makam See **maqam**.

malagueña (Sp.) Andalusian song and dance (similar to the **fandango**) in triple time, which originated in Malaga. The form is also sometimes used for instrumental music.

Malipiero, Gian Francesco (1882-1973) Italian composer and violinist. He studied in Vienna, Venice and Paris. In 1921 he was appointed professor of composition at the Parma Conservatoire. He was later appointed director at institutes in Padua and Venice. He composed operas, including *Venere prigioniera* (1955), 11 sinfonias and three sets of *Impressioni dal vero* (1910-1922). He also composed ballet music, other choral and orchestral works, chamber music, vocal chamber music, pieces for piano, violin and piano and songs.

Malipiero, Riccardo (1914-) Italian composer and critic, nephew of Gian

Francesco **Malipiero**. A strict adherent of the **twelve-note technique**, his works in this mode include the opera *Minnie la Candida* (1942), *Cantata sacra* (1947) for solo voices, chorus and orchestra, his symphony for orchestra (1949) and other works for string quartet, piano and chorus.

mandola Small stringed instrument of the lute family which is now obsolete. It originated during the Middle Ages in Italy, and in the 18th century was replaced by the **mandolin**. An alternative term is mandora.

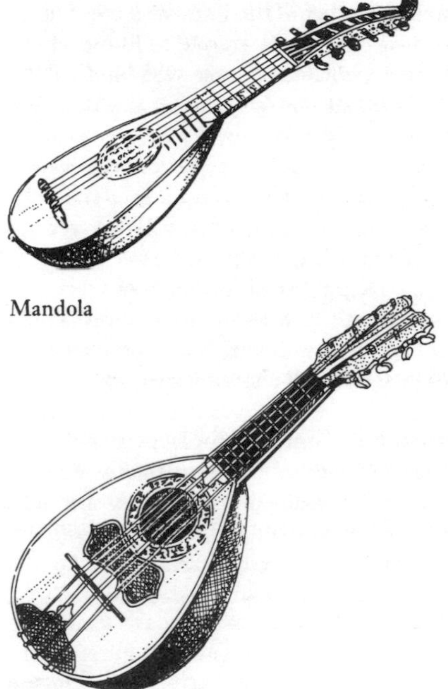

Mandola

Mandolin

mandolin Stringed instrument related to the **lute** which evolved from the **mandola** in Italy during the 18th century. It has a more rounded back than a lute, and has four pairs of wire strings tuned like the violin and played with a plectrum. The fingerboard is fretted to facilitate fingering and **intonation. Beethoven, Mozart** and **Mahler** all composed music for the instrument. An alternative spelling is mandoline.

mandora Alternative term for **mandola**.

Manfredini, Francesco Maria (1684-1762) Italian violinist and composer who studied under **Torelli** and **Perti**. In 1711 he became *maestro di cappella* in Monaco, and in 1727 at the cathedral in Pistoia. His most celebrated works are the six oratorios, but he also composed sinfonias, concertos, concerti grossi and chamber music.

Manfredini, Vincenzo (1737-1799) Italian composer, son of Francesco. He studied under **Perti** in Bologna and Fioroni in Milan. He became court composer in Russia, where he taught Tsar Paul I. His works include several operas, cantatas, a Requiem, ballets and harpsichord sonatas.

Manns, Sir August (1825-1907) German bandmaster and conductor. He played first clarinet in a regimental band until 1848 when he joined Joseph **Gungl**'s orchestra in Berlin, where he advanced to conductor and first violin. In 1855 he was engaged as conductor at Crystal Palace where he organized daily music, Saturday concerts and numerous festivals. He also conducted at the Sheffield and Handel festivals. He was knighted in 1903.

manual Keyboard played with the hands, especially the keyboards of organs and harpsichords as distinct from the pedals.

maqam/makam (pl. **maqamat**) Technical term used throughout the Near and Middle East to mean mode or melody type. Its precise definition depends on the particular performing tradition concerned. In Iran it refers to the scale type, or mode, in which particular tunes or *gusheh* are cast, according to the Persian *dastgah* system. In Iraq, *maqamat* are modes defined more precisely, constituting a melodic entity subject to vocal or instrumental improvisation. Among Arab peoples, *maqam* in common usage refers also to performances of such forms.

maraca Percussion instrument used mainly

in jazz and swing bands. It is a rattle made of a dried gourd containing beads or seeds, although the modern variety is often made of plastic and contains lead shot.

Marais, Marin (1656-1728) French composer and viol player. He studied the viola da gamba under Sainte Colombe and was employed as a musician in royal chamber from 1679. He also studied composition under **Lully** and wrote four operas, including *Alcione* (1706), chamber music and compositions for the bass viol.

Marcello, Alessandro (1684-1750) Italian philosopher, mathematician, singer and composer. His published works include 12 solo cantatas, 12 sonatas for violin and continuo, six concertos for two flutes or violins and other concertos.

Marcello, Benedetto (1686-1739) Italian composer and theorist, brother of Alessandro **Marcello**. A former lawyer who studied music under **Lotti** and **Gasparini**, he began studying the violin but soon devoted his time to vocal music and composition. In 1712 he joined the *Accademia Filarmonica* in Bologna. Apart from his best-known work, *Estro poetico-armonico* (settings for two parts of 25 psalms paraphrased by Giustiniani), he also composed more than 400 cantatas, several oratorios, concertos and sonatas.

march Piece of music in strongly emphasized regular metre (4/4, 2/4 or 6/8 rhythms), primarily intended for use at military parades to keep marching soldiers in step. It is often used for processions of various kinds, especially in operas such as *The Magic Flute* (**Mozart**, 1791) and *Die Meistersinger* (**Wagner**, 1868). Although slower in pace, funeral marches also have a processional purpose, and are found in symphonies, including **Beethoven's** *Eroica Symphony* (1803-1804) and **Elgar's** *Six Pomp and Circumstance Military Marches.*

marche (Fr.) Equivalent of the English **march**.

Marchand, Louis (1669-1732) French organist, harpsichordist and composer. At the age of 14 he was appointed organist at Nevers Cathedral and in 1693 at Auxerre Cathedral. He settled in Paris in 1698 and by 1702 he was organist in three Parisian churches; in 1708 he became court organist. Apart from his works for organ, including the *Grand dialogue* and *Livre d'orgue*, he wrote harpsichord music, a collection of airs and a cantata.

Marenzio, Luca (1553-1599) Italian composer. It is uncertain where or under whom he studied, but it is likely that he was a member of the Cathedral choir in Brescia. In 1574 he moved to Rome where his most notable patrons were Cardinal Luigi d'Este and Virginio Orsini. Between 1596 and 1598 Marenzio was *maestro di cappella* to the King of Poland. Marenzio is noted mainly for his five- and six-voice madrigals, which number well over 200 and were published in Venice between 1580 and 1599. He published further books of madrigals, for three and four voices, a book of twelve-part motets, and a complete series of motets for all church festivals.

marimba Form of **xylophone** found in Central America, which originated in Africa. It is made of tuned strips of wood of various lengths laid out in a frame with resonator-boxes below each strip. The strips are struck with soft-headed sticks.

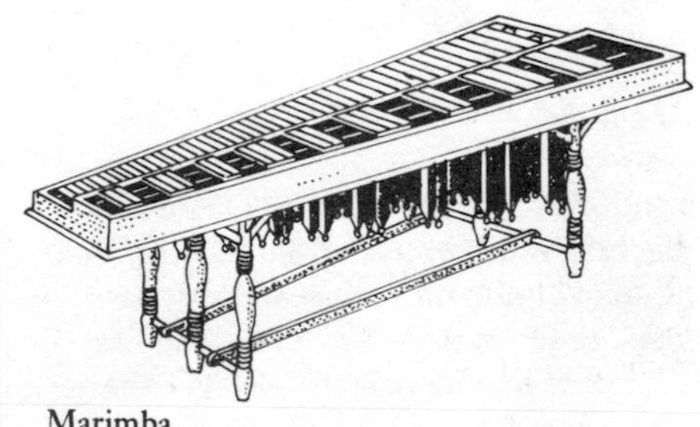

Marimba

The marimba is occasionally used in the modern orchestra. Darius **Milhaud** wrote a concerto for marimba and vibraphone (1947).

Markevich, Igor (1912-1983) Soviet conductor and composer. In 1927 he settled in Paris and studied under **Boulanger**. His compositions were at first greatly influenced by **Stravinsky** but later he found a more personal style. Markevich's works comprise a sinfonietta, a concerto for piano and orchestra, a cantata for soprano and male-voice choir, a serenade, a psalm and a partita. He has also written two ballets, *Rébus* (1931) and *L'Envoi d'Icare* (1932). After 1945 he concentrated more on conducting, and as well as several major American orchestras, he has conducted the Lamoureux Orchestra, Paris (1957-1961), and the Monte Carlo Opera (1968-1973).

Marpurg, Friedrich Wilhelm (1718-1795) German musical theorist and critic. He is noted for his unbounded admiration for J.S. **Bach**, whom he met in Leipzig shortly before the latter's death in 1750. Marpurg wrote a preface to an edition of *The Art of Fugue*, which appeared in 1752, and recommended Bach's contrapuntal techniques in his famous treatise on the fugue, *Abhandlung von der Fuge* (1753-1754). He also introduced the musical theories of the French composer **Rameau** to German readers.

Marriner, Neville (1924-) British conductor and violinist. In 1959 he founded the **Academy of St Martin-in-the-Fields** and remained its director until 1978, when he became conductor of the Minnesota Orchestra. In 1969 he took up the position of conductor to the Los Angeles Chamber Orchestra.

Sir Neville Marriner

Marschner, Heinrich August (1795-1861) German composer and conductor, who studied under Schicht in Leipzig. In 1823, after a successful production of his opera *Heinrich IV und Aubigné*, produced by **Weber** three years earlier, he was appointed joint *Kapellmeister* of the Italian and German Opera in Dresden, and a year later he advanced to *musikdirektor*. However, by 1827 he had settled in Leipzig as *Kapellmeister* of the theatre. From 1831 to 1859 he was conductor of the Hanover Hoftheater. He wrote a total of 13 operas, including *Der Vampyr*, *Der Templer und die Jüdin* and *Hans Heiling*. He also wrote a ballet and incidental music, two symphonies, chamber music, piano music, more than 120 choral pieces for male voices and over 420 songs.

martenot Electrophonic device (an early form of **synthesizer**) invented by Maurice Martenot in 1929. It was more commonly known as *ondes martenot* and was operated by a piano-type keyboard. It was an electronic device using thermionic-valve oscillators to produce sound through loudspeakers. The instrument was used by **Honegger** in *Joan of Arc at the Stake* (1938).

Martin, Frank (1890-1974) Swiss composer. He studied in Geneva under Joseph Lauber, and later in Rome, Zurich and Paris. In 1911, at the Swiss Music Festival, Martin made his first appearance as a composer with a performance of his *Trois Poèmes Payens*. His earlier compositions demonstrate a strong French influence, although he later experimented by combining traditional and popular eastern musical constructions. He was also influenced by **Schoenberg**'s twelve-note music. Martin's works include three ballets, several pieces for chorus, including an oratorio (*Le Vin Herbé*), orchestral works and chamber, piano, organ, and guitar music.

Martini, Giovanni Battista (1706-1784) Italian composer, theorist and teacher, nicknamed Padre Martini. Although an important composer in his own right, his reputation as a teacher was such that J.C. **Bach**, **Mozart**, **Sarti**, Ottani and many others came to study under him. Martini learned to sing and play the harpsichord under Predieri and counterpoint from Riccieri and **Perti**. In 1725 he became *maestro di cappella* of the church of San Francesco, Bologna, where he was also a priest. Apart from his contrapuntal sacred works, he also composed ensemble works, sinfonias, concertos, keyboard music and *intermezzi*.

Martini il Tedesco (1741-1816) Nickname of Johann Paul Aegidius Schwartzendorf, a German composer, organist and teacher. He moved to France in the mid-18th century and settled in Paris in 1764, when he Italianized his name. In 1798 he became an inspector of the Conservatoire and in 1814 director of the court orchestra. His works include military music, symphonies, operas, cantatas and masses.

Martinon, Jean (1910-1976) French conductor, composer and violinist. He studied at the conservatoires in Lyons and Paris. From 1951 to 1957 he conducted the Lamoureux Orchestra, and from 1963 to 1969 the Chicago Symphony Orchestra. His compositions include four symphonies and four concertos.

Martinu, Bohuslav (1890-1959) Czech composer who studied at the Prague Conservatoire from 1906, and by 1913 had joined the Czech Philharmonic Orchestra as a violinist. After World War I he re-entered the conservatoire and became a pupil of **Suk**. A year later (1923), he moved to Paris and studied under **Roussel**. Martinu remained in Paris until 1940, when the threat of Nazi Germany forced him to flee to the United States. In 1946 he accepted a post at the Prague Conservatoire as a professor of composition, only to return to the United States two years later to continue teaching. In 1957 he moved to Switzerland. Martinu's prolific output consists of operas, including *Comedy on the Bridge*, *Julietta*, *The Marriage* and *Ariadne*, ballets, six symphonies, concertos for one and two pianos, pieces for cello, violin and harpsichord, chamber music, a piano quartet and a variety of choral works.

Martin y Soler, Vicente (1754-1806) Spanish composer.He began his career as an organist in Alicante, but soon he turned to the composition of operas. By 1785, when he went to Vienna, he was well established and worked with Da Ponte, producing three operas including *Una cosa rara* (1786). In 1788 Martin travelled to St Petersburg, where he was later to become court conductor to Catherine II. In 1798, after a brief visit to London where he produced two more operas with Da Ponte, he returned to Russia where Tsar Paul I nominated him Privy Councillor. His works include operas, ballets, songs and cantatas.

mārvā/mārwā (India) One of the ten parent scales (**thāt**) in Hindustani music, corresponding to C, D♭, E, F♯, G, A, B, C′.

mārwā See **mārvā**.

Marx, Joseph (1882-1964) Austrian composer, critic and teacher. In 1914 he was awarded a professorship in musical theory at the Imperial Music Academy in Vienna. From 1924 to 1927 he was principal of the Viennese High School for Music. Marx is best known for his songs, but certain chamber works, such as the *Quartetto in modo antico* (1940), represent his style equally well.

marziale (It.) In a martial or warlike fashion.

Mascagni, Pietro (1863-1945) Italian

composer. He studied at the *Instituto Luigi Cherubini* under **Ponchielli**. He became fully established after his opera *Cavalleria rusticana* won first prize in a competition instituted by the publisher Sonzongo, and was produced in Rome in 1890. Mascagni's other operas include *L'Amico Fritz* (1891), *Iris* (1898), *Le Maschera* (1900) and *Nerone* (1935), all in the *verismo* style.

mask Alternative spelling of **masque**.

maske Alternative spelling of **masque**.

Mason, Lowell (1792-1872) American composer, educationist and conductor. He composed, with the help of F. L. Abel, a collection of hymns based on Gardiner's *Sacred Melodies*, which subsequently became popular throughout the United States. In 1832 he established the *Boston Academy of Music*, and by 1838 he had obtained the mandate to teach in every school in Boston, leading to the introduction of music as part of the school curriculum. He published a large number of educational manuals and travelled widely in the United States and Europe, lecturing on educational methods. He also composed glees, children's songs and musical exercises.

masque Stage entertainment cultivated for court occasions in England during the 17th century, but which originated in the Italian *intermedio* and the French ballet. The masque may be said to be the English form closest to Italian opera at this time. It involved the recital of poetry, singing, dancing and spectacle. The subject matter upon which the masque was based was mainly mythological, heroic or allegorical.

One of the most famous masques of the era is *Comus*, with words by John Milton and music by Henry **Lawes**. A second, Thomas **Arne**'s *Alfred* (1740), includes *Rule, Britannia!* Other writers of music for masque include **Campion** and Lanier.

In the 20th century, the term has been applied to pieces such as *The Crown of India*, by **Elgar** (1912), and to *Job, A Masque for Dancing*, by **Vaughan Williams** (1931). Alternative spellings of the term are mask and maske.

mass Most important service of the Roman Catholic Church, which includes the celebration of the Eucharist. The Mass is divided into two main parts: the Proper of the Mass and the Ordinary of the Mass, both of which are sung. The six sections of the Proper are *Introit, Gradual, Alleluia, Tract, Offertory* and *Communion*. (The words of these movements change according to the season of the Christian year.) The Ordinary consists of *Kyrie*, *Gloria, Credo, Sanctus* with *Benedictus*, and *Agnus Dei*. During Advent and Lent, the Gloria is omitted. Works entitled Mass are usually settings of the Ordinary.

The **plainsong** Mass of the Middle Ages consisted of a setting of the Creed and a large number of alternative settings of other musical parts of the liturgy. With the development of **polyphony** in the 15th and 16th centuries, Mass music became integrated, first as a **cantus firmus** work with the plainchant 'held' by the tenor voice, and then as a work based upon a freely composed melody or upon a *cantus firmus* borrowed from secular music.

The Baroque era of the 17th century encouraged the composition of 'cantata masses', with texts broken into set **arias, duets** and **choruses**, often with very elaborate orchestral accompaniment. **Bach's** Mass in B minor (1733-*c*1738) is the greatest of these. Later came **Beethoven's** *Missa solemnis* (1823).

During the 20th century, settings have been made by **Vaughan Willams** (Mass in G minor, 1920-1921), Francis **Poulenc** (Mass in G major, 1937), and Igor **Stravinsky** (Mass for mixed chorus and double wind quintet, 1948).

Massenet, Jules Emile Frédéric (1842-1912) French composer and teacher who entered the Paris Conservatoire at the age of 11 and studied under Laurent Reber and Ambroise **Thomas**. In 1863 he won the Prix de Rome with a cantata, *David Rizzio*.

His first opera, *La Grand' Tante*, was produced in 1867 at the Opéra-Comique, and in the same year his first orchestral suite was performed. In 1878 he was appointed professor of advanced composition at the Conservatoire, where **Bruneau**, **Leroux**, Pierne and **Charpentier** were among his pupils. Massenet wrote a great many operas, including *Manon* (1884), *Werther* (1892) and *Theis* (1894), several ballets, incidental music, a piano concerto (1903) and orchestral suites, including *Scènes Napolitaines* (1876) and *Scènes Alsaciennes* (1881), three oratorios *Marie-Magdeleine* (1873), *Eve* (1875) and *La Vierge* (1880). At 36 Massenet was the youngest member of the Académie des Beaux Arts, in 1876 he was awarded the Legion of Honour.

Mather, Bruce (1939-) Canadian composer and pianist who studied under **Beckwith** at the Toronto Royal Conservatoire and under **Messiaen** and **Milhaud** in Paris. In 1966 he became a teacher of composition at McGill University in Montreal. His works include *Cycle Rilke* (1960) for tenor and guitar, *Ombres* (1967) for orchestra and a sonata for two pianos (1970).

Mathias, William (1934-) Welsh composer and pianist who trained in Aberystwyth and then at the Royal Academy of Music, where he studied composition under Lennox **Berkeley**. From 1959 he was a lecturer and professor of music at Bangor University. His works include pieces for orchestra, concertos, chamber music and church music.

mātrā (India) Smallest metrical unit in Indian music, grouped in **tālas** or rhythmic cycles.

Matsudaira, Yoritsune (1907-) Japanese composer who studied under **Tcherepnin**. His style combines **serial** procedures with Japanese traditional music. His works include two piano concertos (1946), *Ancient Japanese Dance* (1953), *Portrait B* (1968) and *Circulating Movements* (1972).

Mattheson, Johann (1681-1764) German singer, theorist and composer. He studied music in Hamburg and made his first appearance in 1696 with the Hamburg Opera. In 1699 his first opera, *Die Plejades*, was produced soon after he met **Handel**, who arrived in Hamburg in 1703, and they worked together on several operas. In 1719 the Duke of Holstein appointed Mattheson as court *Kapellmeister*. His works include many German oratorios and cantatas, eight operas, sonatas for flute and violin and suites for clavier. He also wrote several books, including some on the subject of the state of music in Hamburg, a collection of biographies of contemporary musicians and theoretical works, including *Das neu-eröffnete Orchestre* (1713), *Exemplarische Organisten Probe* (1719) and *Der Vollkommene Capellmeister* (1739).

Matthews, Colin (1946-) English composer who studied under Whittall and **Maw**. His works for orchestra include *Fourth Sonata* (1974-75) and *Night Music* (1977). He has also written for wind quintet and string quartet, a piece for voice and harp, five studies for piano, and a partita for violin (1975).

Matthews, Denis (1919-) English pianist. In 1935 he entered the Royal Academy of Music and studied under Craxton and **Alwyn**. He held the Thalberg Scholarship for two years and the Blumenthal Scholarship for three. He first appeared in 1939 at a promenade concert in London and at the National Gallery. He played in the RAF orchestra during World War II and in 1945 played with the Royal Philharmonic Society. Although he has a wide repertoire, he specializes in the classics, particularly **Mozart** and **Beethoven**. He became a professor of music at Newcastle University in 1971.

Maw, Nicholas (1935-) English composer who entered the Royal Academy of Music in 1955. From 1958 to 1959 he studied in

Paris under **Boulanger** and Deutsch. His work combines contemporary **serial** procedures with traditional forms and outlook. His works include two operas, *One-Man Show* (1964) and *The Rising of the Moon* (1969), orchestral pieces including *Sinfonia* (1966) and *Sonata* (1967), chamber music and songs.

Mayr, (Johannes) Simon (1763-1845) German opera and church music composer who worked in northern Italy. Born in Mendorf, Bavaria, he went to study in Bergamo and Venice, where his oratorios proved popular. *Saffo*, the first of his 67 operas, was staged in 1794. In 1802 he became *maestro di cappella* at the church of Santa Maria Maggiore in Bergamo. He turned the choir school there into a proper music school, the ancestor of the city's conservatoire, and taught counterpoint, one of his pupils being **Donizetti**. In his later years, faced with the dazzling talent of Rossini, he gave up composing opera in favour of church music. Many of his operas use classical themes, such as *Il ritorno di Ulisse* and *Medea in Corinto*. But his *Amor congiugale* uses the same storyline as **Beethoven**'s *Fidelio*.

Mayuzumi, Toshiro (1929-) Japanese composer who studied in Tokyo and at the Paris Conservatoire. His works combine Japanese sources with avant-garde Western methods. His most well-known pieces are the symphonies *Bacchanale* (1953) and *Mandala* (1960).

mazurka Polish national dance dating back to the 17th century and originating in the Mazovia region around Warsaw. The dance-figures are complicated and subject to much variation. They are performed to improvised music. Groups of four, eight or twelve dancers perform the mazurka, and the music is in moderate 3/4 time. **Chopin** composed 55 mazurkas for piano, which not only illustrate his pianistic virtuosity, but also reflect the many possible moods and speeds of the dance.

mbira (Africa) African keyboard instrument – a tuned idiophone consisting of a sounding board supporting wooden or metal keys

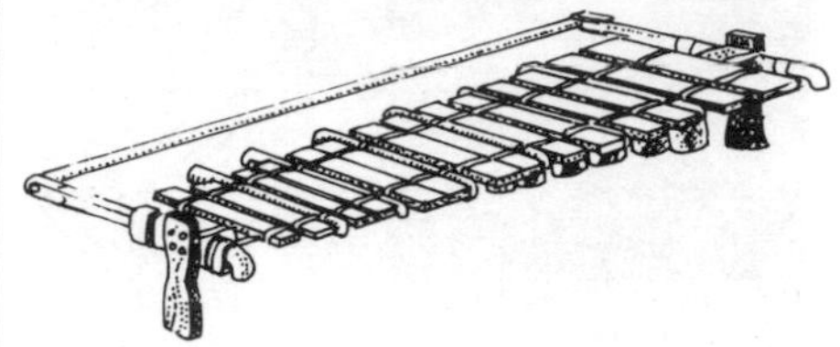

Mbira

over a resonator. The keys are plucked in syncopated stratified rhythms, typical of African musical systems.

me Mediant note in any key in **tonic sol-fa**.

mean-tone temperament Method of 'tuning' an organ so that the major third intervals are as accurate as possible, making the **temperament** of six major keys and three minor keys reasonable. All other intervals are adapted to the major third intervals.

measure In post-17th-century music, the space in time between one accented beat and another. The group of beats within a measure is separated from the next by a bar line.

mediant Third degree of the major or minor scale, so called because it stands half way between **tonic** and **dominant**.

Medtner, Nikolay Karlovich (1880-1951) Russian composer and pianist. In 1892 he joined the Moscow Conservatoire and studied the piano under Pabst, Sapellnikov and Safonov and theory under **Arensky** and **Taneyev**. His career took him to Germany, the United States, France, Canada and, finally England.

Medtner is known mainly for his compositions for piano, particularly the sonatas; however, he also wrote three piano concertos, some chamber music and a large number of works for voice and piano.

Zubin Mehta

Mehta, Zubin (1936-) Indian conductor, violinist and pianist who studied at the Vienna State Academy of Music. From 1961 to 1976 he was director of the Los Angeles Philharmonic Orchestra. In 1978 he became director of the New York Philharmonic Orchestra.

Méhul, Etienne Nicolas (1763-1817) French composer. After gaining some musical instruction from Hauser at the monastery of Val Dieu, Méhul moved to Paris in 1788, where he studied piano and composition under Edelmann. He was greatly influenced by **Gluck**, from whom he received valuable advice and encouragement to write operas. In 1790 Méhul's *opéra-comique*, *Euphrosine* was produced and became popular throughout France. In 1793 he became an inspector of the newly-founded Paris Conservatoire. He wrote more than 30 operas, including *Cora* (1789), *Le Jeune Sage et le Vieux Fou* (1793), *Uthal* (1806) and *Joseph* (1807). He also wrote four ballets, cantatas, patriotic songs, in particular *Chant du départ* (1794), symphonies and piano sonatas.

meistersinger (Ger.) Member of a guild of poets and musicians who cultivated poetry and singing during the 14th to 16th centuries. The members passed through various stages from apprenticeship to mastery. They were middle-class burghers, tradesmen and artisans and not aristocrats such as the earlier *Minnesinger*. **Wagner's** opera *Die Meistersinger von Nürnberg* (1868) is a romanticized view of the *Meistersinger*.

Dame Nellie Melba

Melba, Dame Nellie (Helen Armstrong) (1861-1931) Australian soprano who went to Europe in 1886 and studied in Paris under Marchesi. In 1887 she made her debut at the Paris Opéra. She returned the next summer to Covent Garden before singing at St Petersburg and touring Italy. Two of her most notable tours were those in Canada and the United States in 1903. During these tours she studied the part of Hélène in Saint-Saëns's opera of that name, which she first performed at Monte-Carlo in 1904. Melba became a Dame of the British Empire in 1918.

Melchior, Lauritz (1890-1973) Danish tenor. He studied at the Royal Opera School in Copenhagen and made his debut there in 1913. His powerful voice enabled him to take the heroic **Wagnerian** parts, notably Siegfried and Tristan, but he also sang a number of Italian tenor parts, including **Verdi**'s *Othello*. He was honorary president of the Richard Wagner Society of America.

melisma Group of notes sung to a single syllable. The term sometimes applies to any florid vocal passage in the nature of a **cadenza**. The device came into use in **plainsong**, but became most popular in the 18th century in the works of such composers as **Handel**, being inserted either to emphasize emotion or to give an opportunity to display the technique of a virtuoso singer. The plural of the word, *Melismata*, is also the title of a collection of English vocal pieces by Ravenscroft (1611).

Mellers, Wilfred (1914-) English critic and composer. After studying English and music at Cambridge (1933-1938), he studied composition with **Rubbra** and **Wellesz** at Oxford. He held a variety of teaching posts, including Dartington Hall, Cambridge, Birmingham and Pittsburgh before becoming professor of music at York University in 1964. His reputation as a writer on music grew quickly, and from 1940 he was music editor of *Scrutiny*. His list of published books includes *Music and Society* (1946), *Studies in Contemporary Music* (1948) and *François Couperin and the French Classical Tradition* (1950).

mellophone Brass instrument of circular shape that is a simplified version of the orchestral **horn** and used in marching bands. It is similar to a tenor horn, pitched in E♭ or F.

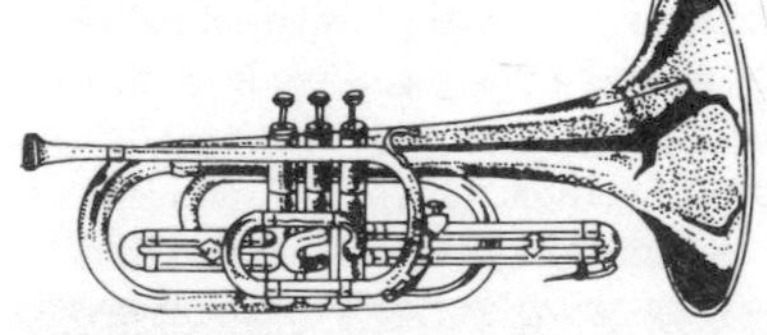

Mellophone

melodeon Type of accordion that is played with both hands. The right hand plays the melody by depressing buttons arranged to play **diatonic** scales in one or two keys.

Melodeon

The left hand has a set of accompanying chords and notes, produced by buttons for each key. Different notes are produced by each button, according to whether the bellows are being closed or opened.

mélodie (Fr.) Melody. Term used since the 19th century for accompanied art song. It is the French equivalent of the German *Lied*.

melodic minor Variation of a **minor** scale in which the third and fourth notes of the upper **tetrachord** are sharpened when the scale is moving upwards. When the scale is moving downwards, these notes are flattened. The melodic minor is more lyrical in its effect than the **harmonic minor** scale. See also **major scale**.

Scale of A melodic minor

melodrama Dramatic use of spoken words against a musical background. This may occur throughout a musical work, or only as part of a work, such as the gravedigging scene in **Beethoven's** *Fidelio* (1814).

melody Intelligible succession of notes defined by **pitch, rhythm** and **harmony**, which are the basic characteristics of Western music. The term is also used as a title for a simple piece, such as Melody in F, by Anton **Rubinstein** (1853).

membranophone Instrument in which the sound is produced by the vibration of a stretched membrane of skin. All forms of drum are included in this classification. See also **chordophone; idiophone**.

Mendelssohn, Felix (1809-1847) German composer, pianist and organist. He was a child prodigy as a pianist, making his debut when he was only nine. At ten his setting for Psalm 19 was performed by the *Berlin Singakademie*. He wrote his first symphony in 1824, the comic opera *Die Hochzeit des Camacho* coming a year later. At 17 he entered Berlin University and studied for three years before determining upon music as his profession. It was around this time that he became an advocate of J.S. **Bach**, conducting the *St Matthew Passion* in 1829. Later in the same year he visited England, where he was received with great enthusiasm. His overture, *The Hebrides* (1830), was inspired by a tour he made of Scotland during this visit.

The following two years he spent touring Germany, Austria and Italy, composing two symphonies. Between 1835-1846 he was conductor of the Leipzig Gewandhaus Orchestra. During this period he wrote *Lobgesang*, a symphonic cantata, the *Scottish Symphony* (No. 3), the *Variations Serieuses* (for piano) and a violin concerto. By 1843 he had founded, with **Schumann**, the Leipzig Cconservatoire, teaching the piano and composition. In 1846 he made his ninth and penultimate visit to Britain, where he conducted the first performance of his oratorio *Elijah* at the Birmingham Festival. As well as his five symphonies, including *The Reformation Symphony* (1830) and *The Italian* (1833), Mendelssohn wrote the overture *Die Schöne Melusine* (1833), several concertos, seven string quartets and a great deal of other chamber music, choral works and partsongs. His style may be compared in its Romanticism with that of **Chopin** and Schumann.

Mengelberg, Willem (1871-1951) Dutch conductor who studied at the conservatoire in Cologne under Wullner. In 1895 he was appointed conductor of Concertgebouw Orchestra of Amsterdam. His particular interpretations of **Strauss**, **Mahler** and **Beethoven** stand at the forefront of his career.

Menotti, Gian Carlo (1911-) Italian composer and conductor. After studying in Milan for four years, Menotti emigrated to the United States at the age of 16. There he studied at the Curtis Institute in Philadelphia under Scalero. His compositions tend towards opera, and his first, *Amelia Goes to the Ball*, was produced in 1937. This opera, along with *The Medium* (1946) and *The Consul* (1950), attained great popularity and demonstrates Menotti's dramatic writing skill as librettist as well as composer. In addition to more than 12 operas, including at least two produced for television (*Amahl and the Night Visitors*, 1951, and *The Labyrinth*, 1963), Menotti has written ballets, a cantata and a piano and violin concerto.

Menuhin, Yehudi (1916-) American violinist and conductor. He was a child

Yehudi Menuhin

prodigy as a violinist, making his debut at the age of eight with a performance of Mendelssohn's violin concerto. He studied in Paris under **Enescu** and was later coached by **Elgar**. **Bartók** composed a solo violin sonata for him in 1942 and **Walton** another in 1950. In 1959 he settled in England and until 1968 he directed the Bath Festival. In 1962 he founded what has become a famous music school at Stoke d'Abernon, near London. Menuhin has recorded widely and his repertory is extensive, including the works of such composers as **Bach**, **Beethoven** and **Brahms**.

Mercadante, Saverio (1795-1870) Italian composer. Mercadante entered the Naples Conservatoire in 1808, studying under **Zingarelli**. After visiting Spain and Portugal (1826-1827) composing for the Italian opera in Madrid. He went to Paris in 1835. There he came under the influence of **Meyerbeer**, whose style replaced Mercadante's previous Rossinian style of composition. From 1840 until his death Mercadante was director of the Naples Conservatoire.

In addition to some 60 operas, including *Elisa e Claudio* (1821), *I Briganti* (1836) and *Orazi e Curiazi* (1846), he wrote 21 masses, four ballets as well as songs, orchestral and chamber music.

Merkel, Gustav (1827-1885) German composer and organist. In 1861 he became a professor at the Dresden Conservatoire, and from 1864 he was appointed court organist. His principal works are nine organ sonatas, but he has also written many choral preludes and other works.

Merulo, Claudio (1533-1604) Italian organist, publisher and composer. In 1556 he was appointed organist at Brescia and later he moved to St Mark's in Venice in the same capacity. In 1584 he became organist at the ducal chapel in Parma. He composed motets, madrigals and organ music (mostly toccatas, ricecares and canzoni).

messa di voce (It.) Placing of the voice. Technique of increasing and decreasing of vocal volume during one long-held note.

Messager, André (1853-1929) French composer, organist and conductor. He studied in Paris under **Saint-Saëns**, becoming the organist at St Sulpice in 1874. From 1901 to 1906 he held the position of art director at Covent Garden. In 1907 he became chief conductor of the Paris Opéra, and a year later was also appointed director of the Paris Conservatoire. His 28 operas include *La Béarnaise* (1885), *Véronique* (1898) and *Béatrice* (1914). He also wrote music for ten ballets, a symphony, some piano pieces, songs and cantatas.

Messiaen, Olivier (Eugène Prosper Charles) (1908-) French composer, organist and teacher whose innovative musical compositions and theories have been among the most influential and individualistic of the 20th century. He was born in Avignon, his father being a university professor and his mother a poet and devout Roman Catholic. Largely self-taught in music, he entered the Paris Conservatoire in 1919 and studied composition with Paul **Dukas**, Marcel **Dupré**, and others. In his spare time he also read of India and ancient Greece. He also wrote down in musical notation the songs of all French birds, categorizing them by region. All these preoccupations, along with his own deep Catholic faith, were to have far-reaching implications for his future musical development. In 1931 he became organist at L'Eglise de la Trinité, Paris, a post he still holds. In 1936 he joined the teaching staff of the Ecole Normale de Musique and the Schola Cantorum and established with André **Jolivet**, Daniel **Lesur** and Yves Baudrier the group of young French musicians known as *Jeune France*. Called up by the French Army at the start of World War II, he was captured in 1940 and held in a German concentration camp for two years. Released in 1942, he was appointed a professor of harmony at the Paris Conservatoire. Five years later he was given the specially created professorship of analysis, aesthetics and rhythm, and in 1966 he also became professor of composition. His pupils have included **Boulez, Stockhausen** and **Xenakis**.

Messiaen's church commitments and teaching have gone hand in hand with a career as an organ recitalist. As a virtuoso of the instrument he has been in demand throughout the world. But it is as a composer and theorist that he has placed an indelible stamp upon the music of the 20th century. Much of his music is of a transcendental character, springing from and depicting his own deep religious faith, his celebration of human love, and his fascination with nature, especially bridsong. His organ works can only gain their full colouristic effects by exploiting the full range of the instrument's contrasting registers and making special use of acoustics and reverberation. His warm and exotic harmonies resemble those of **Debussy** and often use modal techniques. In orchestral works such as the huge *Turangalîla-symphonie* (1946–1948), he utilizes the other-worldly sound of the ondes **martenot**; elsewhere he employs tuned gongs to give his work an oriental flavour. His vast *Et expecto resurrectionem* for orchestra, which should ideally be played on top of a mountain, makes breathtaking use of tamtams and gongs. Irregular rhythms are another innovative feature of his work, arising partly from his study of ancient Greek music. His theoretical work has in part been connected with his own individual approach to modes and the application of modal principles to rhythm.

Messiaen's major compositions include the orchestral works *L'Ascension* (1933), *Oiseaux exotiques* (1955–1956) – both also transcribed for organ – *Chronochromie* (1960) and *Des Canyons aux Etoiles* (1970–1974); the song-cycle *Poèmes pour Mi* (1936); *Rechant* (1949), for 12 unaccompanied voices; the choral piece *La Transfiguration de Notre Seignur Jésus-Christ* (1965–1969); the piano works *Cantique d'oiseaux* (1956–1958) and (for two pianos) *Visions de l'Amen* (1943); *Nativité de Seigneur* (1935) for organ; and the extraordinary *Quattuor pour la fin du temps* (1940). This last work was written while Messiaen was a prisoner of war; it was scored for the only instruments available in the camp – violin, piano and clarinet. Messiaen's crowning achievement to date has been his monumental opera *Saint François d'Assisi*, using his own libretto. Premiered in Paris in 1983, it has a running time of five hours and calls for an orchestra so large that virtually no orchestra pit in any opera house can accommodate all the instrumentalists.

mesto (It.) Sad, gloomy.

metamorphosis Method by which a composer transforms a theme or motif, especially by tempo and rhythm, to represent various moods or poetic ideas. Metamorphosis was first exploited by **Liszt**, who used it regularly in his tone poems, and **Hindemith** wrote an orchestral piece called *Symphonic Metamorphoses on a theme by Weber* (1943).

Metner Alternative spelling of **Medtner**.

metre Rhythmic relationship produced in music between **beats** in a bar and bars in a **phrase**. A similar relationship applies to the syllables in a line of verse or the lines in a stanza. Some musicians differentiate between metre and rhythm, in that the metre covers the fixed number of beats in a bar and their relationship to each other, whereas rhythm covers the configuration of time values given to each note.

metronome Device invented by J.N. **Maelzel** in 1814, consisting of a clockwork-driven upside-down rigid pendulum that may be weighted in different positions along its length, to produce a 'tick' at different rates per minute. It is sometimes used to define the speed of a passage of music. For this purpose, some composers indicate the number of crotchets per minute at the head of a composition, along with the letters MM (Maelzel's metronome)

Meyer, Kerstin (1928-) Swedish mezzo-soprano who studied in Stockholm under Sunnegarth and Skoldorz. She made her debut there in 1952 as Azucena in *Il Trovatore*, then continued her studies in Salzburg and Italy. She has sung in Vienna, Venice, Hamburg and Berlin, making her Covent Garden debut in 1960.

Meyerbeer, Giacomo (Jakob Liebmann Meyer Beer) (1791-1864) German composer and pianist. A child prodigy as a pianist, Meyerbeer first performed in public at the age of seven. After studying in Darmstadt under **Vogler**, he concentrated on writing German opera, and became court composer to the Duke of Hesse. He visited Italy in 1816, where he was strongly influenced by **Rossini**, and this initiated a switch from German to Italian opera. While in Italy he wrote six operas, all successful, particularly *Il Crociato in Egitto* (1824). He then set to work with the librettist Eugene Scribe and they worked together on almost all his remaining operas (which were written for the Paris Opéra), including *Robert le Diable* (1831) and *Les Huguenots* (1836).

From 1842 to 1849 Meyerbeer acted as *Generalmusikdirektor* at Berlin; for the re-opening of the Berlin opera house he composed the *Singspiel*, *Ein Feldlager in Schlesein*, with Jenny **Lind** taking the principal role. Other successful operas include *Le Prophète* (1849), *L'Etoile du Nord* (1854) and *L'Africaine* (1865). He also composed choral, orchestral and piano music and songs.

Meyerowitz, Jan (1913-) German-born composer who became an American citizen in 1951. He studied under **Zemlinsky** in Berlin (1930-1933) and then in Rome under **Casella** and **Respighi** (1933-1937). In 1946 he moved to the United States, teaching at Tanglewood, Brooklyn, and in New York. As well as seven operas, including *Esther* (1957), Meyerowitz has written many choral works, a symphony, a cello sonata and songs.

mezzo, mezza (It.) Half, as in **mezzo-soprano** and **mezza voce**, half voice.

mezza voce (It.) Half voice. A method of producing the singing voice as if under the breath, resulting not only in a soft tone, but in a quality different to that of full voice.

mezzo-soprano Female singing voice, lower in range than **soprano** and higher in range than **contralto**.

mi Alternative spelling of **me**.

Miaskovsky, Nikolai (Yakovlevich) (1881-1950) Russian composer who studied under **Glière**, **Lyadov** and **Rimsky-Korsakov**. From 1921 he taught at the Moscow Conservatoire. His works include 27 symphonies, symphonic poems, a sinfonietta, nine string quartets, three piano sonatas and songs.

Michelangeli, Arturo Benedetti (1920-) Italian pianist who studied at the Milan Conservatoire. In 1939 he won the Geneva International Music Competition. He made his debut in England in 1946. He has toured widely and established a worldwide reputation.

microtonaltiy Method of composing music using a tonal scheme that involves intervals smaller than a semitone (**microtones**).

microtone Interval smaller than a **semitone**. The Mexican composer, Julian **Carrillo**, devised a scale using microtones and also invented special instruments for the purpose. Quarter tones have been used by **Bloch** in some of his chamber music, and by **Bartók**, although the use of microtones has been discussed (and indeed, put into practice) since the 16th century by **Vincentino** and others.

middle C Note of C that appears roughly in the middle of the piano keyboard. It is usually tuned to a frequency of 261.6 hertz.

Middle C

Mighty Five Formal name for the **Mighty Handful**.

Mighty Handful Group of Russian composers led by **Balakirev** and including **Borodin, Mussorgsky** and **Rimsky-Korsakov**, who during the latter part of the 19th century began to promote a national music based on themes and forms taken from Russian folk music. The formal name for the group was the Mighty Five.

Mignone, Francisco (1897-) Brazilian composer and conductor who studied at the Sao Paulo Conservatoire and at the Milan Conservatoire. In 1933 he was appointed official conductor and conducting teacher at the National Music School in Brazil. He pursued an international conducting career and held many other appointments, including directorships of the Teatro Municipal, Radio Ministerio da Educacao e Cultura and Radio Globo. His early works, such as *Suite campestre* (1918), show the influence of his Italian training, whereas in his middle-period works he was attracted by musical nationalism and in pieces such as the ballet *Maracatu de chico rei* (1933) he drew heavily on Brazilian folk and popular traditions. From the late 1950s he turned away from this folk influence and began to use polytonality, tone clusters, atonality and serialism, in pieces such as *Variacoes em busca de um tema* (1972).

Migot, Georges (1891-1976) French composer who studied at the Paris Conservatoire under **Widor** and **d'Indy** and won three consecutive composition prizes (1918-1920). His early works show the influence of **Fauré**, using a linear rather than a harmonic style, which distinguished him from contemporaries such as **Hindemith**, as he struggled against their neo-Classical aesthetic. His later works, such as the *Requiem* (1953), have **diatonic** melodies, while avoiding tonality in the music. Throughout his life he insisted on the close link between text and music, and the larger part of his output was of sacred works, including six oratorios on the life of Christ.

mi-kagura (Japan) Shinto ceremonial. *Kagura* (good music) is the generic term for all Shinto music. *Mi-kagura* comprises two types of song: *torimono*, songs intended to praise or invoke the gods, and *saibari*, songs to entertain the gods. Both are accompanied by an oboe (*hichiriki*), zither (*wagon*), flute and wooden time-marking clappers. See also **sato-kagura**.

Milan, Francisco (*fl* early 15th century) Spanish singer and composer of *villancicos*, muscal compositions akin to choral cantatas. He was employed in the 'chapel' (private musical establishment) of Queen Isabella of Castile and was one of the most popular composer-musicians of his day.

Milan, Luis de (*c*1500-*c*1561) Spanish musician whose most important publication was the *Libro de Musica de Vihuela de Mano Intitulado El Maestro* (1536). This is the earliest collection of vihuela (guitar) music and is unusual because the pieces give indications of tempo. In addition to the instrumental pieces – including more than 40 fantasias, showing a blend of homophony and **polyphony** – *El Maestro* contains a rich repertory of songs in Castilian and Portuguese.

Milford, Robin (1903-1959) English composer who studied under **Holst** and **Vaughan Williams** at the Royal College of Music. He was a prolific composer, and although several of his large-scale works received successful first performances, such as the oratorio *A Prophet in the Land* (Three Choirs Festival, 1931), none of them have been published. He is better known as a composer of songs in a simple, diatonic style, influenced by English folk song.

Milhaud, Darius (1892-1974) French composer. He studied at the Paris Conservatoire under **Dukas**, Gedalge and **Widor**. He was close friends with many contemporary painters and writers (most notably Paul Claudel), and was a member of Les Six. He travelled widely – including two years in South America as Claudel's secretary, which influenced early works such as the ballet *L'homme et son désir* (1918) and the dance suite *Saudades do Brasil* (1920-1921). He composed the ballet *La Création du Monde* (1923) following a tour of the United States, where he heard black jazz in Harlem.

From his earliest works, Milhaud used the technique of **polytonality**. His enormous output included music for chamber groups, often in unusual combinations such as choir, cello and oboe in the sixth of his chamber symphonies, and he used folk material from many countries.

military band Band of brass, woodwind and percussion, originally attached to a military regiment. The range of instruments involved varies in type and number between and in the countries who have bands of this kind. In England the military band usually consists of flute, piccolo, oboe, clarinet, bassoons, saxophones, horns (orchestral), cornets or trumpets, trombones, euphoniums, tubas and percussion. A double-bass is often included when the band is not marching.

Milner, Anthony (1925-) English composer and teacher. He was educated at the Royal College of Music, and after teaching at Morley College was appointed lecturer at King's College, London, in 1965, and then senior lecturer in music at Goldsmith's College, London, in 1971. He is also a professor of composition at the Royal College of Music. His work includes choral and instrumental works, often influenced by his Roman Catholic beliefs, and using many varied contrapuntal devices.

Milnes, Sherrill (1935-) American baritone. His debut with the New York City Opera was in 1964 as Valentin in *Faust*, and his Covent Garden debut was in 1971 in *Renato*. He has appeared throughout North and South America and Europe, and has become one of the most prolific recording artists of his time. His voice has been noted for its brilliant top range and extraordinary command of legato.

Milstein, Nathan (1904-) American violinist of Russian birth. He studied with Pyotr Stolyarsky and made his official debut in Odessa in 1920. Later that year he played **Glazunov**'s concerto under the composer. He was well received in the Soviet Union, often appearing in joint recitals with Vladimir **Horowitz**. It was while on tour in Europe with Horowitz that they decided not to return to their homeland. Milstein became an American citizen in 1942 and in his international career has travelled widely in the United States and Europe.

minim Note that is half the time value of a semibreve and twice that of a crotchet. In the United States it is referred to as a half note.

Minkus, Léon (1826-1891) Composer and violinist of Austrian origin. He worked in Russia as a concert soloist and teacher, and was conductor of the Bolshoi Theatre, Moscow (1862-1872). He collaborated with the choreographer Saint-Leon on several ballets, performed in Paris. He also collaborated with **Delibes** on the ballet *La source* (1866). His ballet *Don Quixote* was well received in Moscow. While holding the post of ballet composer to the Imperial theatre in St Petersburg (1872-1891) he wrote many more ballets, which were popular in their day but have now been all but forgotten.

minor interval Major **interval** that has

been decreased by a semitone.

minor scale One of the two predominant scales of the Western tonal system (the other being the **major scale**). It is constructed of eight notes in the same way as the major scale, but with a sharpened third note in the lower **tetrachord**, and either a sharpened seventh (harmonic minor) or a sharpened sixth and seventh (melodic minor). The melodic minor also differs from the harmonic in that when the scale is played downwards, the seventh and sixth are flattened.

minstrel General term for a travelling entertainer who sang to his own accompaniment. Minstrels existed between the 12th and 17th centuries. See also **jongleur**; **troubadour**; **trouvère**.

Minton, Yvonne (1938-) Australian mezzo-soprano. She studied in Sydney and moved to Europe in 1960, winning a Kathleen Ferrier Prize in the following year. Minton joined the Royal Opera in 1965, where her first important role was as Marina in *Boris Godunov*. She has also regularly visited the Cologne Opera and has also sung at the Chicago Opera, the Metropolitan Opera and the Paris Opéra. Her first Bayreuth appearance was as Brangäne in 1974. In addition to her opera work she has a wide concert repertory, much of which has been recorded.

minuet Dance in triple time of French courtly origin that became popular throughout Europe in the mid-17th century. An instrumental form of the minuet was used as one of the movements in a **suite** during the Baroque period, and during the late 18th and early 19th centuries was incorporated into sonatas, quartets and symphonies, especially by such composers as **Haydn**, **Mozart** and **Beethoven**.

mirliton Instrument consisting of a pipe covered at one end with parchment or tissue-paper, into which the player sings and producing a reedy tone similar to a primitive oboe. The simplest form is the toy kazoo, which consists of a comb and a piece of paper through which a child blows to produce the same type of sound.

Miserere Title of a sacred composition derived from the opening words of Psalm 51, which begins Miserere mei, Deus (Have mercy on me, O God). Settings in polyphonic style have been made by **Josquin**, **Lassus**, **Tye**, **Gabrieli** and **Allegri**, and one was incorporated into Act IV of **Verdi's** *Il Trovatore* (1853). Another text from Psalm 4, beginning with the words *Miserere mihi Domine* has a plainchant melody that was used for innumerable canons and other instrumental settings by Elizabethan composers.

misura (It.) Measure. It is used to refer either to the measure of a piece, (for example, *senza misura*, in free measure) or to a bar.

Mitropoulos, Dimitri (1896-1960) American conductor, pianist and composer of Greek birth. He studied at the Athens Odeion Conservatoire and at Brussels. He was conducting the Berlin Philharmonic Orchestra in 1930 when the pianist failed to appear for a performance. Mitropoulos successfully led the orchestra from the piano in **Prokofiev**'s Piano Concerto No. 3 – a practice that he then repeated in Europe and the Soviet Union. His American debut was with the Boston Symphony Orchestra in 1936. He was conductor of the Minneapolis Symphony Orchestra for 12 years from 1937, and of the New York Philharmonic Orchestra from 1949 to 1958. An international conductors' competition bearing his name was established in New York, 1961.

Mixolydian mode Seventh **mode** and one of the original Ambrosian modes, starting on the note G and proceeding for an octave.

mode System of scales that became established in the Middle Ages and was still accepted up to the 16th century when the modern concept of key was introduced. They are sometimes called church modes or ecclesiastical modes because of their use in sacred **plainsong**. Modes are easily identified by reference to the white notes on a piano keyboard. The ancient Greeks used a modal system, based on the Pythagorean scale, from which the later system is derived. Over the centuries various classifications, named in Greek, evolved which led to the following:

Name	*Range*	*Final*	*Dominant*
Dorian	A-D	D	A
Hypodorian	A-A	D	F
Phrygian	E–E	E	C
Hypophrygian	B-B	E	A
Lydian	F-F	F	C
Hypolydian	C-C	F	A
Mixolydian	G-G	G	D
Hypomixolydian	D-D	G	C
Aeolian	A-A	A	E
Hypoaeolian	E-E	A	C
Ionian	C-C	C	G
Hypoionian	G-G	C	E

This table of modes was devised by Henricus Glareanus in the 16th century. He gave odd numbers to the authentic modes in which a melody always ended on the last note of the scale, called the final. Plagal modes were formed from the same scale as the authentic modes, although the compass was altered, so that the final appeared in the middle of the scale and the dominant became the last note. The plagal modes were given even numbers and had the Greek prefix hypo- (under) added to the corresponding authentic name.

From the 17th-century onwards, the Ionian and Aeolian modes became known as the **major** and **minor scales**, on which most music has since been based.

moderato (It.) Moderate. A direction used either singly or in combination with other terms to indicate tempo. For example, *allegro moderato*, at a moderately lively speed.

modo (It.) Mode or manner. For example, *in modo di*, in the manner of.

modulation Changing from one key to another in the course of a composition by means of logical harmonic progressions. Modulations that are the most natural are those in which the change is to a related key, such as a related major or minor key, to the key of the **dominant** and its relative major or minor, or to the key of the **subdominant** and its relative major or minor.

modulator Diagram used for instruction purposes in **tonic sol-fa**, and also for practice in sight-reading and modulation. It is also an instrument used to modulate sound signals electronically.

Moeran, Ernest John (1894-1950) English composer of Anglo-Irish descent. He studied at the Royal College of Music, and privately under John **Ireland**. His music shows the influence of Ireland and **Delius**, and of the folk music of his native East Anglia. His earlier works tended to be in small genres such as the piano trio and violin sonata, but later he produced a series of large-scale works, such as the Symphony in G minor, which began to show the influence of **Sibelius**.

Moiseiwitsch, Benno (1890-1963) British pianist of Russian birth. He studied in Russia and at Vienna, and made his official debut in Reading in 1908 after his family had settled in England. His career took him throughout Europe, the United States, the Far East, Africa and South America. He admired **Rachmaninov** greatly and was best known for performance of his music.

mokugyo (Japan) Wooden, fish-mouthed, slit gong, also known as the Chinese temple block. It is tapped with a padded stick and is used in Buddhist temple worship as a meditative aid during the incantation of the name of Buddha.

Molinari, Bernardino (1880-1952) Italian conductor. Between 1912 and 1943 he was artistic director of the Augusteo Orchestra in Rome and initiated popular open-air summer concerts there from 1929. He conducted mainly in Italy, only occasionally appearing in the rest of Europe and the United States. He made many transcriptions for symphony orchestra, including **Debussy**'s *L'isle joyeuse*.

moll (Ger.) Minor. For example, A moll, A minor.

Molter, Johann Melchior (1696-1765) German composer. He held posts as *Kappellmeister* at the courts of the Margrave Carl Wilhelm of Baden-Durlach, Duke Wilhelm Heinrich of Saxe-Eisenach and the Margrave Carl Friedrich of Baden-Durlach. He visited Italy on two occasions, having the opportunity to meet **Vivaldi, Albinoni, Scarlatti, Pergolesi** and **Sammartini**. His works reflect the many influences to which he was exposed and show a steady development from the late **Baroque** style to the **galant**. He worked with court musicians, many of whom could play several instruments, and this enabled him to experiment with unusual and new instruments, such as the clarinet and the **chalumeau**.

molto (It.) Much, very. For example, molto allegro, very quickly.

moment Structural concept devised by **Stockhausen** as an attempt to help the listener to overcome some of the difficulties of listening to serial music. A 'moment' is a brief segment of a composition with its own musical characteristic. Each moment is equal in status and equally dispensible. As the composer does not move forwards from a fixed point in time, but moves in all directions within cyclic limits, the moments may be arranged in any order to achieve an indeterminate open form. An example of this is **Stockhausen's** work *Moments* (1962-1964) for soprano, four choirs and 13 instruments.

Mompou, Federico (1893-) Spanish composer who initially studied the piano in Paris, but devoted his later career to composition. He was much influenced by **Debussy, Satie** and the new French school. His work is almost entirely restricted to intimate piano miniatures or slow songs of very similar style.

Monckton, (John) Lionel (1861-1924) British composer and music critic. He studied at Oxford and trained as a lawyer. While a critic on the *Daily Telegraph*, he wrote music for several successful Edwardian musical comedies, including *The Arcadians* and *The Quaker Girl*.

Moniuszko, Stanislaw (1819-1872) Polish composer whose first fame came with the publication of his *Songbook for Home Use* (1842). He became a popular opera composer, his first great success being the final version of *Halka* which was performed in 1858. In 1859 he was appointed as the opera conductor at the Grand Theatre in Warsaw, where he composed several more operas. He is the most representative opera composer of the Polish 19th-century national school, and his use of material from Polish national music links him with composers such as **Smetana, Glinka, Weber** and **Rossini**.

Monk, William Henry (1823-1889) English church musician and composer. He held the post of organist and choir master in several London churches. He was also professor of vocal music at King's College, London, the National Training School for Music and at Bedford College, London. He was the editor of *Hymns Ancient and Modern* (1861), for which he wrote *Eventide*, the famous tune for *Abide with Me*. He wrote many other popular hymn tunes, anthems and service music.

Monn, Georg Matthias (1717-1750) Austrian composer and organist. He was organist at St Charles' Church in Vienna, and was also a teacher. None of his music was published during his lifetime, but he had a substantial local reputation. His output included symphonies and concertos which are in the early Classical style, and more conservative chamber music and keyboard sonatas. He was the first composer to write a four-movement symphony with a third-movement **minuet** (1740), and his treatment of fast movements (with development sections and full recapitulations in the tonic) heralded the emergence of the **sonata form** in the symphony.

monodrama Stage work for one character, such as **Schoenberg's** *Erwartung* (1909), a monodrama for soprano and orchestra.

monody Compositon that comprises a single melodic part presented over a simple chordal accompaniment, which formed the basis of the first **operas**. The earliest use of this type of composition can be found in Giulio **Caccini**'s *Le Nuove Musiche* (1601).

monophony Music in a single melodic part, without harmony, as distinct from **homophony**, which is a form of sound in which the music moves by step in all the parts, with no variation in rhythm between the parts. See also **monody, polyphony**.

monothematic Describing a composition based on a single theme. The term may apply to one movement or to a larger composition having several movements. Monothematic movements occur in the finale of **Haydn's** Symphony No. 103 in E♭ (1795), and in the first movement of his Symphony No. 104 in D major (1795).

Monsingy, Pierre-Alexandre (1729-1817) French composer who began to study composition at the relatively late age of 30, under Gianotti. His first complete *opéra-comique*, *Les aveux indiscrets*, was performed in 1759. In 1761 he started a long collaboration with the librettist Sedaine. After several more works for the comic opera he had an immense success with *Felix ou l'enfant trouvé* (1777).

Monte, Phillippe de (1521-1603) Flemish composer. He held various positions in Italy, and from 1568 became choirmaster to the Habsburg court, spending the rest of his life in the post at Vienna or Prague. He had a wide circle of friends, including **Lassus** and **Byrd**. He composed around 260 sacred works, including 40 Masses, but is best known for his even larger secular output, comprising more than 1,100 madrigals which span his entire career. He was one of the most renowned and prolific composers of the 16th century.

Montéclair, Michel Pinolet de (1667-1737) French Baroque composer, teacher and double-bass player. From 1699 he was employed as a double-bass player at the Paris Opéra. The Opéra put on two stage works by him, *Les Festes d'été* (1716) and *David et Jonathan* (1732), unusual for the period because of its biblical content. His other surviving works include three fine orchestral *Sérenades* (suites) and a few *cantates* (chamber cantatas). He also wrote a number of books about the theory and teaching of music, including one of the first violin 'methods'. Both his music and his theoretical writings influenced **Rameau**.

Monteux, Pierre (1875-1964) American conductor of French birth. He studied at the Paris Conservatoire and played viola at the Opéra-Comique while still a student. His many conducting posts included Diaghilev's *Ballets Russes* (1911-1914), for which he directed the premieres of Stravinsky's ballets, the Metropolitan Opera (1917-1919), the Boston Symphony Orchestra (1920-1924), the Amsterdam Concertgebouw Orchestra (1924-1934, as second conductor), the San Francisco Symphony Orchestra (1936-1952), and finally the London Symphony Orchestra (1961-1964). He made many successful recordings, but much preferred live performance, and continued to conduct until the end of his life.

Monteverdi, Claudio Giovanni Antonio (1567-1643) Italian composer who served at the court of the Gonzagas in Mantua (1592-1612) and spent the rest of his life as *maestro di cappella* at St Mark's, Venice.

Monteverdi was a prolific composer, and throughout his life kept abreast of the latest ideas. He published many books of madrigals, but he is best known for his dramatic works. In this respect, he occupies a highly significant position in the development of opera. His first opera was *L'Orfeo* (1607). The first public opera houses opened in Venice in 1637 (when Monteverdi was 70 years old) and he composed four more operas, of which only two survive, *Il Ritorno d' Ulisse in Patria* and *L'incoronazione di Poppea*. These are masterpieces in a then modern style, portraying people in realistic situations, the musical units being woven into a continuous pattern rather than being self-contained, with emphasis on the drama. His best known sacred work is the *Vespers* (1610), in which he used a secular style to bring meaning to the text.

Montgomery, Kenneth (1943-) British conductor who studied at the Royal College of Music under **Boult** and later in Siena. He was director of the Bournemouth Sinfonietta (1973-1975), but was already working mostly in the field of opera, with Glyndebourne, Sadler's Wells and the Netherlands Opera. He made his Covent Garden debut in 1975 with *Le nozze di Figaro* and was appointed musical director of Glyndebourne Touring Opera in 1976. Later that year he moved to the Netherlands Radio Orchestra.

Moog, Robert Arthur (1934-) American inventor of the 'Moog synthesizer' and other instruments, in collaboration with many composers. He founded the R.A. Moog Company in New York in 1954 to manufacture thérémins, and started the manufacture of synthesizers in 1965. His instruments became very popular following the success of Walter Carlos's *Switched on Bach* recording (1969), and Moog is still active in the development of new instruments.

Moore, Douglas Stuart (1893-1969) American composer, teacher and writer. His first compositions, while still a student at Yale, were popular songs. He studied with **d'Indy** and Nadia **Boulanger** in Paris in 1919. He held a teaching post at Barnard College, Columbia University, from 1926 until his retirement in 1962. Moore composed several operas, of which *The Ballad of Baby Doe* and *The Devil and Daniel Webster* are the best known. He also composed choral, orchestral and chamber works.

Moore, Gerald (1899-1987) English pianist who started a career as a recording artist in 1921, and began to specialize in piano accompaniment from 1925. From that time until his retirement in 1967 he accompanied virtually every eminent solo singer and instrumentalist in England and abroad, and had raised the art of accompaniment to one of the highest prestige. His recordings include more than 500 **Schubert** songs with artists such as **Fischer-Dieskau** and **Schwarzkopf**. He was awarded the Grand Prix du Disque four times and, among other honours, he was made a CBE in 1954.

Moore, Thomas (1779-1852) Irish poet and musician. He trained and practised as a lawyer, but even as a law student in London he wrote songs, and the libretto for Michael Kelly's opera *The Gipsey Prince* (1801). He became very popular for the serial publication of *Irish Melodies* (1808-1834), in which he added new texts to old tunes. Apart from other collections of poems and songs, he was best known for *Lalla Rookh* – a story with four interpolated poems (1817). He also published lives of Sheridan (1825), Byron (1830) and Fitzgerald (1831).

Morales, Cristóbal de (*c*1500-1553) Spanish composer of churh music. He was born in Seville and trained there as a choirboy. From 1526 to 1531 he held the post of chapel-master first at the cathedral of Avila and then at Plasencia in western Spain. From 1535 to 1545 he sang in the Papal choir in Rome and wrote most of his finest church pieces for it. His two volumes of masses (1544) and popular Magnificat cycles rank him with **Palestrina** and **Victoria** in terms of the quality of their construction. Returning to Spain in 1545, he successively held the posts of chapel-master in Toledo and Malaga. In all he wrote some 23 masses and about 90 motets. He thus ranks as Spain's first internationally famous composer.

morbido (It.) Gentle or delicate, but not morbid.

morceau (Fr.) Piece. For example, *morceau symphonique*, symphonic piece.

mordent **Ornament** written over a note to indicate that three notes are to be played in the time-value of the principal note. The **upper mordent**, consists of the principal note, then the next note up, then the principal. The lower, or **inverted mordent**, is constructed in the same way, but using the note below the principal.

Upper mordent (above); inverted mordent (below)

Moreau, Jean-Baptiste (1656-1733) French composer and teacher. He served alongside Clérambault as *musicien ordinaire* at a school for young noblewomen established at St Cyr in 1686. While there he collaborated with Racine on several works, including a setting of Racine's *Esther* (1689) which delighted the King, Louis XIV. Moreau was persuaded to write music of a popular nature by Lainez for his divertissement *Zaïre*, for which he gained much public success.

morendo (It.) Dying. It indicates that a phrase is to be allowed to die away. It may mean not only a decrease in volume and tone, but also in pace.

Morley, Thomas (1557-1602) English composer and music publisher, a master of the English madrigal tradition. He was probably born in Norwich. A student of William **Byrd**, he graduated from Oxford University in 1588 and travelled to London where he became organist at St Paul's Cathedral and also a Gentleman of the Chapel Royal. In 1598 he won a 21-year monopoly on the printing of song books and music paper and published *The Triumphs of Oriana*, a collection of madrigals dedicated to Queen Elizabeth I, to which he also contributed. He also composed sacred music and lute songs, and wrote *A Plaine and Easie Introduction to Practicall Musicke*. Morley is best known for his balletts, of which *Now is the Month of Maying* and *It was a Lover and his Lass* are among the finest examples.

morris dance English folk dance which derived its name from the Moorish *moresca*, and was introduced into England in about the 15th century. It is danced in various kinds of symbolic fancy dress, with jingles tied to the dancers' legs and performed in two groups of six. Two of the dancers represent traditional characters, such as the Fool and the Queen of the May. The music is played by a pipe and tabor and sometimes a violin.

Moscheles, Ignaz (1794-1870) German pianist, conductor and composer of Czech birth. He studied piano in Prague then moved to Vienna, where he became a popular pianist. He then moved to London, teaching piano at the Royal Academy of Music and conducting the Philharmonic Society. He was a close friend of **Mendelssohn**, whom he taught, and he moved to Leipzig in 1846 to be principal professor of the piano at the conservatoire which Mendelssohn founded there. Most of his compositions are for piano. Many are salon pieces, but **Schumann** considered him one of the best **sonata** composers of the time.

Mosolov, Alexandr Vasilyevich (1900-1973) Russian composer, born in Kiev. A student of **Miaskovsky** and **Glière** at the Moscow Conservatoire, he began a promising career as a concert pianist and composer. A hero of the 1917 Revolution, he early espoused the creed of socialist realism (then known as constructivism) with his 1927 ballet *Zavod* (*The Factory*), also performed as a concert piece under the title (in English) *The Iron Foundry*. However, his avant-garde style incurred the displeasure of the Stalinist authorities and kept him out of favour for more than a decade. He regained official recognition during World War II, when he was commissioned to write patriotic songs, but he never attained musical eminence. His works include six symphonies, cello, violin and piano concertos, chamber music and songs. Some of his early songs use newspaper advertisements as texts.

mosso (It.) Animated. Usually proceeded by *piu* or *meno*.

Moszkowski, Moritz (1854-1925) German pianist and composer of Polish descent. He studied at Dresden and in Berlin, where he taught for many years while touring extensively as a pianist. He is best known for two books of piano duets, *Spanische Tanze*.

motet Short vocal composition for sacred use which evolved from 13th-century clausulae. Originally it appeared as an elaboration of a given **plainsong** melody with the contrapuntal addition of other melodies with a different text. The earliest motets were often written for three voices: *triplum*, *motetus*, and tenor, which was the lowest part.

In the 14th century the motet became **isorhythmic**, especially in the works of such composers as **Dufay**, **Machaut** and **Dunstable**. Dufay also introduced secular melodies into the motet form as a *cantus firmus*.

During the 15th century the motet form became more independent, and gradually developed into an elaborate form of **polyphonic** sacred composition set to Latin words not in the Mass. By the end of the 16th century this style reached full fruition in the motets of **Palestrina, Lassus, Victoria, Tallis** and **Byrd**. At times during the 18th century it was difficult to distinguish the motet from the **cantata**, but between 1723 and 1729 the motet proper reached its climax with the composition by J.S. **Bach** of motets for a five-part chorus and two eight-part choruses. Among the 19th-century composers whose works included motets were **Brahms, Bruckner, Liszt** and **Gounod,** who were followed in the 20th century by **Franck, Poulenc, Vaughan Williams** and **Stanford**.

motif Alternative spelling of **motive**.

motion Movement upwards or downwards of a line of music. There are six forms of motion.

In a single part, a conjunct motion moves by steps of adjoining notes. Conversely, a disjunct motion occurs when the part moves by larger steps.

If two or more parts move together in the same direction they are said to be in similar motion, and if they move in opposite directions they are in contrary motion.

In oblique motion, one part moves while the other stands still. Parallel motion is similar motion in which the parts preserve a constant interval between them.

motive Brief melodic or rhythmic figure, too short to be called a theme. Some composers have used a motive in programme music or in opera in association with a character, object or idea. In such cases it becomes a leading motive, such as the **leitmotiv** associated with **Wagner**.

moto (It.) Movement, pace.

Mottl, Felix Josef (1856-1911) Austrian conductor, composer and editor. He was appointed conductor at the court opera and the Philharmonic Society, Karlsruhe in 1881. His conducting debut at Bayreuth was in 1886 with *Tristan und Isolde* and *Parsifal*, and he was a regular guest conductor there. He conducted Wagner's *Ring Cycle* at Covent Garden in 1890 and 1898, and prepared the first performances of *Parsifal* for New York in 1903. In the same year he took charge of the Munich opera house. He also edited vocal scores of Wagner's operas, made orchestral arrangements of songs by many composers, arranged ballet suites and composed some pieces of his own.

motto Musical theme or figure that usually occurs at the opening of a composition and again during its course (in its original form or altered), in the manner of a quotation or allusion to some definite idea. The opening themes in **Tchaikovsky**'s Symphonies No. 4 (1877) and No. 5 (1888) are examples of this. The motto may also be called a motto theme.

Moussorgsky, Modeste Petrovich Alternative transliteration of **Mussorgsky, Modeste Petrovich**.

mouth music (Scotland) Highland term for vocal music that is used to accompany dance when instrumental accompaniment is not available or permitted. Words are often personal, derogatory or humorous in nature. Also known as *port à beul*. See also **diddling**.

mouth organ Alternative term for **harmonica**.

mouthpiece Part of a woodwind or brass instrument that a player takes into the mouth or to which he or she applies the lips in order to produce a sound. Each different type of mouthpiece provides the right kind of medium for directing a player's breath in order to set a column of air within the instrument's tube vibrating to produce a note.

There are many different types of mouthpiece. An oboe's mouthpiece consists of a double reed of cane or flexible plastic, the tip of which the player takes between his or her teeth. In a clarinet the single cane reed is clamped over a slot on the underside of a plastic or ebonite mouthpiece by means of a ligature. The reed is placed on the player's bottom lip, with his or her top teeth resting on top of the mouthpiece. A recorder mouthpiece has a slot with a sharp edge cut in it at an angle so that the breath can be directed downwards but actually flows over the top of the tube as in a flute. A flute's mouthpiece is a hole near one end of the instrument, and the player blows across it as someone might blow across the open top of a bottle. In a brass instrument a cup- or funnel-shaped metal mouthpiece made from a single casting fits into the top of the air column. It is pressed against the player's lips. The deeper and larger the cup, the more suitable the mouthpiece is for the mellow tones of the larger instruments, such as the tuba or horn. A shallow cup is ideal for the brilliant penetrating tones of the trumpet.

Mouton, Jean (1459-1522) French composer, one of the most important writers of motets of the early 16th century. He spent the earlier part of his life in various church positions and studied under **Josquin des Prés**. He joined the French court in 1502, serving Louis XII and Francis I. More than 100 motets, about 15 masses and 20 chansons by Mouton survive. He is also important as the teacher of Adrian **Willaert**.

movable doh In the tonic sol-fa system, the concept that the scale, beginning with the tonic (doh) may start on any note.

movement Independent section of a large composition, such as a symphony, concerto or sonata. The French word *mouvement* is also used for **tempo** or speed, although each movement of a large composition usually has a different tempo. **Stravinsky** included the word in his work entitled *Movements for piano and orchestra* (1959).

Mozart, (Johann Georg) Leopold (1719-1787) Austrian composer and violinist, father of Wolfgang Amadeus **Mozart**. He was a violinist in the orchestra of the Archbishop of Salzburg (1743-1787). He recognized his son's genius, taking him on concert tours at a very early age, and has often been criticized for exploiting his son's talents. He composed sacred music, symphonies and keyboard sonatas. He is best known for his *Peasant Wedding Divertimento* and *Sinfonia da Caccia* (Toy Symphony), in which he included such 'instruments' as whistles and pistols. He also wrote a textbook on violin technique (1756) which was widely used.

Mozart, Wolfgang Amadeus (1756-1791) Austrian composer, who received his earliest musical training from his father,

Wolfgang Amadeus Mozart

Leopold. His musical talent was evident from infancy, through an outstanding musical memory and the facility of absolute pitch. As early as the age of five he was composing minuets, and at the age of six he and his sister, Anna Maria (then aged ten), visited the courts of Europe, delighting audiences with virtuosic performances on the harpsichord.

Later he undertook an extended tour of Europe accompanied by his mother, but by this time public interest in the young musician was already on the wane. He took a position in the household of the Archbishop of Salzburg. He was expelled from this post, but eventually found moderate favour with the nobility and the Emperor of Vienna. It was in Vienna that at the age of 26 he married the singer Constanze Weber, and two years later joined the Freemasons, a connection which was to influence several of his later works, most notably the Masonic cantata *Die Maurerfreude* (1785). However, Mozart never regained the popularity he had enjoyed as a child, and died a pauper in 1791.

Although Mozart lived for only a short time, he was nevertheless a prolific composer, contributing substantially to all the contemporary genres. He wrote about 20 operas, including *Bastien und Bastienne* (1768), *Lucio Silla* (1772), *Idomeneo* (1781), *Le Nozze di Figaro* (1786), *Don Giovanni* (1787), *Così fan Tutte* (1790), *Die Zauberflötte* (1791).

Of 41 symphonies, probably the three most famous (No. 39 in E♭ major, No. 40 in G minor and No. 41 in C major, *Jupiter*) were written in 1788, while some of the others reflect his travels: the *Paris Symphony* (No. 31 in D major), written during his visit to the city, and the Prague Symphony (No. 38 in D major).

His contribution to the chamber repertory includes, among others, the famous serenade *Eine Kleine Nachtmusik*.

Mozart often exploited the new instruments of the era, most notably the piano, for which he wrote 21 concertos. The clarinet also features in his orchestral, concerto and chamber ensemble compositions.

His chamber music for strings includes six string quintets, (with two violas), 27 string quartets (of which six, including the *Hunt Quartet* of 1784, are dedicated to **Haydn**) and more than 40 violin sonatas.

His sacred music includes 18 Masses, litanies and motets.

In its purity of form, Mozart's music exhibits clearly the classical ethos, emphasizing formal scheme and proportion, clarity of articulation in melody, rhythm and harmonic colouring. His early works were influenced by Haydn, whom he met in Vienna, and who, in turn, took his inspiration from C.P.E. **Bach**, effecting the transition from Baroque to Classical.

Muffat, Georg (1653-1704) German composer and organist of French birth. He studied with **Lully** and others in Paris and later with **Pasquini** in Rome. He spent much of his life in Salzburg, and the last 15 years as *Kapellmeister* at the court of Johann Philipp of Lamberg. He composed several orchestral suites, concerti grossi, violin sonatas and organ music. He is best known, however, for bringing the French style of Lully and the Italian style of **Corelli** to German performers.

Muffat, Gottlieb (1690-1770) German composer and organist. He entered the musical establishment at the Viennese court early in his career and remained there for more than half a century. He wrote exclusively for the keyboard, and these works never desert traditional Baroque structures, such as the toccata, prelude, capriccio, canzona, fugue, dance suite and ciaccona.

muffle Means of reducing the volume of sound made by a **drum**, either by covering the membrane with a piece of cloth, or by using sponge-head drumsticks.

Muldowney, Dominic (1952-) English composer who studied with **Harvey**, **Birtwistle**, Rands and **Blake**. He was composer in residence for the Southern Arts Association (1974-1976) and was appointed resident composer to the National Theatre, London, 1976.

multimedia Performance of a composition that includes music, poetry, drama, dancing and other events, but excludes opera and ballet. It was a form of music practised in the 1960s, particularly by Luciano **Berio**, who sometimes used electronics in his compositions.

Mumma, Gordon (1935-) American composer, performer of electronic music and horn player. He studied at the University of Michigan. Mumma collaborated with Ashley and Milton Cohen to create mixed-media 'Space Theater' productions, involving light projections, dance, sculpture and electronic sound, and was co-founder with Ashley of the Co-operative Studio for Electronic Music in Ann Arbor. In 1966 he joined Merce Cunningham's Dance Company as a composer and performer.

Münch, Charles (1891-1968) French violinist and conductor. He studied at the Strasbourg Conservatoire, with Flesch in Berlin and with Capet in Paris. He became professor of violin at Strasbourg and then at Leipzig, where he led the Gewandhaus Orchestra under **Furtwängler** (1926-1933). His conducting debut was made in 1933 in Paris, where he was based for many years and where he made a name conducting many first performances by French composers. He was chief conductor of the Boston Symphony Orchestra from 1948 to 1962, introducing much French music to the American public and conducting first performances of many American works.

Mundy, John (1555-1630) English composer and organist, son of William **Mundy**. He studied at Oxford, and was the organist at St George's Chapel, Windsor, for more than 40 years. He was a versatile composer, and his output includes sacred and secular choral works, and keyboard pieces found in the *Fitzwilliam Virginal Book*.

Mundy, William (1529-1591) English composer, father of John **Mundy**. After holding posts at several London churches, he was made a Gentleman of the Chapel Royal in 1564. He was highly regarded by his contemporaries and composed many sacred works. However, most manuscripts are marked simply 'Mundy', and it is impossible to know whether much of this music was by father or son.

Munrow, David John (1942-1976) English player of early wind instruments. He studied at Cambridge and Birmingham Universities and lectured at Leicester University and the Royal Academy. In 1967 he formed the Early Music Consort of London, and the group brought polished performances of medieval and Renaissance music to wide audiences. He was much in demand as a recorder player, and was very influential in the growth of 'authentic' performances.

Murrill, Herbert Henry John (1909-1952) English composer and administrator. He studied at the Royal Academy of Music (1925-1928) and at Oxford (1928-1931). He acted as music director for the Group Theatre, London, and after holding various posts at the BBC he became head of music there in 1950. He was also professor of composition at the Royal Academy from 1933 until his death.

Musgrave, Thea (1928-) Scottish composer who studied at Edinburgh University and in Paris with Nadia **Boulanger** (1950-1954). Her earliest pieces were predominantly **diatonic** in style, but her style changed gradually through **chromaticism** into an orthodox **serial** technique by 1960. Her style changed again during the 1960s, becoming less conservative, more atonal and rhythmic. Her output covers a wide range, from full-length stage works such as the opera *The Decision* (1965) to *a cappella* choral motets, music for brass band and piano duets.

musica ficta Practice in medieval and Renaissance music of treating certain notes in a performance as though they were marked with **flat** or **sharp** signs. In order to make harmonic sense between the parts or to avoid awkward intervals such as the **tritone** between F and B, the leading note of the scale was often sharpened and the B often flattened, the latter especially in the **Dorian mode**. An alternative term is *musica falsa*.

musica figurata **Plainsong** decorated by auxiliary notes, or the addition of a **descant** sung against a fundamental melody.

musical bow One of the most basic and primitive of stringed instruments which consisted of a single string attached to a flexible stick. By flexing the bow, the tension of the string was altered and this allowed a change of note. The string was normally plucked, although in some cases it was bowed with a smaller bow. The musical bow was the predecessor of the lute and harp, and is still used in some parts of Asia and Africa.

musical glasses Alternative term for **glass harmonica**.

musica reservata 16th-century term for music intended for connoisseurs and private occasions, especially vocal music which faithfully interpreted the words. It was a term used in the 1550s to describe the music of **Lassus**.

music drama Alternative term for opera used by composers, especially **Wagner** who thought that the older term implied obsolete methods and forms. His view of opera was that it should be a fusion of stagecraft, literature and music. Wagner exploited the **leitmotiv**, a device to enhance the drama and unify the music. He expressed his ideas on music and drama in *The Artwork of the Future* and *Opera and Drama* (1851). His musical dramas include *Der Ring des Nibelungen* (1869-1876), *Tristan und Isolde* (1857-1859), *Die Meistersinger von Nürnberg* (1862-1867) and *Parsifal* (1877-1882).

music theatre Dramatic work performed on the concert platform that involves action, although less grand in production than opera.

musicology 20th-century word that applies to the scientific and scholarly study of music in all its aspects. The branches of musicology include acoustics, aesthetics, bibliography, history, biography, instruments, harmony and notation.

Mussorgsky, Modeste Petrovich (1839-1881) Russian composer, a member of the **Five**. In his early life he was in the guards, and he later entered the Civil Service. Although a good pianist, he suffered from a lack of early musical training in harmony and composition. Many of his works were left unfinished or poorly orchestrated and **Rimsky-Korsakov** 'corrected' a large number of these when he arranged for them to be published following Mussorgsky's death.

He is best known for his operas *Boris Godunov* and *Khovanshchina*, his orchestral piece *Night on the Bare Mountain*, and his piano suite *Pictures at an Exhibition*. Alternative transliterations of his name are Moussorgsky or Musorgsky.

Modeste Mussorgsky

Mustel organ Reed organ similar to the American organ. It was invented by Victor Mustel (1815-1890) in Paris. The Mustel organ has a special device by which the top and bottom halves of the keyboard may be separately controlled for dynamic expression.

muta (It.) Change. Indication that a performer has to make a change between instruments. For example, A and B♭ clarinet, or in tunings of kettledrums or strings of the violin family temporarily tuned to abnormal notes.

mute Any of various devices that serve to reduce the volume of sound (and with it the tone) produced by an instrument. On bowed stringed instruments the mute is in the shape of fork whose prongs are made to grip the bridge and reduce its vibration, and with it the vibration of the strings. In brass wind instruments the mute consists of coned-shaped piece of wood, metal or plastic inserted into the bell, although other forms of mute are also used, especially in jazz music. To depress the soft pedal of a piano or to muffle a drum are other forms of applying a mute.

Muti, Riccardo (1941-) Italian conductor who studied in Naples and in Milan. He made his debut in Florence in 1966 and his Covent Garden debut came in 1977 (*Aïda*). From 1977, he has acted as the principal conductor of the Philadelphia Orchestra.

N

Nabokov, Nicolas (1903-1978) Russian-born composer, author and administrator who became an American citizen in 1939. He worked with **Diaghilev's** *Ballets Russes* in the 1920s, and in 1928 his own ballet-oratorio *Ode* (1928) was performed by the company in Paris, London and Berlin. In 1947 he became chief of the first broadcast unit of the Voice of America, was secretary-general of the Congress for Cultural Freedom, and director of the (West) Berlin festival. He composed ballets, orchestral and choral works, a piano concerto, a flute concerto, a string quartet, and two piano sonatas. His publications include *Old Friends and New Music* (1951) and *Igor Stravinsky* (1964). He was the cousin of the writer Vladimir Nabokov.

Nachschlag (Ger.) After-stroke, referring to the two extra notes that conventionally form the end of some kinds of **trill**. The term also refers to a note or notes (shown in smaller print) added after a given note.

Nachtanz (Ger.) After-dance. For example, a quicker dance following a slower one, such as a **galliard** following the **pavane**.

Nachtmusik (Ger.) Night music, a composition played in the open air during the evening as a serenade to a loved one. The most famous example of this type of composition is **Mozart's** *Eine Kleine Nachtmusik*, for strings (1787).

nagauta (Japan) 'Long song', used to accompany **kabuki** dances, usually with **shamisen** (lute), flute and three drums: *ō-tsuzumi*, *ko-tsuzumi* and *taiko*. *Nagauta* was influenced by the *jōruri* song form, and evolved alongside *kabuki* dancing. It is now also performed in concerts and as domestic music. See also **tsuzumi**.

nai (Romania) Panpipes consisting of 20 or more bamboo tubes, open at the upper end and set in a concave row in order of size. They are glued together and fixed to a curved stick, the lower end plugged with beeswax in order to tune them to a **diatonic** scale. The instrument has a distinctive sound quality, with characteristic *portamenti* in slow solo melodies. Made popular by the Romanian virtuoso Gheorghe Zamfir in film and television theme music, such as *Picnic at Hanging Rock* and *The Light of Experience*.

Nápravnik, Eduard (1839-1916) Czech conductor and composer, who studied in Prague but moved to St Petersburg and was considered a Russian conductor. In 1869 he became principal conductor at the Imperial Russian Opera in succession to **Lyadov**. His own opera *Dubrovsky* (1895) was successful in his time, but he was best known as a conductor, particularly of Russian opera. He was very influential in raising the standard of performance at the Mariinsky Theatre, and was admired for his strict discipline in conducting.

Nares, James (1715-1783) English composer, organist and teacher. He studied under **Pepusch** as chorister in the Chapel Royal, London. In 1735 he became organist at York Minster, and in 1757 succeeded Gates as Master of the Children of the Chapel Royal. He composed church and keyboard music, songs, and wrote treatises on the harpsichord and on singing.

Nash, Heddle (1896-1961) English tenor who studied in London and Milan. He made his debut in Milan as Almaviva in *The Barber of Seville* in 1924. He sang for all the leading British opera companies and was at his best in **Mozart** – especially as Ottavio in *Don Giovanni*.

Nathan, Isaac (1790-1864) Australian composer of Polish-Jewish descent and English birth. He collaborated with Lord Byron on Hebrew Melodies (1815-1819) by adapting ancient Jewish chants to Byron's poems. These were very popular, and remained in print until 1861. He was the music librarian to George IV until 1841, when he was forced to emigrate to Australia because of financial difficulties. In Sydney he opened a singing academy and wrote patriotic music: *Australia the Wide and Free* (1842) and *Song to Freedom* (1863). He wrote the first European operas in Australia, *Merry Freaks in Troublous Times* (1843) and *Don John of Australia* (1846), and as a teacher and conductor he assisted early colonial musicians in their concert careers. He also made precise observations of Aboriginal musical practice, and transcribed it into such works as *Koorinda Braia* (1842).

Natra, Sergiu (1924-) Israeli composer, Romanian by birth. He studied at the Bucharest Academy of Music under Leo Klepper, but settled in Tel Aviv in 1961 and was made professor at Tel Aviv University in 1976. His early music was influenced by **Stravinsky**, **Prokofiev** and **Hindemith**, although all these composers were banned in Romania. After World War II Natra and his contemporaries tried to compose music based on folk song, but it was not well received by the 'proletariat' – those they were trying to reach. His Israeli compositions are atonal.

natural Accidental (♮) that indicates that a note raised by a sharp or lowered by a flat (either in the key signature or previously in the written music) should be restored to its original position.

naturale (Fr.) Natural, indicating that a voice or instrument, after performing a passage in some unusual way (for example, falsetto or muted), is to return to the normal style of playing.

Naumann, Johann Gottlieb (1741-1801) German composer who lived and travelled extensively in Italy, where he studied under **Tartini** and **Hasse**. In 1764 he became court composer of church music at Dresden, and *Kapellmeister* in 1776. In 1777 he was asked by Gustav III to develop the National Opera in Stockholm, and in 1782 the New Royal Opera House opened under his direction. His compositions include 26 operas, the best known being *Orpheus og Eurydik* (1786) influenced by **Gluck**, sacred music, and several works for the glass harmonica. He was aware of the *Sturm und Drang* movement of the early Romantics, and was one of the most esteemed composers of Europe in the late 18th century.

Navarra, André-Nicholas (1921-) French cellist who studied at the Paris Conservatoire with J. Loeb and **Tournemire**, and played with the Krettly String Quartet (1929-1935), formed while he was still a student. In 1931 he made his solo debut with **Pierné** conducting, at the Colonne Concerts in Paris. He has been associated with **Elgar**'s Cello Concerto, having performed this work with great success for his British debut (1950) at the Cheltenham Festival.

Naylor, Bernard (1907-) English composer, the son of organist and composer Edward Naylor (1867-1934). He studied at the Royal College of Music with **Holst**, **Vaughan Williams** and **Ireland**. He spent much time in Canada as a teacher and conductor. His own music was deeply rooted in the English choral tradition but included a setting of Elizabeth Barrett

Browning's *Sonnets from the Portuguese* for voice and string quartet.

Neapolitan sixth Chord comprising the notes F, A♭ and D♭, and correspondingly in other keys. The origin of the term is obscure, but it appears as early as the time of **Purcell** (1658-1695).

Neel, (Louis) Boyd (1905-1981) English conductor who founded the Boyd Neel Orchestra (1932), which was later renamed Philomusica of London. The orchestra was noted for its revival of Baroque string music, little known at this time. **Britten** composed *Variations on a Theme of Frank Bridge* for the orchestra, which performed it at the Salzburg Festival (1937). This established the international reputations of Britten and the orchestra. Neel conducted the **Sadler's Wells** Opera (1945-1946) and the D'Oyly Carte Opera (1948-1949). He was made a CBE in 1953.

negro spiritual Afro-American religious song whose lyrics are adapted from passages of the Bible. Many stanzas consist of repetitions of lines with short, recurrent, interjected refrains or responses for communal involvement. Frequent use is made of extemporization in the song's verses. Although patterned on white American models, negro spirituals nevertheless conform to African musical practice and are characterized by rhythms associated with the swinging of the head and upper body.

neighbour note American term for **auxiliary**.

neo-Classicism Movement in musical style that began in the 1920s and continues to be a dominant trend today. Generally, it implies a return to pre-Romantic ideals of objectivity and clarity of texture, although not confined to 18th-century Classicism. It includes the revival of contrapuntal textures and forms (fugue, passacaglia, toccata and madrigal) from the Renaissance and Baroque while employing modern harmony, rhythm, tonality, melody and timbres. The principal neo-Classical composers are **Stravinsky** (from the ballet *Pulchinella*, 1920, to the opera *The Rake's Progress,* 1948-1951), **Prokofiev** (Symphony No. 1, *Classical*, 1916), and **Hindemith** (*Ludus Tonalis*, for piano, 1943).

Neri, St Philip (San Filippo) Italian saint and religious leader. He introduced the singing of the *Lauda Spirituale* which he developed from informal spiritual exercises. He placed great stress on music for attracting people to his services. **Palestrina** and **Victoria** probably participated in these. In 1575 his gatherings were recognized by Pope Gregory XIII as an official community – *Congregazione dell' Oratorio* – and his spiritual exercises became an important aspect of the Catholic reform movement in Rome.

netori (Japan) Serene musical prelude to a performance of **gagaku** court music and dance. It is used to establish the mode of the composition and might be regarded as a formalized tuning of the orchestra, with instruments entering one by one in a fixed sequence, beginning with the **shō** mouth organ, followed by the **hichiriki** oboe, a flute and the **kakko** drum.

neum(e) Sign used, originally in the 7th century, indicating the single notes or groups of notes to which each syllable was to be sung. Neumes were marked above the words of the text to serve merely as reminders of the general upward or downward direction of a melody already known to the singer.

Neumann, Václav (1920-) Czech conductor who studied conducting with Pavel Dedecek and Metod Dolezil at the Prague Conservatoire. He also formed the Smetana Quartet, in which he played first violin, and later viola, giving concerts from 1945. In 1956 at the invitation of Felstein he conducted **Janáček**'s *The Cunning Little Vixen*, which was very successful, and gave more than 200 performances. He became chief conductor of the Czech Philharmonic Orchestra in 1968, and is concerned with promoting Czech Classical music.

Neveu, Ginette (1919-1949) French violinist who studied at the Paris Conservatoire under Carl Flesch and made her debut in Paris in 1926. Neveu was considered best known for her performances of the concertos of Sibelius. She was killed in an air crash.

new music Term with three meanings.

First, it is a 'new' form of expressive music, a style first used Giulio **Caccini** in the 17th century, published in his work *Nuove musiche* (new music), containing madrigals and arias for voice and thorough-bass.

Second, it refers to the style of the music of **Liszt** and **Wagner** and their followers during the period 1850-1900, as opposed to the more traditional music of **Brahms**.

Third, it refers to the various new techniques adopted for composition in the early 20th century, such as **serialism** and **atonality**.

New Orleans style Original style of jazz that originated in the 1890s when black people played lively marches for processions leaving cemeteries after funerals, or for dancing and entertainment in Storeyville, the red light district of New Orleans. The bands usually consisted of a cornet, trombone, clarinet, banjo and drums. As the majority of the players could not read musical scores, they improvised on a given tune such as *When the Saints Come Marching In* and *Oh Didn't He Ramble*. After the Storeyville district was closed in 1917, the centre of jazz activity moved from New Orleans to Chicago.

New Philharmonia Orchestra British symphony orchestra founded by Walter Legge (1945), when it was known as the Philharmonia Orchestra (renamed the New Philharmonia Orchestra, 1964). It reverted to its original name in 1977. Under Walter Legge its main objective was to make recordings, although as its reputation grew, it gave several concerts both in London and abroad. With the departure of Walter Legge in 1964, the orchestra became self-governing. Among its many famous conductors have been Richard **Strauss** and Arturo **Toscanini**. In 1950, Otto **Klemperer** conducted a series of concerts with the orchestra which led to his being made 'conductor for life' (1964).

New York Philharmonic Orchestra American symphony orchestra founded in 1842. It was originally known as the Philharmonic Symphony Society of New York, when about 60 playing members shared the financial risks and conductor's duties. It is the oldest orchestra in the United States. In 1928 it merged with the New York Symphony Orchestra (founded in 1878 by Leopold **Damrosch**). From the time of its first permanent conductor, Carl Bergmann (1865-1877), it has attracted conductors of the highest international repute. They included Walter **Damrosch**, Emil **Paur**, Gustav **Mahler**, Arturo **Toscanini**, Bruno **Walter**, Leopold **Stokowski**, Leonard **Bernstein**, Pierre **Boulez** and Zubin **Mehta**. The orchestra has visited Britain several times, including appearances at the **Edinburgh Festival**.

Nicolai, (Carl) Otto (Ehrenfried) (1810-1849) German composer and conductor. He studied in Berlin and Rome and was the last of the important composers to study seriously in Italy. His most famous work, *The Merry Wives of Windsor* (1849, *Die lustigen Weiber von Windsor*), is an example of early Romantic German comic opera. He was the first *Kapellmeister* of the Court Opera in Vienna (1841-1847) and in 1847 became director of the Court Opera, Berlin.

Nielsen, Carl August (1865-1931) Danish composer who studied at Copenhagen Conservatoire under Niels **Gade** and joined the Royal Orchestra as a violinist in 1891. He later became director of the Conservatoire and conductor of the Musical Society (1915-1927). He wrote six

Carl Nielsen

symphonies, the first of which in 1892 made history by beginning in one key and ending in another, a technique called 'progressive tonality'. His fourth symphony became known as *The Inextinguishable* (1914-1916). He also wrote the operas *Saul and David* (1902), *Maskarade* (1906), and chamber works such as the Wind Quintet (1922). This work made him aware of the individual tonal potentials of each instrument, and he wrote a Flute Concerto (1926) to explore these possibilities. In 1931 he composed an important organ work, *Commotio* Op. 58, which started from Baroque toccata form, extending through other forms, summing up his thematic, tonal and structural style. His music shows the influence of the Danish romance tradition of Heise and Lange-Müller as well as harmonic influences traceable to **Brahms** and **Grieg**.

Nigg, Serge (1924-) French composer. He studied at the Paris Conservatoire with **Messiaen** and later studied twelve-note serial technique with **Leibowitz**. He was one of the first French composers to master this technique, as seen in his Variations (1947). With Désormière he founded the French Association of Progressivist Musicians, making journeys to Eastern Europe. His own music, with its combination of tenderness and aggressiveness as in *Visages d'Axel* (1967), shows an affinity with that of **Ravel**.

Nikisch, Arthur (1855-1922) Austro-Hungarian conductor who started his career as a violinist in the Vienna Hofkappelle, playing under **Brahms**, **Liszt**, **Verdi** and **Wagner**. In 1879 he became the first conductor of the Leipzig Opera. He also conducted the Boston Symphony Orchestra, the Royal Opera Budapest, the Leipzig Gewandhaus (in succession to Reinecke) and the Berlin Philharmonic Orchestra. He had a clear, unostentatious technique and influenced many who followed him, including **Furtwängler** and **Boult**.

Nilsson, Märta Birgit (1918-) Swedish soprano. She studied at the Royal Academy in Stockholm and made her operatic debut in 1946 as Agathe in *Der Freischütz*. She then gradually established herself as the leading **Wagner** soprano of the day. In 1954-1955 she appeared as Brünnhilde in *The Ring* at Munich, became associated with this role and recorded it with Sir George **Solti**. In 1959 she made her debut at the Metropolitan Opera, New York, as Isolde in *Tristan und Isolde*. She is noted also for the title roles in **Strauss**'s *Salomé* and *Elektra* and **Puccini**'s *Turandot*. Her range is phenomenal and easily heard above the large Wagner and Strauss orchestra.

Nilsson, Bo (1937-) Swedish composer who was largely self-taught. There are influences of **Boulez** and **Stockhausen** in his music but he has his own distinctive combination of percussive and melodious sounds of voice or instrument, often using the alto flute. He became well known when his *Frequenzen* for eight instrumentalists was performed in Darmstadt (1956). His *Nazm* (1973) combines free form with specified formulae based on Turkish folk music and jazz. It is scored for solo voices, chorus and orchestra, all amplified.

Nin (y Castellanos), Joaquín (1879-1949) Cuban pianist and composer, the father of Nin-Culmell. He studied piano under Carlos Vidiella in Barcelona and **Moszkowski** and **d'Indy** in Paris. He was famous for his performances of **Bach** and early Spanish works and his opposition to the performance of these on the harpsichord resulted in a celebrated exchange with **Landowska**. His compositions, including works for violin, piano, a ballet and songs for voice and orchestra, show his enthusiasm for Spanish Baroque music.

Nin-Culmell, Joaquín Maria (1908-) American composer, pianist and conductor of Cuban descent. He studied in New York, in Paris under Paul Brand and **Dukas**, and in Granada under **Falla**. He later became professor and chairman of the University of California, Berkeley, Music department (1940-1956). His music, which is clearly influenced by Spanish rhythms, includes a quintet for piano (1934-1937), a piano and violin concerto, a ballet, *El Burlador de Sevilla* (1957-1965) and an opera.

ninth Interval of nine notes (counting the bottom and top notes). See also **dominant ninth**.

no See **noh**.

nobile, nobilmente (It.) Noble, nobly.

nocturne Night piece or instrumental serenade, generally of a quiet lyrical character, especially for the piano, in one movement. During the 18th century the term applied to short works such as **Mozart's** *Serenata notturna*. **John Field** (1782-1837) is believed to have been the first composer of nocturnes and composed more than 20 for the **piano**, although it was **Chopin** who expanded the scope of the nocturne with 21 examples expressing a wide range of moods. Other notable composers of nocturnes were **Mendelssohn** (*A Midsummer Night's Dream*, 1826), **Debussy** (*Nocturnes*, 1900) and **Britten** (*Serenade*, a song-cycle for tenor, horn and strings, 1943).

node Point in a vibrating string or air-column that is stationary and about which the vibrating string or column divides itself into separately vibrating segments.

noh/no (Japan) Theatre form originating from song-dances and folk theatre of the 14th century. *Noh* performances embody the essence of Buddhism – simplicity, serenity, meditation and mental control - the central focus being the symbolic dance imbued with mystical power. There are usually two actors, the *shite* (principal) and the *waki* (secondary), who wear masks and elaborate, symbolic costumes. A performance consists of alternate recitation and singing between the main actors, interspersed with dance and chorus. The vocal parts, showing the influence of Buddhist liturgical chant, comprise recurring melodic patterns which are shaped by a rigid metrical scheme in which 12 syllables, divided into groups of seven and five, are contained within a rhythmic period of eight beats. The instruments of the *noh* drama, the **hayashi** ensemble, are *noh* flute (*nohkan*) and three drums (two **tsuzumi** and one *taiko*). A full *noh* programme consists of five plays separated by comic interludes (*kyōgen*) and can last all day.

nonet Composition for nine instruments or voices. A group performing this type of composition often includes a mixture of stringed and wind instruments. An example is **Webern's** *Concerto for Nine Instruments* (1934) which includes flute, oboe, clarinet, horn, trumpet, trombone, violin, viola and piano.

non-harmonic note Note that is not harmonically associated with the chord which it precedes or follows. See also **auxiliary note; passing note**.

Nono, Luigi (1924-) Italian composer. He started his studies in law and then began to compose under the influence of **Malipiero**. **Maderna** and Scherchen introduced him to serial methods and he won attention outside Italy with his *Orchestral Variations on a Note Series by Schoenberg* Op. 41 performed at Darmstadt in 1950. His other notable works are *Epitaph for Frederico García Lorca* (1951-1953) for speakers, singers and orchestra, *Incontri* (1955) for chamber ensemble, *Intolleranza* (1960), an opera combining live and recorded performances and using actors and film sequences and *Sul Ponte di Hiroshima* (1962) for soprano, tenor and orchestra. His music became increasingly dry and didactic as he tried to use it to portray left-wing political views, such as *Non Consumiamo Marx* (1969) scored for voices and tape. He has also organized concerts in factories.

Nordheim, Arne (1931-) Norwegian composer who was concerned with novel sound combinations and a free atonal style. *Katharsis* (1962), commissioned by the Norwegian State Opera, was his first composition using electronics in combination with a live orchestra. His major work *Colorazione* (1968) combined instruments (Hammond organ and percussion) and equipment including a ring modulator and a tape delay. In 1975 he collaborated with Arnold Haukeland in the creation of *Sound Sculpture* – sounds are produced on 13 points of the sculpture which begins to sing when daylight hits its photosensitive cells.

Nordraak, Rikard (1842-1866) Norwegian composer who studied music in Copenhagen and Berlin under Theodor **Kullak** and Frederick Kiel. In 1861 he met **Grieg**, Emil Horneman and Gottfred Matthison-Hansen and with them founded the music society Enterpe, aimed at performing works by young Scandinavian composers. He was influential on Grieg in his strong sense of the importance of Norwegian national music.

Nørgård, Per (1932-) Danish composer who was a pupil of Vagn **Holmboe** and Nadia **Boulanger**. His *Fragment VI* for six orchestra groups won the international first prize at the Dutch music week, Gaudeamus (1961). His music is influenced by **Sibelius, Ligeti** and the American minimalists. Per Nørgård was head of the Danish section of International Society for Contemporary Music (ISCM), between the years 1965-1967.

Norman, Jessye (1945-) American soprano who made her operatic debut in Berlin as Elisabeth in *Tannhäuser* (1969), and opera appearances followed in Rome, Florence and Covent Garden. Her performances of Berg's *Der Wein* were acclaimed internationally. Recordings include *Lieder* by **Schubert and Mahler**, and the works of **Mozart** and **Verdi**. Her tone is opulent and particularly vibrant in the lower registers.

nota cambiata (It.) Device in strict counterpoint by which a dissonant note is used on an accented beat instead of falling to the note below, as normal, but by first rising or falling by the interval of a third and then only resolving in the conventional way.

notation Method of writing down music so that it can be read for performance. This can be done by means of symbols, such as specially devised letters as in Greek music; by **neumes** as in the early Middle Ages; in **tablature** for old lute and organ music; in notes according to the present system, or in the special syllable form of the **tonic-sol-fa system**. A simple harmonic notation is used in jazz and other popular music, whereby the harmonic sequence is shown by abbreviations for the names of the chords. See also **graphic notation**.

note Term with three meanings.

First, it is a single sound of a given **pitch** and precise duration.

Second, it is a written sign for such a sound.

Third, it is an alternative term for the key of a **keyboard**.

note-row Alternative name for the **twelve-note technique**.

notturno (It.) Equivalent of **nocturne**.

Novák, Vítézslav (1870-1949) Czech composer and teacher who studied under **Dvorák** at Prague Conservatoire; he was appointed professor there in 1909. He made a study of Slovakian and Moravian folk melody and in his own composition was concerned with exploring the metamorphosis of a single theme as in *Pan* (1910). He also wrote symphonic poems, ballets, *Lucerna* (1922) and operas. **Debussy**, **Strauss** and **Dvorák** were important influences on his style.

Novello, Clara Anastasia (1818-1908) The daughter of Vincent **Novello** who became one of the most famous sopranos of her day, earning the praise of **Mendelssohn** and **Schumann**. In 1838 Mendelssohn arranged for her to sing at the Gewandhaus concerts in Leipzig, which launched her career in Germany. She was a friend of **Rossini**'s and sang in the title role of his *Semiramide* (1841) and in the first performances of *Stabat Mater* (1841). In 1851 she returned to England and established herself as an oratorio singer.

Novello, Ivor (David Ifor Davies) (1893-1951) British composer, the son of Madame Novello Davies, well-known in Wales and London as a teacher of singing. He began composing songs at the age of 15 and his greatest success was in 1914 with *Keep the Home Fires Burning* (*Till the Boys Come Home*). He wrote many operettas in an anglicized Viennese style; the most popular, *The Dancing Years* (1939), ran almost continuously in London and on tour for ten years.

Novello, Vincent (1781-1861) London publisher, editor, organist and composer. He was organist at the chapel of the Portuguese Embassy (1797-1822). In 1811 he founded the music publishing firm of Novello & Co., whose first publications were two volumes of *Sacred Music* (1811) and *Twelve Early Masses* (including three of his own) by **Haydn** and **Mozart**. These were issued in vocal score with fully written-out piano and organ accompaniment rather than figured bass. His concern was to make music more accessible to less skilful musicians. He enriched music-making by making scores available and affordable.

number Self-contained musical piece in an **opera** or musical, (so-called because originally each piece was separately numbered in the written score).

Nunc Dimittis Text from St Luke's Gospel ("Lord, now lettest Thou Thy servant depart in peace") which is sung in the Roman Catholic Church and in the Anglican Church at Evensong. It is often set by composers as a second part following the **Magnificat**.

Ivor Novello

nut Ridge at the end of the fingerboard of a stringed instrument just below the pegs, serving to raise the strings clear of the board. It is also the head of a screw attached to the heel of a violin bow to enable the hairs to be tightened.

Nyström, Gösta (1890-1966) Swedish composer who went to Paris in 1920, became a pupil of **d'Indy** and remained in the company of Scandinavian and French artists. He was also a talented painter. His early music such as *Ishavet* (1924-1925) was influenced by **Debussy, Ravel** and **Stravinsky**'s *The Rite of Spring*. His *Sinfonia Breve* (1929-1931) combined polyrhythms and harsh dissonance, a style found shocking at the time. His music later became more harmonic and lyrical in conception, often referring to nature and the sea. An example of this is *The Tempest* (1934).

O

obbligato (It.) Used on a musical score to indicate that a certain instrumental part must not be omitted in a performance. For example, an oboe obbligato is an oboe part that must be played. On some occasions it can be used in the opposite sense whereby the playing of the same instrument can be optional.

oblique motion In harmony, movement in one of the parts while the other parts remain stationary. See also **contrary motion; similar motion.**

oboe Double-reed woodwind instrument, formerly called the **hautboy**, developed in France during the 17th century from the **shawm**. An oboe dating from about 1690 was equipped with six finger-holes and three keys. The bore was much wider at the top and expanded more gradually than modern instruments. During the 19th century a complicated system of keys was added. Today, the regular oboe has a range of two and a half octaves from B♭ below middle C.

Other members of the oboe family include the *oboe d'amore*, a **transposing** instrument sounding a minor third below the regular oboe; the **cor anglais**, which sounds a fifth below and is much bigger than the oboe, and was sometimes known as an English horn. Other oboes that are not often used are the baritone oboe and the **heckelphone**, or bass oboe.

The oboe is a standard instrument in an orchestra, and it is often used as a solo instrument. Because the oboe is one of the most difficult instruments to tune, it is used as the norm against which all the other orchestral instruments are tuned. The most famous oboist was Leon Goossens (1897-1988), who was principal oboe player for the Queen's Hall Orchestra when he was only 17 years of age.

Oboe

Obrecht, Jacob (*c*1450-1505) Flemish composer who spent some time in Italy and eventually died there in Ferrara. He held important church-music positions in Bruges, Cambrai and Antwerp, succeeding Barbireau at Notre Dame, Antwerp, in 1492. He wrote masses, motets and chansons to Dutch, French and Italian words. His music revealed a later style than **Ockeghem**'s, employing the use of imitation between the parts and definite cadences. As a northerner he was not as popular as **Josquin des Près** and the other southern composers.

ocarina Pear-shaped wind instrument with finger holes and a protruding mouthpiece, usually made of terracotta. It was invented by Giuseppe Donati in about 1860. It is mainly used as a toy and was featured in the musical play entitled *Call Me Madam* by Irving **Berlin** (1950).

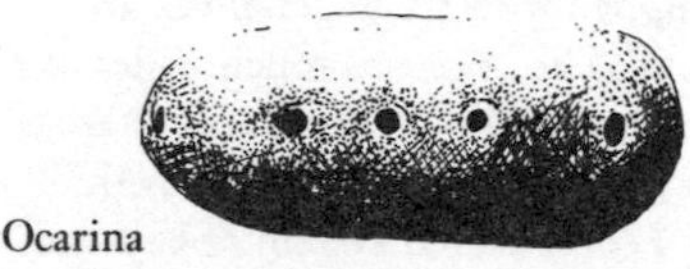

Ocarina

Ockeghem, Jean de (*c*1430-1495) The first famous Flemish composer, recognized during his lifetime as a master, the teacher of **Josquin des Près** and **Busnois**. In the mid-1440s he entered the service of Charles I, Duke of Bourbon, and became *maître de chappelle* to the King of France in 1465. He composed masses, motets and chansons which explored new sonorities and have a distinctive flowing and continuous style. His polyphonic *Requiem* is of importance as the earliest existing setting. Along with Josquin and **Dufay** he is one of the most important composers of the second half of the 15th century.

octave Interval of eight notes on the **diatonic scale**, the upper note having exactly twice the frequency (number of vibrations) of the lower note. Notes separated by an octave are denoted by the same letter.

octet Composition for eight voices, instruments or a combination of both. In **Mendelssohn's** String Octet in E♭ major (1825) it was limited to strings, whereas **Beethoven's** Octet in E♭ (1834) was for two oboes, two clarinets, two horns and two bassoons.

octobass Three-stringed **double bass** measuring 12ft (4m) high, invented by Jean-Baptiste Vuillaume of Paris in 1849. It was very unwieldy and the strings were so thick and heavy that they had to be stopped by levers and pedals. The octobass was not considered a practical instrument.

octuor (Fr.) French equivalent of the English **octet**.

ō-daiko (Japan) Large, convex drum with two tacked skin heads. It is struck with sticks, but these differ according to the situation in which it is being used. In the **geza** percussion of the **kabuki** theatre, it is struck with two long, tapered sticks on both heads, generally as a representation of wind and rain. It is also struck one hour before the curtain rises, a ceremony known as *ichiban-daiko*' to indicate a performance is due to take place.

In the Buddhist temple, only one head is struck with a single stick, and it is used as an accompaniment to the singing towards the end of a ceremony.

Finally, a crude version is used in the folk **hayashi** ensemble: it is placed on a crate with one head tipped towards the player and hit on the skin or rim with two blunt sticks.

ode Musical setting of a poem with alternating solos and choruses which are often dedicated to a monarch or deity. During the 17th and 18th centuries there were several English settings of odes in the form of **cantatas**, such as those by **Purcell** (*Come Ye Sons of Art* composed for Queen Mary's birthday, 1694) and **Handel** (*Ode for St Cecilia's Day*, 1739). A 19th-century example is **Parry's** setting of Milton's *Ode at a Solemn Music* (1887).

Offenbach, Jacques (1819-1880) French composer born in Cologne and educated in Paris, where he spent the rest of his life. He was largely responsible for the development and popularity of the operetta, which became an established international genre. Most of his career was spent working in theatres such as Théâtre Français, Bouffes Parisiens and Théâtre Gaité, which he managed. His best-known works are *Orphée aux Enfers* (1858), *La Belle Hélène* (1864), *La Vie Parisienne* (1866) and finally *Les Contes d'Hoffmann*. This was unfinished at the time of his death, but was completed by **Guiraud** and produced in 1881.

offertorium (offertory) Part of the Proper of the Mass following the gospel or the Credo. It was originally an antiphonal chant, sung with a complete psalm and accompanied the offering of bread and wine. In the 10th century the chants became more elaborate, with **melismas** in the responsorial style.

Ogdon, John (Andrew Howard) (1937-) English pianist and composer. His compositions include a piano concerto, a sonata, and preludes for piano, but it is as a performer that he is best known. In 1962 he was a joint winner (with Vladimir **Ashkenazy**) of the International Tchaikovsky Competition in Moscow. His technique is powerful and agile, and his repertory vast, encompassing the Viennese classics, Romantics, Slavonic nationalists and, particularly, 20th-century works.

Oistrakh, David (Fedorovich) (1908-1974) Soviet violinist who did not travel extensively in the West until the 1950s, even though he had won the Ysaye Prize in Brussels in 1937. His performances were characterized by his extraordinarily sweet tone, and many Soviet composers wrote works for him, including **Khachaturian** and **Shostakovich**. In 1945 he performed **Bach**'s double violin concerto with **Menuhin** in Moscow – the first foreign artist to visit the Soviet Union after the war. His students included his son Igor, Valery and Klimov. In 1954 he was named 'People's Artist of the USSR' and received the Lenin Prize in 1960.

David Oistrakh

Oistrakh, Igor (1931-) Soviet violinist somewhat overshadowed by his father and teacher David **Oistrakh**, but with a distinctive, less emotional and more modern style than his father's. In 1958 he was appointed to the staff of the Moscow Conservatoire and became a lecturer there in 1965. There are many recordings of father and son duos and double concertos, as well as performances with Igor as soloist and David as conductor.

oliphant Medieval horn made from an elephant's tusk or of gold. The oliphant was considered a symbol of high dignity by African kings during the 10th-12th centuries.

Oliver, Stephen (1950-) British composer. He was a pupil of Leighton and Sherlaw Johnson and studied electronic music at Oxford. He has written the operas *Duchess of Malfi* (1971), *Ricercare* (1974), *Tom Jones* (1976), *Exchange* (1978) and a symphony. He also wrote the music for the Royal Shakespeare Company's *Nicholas Nickleby*.

ondes martenot More common name for **martenot**.

Onslow, André Georges Louis (1784-1853) French composer of English descent who wrote operas, symphonies and chamber music including more than 30 string quintets. He studied composition under Reicha in Paris. In 1842 he was elected to the Institut de France in succession to **Cherubini**. His compositions are not heard any more, but he is known for his *Bullet Quintet* Op. 38.

Op. Abbreviation of **opus**.

open **Organ** pipes whose upper ends are left open and which, unlike the stopped pipes, produce notes corresponding to their full length.

open form Compositions that can begin or end at any point in the score, at the performer's discretion. An example is **Stockhausen's** *Zklus* (1959) for solo percussionist, where the percussion instruments are arranged in a circle and the score is on spiral-bound pages, so that the player has freedom of choice to begin at any point and continue in a circular fashion until he or she reaches that point again.

Oper (Ger.) **Opera**, opera house or opera company.

opera Theatrical entertainment in which music, drama, poetry, spectacle and, often, dancing play a part. Its Western origins have been traced to Ancient Greece, when Greek tragedies used choruses and dances, and dialogue may have been sung. There was an element of music in medieval liturgical dramas, mystery plays and miracle plays, in which some sections were partly sung. The actual source of opera was in Florence where, at the end of the 16th century, a group of young poets and musicians known as the Florentine **Camerata** sought to re-create Greek tragedy in terms of contemporary poetry and music. The first opera is believed to be *L'Euridice*, with text by Rinuccini and music by **Peri** and some choruses by **Caccini**, performed at the Pitti Palace, Florence, in 1600.

The invention of **recitatives** allowed the story to move forward through the medium of music. In 1607 Claudio **Monteverdi** brought to the composition of his first opera, *La Favola d'Orfeo*, a mastery of every kind of music practised at that time. It is known that the orchestra consisted of 36 players and most of the music was for keyboard instruments, lutes and harps.

In 1637 the San Cassiano theatre in Venice opened as the world's first public opera house. By the middle of the 17th-century operas became more formalized, and the Italian **overture**, called **sinfonia**, was established. The **aria** emerged as a distinct form, and **castrati** (male **sopranos**) reigned supreme as the opera stars of the day.

The new Italian opera quickly spread to Vienna and France. French opera was strongly influenced by the court **ballet** and the dramas of Corneille, Racine and Molière. An Italian, Giovanni Battista Lulli (1632-1687), who became a naturalized French subject and changed his name to **Lully**, created a French operatic style. Among his operas were *Cadmus et Hermione* (1673), *Alceste, ou le triomphe d'Alcide* (1674) and *Amadis de Gaule* (1684). The style and orchestral brilliance originated by Lully was continued by Jean-Philippe **Rameau** (1683-1764) with his work *Castor et Pollux* (1737).

During the 17th-century, opera made very little impact in England. The only true operas of that period were **Blow's** *Venus and Adonis* (1684) and **Purcell's** *Dido and Aeneas* (1689). In Germany a form of opera known as **singspiel** was popular during the 18th century. **Hiller's** *Die Jagd* (1770) was an example of this type of work. **Gluck** (1714-1787) inspired what became known as the reform operas with his works *Orfeo ed Euridice* (1762) and *Alceste* (1767), which drew music and drama closer together. Towards the end of the 18th century comic opera became more common, such as **Mozart's** *The Marriage of Figaro* (1786) and *Don Giovanni* (1787). Mozart, with his extraordinary powers of dramatic and musical characterization in all forms of opera, composed **opera seria** (*Idomeneo*, 1781) and *singspiel* (*The Magic Flute*, 1791).

Grand opera was established in France in the early 19th century when grandiose plots, larger ensemble scenes and expanded orchestras were introduced. The principal composers at that time were **Rossini** (*William Tell*, 1829), **Meyerbeer** (*Les Huguenots*, 1836) and **Berlioz** (*The Trojans*, 1863). At the same time lyric opera appeared in the form of **Gounod's** *Faust* (1859), which combined the melodic appeal of comedy opera and some aspects of grand opera.

Italian opera in the 19th century was dominated by the works of Verdi, such as *Il Travatore* and *La Traviata* (both 1853), *Aïda* (1871), *Otello* (1887) and *Falstaff* (1893).

German opera rose to a position of eminence during the 19th century, with the first half of the century being dominated by Romantic opera, such as **Weber's** *Der Freischütz* (1821) and *Oberon* (1826), and **Beethoven's** *Fidelio* (1803-1814). In the second half of the century, **Wagner** emerged as the main German composer. His Romantic operas included *The Flying Dutchman* (1843), *Tannhäuser* (1845) and *Lohengrin* (1851), which was followed by his music dramas, such as *Der Ring des Nibelungen* (1869-1876).

In the early 20th century, a degree of decadence was reflected in the operas of Richard **Strauss**, such as *Salomé* (1905), based on Wilde's tragedy, and *Elektra* (1909).

Verismo opera (based on contemporary events and characters) appeared in the form of **Puccini's** *La Bohème* (1896) and *Tosca* (1900) and also **Impressionism** (**Debussy's** *Pelleas et Melisande*, 1902).

Since the 1950s **Stravinsky** sought to revive the 18th-century **neo-Classical** form with *The Rake's Progress* (1951). Other notable composers of opera in the post-war period are **Britten** (*Peter Grimes*, 1945, *Albert Herring*, 1947, *Billy Budd*, 1951 and *Death In Venice*, 1973); **Bliss** (*The Olympians*, 1949); **Walton** (*Troilus and Cressida*, 1954) and **Tippett** (*The Midsummer Marriage*, 1952, and *The Ice-Break*, 1976).

Although today it may appear that operas are too often plays with musical accompaniment, rather than dramas presented through music, it is indicative of their popularity – and that of those composed more than 300 years ago – that opera in general continues to attract wide audiences throughout the world. See also **ballad opera; bel canto; libretto; opera-ballet; opéra bouffe; opera buffa; opéra-comique; opera-oratorio; opera semi-seria; opera seria; operetta; Peking opera.**

opera-ballet Combination of opera and ballet that originated in France during the 17th and 18th centuries, examples of which may be found in the work of such composers as **Lully** and **Rameau.**

opéra bouffe (Fr.) French comic opera of the 18th century, largely derived from the Italian **opera buffa**, such as **Offenbach's** operettas *Orphée aux enfers* (1858) and *La Belle Hélène* (1864).

opera buffa (It.) Italian comic opera of the 18th century, which originated from the **intermezzo**. It is characterized by the use of recitative rather than dialogue and the appearance of a chorus finale. The most famous operas of this type are **Pergolesi**'s *La Serva Padrona* (1733), **Rossini**'s *Barber of Seville* and **Mozart**'s *Don Giovanni*. The French rough equivalent is *opéra bouffe*, which is closer to musical farce than *opera buffa*.

opéra-comique (Fr.) French opera of the 18th century that was not necessarily humorous, but always involved spoken dialogue. One of the most notable exponents of this type of opera was François André **Philidor** (1726-1795), whose works included *Le Sorcier* (1764) and *Tom Jones* (1765). Other examples are **Gounod's** *Faust* (1859) and **Bizet's** *Carmen* (1875).

opera-oratorio Term used by **Stavinsky** to describe his *Oedipus Rex* (1927), in which the singers are placed in a static position on the stage so that the work is half-way between an opera and an oratorio.

opera semi-seria (It.) Italian opera that is

neither wholly comic nor wholly tragic. An example of this is **Mozart's** *Don Giovanni* (1787), in which the plot is serious, although there are also comic elements.

opera seria (It.) Opera of the 18th and early 19th centuries in which the plot is heroic, mythological or tragic. Apostolo Zeno (1668-1750), the librettist, is seen as one of the founders of *opera seria*.

operetta Light opera or musical comedy, normally with spoken dialogue.

ophicleide Large 19th-century bass instrument similar to the key bugle, with a cup-shaped mouthpiece and holes in the side covered with keys. It was a baritone instrument made in C or B♭, and was superceded by the **tuba** in about 1850.

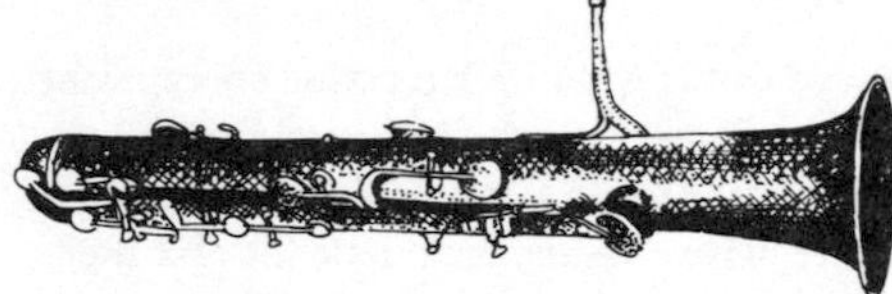

Ophicleide

opus (Lat.) Work. Used for the enumeration of a composer's works. Its abbreviated form is Op. Originally it was used by music publishers (not composers) in the early 18th century and more often for instrumental works. It was used for the works of **Handel**, but not for those of **Mozart**, and from the time of **Beethoven** it began to be used regularly. The number of the opus does not necessarily indicate the date of its composition. Because there was some confusion with the number system, the works of some composers are classified differently. These include J.S. **Bach** (BWV), Mozart (K), **Haydn** (Hob.) and **Vivaldi** (RV).

oratorio Large-scale composition for solo voices, chorus and orchestra with a libretto based on sacred words from the Bible or paraphrased from it. The form took its name from the Oratory of St Philip Neri in Rome, where scenes from the scripture were enacted with music in the 16th century. It was there in 1600 that **Cavalieri**'s *Rappresentazione di Anima e di Corpo*, an operatic morality play demanding acting and ballet, was produced. Acting and dancing were soon abandoned, so that the oratorios of **Carissimi**, such as *Jephtha* (1650), are dramatic works sung with massive choruses.

The culmination of Baroque oratorio was achieved by **Handel** with his mastery of choral technique. Altogether he composed more than 20 oratorios, including *Israel in Egypt* (1739), *Messiah* (1741), *Samson* (1743), *Belshazzar* (1745) and *Solomon* (1749). Oratorios that followed included **Haydn**'s *Seven Last Words* (1797) and *The Creation* (1797), **Mendelsohn**'s *St Paul* (1830), **Liszt**'s *Christus* (1866), **Parry**'s *Job* (1888) and **Elgar**'s *The Apostles* (1903).

Orchésographie Title of a French treatise on dancing published in 1588 by Thoinot Arbeau. The treatise is an important source of information about contemporary dance music.

orchestra In ancient Greece, the orchestra was the space between actors and audience reserved for the dancers and musicians. In modern terms it means a mixed group of instrumentalists playing stringed instruments, often with wind and percussion instruments as well. Apart from a symphony orchestra, there are also string, chamber and theatre orchestras.

The modern orchestra originated in the ballets and operas of the early 17th century, and at that time groups of strings and brass were used separately, but gradually they were combined. During the course of the same century, trumpets and timpani were introduced, to be followed in the early 18th century by flutes, oboes, bassoons and horns, although recorders were often used as alternatives to flutes. Throughout this period keyboard instruments were also in use, and in the course of the same century clarinets were added, although the keyboard **continuo** disappeared. The use of trombones was limited to sacred music and to certain operatic scenes.

As other instruments were developed and improved in the 19th century, they were added to the orchestra. These include the piccolo, English horn, bass clarinet, double bassoon, tuba and harp. The older, natural trumpets and horns were replaced by valve instruments at this time.

The 20th-century symphony orchestra is a group of many varied instruments, and could amount to more than 90 instrumentalists.

orchestration Art of blending and contrasting the tonal qualities of the various orchestral instruments. Some composers work out their first ideas in a **short score** by indicating the most important colouring of the instruments and their combinations. Upon completion in this form, they apply it to the final score.

Orchestre de Paris French symphony orchestra founded in 1967, whose conductors have included Charles **Munch**, Herbert von **Karajan**, Georg **Solti** and Daniel **Barenboim**.

Ord, Boris Bernhard (1897-1961) English organist and conductor. He founded the Cambridge University Madrigal Society and was responsible for making the choir of King's College internationally famous through its Christmas Eve broadcasts. He was made a CBE in 1958.

ordre (Fr.) 17th- and 18th-century French equivalent of suite.

Orff, Carl (1895-1982) German teacher, editor and composer, born in Munich. As a composer he is best known for *Carmina Burana* (1938), a 'scenic cantata' which gained its effect through exploration of rhythm, reiterated short motifs and plainsong. He strove for the creation of 'total theatre' with music, words and dance united as in Greek tragedy. In 1924 he formed the Günterschule for Gymnastics, Music and Dance in Munich. He wanted to explore and teach new relationships between dance and music, and was influenced in this by Mary Wigman, a pupil of Emile **Jacques-Dalcroze.**

organ Keyboard instrument of great antiquity, the earliest of which originated with the mouth-blown **panpipes**. The first mechanically-blown organ was the ancient Greek **hydraulis**, invented in the 3rd century BC by Ctesibios of Alexandria. The organ can be the simplest and the most complex of musical wind instruments. It is simple because every pipe produces only a single note when a mechanical valve admits compressed air to it. It is complex because, in its fully developed form, it is a vast combination of mechanisms controlling a huge number of tonal combinations.

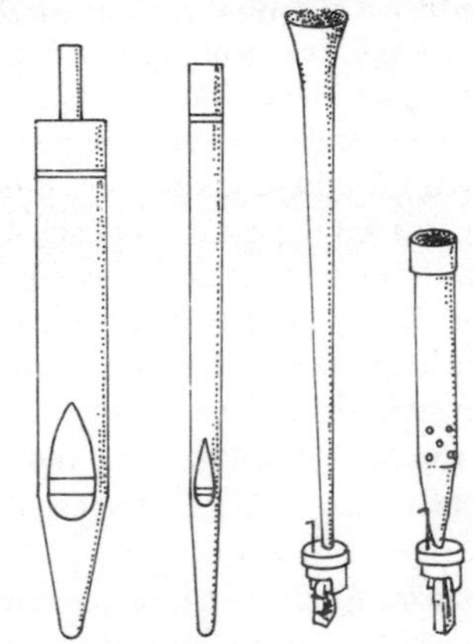

Four types of organ pipe

With the introduction of bellows, air was blown into the **pipes**. These were opened and closed by an action of keys, and a keyboard of pedals, operated by the feet, was added to control the largest bass pipes. The number of pipes, measuring from 32ft down to less than an inch, was increased. They were made in a variety of shapes, with different speaking-mechanisms, each range being controlled by stops which could be brought into action or shut off at the performer's discretion. The number of **manuals** (hand keyboards) increased to three or more, which meant that a greater number of stops drawn before the performance could be controlled and varied.

During the late 19th century, the bellows – previously blown by hand – were operated mechanically and devices by which whole ranges of stops could be activated in various combinations were invented. By using **couplers** which interlock the mechanisms of the keyboards, it was possible to play two or more sections at once from a single manual, and so bring into use the immense resources of the whole instrument, or to link certain stops on different manuals in new tonal combinations. Expression was added by swell pedals which produced crescendo and diminuendo, but beyond that the player's hands and feet have no power to vary the tone either in strength or in quality.

The use of the organ has varied considerably since it was invented more than 2000 years ago. It was introduced into the English Church by the 8th century, and up to the 19th century it was still primarily associated with the Church. During the course of its development it was able to emulate the orchestra, and as a result its repertory became wider. It not only became part of a major concert hall, but a popular instrument in the cinema and theatre during the 1920s and 1930s. See also **electric organ**.

organistrum Alternative term for **hurdy-gurdy**.

organ point Keys (pedals) of an organ that are played with the feet.

organum Earliest type of medieval polyphony from the 9th through to the 13th century which appeared in sacred music and was based on **plainsong**. There are three basic types of organum.

In parallel organum the added voice moves wholly or mainly in parallel fourths or fifths with the chant, note for note.

In the 11th century, strict parallel organum was replaced by free organum, in which the added voice moves in a free succession of intervals, still moving note against note.

A new type of organum emerged in the early-12th century, called melismatic organum. A plainsong, or part of one, was assigned to one voice in long sustained notes to which was added a higher voice in faster moving notes values.

orgel (Ger.) **Organ**.

Ormandy, Eugene (1899-1985) Hungarian-born conductor who settled in the United States and became an American citizen in 1927. He became principal conductor of the Minneapolis Symphony Orchestra in 1931, and in 1938 succeeded **Stokowski** as conductor of the Philadelphia Orchestra. His repertory is concentrated on late Romantic and early 20th-century composers, and his recordings include **Mahler**'s 10th Symphony in the performing version by Deryck Cooke. In 1948 he conducted the first symphony concert shown on American television – beating **Toscanini** on a rival network by $1\frac{1}{2}$ hours. He was made an honorary KBE in 1976.

Eugene Ormandy

ornament Something that is added to a piece for decorative purposes and often incidental to the main composition. It can apply either to vocal or instrumental music, and is included as an improvisation by the composer or the performer. Ornaments appear on a score either as a symbol or by notes in small type. The most common musical ornaments are **appoggiatura, acciaccatura, upper** and **lower mordents**, the **turn, slide** and **trill**.

Orozco, Rafael (1946-) Spanish pianist who studied with Alexis Weissenberg at the Academia Chigiana in Siena and gained the diploma of merit in 1964. In 1966 he won the Leeds Piano Competition and is particularly well known for his interpretation of **Rachmaninov**'s concertos.

Orr, Robin (1909-) Scottish composer. He was a pupil of **Casella** in Siena and Nadia **Boulanger** in Paris. He was a professor at Glasgow University until 1965 and thereafter at Cambridge. His compositions include two operas, *Weir of Hermiston* (1975) and *Full Circle* (1968), orchestral and chamber works, song-cycles and church music.

Orrego-Salas, Juan Antonio (1919-) Chilean composer and musicologist. He was a student of Thompson and **Copland** and was appointed professor of composition at the University of Chile in 1947. He was the founder and director of the Latin American Music Centre (1961), promoting Latin American music through festivals, broadcasts and setting up the largest existing library of scores and recordings of 20th-century music from this area. His own music involves a free style incorporating formal procedures taken from all periods after the Middle Ages.

ossia (It.) Or, maybe. Indication used either by the composer or an editor to introduce an alternative musical passage to the main text, which is normally easier to play than the original theme.

ostinato (It.) Persistent. A figure that is repeated throughout a composition. For example, if it is in the bass, it is called *basso ostinato* (ground bass). An ostinato occurs in the final section of **Stravinsky's** *Symphony of Psalms* (1930).

Ostrčil, Otakar (1879-1935) Czech composer, conductor and administrator with a strong intellectual background, having started his career as a language professor. As a conductor he was concerned with encouraging modern music, and in 1924 he founded The Society for Modern Music in Prague. He was responsible for introducing audiences to national composers such as **Janáček** and **Fibich**, and to international composers including **Stravinsky** and **Schoenberg**. In this way he was influential in moving Czech music away from the purely nationalistic towards a more international avant-garde. His own compositions include operas – *Legenda z Erinin* (The Legend of Erin, 1921) – but were largely orchestral, and, like his conducting, were analytical rather than romantic in style.

ottoni (It.) Brass instruments.

Ouseley, Sir Frederick Arthur Gore (1825-1889) English church musician, scholar and composer. As a child he was very precocious, composing from the age of three and developing an accurate musical ear – at the age of five he could recognize the key in which he father blew his nose. Educated at Oxford, he then went into the Church, returning to Oxford in 1855 as a professor. He was keen to purge religious music of all contemporary secular influences and modelled his own style on the classics of **Mozart** and **Handel**. In 1854 he founded the Church of St Michael and All Saints, Tenbury, which now houses his very valuable collection of manuscripts, books and scores.

overblowing Playing of a wind instrument in such a way that the upper harmonics are produced instead of the fundamental notes.

Unwanted overblowing may occur in organ pipes if the wind pressure is excessive, but safety valves have been invented to prevent this.

overstrung Positioning of piano strings such that they are made in two ranges, crossing each other diagonally to save space and to secure greater length in the strings.

overtone Any note of the harmonic series except the first harmonic (fundamental). Sometimes also known as a partial. See also **acoustics**.

overture Instrumental composition that introduces an **opera**, **oratorio** or play. Some operas of the early 17th century incorporated the overture, but usually it was to alert the audience that the opera proper was about to begin.

Later in same century the French overture was introduced by **Lully**, and the Italian overture by **Scarlatti**. Lully's French overture had as its basic principal a slow introduction, with a predominance of dotted rhythms, followed by a quick movement of a somewhat lightly and freely treated contrapuntal style. The overture to **Handel's** *Messiah* is a typical example of the French style. The Italian type of overture was often called **sinfonia**. It had three sections, arranged quick-slow-quick.

During the 18th century the French type of overture became a simple movement in **sonata**-like form, such as **Haydn's** *Creation* (1798) and **Mozart's** *The Magic Flute* (1791). With **Gluck's** opera *Iphigenie en Tauride* (1779), his overture anticipated the mood of the first scene in which a storm is represented. The same process of integrating the overture into the opera as a whole was followed in the 19th century by **Weber** (*Der Freischütz*, 1821) and in the preludes to **Wagner's** music dramas.

The concert overture is an independent orchestral composition. Examples of these are **Berlioz'** *Le Carnaval Romain* (1844) and **Brahms's** *Academic Festival Overture* (1880). **Beethoven's** operatic or dramatic overtures, *Leonora* (1814) and *Coriolanus* (1807), are played as concert overtures.

Ozawa, Seiji (1935-) Japanese conductor who went to Europe in 1959. He was noticed by **Bernstein** while working with von **Karajan** in Berlin, and was invited to be assistant conductor of the New York Philharmonic Orchestra (1961-1962). He has been music director of the Chicago Symphony Orchestra's Ravinia Festival, of the Toronto Symphony Orchestra, of the San Francisco Symphony Orchestra, and in 1973 was appointed director of the Boston Symphony Orchestra. In 1974 he made his Covent Garden debut with *Eugene Onegin*. He has a flamboyant but clear style, focusing on large 19th-century and early 20th-century works.

Seiji Ozawa

P

Pachelbel, Johann (1653-1706) German organist and composer who, after studying under Heinrich Schwemmer, went on to hold several important posts including that of organist at St Sebaldus's church in Nuremberg. He was one of the most productive and progressive composers of the 17th century, whose work has never been entirely forgotten and has recently been highly revalued. His works include 94 organ fugues on the Magnificat, 78 choral preludes, chamber music and numerous suites and variations for the keyboard of which his 11 concertato settings of the Magnificat and the *Hexachordum Appollinis* (1699) are perhaps best known. His keyboard compositions are of particular importance in their influence on J. S. **Bach**.

Pachmann, Vladimir (1848-1933) Ukranian pianist, who studied first under his father, a celebrated amateur violinist, and later at the Vienna Conservatoire. After a highly successful debut in Odessa in 1896, he became dissatisfied with his performances and retired only to resume his career 10 years later playing in all the principal cities of Europe and the United States. A particularly fine exponent of the work of **Chopin**, he was well known for his eccentric platform manner, often making remarks to his audience.

Pacini, Giovanni (1796-1867) Italian composer, whose first performed opera *Annetta e Lucindo* (1813) was written at the age of 17. He wrote music with extraordinary speed and composed 90 operas, mostly in the comic **Rossini** manner, and was also a prolific composer of sacred music. In 1834 he settled at Viareggio in Italy, where he opened a music school which later transferred to Lucca. His best known and most successful opera was *Sappho*, first performed in Naples in 1840, but he is also remembered for his lively memoirs, a valuable source of information on opera of the period.

Paderewski, Ignacy (Jan) (1860-1941) Polish pianist and composer who studied in Warsaw and Vienna, where he was once advised by his teacher Leschetizky to give up his career as a pianist, but went on to become a successful concert pianist who played throughout the world and was a particular favourite with British audiences. His compositions include the romantic opera *Manru* (1901) and many works for the piano, of which his piano concerto, *Fantasie Polonaise* and the *Minuet in G* are still part of the modern concert repertory. After the outbreak of World War I he collected large sums of money for the Polish relief fund and later became prime minister and minister of foreign affairs in Poland (1919), returning to his concert career and teaching in 1922. In 1936 he appeared in the British film, *Moonlight Sonata*.

Paer, Ferdinando (1771-1839) Italian composer, originally a violinist who became *maître de chapelle* to Napoleon, for whom he wrote the bridal march for his wedding to Marie Louise of Austria. Napoleon appointed him director of the Opéra

Comique and later the Théâtre Italien in Paris, where Paer settled (1807). He wrote 53 operas, including *Leonora* (1804) based on the same plot **Beethoven** was to use in his opera *Fidelio* the following year, and also composed oratorios, masses, motets and many instrumental works. In 1820 he numbered **Liszt** among his composition pupils.

Paganini, Niccolò (1782-1840) Italian violinist and composer whose virtuosity and personal magnetism brought him fame throughout Europe. At the age of 15 he was already playing his own compositions in order to display his own virtuosity, pioneering the use of harmonics and retuning his instrument to obtain special effects. His career included a number of triumphant European tours (including France, Germany and England) during which he made a considerable personal fortune. His virtuosity encouraged other composers – such as **Liszt, Schumann** and **Chopin** – to expand the technical and expressive limits of their instruments, and his own compositions, in particular his bravura variations *Le Streghe* (1813), are a considerable creative achievement. **Rachmaninov**'s *Rhapsody on a Theme by Paganini* is based on Paganini's famous A minor Caprice for solo violin.

Paine, John Knowles (1839-1906) American organist, composer and teacher who studied in Germany, and used the German style and manner in his compositions. He became the first American professor of music at Harvard in 1875. His larger composition, the Mass in D Major, the oratorio and the two symphonies attracted massive attention in his lifetime.

Paisiello, Giovanni (1740-1816) Italian composer most successfully of **opera buffa**. Between 1764 and 1784 he produced many works in Modena, Naples, Venice and at the Russian Court of Catherine II at St Petersburg, and became musical director to Napoleon Bonaparte, who greatly admired his music. His compositions include sacred music, symphonies, concertos and 100 operas, the most famous of which are *Il Barbière di Siviglia* (which was later upstaged by **Rossini**'s setting of the same story) and *Il re Teodoro in Venezia*, which are known to have influenced **Mozart**'s own style in *Le Nozze di Figaro* and *Don Giovanni*.

pakad (India) Short, melodic catch phrase in a composition which is characteristic of, and therefore identifies, a particular **rāga** melody.

pakhāvaj/pakhāwaj (India) Double-headed barrel drum from northern India, played in a horizontal position with the hands. Used in **dhrupad** and to accompany the **bin**.

pakhāwaj See **pakhāvaj**.

pan calypso See **calypso; steel band**.

Palestrina, Giovanni Pierluigi da (*c*1525-1594) Italian composer, organist and choirmaster who was one of the most important figures in 16th-century music. He spent his musical life in the service of the Church and was appointed *maestro di cappella* of the Julian Chapel at St Peter's, Rome and also became a member of the Sistine Choir. He later held several other important appointments. Much of his music was published during his lifetime, including four volumes of motets and six volumes of masses. He was a good businessman and his second marriage to a rich widow enabled him to publish 16 collections of his music during the last 13 years of his life.

Pallavicino, Benedetto (1551-1601) Italian composer, a monk who was a prolific and popular madrigalist, whose work was much published, and much esteemed by his contemporaries. He also wrote sacred music including psalms, motets, and four masses which were published posthumously. He was appointed *maestro di cappella* in Mantua (1596-1601) preceding **Monteverdi**, and later retired to a monastery in Tuscany.

Pallavicino, Carlo (1630-1688) Italian composer, chiefly of opera, and one of the leading and most popular in Venice between 1675 and 1685, where all but one of his 20 operas were produced. He also wrote sacred music. Pallavicino divided his time between Venice and Dresden where he was *Kappelmeister*, and in which city he died.

Palmgren, Selim (1878-1951) Finnish pianist, conductor and composer, who studied at Helsinki Conservatoire and then in Germany and Italy under **Busoni**. He toured and taught in the United States and Europe, where he was accompanied by his first wife, the singer Maikki **Järnefelt**. His works include many short piano pieces, two operas, choral works, five piano concertos and songs. His music is characterized by its technical mastery and pictorial quality, sometimes with a strong national flavour.

pandora 16th-century English stringed instrument similar to the **cittern**, with six or seven metal strings that were plucked with the fingers. It was often used as a **continuo** instrument.

panpipes Set of simple flutes of different lengths fixed side by side to give a scale when blown. Panpipes date back to antiquity and were also known as syrinx.

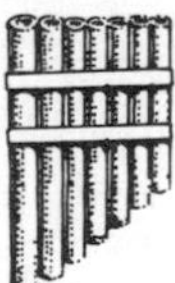

Panpipes

p'ansori (Korea) Dramatic narrative form, performed by a narrator who sings, speaks and gesticulates, accompanied by a drummer. It probably developed from an archaic form of shamanistic folk drama which may have included theatrical performance, but since the 18th century has been refined for courtly use. Musical resources include a variety of modes and rhythmic patterns which denote particular characters or moods. A full open-air performance, lasting up to eight hours, makes heavy demands on the narrator, who maintains a forced vocal delivery throughout.

pantomine Derived from the Greek 'all-imitating', and was probably a play in dumb-show. Since the 18th century, pantomine has been a popular form of stage entertainment in England. It is still based mainly on fairy tales, and was no doubt influenced by the characters and forms of the Italian *commedia dell'arte*, including Harlequin, Pantaloon and Clown. Modern pantomines are now costly and showy productions, often including popular songs of the day.

pantonality 20th-century term for **atonality** in which music is not written in any definite key. Pantonal harmony is a feature of the music of such composers as **Ligeti**, **Schoenberg**, **Stockhausen** and **Webern**.

Panufnik, Andrzej (1914-) Polish composer and conductor who studied with Sikorski at the Warsaw Conservatoire, and later became conductor of the Krakow and Warsaw Symphony Orchestras. He left Poland in protest against political regimentation, settling in England in 1954. He became conductor of the City of Birmingham Symphony Orchestra between 1957 and 1959, resigning to concentrate on composition. His works include six symphonies of which the *Sinfonia Rustica* and *Sinfonia Sacra* are best known, film music, Polish folk song settings and works for the piano. Panufnik has also recently published his autobiography.

Papaïoannou, Yannis (1911-) Greek composer who studied with **Honegger** and at the Hellenic Conservatoire, where he later taught counterpoint and composition. He was almost solely responsible for encouraging Greek composers to adapt to avant-garde techniques using **twelve-note** and total **serial** methods in his own compositions, which also reflect his interest in tribal music and Byzantine chants. His works include five symphonies, chamber music, songs and an orchestral tone poem after the poet Shelley, *Hellas*.

parallel motion In harmony, the movement of two notes from one chord to the next in the same direction and by the same interval. In Classical harmony, movement by parallel motion is generally undesirable. Consecutives is a common alternative term for parallel motion. See also **conjunct motion; contrary motion; disjunct motion; oblique motion; similar motion**.

Parker, Horatio (William) (1863-1919) American organist and composer whose music is now largely neglected, despite its success during his lifetime. He studied in Boston and Munich where he was a pupil of **Rheinberger**. He held organ posts in New York and taught at the National Conservatoire when **Dvorák** was director, and later became professor of music at Yale. The oratorio, *Hora Novissima* (1893), brought him to national prominence and his other works include cantatas, choral ballads, songs and anthems and other orchestral pieces. His second area of composition was theatre music, both incidental music for plays and two operas, *Mona* (1910) and *Fairyland* (1914).

parlando (It.) Speaking, used to indicate that a performer should speak rather than sing, or to reverse the procedure and give the impression of singing when speaking.

parody Substitution of a composition known to be serious, with one that is comical or satirical. It also refers to altering or revising a composition designed for a specific medium to suit the needs of another.

Parrott, (Horace) Ian (1916-) English composer and teacher who identified himself closely with the language, culture and music of Wales. He studied at the Royal College of Music and later became professor of music at University College, Aberystwyth. His works include the opera *The Sergeant Major's Daughter*, a folk opera *The Black Ram* (1952), a ballet *The Maid in Birmingham*, three symphonies, choral works, songs and other instrumental pieces.

Parry, Sir (Charles) Hubert (Hastings) (1848-1918) English composer, writer and teacher, who did not make his mark in public until his Piano Concerto was played in 1880 by Dannreuther, with whom he studied, and when in the same year his choral scenes from Shelley's *Prometheus Unbound* appeared. He wrote prolifically and his works include *Blest Pair of Sirens*, *Songs of Farewell* and in 1916, wrote the unison setting for Blake's *Jerusalem*, which has become a national song. He was the author of several books that helped to restore the place of music in literary, academic and national life, including a study of **Bach** and a volume of the Oxford History of Music. From 1894 until his death he was director of the Royal College of Music and from 1900 to 1908 he was professor of music at Oxford University. He was knighted in 1898 and made baronet in 1903.

part Term with three meanings.

First, it is the music written for a particular voice (e.g. the tenor part) or instrument (e.g. the flute part) in an ensemble, orchestra or choir.

Second, it is a strand of melody in polyphonic music, e.g. fugue in four parts or four-part fugue.

Third, it is a section of a cantata or oratorio which corresponds to an act in an opera.

Partch, Harry (1901-1976) American composer and instrument-maker who, having destroyed all his previous compositions at the age of 25, spent the depression years wandering across the United States as a hobo and worked for some time as a lumberjack. His compositions include *Eight Hitchhiker Inscriptions from a California Highway Railing* and *US Highball, a*

Musical Account of a Transcontinental Hobo Trip. Largely self-taught, he experimented with **microtonal** scales (using a system of intonation with 43 notes to the octave) and new experimental and often theatrical instruments, including the **marimba** eroica and chromelodeon.

partials Name given to the notes of the **harmonic series** produced when a string or column of air vibrates. The lowest note heard is known as the first partial, or fundamental tone, and the higher ones are upper partials or **overtones**.

partita 18th-century term for a **suite** or set of variations. It also referred to a set of variations on a chorale tune, known as a chorale partita. Examples include J. S. **Bach**'s chorale partitas for organ.

pas de deux In ballet, a dance for two, or music for such a dance.

pasodoble Spanish dance in a martial 2/4 time, in which the movements of the dancer imitate the actions of a toreador and his cape.

Pasquini, Bernardo (1637-1710) Italian composer, harpsichordist and organist who was renowned in his day as a virtuoso keyboard player. He was also a considerable composer, mainly for the keyboard. He was the organist of Santa Maria Maggiorè, Rome, where he also played harpsichord continuo in the opera house orchestra with **Corelli** as his first violinist. Pasquini's output included 14 operas, suites for the harpsichord, oratorios, cantatas, sonatas, arias and motets, but despite his reputation, little of his music was published.

passacaglia Originally a Spanish or Italian dance, similar to the **chaconne**. It is more commonly known as an instrumental piece consisting of continuous variations in slow triple time above a **ground** bass. One of the best-known examples is **Bach**'s Passacaglia in C minor for organ. The last movement of **Brahms**' Symphony No. 4, although not so entitled, is also in this form.

passage Any melodic or decorative feature in a composition, e.g. a fortissimo or staccato passage.

passage work **Passage** in a composition that is designed to display the virtuosity of the soloist.

passing note Incidental note in a composition that moves between notes a third apart and creates a temporary **dissonance** with the prevailing harmony. See also **auxiliary note**.

Pasta, Giuditta (1798-1865) Italian soprano whose combination of lyric and dramatic genius brought her almost legendary fame in Europe. Her voice, though unequal, ranged from A to D''' and her sincerity of interpretation in creating roles such as Anna Bolena (**Donizetti**) and Desdemona (**Rossini**) held audiences spellbound. Her special talents inspired several works by **Bellini**, including the opera *La Somnambula*. Her real success dates from the Paris season of 1821 and she appeared regularly in London, Paris and St Petersburg until 1837.

pastoral Light-hearted English madrigal with words of a rustic or pastoral character. The term also describes a flowing melodic piece for instruments or voices in 6/8 or 12/8 time that originated in rural Italy.

Patterson, Paul (1947-) English composer who studied at the Royal Academy of Music, where he later became a teacher. His orchestral, ensemble, and vocal works, some using electronic tapes and aleatoric methods, include a Requiem in memory of President Kennedy. The performance of his Trumpet Concerto by Wilbraham first brought him to public notice in 1969. More recently his *Mass of the Sea* has achieved wide public acclaim.

patter song Comic song in which the words are sung as fast as possible. Many examples appear in **Sullivan**'s operettas, such as 'The Chancellor's Nightmare Song' from *Iolanthe* (1891).

Patti, Adelina (1843-1919) Italian soprano who was the most famous member of the Patti family of singers. Taken to New York as a child, she made her debut there in 1859 under the stage name Little Florinda. Essentially a coloratura soprano with a talent for dramatic interpretation, she sang in North and South America and the capital cities of Europe, making her London debut as Amina in *La Sonnambula* at Covent Garden, where she sang 25 consecutive seasons. She became legendary for the enormous sums paid to her, the jewels she wore and her refusal to attend rehearsals. She retired to a castle in Wales but was able to make a number of recordings at the age of 60, testifying to the tone, flexibility and the exemplary care she took of her voice.

patting juba American dance form that involves hitting the body in complex, syncopated patterns, typical of African rhythmic interplay, and suggests the rhythmic basis of **ragtime** and early jazz. It probably originated from the Afro-Caribbean juba dance, and may well be a rhythmic hand-and-body version of the kalinda stick dance. It was often seen in 19th-century religious meetings in Louisiana.

Patzak, Julius (1898-1974) Austrian tenor who began by studying conducting in Vienna but turned to singing in 1926, making his debut at Reichenberg Opera as Radamés in *Aïda*. His greatest roles were considered to be Florestan in *Fidelio* and the title role of **Pfitzner**'s *Palestrina*, and although his voice was never considered to be outstanding, his intelligence, musicianship and style made him one of the great singers of *Lieder* and oratorio.

pausa (It.) Rest.

pause Sign indicating that the note, chord or rest over which it is placed is to be held longer than its written value. The length of time for which it is held is normally left to the conductor's or performer's discretion.

pavane Slow courtly dance of the 16th and 17th centuries, normally in quadruple or duple time, that originated in the Padua region of Italy. It was serious and stately in character and was often followed by a **galliard** based on the same thematic material. **Ravel** revived the form in his *Pavane pour une infante défunte* for piano in 1899, which was later orchestrated and now sometimes played on guitar.

Pavarotti, Luciano (1935-) Italian tenor who is noted for his vocal technique and a bright, vibrant voice of considerable beauty. He studied with Pola and Campogalliani, making his debut at Reggio Emilia in 1961, where he won the international competition. He made his first London appearance at Covent Garden in 1963 as Rodolfo, and the next year toured Australia with Joan **Sutherland**, with whom he has sung frequently. Pavorotti specializes in *bel canto* repertory and has recorded extensively, his finest performances on disc being his Rudolfo for **Karajan**, and Arturo in *I Puritani* with Sutherland. He is now one of the most famous of tenors.

pavillon Bell of a horn, trumpet or trombone, named from its pavilion-like shape. In musical scores the direction *pavillon en l'air* occurs where the composer wishes the bell to be raised to increase the power of the tone.

Pears, Sir Peter (1910-1986) English tenor and organist, who studied at the Royal College of music and took lessons from Gerhardt. He sang with the BBC chorus and later with the Glyndebourne Chorus, making his stage debut in 1942 as Hoffmann in *The Tales of Hoffmann* at the Strand Theatre, London. He is closely associated with the music of Benjamin **Britten** who wrote all his major tenor roles and many of his solo vocal works with

Sir Peter Pears

Pears's voice in mind. Parts he sang in Britten operas include Peter Grimes, Albert Herring, and Captain Vere in *Billy Budd*. He was also a notable singer of **Schubert** and **Bach**. He was knighted in 1978.

Pearsall, Robert Lucas (1795-1856) English composer, whose main interest was in the revival of Renaissance music. He studied as a lawyer, but turned to music when living in Germany, eventually settling in the Castle of Waternsee on Lake Constance. He wrote mostly vocal music, part songs, including the well known *In Dulci Jubilo*, and Anglican and Roman Catholic music. His madrigals are perhaps the nearest musical equivalent to Gothic Revival and the pre-Raphaelite school of painting in England.

ped. Abbreviation of **pedal**.

pedal Device in composition whereby a **bass** note is sustained over a passage that includes some chords with which it is dissonant. The note held is normally the **tonic** or **dominant** of the prevailing key, which is called tonic pedal or dominant pedal respectively.

The term also occurs in piano music (often abbreviated to ped.), where it indicates that the sustaining pedal is to be depressed until a point when its release is shown. It also occurs as an instruction in organ music to indicate which notes or passages are to be played on the pedals.

pedalboard Keyboard of an organ that is played with the feet.

pedal clarinet Alternative term for double-bass **clarinet**.

pedal drum **Kettledrum** that is tuned by use of a pedal.

Peerson, Martin (1571-1651) English composer, virginalist and organist, who wrote mostly sacred and vocal music, but also works for viols and keyboard. He was organist at St Paul's Cathedral, London, from about 1624.

Peeters, Flor (1903-) Belgian organist, composer, musical editor and a renowned teacher who has toured worldwide as an organ recitalist. He wrote piano works, songs and sacred choral music, but his most characteristic compositions are for the organ for which instrument he wrote a three-volume book on organ method.

peg Device by which a stringed instrument is tuned. The strings are wound around the pegs, which rest in the pegbox at the end of the instrument's neck. The strings are tuned by a turn of the peg. A **machine head** is fitted to the double-bass and modern **guitar** in place of a pegbox.

Peking opera (China) Traditional Chinese theatre which incorporates aspects of regional entertainment forms from the environs of Beijing (formerly Peking). It now involves both male and female actors, and consists of four main dramatic elements: singing, recitation, acting and acrobatics. Costumes are intricate and colourful, certain colours having associative and symbolic meaning. Two basic groups of instruments are used in Peking opera. The first is employed for military and battle scenes and comprises the double-reed *sona* and a variety of drums, gongs and cymbals, the latter of which are used to punctuate recitatives. The second ensemble generally accompanies arias and varies enormously according to the nature of the scenario. However, its most common instruments are bowed and plucked lutes, time-beating clappers and wood-blocks, and occasionally the **ti** flute.

pélog (Indonesia) One of two tonal systems, consisting of seven unequal intervals within an octave. In Java, there are three hemitonic **pentatonic** modes or *patet* drawn from the *pelog* scale: *barang*, *nem* and *lima*, each corresponding to specific times of the day. See also **slèndro**.

Penderecki, Krzysztof (1933-) Polish composer who was one of the first avant-garde composers to experiment with sounds such as hissing, screeching, sawing wood, typewriters and rustling paper. He has travelled widely to supervise and conduct his own work, and his compositions include a canon for 52 instruments and tape, *De Natura Sonoris II* (1971) and an opera, *The Devils of Loudon* (1968-1969), as well as works for orchestra and voices. He became teacher at the Yale school of music from 1975 and is much in demand as a consultant.

penhillion Ancient Welsh form of singing, usually performed to a harp accompaniment. The words and music are often improvised and sung as counterpoint or descant to the harp. The form is still practised, although the modern tendency is to rely on traditional tunes rather than improvisation.

penny whistle Alternative term for **tin whistle**.

pentatonic Scale of five notes within the octave. Pentatonic scales are frequently associated with Oriental music, but are also widespread throughout European folk music, particularly in the anhemitonic mode, corresponding to C-D-E-G-A. See also **Japanese scales**.

Pentatonic scale

Pentland, Barbara (1912-) Canadian composer and university teacher who was a pupil of **Copland**. She began composing at the age of nine, and her works include four symphonies, three string quartets, a piano concerto, a violin sonata and several piano works for children.

Pepin, Clermont (1926-) Canadian composer and educationist who studied with **Honegger**, **Jolivet** and **Messaien**. Many of his compositions reflect his interest in physics and mathematics, and include the symphonic poems *Guernica* (1952) and *Le Rite du Soleil Noir* (1955), and the ballets, *At the Gates of Hell* (1953) and *The Phoenix* (1956). From 1967 to 1972 he was director of the Montreal Conservatoire and was also president of Jeunesses Musicales du Canada.

Pepping, Ernst (1901-1981) German composer who devoted himself to the cultivation of Protestant church music. He studied at the Berlin Conservatoire, and later became professor at the Kirchenmusikschule, Spandau. He wrote for organ, piano and orchestra and composed a large number of choral works including a *St Matthew Passion*.

Pepusch, Johann Christoph (1667-1752) German-born composer, who settled in London in 1704. Largely self-taught, he wrote music for operas and masques at Drury Lane and Lincoln's Inn theatre and arranged music for the original production of Gay's *The Beggar's Opera* and its sequel *Polly*. An expert in music theory and history, he wrote a treatise on harmony and theoretical books and was a founder of the Academy of Ancient Music.

Perahia, Murray (1947-) American pianist. Born in New York, where he also studied at Mannes College, he shot to fame after winning the Leeds Piano Competition in 1972, making his London debut as a recitalist in the following year. Since then he has won international acclaim as a concert artist, appearing with many of the world's leading orchestras. He is particularly noted as an exponent of Mozart's piano concertos, which he frequently directs from the keyboard. Perahia has also been involved in the artistic direction of the Aldeburgh Festival.

percussion instruments Musical instruments that produce sound when struck. They include instruments that may be tuned to a definite pitch, such as kettledrums, glockenspiel, vibraphone, xylophone and tubular bells, and instruments that produce sounds of indefinite pitch, such as the side drum, bass drum, triangle and cymbals. Within the percussion section of an orchestra, special effects are obtained by use of such instruments as castanets, anvil, thunder sticks, motor-horn, whip and chains.

perdendosi (It.) Losing, an indication that the sound of a note or a passage is to be become gradually weaker until it fades away.

perfect cadence **Cadence** in which the progression of chords is V-I, giving the impression that the phrase is complete.

perfect interval **Interval** of a fourth, a fifth or an octave.

perfect time Alternative term for triple time. Perfect time was represented by a full circle, and imperfect time by a half-circle. See also **time signature**.

Pergolesi, Giovanni Battista (1710-1736) Italian composer who wrote comic operas and is remembered for his intermezzo *La Serva Padrona* from the opera *Il Prigioner Superbo* (1733) and his Stabat Mater (1736) written shortly before his early death from tuberculosis. Some of his works were later rewritten by **Stravinsky**.

Peri, Jacopo (1561-1633) Italian composer, who was one of the founding fathers of opera. A prominent member of the group of poets and musicians known as the **Camerata**, whose interest was in revising Greek drama, he wrote what is considered the first opera, *Dafne* (1597), and later *Euridice* (1600). He was a musician at the Medici court and won considerable fame as a singer. He wrote several other operas, madrigals and ballets, of which few survive.

Perlman, Itzhak (1945-) Israeli violinist who by the age of 10 had already given several broadcasts with the Israel Broadcasting Orchestra and a recital on American radio. He made his professional debut at Carnegie Hall in 1963 and his London debut in 1968, and has played with the London Symphony Orchestra, the New York Philharmonic Orchestra and other major American orchestras.

Itzhak Perlman

Persichetti, Vincent (1915-) American composer, conductor and teacher, who studied at the Philadelphia Conservatoire and Curtis Institute, and was a pupil of Roy **Harris**. He later became a teacher at Philadelphia and at the Juilliard School of Music, New York. Composing in a wide range of styles, he has produced an important body of keyboard works as well as a ballet, *King Lear*, and symphonias, cantatas and songs.

Perti, Giacomo Antonio (1661-1756) Italian composer who wrote 26 operas, later devoting himself to religious works through which he achieved fame both as a composer and teacher. He was *maestro di cappella* at San Pietro at Bologna for 60 years.

pesindhèn (Java) Female singer of the **gamelan** ensemble. She is the only woman in this all-male domain, and often found in the 'soft style' of Javanese *gamelan* playing, singing sustained melodic lines, with *suling* (flute), *rebab* (spiked fiddle) and with a counter melody by the male chorus.

Petrassi, Goffredo (1904-) Italian composer who was educated at choir school but did not undertake systematic studies until the age of 21. He studied at the Santa Cecilia Academy, Rome (1928-1932), where he became professor of composition in 1939. His compositions are neo-Classical in style, but he also makes individual use of twelve-note methods. His works include the operas *The Spanish Scream* and *Death in the Air*, ballets *Portrait of Don Quixote* and *Orlando's Madness*, a piano concerto and choral works (including *Nonsense*, based on poems by Edward Lear).

Petrucci, Ottaviano dei (1466-1539) Italian music printer who issued many famous collections, which represent the most important body of music issued at the beginning of the 16th century. He was the first to print polyphonic music from movable type, and his successful method began the widespread circulation of **polyphonic** music.

Petterssen, Gustaf Allan (1911-1980) Swedish composer and violist who studied at Stockholm Conservatoire (1930-1939) and also with **Honnegger** and **Leibowitz**. He was violist with the Stockholm Philharmonic Orchestra from 1940 to 1950, his career ending with the onset of rheumatoid arthritis. His music came to public notice with the first performance in 1968 of his Symphony No. 7 and the *Barefoot Songs*, written 25 years earlier.

Pfitzner, Hans (1869-1949) German composer and conductor born in Moscow who was well known as a writer and critic of modern tendencies in music. His own music is Romantic and traditionalist and he achieved a considerable success with his opera *Palestrina*, first performed in Munich in 1917.

Philadelphia Orchestra American symphony orchestra founded in 1900. It was established by Fritz Scheel who was also its first conductor, who was then followed by Karl Pohlig. The orchestra became one of the finest in the world under Leopold **Stokowski** (1912-1938), and this tradition was continued during the time (1938-1978) when Eugène **Ormandy** was conductor. In 1981 Riccardo **Muti** was appointed musical director. The orchestra has introduced many new works to the United States, including some by **Mahler**, **Scriabin**, **Stravinsky** and **Schoenberg**.

Philharmonia Orchestra See **New Philharmonia Orchestra**.

philharmonic From the Greek 'friendly to harmony', a term used as a title of some orchestras and other musical organizations. It does not identify a particular type of orchestra, but just its name, such as the London Philharmonic Orchestra.

Philidor, François André Danican (1726-1795) French composer, the most famous member of a large family of musicians of the same name. Better known to his contemporaries as a chess player, he was nevertheless a gifted composer of *opéra-comique* and had success with *Tom*

Jones (1765) and *L'Amant désguisé* (1769). His major choral work *Carmen seculare* (1779) was greatly admired in London and Paris, and is his most frequently revived work.

Philips, Peter (*c*1560–1628) English organist and composer, who left England to live in the Low countries because he was Roman Catholic yet always described himself as Inglese or Anglo. His best works are his madrigals and motets, and apart from **Byrd**, he was the most publicized English composer of his time. He was appointed organist at the Chapel Royal, Brussels, and was famous as an organist throughout the Netherlands.

Philomusica of London London chamber orchestra which partly evolved from the Boyd Neel String Orchestra in the late 1950s under the direction of Thurston Dart.

phrase More or less small group of notes or chords that constitutes a definite melodic or thematic feature in a composition. Phrases are a form of punctuation in music because they allow a performer to correctly apply stresses as indicated by a composer's phrase marks.

Phrygian mode One of the authentic **modes**.

piangendo (It.) Weeping or plaintive.

piano Term with two meanings.

First, it is a keyboard instrument (originally known as the fortepiano or pianoforte) derived from the **harpsichord**, which produces its sound by striking the strings with hammers, an action based on that of the **dulcimer**. It was invented in 1709 by Bartolommeo **Cristofori** (1655–1731) in Florence and he called it a *gravicembalo col piano e forte*. The piano was not in general use until late in the 18th century, and by then had almost superseded the harpsichord.

Improvements to the piano continued in the 18th century, especially by Johannes Zumpe who introduced the square piano which had strings running parallel to the keyboard. Grand pianos with horizontal strings were developed in the late 18th century and grand pianos are now made in three varieties: baby grand, boudoir grand and concert grand. They all have about 88 keys, starting on G and ending on A, striking strings of ascending pitch from left to right. In 1800 John Hawkins of Philadelphia developed the upright piano with vertical strings.

Second, it is an Italian term meaning quiet. See also **pianissimo**.

piano accordian Instrument of the reed organ family, which differs from the **accordian** in that the original buttons are replaced by a keyboard similar to that of a piano. This innovation was made by Bouton in 1852, and by the 1920s this model had superseded its predecessors.

pianoforte Alternative term for **piano**.

pianola Trade name for a mechanical device (patented in 1897) attached to an ordinary **piano** whereby the hammers are made to strike the strings not by action of the hands on the **keyboard**, but by air pressure. A piece of music is represented by a roll of perforated paper, and the holes in it correspond to different notes. When the

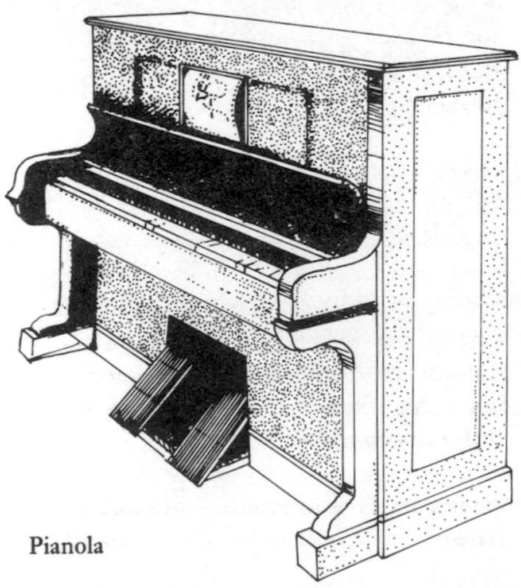

Pianola

instrument is played, air passes through the holes in the paper and along tubes, and this makes the piano's hammers strike the strings. The mechanism and the air pump is set in motion by foot pedals or by an electric motor. With the introduction of the gramophone, pianolas had lost their popularity by the 1920s. Also known as a player piano.

piano score **Score** that reduces orchestral parts to a version that is playable on the piano.

pianissimo (It.) Instruction to play very quietly. See also **piano**.

Piatigorsky, Gregor (1903-1976) Russian cellist, who studied at the Moscow Conservatoire and became principal cellist for Moscow Opera Orchestra. In 1921 he left Moscow to become first cellist with the Berlin Philharmonic Orchestra. He made his American debut in 1929 and later settled in the United States, being naturalized in 1942. He was internationally known both as a soloist and a chamber music player, and was dedicatee and first performer of **Walton**'s Cello Concerto (1957).

pibroch (Scotland) Type of bagpipe music falling into the **ceòl mor** or 'big music' category. Includes laments, salutes and compositions in honour of important historical events. The form is basically a theme with specific variations and ornamentation. The term is derived from the Gaelic, *piobaireachd*.

Picardy third English equivalent of **tierce de Picardie**.

piccolo Small **flute** pitched one octave above the normal instrument.

pien (China) Extra auxiliary tones in a Chinese **pentatonic** scale. Often referred to as 'changing' tones, they are used as passing notes or to facilitate a change of mode.

Pierné, Gabriel (1863-1937) French conductor and composer who studied at the Paris Conservatoire from the age of eight. He won the Prix de Rome (1882) and succeeded **Franck** as organist of St Clotilde (1890). He became second conductor of Colonne's Orchestra (1903), becoming principal conductor in 1910. He is best known for his oratorio *The Children's Crusade* and the ballet *Cydalise and the Satyr*, from which comes the *The Entry of the Little Fauns*.

Pierson, Henry Hugo (1815-1873) English composer, who studied with **Attwood** and Corfe, interrupting his musical career to continue his musical studies in Leipzig where he met **Schumann** and **Mendelssohn** among others, settling in Germany in 1844. His reputation in Germany was considerable and his music continued to be performed after his death, but was not well received in England. A composer of opera, oratorio, songs and part songs, his most successful works were the *Music for Goethe's Faust* and his symphonic poem *Macbeth*.

piffero (It.) Rustic Italian flute-like instrument of the **shawm** family. It was often played in Italian cities, such as Rome and Naples, by pipers from the hills who played tunes similar to those of the pastoral symphony in **Handel's** *Messiah*, which has the word *pifa* written above the music.

Pijper, Willem (1894-1947) Dutch composer, who was the most prominent composer of his country in the first half of the 20th century. Having studied with Wagenaar, he became professor at the Amsterdam Conservatoire in 1925, and director of the Rotterdam Conservatoire in 1930. Works such as his *Septet* (1920) and the Symphony No. 2 caused a sensation when first performed, and the Symphony No. 3, Piano Concerto and *Zes Symfonische Epigrammen* are major contributions to Dutch orchestral repertory of the period.

Pilkington, Francis (1562-1638) English

composer, who described himself as a lutenist, and whose songs with lute are of particular quality. He was also a writer of madrigals, contributing one to *The Triumphs of Oriana*. He was chorister at Chester Cathedral and later a minor canon, remaining there until his death.

Pinza, Ezio (Fortunato) (1892-1957) Italian bass known for his noble voice and fine looks as well as his considerable dramatic ability. He had a repertory of nearly 100 roles, singing at La Scala, Milan (1921-1924), New York Metropolitan (1926-1948), Covent Garden (1930-1939), and was a particularly fine Don Giovanni. After his operatic career finished he appeared in television, films and musicals, including *South Pacific* on Broadway (1949).

p'ip'a (China) Four-stringed lute, the body of which is made of hardwood and the top of tung wood. The modern version has 24 chromatically divided frets, six upper and 18 lower. Originally the *p'ip'a* was plucked with a plectrum, but now fingers and fingernails are used.

pipe Hollow tube used to produce a musical sound when air is vibrated through it, such as in an organ or a blown wind instrument. It is also a one-handed whistle flute played in some folk music with a **tabor**.

pi'phat (Thailand) Percussive Thai orchestra of 6 to 14 players, which includes pairs of wooden-keyed xylophones and metallophones, circles of gongs, a hanging gong, a hand-hit, laced-head drum and a tacked-head drum hit with sticks. The only non-percussive instrument is the *pi pai*, a bulging oboe with a quadruple reed. It is an urban ensemble, often used to accompany theatre performances.

p'iri (Korea) Double-reed bamboo aerophone, with eight finger holes and a wide, dynamic and expressive range, played with a distinctively wide vibrato. Used in the **hyangak** and **tangak** orchestras and the **kagok** and **sijo** ensembles.

Piston, Walter (1894-1976) American composer and writer who studied at Harvard University and in Paris with Nadia **Boulanger**. He was professor of music at Harvard from 1944 to 1960. He was author of three important books, on harmony (1941), counterpoint (1947) and orchestration (1955), and composed instrumental music, his most popular work being the suite from the ballet *The Incredible Flutist* (1938).

piston Valve on a brass wind instrument which when depressed increases the effective length of the tube and thus alters the range of notes available to the player. It is also the abbreviation for the *cornet à pistons*, the French name for **cornet**.

pitch Height or depth of a note, according to the number of vibrations that produce it. The standard pitch of the A above middle C (from which all other notes are now reckoned and tuned in Western music) is at a frequency of 440 vibrations per second (hertz), which was fixed by international agreement in 1939. Prior to that time the accepted standard pitch varied to such an extent that until the middle of the 18th century there were at times three or four different pitches in use for different types of musical performance.

Pittsburgh Symphony Orchestra American orchestra of international reputation which was founded in 1895 and made its debut appearance under the baton of Frederic Asker. In 1910 the orchestra was disbanded and it was not until 1926 that it was reformed. In 1937 Otto **Klemperer** reorganized the orchestra. Guest conductors have included Richard **Strauss** and Edward **Elgar**, and such names as **Steinberg** and **Previn** have appeared as principal conductors. The orchestra has toured throughout the world, including Japan and Korea (1972), and the Middle East (1963).

pizz. Abbreviation of **pizzicato**.

Pizzetti, Ildebrando (1880-1968) Italian composer and conductor, a noted critic and teacher who was the most respected conservative Italian musician of his day. His works include the operas *Ifigenia* (1950), *Phaedra* (1909-1912) and *Murder in the Cathedral* (1958), and he was also a composer of incidental music for plays, instrumental and choral works.

pizzicato (It.) Plucked, indicating that the strings of an instrument should be plucked with a finger of the right hand, or occasionally with fingers of the left hand between bowed notes.

plagal cadence **Cadence** in which the progression of chords is IV-I, giving the impression of an Amen.

plagal mode Any of the series of modes in which the compass of the melody cast in that mode extends from dominant to dominant, rather than from final to final as it does in the authentic modes. Each plagal mode is linked to a corresponding authentic mode in that the same notes are used in each but the span of the notes involved in the plagal mode lies a fifth above the corresponding authentic mode when the modes are conceived of as equivalent to scales played on the white keys of the piano. (It should be noted that modes are orderings of pitch intervals and can be transposed from one key to another.) Plagal modes have the final in the middle, with a new dominant established three notes below where the dominant in the authentic mode is. Plagal modes are distinguished by the use of the prefix *hypo-*. For example, the Lydian mode is an authentic mode extending from F to F, with the final on F and the dominant of C. The Hypolydian mode is a plagal mode running from C to C with the final at F and a new dominant at A. See also **modes**.

plainsong Body of unison sacred music in the West, dating from early Christian times. The term comes from the Latin, *Cantus planus*, and frequent alternatives are plainchant or Gregorian chant. Plainsong was written as settings of psalms or responses for Christian services and may have been derived from similar Jewish and Greek systems. Originally unaccompanied, the piece was structured around the spoken rhythm of the prose works set (for example, the psalms) and the melody centred around a monotone, the dominant note (see **modes**). The melody was generally constructed in five sections: the intonation, dominant, meditation, recitation and ending. The dominant and recitation sections were normally chanted on the dominant while the other sections provided cadences.

Plainsong preceded Western harmony, and gave rise to the **Anglican chant** and the more modern forms of sacred music and eventually fell out of use. The 20th century has, however, seen a revival of interest in plainsong. See also **Gregorian chant**; **madrigal**; **motet**.

player piano Alternative term for **pianola**.

plectrum Device made of wood, metal or plastic used to pluck the strings of some stringed instruments, including the lute, mandolin, electric guitar, zither and banjo. It is also attached to the jack of a harpsichord.

Pleyel, Ignaz Joseph (1757-1831) Austrian pianist, piano-maker and composer, who was enormously popular in his day and whose music was much published. A pupil of **Haydn**, he also studied in Rome, later becoming *Kapellmeister* in Strasbourg (1789). He settled in Paris (1795) where he founded a piano factory. His prolific output of music included two operas, 29 symphonies, 45 string quartets and other chamber music. Although his early works display inventiveness, his later compositions often re-used earlier works and were aimed largely at pleasing his popular audience.

pneuma Vocal ornament sung to a single vowel in **plainsong**. An example is the word Alleluia when the final 'a' provided a vowel over which a melody was embellished.

pochette (Fr.) Small pocket-sized violin formerly used by dancing masters in the 17th and 18th centuries.

poem Term introduced by various romantic composers, especially the symphonic poems written by **Liszt** and **Chausson** (*Poème*, for violin and orchestra, 1896).

point End of the bow of a stringed instrument opposite to that held by the hand (the heel).

point d'orgue (Fr.) Pause in music marking the traditional place for the insertion of a **cadenza**.

pointillism Style of musical composition in which the notes appear to be disposed as isolated dots rather than in flowing melodic lines. It is a term derived from the school of painting in which dots of colour are painted on a canvas. Certain music by **Stockhausen** and **Webern** is described as pointillist.

pointing Distribution of the syllables of the psalms in **Anglican chant** according to the rhythm of the words as spoken.

pokok (Bali) Principal melody upon which the instruments of the Balinese **gamelan** orchestra elaborate, somewhat similar in concept to the Western **cantus firmus**.

polka Dance originating in Bohemia in the early 19th century, written in 2/4 time with vigorous rhythms.

Pollini, Maurizio (1942-) Italian pianist and conductor, who is known for a modern as well as classical repertory. He made his debut at the age of nine and studied at the Milan Conservatoire until 1959. He has worked in the United States and Europe, and is in particular association with Claudio **Abbado**. He often conducts from the keyboard and made his debut as a conductor in **Rossini**'s *La Ponna del Cago* (1981).

polonaise Polish dance of stately character that originated in the 16th century. The music is in 3/4 time and is characterized by **feminine cadences** at the end of each section, and also by dotted rhythms. **Beethoven**, **Schubert** and **Liszt** have used these features in their polonaises for piano. Between 1817 and 1846, **Chopin** composed 16 polonaises which expressed his strong patriotic sentiments.

polymodality Music that is based on more than one **mode**. An illustration of this is **Vaughan Williams**' *Pastoral Symphony* (1921).

polyphonic Music that combines two or more independent melodic lines. Following the polyphonic period (13th to 16th centuries), when harmonic progressions were controlled by the independent melodies, the later polyphony of **Bach** was governed by the harmonic structure of the composition.

polyrhythmic Music in which different parts, based on different rhythms, are performed simultaneously. For example, in the movement 'Dance' in **Copland**'s *Music for the Theater* (1925), there are as many as five different rhythmic patterns.

polytonality System of composing music in which more than one key is used simultaneously. It was a system used by **Holst** and **Milhaud**. See also **atonality**.

Ponce, Manuel (1882-1948) Mexican composer, who studied in Italy, Germany and in Paris under **Dukas**. At the age of 14 he composed the gavotte made famous by the dancer Argentina. His other compositions include the well-known song *Estrellita* and classical works for guitar, which have been made part of the standard repertory by **Segovia**.

Ponchielli, Amilcare (1834-1886) Italian composer and organist, who despite the accepted importance of his work was never popular. Of the operas he wrote, only *La Giaconda* (1876) has survived into the modern repertory, from which comes the well known *Dance of the Hours*. He was choirmaster at Bergamo Cathedral (1881) and taught composition at Milan Conservatoire from 1880.

ponticello Bridge of a stringed instrument over which the strings are stretched so that they are kept clear of the belly of the instrument. *Sul ponticello* indicates that the player should play the instrument as close as possible to the bridge.

Poot, Marcell (1901-) Belgian composer and critic, who was one of the pupils of **Gilson** who in 1925 founded *Les Synthetistes* dedicated to new ideas in music. Also a pupil of **Dukas**, he wrote music for silent film, radio, plays and discovered the possibilities of using jazz in his first ballet *Paris in Verlegenheid* (1925). He also composed operas, three symphonies and a symphonic poem *Charlot* (1926).

pop music Common name given to any form of popular music, probably coined in the 1950s to describe such performers as Elvis Presley and the Everley Brothers. Music is generally in a fast 2/4 or 4/4 time with syncopated rhythms. The structure of a pop song is often verse and refrain, with an eight-bar bridge. The regular formation was a group of four: a drummer, bass guitarist and second and lead guitarist. One or all of the band members provided the vocals. Sometimes, however, bands use more people and a great variety of combinations of instruments, including large brass sections. Because of the rise of the recording industry (which for the greater part determines the quality and content of the music released), pop music has become a dominant and all-pervasive form in many countries of the world. The term is now also used to describe collections or concerts of the most popular classical music. See also **jazz**; **punk rock**; **reggae**; **rock**.

Popp, Lucia (1939-) Austrian soprano born in Czechoslovakia, who studied at the Bratislava Music Academy. She made her debut as the Queen of the Night (1963) and was principal soprano with the Vienna State Opera. She has made a number of recordings and has sung throughout Europe as a recitalist and in opera.

portamento (It.) Direction in vocal music or music for a bowed instrument to carry the sound from note to note without a break. It is also possible to achieve this effect on a **trombone**.

portative organ Small **organ** with a single keyboard and flue pipes which could be suspended from the shoulder by a strap so that it could be carried in a procession.

Portative organ

Porter, Cole (1891-1964) American composer of popular songs, noted for the wit of his lyrics on songs such as *Let's Do It*, *Night and Day* and *I Get a Kick Out of You*. He also wrote successfully for musicals such as *Kiss Me Kate* (1948) and *Anything Goes* (1934). One of the most thoroughly trained popular song writers of the 20th century, he studied harmony and counterpoint at Harvard (1915-1916) and with **d'Indy** at the Schola Cantorum, Paris (1919). After the death of his wife in 1954 he spent the last ten years of his life in New

Cole Porter

York where he became a semi-recluse. His shows and songs have often been revived.

Porter, Quincy (1897-1966) American composer, violinist and educationist who was a pupil of **d'Indy** in Paris and **Bloch** in New York. He later became dean of the faculty of the New England Conservatoire (1938) and then professor at Yale (1946-1965). His works include incidental music for Shakespeare's *Antony and Cleopatra* and T.S. Eliot's *Sweeney Agonistes*, two symphonies, two piano concertos, ten string quartets and other chamber music.

Porter, Walter (1595-1659) English composer who wrote madrigals, motets and other sacred music. Possibly a pupil of **Monteverdi**, he was choirmaster of Westminster Abbey until choral service was suppressed in 1649, and he came under the patronage of Sir Edward Spencer.

position Term with two meanings

First, it is the place at which the strings of a stringed instrument are stopped (or the slide of a trombone is held) to produce the note required.

Second, in harmony it is the particular configuration of the notes available in a chord. The most usual position is root position, in which the generating note of the chord is in the bass. The other two positions are known as the first and second **inversions**. See **triad**.

positive organ Small organ used from the 10th to the 17th century that could be placed on a floor or a table, but unlike the **portative organ** could not be carried.

post-horn Brass instrument (similar to the **bugle** rather than the **horn**) which was able to produce only its fundamental note and the relative **harmonic series**. Post-horns were used by guards of the early mail coaches to announce their arrival when approaching towns or villages.

postlude Piece of **organ** music played at the end of a church service. It means the opposite of **prelude**.

Poston, Elizabeth (1905-) English composer and pianist who studied at the Royal Academy of Music and with Harold Samuel. She has worked in a wide field of musical activities and she was director of music in the Foreign Service of the BBC (1940-1945). She has written music for radio programmes, choral music, songs and film music, notable for *Howards End* (1970). She was president of the Society of Women Musicians (1955-1961).

post-Romanticism Music of a style (represented by **Brahms, Liszt** and **Wagner**) written immediately after that of the Romantic period of the late 18th and early 19th century. The term has also been applied to the music of early 20th-century composers such as **Elgar, Mahler**, and **Sibelius**.

Poulenc, Francis (1899-1963) French composer who received a classical education studying with Ricardo Vines and **Koechlin** among others, but did not study counter-point or orchestration, relying on his own instinctive sense of form. Vines introduced him to **Satie** who was a particular influence on his early work, and he was also encou-ranged by Jean Cocteau as one of a number

Francis Poulenc

of new composers known as *Les Nouveaux Jeunes*. From these Henri Collet (the music critic) selected six, Poulenc being one of them, becoming known as *Les Six*. Influenced by Parisian folklore and jazz, he wrote operas and ballets, combining with Diaghilev on the ballet *Les Biches* (1923), also choral, piano works, concertos and chamber music. Among his best works are the songs written after 1935, at which time he began accompanying the great French baritone Pierre **Bernac**. His works include the opera *Les Mamelles de Tiresias* (1944), much sacred music and works for voice, along with many orchestral works.

Pousseur, Henri (1929-) Belgian composer, who having studied at the Brussels Conservatoire wrote electronic music, influenced by the methods of **Webern**, **Stockhausen** and **Boulez**, the latter of whom he also studied with. He has written operas, symphonies, chamber music, a quintet in memory of Webern and music for tape, such as *Trois Visages de Liège* (1961). In 1958 he founded a studio for electronic music in Brussels.

praeludium Alternative term for **prelude**.

Pralltriller (Ger.) German equivalent of upper **mordent**.

precentor Ecclesiastical dignitary in an Anglican church who is in charge of the vocal church music. He is superior to the organist.

pre-Classical Style of composition that followed the Baroque music of the 18th century and preceded the Classical music of the late 18th century. Composers such as C.P.E. **Bach** and J.C. **Bach** were active during the pre-Classical period.

prelude Instrumental piece played as an introduction to a church service, preceding a **fugue**, or forming the first part of a **suite**. In addition, it sometimes forms the introduction to an act of an opera.

preparation In harmony the process of sounding a note first in a chord with which it is **consonant** and then again in a chord against which it is **dissonant**. The dissonance is then said to be prepared, or if it has not been treated in this way, it is said to be an unprepared dissonance.

prepared piano Piano that has been altered by placing various objects on the strings to produce special effects. John **Cage** is especially noted for the form of music produced by prepared pianos. One example is his work *A Book of Music* (1944) for two prepared pianos.

prestissimo (It.) Very fast indeed. See also **presto**.

presto (It.) Fast. Indication that the music should be played very fast. *Presto* indicates a speed faster than **allegro**.

Preston, Simon John (1938-) English organist and harpsichordist who is noted for his perfectionism and virtuosity. He has held a number of important organ posts and was appointed organist of Westminster Abbey in 1981. A particularly fine interpreter of **Liszt** and **Messaien**, he has made a number of recordings including a much admired version of **Handel**'s organ concertos.

Prêtre, Georges (1924-) French conductor who studied at the Paris Conservatoire and with Clatyens. He made his debut in 1946 at the Opéra-Comique and has since worked throughout Europe and the United States, most successfully in opera. He often worked with **Callas**, recording *Tosca* and *Carmen* with her. A conductor of both Classical and modern music, he is particularly dedicated to **Poulenc**'s music, conducting the first performances of the *Voix Humane* and *Gloria*, and he has recorded most of Poulenc's orchestral music.

Previn, André (1929-) American (naturalized) pianist, conductor and composer who studied in Berlin and Paris before moving with his family to the United States (1939).

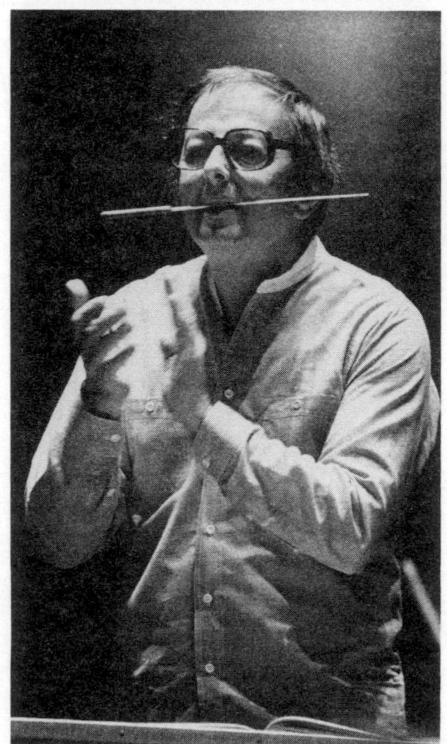

André Previn

He became a successful jazz pianist, making a number of recordings, and worked as a composer and arranger of film music in Hollywood. He later settled in England where he has won fame as a presenter of music on television, and he is a noted champion of English music, in particular **Walton** and **Vaughan Williams**. His compositions include a symphony, concertos, chamber music and piano works, and he has also written scores for the musicals *Coco* (1969) and *Good Companions* (1974).

Prey Hermann (1929-) German baritone, who studied at the Berlin Music Academy, making his debut at the Wiesbaden State Theatre in 1952. He is internationally known as an opera singer, his more notable roles being Figaro and Papageno, but he is also a particularly fine *Lieder* singer who has made a number of recordings.

Price, Leontyne (1927-) Amcrican soprano, who studied at the Juilliard School, New York. She began her career as a concert performer, but after her television appearance as *Tosca* (1955) she became a highly successful opera singer, one of the finest **Verdi** sopranos of her day. She has sung in Europe and the United States, making her debut at Covent Garden in 1958 and at the Metropolitan, New York, in 1961.

Price, Margaret (1941-) Welsh soprano, who studied at Trinity College and made her debut with the Welsh National Opera in 1962 as Cherubino. She is a noted *Lieder* singer and has been a guest at many European opera houses, especially in **Mozart** roles. She has appeared on television as Salud (*La Vida Breve*) and as Tatyana. She was awarded a CBE in 1982.

prick song 15th- to 18th-century term for written ('pricked') rather than improvised music.

prima donna (It.) First lady. The chief female singer in an opera.

Primrose, William (1903-1982) Scottish violist, who began his career as a violinist, but changed to viola on advice from his teacher, Ysayë, becoming the world's foremost virtuoso. He appeared as a soloist in Europe and the United States. He settled in the United States in 1937 and was principal viola with the NBC Symphony Orchestra from 1938 to 1942. In 1944 he commissioned a viola concerto from **Bartók** and inspired other composers such as **Rubbra**, **Fricker** and **Hamilton** to write for him. He was awarded a CBE in 1953.

principal Term with three meanings.

First, it is the leading player of a section in an orchestra, who usually takes solo parts when necessary.

Second, it is one of the singers who take the leading parts in an opera, as opposed to members of the chorus. However, a principal **tenor** is someone who takes principal roles, but is not necessarily the leading tenor of the opera company.

Third, it is an organ stop of the open **diapason** type, but sounding an octave higher.

Pritchard, (Sir) John (1921-) English conductor, whose career is divided between opera and concerts. He was *répétiteur* at Glyndebourne and later its musical director (1969-1977). A guest conductor at leading European opera houses, his other appointments include conductor of the Royal Liverpool Philharmonic Orchestra and in 1983 he was appointed chief conductor of the BBC Symphony Orchestra. He has always been a champion of new music, conducting premieres of **Britten**'s *Gloriana*, **Tippett**'s *The Midsummer Marriage* and *King Priam*, and **Henze**'s *Elegy for Young Lovers*. He was knighted in 1983.

Sir John Pritchard

programme music Music that represents a story, picture or other extra-musical sounds. The earliest examples of this type of music are the 14th-century **caccias**, which often depicted hunting scenes in a colourful manner. The **chansons** of **Jannequin** attempted to convey extra-musical sounds such as bird songs. **Beethoven's** *Pastoral Symphony* (1808) portrays the feelings of the countryside, which was a new approach to programme music. Other composers who have used this form include Richard **Strauss** (tone poems), **Debussy** (*La Mer*, 1903-1905) and **Honegger**'s steam-locomotive epic (*Pacific 231*, 1923).

progression Movement from one **note** or **chord** to its successor. See also **harmony**.

progressist Group of French Communist composers, such as **Durey** and **Nigg**, who after 1945 became active in composing music in accordance with Communist doctrine. One of Durey's works was entitled *La Longue Marche*, to words by Mao Tse-tung.

progressive tonality Type of music in which the work or movement opens in one key and, progressing through other keys, ends in another. It was a system used by **Mahler** and C. **Nielsen**.

Prokofiev, Sergei (1891-1953) Russian composer, who was taught by his mother from the age of three and had already tried his hand at an opera by the age of nine. He

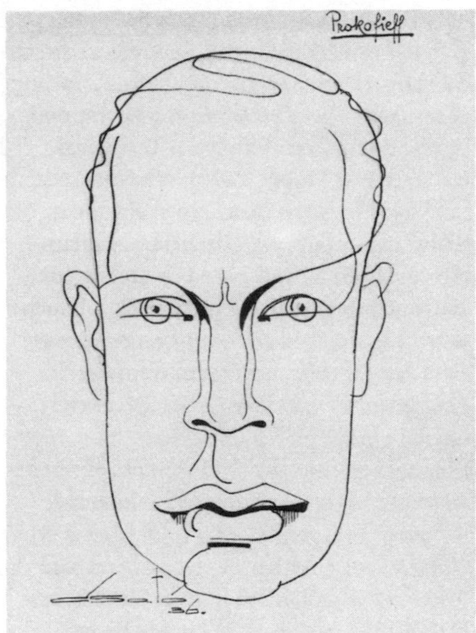

Sergei Prokofiev

entered St Petersburg Conservatoire (1904), and was a pupil of **Rimsky-Korsakov**, composing and publishing several works while still a student, including the Piano Sonata No. 2 and his Piano Concerto No. 1. From 1918 he lived abroad, working as a solo pianist in his own works in New York, where he composed the opera *The Love of Three Oranges*, and later in Paris where he composed three ballets for Diaghilev. Never fully at home in the West, he returned to the Soviet Union in 1934 where he suffered under Stalin's doctrine of social realism, condemned with others as a formalist, which lead to a tendency to popularize his style in works such as *Peter and the Wolf*. He found outlets for his music in film scores such as for *Lieutenant Kijé* and *Alexander Nevsky*, and in ballets such as *Romeo and Juliet*, and *Cinderella*. His opera *War and Peace* was performed in its complete version (1957) only after his death, despite his numerous revisions in an attempt to secure a performance. Although regarded as avant-garde in his youth, he was fundamentally a Romantic melodist and was successful in a wide range of works which are crucial to the 20th-century repertory.

prolation Division of the **semibreve** into **minims** in old notation, where according to the **time-signature** a semibreve could be equal to two minims (minor prolation) or three minims (major prolation).

promenade concert Originally an orchestral concert at which the audience walked about during the programme. Modern promenade concerts now usually entail a large part of the audience standing or sitting on the floor of the main body of the auditorium (having bought lower priced tickets). The most famous of this type of promenade is the summer series at the Royal Albert Hall, London, started by Sir Henry **Wood** in 1895. Originally held at the London Queen's Hall, they continued there until the building was destroyed by bombs in 1941. They are now held almost exclusively at the Royal Albert Hall, where they are affectionately known as the 'Proms'. The programme of music is very varied, sometimes arranged around a theme, and often including specially commissioned works. Performers include many famous orchestras and soloists. The opening and last nights of the Proms are special occasions where the mainly young audience show much enthusiasm.

psalm Text taken from the Book of Psalms in the Old Testament, usually sung as part of the offices of the Roman Catholic Church and of the Anglican morning and evening services. In the Catholic Church they are set to **plainsong** and **chants**, and other musical settings in the Anglican services. Psalms have also been set as **anthems** or **cantatas** by composers such as **Bach** and **Mendelssohn**.

psalter Book that contains the psalms as used in the Christian Church as part of the liturgy. The earliest surviving psalters are those by Miles Coverdale, *Goostly Psalmes and Spirituall Songes* (*c*1538), and *The Psalter of David Newely Translated into Englyshe Metre* (1549), by Robert Crowley. The psalter often indicates the chant to which the psalm is to be sung.

Puccini, Giacomo (1858-1924) Italian composer who was in his youth a Church musician, later studying at Milan Conservatoire. Despite his original bias towards symphonic works he was persuaded by his teacher, Ponchielli, to write opera, and his first opera *Le Villi* was heard by **Verdi**'s music publisher who commissioned the operas *Edgar*, *Manon Lescaut* and *La Bohème*, the latter of which remains one of the most popular operas ever written. The power of his characterizations, his instinctive theatrical skill, and original harmonies and orchestration are also shown in his next operas, *Tosca*, *Madama Butterfly*, *The Girl of the Golden West*, *Trittico* (composed of three one-act operas), and *Turandot* (beforē the completion of which Puccini died). His compositions have remained in the regular repertory of the world's opera houses.

Pugnani, Gaetano (1731-1798) Italian violinist and composer, who travelled widely and spent long periods in London and Paris, otherwise working for most of his life at the Turin court where he became leader and teacher from 1770. His compositions include violin sonatas, operas, ballets and cantatas. His playing was known for its power and eloquence, and he was probably partly responsible for the development of the modern bow.

punk rock Style of music that became popular during the 1970s, characterized by harsh sounds, very loud shouting and discords. Punk rock spoke to the young people of the decade of violence and frustration, and made its own protest against urbanization and the economic recession of the time. The music of punk cannot be extricated from the costume of its adherents, being very intimidating in style, with grotesque make-up (for boys as well as girls), black leather, ragged jeans, chains and junk jewelry. Some punk songs were banned by radio and television, because they were considered offensive.

Purcell, Henry (1659-1695) One of the greatest of English composers whose music was largely ignored for more than 200 years, and whose reputation was restored by the composers **Vaughan Williams**, **Britten** and **Holst**, and the Purcell Society. He was a choirboy at the Chapel Royal and a pupil of **Humfrey** and later **Blow** whom he succeeded as organist at Westminister Abbey (1679). The following year he published the well-known *String Fantasias* and from then on composed a long series of *Welcome Odes* and other official choral pieces, including the coronation anthem for James II *My Heart is Inditing*. He also wrote incidental music for plays by, among others, Dryden and Congreve, a number of semi-operas and the first great English opera *Dido and Aeneas*. During the last years of his life he was increasingly prolific, writing some of his greatest church music, such as the Te Deum and Jubilate in D, and a large quantity of secular music, particularly songs, but it is his instrumental works which best demonstrate Purcell's subtle rhythms and harmonies.

pūrvi (India) One of the ten parent scales (**thāt**) in Hindustani music, corresponding to C, D♭, E, F♯, G, A♭, B, C′.

Puyana, Rafael (1931-) Colombian harpsichordist who was a pupil of Wanda **Landowska**, studying at the New England Conservatoire. He made his first European tour in 1955, making his New York debut in 1957 and his London debut in 1966. His wide repertory includes music from the 16th to the 18th centuries as well as modern works. He has made many recordings and has had several works written for him by composers such as Evett, **McCabe**, Houpon and Orbon.

p'yŏngjo (Korea) One of the most common **pentatonic** modes, corresponding to C, D, F, G, A.

Q

qawalī (India) Muslim devotional song of northern India and Pakistan.

qin (China) See **ch'in**.

quadrille Square dance originating from military horse displays which was introduced to French ballet during the 18th century. It was taken to England at the beginning of the 19th century, where it became a ballroom dance with five different sections. Each section has different music, mainly drawn from popular songs and fashionable operatic tunes. The Lancers is a type of quadrille.

quadruple counterpoint Four-part **invertible counterpoint**.

quadruplet Four notes played in the time of three.

Quantz, Johann Joachim (1697-1773) German composer of about 500 concertos and other works for the flute. He also taught King Frederick the Great of Prussia to play the flute, made technical improvements to it and wrote a treatise on the subject.

quarter note Alternative term for **crotchet**.

quarter tone Note whose pitch is half-way between two adjacent semitones. Quarter tones were not used in Western music until the 20th century, when they have been used by such composers as **Haba, Bartók** and **Bloch**. See also **microtone**.

quartet Any composition written for four vocalists or instrumentalists or the group that performs such a piece. For example, a string quartet normally consists of two violins, viola and cello. Strictly speaking, a string quartet is normally in the form of a **sonata** for four stringed instruments. A piano quartet is usually written for **piano**, violin, viola and cello. A vocal quartet normally consists of the voices soprano, alto, tenor and bass.

quaver Note that has half the time value of a **crotchet** or an eighth that of a **semibreve**. In the United States it is known as an eighth note.

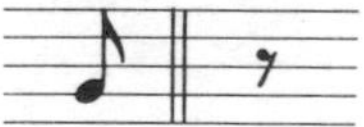

Quaver Quaver rest

Quilter, Roger (1877-1953) English composer best known for his songs, mainly settings of Shakespeare and other English poets, and his attractive *A Children's Overture* for orchestra based on traditional nursery rhyme tunes.

quintet Any composition written in five vocal or instrumental parts, or the group that performs such a piece. For example, a string quintet is the same as a string **quartet**, with an extra viola or cello. A piano quintet consists of a piano and a string quartet, and a clarinet quintet has a clarinet and a string quartet.

quintuplet Group of five notes of equal time value played in the time of three or four notes.

Quintuplet

quodlibet Composition compiled from existing tunes used against one another.

R

Rabaud, Henri (1873-1849) French composer who was a pupil of **Massenet**, among others, at the Paris Conservatoire, where he later became professor of harmony, succeeding **Fauré** as director in 1920. He was known for his catch phrase "modernism is the enemy", and his cantata *Daphne* won him the Prix de Rome (1894). After travelling in Europe he became gradually reconciled to the modern movement and enjoyed an immense success with the oratorio *Job* (1900). He was also a frequent conductor at both the Opéra and the Opéra-Comique in Paris, and himself composed eight operas, including *L'Appel de la Mer*, based on Synge's *Riders to the Sea*.

Rachmaninov, Sergei Vassilievich (1873-1943) Russian composer and pianist who was one of the greatest of pianists, but is remembered for his compositions and as the last great representative of Russian Romanticism. He studied at the St Petersburg Conservatoire (1882) and later the Moscow Conservatoire (1885), and had his first real success in 1892 with the Prelude in C♯ Minor, which became his most celebrated composition. He suffered a brief lapse in confidence due to the failure of his first symphony, but later had further successes with the 2nd Piano Concerto and Symphony No. 2, and in 1913 wrote his masterpiece, the choral symphony *The Bells*.

His reputation was now established as both composer and pianist. The following period was marked by his increasing unease with the political situation in Russia, and in

Sergei Rachmaninov

1913 he finally left his homeland and settled in the United States, where he made his career as a concert pianist, making a number of recordings but leaving little time for composition. However, in 1934 he wrote one of his finest compositions, the *Rhapsody on a Theme by Paganini*, followed by his Symphony No. 3 (1936). Rachmaninov's compositions remain an indispensable part of the Romantic repertory.

racket Double-reed woodwind instrument that was in use between the 16th and 18th centuries. Its long tube was folded many times, so that the actual size of the instru-

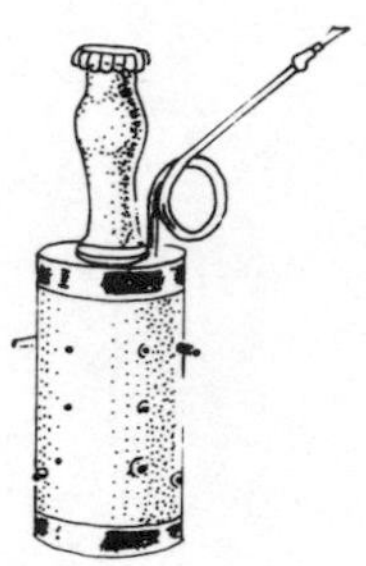
Racket

ment seemed small. Alternative names for the racket are ranket and sausage bassoon.

rāga (India) Melodic material that forms the basis for composition and improvisation. The term means colour.

A *rāga* is designated by a name that often includes reference to its scale or mode. Its melodic substance is defined by characteristic ascending and descending tone patterns, ornamentation and embellishment, particular tonal emphases, mood or **rasa**, and an associated time of day.

The term also applies to a performance, generally an improvisation, of a *rāga* as defined above. Most *rāgas* comprise two principal movements, an unmeasured introductory section (**ālāp**), followed by a fixed composition (**gat**), with improvisation, in a fixed temporal cycle (**tāla**).

ragtime Style of piano music that probably originated in the **minstrel** shows of the late 19th century. It was popular until about 1919 and then replaced by **jazz**. Ragtime has a syncopated melodic line usually accompanied by a 2/4 march-type bass. Classic examples are Scott **Joplin**'s *Maple Leaf Rag*, and Zez Confrey's *Kitten on the Keys*.

Raimondo, Pietro (1786-1853) Italian composer and opera director who, having studied in Naples, wandered Italy in great poverty, finally producing a successful opera in Genoa (1807). He had further successes as an opera director in Rome, Naples and Milan, and was appointed professor of composition at Palermo Conservatoire (1832). His compositions include sacred music, ballet, some 60 operas such as *Le Bizzarie d'Amour*, and oratorios, including *Giuseppe*.

Raimondi, Ruggero (1941-) Italian bass, who is considered to be one of the finest interpreters of the 19th-century repertory. He studied in Rome, making his opera debut at Spoleto in 1964, and has since sung at **Glyndebourne** (1969) and the New York Metropolitan (1970). He has been a member of La Scala, Milan since 1970 and has won great praise, particularly in the role of Don Giovanni.

Rainier, Priaulx (1903-) South African composer and violinist, whose music particularly reflects the language and music of the Zulus. Having studied at the South African College of Music, in 1920 she won a violin scholarship to London, where she settled, concentrating on composition from 1935. Her works include *Barbaric Dance Suite* (1949) and *Requiem* (1955-1956). She was professor of music at the Royal Academy of Music (1943-1961).

rallentando (It.) Indication that the music is to decrease in tempo. Often abbreviated to rall.

Rameau, Jean-Philippe (1683-1764) French composer and theorist who worked as an organist in France (1702-1722), when he came under the wealthy patronage of La Pouplinier. He wrote a number of important theoretical works, including the treatise *Traité de L'Harmonie*. In 1733 he began a second career as an opera composer and quickly established himself as the leading French composer for the stage, writing more than 20 operas and opera-ballets, such as *Les Indes Gallantes* (1735) and *Castor et Pollux* (1737). He was the champion of French music against the Italian party lead by **Pergolesi** in the so-called *Guerre des Bouffons*.

Rameau, Jean-Pierre (1922-) French flautist, who is well known as a soloist specializing in 18th-century chamber music, and for whom composers such as **Poulenc** and **Jolivet** have written. He was founder of the French wind quintet (1945) and the Paris Wind Ensemble (1953), and is author of *Ancient Music for the Flute*. He was appointed professor of flute at the Paris Conservatoire.

Randegger, Alberto (1832-1911) Italian conductor, singing teacher and composer who studied in Trieste with **Ricci**, becoming known locally as a composer of sacred music and operas such as *Il Lazzarone* and *The Rival Beauties*. He settled in London, where he became professor of singing at the Royal Academy of Music (1860) and was also conductor at Drury Lane and Covent Garden (1887-1898).

Rands, Bernard (1935-) English composer of avant-garde music who studied in Wales at University College, Bangor, and in Italy with **Dallapiccola, Boulez** and Naderna, among others. He spent two years in the United States as visiting fellow at Princeton and Illinois universities. He has also held the position of lecturer at Bangor (1961-1970) and York University (1970). His compositions have involved work in electronic music studios in many cities, and they include the orchestral piece *Wildtrack One*, *Refractions* for 24 performers and *Expressione IV* for two pianos. In 1984 he was awarded the Pulitzer prize for *Canti del Sole*.

Rangström, Ture (1884-1947) Swedish conductor, critic and composer who was largely self-taught, and a number of whose works are associated with August Strindberg, including the Symphony No. 1, *In Memoriam Strindberg*, and incidental music written to Strindberg's *Till Damaskus*. He was also one of the most important Swedish song writers, writing more than 50 songs with orchestral accompaniments. In 1907 He settled in Stockholm as a critic and was conductor of the Göteburg Symphony Orchestra (1922-1925). He was founder of the Society of Swedish Composers (1918).

rank Set of organ pipes of the same quality arranged in an ascending scale, one pipe for each note of the organ keyboard. An alternative term is stop.

ranket Alternative term for **racket**.

Rankl, Karl (1898-1968) Austrian conductor and composer, who was a pupil of **Schoenberg** and **Webern**. He worked in Germany and Austria as a conductor of opera from 1925 to 1938, becoming a resident in Britain from 1939 where he was musical director at Covent Garden from 1946 to 1951. His works include eight symphonies and the opera *Deidre of the Sorrows*, based on the play by Synge.

rant 17th-century term that was applied loosely to many different English dances. The term may have been a corruption of **courante**.

ranz des vaches Swiss cowherds' song or alphorn signal used in mountainous districts to call cattle. There are many different tunes, varying according to each locality. A *ranz des vaches* has been used by some composers, such as **Rossini** in the overture to *William Tell* (1829) and **Beethoven** in the *Pastoral Symphony* (1809).

rasa (India) Aesthetic concept in the Indian arts. In music there is said to be a direct connection between musical expression in a particular **rāga** and the evocation of one or more of the nine *rasas* (love, humour, sadness, anger, heroism, fear, horror, surprise, peace). While music is particularly suited to the expression of the more profound *rasas*, good musicians often demonstrate their skill and personality by portraying a variety of *rasas*.

rattle Noise-producing toy occasionally used as an orchestral percussion instrument.

Rattle, Simon (1955-) English conductor who studied at the Royal Academy of

Music (1971-1975) and founded and conducted the Liverpool Sinfonia (1970-1972). In 1974 he won the John Player International Conducting award and has since worked at Glyndebourne and with the London Sinfonietta. From 1980 he has been principal conductor of the City of Birmingham Symphony Orchestra.

Ravel, Maurice (1875-1937) French composer, whose compositions are remarkable for their impressionist techniques and mastery of orchestration in works such as *Boléro*, *Spanish Rhapsody* and *La Valse*. He studied at the Paris Conservatoire and under **Fauré**, and in 1899 the Société Nationale performed his overture *Schéhérezade* and the *Pavanne Pour un Infante Défunte*. Although he produced some of his best works in the following ten years, his first public success did not come until 1911 when the Opéra-Comique produced *L'Heure Espagnole*, and the following year Diaghilev's *Ballets Russes* produced *Daphnis et Chloé*.

Maurice Ravel

Ravel was one of the great innovators in writing for piano, exploiting the sonorities of the instrument in works such as his *Concerto for Left Hand*, *Miroirs* (1905) and *Gaspard de la Nuit* (1908). He never held an official post, and had few pupils, **Vaughan Williams** being the best known of them.

Ravenscroft, Thomas (*c*1590-1633) English composer and publisher who wrote sacred music, madrigals and part songs, but is best known as a collector and editor of popular songs, published in the books *Pammelia*, *Deuteromelia* (in which the round *Three Blind Mice* is to be found) and *Melismata*. Some of the songs included were his own compositions. He was also editor of the London edition of the psalter *The Whole Booke of Psalmes* (1621), in which 55 of the 105 settings were his own.

Rawsthorne, Alan (1905-1971) English composer, who began to study dentistry but turned to music at the age of 20. Largely self-taught, he wrote mostly instrumental works, including three symphonies, the ballet *Madame Chrysantème*, overture *Street Corner*, fantasy overture *Cortèges* and music for film and radio.

ray Second note of the **tonic sol-fa** scale.

re The old name for the note D in **solmization**, which is still used in Latin countries.

Read, Gardner (1913-) American composer who studied with **Pizzetti** and **Copland**. He has taught at several American universities and has worked as a radio commentator and writer on music. His compositions include four symphonies, piano and organ music and the operas *Villon* and *The Golden Journey to Samarkand*.

realism Term with two meanings.

First, it is the use of real sounds in music, such as birdsong calls, bells, anvils and cannon fire. In some instances recordings of these sounds are played, while in others musical instruments are used to imitate them.

Second, it is an alternative term for the Italian **verismo**.

realization Act of writing out a full version of a piece of music that was left incomplete by the composer. This might, for example, involve completing the harmony of a 17th-century piece from the basso **continuo** line. Realization involves more than editing, but less than arranging.

rebab Spiked fiddle, with one or more strings, widespread throughout Asia and the Far East. It is held vertically and balanced on a long spike.

rebec Obsolete stringed instrument, similar to the violin, which was of Arab origin and an ancestor of the violin family. It was a pear-shaped instrument with three gut strings played with a bow. The rebec survived in France until the 18th century, but its use was limited to the accompaniment of singing and dancing by **troubadours**.

recapitulation Section of a composition in which the original subjects are restated after their development. See **sonata form**.

recit. Abbreviation of recitative.

recital Musical performance given by a solo instrumentalist, a singer with piano accompaniment or duettists. Other musical performances without action are known as concerts, although in popular music the term concert is now used even for performances by solo singers.

recitative Form of speech singing used in **opera** and **oratorio**, described by **Caccini** at the beginning of the 17th century as speaking in music. The words are declaimed on a fixed note and without rhythm or metre, although recitative is generally written by convention in 4/4 time, with bar-lines. There are two kinds of recitative: recitativo secco and *recitativo accompagnato* (often also known as *recitativo stromentato*). The recitative was used to advance the action of the piece.

Recitativo secco consists of the rapid declamation of words, punctuated by chords on the keyboard and possibly another instrument such as the *viola da gamba*. The accompaniment is often only at the cadence points.

Recitativo accompagnato has an orchestral accompaniment and was used not only to move the action of the plot forward, but also to modulate to the key of the **aria** that followed it.

Handel's *Messiah* is an example of an oratorio in which recitative is used extensively. The work tells of the life of Christ, and the words to the recitative sections are drawn directly from the Bible. These lead to arias which, by contrast are used to comment upon the action.

recorder Whistle-headed flute that was used throughout Europe between the 16th and 18th centuries. It was formerly known as the English flute. The recorder is held vertically and blown through a mouthpiece in which the air is diverted by a block of wood (the fipple). This produces a milder tone than the flute. The most widely used recorders are the treble, tenor, descant, soprano and bass. In the 20th century the instrument was revived by Arnold **Dolmetsch** as a relatively inexpensive and easy way to teach children the basics of music.

Recorder

recte et retro (Lat.) Form of **canon** in which the imitating voice plays or sings the first theme backwards. The Italian equivalent is *al rovescio*.

reed instrument Musical instrument in which the sound is produced by the vibration of the reed (a tongue of thin cane or metal). In beating-reed instruments, such as the clarinet, the reed vibrates against an air slot; in free-reed instruments (harmonica, accordian and concertina), it vibrates through a slot, and in the double-reed instruments (oboe and bassoon) two reeds vibrate against each other. With the exception of the flute, all the woodwind instruments of an orchestra are reed instruments.

reed organ Types of keyboard instrument that uses free-beating reeds to produce individual notes. As there are no pipes, the reeds are activated by air blown across them. Among the instruments in this group are the harmonium and the American organ, in which the air pressure is produced by pedal-operated bellows or an electric motor. The air pressure to an accordian is produced by pumping bellows with the arms, and with the mouth organ the player blows air directly over the reeds. See also **reed instrument**.

reed pipe Organ pipe in which sound is produced by causing a reed to beat regularly against an opening into the pipe. The reeds are all of the single-beating type, similar to that of the clarinet. The actual tone quality produced by reeds range from the **diapason tone** of the basic flute-work to brilliant and powerful reeds of marked individual character. See also **reed instruments**.

reel Irish or Scottish dance, also found in North Yorkshire as part of the Long Sword dance, the influence of which can be traced in dances as far afield as the Caribbean and United States. It is a rapid dance performed by two or more couples, the music flowing smoothly in quadruple metre. The Irish version is generally faster than the Scottish.

refrain In verse songs and anthems, a strain that returns with the same words at the beginning, middle or end of each verse.

regal Small portable reed organ that was in use from the 15th to 17th centuries. It was used in churches to accompany the singing. Some models could be folded like a book, and were named Bible-regal. The regal was said to have been invented by Heinrich Traxdorff of Nuremberg in about 1460.

Reger, (Johann Baptist Joseph) Maximilian (1873-1916) German composer and pianist who was the most important composer of organ music after **Bach**, and whose work has been made the subject of study by composers such as **Hindemith**, **Honegger** and **Schoenberg**. He became organist of the Catholic Church of Weiden in Bavaria at the age of 13 and later toured Europe and Russia as an organist, but had little immediate success with his compositions. He made a reputation as a remarkable teacher of composition and was professor at the conservatoire in Leipzig from 1907. His prodigious output in a working life of only 26 years includes *Variations on a theme by Mozart*, an unfinished requiem and the choral work *Die Nonnen*.

reggae (Caribbean) Highly rhythmic Jamaican song form popular from the late 1960s onwards. It is a synthesis of Afro-American popular music and Afro-Jamaican traditional music, containing traces of African religious music and Christian revivalist songs. The lyrics are often concerned with political and social comment, and frequently imbued with Rastafarian values.

The form originated in the urban lower-class music of the 'rudie boys' and is associated with its forerunners **ska** and rock-steady.

register Part of the compass of an instrument or the human voice that is said to have its own particular tone-quality. Examples are the human head and chest registers.

Reich, Steve Michael (1936-) American

composer whose work deals with very gradual changes in time and the possibilities of using multiples of the same instrument, making use of minimal material (such as a single chord in *Four Organs*) to construct his music. In 1966 he founded the group Steve Reich and Musicians and he has established his own electronic studio in New York. Other works include *Pitch Charts* (1963), *Piano Phrase* (1967) and *Music for 18 Instruments* (1975).

Reichardt, Johann Friedrich (1752-1814) German composer, who was author of several books on composition and criticism, and also published collections of music. He was musical director at the Prussian court of Frederick the Great and Frederick II until his dismissal in 1793 for his sympathy with the French Revolution. A forerunner of **Schubert** in song composition, he wrote some 100 songs and 12 operas, including *Hänschen and Gretchen* and a setting of Milton's *Morning Hymn*.

Reimann, Aribert (1936-) German composer, who is also well known as an accompanist to singers, and in particular to **Fischer Dieskau**. He studied with **Blacher** and Rausch in Berlin and his works include the opera *A Dream Play* (after Strindberg), songs and choral pieces. He has also set texts by Shakespeare and Shelley.

Reincken, Hohann Adam (1623-1722) German organist and composer, of whom it is said that **Bach** often walked from Lüneberg and later Cöthen to Hamburg to hear play at St Catherine's, where he was organist from 1663. A pupil of Heinrich **Scheidemann** and masterful technician, his best known compositions are his keyboard arrangements from *Hortus Musicus*.

Reiner, Fritz (1888-1963) Hungarian-born conductor who was a particularly famed interpreter of Richard **Strauss, Wagner** and **Bartók**. He was principal conductor at Dresden Staatsoper, later settling in the United States where he was principal conductor with the Cincinnati Symphony Orchestra (1922-1931) and then the Chicago Symphony Orchestra (1953), which under his direction became in **Stravinsky**'s opinion the most precise and flexible orchestra in the world. He also taught at the Curtis Institute, Philadelphia, where Leonard **Bernstein** was among his pupils.

Reizenstein, Franz (1911-1968) German composer and pianist who studied in Berlin with **Hindemith**, settling in England 1934 in order to escape the Nazi regime, where he studied with **Vaughan Williams**. From 1958 he taught piano at the Royal Academy of Music. His compositions include the oratorio *Genesis*, the cantata *Voices of Night* and two Hoffnung concert pastiches *Let's Fake an Opera* and *Concerto Popolare*.

related keys Keys that are harmonically close so that **modulation** between them is relatively simple and concordant. For example, major and minor keys that share the same key signature (e.g. C major and A minor) are said to be related.

relative pitch Ability to identify a tone to the nearest semitone. See also **absolute pitch**.

reminiscence-motive Recurring theme in the composition of an **opera**, linked to a specific character or an emotion.

repeat Restatement of a section of a composition, not written out a second time, but indicated by signs or marks used in conjunction with a **double bar**. In Classical music the expositions of movements in **sonata form** are nearly always marked for a repeat, with or without the **coda**.

Two methods of indicating a repeat

répétiteur (Fr.) Member of an operatic or choral company (sometimes a keyboard player) whose function is to rehearse the singing parts before rehearsals with the conductor. The *répétiteur* often also acts as prompter during operatic performances.

reprise Term with three meanings.

First, it is a repeated section of a composition.

Second, it is the reappearance of the first subject in a **sonata form** movement at the point where the **recapitulation** begins.

Third, it is the reappearance of a song or dance number in a musical or operetta.

requiem Roman Catholic Mass for the dead. Some requiems are set in plainsong, whereas more recent settings are through-composed. Some of the finest settings, although originally written to order (**Mozart**) or intended for a special religious occasion (**Berlioz**, 1837, and **Verdi**, 1874), are now fit mainly or solely for concert use, and some were written for that purpose (**Dvorák**). **Britten**'s *War Requiem* (1961) combines the liturgical text with settings of poems by Wilfrid Owen.

Resnik, Regina (1922-) American mezzo-soprano who formerly sang soprano and has sung at the New York Metropolitan and at Covent Garden in both voices. She made her debut in New York (1942) in *Lady Macbeth* and has since been a notable interpreter of the roles of Amneris, Klytemnestra and Carmen, in which opera she also made her debut as director in Hamburg (1971).

resolution Process by which a chord that is a **discord** is made to pass into a **concord** in harmony.

resonance Characteristic of an object whereby it vibrates to a note of a certain pitch. A resonator may be the cavities in the human skull, the hollow in a musical instrument such as a guitar, or a concert hall.

Respighi, Ottorino (1879-1936) Italian composer, conductor, string player and pianist, who was probably the most internationally successful Italian composer of his generation. He studied with **Rimsky-Korsakov** in St Petersburg and later in Berlin with **Bruch**. From 1903 to 1908 he pursued a career as a violinist and violist, and later became professor of composition at Liceo di S Cecilia, Rome (1913). Among his compositions, which include operas, orchestral works, concertos and chamber music, his best work is to be found in his short vocal pieces such as *Aretusa* (1911), *La primavera* (1918-1919) and *Lauda per la nativita del signore.*

response In Anglican church music the choral and congregational cadences answering the versicles read or chanted by the priest, such as "Amen", or "Have mercy upon us..." in the Litany.

rest Period of silence on the part of a performer corresponding to a given number of beats or bars. If the performer is to rest for an entire movement, the word tacit (silent) appears in the music.

Two bars and 16 bars rest

resultant tone Alternative term for **combination tone**.

retenu (Fr.) Retained, a direction indicating that the tempo should be held back.

Reuske, Julius (1934-1950) German pianist and composer, whose early death cut short a promising career. The son of Adolf Reuske the organ builder, he was a pupil of **Liszt**. The works published before his death include the organ sonata *The 94th Psalm*, piano works and songs.

Reutter, Herman (1900-1985) German composer and pianist, who was a highly successful accompanist to singers such as

Sigrid Onegin, **Schwarzkopf**, Hotter and **Fischer Dieskau**. He held a number of appointments at the German music schools including director of the Stuttgart Academy (1956-1966). A composer in many genres, Reutter is particularly admired for his stage works, such as the opera *Saul* (1928) and songs, and is considered to be one of the foremost proponents of the *Lied* tradition in the 20th century.

Revelueltas, Silvestre (1899-1940) Mexican violinist, conductor and composer whose compositions were greatly influenced by Mexican folksong, although he did not directly quote from them. He studied and worked in both Mexico and the United States and from 1929 to 1935 was assistant conductor of the Mexican Symphony Orchestra. His compositions include the much played symphonic *Sensamayá* (1938).

Reyer, Ernest (1823-1909) French composer and critic who championed composers such as **Wagner, Berlioz** and **Bizet**. He began his musical career in Paris in 1948, and over the next 14 years composed a substantial body of music, including the successful *Oriental Symphony* (1850) and *Le Sélam*. His activities as a critic account for his very small output over the next 46 years of his life, but he had successes with the operas *Sigurd* (1844) and *Salammbô* (1890), based on the novel by Flaubert.

rfz. Abbreviation of **rinforzando**.

rgya-gling (Tibet) Oboe used in Buddhist ritual, with a conical wooden body about 60 cm (23 in) in length, seven finger holes and a single thumb hole. The mouthpiece, which grips the double reed, has a disc against which the player rests his lips. It resembles the more ubiquitous **zurna**, with the exception of the large, flared silver or copper bell, which gives it a sweeter, yet still powerful sound. In rituals pairs of *rgya-gling* play short pieces, which are usually themes subject to much variation.

rh Abbreviation for right hand. The letters are written above or below the bass staff in piano music, to indicate that the section is to be played by the right instead of the left hand.

rhapsody Musical form that came to prominence in the 19th century. Usually free in form, the rhapsody often made use of elements derived from folk music. Typical examples include **Liszt**'s *Hungarian Rhapsodies* (1852) and **Dvorák**'s *Slavonic Rhapsodies* (1878). Among more recent rhapsodies are **Gershwin**'s *Rhapsody in Blue* (1924) and **Rachmaninov**'s *Rhapsody on a Theme of Paganini* (1934).

Rheinberger, Joseph (Gabriel) (1839-1901) German organist, composer and conductor who held his first organ post at the age of seven. He studied and taught at Munich Conservatoire, composing a number of operas, symphonies and chamber music, but is remembered for his elaborate and challenging organ compositions, in particular the 20 organ sonatas. Rheinberger achieved lasting fame as a teacher of the organ.

Rhodes, Helen See **Hardelot, Guy d'**

rhythm One of the three basic elements that go to make up Western music, rhythm is the combination of all those constituent parts that are involved in the time aspect of a composition (rather than its pitch, covered by the other two basic elements, melody and harmony). The constituent parts include metre, tempo, accents and phrasing. In some forms of Western music, rhythm is the predominant element (for example in jazz and some rock music), whereas in others it is much less important (for example, plainsong). In many Eastern forms of music, rhythm takes a completely different role.

rhythm and blues Style of popular music that developed from traditional **blues**, with the more emphatically rhythmic elements of modern rock music. The popularity of rhythm and blues grew with the acceptance by young whites of the music of black American singers such as Bo Diddley and Chuck Berry. In the 1960s their music also influenced many leading British pop groups.

ribible Alternative term for **rebec**.

Ricci, Ruggiero (1918-) American violinist, who made his debut at the age of ten in New York, making his first tour of Europe in 1932 and going on to have a brilliant international career. He is a notable interpreter of the works of **Paganini** and reintroduced the recently discovered Concerto No. 4 in 1971. He has had a number of works written for him by **Ginastera** and von Einem. He has been teacher at the Juilliard School since 1975.

ricercare (It.) To search out. A 16th-18th-century instrumental piece in the style of a fugue, using all forms of variation technique available to ornament the principal theme.

Richter, Franz (1709-1789) Bohemian composer, who entered the service of the Mannheim court (1747) first as a singer and violinist and then as court composer. He was later appointed choirmaster at Strasbourg Cathedral (1769-1789). He was one of the leaders of the Mannheim School of symphonists, and also wrote some 30 masses, two requiems and two passions.

Richter, Hans (1843-1916) Austrian-Hungarian conductor who was particularly associated with **Wagner**, who chose him to conduct the first performance of *The Ring* at Bayreuth (1876). He held a number of important conducting appointments and in 1877 travelled to London with Wagner and continued to work in England until 1910, giving an annual series of Richter Concerts in London. He was the permanent conductor of the Hallé Orchestra, Manchester, (1900-1911) and was champion of several English composers, including **Elgar**.

Richter, Karl (1932-) German organist, harpsichordist and conductor who is a specialist in the choral works of Bach. He joined the staff of the Munich Academy in 1951 and was appointed professor in 1956.

Richter, Sviatoslav (Teofilovitch) (1915-) Soviet pianist and conductor who is among the outstanding pianists of the 20th century. Largely self-taught he was *répétiteur* at Odessa Opera at the age of 15 and assistant conductor by the age of 18. A specialist in the works of **Prokofiev**, he has toured throughout Europe and the United States and has appeared at the Aldeburgh Festival a number of times in association with **Britten** and **Rostropovich**.

ricochet In violin playing, **staccato** effect produced by letting the bow bounce on the strings, whereas in ordinary staccato it remains on the string and is moved in rapid jerks.

Ridout, Alan (1934-) English composer who studied at the Royal College of Music and went on to become lecturer at Cambridge University (1937), and then professor at the Royal College of Music (1969). His work as a composer is closely linked with his residence in Canterbury and includes the opera *The Pardoners Tale*, based on Chaucer.

Riegger, Wallingford (1885-1961) American composer and conductor, who worked and studied in Germany, eventually settling in the United States, where he established his reputation with his first major work, a piano trio (1920). He wrote for Martha Graham's dance company and a number of scores for other American choreographers. Other works such as the *Study in Sonority* and *Music for Brass Choir* demonstrate the originality and importance of his compositions, which made a significant impression on his contemporaries although he achieved no real fame.

Ries, Ferdinand (1784-1838) German pianist, conductor and composer. He was the son of Franz Anton **Ries** and a pupil of **Beethoven** in Vienna (1801-1805), collaborating with Wegeler on one of the most important early biographies of Beethoven, *Biographical Notices of Beethoven* (1838). He toured Europe and Scandinavia as a pianist, and worked in London (1813-1824), retiring to Germany where he conducted eight Lower Rhine Fests (1825-1837). His compositions include three operas, 18 symphonies, nine piano concertos and other instrumental works.

Ries, Franz Anton (1755-1846) Violinist who was a member of the German family of musicians of the same name. He was able to take his father Johann's place in the orchestra at the age of 11 and went on to become leader of the electroal court orchestra. He was a friend and teacher of **Beethoven**.

Ries, Hubert (1802-1886) German violinist, the youngest son and pupil of Franz Anton **Ries**. His appointments included member of the court orchestra in Berlin and leader of the Berlin Philharmonia Society. Among other works, he published two violin concertos but is best known for his *Violin School for Beginners*, published in England (1873).

Rieti, Vittorio (1898-) Italian composer, who studied with **Casella** and **Respighi** among others. He lived in Paris from 1925, where he formed close ties with Les Six and was founder-director of the group *La Sérénade* dedicated to modern chamber music (1931-1940). He wrote a number of ballets for **Diaghilev**, later choreographed by Balanchine, the most successful of which being *Barabau*. He settled in the United States in 1939, where he taught at a number of American colleges.

riff Jazz term for a short written phrase or figure that is constantly repeated.

Rifkin, Joshua (1944-) American musicologist, pianist, conductor and composer

Joshua Rifkin

whose principal areas of research are Renaissance and Baroque music. As a pianist and conductor he has made several recordings, including most of the rags of Scott **Joplin**, and his compositions include chamber music and songs. He has also worked with **Stockhausen**.

rigaudon 17th-century French dance in duple time, probably originating in Provence or Languedoc.

Riley, Terry (Mitchell) (1935-) American composer and performer whose interest is in the quality of sound rather than thematic development using repetition of short phrases, sometimes freely combined by the performer with other repeated motifs, creating constantly changing relationships between the parts. He has frequently toured Europe performing his own works, such as *Mescalin Mix* and *Dorian Reeds*. Since 1970 Riley has devoted much of his time to Indian music.

Rimsky-Korsakov, Nikolai (Andreyevich) (1844-1908) Russian composer and conductor who in early life was consumed by his ambition as a naval officer, but was persuaded to pursue a career as a composer

Nikolai Rimsky-Korsakov

by **Balakirev**. While still ignorant of the basic rules of harmony and counterpoint he composed his Symphony No. 1 in E♭ minor, the first of real importance by a Russian composer. He also produced the opera *The Maid of Pskov* (1868-1872). On the strength of these compositions, he was appointed professor of the St Petersburg Conservatoire, and continued to teach himself in secret.

He was then appointed Inspector of Naval Bands (1873), a post created entirely for him, allowing him time to undertake his own education, producing a number of academic compositions including *Six Piano Fugues* (1875).

His compilation of two collections of Russian folk songs led him to a new and successful phase in composition, blending fantasy and the comic in the operas *May Night* (1870) and *Snow Maiden* (1882).

After the death of his friend **Mussorgsky** he devoted himself to setting the composer's works in order, including revisions to the operas *Prince Igor* and later *Boris Gudunov*, only interrupting this work to write two of his most colourful compositions, the *Spanish Caprice* (1887) and *Schéhérezade* (1888). In 1905, Rimsky-Korsakov came into conflict with the authorities because of his sympathy with revolutionary students, and he reflected these conflicts in his last satirical opera *The Golden Cockerel*.

Rimsky-Korsakov's compositions are distinguished by their rich orchestration and literary references. Many of them have become very popular, and have influenced such composers as his best-known pupil, **Stravinsky**.

rinf. Abbreviation of **rinforzando**.

rinforzando (It.) Reinforcing. Indication that a particular note or phrase is to be emphasized. It is often abbreviated to rinf. or rfz.

ring shout Afro-American call-and-response religious song and dance. A circle of people move in single file singing and stamping their feet in a repetitive fashion, the tempo gradually building up until participants are seemingly entranced or 'possessed by spirits'. The ring shout represented an attempt to provide an acceptable form of dance, an integral part of African worship, within a Christian context. It was prevalent in the United States from the 1860s.

ripieno (It.) Replenished. Term with two meanings.

First, in *concerti grossi*, it is the group of instrumentalists apart from the soloists (the *concertino*). An alternative term is *tutti*.

Second, it is a part that fills in or supplements another.

rit. Abbreviation of **ritardando**.

ritardando (It.) Slowing. Indication that the music is to decrease in tempo, often abbreviated to rit.

ritsu (Japan) One of the two basic **pentatonic** scales in Buddhist music theory and

gagaku court music. See **Japanese scales**.

Rochberg, George (1918-) American composer and critic, who studied at the Mannes School and Curtis Institute where he later taught. Influenced by **Schoenberg** and **Mahler**, he developed an individual form of **serialism** in works such as the String Quartet No. 2, later broadening his range to include tonal idioms, for instance in his *Contra Mortem et Tempus*. Several of his works contain Jewish references, including his choral psalm settings in Hebrew.

rock music Type of popular music that originated in the rock 'n' roll of the American 1950s. Rock covers many varieties and forms of vocal and sometimes purely instrumental music, usually played by bands of anything from two to twelve or more players. The minimum configuration usually consists of guitars and drums, but many bands also use brass, woodwind, piano and other instruments. Rock is normally divided into types, such as jazz-rock, funk-rock, heavy rock, etc.

rock 'n' roll Style of music that first appeared in the 1950s, probably originating in the twelve-bar blues of New Orleans jazz, and forming the beginning of pop music. Rock 'n' roll involved a vocalist and guitar (often electric guitar) and originally the term covered all styles of pop music. Early examples are Bill Haley's *Rock Around the Clock* (1955), and Elvis Presley's *Blue Suede Shoes* (1956). The term is now used to mean a specific form of popular music, with characteristic rhythms and sequences. Rock 'n' roll eventually gave birth to **rock music**, with all its sub-types.

rococo music Style of music of the early and mid-18th century that was characterized by a light and delicate elegance in the homophonic style. It is said to relate to a style of visual art that evolved in France at that time. Some of the music by **Couperin**, **Telemann**, J.C. **Bach** and **Mozart** was associated with this form.

Richard Rodgers

Rodgers, Richard (1902-1979) American composer whose partnership with lyric writers Lorenz Hart and Oscar **Hammerstein** II led to a series of stage musicals and songs which enjoyed unprecedented success. With Hart he had a number of Broadway hits including *Babes in Arms* (1937) and *Pal Joey* (1940) with songs such as *My Funny Valentine*, *The Lady is a Tramp* and *Bewitched, Bothered and Bewildered*, and by the time of Hart's death (1943), their collaboration had produced 30 stage musicals and a number of films and film versions of their stage shows. Rodgers continued his success with Hammerstein, with whom he wrote the "first American vernacular opera" *Oklahoma!* and had further successes with *South Pacific*, *The King and I* and *The Sound of Music*. He was made a member of the National Institute of Arts and Letters and was presented with numerous doctorates by American universities.

Rodrigo, Joaquin (1901-) Spanish composer who, blind from the age of 3, studied with **Dukas** and was much encouraged by **Falla**. He was appointed professor of music history at Madrid University. Rodrigo is best known for his works for guitar and orchestra, *Concierto de Aranjuez* and *Fantasia Para Un Gentilhombre*. Although sometimes regarded as a retrogressive figure, his compositions, which combine agreeable tunes with picturesque Spanish ambience and folklore, were immensely influential among contemporary Spanish composers.

Roger-Ducasse, Jean Jules Aimable (1873-1954) French composer who was a pupil of **Fauré**. He studied at the Paris Conservatoire, where he was later appointed professor of composition (1935-1940). His compositions include the mime drama *Orpheus*, a comic opera *Cantegril* and he completed and orchestrated **Debussy**'s *Rhapsody for Saxophone and Orchestra*.

Roger, Florimond French composer who wrote under the pen-name of **Hervé**.

Rogers, Bernard (1893-1968) American composer who studied at the New York Institute of Music Art and was a pupil of **Bloch**. He was chief critic of *Musical America* (1913-1924) and professor of composition at the Eastman School (1929-67). His compositions include the opera *The Warrior* (1944). His treatise *The Art of Orchestration* is a standard work.

Rogg, Lionel (1936-) Swiss organist who is best known for his recordings of **Bach**'s complete organ works on 18 records, laying the foundation for a career as an international recitalist who specializes in Bach. He was appointed professor at the Geneva Conservatoire in 1960.

Roldján, Amadeo (1900-1939) Cuban composer and conductor was much influenced by African music, making liberal use of Afro-Cuban rhythms and themes in his music. His works include the ballet *Rebamberamba*, the orchestration of which includes indigenous Cuban instruments, and *Overture on Cuban Themes*. He was conductor of the Havana Philharmonic Orchestra and professor at the Havana Conservatoire (1935).

roll Technique in percussion playing whereby an instrument (drums or cymblas) is struck by the two drumsticks in very rapid succession, to produce a virtually continuous sound. The technique is used in many ceremonial works, for example (usually) at the start of *God Save The Queen* and in Haydn's *Drum Roll Symphony*.

rol-mo (Tibet) Music, especially instrumental music, associated with Buddhist ritual. More specifically, it refers to the loud, large-bossed cymbals, also known as *sbub-chal*. With the frame drum (*rnga*), these punctuate the syllables of sung texts, whether measured or not. In unison measured hymns, the cymbals and drum function as time-beaters, whereas in unmeasured **dbyangs**, they merely mark time. In instrumental interludes, the cymbals also provide various rhythmic patterns, either solo or as part of the ensemble (which may include **rgya-gling**, **dung-chen**, trumpets made from shell or bone, bells and drums).

Roman, Johan Helmich (1694-1758) Swedish composer who acted as leader of the court orchestra in Stockholm, studying in London under **Pepusch** and Atioste from 1714 until his return to Stockholm in 1720, where he became *Kapellmeister* (1729). His works include a Swedish setting of the Mass and his most performed composition *Drottingholmsmusiquen*.

romance Term with only a vague meaning in music. It normally implies a short piece of emotional and quiet nature. The French equivalent (also spelled romance) sometimes means a short song for solo voice, and the term has also been used for the slow movement of some concertos. The Italian and German forms are *romanza* and *Romanze*, respectively.

Romantic music School of thought that arose in the 18th and 19th centuries, in parallel with movements of the same kinds in art and literature. It is said that the movement began with the work of **Weber**, and continued with such great composers as **Beethoven, Berlioz, Brahms, Liszt, Mendelssohn, Schubert** and **Schumann**.

To define Romanticism is difficult in any of the fields it affected, but it may be said that the most important change it brought about was the subordination of form to content. This gave rise to (among other things) pieces inspired by pictures, landscapes or literary themes (programme music). Needless to say, much Romantic music is highly emotional and at times intensely lyrical.

Romanticism has been continued into the 20th century by such composers as **Elgar, Mahler** and **Sibelius**.

Romberg, Sigmund (1887-1951) Hungarian born composer, who was best known as a writer of popular operettas such as *Maytime* (1917), *The Student Prince* (1924) and *Desert Song* (1926). Having studied in Vienna with Heuberger, he settled in the United States (1909), becoming an American citizen. In the 1930s he moved to Hollywood, where he wrote film scores.

rondeau (Fr.) Term with two meanings.

First, it is a 13th-century poetic and musical structure derived from the monophonic *trouve* form which had a recurrent **refrain** with the same words and music. In the 14th century **polyphonic** settings were made by **Machaut** in three parts for voice and two instruments.

Second, it is an alternative term for **rondo**.

rondo (It.) Composition in which one theme (known as the rondo theme) recurrs intermittently. A rondo normally appears in the form ABACADA, and sometimes makes up the final movement of a sonata or concerto. The other sections (B,C,D, known as episodes) are usually written to contrast with the theme, which may be varied each time it appears.

A simple rondo form combined with **sonata form** (known as sonata-rondo form) has a structure that can be expressed as ABACABA, where A and B represent the exposition and recapitulation, and the episode C, the development. An outstanding example of the rondo form is the **adagio** from **Beethoven**'s Piano Sonata No. 8, *Pathétique* (1799). Other works in rondo form include **Mendelssohn**'s *Rondo capiccioso in E for piano* (1837), and the tone poem *Till Eulenspiegel* (1895) by Richard **Strauss**.

root Lowest note of a triad or four-note chord in root position. When the chord is inverted, the note that was originally the root is still considered as such, although it is no longer at the bottom of the chord. See also **inversion; triad**.

Ropartz, Joseph Guy (Marie) (1864-1955) French composer who studied at the Paris Conservatoire with **Massenet** and also with **Franck**. He was director of the Nancy Conservatoire from 1894 to 1919, and then conductor of the Strasbourg orchestra until 1929. He is best known for his symphonies *Le Cloche des Morts* (1587) and *La Chasse du Prince Arthur* (1912), and the opera *Le Pays* (1910).

Rore, Cypriano de (1516-1565) Flemish composer, who is best known as a writer of Italian madrigals. A pupil of **Willaert** in Venice, he lived in Italy and held several church and court posts, succeeding Willaert as choirmaster of St Marks, Venice (1563). His compositions also include sacred music, such as *St John Passion* (1557).

Rorem, Ned (1932-) American composer who is best known as a writer of many songs, such as the song-cycles *Poems of Love*, *The Rain* (1963) and *Sun* (1967). He studied under such teachers as Dagenaar and **Honegger**, and was particularly influenced by **Poulenc**. He has also written the books *The Paris Diary of Ned Rorem* (1966) and *Critical Affairs, a Composer's Journal*.

Rosbaud, Hans (1895-1862) Austrian conductor and pianist who was a renowned interpreter and champion of 20th-century music, conducting first performances of **Bartók**'s Piano Concerto No. 2 and **Schoenberg**'s *Moses und Aron*. He held numerous conducting posts, including the Strasburg Opera (1941-1944), the Munich Philharmonic Orchestra (1945-1948), and chief conductor at the Aix-en-Provence Festival (1947-1959). He toured widely as a guest conductor in Europe, South America and Africa.

Rose, Leonard (1918-1984) American cellist who is known as a particularly fine player of the Romantic repertory, most of which he has recorded. He was principal cellist with the New York Philharmonic Orchestra from 1943 to 1951 and has toured widely as a soloist, including the London Festival Hall (1958). He taught at the Juilliard School from 1947 and at the Curtis Institute until 1962.

Rosen, Charles (1927-) American pianist who studied at the Juilliard School between the ages of 7 and 11 and has become a noted performer of the works of **Debussy**, **Beethoven** and, in particular, of **Bach**'s *Goldberg Variations*. He was professor of music at the State University of New York from 1971 and has written two books, *Classical Style* (1971) and *Schoenberg* (1975).

Rosenberg, Hilding (Constantin) (1892-) Swedish composer, pianist and conductor who is held by many to be a leading figure in 20th-century Swedish music. He spent a number of years writing incidental music for the theatre, the scores of which gave rise to several large-scale works, including the opera *The House with Two Doors* (1969). His other works include the opera *Journey to America* (1932) in which the celebrated *Railway Fugue* is to be found, a ballet *Orjheus in Towol* and a tetralogy of stage oratorios after Thomas Mann's *Joseph and His Bretheren*. He taught theory and piano in Stockholm (1916-1930) and was conductor of the Royal Swedish Opera (1932-1934).

Rosenmüller, Johann (1619-1684) German composer who taught in Venice for nearly 20 years. He wrote masses, other sacred music and suites of instrumental dances. Rosenmüller's music, much respected in Germany, was of particular importance in transmitting the Italian style of composition to the north.

Rosetti, Francesco Antonio (Franz Anton Rössler) (1746-1792) Prolific Bohemian composer who wrote mostly orchestral and chamber music. He held posts as conductor of the orchestra of Prince Ottingen-Wallerstein and later at the court of Ludwiglust. His contemporaries compared him with **Mozart** and **Haydn**, although his work is now largely forgotten.

rosin Preparation made of gum of turpentine rubbed onto the hair of the bows of stringed instruments to produce the required friction on the strings.

Rossellini, Renzo (1908-1982) Italian composer and critic, who composes in the 19th-century Italian tradition and is a noted opponent of innovation. He has written several film scores for his brother Roberto Rossellini and others, including *Rome, Open City* (1945). He has also composed operas, such as *Una Squardo dal Ponte* (1961) based on Arthur Miller's *A View From the Bridge*, and he has been director of Monte Carlo Opera since 1973.

Rosseter, Philip (1568-1623) English lutenist, composer and theatrical manager who was appointed to the court of James I. He was a composer of airs with lute and other accompaniment, published in the *Booke of Ayres* (1601), the first half of which is devoted to works by Thomas **Campion**. He also published *Lessons for Consort* (1609). He was the manager of a company of boy actors called *Children of the Revels*.

Rossi, Luigi (1598-1653) Italian singer, organist and composer, who was recognized as one of the leading musicians of his time.

His fame was largely due to his chamber cantatas, his major achievement. He also played a role in the development of opera, in that his opera *Orpheus* was the first Italian opera to be heard in Paris (1647).

Rossi, Salomone (1570–1630) Italian composer, who was important in the history of music for his pioneering of the trio-sonata and chamber duet. He was a colleague of **Monteverdi** at the court of Mantua, where he spent most of his working life (1587–1628). Among other works he wrote seven books of madrigals and Hebrew psalms.

Rossi-Lemini, Nicola (1920–) Italian bass singer, of mixed Italian and Russian parentage. He made his debut in Venice in *Boris Godunov* (1946) and has since sung regularly at La Scala, Milan, and in New York and London, specializing in Russian and modern opera. Rossi-Lemini sang in the first performance of **Pizzetti**'s *L'Assassino nella Cathedrale* (1958). He has also worked as an operatic stage director.

Rossini, Gioacchino Antonio (1792–1868) Italian composer, who is best known as the last and greatest composer of comic opera in the **buffo** style, but is historically more important as a composer of **opera seria**. Apprenticed as a child to a blacksmith, he sang in church choirs and by the age of 15 was playing harpsichord in theatres, entering Bologna Academy in 1806.

He was first commissioned in 1810 to write the comic opera *La Cambiale di Matrimonio* and in 1813 he established his reputation with two operas, *Tancredi*, an *opera-seria*, and *L'Italiana in Algeri*, an *opera buffa*. He was appointed musical director of both Neapolitan opera houses (1814), for which he wrote the operas *Otello*, representing a real development in Rossini's dramatic music, and perhaps his best known work *Il Barbiere di Siviglia*, which at first had a disastrous reception in Rome (1816). His last opera of the Italian cycle was *Semiramide* (1823), Rossini settling in Paris in 1824 as director of the Théâtre Italien, where he wrote three operas including *Guillaume Tell* (1829).

This marked the end of his career as a writer of opera and during the next 19 years which he spent back in Italy he wrote only three sacred works and some occasional pieces, partly due to poor health. He returned to Paris in 1855 where he remained the centre of artistic and intellectual life until his death, during which time he again began to compose, writing a number of pianoforte works, the *Petite Messe Solennelle* (1863) and ensembles which he called *Péchés de Vieillesse* (Sins of Old Age) (1857–1868), many of which were performed at Rossini's 'Samedi Soirs'.

Rostal, Max (1905–) Austrian violinist, teacher and composer, who is a noted exponent of contemporary music and is much sought after as a teacher. His teaching posts have included professor at Berlin State Academy (1927–1930), professor at Guildhall School of Music (1944–1958) and professor at Cologne State Academy and Berne Conservatoire from 1957. He settled in England in 1934, and was recognized as one of the leading violinists of his day. He was awarded the CBE in 1977.

Rostropovich, Mstislav Leopolovich (1927–) Soviet cellist, who is recognized as one of the greatest of the 20th century,

Mstislav Rostropovich

achieving international success, and for whom **Shostakovich, Britten** and **Prokofiev** have all written. Rostropovich completed Prokofiev's cello concerto after the composer's death. He has worked as a pianist, accompanying his wife, the soprano Galina Vishnevskaya, and also held posts as a conductor, including conductor of Moscow Bolshoi (1968) and the Washington National Symphony Orchestra (1977). He left the Soviet Union in 1974 and was deprived of Soviet citizenship in 1978. His compositions include piano concertos and a string quartet.

rota Occasional alternative for **round.**

Rothwell (Barbirolli), Evelyn (1911-) English oboist and teacher, who studied at the Royal College of Music. She has worked with a number of orchestras including the Scottish Orchestra (1937) and the London Symphony Orchestra (1935-1939), and has since performed as a soloist and recitalist. Several works by composers such as **Rubbra** and **Benjamin** have been dedicated to her, and in 1948 she gave the first performance in modern times of **Mozart**'s Oboe Concerto. She is author of several books, including *Oboe Technique* (1953), and from 1971 has been professor of oboe at the Royal Academy. She was awarded the OBE in 1984.

round Short canon for unaccompanied voices, in which the voices, entering in turn, all sing the same melody at the same **pitch** or an octave apart. *London's Burning*, a popular round dating from the 16th century, is an example.

Rousseau, Jean Jacques (1712-1778) Swiss philosopher, composer and writer on music, who was important for two of his poetical-musical creations, *Le Devin du Village* (1752) which anticipated French *opéra-comique*, and *Pygmalion* (1770), which inaugurated the genre of spoken drama with instrumental interjections known as melodrama. He also devised a new system of musical notation published in *Dissertation sur la Musique Moderne* which, however, proved inadequate. His extreme hostility to French music was demonstrated in his infamous *Lettre sur la Musique Française* (1753) taking the Italian side in the *Querelle des Bouffons*. In 1768 he published the *Dictionnaire de Musique*.

Roussel, Albert (1869-1937) French composer who is best known for his ballet *Bacchus et Ariane*. He began his career as a naval officer, serving in Indochina, resigning his commission to study music in 1894. He studied with **Gigout** and later **d'Indy** at the newly created Schola Cantorum, where he later became professor (1909-1914). Roussel was one of the few 20th-century composers able to create a highly personal and modern symphony idiom based on a traditional foundation, exemplified especially in works such as his third and fourth symphonies.

Royal Academy of Music College of music founded in London in 1822 by John Fane, Lord Burghesh, later 11th Earl of Westmorland. The academy was granted a royal charter in 1830, and it provides a wide range of courses for performers, composers, teachers and students and boasts many highly-respected past pupils and teachers.

Royal Albert Hall Concert hall built in London in 1871 on the site of part of the Great Exhibition. It is now used for many types of entertainment, from rock concerts and beauty contests to the Henry Wood Promenade Concerts that continue each night throughout the summer season. The hall is oval in shape and seats 10,000 people.

Royal College of Music British school of music established in 1873 as the National Training School of Music and reorganized under its present name in 1882, the date at which it received its Royal charter. The Royal College's directors have included **Parry** (1895-1918) and Grove (1883-1884) and it is renowned for its fine library and collections.

Royal Festival Hall

Royal Festival Hall Concert hall built in London in 1951 as a permanent monument to the Festival of Britain. The main hall is used for orchestral concerts, and the two adjoining halls (Queen Elizabeth Hall and the Purcell Room, both opened in 1967) are used for chamber music and recitals.

Royal Liverpool Philharmonic Orchestra British symphony orchestra founded in 1840 in association with the Liverpool Philharmonic Society. Its first conductor was J.Z. Hermann. Other conductors have included Alfred Mellon, Maz **Bruch**, Charles Hallé, Henry **Wood**, Thomas **Beecham**, Malcolm **Sargent**, Hugo Rignold, John **Pritchard**, Charles Groves, Walter **Weller** and David Atherton.

Royal Opera House Opera house in Covent Garden, London (sometimes referred to as Covent Garden), used mainly for opera and ballet. The first opera house on this site was opened in 1732, and the current building is the third.

Royal Philharmonic Society Society formed in London in 1813 by J.B. Cramer,

Royal Opera House

P.A. Corri and W. Dance, for the cultivation of good orchestral music. The inaugural concert was given at the Argyll Rooms, conducted by Muzio Clementi. Throughout its history the RPS has continued to promote concerts, engaging a variety of orchestras and conductors, and presenting new works to London audiences. The society has always been closely connected with **Beethoven** (on his deathbed the RPS sent him a cheque for £100). To commemorate his centenary they performed all his symphonies and had a special Gold Medal made. Among some of the winners of the medal were **Brahms**, **Sibelius**, **Rachmaninov**, **Stravinsky** and **Shostakovich**.

Rozhdestvensky, Gennady Nikolayevich (1931-) Soviet conductor who has toured the United States and worked in Europe, and among other appointments acted as principal conductor of the Bolshoi Theatre Moscow (1965-1967). He was also chief conductor of the Vienna Symphony Orchestra (1981-1983).

Rózsa, Miklos (1907-) Hungarian-born composer, best known for his scores for films such as *The Thief of Bagdad* (1940), *The Jungle Book* (1942), *Spell Bound* (1945), *Double Indemnity* (1944) and *Ben Hur* (1959). He studied at Leipzig Conservatoire (1925-1929) and Trinity College London (1930-34) emigrating to the United States in 1940, where he was composer for MGM (1948-1962).

rubato (It.) Robbed. Indication that the tempo of the music may be 'robbed' in order to add expression to a bar, or more likely, a phrase. This is done by interpreting liberally the tempo of the written notes, by a slight retardation or acceleration. A good performer is said to be able to return to the strict time of the piece by the time a rubato section ends.

Rubbra, Edmund (1901-) English composer and pianist who studied with **Holst**, **Vaughan Williams** and Morris, among others, and became a leading English exponent of the symphony, writing 11 symphonies in all. He worked as a teacher and music critic and wrote music for a travelling theatre company before recognition came with the performance of his first symphony (1935-1937). During World War II, he formed a piano trio, giving concerts to service men and women throughout Great Britain. He was lecturer in music at Oxford University (1947-1968) and professor of composition at the Guildhall from 1961. His prolific output as a composer covers music in all forms, including vocal and chamber music.

Rubinstein, Anton Gregorevich (1829-1894) Russian pianist and composer, who was one of the greatest pianists of the 19th century. He was also a prolific composer whose works are now largely forgotten, but who is remembered for the *Melody in F* for piano and the opera *The Demon* (1871). He studied under **Liszt** among others and toured as a soloist throughout Europe and the United States. He held the position of court pianist at St Petersburg and conductor of the Vienna Philharmonic Orchestra (1871-1872). He was founder of the St Petersburg Conservatoire (1862).

Rubinstein, Arthur (1887-1982) Polish pianist, who made his first appearance in Kódz at the age of seven, and is now recognized as one of the great players of the century. He studied in Berlin, where he was supervised by **Joachim**, making his debut in 1900. He made extensive overseas tours, making his London debut in 1912, visiting Spain and South America (1916-1917), where he achieved a life-long enthusiasm for the works of **Falla** and was said to have played in every country except Tibet.

He frequently played in the United States and he settled in Hollywood in 1939 and became an American citizen in 1946. He continued to play seemingly with undiminished power until his 90th birthday. The numerous honours bestowed on him include the KBE (1977) and the United States Medal of Freedom.

Ruckers Family Flemish family of harpsichord and virginal makers, whose instruments influenced the manufacture of stringed keyboard instruments throughout Western Europe. Over 100 Ruckers instruments still exist, their sound being much emulated by 20th-century harpsichord makers. The firm was founded in 1579 by Hans Ruckers (1550-1625), who was succeeded by his sons, Joannes (1578-1642), Andries (1579-1645), production continuing until 1667.

Ruggles, Carl Sprague (1867-1971) American composer and painter who as a youth earned his living playing in Boston theatre orchestras, going on to study at Harvard University with J.K. **Paine** among others (1903-1907). He wrote a few works, which he constantly revised, including *Evocations* for piano and an *Organum* for orchestra. In the last years of his life he devoted his creative energies to painting.

Ruhrtrommel (Ger.) German equivalent of **tenor drum**.

rumba Cuban dance of African origin in quick 2/4 time. It became popular in European and American ballrooms in the 1930s.

Russolo, Luigi (1885-1947) Italian composer who used a variety of sounds and materials in his compositions, and who in his futurist manifesto (1913), *L'arte dei Rumore*, included in the orchestra explosions, shrieks, screams and groans. He developed a number of instruments, including the Russolophone, for which he also invented **graphic notation**. His compositions include *Meeting of the Automobiles and Aeroplanes* and *Awakening of a City*.

RV Abbreviation for *Ryom Verzeichnis*, used as a prefix by Peter Ryom when compiling a catalogue (1974) of **Vivaldi**'s works.

ryo (Japan) One of the two basic **pentatonic** scales in Buddhist musical theory and **gagaku** court music. See **Japanese scales**.

Rysanek, Leonie (1926-) Austrian soprano, who is noted as a singer of Richard **Strauss** roles. She made her debut in Innsbruck (1949) and has since sung at Covent Garden (1953) and at the New York Metropolitan (1959). She has appeared regularly at the Bayreuth Festival since her debut there in 1951.

Rzewski, Frederik (1938-) American composer and pianist who studied at Harvard University, working as a professional pianist from 1960. He has taught courses in new music at Cologne and is co-founder of the music studio *Musica Elettronica Viva* in Rome. Influenced by **Cage** and **Stockhausen**, with whom he has worked, he has written compositions involving dancers, film and tape and has also explored collective improvisation.

S

Sabata, Victor de (1892-1967) Italian conductor and composer who studied in Milan with Saladino and Orefice. Between 1929 and 1953 he was at La Scala, first as conductor and then as musical and artistic director. He made appearances in the United States (1938), Bayreuth (1939) and London (1946). Sabata is especially associated with the operas of **Verdi** and **Wagner**, his interpretations of which have been compared to **Toscanini**'s. As a composer, his works include operas, symphonic poems and incidental music.

sacbut Alternative spelling of **sackbut**.

Sacchini, Antonio (Maria Gasparo) (1730-1786) Italian composer who, after early successes in Italy, went to London (1773-1782) where he produced 17 operas. In 1782 he settled in Paris where his work was influenced by **Gluck** and he became a rival to Piccinni with his comic and serious operas. His most notable success was the opera *Oedipe à Colonne* (1785). Altogether he wrote about 60 operas. His other works included string quartets, church music, symphonic poems, violin sonatas and songs.

Sacher, Paul (1906-) Swiss conductor who founded the Basle Chamber Orchestra in 1926, for which he commissioned works from many composers such as **Bartók**, Richard **Strauss**, **Hindemith**, **Stravinsky**, **Martinu**, **Honegger** and **Tippett**. Sacher also founded the distinguished chamber ensemble Schola Cantorum Basiliensis (1933).

sackbut Name given to the **trombone**. The sackbut differed from the modern trombone mainly in the fact that the bell of the latter has a slightly wider flare. The instrument was often associated with the *cornett*, being used in outdoor ceremonies such as those at St Mark's, Venice. In England, the King had "his majesties cornetts and sackbuts". Alternative spellings are sacbut, sagbut and sacquebot.

Sadie, Stanley (1930-) British musicologist, editor and critic who, after teaching at Trinity College of Music, London (1957-1965), became music critic to *The Times* (1964) and editor of *The Musical Times* (1967). Later (1970) he became editor of *The New Grove Dictionary of Music and Musicians*.

Sadler's Wells English theatre and opera house, situated in north London. The present theatre was opened in 1931, and was built by Lilian Bayliss to present opera, ballet and drama in conjunction with the Old Vic. It stands on the site of the theatre built in 1765 to replace gardens and a building (called the 'musicke house') erected in the 17th century by a Mr Sadler. The opera and ballet companies became Sadler's Wells Opera (renamed **English National Opera** in 1974) and Sadler's Wells Ballet (renamed Royal Ballet in 1956), but they are no longer resident in the theatre.

Saeverud, Harald (Sigurd Johan) (1897-) Norwegian conductor and composer who studied at Bergen and

Berlin. He wrote nine symphonies, including the *Minnesota Symphony*, concertos for piano, violin, oboe and cello, variations for chamber orchestra, and incidental music for Shakespeare's *Rape of Lucrece* and Ibsen's *Peer Gynt*.

sagbut Alternative spelling of **sackbut**.

saibara (Japan) Folk song form adapted for use as court music and accompanied by the **gagaku** ensemble.

Saint-Saëns, (Charles) Camille (1835-1921) French composer, conductor, organist and pianist. At the age of 10 he made his debut as a pianist, and in 1848 went to the Paris Conservatoire and entered Halévy's composition class in 1851. He was also a pupil of **Gounod**. In 1855, Saint-Saëns' first symphony was performed, and from 1857 until 1877 he was organist at the Madeleine, Paris. Between 1861 and 1865 he taught at the Ecole Niedermeyer, where his pupils included **Fauré** and **Messager**. Together with Romain Bussine he founded the Société Nationale de Musique in 1871. Saint-Saëns often performed in England, and in 1892 he received an honorary doctorate at Cambridge. He also made extensive tours of Europe, the United States, South America and the Far East.

He was a prolific composer, and among his works were 12 operas, including the biblical opera *Samson and Delilah* (which was prohibited on the French stage on account of its subject, but was produced at Weimar in 1877 and has remained in the repertory) and *Henry the Eighth* (1883). He was the first French composer to make use of the form of the tone poem, probably influenced by his friendship with **Liszt**. Works in this form include *Omphale's Spinning-wheel* (1871), *Phaeton* (1873) *Danse Macabre* (1874) and *La Jeunesse d'Hercule* (1877). His other compositions include five symphonies (No. 3 is with organ and two pianos and was dedicated to Liszt), five piano concertos, three violin concertos, two cello concertos, chamber, church and choral music. Although it was not performed during his lifetime, *Le Carnaval des Animaux* (1886), has become very popular and is often played by youth ensembles. After 1890 Saint-Saëns devoted less time to musical composition and turned his attention to writing plays and books of music criticism and essays.

Salieri, Antonio (1750-1825) Italian composer, conductor and teacher who lived mainly in Vienna where he was a pupil of Gassmann (1766), and later became court composer and conductor of the Italian opera (1774) and court *Kapellmeister* (1788). It was said that he intrigued against **Mozart**, but the suggestion that he poisoned him is probably false.

Salieri was conductor of the Tonkunster Society until 1818, and played the continuo in the first performance of **Haydn**'s *Creation* in 1798. Among his pupils were **Beethoven, Hummel, Liszt** and **Schubert**. He composed about 40 operas, including *Armida*, *Tarare, Falstaff* (after Shakespeare) and *Angiolina*. His other works include three symphonies, concertos, chamber music, sinfonias, masses, a Requiem, litanies and other church music.

Sallinen, Aulis (1935-) Finnish composer who studied at the Sibelius Academy, Helsinki (1955), and later (1965) became a member of the staff when he divided his time between teaching and composing. At one stage he was also manager of the Finnish Radio Symphony Orchestra. His works include four symphonies, two operas (*The Red Line*, 1978, and *The King Goes Forth to France*, 1983), four string quartets, a violin concerto (1968), a cello concerto (1976) and four choral pieces.

Salomon, Johann Peter (1745-1815) German composer, violinist, conductor and impresario. After studying at Bonn, he joined the electoral orchestra (1758), and in 1765 he became court musician at Rheinsberg to Prince Henry of Prussia. Having settled in London (1781), where he became a concert violinist and conductor, he organized concerts at the Hanover

Square Rooms during the two visits made by **Haydn** (1791-1792 and 1794-1795). As a result of these visits, Haydn dedicated 12 symphonies (Nos. 93-104) to Salomon, and these became known as the *Salomon Symphonies*. He also wrote four French operas and an English one (*Windsor Castle*, for the marriage of the Prince of Wales, 1795), symphonies, cazonets and chamber music. In 1813 he became a founder member and leader of the Philharmonic Society.

saltando (It.) Bowing technique whereby the bow rebounds on and off the string while continuing to move in the same direction.

saltarello (It.) Italian dance of the 16th century that involves a series of jumps. It is similar to the Neopolitan tarantella, and is usually in compound duple time.

Salzburg Festival Annual summer festival of music and drama founded in 1877 in Salzburg, Austria, the home town of **Mozart**. The Festival presents operas, concerts and recitals, with the works of Mozart and Richard **Strauss** filling most of the repertory. In 1949 the old riding school (*Felsenreitschule*) was used for opera for the first time, and in 1960 the new *Festspielhaus*, adjoining the old *Festspielhaus*, was opened with a performance of *Der Rosenkavalier*. Among the many famous conductors who have appeared at the summer Festival are **Böhm**, **Furtwängler**, **Krauss**, **Strauss** and **Toscanini**.

An Easter Festival, under the direction of Herbert von **Karajan**, was inaugurated in 1967.

Salzedo, Carlos (1885-1961) French-born American composer and harpist who studied at the Paris Conservatoire. He moved to the United States in 1909 at the invitation of **Toscanini** to become first harp at the Metropolitan Opera, New York. His interest in modern music is reflected in his compositions for the harp, which emphasize the instrument's potential in contemporary music. In collaboration with Edgard **Varèse**, he founded the International Composers' Guild in 1921. Salzedo's works include concertos, solos, duets, chamber music, sonatas, and songs with harp accompaniment.

Salzedo, Leonard (1921-) English composer and former pupil of Herbert Howells. He is best known for his ballet music, such as *The Fugitive* (1944) and *Witch Boy* (1956), although his other works include seven string quartets, two symphonies, a concerto for percussion (four players without orchestra) and film music.

Salzman, Eric (1933-) American writer and composer who was a pupil of **Sessions** and **Stockhausen**, among others. He is particularly known for the use of electronic music and his interest in multimedia theatrical works and environmental music. Some of his works include *Verses and Cantos* (1967), *The Nude Paper Sermon* (1968-1969), *The Conjurer* (1975) and *Noah* (1978).

sam (India) Principal beat (**mātrā**) of the rhythmic cycle (**tāla**); the point in time at which the rhythmic and melodic phrases coincide, indicated by a hand-clap on count one when beating time.

Saminsky, Lazare (1882-1959) Russian-born composer and conductor who now lives in the United States. He was a pupil of **Lyadov** and **Rimsky-Korsakov** at St Petersburg Conservatoire, and later became a director of the People's Conservatoire at Tiflis. Following a period in London, he went to the United States and later became naturalized. In 1924 he was one of the founder members of the League of Composers, and was also appointed director of the Jewish Temple of Emanu-El. Saminsky's works include the opera-ballets *The Vision of Ariel*, *Lament of Rachel* and *The Daughter of Jephtha*, the chamber opera *Gagliarda of the Merry Plague*, five symphonies, symphonic poems, and music for Jewish worship.

samisen See **shamisen**.

Sammartini, Giovanni Battista (*c*1700-1775) Italian composer who spent his whole life in Milan as a church musician where, from 1730, he became *maestro di cappella* at Milan cathedral and one of the founders of the Philharmonic Society (1728). **Gluck** was one of his pupils (1737-1741). During his musical career, he was Italy's most important symphonist and made a major contribution towards the founding of a modern style of instrumental music. He was much admired by **Mozart**, J.C. **Bach**, **Boccherini** and **Haydn**, who later took up the style created by Sammartini. He was a prolific composer whose output consisted of 77 symphonies (the earliest are similar in form to trio sonatas, with only three parts written out); two operas; two oratorios; three masses and other church music; six string quintets; 20 string quartets and almost 200 trios.

Sammartini, Giuseppe (1695-1750) Italian oboist and composer, brother of Giovanni. Before leaving Italy in 1728 for London, where he spent the rest of his life, he was an oboist of the Teatro Regio Ducal, Milan. He played in London with **Handel** and **Bononcini** from 1728, and between 1732 and 1744 was director of the Hickford's Room concerts with Arrigoni. He was also appointed director of chamber music to the Prince of Wales (1736).

Among his works was a setting of Congreve's masque *The Judgement of Paris*, 112 concerti grossi (1728-1747), the four *Giuseppe St Martinis Concertos* (1754), concertos for harpsichord and for violin, many sonatas for various instruments, and nine cantatas and other vocal pieces. Sammartini's works only became well-known after his death.

samvādī (India) Consonant tone of a **rāga** which acts as the complement of the sonant (**vādi**) and usually lies at an interval of a fourth or fifth above it.

Sandor, Gyorgy (1912-) Hungarian-born pianist who settled in the USA in 1939. He studied at the Budapest Conservatoire with **Bartók** and **Kodály**, and he is particularly noted for his performances and recordings of the works of both of these composers. In 1945 Sandor gave the first performance of Bartók's Piano Concerto No. 3.

san-hsien (China) Plucked stringed instrument with a hollow cylindrical body, both sides of which are covered with snakeskin. It has a long flat neck, no frets and three strings. It is played either with the fingernails or with a plectrum. The *san-hsien*'s Japanese relative is the **shamisen**.

sanjo (Korea) Solo instrumental genre of 19th-century origin, consisting of 3-6 movements based on folk tunes, which the soloist (usually a **kayagŭm** player) uses as a basis for improvisation. The accompanying **changgo** drum provides the rhythmic patterns which change between movements, becoming gradually faster and more complex. Various instrumental *sanjo* styles are maintained in traditional schools of playing.

sankyoku (Japan) Chamber music ensemble, literally 'music for three'. It consists of **koto**, **shamisen** and **shakuhachi**, the latter having replaced a bowed lute.

santoor (India) See **santur**.

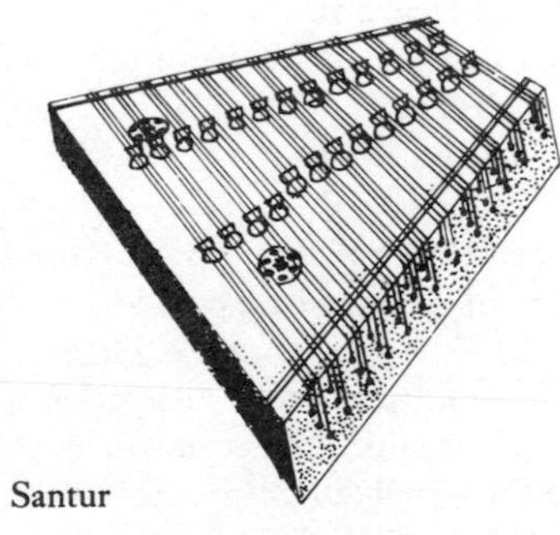

Santur

santur/santoor (India) Trapezoid board zither from Kashmir which has 25 quadruple courses of strings, played with two light wooden hammers. Used throughout northern India.

Sanz, Gaspar (1640-1710) Spanish composer and guitarist. Following graduation as a theology student, he studied music in Rome under various tutors, including Orazio **Benevoli**. He wrote several instructional pieces for the guitar and also a treatise.

sarabande 16th-century Spanish dance in a slow 3/2 time which became popular throughout Europe in the 17th and 18th centuries. There is a characteristic stop of rhythmic flow on the second beat of alternate bars.

sārangī (India) Bowed, fretless lute with a parchment belly and sympathetic strings, probably of central Asian origin. Its distinct vocal quality makes it ideal as an accompaniment to the voice in the classical genres of northern Indian music.

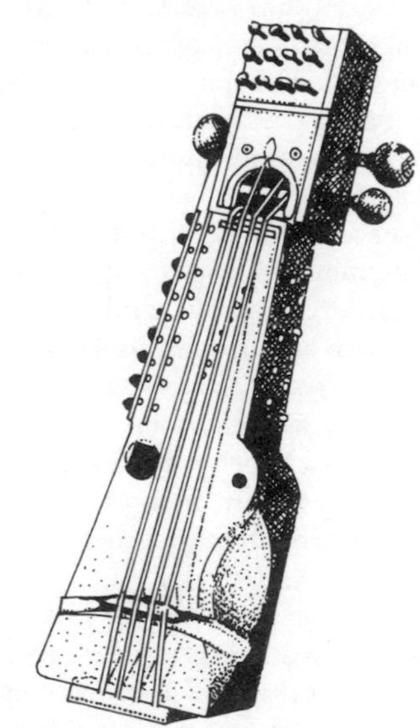

Sarangi

Sarasate (y Navascues), Pablo (Martín Meliton) (1844-1908) Spanish violinist and composer who was among the most famous virtuosi of his time. He gave his first public concert when he was eight years old, and in 1856 went to Paris to study at the conservatoire as a pupil of Alard. For the rest of his life he gave concert tours throughout Europe and the United States. He first appeared in London in 1861. Sarasate's compositions included *Zigeunerweisen*, an orchestral fantasy, four books of Spanish dances and many other pieces for violin.

sargam (India) System of *solfège* used to memorize or notate melodies. The name is taken from the first four mnemonics of the native scale, represented by the syllables Sa Re Ga Ma Pa Dha Ni. *Sargams* are also set compositions sung to these syllables, either as independent exercises or as passages in vocal improvisations. See also **khyāl**.

Sargent, Sir (Harold) Malcolm (Watts) (1895-1967) British conductor and organist. Following his studies at the Royal College of Organists, where he was awarded the Sawyer Prize (1910), he became assistant organist at Peterborough Cathedral. He made his debut at a Promenade Concert in 1921, where he conducted his own work *Impressions of a Windy Day*, which attracted the attention of Sir Henry

Sir Malcolm Sargent

Wood, who advised him to take up conducting as a career. He subsequently conducted the Royal Choral Society (from 1928), the Hallé Orchestra (1939-1942), the Liverpool Philharmonic Orchestra (1942-1947) and the BBC Symphony Orchestra (1950-1957). Sargent's impeccable appearance and his extraordinarily effective control of an orchestra attracted a wide and enthusiastic following, especially at the Henry Wood Promenade Concerts.

sarod (India) Plucked, fretless lute with a parchment belly and sympathetic strings, used throughout northern India, but probably of central Asian origin.

saron (Java) One-octave, bronze metallophone of the **gamelan** ensemble, with keys resting over a sound box. It is struck with a wooden or bone mallet and is found in three sizes, *panerus*, *barung* and *demung*. Together they play versions of the basic melody line.

sarrusophone Brass wind instrument with a double reed mouthpiece (a member of the **oboe** family), invented in 1856 by the Frenchman, Sarrus. Various sizes have been used by some continental military bands, but the double-bass sarrusophone was the only instrument of this type that had any success. Compositions that demand the use of the sarrusophone include Delius' *Dance Rhapsody No. 1* (1908) and Saint-Saëns' *Requiem* (1878).

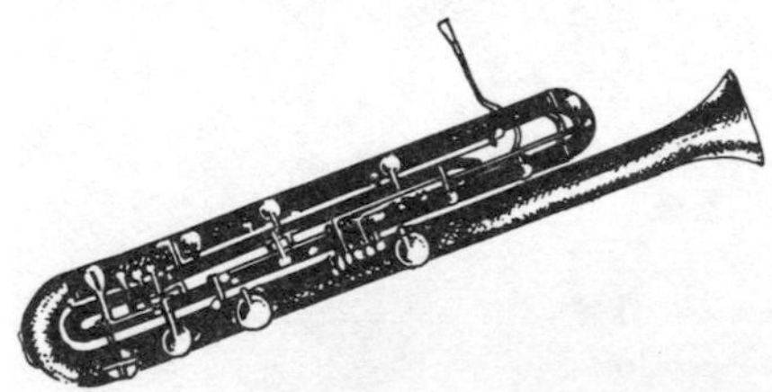

Sarrusophone

Sarti, Giuseppe (1729-1802) Italian conductor and composer who studied at Padua and Bologna. He became organist at Faenza Cathedral, Bologna (1748-1752). In 1753 he went to Copenhagen as director of the Mingotti opera company, and in 1755 was appointed court *Kapellmeister*, a position he held (apart from three years in Italy) until 1775. He acted as *maestro di cappella* at Milan Cathedral (1779), and in 1784 was made musical director to the Russian court in St Petersburg. While in Russia he collaborated with Empress Catherine II in one of the country's earliest operas, *The First Government of Oleg* (1790). Although Sarti wrote more than 70 operas, most of them are now forgotten, apart from a single air (*Fra due litiganti*) which **Mozart** used as part of the hero's supper-music in *Don Giovanni*. He also wrote church music and harpsichord sonatas.

Satie, Erik (Alfred Erik Leslie) (1866-1925) French composer whose parents were both musicians, although his rebellious approach to his musical education meant that he spent only a year at the Paris Conservatoire (to the surprise of his contemporaries). At the age of 40 he returned to study at the Schola Cantorum under **d'Indy** and **Roussel** (1905-1908). In the 1890s he made a precarious living playing at cafés and composing music for the Rosicrucian Society.

Satie had considerable influence upon Les **Six**, a group of French composers who were endeavouring to avoid elements of **Romanticism** and **Impressionism** in French music. Jean Cocteau was also associated with the same group, and it was through him that Satie's works were performed more widely. It also allowed him to collaborate with **Diaghilev** and Picasso in the ballet *Parade* (1917).

He was an eccentric composer who often dispensed with bar lines altogether, adopted a mocking satirical air and gave his compositions strange titles such as *Deux pièces froides* (1897), *Trois Morceaux en Forme de Poire* (1903) and *Choses vues à droite et à gauche (sans lunette)* (1912). Some of Satie's other works include a symphonic drama, *Socrates* (1918), for four sopranos and orchestra, many piano pieces and two further ballets, *Mercure* and *Relâche* (1924). Possibly his most famous work is the collection of *Trois Gymnopédies* (1888) for piano.

Erik Satie

sato-kagura (Japan) Shinto folk and festival music. *Kagura*, literally 'good music', is the generic term for all Shinto music. The repertory embraces both song and dance music and it is played by the folk **hayashi** ensemble, comprising three drums and flute. See also **mi-kagura**.

Satsuma-biwa (Japan) Type of **biwa** or lute.

satz (Ger.) Setting. In German, the term has several meanings.

First, it is a musical setting or composition (*Tonsatz*).

Second, it is a movement.

Third, it is a main theme (*Hauptsatz*).

Fourth, it is a secondary theme (*Nebensatz*).

Sauguet, Henri (Jean Pierre Poupard) (1901-) French composer and critic who studied the piano and organ at Bordeaux and was a pupil of **Canteloube** and **Koechlin**. His introduction by **Milhaud** to **Satie** led to the formation of the school at Arcueil in 1923. In 1936 he succeeded **Milhaud** as music critic to *Le Jour-Echo de Paris*. His works were mainly in a lighter vein and included the opera *Les Caprices de Marianne* (1954), the ballets *Les Forains* and *La Chatte* (1927), the song cycle *La Voyante*, three symphonies and two string quartets.

saung-gauk (Burma) Arched harp with 13, 14 or 16 strings stretched between a curved acacia root and a decorated bowl resonator. Of ancient origin, it may have been brought from Buddhist India by the Mon hill-tribe, who still play a five- to seven-stringed harp. The royal harp, however, formed the basis of Burmese music theory, and is associated with an extensive repertory of court songs. It is held in the player's lap, the right hand plucking the strings from the outside, leaving the left hand to add any embellishments by pulling on the strings at the arch. Usually accompanied by hand cymbals and clappers.

Sauret, Emile (1852-1920) French violinist and composer who was a pupil of **Bériot**. His career began at the age of 10, when he visited London. He played in the United States from 1872 as well as in Scandanavia and other European capitals. Sauret taught at the Royal Academy of Music in London (1891) when he succeeded Sainton as violin professor, and in 1903 he took up a similar post at Chicago. His works include two concertos, *Ballade* and *Legende*, and many pieces for the violin.

sausage bassoon Alternative term for **racket**.

sautillé (Fr.) Alternative term for **saltando**.

Savoy Operas Name for the operettas composed by **Sullivan** with librettos by W.S. Gilbert, and produced by Richard D'Oyly Carte at the Savoy Theatre, London. These operettas included *Iolanthe* (1882), *Princess Ida* (1884), *The Mikado*

(1885), *Ruddigore* (1887), *The Yeoman of the Guard* (1888) and *The Gondoliers* (1889).

Sawallisch, Wolfgang (1923-) German conductor who studied at the Munich Hochschule für Musik with Joseph Haas. He made his debut in Augsburg (1947) where he remained until 1953, when he became musical director at the opera in Aachen. From 1957 to 1959 he conducted at the Wiesbaden opera; from 1959 to 1963 in Cologne, and between 1957 and 1962 at the **Bayreuth** Festival. Since 1971 he has been music director of the Bavarian State Opera, Munich.

Sax, Adolphe (1814-1894) Belgian instrument maker who continued the business started by his father. He studied the flute and the clarinet at the Brussels Conservatoire before establishing himself in Paris (1842), where he made several improvements to wind instruments. His chief inventions were the **saxhorn** and the **saxophone**.

saxhorn Group of instruments of the brass family, invented by Adolphe **Sax** who patented them in 1845. They are made in seven different pitches, covering between them a range of some five octaves. They are: the soprano in E♭, alto in B♭ (both also called **flugelhorns**), tenor in E♭, baritone in B♭ (both also called althorns), bass in B♭ (**euphonium**), bass **tuba** in E♭ (**bombardon**) and contrabass in B♭.

saxophone Brass wind instrument, with woodwind characteristics, invented by Adolphe **Sax** in the 1840s. It is a cross between the **clarinet** and the **oboe**, having a single reed clarinet-type mouthpiece and a conical bore like the oboe.

There were originally 14 instruments in the family, but today they are limited to the following: soprano in E♭ (occasionally used in military bands); soprano in B♭ (sometimes used in jazz bands); alto in E♭; tenor in B♭; baritone in E♭ and contrabass in B♭, which is rarely used.

saz (Persia) General term for a stringed instrument, covering various types of plucked lute in Iran, Turkey, Armenia, Azerbaijan, Albania, Greece and Yugoslavia. The *saz* appears in different sizes and tuning, but all have a pear-shaped, wooden resonator and usually eight to ten strings (including drones) in two or three courses.

scale Stepwise succession, ascending or descending, of notes within an octave. See also **chromatic; diatonic; major scale; minor scale; mode; pentatonic; temperament; twelve-note; whole-tone**.

Scarlatti, Alessandro (1660-1725) Italian composer who, upon the success of his first opera, *Gli equivoci ne sembiante* (1679), was appointed *maestro di cappella* to Queen Christina of Sweden. He moved to Naples as conductor of the San Bartolomeo opera (1683-1684), and *maestro di cappella* to the court (1684) where he remained for nearly 20 years, although in 1702 he went to Florence with his son, Domenico, to enjoy the patronage of the Medicis.

For two years he was *maestro di cappella* at Santa Maria Maggiore, Rome, before

Saxophone

finally returing to his old position in Rome in 1709.

Alessandro Scarlatti is considered to be one of the founders of the Neopolitan school of opera, and formulated some of its notable characteristics, such the da capo aria which was to dominate opera for two centuries. In addition, he was one of the last composers to write chamber cantatas, but one of the first to write a string quartet in its modern form. Probably his greatest work was for Ferdinand de' Medici, *Mitridate Eupatore* (1707), which is considered a great Classical document. Altogether Scarlatti wrote 115 operas – many of which are now lost – about 600 chamber cantatas for solo voice and continuo, 200 masses and 14 oratorios.

Scarlatti, (Giuseppe) Domenico (1685-1757) Italian composer, harpsichordist and organist. After studying with his father Alessandro, he was appointed organist and composer to the court in Naples (1701) where he composed his first two operas, *Ottavia ristituita al trono* and *Giustina* (1703). He travelled widely, visiting Florence, Venice (1708) and Rome, where it is said that he engaged with **Handel** in a contest in harpsichord and organ playing. While in Rome (1709-1714) he became *maestro di cappella* to the exiled Queen of Poland, and of the Cappella Giulia (1714-1719). In about 1720 he became *maestro* to the royal court in Lisbon, returning to Italy in 1724 before moving to Madrid in 1729 where he spent his remaining years in the service of the Spanish court.

Domenico Scarlatti was the greatest Italian composer for harpsichord of his age. He wrote more than 550 sonatas, mostly in one movement in binary form, of which the first pieces were published in the *Essercizi per gravicembalo* (1738). They have been catalogued by Ralph Kirkpatrick. Scarlatti's other works include 12 operas, cantatas and church music, including a Stabat Mater. His sonatas were important influences on **sonata form** and considerably expanded the virtuosity of the keyboard instrument, using cross-handed techniques and *acciaccature* (a technique in which chords are sounded with extra dissonances, immediately released).

scat singing Vocal style adopted by jazz singers in which syllabic sounds are used instead of words.

scena Extract from an opera used in a concert performance during the 18th century. In the 19th century it developed into a concert work for solo voices on a large scale, usually a **recitative** followed by **arias** with orchestral accompaniment.

Schaeffer, Pierre (1910-) French composer and writer who trained as a radio technician, and in 1948 became associated with Pierre **Henry** (1927-). Together they pioneered the concept of musique concrète. Their first major work in this medium was *Symphonie Pour un Homme Seul* (1950), and in 1951 they founded the *Groupe de Musique Concrète* studio. The experimental opera *Orphée* was produced by Shaeffer in 1953.

Schafer, R. Murray (1933-) Canadian composer who was a pupil of Weinzweig, Guemerov and **Fricker**, and resident composer at the Simon Fraser University, Vancouver. He is an active promoter of modern music, and his interest in mixed media and ecology led him to initiate the World Soundscape Project to fight noise pollution. Among his works are *Loving/Toi* (1965), *Requiem for a Party Girl* (1972), *East* (1973), *North/White* (1973), *Waves* (1976), and *Apocalypsis* (1976, for 500 performers).

Scheidemann, Heinrich (*c*1595-1663) German composer, organist and teacher who was pupil of his father and later of **Sweelinck**. He succeeded his father as organist at St Catherine's Church, Hamburg, in 1625 until his death from the plague when he was succeeded by **Reinken**, one of his pupils. Scheidemann, as leading composer of the north German school of organists, produced many fine works, especially his chorale arrangements, and he also contributed to Part V of **Rist**'s hymn-book *Neue himmilische Lieder* (1651). Some of his other works include Magnificat settings, chorale fantasias and the Toccata in G.

Scheidt, Samuel (1587-1654) German organist and composer who studied with **Sweelinck** in Amsterdam. In 1609 he became court organist at Halle to the Margrave of Brandenburg, and *Kappellmeister* in 1619, a position he lost in 1625 as a result of the Thirty Years War, but was resumed in 1638. Scheidt was a prolific composer whose works included madrigals, motets and organ music. His most notable work was *Tabulatura Nova* (1624).

Schein, Johann Herman (1568-1630) German composer who became a choirboy in the court chapel at Dresden (1599), and later studied at Leipzig University (1607). In 1615 he was appointed *Kappellmeister* at the court of Weimar and in 1616 became cantor at St Thomas's School, Leipzig, where he remained until his death.

He composed mainly vocal music such as *Fontana d'Israel* (1623), which contains biblical words set for 4-5 voices and instruments, *Cantional* (1627), an important collection of Lutheran hymns with a figured bass part, instrumental dances and wedding and funeral cantatas.

Schenker, Heinrich (1867-1935) Austrian musical theorist and writer who studied with **Bruckner** at the Vienna Conservatoire. As a writer, he wrote several books, including *Neue musikalische, Theorien und Phantasien* and *Das Meisterwerk in der Musik*, in which he analyses works composed in the period from **Bach** to **Brahms**. His most influential work is *Der freie Satz*, containing graphic analyses which have been highly important to the analysis of subsequent theorists.

scherzando (It.) Direction to indicate a light-hearted manner of performance.

scherzo (It.) Joke. One of the two middle movements, more usually the third, of a four-movement **symphony, sonata** or other **sonata-form** work, in which it displaced the **minuet**. It is a movement of a vigorous and bustling nature (3/4 time) and was first fully characterized by **Beethoven**, closely followed by **Schubert** and **Bruckner**. Composers do not always conform to the Classical form of the scherzo, such as the piano pieces composed by **Brahms** and **Chopin**, which express drama, intensity and lyricism, as well as humour.

Schibler, Armin (1920-) Swiss composer who studied at Zurich Conservatoire, and in 1942 he became a pupil of **Burkhard**. Among his compositions are three operas (*The Spanish Rose-tree, The Devil in the Winter Palace* and *The Feet in the Fire*); an oratorio (*Media in Vita*); three symphonies; violin, piano, trombone and horn concertos; and string quartets.

Schikaneder, (Johann Josef) Emanuel (1751-1812) German actor, singer, playwright and theatre manager. He wrote the libretto for **Mozart**'s *The Magic Flute* (1791), which he also produced and performed in as Papageno.

Schipa, Tito (1889-1965) Italian tenor who began his career as a composer of piano pieces and songs, but later studied singing with Piccoli in Milan.

He made his debut as a tenor in Vercelli (1912). Between 1920 and 1932 he was a member of the Chicago Civic Opera, and from 1932 and 1935 and in 1940-1941 he sang at the New York Metropolitan. Returning to Italy, he continued to appear at La Scala, Rome and other places until 1950 and later in the Italian provinces, but he never appeared in England.

Schippers, Thomas (1930-1977) American conductor who first appeared in public playing the piano at the age of six, and became a church organist when only 14. He studied at the Curtis Institute, Philadelphia, and with Olga Samaroff. In 1948 he made his debut with the Lemonade Opera Company, and after appearances with the New York City Opera Company and the New York Philharmonic Orchestra he appeared at the New York Metropolitan and La Scala in 1955.

At the opening of the new Metropolitan at the Lincoln Center in 1966, Schippers conducted the premiere of **Barber**'s *Antony and Cleopatra*. Other appearances have been at La Scala, Milan (1967), Bayreuth (1963) and Covent Garden, London (1968). Between 1970 and 1977 he was conductor of the Cincinnati Symphony Orchestra.

schleppend (Ger.) Direction that the pace of the music should not be allowed to drag.

Schlick, Arnolt (*c*1460-*c*1521) German organist, composer and theorist. Having travelled widely from his home in Heidelberg, he went to Frankfurt in 1486 where he was organist for the coronation of Maximilian I. Further travels took him to Holland, Strasburg, Worms and in 1511 he became a member of the Heidelberg court chapel. During this time he gained a reputation for testing new organs, and in 1511 he published a treatise on organ-building and playing entitled *Spiegel der Orgelmacher und Organstein*. Schlick's works include sacred organ music and pieces for lute. He also wrote the music for the coronation of Charles V in Aachen (1520).

Schmelzer, Johann Heinrich (*c*1623-1680) Austrian composer and violinist. Little is known about his early life, although it is known that he was a chamber musician at the Austrian court in Vienna from 1649, assistant conductor from 1671 and first conductor from 1679 until his death from the plague the following year.

His works include ballet music, church music, trumpet fanfares, trio sonatas and *Sonatae Unarium Fidium* (1664) for violin and continuo.

Schmidt, Franz (1874-1939) Austrian cellist, pianist and composer who studied at the Vienna Conservatoire, and in 1896 became cellist in the Court Opera orchestra. His distinguished teaching career began when he taught the cello at the Conservatoire from 1901 to 1908. In 1922 he was appointed professor at the Vienna Staatsakademie, a director from 1925 to 1927, and director of the Musikhochschule from 1927 to 1931. His works include four symphonies, two operas (*Notre Dame*, 1902-1904 and *Fredigundis*, 1916-1921), chamber and organ music.

Schmidt-Isserstedt, Hans (1900-1973) German conductor who studied with **Schreker** and at the University of Cologne, where he graduated in 1923. He began his career at the Wuppertal opera, and from 1928 to 1931 conducted at Rostock. He appeared as principal conductor at the Hamburg State Opera (1935-1942) and then director of the German Opera in Berlin (1942-1945).

Schmidt-Isserstedt also founded and directed the Northern German Radio Symphony Orchestra (1945-1971).

Schmitt, Florent (1870-1958) French composer who began his studies in Nancy before going to the Paris Conservatoire, where he was a pupil of **Dubois**, Lavignac, **Massenet** and **Fauré**. At his fifth attempt he won the Prix de Rome (1900). He became director of the Lyons Conservatoire (1922-1924) and music critic of *Le Temps* (1929-1939). Among his works were two symphonies, three ballets, including *La Tragédie de Salomé* (1907), orchestral and chamber music and piano pieces.

Schnabel, Artur (1882-1951) Austrian pianist and composer who studied with Essipova and Leschetizky, and with Mandyczewski in Vienna. He appeared in many solo recitals and also accompanied artists such as **Casals, Szigeti** and **Primrose**. He was considered a thoughtful interpreter, especially in his playing of **Beethoven, Schubert** and **Brahms**. His compositions include orchestral and chamber music, one piano concerto and other piano pieces.

Schnebel, Dieter (1930-) German composer whose compositions reflect his tendency to experiment with new choral techniques, variable form and aleatoric music. Examples of his methods include *Nostalgia*, which is for conductor alone, *Drei Klang* (1977), for three simultaneously-broadcast ensembles, and his symphonic improvisations, *Thanatos-Eros* (1979).

Schnittke, Alfred (1934-) Soviet composer who studied at the Moscow Conservatoire until 1958, and then joined the staff there to teach instrumentation and composition. He later resigned his post to devote time to composing. He has experimented with serial procedures and unusual instrumental textures, which in some instances involved electronic music. Among his works are two symphonies, three violin concertos, *Dialog* for cello and seven instruments (1965), *Pianissimo* for large orchestra (1968), *Passacaglia* for orchestra (1979-1980), *Two Little Pieces for Organ* (1981) and *Schall und Hall* for trombone and organ (1983).

Schobert, Johann (*c*1735-1767) German composer and harpsichordist who lived in Paris, where he was in the service of the Prince of Conti from about 1720. As a result of his development of keyboard technique, he greatly influenced some of **Mozart**'s early piano sonatas and concertos, and Mozart also used one of Schobert's sonata movements as the second movement of his Piano Concerto (K39, 1767). Apart from keyboard music, Schobert also composed chamber works, concertos, sinfonias and comic operas.

Schoenberg, Arnold (1874-1951) Austrian composer who started his working life in a bank before becoming a chorus-master in 1895. The only formal music training he received was from his friend **Zemlinsky**, who introduced him to the music of **Wagner**, which had a profound effect upon the young Schoenberg. Towards the end of the 19th century he earned his living by conducting theatre orchestras, and in 1901, with the help of Richard **Strauss**, he obtained the Liszt Scholarship. He taught for a brief period at Stern's Conservatoire, Berlin, and in 1903 went to Vienna where two of his many pupils were **Webern** and **Berg**. In 1911 he returned to Berlin and, after serving in World War I, began his most successful period as a composer. His teaching continued at the Prussian Academy of Arts, Berlin, until 1933, when he found life under the Nazi regime intolerable and moved to the United States, where he became an American citizen in 1940.

In the early 1920s, Schoenberg formulated what became known as **twelve-note composition**, which was basically a return to **polyphony** and was described by him as a 'higher and better order'. His works from 1921 to 1933 especially exemplified this style, although some of his later works written in the United States show a tendency to return to a more traditional handling of form and tonality.

Among Schoenberg's works are *Erwartung*, a monodrama for soporano and orchestra (1909); the operas *Die Gluckliche Hand* (1910-1913) and *Von Heute auf Morgen* (1929); *Pelleas und Mélisande*, suite for orchestra (1903); *Gurrelieder*, for chorus, soloists and orchestra (1900-1913); *Pierrot Lunaire*, song-cycle of 21 poems (1912); *Ode to Napoleon*, for speaker, strings and piano (1943); concertos for violin and piano; four string quartets and a string sextet, *Verklärte Nacht* (1899). He also wrote several influential theoretical works, including *Counterpoint* (1911) and *Structural Functions of Harmony* (1954).

Schonbach, Dieter (1931-) German composer whose music often includes visual aspects, such as film and dance. Apart from the conventional orchestral and chamber music, his output also includes numerous multimedia works.

schottische Ballroom dance in 2/4 time,

fashionable during the 19th century, similar to but slower than the **polka**. It is not to be confused with the écossaise.

Schrecker, Franz (1878-1934) Austrian composer and conductor who studied with Fuchs and Gardener in Vienna, where he founded the Philharmonic Choir (1911). He was director of the Berlin Hochschule für Musik (1920-1932) until the Nazis dismissed him from his position. His first serious opera, *Der Ferne Klang* (1901-1910), made a powerful impression on his contemporaries, although two subsequent operas, *Die Gezeichneten* (1918) and *Der Schatzgraber* (1920), received wider acclaim. Among his other works were a ballet, *Rokoko* (1908), *Chamber Symphony* (1916) and songs.

Schreier, Peter (1935-) German tenor and conductor who studied with Polster in Leipzig and with Winkler in Dresden. He made his debut in Dresden (1959) as the First Prisoner in **Beethoven**'s *Fidelio*. Since then he has appeared in Berlin, New York, Vienna, Salzburg, London and Hamburg. Apart from being a gifted singer and actor, he is also considered an outstanding **Mozart** singer and has been compared with **Tauber** and Wunderlich.

Schubert, Franz (Peter) (1797-1828) Austrian composer who was taught the violin by his father and the piano by his eldest brother. He had a few lessons in counterpoint from his choirmaster Michael Holzer, and when aged 11 he was admitted to the Imperial Choristers' School, Vienna, where he attracted the attention of **Salieri**. Leaving school in 1814, Schubert joined his father's school as an assistant master, but he had no enthusiasm for teaching and left his post after four years at the suggestion of his friend Michael Vogl, the singer. Apart from two visits to Hungary in 1818 and 1824, where he acted as a domestic musician to the Esterházy family, Schubert spent all his life in Vienna.

In 1814 he wrote his first great song, *Gretchen am Spinnrade*, and completed his first opera, *Des Teufels Lustschloss*. He always wanted to compose a successful opera, and continued to compose in this form throughout his life, but the nine he wrote were not popular and some not even performed. He made one public concert appearance (1828) which was sufficiently successful for him to buy his own piano. Sadly he gained no financial success in his lifetime from the nine symphonies, chamber music, numerous piano sonatas and duets, and the songs (nearly 600) that he composed. He was inventor of the *Lied* which forms part of his famous song-cycles such as *Die Schöne Mullerin* (1823), *Die Winterreise* (1827) and *Schwanengesang* (1828). Among his symphonies, No. 8 in B minor, *Unfinished* (1822), and No. 9 in C major, *The Great* (1828), are considered two of the greatest symphonies of all time, although neither was performed during his lifetime. He wrote a great deal of music for solo piano, as well as piano duets. Impromptus and *moments musicaux* feature among the shorter pieces but there are also sonatas. In particular his last sonata, No. 21 in B♭, is considered his greatest, although No. 18 in G major and No. 20 in A major are also outstanding pieces.

Schüller, Gunther (1925-) American composer, horn player and conductor who studied at St Thomas' Choir School (1938-1942), and taught at the Manhattan School of Music (1950-1962), Yale School of Music (1964-1967) and the New England Conservatoire, of which he was president from 1967 to 1977. In the 1950s he played with Miles Davis and in 1957 he coined the phrase 'third stream', a form of music that incorporates the virtues of both jazz and classical styles. His works include a *Horn Concerto* (1944), *Symphonic Tribute to Duke Ellington* (1955), the opera *The Visitation* (1966), a double-bass concerto (1968), *The Five Senses*, a television ballet (1967), a violin concerto (1976), various orchestral pieces, and film music.

Schuman, William (1910-) American composer who studied at Columbia

University and at the Mozarteum, Salzburg. He was director of the Juilliard School of Music, New York (1945-1961), and holds honorary doctrates from 20 American colleges and universities. Schuman's interest in early American music and themes is reflected in his romantic, rhapsodic style. His works include ten symphonies (composed 1936-1976), concertos, string quartets, a ballet, *Undertow* (1945), an opera, *Mighty Casey* (1953), a fantasy entitled *Song of Orpheus* (1962), and *To Thy Love*, a choral fantasy (1973).

Schumann, Clara (1819-1896) German pianist and composer who was taught by her father, Friedrich Wieck. She made her first public appearance at the age of nine, and gave her first concert just before her 11th birthday at the Leipzig Gewandhaus. Her marriage in 1840 to Robert **Schumann** was violently opposed by her father. After her husband's death (1856), she lived in Berlin and Baden-Baden until her appointment (1878) as chief piano professor at the Hoch Conservatoire, Frankfurt. Her works include a Piano Concerto in A minor, a Piano Trio in G minor, Variations on a theme by Robert Schumann, other piano pieces, and several sets of songs. She was internationally noted as a perfomer and made many visits to England.

Schumann, Elizabeth (1888-1952) German soprano who studied in Berlin, Dresden and Hamburg where she made her stage debut in 1909, remaining with the opera there until she joined the Vienna Opera (1919-1937). She made her first appearance in the United States in 1921 and at Covent Garden, London in 1924. In 1938 she settled in the United States where she taught at the Curtis Institute, Philadelphia, and became an American citizen in 1944.

She possessed a voice of superb clarity and her performances of works by **Mozart** and **Strauss** were considered incomparable.

Schumann, Robert (Alexander) (1810-1856) German pianist and composer who began to learn the piano at the age of eight. In 1828 he studied law at Leipzig University, where he met Wieck from whom he took piano lessons (1830), having neglected his legal studies.

In 1832 Schumann permanently injured his right hand, so he gave up a career as a pianist and devoted his time to composing. In 1840 he married Clara Wieck (see **Schumann, Clara**) and she encouraged him to write symphonies and chamber works in addition to songs and piano pieces. He suffered a mental breakdown in 1844, and at the end of the year the Schumanns settled in Dresden. In 1850 he accepted the post of director of music in Dusseldorf, but was forced to resign in 1853 because his mental health was declining rapidly. An attempted suicide by drowning in the Rhine led him to go voluntarily to an asylum at Endenich, where he died in 1856. Schumann is especially known for his songs and piano compositions, such as the *Abegg Variations* (1830), *Papillons* (1829-1831), *Paganini Studies* (1832-1833), *Phantasie in C major* (1836), *Kriesleriana* (dedicated to **Chopin**, 1838), and *Kinderscenen* (1838).

Elizabeth Schumann

He also wrote four symphonies: No. 1, in B♭ major – *Spring* – (1841), No. 2 in C major (1846), No. 3 in E♭ major – *Rhenish* – (1850), and No. 4 in D minor (1841, rewritten in 1851). His other works include the opera *Genoveva* (1847-1850), string quartets, violin sonatas, and several choral works, including *Paradise and the Peri* (1843) and *Scenes from Goethe's Faust* (144-1853). In 1834 he was founder of *Die Neue Zeitschrift für Musik* which he edited for ten years.

Schurmann, Gerard (1928-) Dutch composer, born in Indonesia and now resident in England. He was a pupil of **Rawsthorne**. Although his compositions are not quite serial, they show a high degree of large-scale integration with much use of repetition. His works include the song-cycle *Chuench 1* (1966), *Variants* (1970), a piano concerto (1973), a violin concerto (1978), the cantata *Double Heart* (1977) and the opera-cantata *Piers Plowman* (1980).

Schutz, Heinrich (1585-1672) German composer who started his career studying law at Marburg University, but then went to Venice (1609-1612) where he studied music under Giovanni **Gabrieli**. Returning to Cassel as court organist, he left for Dresden in 1614 where he was appointed *Kappelmeister* to the Elector of Saxony. Apart from further visits to Venice and also a period in Copenhagen (1633-1641), he spent the rest of his life in Dresden.

It is said that Schutz was the greatest German composer before J.S. **Bach**, and has been described as the "Father of German Music". Influenced by the works of Gabrieli, and to a certain extent by those of **Monteverdi**, he was able with his later compositions to strike the perfect balance between Italian and German styles. Such an achievement made a very significant contribution to the development of the **oratorio**. His Four Passions (*Matthew, Mark, Luke* and *John* – 1665-1666), reveal very little use of chorale melodies. His only opera, *Dafne* (1627), is lost but it is held to have been the first German opera ever written. Some of his other works include *Psalmen Davids* for two, three or four choirs of voices and instruments (1619), *Resurrection Oratorio* (1623), *Symphoniae sacrae* (Parts I, II & II, 1629, 1647, 1650), a ballet, *Orpheus and Euridice* (1638), *The Seven Words from the Cross*, choral (1645) and *Deutsches Magnificat* (1671).

Schwarz, Rudolf (1905-) Austrian conductor who studied the violin and piano, playing the viola in the Vienna Philharmonic Orchestra. In 1923 he became an assistant conductor at the Dusseldorf Opera, and later (1927-1933) conductor at the Carlsruhe Opera. He then became musical director of the Jewish Cultural Union in Berlin until 1941, when he was sent to Belsen concentration camp. As a survivor, he came to England through Sweden and in 1947 became musical director of the Bournemouth Symphony Orchestra, and later directed the City of Birmingham Symphony Orchestra (1951-1957), the BBC Symphony Orchestra (1957-1962) and the Northern Sinfonia (1964-1973).

Schwarzkopf, Elizabeth (1915-) German soprano who studied with Lula Mysz-Gmeiner and Maria Ivogun. She made her

Elisabeth Schwarzkopf

debut at the Berlin State Opera (1938) where she soon established herself as a brilliant soprano in the opera *Ariadne auf Naxos* by Richard **Strauss**. In 1943 she joined the Vienna State Opera and moved from there in 1950 to La Scala in Milan. Previously she had appeared in England at Covent Garden for the 1947-1948 season, where she confirmed her position as one of the leading sopranos of her generation. She created the role of Anne Truelove in **Stravinsky**'s *The Rake's Progress*, and is equally famous as a *Lieder* singer.

Schweitzer, Albert (1875-1965) Alsatian theologian, medical missionary, organist and musical scholar. He studied the organ at Strasbourg and with **Widor** in Paris. He became an authority on **Bach**, writing a biography which was published in France (1905) and an enlarged version in Germany (1908). Most of his life after leaving his post as principal of the theological college in Strasbourg was spent in Africa as a medical missionary. He visited Europe periodically to give organ recitals of Bach's works, and in 1952 was awarded the Nobel Peace Prize.

scoop Fault in singing in which a note is approached from below its true pitch instead of being attacked cleanly.

scordatura Tuning of a stringed instrument to notes other than those to which they are customarily tuned. This may be done to facilitate the playing of chords, to change the tone quality or to alter the instrument's range. An example of scordatura is in Mozart's Sinfonia Concertante in E♭ for violin and viola (K364), in which the viola is tuned in fifths from C♯ sharp instead of the usual C.

score Copy of any musical composition written in several parts on separate staves, with the coincident notes appearing vertically over each other. Players in orchestras or other ensembles normally read from music giving only their own parts, whereas the conductor has a full score showing all the parts combined. The usual layout of orchestral scores is to show the woodwind at the top, brass in the middle, and strings at the bottom. Harps and percussion are placed between brass and strings.

On a vocal score, the voice parts for operas and operettas are usually given with piano accompaniment.

On a piano score, the orchestral and vocal parts are reduced to a simple piano transcription.

Short scores are composers' sketches reduced to a few staves, to be elaborated and fully written out later.

Scotch snap Technical name for rhythmic figures inverting the order of dotted notes, the short note coming first instead of last. It is found in many Scottish songs, such as *Coming through the Rye*, and in the **strathspey**. During the 17th and 18th centuries the Scotch snap was a device popular in Italy, and it was called by German and French writers the 'Lombardic rhythm'.

Scott, Cyril Meir (1879-1970) English composer and poet who went to the Hoch Conservatoire, Frankfurt at the age of 12 for a period of 18 months. Returning there in 1895, he became a member of the Frankfurt Group with **Grainger, Gardiner**, O'Neill and **Quilter**. In many respects his works had a greater following abroad than in England, possibly explained by the fact that his work did not lie in the stream of traditional English music. He was basically a melodist and lyricist with a very individual taste in harmony that had its roots in French impressionism. His works include an opera, *The Alchemist* (1917), three symphonies (1900, 1903 and 1939), concertos for violin, piano and horn, chamber music and songs. He also wrote books on occultism, naturopathy, osteopathy and homoeopathy, and several volumes of poetry.

Scotta, Renata (1933-) Italian soprano who studied in Milan with Ghirardini and Llopart. She made her debut as Violetta in

Verdi's *La Traviata* (1953) at La Scala, and has since toured throughout Europe, specializing in the operas of **Verdi** and **Puccini**.

Scottish National Orchestra Symphony orchestra founded in 1891 and established in Glasgow in 1893 under Sir George **Henschel** as the Scottish Orchestra, and renamed in 1951. It is a permanent orchestra that operates all the year round, giving concerts in Edinburgh, Glasgow and other Scottish towns. Its conductors have included Frederick **Cowen**, John **Barbirolli**, Walter **Susskind**, Karl **Rankl** and Neeme Jarvi.

Scriabin, Alexander (1877-1915) Russian pianist and composer who gave up a military career to study music at the Moscow Conservatoire under Safonov and **Taneyev**. He was a professor of piano (1898-1903) at the Conservatoire following a brilliant series of concert tours in Europe. Later in life he devoted himself entirely to composition and occasional appearances as a pianist. He invented a new system of harmonics based on the 8th to the 14th notes of the **harmonic series** but missing out the 12th, and usually arranged in fourths. The influence of **Chopin** can be seen in his early piano works, and in his orchestral works that of **Wagner** is evident.

Scriabin's works include a piano concerto (1894), three symphonies (1895, 1901 and 1903), *Poem of Ecstasy* (1908), *Poem of Fire – Prometheus* (1909-1910), and many other piano pieces.

Sculthorpe, Peter (1929-) Australian composer who studied at Melbourne University Conservatoire, and was a pupil of **Rubbra** and **Wellesz** at Oxford. His rejection of European music techniques in search of an Australian nontonal style led him to study eastern music, especially that of Bali and Tibet. The influence of this music is reflected in some of his works.

Among his compositions are nine string quartets, *Music for Japan* (1970), the opera *Rites of Passage* (1973) and *Lament for Strings* (1976). He has also written much film and stage music.

Seaman, Christopher (1942-) British conductor who was formerly a percussionist. He is principal conductor of the BBC Scottish Symphony Orchestra (1971-), and the Northern Sinfonia (1974-). He has gained a wide following as a frequent conductor of the National Youth Orchestra and the Robert Mayer Concerts for Children.

sean-nós (Ireland) Literally the 'old style', a slow, lyrical song or air sung in Gaelic. Generally it is unaccompanied, with improvised variations and melismatic embellishments. It survives today mainly in the Connemara region.

Searle, Humphrey (1915-1982) British composer and writer on music who studied music with **Ireland** in London and in Vienna under **Webern**. His works include five symphonies, chamber music, such as *Intermezzo for Eleven Instruments* (1947), ballets and a piano concerto. He also wrote operas, the first of which was a one-act setting of a Gogol story, *The Diary of a Madman* (1958), which made use of electronic music as well as a traditional orchestra.

sebell Alternative spelling of **cebell**.

secco (It.) Dry. Used either as a direction to players or to mean a form of **recitative** (*recitativo secco*).

second Interval of one tone between two notes (major second) or one semitone (minor second).

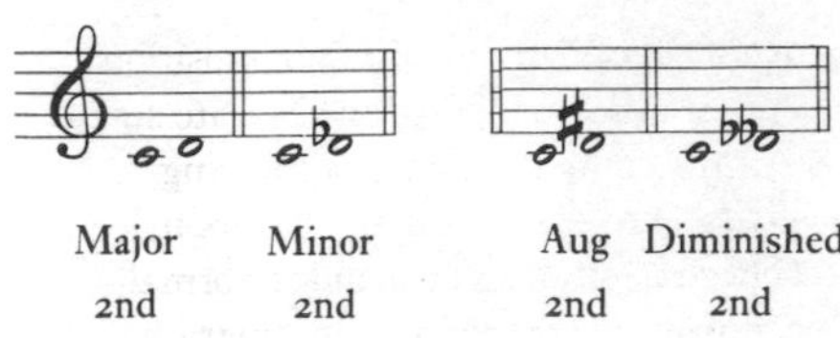

secondary dominant The **dominant** in the key of the dominant; that is, if the composition is in C major, the dominant is G, and the dominant of the key of G major is the chord of D (termed the secondary dominant of C major).

secondo (It.) Second, usually referring to the lower of the two parts in a duet.

sedenka song (Bulgaria) Song performed on an evening occasion when women gather together for communal sewing, knitting and embroidering.

Seefried, Irmgard (1919-) German soprano who studied at the Augsburg Conservatoire and joined the Aachen Opera under **Karajan** (1939) where she made her debut (1940) as the priestess in **Verdi**'s *Aïda*. She joined the Vienna State Opera in 1943 and was chosen by **Strauss** to sing the Composer in *Ariadne auf Naxos* during his 80th birthday celebrations. Seefried is especially well known as a **Mozart** singer and has performed throughout the world.

Segovia, Andrés (1893-1987) Spanish guitarist who was self-taught and first appeared in public at the age of 14. From his first concert appearance in Paris (1924), he was received with international acclaim and regarded as foremost among modern guitarists. His influence on the younger generation was considerable. Composers such as **Falla**, **Casella**, **Villa-Lobos** and **Castelnuovo-Tedesco** have written works especially for him. He himself arranged for the guitar many pieces by J.S. **Bach** and others originally written for the lute.

Andrés Segovia

segue (It.) Direction which indicates to the performer to proceed with the next section without a break.

seguidilla (Sp.) Dance in triple time dating back to at least the 16th century. The original form, *seguidilla Manchega*, came from La Mancha, although it is possible that it was of Moorish origin. The seguidilla is played on guitars, often accompanied with castanets, and sometimes with violin and flute. The vocal accompaniment usually consists of four-line verses followed by three-line **refrains**.

Seiber, Mátyás (1905-1960) Hungarian cellist, composer and conductor who studied with **Kodály** at the Budapest Academy of Music (1919-1924). He joined the staff of the Hoch Conservatoire, Frankfurt (1928-1933), and then settled in London (1935) where he spent the rest of his life. In 1943 he founded, with **Chagrin**, the Society for the Promotion of New Music, and taught at Morley College (1942-1957). His style of music developed from a Hungarian mode to incorporate elements of oriental music and jazz. Seiber's works include the opera *Eva spielt mit Puppen* (1934), *La Blanchisseuse*, ballet music (1942), the cantata, *Ulysses* (1947), three string quartets, *Improvisation for Jazz Band and Symphony Orchestra* (with Johnny Dankworth, 1959), piano music and film music.

Seixas, (Jose Antonio) Carlos de (1704-1742) Portuguese organist and composer who was taught by his father, whom he succeeded as organist at Coimbra Cathedral (1718). From 1720 until his death he was organist to the court in Lisbon, at first serving under Domenico **Scarlatti**. He is mainly remembered for his keyboard sonatas and choral works.

semibreve Note that is half the length in time of a breve and double the length of a minim.

semichorus Group of singers detached from a chorus for the purpose of obtaining **antiphonal** effects or changes of **tone colour**. It does not comprise half of the chorus, but perhaps represents only a segment of it.

semi-opera Modern term for certain 17th- and 18th-century operas in which music (rather than the spoken word) plays a less dominant part than in the full opera form. An example is **Purcell's** opera *King Arthur* (1691). See also **masque**.

semiquaver Note having half the value of a **quaver** and a sixteenth of a **semibreve**. It is shown as a filled-in circle with a tail to which two bars, or hooks, are attached. In American terminology, it is also known as a sixteenth note.

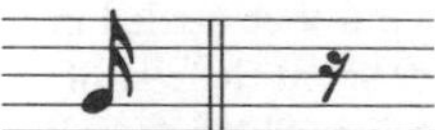

Semiquaver Semiquaver rest

semitone Smallest interval commonly used in Western music. It is the interval between one key and the next on the piano, whether a black or white note. Also known as a minor second.

semplice (It.) Simple. Direction indicating that a passage or whole composition is to be performed in an unaffected manner.

sempre (It.) Always, as in *sempre piu mosso*, always getting faster.

Senfl, Ludwig (*c*1486-*c*1543) Swiss composer who was a pupil of Heinrich Isaac, whom he succeeded as *Kapellmeister* to Maximilian I (1496-1519). When the emperor died, Senfl joined the Bavarian court in Munich. His works included masses, magnificats, motets and about 150 German songs.

senza (It.) Without, as in *senza sordini*, without mutes.

septet Composition for seven voices or instruments, or the group that performs such a work.

Septuplet

septulet Group of seven notes to be fitted into the time of four or six.

serenade Song or operatic air sung in the evening, by a lover at the window of his mistress, the accompaniment often imitates that of a guitar. In the 18th century the serenade took the form of a **suite**.

serenata 18th-century term for a type of **cantata** approaching operatic form, such as **Handel's** *Acis and Galatea* (*c*1720).

serialism Music constructed on the basis of a recurrent series of tones, which arose in the 1920s from **Schoenberg's twelve-note system**, (itself derived from his experiments with **atonality**). The system worked in the following way: all twelve notes on the staff were used in an order laid down by the composer. No note could be repeated until each of the other 11 had sounded (with certain exceptions). Composers such as **Berg** and **Webern** composed in this form and slightly modified the technique, until **Messiaen** greatly enlarged its scope by adding other musical components (for example, rhythmic figures, etc.) as material to be serialized. This enlarged form has come to be known as total serialism. The rise of **electronic** music (with its ability to create new sounds and to programme-in motifs and repetitions) and **aleatory** music has now shed doubts on the future of serialism, but it remains as the first real break from traditional methods of composition that has radically altered the range of techniques open to the present-day composer.

Serialism is also known as the serial technique or serial music.

Serkin, Rudolf (1903-) American pianist of Russian parentage who studied in Vienna with **Schoenberg** and others. He excels particularly in his interpretations of **Bach, Mozart, Beethoven** and **Schubert**. Serkin appeared frequently with the violinist Adolf Busch, whose daughter he married. From 1939 he taught at the Curtis Institute, Philadelphia.

Serocki, Kazimerz (1922-1981) Polish pianist and composer who was a pupil of Sikorski and Nadia **Boulanger** (1947-1948), and was active in promoting modern music, with a special interest in instrumental sounds, spatial composition and **aleatoric** techniques. During the early 1950s he toured Europe as a pianist, but then devoted himself to composition. His works include *Musica Concertante* (1958), *Segmenti*, for chamber ensemble and percussion (1961), *Swinging Music* (1970), *Ad Libitum* (1974) and *Pianophonie* (1978).

Serov, Alexander Nikolaievich (1820-1871) Russian composer and critic who was originally in the civil service and studied music by taking a correspondence course. He later became a music critic, and following a visit to Germany (1858) became an ardent admirer of **Wagner**. A series of articles by Serov paved the way for Wagner's 1865 visit to Russia, in which he organized the country's first performance of *Tannhäuser*. Serov achieved considerable success with his first opera, *Judith* (1863), and he followed it with the still more successful *Rogneda* (1865).

serpent Brass instrument of the cornet family, often made of *papier-mâché*, introduced in the 16th century. It is eight feet long and wound in a series of curves to form a snake-like shape. The lowest note the serpent is capable of is the B♭ below the bass staff, and its compass is three octaves. The serpent fell out of use in the 19th century.

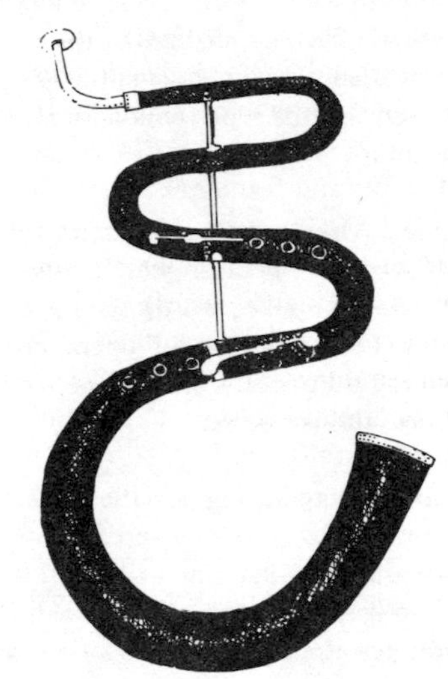

Serpent

service Musically unified setting of the Anglican **canticles** and responses from the Book of Common Prayer. These include English translations of the Venite, Te Deum, Benedictus, Benedicite or Jubilate at Matins, and of the Magnificat, Nunc Dimittis, Cantate Domino or Deus Miserator at Evensong. For the service of Holy Communion the settings are of the Kyrie, Credo, Sanctus, Benedictus, Agnus Dei and Gloria. During the 16th and 17th centuries the terms short service and great service were used to distinguish between less and more elaborate settings of the service.

sesquialtera Mixture stop on an organ containing ranks sounding a twelfth (one octave and a fifth) and a seventeenth (two octaves and a third) above written pitch.

Sessions, Roger (1896-1985) American composer who studied with **Bloch** and then went to Europe (1925-1933). Returning to the United States, he held several teaching posts at Princeton, Berkeley and Harvard. His early compositions became progressively more chromatic and expressionistic, although in the 1950s he adopted **serial** procedures. With his later works he has shown greater brevity. His compositions include the operas *Montezuma* (1941-1963) and *The Trial of Lucullus* (1947), nine symphonies, a cantata, *When Lilacs Last in the Dooryard Bloom'd* (1970), and chamber and piano music.

seventh Interval of seven notes (counting the lowest and highest notes), or eleven semitones for a major seventh (say, C-B) and ten semitones for a minor seventh (say, C-B♭). A diminished seventh is equivalent to a major sixth (C-A).

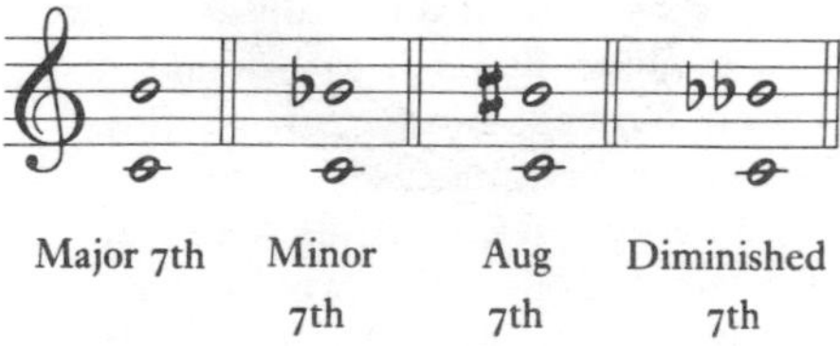

Major 7th Minor 7th Aug 7th Diminished 7th

sextet Composition for six voices or instruments, or a group that performs such a work.

sextolet Alternative term for **sextuplet**.

sextuplet Group of six notes of equal time value played in the time of four. Also known as a sextolet.

sforzando (It.) Direction indicating that a note or chord is to be strongly emphasized by adding an accent. An alternative spelling is sforzato, and the term is often abbreviated to Sf.

sforzato Alternative spelling of **sforzando**.

shake Alternative English term for **trill**.

shakuhachi (Japan) Long, bamboo flute of Chinese origin. It is made from a piece of bamboo that tapers from the bell towards the mouthpiece and is also slightly bowed so that the bell curves gently upwards. The *shakuhachi* has four finger-holes on top and one below, and is blown across the end. It has a mouthpiece which is cut obliquely outwards, with a piece of bone or ivory inserted into the playing edge. Holes can be half-covered to produce microtonal inflections known as *meri-kari*. The

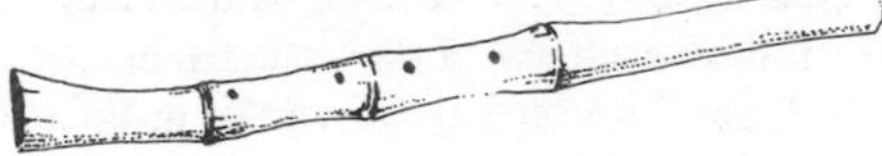

Shakuhachi

shakuhachi, as a solo instrument, was played by both Buddhist priests and itinerant *samurai*, and eventually found its place in the chamber **sankyoku** trio and in the **kabuki** ensemble.

Shaliapin, Feodor Ivanovich (1873–1938) Russian bass singer who, after a childhood spent in poverty, joined a provincial opera company and then studied briefly with Dmitri Usatov in Tiflis (1893). In 1894 he made his first appearance at St Petersburg, and in 1896 joined the Mamontov's Company, Moscow, which was the beginning of his future fame. His first

Feodor Shaliapin

appearance abroad was at La Scala, Milan (1901), and later (1913) he was engaged by **Diaghilev** to sing in Paris and London. Shaliapin left the Soviet Union in 1920, and from 1921 to 1925 sang at the New York Metropolitan Opera. His last stage appearance was at Monte Carlo in 1937. In his day, he was considered unrivalled as a singing actor. An alternative transliteration of his surname is Chaliapin.

shamisen/samisen (Japan) Plucked stringed instrument with a long neck and a body made of four pieces of wood. The square sound-box is covered with catskin. An additional piece of skin is attached to provide reinforcement against the percussive blows of the large, fan-shaped, ivory plectrum (*bachi*). It has three strings of twisted silk which pass over an ivory bridge to a rope tailpiece. The upper two strings pass over a metal bridge at the top of the neck, where they are then attached to tuning pegs, but the lowest string passes through a notch in which it vibrates, providing the characteristic buzzing sound. There are three basic tunings. The *shamisen* may be found in the **sankyoku** trio, the **bunraku** puppet theatre, the **kabuki** theatre and in the **nagauta** ensemble.

Shankar, Ravi (1920-) Indian sitarist and composer who has had a highly successful international career spanning more than 50 years, and is widely acclaimed as one of the greatest living sitarists. He received his early musical training from Ustad Allanddin Khan, subsequently becoming very active as a composer, performer and producer in India. Since his first major European tour in 1956-1957, he has captured a worldwide audience, delighting them with his virtuosic technique. He has appeared with Western artists (including Yehudi **Menuhin** and George Harrison), and has made educational films, which has done much to popularize Indian music and to improve the appreciation of it in the West. His book *My Music, My Life* was published in 1969.

Ravi Shankar

shanty Sailors' work song with a strong rhythmical element, sung in the days of sailing ships, to aid the rhythmic movements required when pumping, hauling ropes, hoisting sails, etc. The probable derivation is from the French word *chantez*, sing. An alternative spelling is chanty.

Shapero, Harold (1920-) American composer who studied intitially at Malkin Conservatoire, Boston, and then under **Piston, Krenek, Hindemith** and **Boulanger**. From 1970 to 1971 he was composer-in-residence at the American Academy in Rome. His works include *Symphony for Classical Orchestra* (1947), a cantata, *Poems of Halevi* (1954), *On Green Mountain*, for jazz combo (1958), two ballets and several piano pieces, two of which involve the use of a synthesizer.

shape note Notation system in white spiritual singing, common in the United States during the 18th century. In order to facilitate the learning of part-singing, each syllable in the system known as **fasola** was given a distinctively shaped note head. Two systems were in widespread use: the Little and Smith system, and the Law system, which could be used without staff notation. Also known as buckwheat notation.

Shaporin, Yury Alexandrovich (1887-1966) Russian composer who graduated in law at St Petersburg University, and in 1913 entered the Conservatoire there to study under Sokolov, **Steinberg** and **Tcherepnin**. On leaving he became interested in stage music and founded the Great Dramatic Theatre with Gorky and Blok. Among his works are a symphony (1911), chamber music, incidental music for films and the stage, and one opera, *The Decembrists* (1953), based on a revolutionary incident in 1825.

Sharp, Cecil James (1859-1924) British folklorist and composer who, after a period in Australia (1889-1892), returned to London where he became principal of the Hampstead Conservatoire (1896-1905). In 1899 he began collecting folksongs and dances, which eventually totalled nearly 5,000. He founded the English Folk-Dance Society (1911) and visited the United States (1916-1918) collecting songs in the Appalachian Mountains, where many English songs were still preserved in their primitive form by descendants of 17th-century emigrants.

sharp Term with two meanings.

First, it is a sign (♯) that raises a note by a semitone.

Second, it is a note that, either through fault or design, sounds of higher pitch than written. Thus, a singer may be said to be singing sharp.

sharp keys Keys that have sharps in their **key-signatures**. The key of G major has one sharp, D major has two sharps, A major has three sharps, E major has four sharps, B major has five sharps, F♯ major has six sharps and C♯ major has seven sharps. In each case the relative minor keys have the same signatures as the major keys given.

Shaw, Martin (Fallas) (1875-1958) British organist and composer who studied at the Royal College of Music, London, and became organist at several London churches. In association with **Vaughan Williams** he edited the hymn book *Songs of Praise*, and in 1935 became musical director to the diocese of Chelmsford. His works include the opera *Mr Pepys* (1926), a choral, *The Seaport*, motets, string quartets, and about 100 songs.

shawm Primitive woodwind instrument originating in the Middle East, with a double-reed mouthpiece and a wide bell.

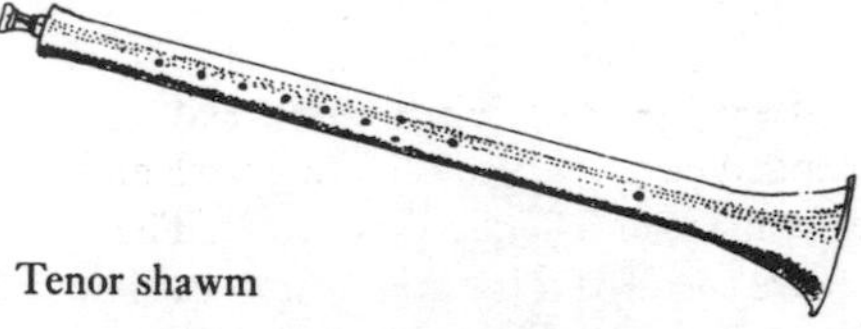

Tenor shawm

The largest types had bent tubes and were therefore similar to the **bassoon**. By the 13th century shawms were in use in Europe, and during the 17th century, with the addition of keys, they evolved into the modern **oboe**. The shawm in its original form is still used in folk music in such countries as Tibet.

Shchedrin, Rodion (Konstantinovich) (1932-) Soviet composer who attended the Moscow Choral School (1948), where he began to compose, and in 1951 went to the Moscow Conservatoire with Shaporin. He is one of the most prominent Soviet composers, although his works are rarely heard in the West. His output includes the ballet *The Little Humpbacked Horse* (1956), an opera, *Not Love Alone* (1961), two symphonies, two piano concertos, three string quartets, incidental music and film scores.

sheng (China) Wind instrument, belonging to the mouth organ family, which consists of a gourd wind box and 17 tubes with brass reeds. It is used both in Chinese folk music and in the classical Chinese orchestra. It is believed to have originated from the **khaen** of Laos, but predates its other relative, the Japanese **shō**. Variations are: in southern music – the wind chest is made of red wood, there are 17 pipes but only 13 have reeds; in northern music – the wind chest is copper and 14 out of the 17 pipes

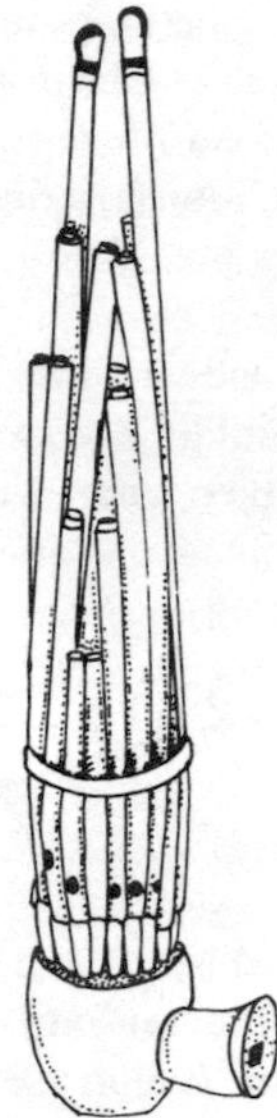

Sheng

are reeded. The inclusion of the silent pipes is said to maintain an aesthetic visual balance.

Sheppard, John (*c*1515-*c*1560) British composer who learned his music as a choirboy at St Paul's Cathedral, London, under Thomas Mulliner. In 1542 he became organist and choirmaster at Magdalen College, Oxford, and later was a member of Queen Mary's Chapel Royal. His five masses include *The Western Wynde, The French Masse* and *Playn Song Mass for a Mene*. He also composed Latin and English church music.

Shield, William (1748-1829) British violinist and composer who studied music with **Avison** in Newcastle, where he appeared as a solo violinist from 1763. In 1772 he came to London as second violinist of the opera orchestra. Following the success of his first opera, *The Flitch of Bacon* (1778), he was appointed composer to the Covent Garden Theatre, and in 1817 he was appointed Master of the King's Music. Apart from his operas and other dramatic works, Shield also wrote string quartets, trios, songs and two treatises on harmony and thorough-bass (1800 and 1817).

shimmy American ballroom dance that became popular after World War I. It was accompanied by jazz music and involved shaking the hips and shoulders.

Shirley-Quirk, John (1931-) British baritone who studied with Roy Henderson, and sang in St Paul's Cathedral choir (1961-1962). He made his debut at **Glyndebourne** (1962) in **Debussy**'s *Pelleas et Mélisande*, and has since created various roles in **Britten's** operas such as *Death in Venice* (1973). His repertory is vast, and he is considered a thoughtful and sensitive artist.

Shnitke, Alfred Garyevich (1934-) Soviet composer and teacher. He was born at Engels, in the western Soviet Union. Following private tuition in music in Vienna between 1946 and 1948, he attended the Moscow Conservatoire from 1953 to 1961. He taught counterpoint and composition there from 1961 to 1972, working also at the Moscow Experimental Studio of Electronic Music. Influenced by writers of serial music as well as by such composers as **Stockhausen**, Ligeti and **Cage**, Shnitke has since the mid-1960s composed works in a dramatic framework. His works include the opera *The 11th Commandment* (1962); the ballets *The Labyrinth* (1971) and *Yellow Sound* (1974); a number of orchestral works including two symphonies and four violin concertos; several choral works, including the oratorio *Nagasaki* (1958), *Requiem* (1974) and *Seit Nüchtern und Wachet* (1982); several chamber works; and *The Stream* (1969) for tape.

shō (Japan) Close relative of the Chinese **sheng**, this mouth organ has 17 reed pipes joined to a cup-shaped wind chest. It is said to be modelled after the wings of a phoenix, the pipes being divided into two symmetrical sets in balancing pairs, two being silent to give an aesthetic visual balance to the instrument. The player blows through a mouthpiece set into the wind chest and covers selected holes in the pipes to produce a variety of chords. The result is an ethereal sound which blows through the **gagaku** orchestra. Its pipes are susceptible to moisture so the *shō* is regularly rotated over a charcoal burner during breaks in a performance to dry the reeds.

shōko (Japan) Bronze gong that is suspended in a standing frame, and appears in three sizes. It is played on the inside (back) with two hard tipped sticks in the **gagaku** court orchestra, where it is used to subdivide the musical phrase by single beats.

shōmyō (Japan) Buddhist chant imported from China, based on sacred texts (*sutras*) and hymns. It is recorded in neumatic script and consists of stereotyped melodic patterns which vary between sects.

short score **Score** that is one of the composer's first drafts, in which he or she roughs out ideas for arrangement, etc.

Shostakovich, Dmitri (Dmitrievich) (1906-1975) Russian composer who entered St Petersburg Conservatoire in 1919, where he studied with **Steinberg** and **Glazunov** and became an outstanding pianist. At the age of 18 he won international acclaim with his Symphony No. 1 in F minor. While his works received a good reception from audiences, his second **opera**, *Lady Macbeth Mtsensk* (1934), came under bitter attack from the Soviet authorities. The opera was not heard again until 1963 when it appeared under the name *Katerina Ismailova*. His Symphony No. 5 in D minor (1937), which was subtitled *A Soviet Artist's Reply to Just Criticism*, was well-received by the authorities and the public alike. The Symphony No. 7 (1941), known as the *Leningrad Symphony*, was written while the city was under seige and made him a war hero. In 1948, Shostakovich again came under criticism from the authorities, but with the

Dimitri Shostakovich

death of Stalin (1953) the cultural atmosphere in the Soviet Union relaxed and he was able to pursue his work with less restraint.

He was a prolific composer, and his works included 15 symphonies, which established him as the leading symphonist of the mid-20th century, 15 string quartets and sonatas for violin, viola and cello, together with ballet, film and theatre scores, vocal and piano music. Shostakovich received the Stalin and Lenin Prizes, and an honorary doctorate from Oxford University.

shruti/sruti (India) Smallest pitch interval thought to be perceivable in Indian musical theory. There are said to be 22 *shrutis* to one octave, but in practice they are never used to form a scale in this way. Particular *shrutis* are selected in a **rāga** to produce the correct intonation or 'colour' peculiar to the latter.

Sibelius, Jean (Julius Christian) (1865-1957) Finnish composer and conductor who began his higher education by studying law in Helsinki, where he formed a life-long friendship with **Busoni**. With a government grant he was able study counterpoint with **Becker** in Berlin and, later, orchestration with Fuchs in Vienna.

Returning to Finland in 1891, Sibelius became a passionate nationalist. The *Kalevala* (a series of myths and folk tales) had a strong influence on the themes Sibelius was to chose for his music. This can be seen in such works as *Kullervo* (1892), *En Saga* (1892), *Karelia* (1893), *The Swan of Tuonela* (1893) and *Finlandia* (1900).

Altogether Sibelius wrote seven symphonies (No. 7 in C major, in one movement), although an eighth (1929) was destroyed by Sibelius for reasons which are not too clear. Some of the symphonies display a typically Sibelian method, by which he would allow thematic material to come together gradually in fragments, appearing only later in completed form. This method has been called the synthetic principle.

Some of Sibelius' other works include *King Christian II* (1898), *Kuolema*, which

Jean Sibelius

includes *Valse Triste* (1904), *Belshazzar's Feast* (1907), *Suite Mignonne* (1921), *The Tempest* (1926), songs and piano pieces.

Early in his musical career, Sibelius was accepted as the foremost Finnish composer of his time and his works are still universally popular.

siciliana (It.) Sicilian dance form in slow 6/8 or 12/8 time, usually in a minor key. Arias in siciliana rhythm were common in the 18th century.

side drum Small drum of indefinite pitch, with two heads tightly stretched over a metal shell. The lower head has strings of catgut (called snares) stretched across it, which give the instrument its characteristic rattling sound. The player strikes the top head with two sticks made from hard wood.

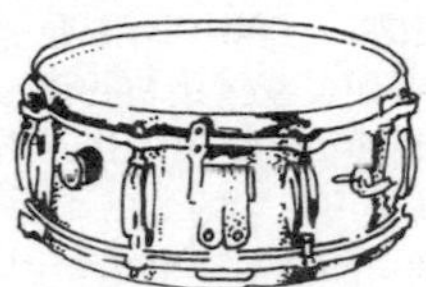

Side drum

They are used in the percussion section of an orchestra, in military and jazz bands. In marching bands, the drum is supported to the side of the body. Also known as a snare drum.

Siepi, Cesare (1923-) Italian bass singer who studied at Milan Conservatoire. He made his debut in **Verdi**'s *Rigoletto* in Schio, near Venice (1941), but his career was interrupted by World War II, during which he sought refuge in Switzerland because of his anti-Fascist activities. After the war he resumed his career, appearing in Venice, Covent Garden, London and Milan. Between 1950 and 1974 he was a member of the New York Metropolitan Opera, where he sang in most of its repertory.

sight reading Art of playing or singing music at the first reading.

signature Directions placed on a score to indicate time (**time- signature**) or key (**key-signature**).

sijo (Korea) Short lyric song form, which is similar in style to **kagok** (except for a distinctive use of falsetto), but with a more simple structure. The verse form of three-line stanzas dates from early dynastic times (7th-8th centuries), but the tunes in the current repertory are of much more recent origin. The *sijo* was traditionally accompanied by the **changgo** drum, but is now often complemented by a small instrumental ensemble, such as **p'iri**, **taegŭm** and **haegŭm**.

Silja, Anja (1940-) German soprano who studied with her grandfather Egon von Rijn, and made her debut at the age of 10 in Berlin. She was greatly influenced by Wieland **Wagner**, and closely associated with the Bayreuth Festival from 1960 where she appeared in *Wozzeck*, *Lulu*, *Otello*, *Salomé* and *Elektra*, as well as in the operas of **Wagner**. Silja is a vivid and forceful singing actress.

Sills, Beverly (Belle Silverman) (1929-) American soprano who studied in New York with Estelle Liebling, and made her debut in Philadelphia (1947). She joined the New York City Opera in 1955, Covent Garden, London in 1970 and the New York Metropolitan in 1975. She became director of the New York Metropolitan in 1979. Sills has a repertory of more than 60 roles, including Cleopatra in **Handel**'s *Julius Caesar*, and Elizabeth in **Donizetti**'s *Roberto Devereux*. She also sings successfully in contemporary American operas, and is probably the most popular American soprano since Grace Moore.

silver band Band with a similar configuration of instruments to the **brass band**, but in which the instruments are coated with a laquer that makes them look as if they are made of silver.

similar motion In harmony, the movement of two parts in the same direction.

The opposite is **contrary motion**. See also **oblique motion; parallel motion.**

simile (It.) Direction indicating that the manner of performance should continue as already indicated.

simple interval **Interval** between two notes of an **octave** or less. See also **compound interval**.

simple time Any **metre** in which the beats can be subdivided into two. Simple duple time is the name given to the signatures 2/2, 2/4, 2/8. Simple triple time applies to the signatures 3/2, 3/4, 3/8. Simple quadruple time applies to 4/2, 4/4, or 4/8. See also **compound time**.

Simpson, Robert (Wilfred Levick) (1921-) British composer and musicologist who originally intended to become a doctor of medicine, but after two years began to study music under **Howells** (1942-1946). He joined the BBC (1951-1980) as a writer on music, especially that of **Bruckner, Nielsen** and **Sibelius**.

His works include eight symphonies, 11 string quartets, a clarinet quintet (1968), a horn quartet (1977), and the motet *Media Morte* (1975).

Sinding, Christian (August) (1856-1941) Norwegian pianist and composer who trained as a violinist, but in 1874 abandoned the violin and went to Leipzig University to study composition. He spent 40 years in Germany and a brief time in the United States (1920-1921), where he taught theory and composition at the Eastman School, New York.

His works include an opera, *Der heilige Berg* (1912), orchestra chamber and piano music and about 250 songs. Probably his best-known work is the piano piece *Rustle of Spring* (1896).

sinfonia Term with several meanings.

First, it is an alternative term for **symphony**.

Second, it was used by **Bach** for many of his three-part compositions.

Third, it was used during the early Baroque period to refer to an instrumental piece played at the beginning of an opera, what we now call the **overture**.

Fourth, it is a small symphony orchestra.

sinfonia concertante (It.) Used by Haydn and Mozart to refer to an orchestral piece that featured one or more solo instruments.

sinfonietta (It.) Term with two meanings.

First, it is a small-scale **symphony** in symphonic form.

Second, it is used (especially in the United States) to refer to a small symphony orchestra.

singspiel (Ger.) Form of popular **opera** in Germany and Austria during the 18th century. The first *singspiels* were translations of English ballad opera, but in the second half of the 18th century they were originally-composed works. The French equivalent of the singspiel was the **opéra-comique**.

The principal composer of the *singspiel* was Johann Adam **Hiller** (1728-1804) whose work *Die Jagd* (1770) had popular and comic plots. In **Mozart**'s operas *The Seraglio* (1782) and *The Magic Flute* (1791) the score often included features of both *singspiel* and **opéra-seria**.

sitār (India) Stringed instrument predominant in northern India, related to the **bīn**,

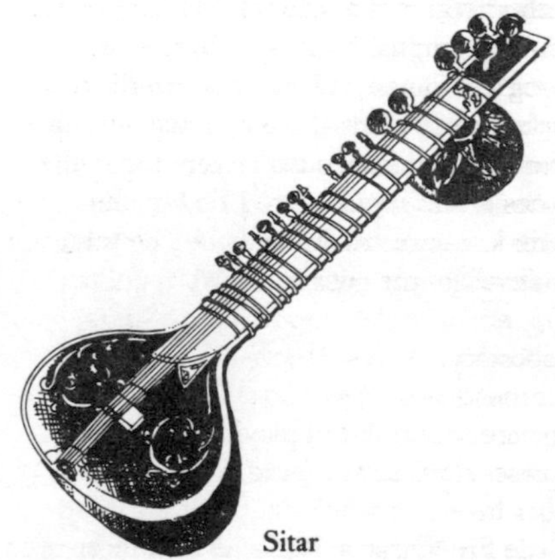

Sitar

which it has almost superseded. It is a long-necked, plucked lute and occasionally has a small gourd fastened to its upper end. It has movable frets, with additional **drone** and sympathetic strings.

Six, Les Group of six French composers who, in 1917, formed an anti-Impressionist movement of a **neo-Classical** nature. The Six were Darius **Milhaud**, Arthur **Honegger**, Francis **Poulenc**, Germaine **Taillferre**, Georges **Auric** and Louis **Durey**. Erik **Satie** and Jean Cocteau were associated with the group.

sixth Interval of six notes (counting the lowest and highest notes). A major sixth consists of nine semitones (say, C-A), and a minor sixth consists of eight semitones (say, C-G♯). See also **augumented sixth; Neopolitan sixth.**

sixty-fourth note Alternative term for **hemidemisemiquaver.**

Sjören, (Johann Gustav) Emil (1853-1918) Swedish composer and organist who studied at the Stockholm Conservatoire and later in Berlin. He became organist at St John's Church, Stockholm (1891), but devoted most of his time to teaching and composing. His main works were for piano and organ.

ska (Caribbean) Jamaican popular dance music, which originated in the late 1950s, with rhythms characterized by a persistent off-beat emphasis adapted from American **boogie-woogie** and **rhythm and blues** styles, particularly those of black musicians from the southern states. From the mid-1960s it was replaced by a slower, modified form known as rock-steady, which soon was to develop into **reggae**.

Skalkottas, Nikos (1904-1949) Greek composer who began studying the violin at the age of five and entered the Athens Conservatoire at 10, graduating in 1920. In 1921 he won a scholarship to the Hochschule für Musik in Berlin, where he studied with **Schoenberg, Weill** and Jarnach.

Although he had a promising career as a violinist, he concentrated on composition. Returning to Athens in 1933, poor and ill, he played the violin in an orchestra and composed in his spare time. Some of his works show the influence of Schoenberg, whereas others have been influenced by his collection of Greek folk music.

Skalkottas's works include three piano concertos, the ballet *The Maiden and Death* (1938), *36 Greek Dances* (1931-1936), an overture entitled *The Return of Ulysses* (1942-1943), chamber works, and piano pieces.

sketch Term with two meanings.

First, it is a short instrumental piece usually for the piano, which describes some scene in musical terms.

Second, it is often used to refer to the first draft of a composition.

Skinner, James Scott (1843-1927) Scottish violinist and composer. After studying in Manchester, he settled in Aberdeen as a dancing master and wrote popular dance music based on Scottish reels, strathspeys and other national dances.

slatt Norwegian folk tune played on a **Hardänger fiddle**. Originally it was in the form of a march. **Grieg** and other Norwegian composers have transcribed the slatt for other instruments.

slèndro (Indonesia) One of two tonal systems, consisting of five nearly equal tones within an octave. In Java, there are three *patet* (modes) in *slèndro* tuning: *manyura*, *sanga* and *nem*, corresponding to specific times of the day. See also **pélog**.

slentem (Java) One-octave, bronze metallophone of the **gamelan** ensemble, with thin keys resting over bamboo resonating chambers. It is struck with a padded disc attached to the end of a stick. In the 'soft style' of Javanese *gamelan* playing, the *slentem* carries the basic melodic line, while other instruments elaborate upon it.

slide Term with three meanings.

First, it is the technique of passing from one note to another on stringed instruments by moving the finger along the string instead of lifting it; a **glissando**.

Second, it is a device on a **trombone** for changing the length of the tube in order to make available different ranges of harmonics.

Third, it is an **ornament** consisting of two notes leading up to a principal note.

Slonimsky, Nicolas (1894-) Russian author and composer who studied at St Petersburg Conservatoire, and in 1923 settled in the United States where he became a naturalized citizen in 1931. He was conductor of the Boston Chamber Orchestra (1927-1934), and conducted his own work *Fragment from Orestes* in 1933. Another of his works was *Suite in Black and White* for piano. He is particularly well-known as editor of the *International Cyclopaedia of Music and Musicians*, a position he first held in 1946.

slur Arching stroke written over two or more notes indicating that they are to be played **legato**, or with one stroke of the bow. It is also used in vocal music where two or more notes are to be sung in the same syllable.

Slur

Smalley, Roger (1943-) British composer and pianist who studied with **Fricker** and attended **Stockhausen**'s courses in Cologne. In 1967 he was artist-in-residence at King's College, Cambridge, and in 1970 he founded Intermodulation, a modern-music ensemble. Since 1976 he has lived mainly in Australia.

For a period Smalley experimented with Renaissance material and procedures, but later followed Stockhausen by adopting moment form, improvisatory elements and electronic music. His works include *Missa brevis* for 16 solo voices (1967), *Pulses* (1969), *Beat Music* for 55 players (1971), *Accord* (1975) and *Echo I- III* (1978).

Smetana, Bedrich (1884-1884) Czech composer, pianist and conductor who started playing the violin at the age of five and gave a piano recital at the age of six. His father opposed a musical career, but after studying in Prague Smetana became music teacher (1844) to Count Leopold Thun's family, and during that time met **Berlioz** and the **Schumanns**. In 1848 he took part in the revolution against Austria, and established a music school in Prague with **Liszt**'s encouragement. He became conductor of the Göteborg Philharmonic Society (1856) in Sweden, where he found immediate success as a conductor, pianist and teacher. In 1861 he returned to Prague where he helped to establish the national opera house, for which he composed his two most famous operas, *The Brandenburgers in Bohemia* (1863) and *The Bartered Bride* (1866). Between 1866 and 1874 Smetana conducted the Czech National Opera and formed a strong friendship with **Dvorák**, one of the viola players.

Smetana's music is distinctly Czech in character, and this can be seen in such works as the symphonic poem cycle *Má Vlast* (1874) and the string quartet *From My Life* (1876). Some of his other works include the operas *Dalibor* (1868), *The Two Widows* (1874), *The Kiss* (1876) and *Libuse* (1881), chamber music, piano pieces and many songs.

Smyth, Dame Ethel (1858-1944) British composer who entered Leipzig Conservatoire in 1877, where she also studied privately with **Herzogenberg**. Her earlier operas (*Fantastic*, 1898, and *The Forest*, 1903) were produced in Germany, but her best were probably *The Wreckers* (1906) and *The Boatswain's Mate* (1916). Smyth's works were full of strong rhythms and well orchestrated, and in spite of her strong belief in English musical nationalism, the influence of earlier training in Germany is evident.

On her return to England in 1910 she became active in the movement for women's suffrage, and in that cause she spent two months in prison (1911). She composed *The March of Women* (1911) as the battle song of the militant suffragettes. During this period, other works include orchestral pieces, chamber music and songs. She was created a DBE in 1922.

snare drum Alternative term for **side drum**.

soave (It.) Sweet, gentle.

Söderström, Elisabeth (1927-) Swedish soprano who studied in Stockholm with Andreyeva-Skilondz, where she made her debut in 1947. Since joining the Royal Swedish Opera, Stockholm (1950), her highly successful career has taken her to Glyndeboure, Salzburg, Covent Garden and the Metropolitan Opera, New York. She was one of the finest singing actresses of the 1960s and 1970s, and is especially

Elisabeth Söderström

well-known for her roles in the operas of **Mozart, Strauss, Henze** and **Tchaikovsky**.

soh Name given to the fifth note of the scale in the **tonic sol-fa** system.

Sohal, Naresh (1939-) Indian composer who studied in England with Alexander **Goehr**. His works include a harmonica concerto, a piece for unaccompanied soprano saxophone, a piece for unaccompanied flute and vocal pieces.

Soler, Antonio (1729-1783) Spanish friar, organist and composer who was a pupil of Domenico **Scarlatti** (1752-1757). He was a chorister at Montserrat and in 1750 was appointed *maestro di cappella* at Lerida Cathedral. In 1752 he entered the Escurial monastery, becoming organist and choirmaster there the following year. Soler's works include masses, motets and other sacred music, quintets and concertos for organ and sonatas for harpsichord.

sol-fa See **tonic sol-fa**.

solmization Designation of the musical **scales** by means of syllables. The notes of the Greek **tetrachords** were already designated by syllables, but in the 11th century Guido d'Arezzo replaced them by the **hexachords** and used the Latin syllables Ut, Re, Mi, Fa, Sol, La for their six notes, Si being added later for the seventh and Ut being replaced by Do (except in France).

The syllables were derived from the hymn for the festival of John the Baptist (770), the first syllable beginning on successive notes of the hexachord: *Ut* queant laxis; *Re*sonare fibris; *Mi*ra gestorum; *Fa*muli tuorum; *Sol*ve polluti; *La*bii reatum; *S*ancte *I*oannes.

The seventh syllable, Si, was derived from the initial letters of the last line. The **tonic sol-fa** is a modern derivative of this system.

solo Composition or part of a composition

Sir George Solti

played by a single performer with or without accompaniment.

Solomon (Solomon Cutner) (1902-) British pianist who made his debut at the age of eight when he appeared at the Queen's Hall, London, playing **Tchaikovsky**'s Piano Concerto No. 1 in G minor. Later he studied in Paris, beginning his true career in 1923. Solomon's brilliant technique and musicianship have made him one of the finest pianists of the 20th century. He was forced to retire in 1965 because he became incapacitated by paralysis.

Solti, Sir Georg (1912-) Hungarian-born conductor and pianist who studied piano with **Dohnányi** and composition with **Kodály** and **Bartók** at Budapest Conservatoire. He conducted at the Budapest Opera (1930-1939) and spent the years of World War I in Switzerland, where he was active as a pianist and conductor. Subsequent appointments include conductor of the Munich State Opera (1946), director of the Frankfurt Opera (1952-1961), and in 1959 he made his debut at Covent Garden, of which he became director (1961-1971). He has also conducted the Chicago Symphony Orchestra, the Orchestre de Paris (1971-1975), and the London Philharmonic Orchestra (1979-1983).

Solti has made many highly successful recordings, including the first complete recording in stereo of **Wagner**'s *Der Ring des Nibelungen*. He became a British citizen, and was knighted in 1972.

Somers, Harry (Stewart) (1925-) Canadian composer who was a pupil of **Milhaud** in Paris. His opera, *Louis Riel* (1967), is considered to be the finest by a Canadian. It was commissioned by the Canadian Opera Company in Toronto, and has since been broadcast on both radio and television. Somers wrote two other operas, *The Fool* (1953) and *The Homeless Ones* (1955). He has also written three string quartets, orchestral and vocal pieces.

Somervell, Sir Arthur (1863-1937) British composer and educationist who was a pupil of Charles **Stanford** and **Parry**. In 1894 he became a professor at the Royal College of Music, and in 1901 an inspector of music in schools, for which work he was knighted in 1929. His works include choral music, songs and piano pieces.

sona (China) Wind instrument, literally 'brass mouthed horn', because of its wide, open brass mouth. It is a folk instrument with a small, double-reed mouthpiece, fixed to a wooden pipe, with six upper finger-holes and one behind.

sonata Orignally, a piece of music that was 'sounded' on wind or strings as opposed to a cantata which was sung. An example of the early sonata was Giovanni **Gabrieli**'s *Sonata Pian' e Forte* (1597) for violin, cornett and six trombones.

By the 17th century the sonata had developed into two forms: the *sonata da chiesa* (church sonata) and the *sonata da camera* (chamber sonata). The *sonata da chiesa* was mostly in four movements, with tempi indicated according to the plan slow-fast-slow-fast. The *sonata da camera* was in the form of a suite with an introduction followed by three or four dances. Both forms of sonata can be divided into four categories according to the number of parts: solo; two parts (*a due*); three parts (*a tre*); four or more parts (*a quattro*).

Among the early keyboard sonatas were those by Johann **Kuhnau** (1660-1722), Bernardo **Pasquini** (1637-1710) and Domenico **Scarlatti** (1683-1757), who wrote over 550 one-movement pieces for harpsichord.

During the second half of the 18th century the sonata developed into the form common today. In its normal shape it has three movements: an **allegro** in **sonata form**; a slow movement; and an allegro, usually in **rondo** form. These are for a solo instrument, or solo instrument with keyboard accompaniment. This arrangement of movements was carried over into the trio, quartet, quintet and symphony.

C.P.E. **Bach** and J.C. **Bach** composed notable solo keyboard sonatas during the 18th century, and they both influenced **Haydn** and **Mozart. Beethoven** added a **scherzo** (*Pathétique*, 1799) and developed the sonata both in the number of movements and their construction.

Among 19th-century composers, **Schubert, Schumann, Chopin** and **Liszt** wrote piano sonatas.

sonata form Structure that evolved during the second half of the 18th century which applies to virtually all instrumental media in the classical period and, therefore, includes concertos, sonatas, symphonies, chamber music, quartets and arias.

The form is in three main sections: exposition, development and recapitulation. The exposition has two subjects, the first in the **tonic** and the second in a **related key**. These subjects are then developed or displayed in various ways (but in no prescribed order) in the development section. The recapitulation then states the first and second subjects again, this time with both in the **dominant**, and rounds off the sonata, sometimes with an added **coda**.

song Composition for solo voice (or a group) with or without accompaniment. The earliest known song was Summerian; when deciphered in 1972, it was found to have been written more than 3,700 years ago.

In western Europe, the earliest songs date from the 12th century. These included the music of the **troubadours, trouvères**, Meinnesingers and **Meistersingers**.

Instrumental accompaniment emerged in the 14th century, especially in France and Italy, and the part-song became established in the mid-15th century.

The lute-song was popular in England during the early 17th century, possibly reaching its highest form in the works of

John **Dowland**.

In Italy a new kind of declamatory song (**recitative**) was being developed by composers such as Jacopo **Peri** (1561-1633). These developments rapidly became part of the new genres of **cantata, opera** and **oratorio**.

The next great impetus occurred in the late 18th and early 19th century with the Romantic movement. One of the most prolific song composers was Franz **Schubert** who wrote more than 600 songs, and together with other composers such as **Schumann, Brahms** and Hugo **Wolf**, is associated with the German *Lied*. The French composers **Debussy, Duparc** and **Fauré** were notable song writers, and so were the Russians **Glinka** and **Tchaikovsky**.

Major English song composers of the 20th century include **Britten, Holst, Vaughan Williams** and **Warlock**.

song cycle Group of songs set to a number of poems with a connecting narrative or other unifying feature. Examples include **Schubert's** *Fair Maid of the Mill* (1823), **Beethoven's** *An die ferne Geliebte* (1816), **Debussy's** *Chansons de Bilitis* (1897) and **Vaughan Williams'** *On Wenlock Edge* (1909).

sopila (Yugoslavia) Conical oboe with six finger holes. On the island of Krk, where they are most commonly used, two different sizes are paired, playing in a narrow interval style. See also **diaphonic song**.

soprano Highest female voice, with an effective range of more than two octaves, the lowest note being around middle C. The soprano voice has three categories and they are classified as either dramatic, lyric or coloratura. Boy sopranos are known as trebles. Soprano also refers to instruments that sound in that range, for example the soprano saxophone.

Sor, Fernando (1778-1839) Spanish guitarist and composer who was educated at the choir school of the monastery at Montserrat. He went to London (1815), to Russia to see the performance of his ballet *Cendrillon* (1822), and finally to Paris (1826).

Sor became a celebrated guitarist and teacher who composed mainly for his instrument. His other works include the operas *Telemaco* (1797) and *Don Trastillo* (1797, now lost), and seven ballets (three of which have been lost), the most notable being *Cendrillon* (1822), two symphonies and three string quartets.

Sorabji, Kaikhosru Shapurji (Leon Dudley Sorabji) (1892-) British-born composer and pianist, son of a Parsee father and Spanish mother who was mainly self-taught. He has appeared in London, Paris and Vienna as a pianist in performances of his own works. His compositions include many works for piano such as a two-hour *Opus clavicembalisticum* (1929-1930), orchestral and organ pieces. Since 1940 he has banned public performances of his compositions, with the exception of works involving two performers.

sordino (It.) **Mute**. For example, *con sordino* indicates that a passage should be played with the mute, and *senza sordino*, is without the mute.

sostenuto (It.) Sustained, a direction to indicate either style or tempo of performance.

sotto voce (It.) Indication that a passage is to be performed in an undertone. Originally it was applied to vocal music, but it has also become current for instrumental music.

soubrette (Fr.) In opera and operetta, a stock, but secondary, role, such as a maid or serving girl, played by a singer with a light soprano voice. An example is Despina in **Mozart**'s *Così fan tutte* (1790). Occasionally a *soubrette* may assume a principal role, such as Serpina in **Pergolesi**'s *Serva padrona* (1733).

soul music Form of black American

popular music, derived from gospel music blended with **rhythm and blues**. Its popularity since the 1960s has given international fame to such artists as Ray Charles, James Brown, Otis Redding and Aretha Franklin.

Sousa, John Philip (1854-1932) American bandmaster and composer whose early career was as an orchestral violinist. In 1880 he became master of the US Marine Corps Band and in 1892 formed his own band which achieved international fame and popularity. He composed several operettas, including *El Capitan* (1895), but he is mainly known for his marches such as *The Thunderer* (1889), *The Washington Post* (1899), *King Cotton* (1895), *The Stars and Stripes Forever* (1897) and *Hands Across the Sea* (1899).

sousaphone Instrument of the **tuba** family, mainly in use in the United States. It sounds in the bass register and has an enormous bell turned upwards and through two right angles. Invented for use in the band of John **Sousa** in 1899.

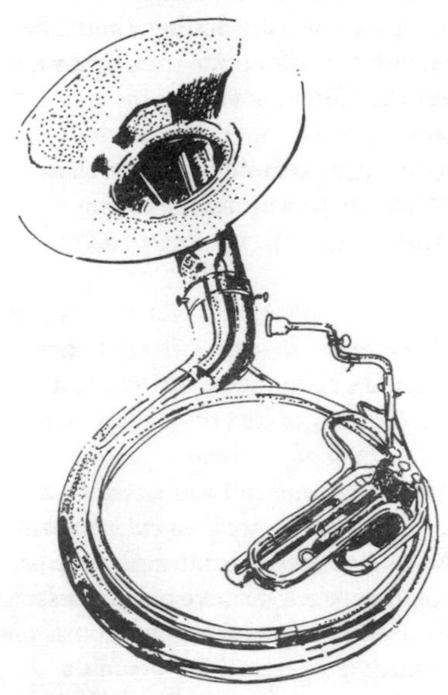

Sousaphone

Souster, Tim (1943-) British composer who was a pupil of **Stockhausen, Berio** and Richard Rodney **Bennett**, and formerly a BBC producer. His works were very much influenced by rock music and group improvisation techniques. Together with **Smalley**, he founded the ensemble Intermodulation (1970). His works include *Chinese Whispers*, for percussion and three synthesizers (1970), *Triple Music*, for three orchestras (1970), *Spectral* (1972), *Arcane Artifact* (1976) and *Arboreal Antecedents* (1978).

soutenu (Fr.) Sustained. Alternative term for the Italian **sostenuto**.

Souzay, Gerard (1920-) French baritone who studied with Pierre **Bernac** and in many respects has followed the same excellent techniques as his tutor when singing *Lieder*. His repertory includes German works and earlier music, such as that of **Monteverdi**. His accompanist since 1954 has been Dalton Baldwin.

species counterpoint Counterpoint is taught in five progressive stages, known as the five species. In each, the student adds one or more lines above, or below, a **cantus firmus**, of one note to the bar, and works within a limiting set of grammatical rules.

In the first species, one note is written against each note of the *cantus firmus*. The second species consists of two notes against each *cantus firmus*; third species, four against one. The fourth species is concerned with **suspensions** and the fifth species allows a combination of any of the preceding species.

speech song Form of singing midway between speech and song. It is used especially by **Schoenberg** in his *Pierrot Lunaire* (1912), a song cycle of 21 poems.

Speer, Daniel (1636-1707) German composer, theorist and writer who composed mainly church music and quodlibets. He is probably best known for his theoretical writings, such as *Grund-rich-tiger* (1687), which deals with performance practice.

spiccato Light **staccato** produced on stringed instruments by the bow bouncing on the string with alternating up and down bowing.

spinet Instrument of the **harpsichord** family, in use between the late 17th century and the end of the 18th century. It was wing-shaped, with strings running away from the keyboard (as opposed to parallel to the keyboard, as was the case with the **virginals**).

Spinet

An alternative name for the spinet was the couched harp. The term spinet is also incorrectly used to mean a square piano.

spinto (It.) Pushed. Operatic style in which the voice (especially one with highly lyrical qualities) is pushed into a more forceful manner. See also **verismo**.

spirito (It.) Indication that a movement or passage is to be performed briskly and energetically (*con spirito*).

spiritual Type of religious folk song developed by black American slaves, originally during the American religious revival which began in the 1740s. Many follow a structure in which lines sung by a soloist alternate with choral refrains, as in *Swing Low, Sweet Chariot*. Spirituals such as *Go Down Moses* reflect the sense of identity that blacks have felt with the Israelites in bondage in Egypt. Sir Michael Tippett used five very popular spirituals as chorales in his oratorio *A Child of Our Time*. They included *Steal Away*, *Nobody Knows the Trouble I See*, *Go Down Moses*, *By and By* and the intensely devotional *Deep River*.

Spohr, Louis (Ludwig) (1784-1859) German composer, violinist and conductor who first learned music from his parents. He was employed as a violinist at the court of the Duke of Brunswick who paid for his private tuition and arranged for him to go on a concert tour with Franz Eck. Returning to Brunswick (1803) as a celebrated violin virtuoso, he became leader in the Duke of Gotha's orchestra (1805-1812), and then musical director of the Theater an der Wien, Vienna (1812-1815). He was also conductor of the Frankfurt Opera (1817-1819) and from 1822 musical director at the court of Cassel. In 1842 Spohr became the first musician of importance to support **Wagner** when he helped him to produce *The Flying Dutchman* (1843) at Cassel. It is said that Spohr was one of the first orchestral conductors to use a **baton**.

Spohr's output was extremely varied and he is considered a leading early romantic. He wrote 11 operas including *Faust* (1816), the premiere of which was conducted by **Weber**, and *Jessonda* (1823), his greatest operatic success. Spohr also wrote 15 violin concertos, nine symphonies, four clarinet concertos, chamber music, 34 string quartets, seven string quintets and more than 90 songs.

Spontini, Gasparo (1774-1851) Italian composer and conductor who studied at Naples Conservatoire (1793-1795). His first opera (*Li Puntigli delle donne*, 1796) was produced in Rome and was an immediate success. In 1798 he went to Palermo with the Neapolitan court as musical director, and in 1802 to Paris where his opera *La Vestale* (1807) led to his recognition as one of the leading opera composers of the day. Spontini became musical director to the court of Frederick William III in Berlin (1820), and although he introduced excellent reforms at the court opera, his success was overshadowed by the acclaim given to **Weber's** *Der Freischütz* (1821), and the acceptance of German opera in general. In addition, he continued to have personality clashes with court officials, and he was pensioned off in 1842 and went to live in Paris. He became deaf in 1848 and returned to his birthplace. founding a music school in Jesi. His other operas include *Milton* (1804), *Julie* (1805), *Ferdinand Cortez* (1809), *Olympie* (1819) and *Agnes von Hohenstaufen* (1829).

springer **Ornament** in which an extra note is inserted between two other notes. It is the opposite of an **appoggiatura**, because it robs the preceding note of part of its time value.

Two ways of writing a springer

square piano Form of **piano** that is square (horizontal) in shape with strings running at right angles away from the keyboard. Also known as a table piano and sometimes (incorrectly) as a **spinet**.

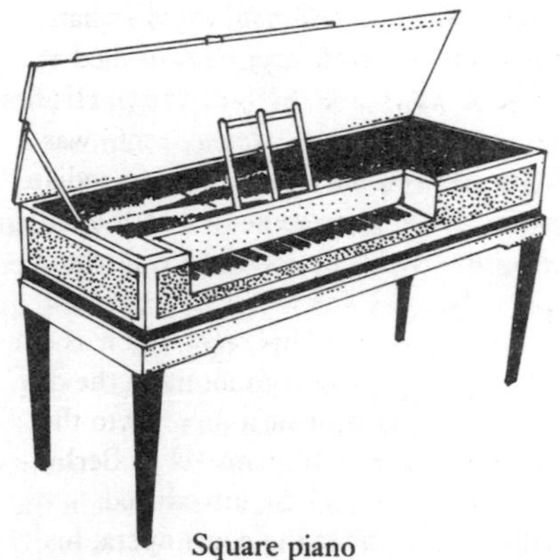

Square piano

sruti (India) See **shruti**.

stabile (It.) Orchestra that is permanent, regular or resident.

staccato (It.) Indication that notes marked with dots above them should be played slightly shorter than their normal time value with a brief pause between notes. As a result, notes of a staccato passage become detached from each other.

Stadler, Anton (1753-1812) Austrian clarinettist and basset-horn player who was a member of the Vienna Court Orchestra. He was a close friend of **Mozart**, who wrote for him the Piano Trio in B♭ Major, K498, for piano, clarinet and viola (1786), and the Clarinet Concerto in A Major, K622 (1791).

Stadtische Oper (Ger.) Municipal Opera, either a house or a company.

staff Set of five horizontal lines on which music is commonly notated. The position of a note on or between the lines (along with the key-signature) denotes its pitch. The system of time signature and bar lines indicates the rhythmic component. Also written stave. See also **score**.

Stainer, Sir John (1840-1901) English composer, organist and scholar who became a chorister in 1848 at St Paul's Cathedral, and in 1854 an organist, first in London, then in Tenbury. He studied at Christ College, Oxford (1859-1866), and founded the Oxford Philharmonic Society. He was organist at St Paul's Cathedral (1872-1888), but because of failing eyesight had to resign. He was knighted in 1888 and the following year was appointed professor of music at Oxford. From 1881 he was principal of the National Training School for Music.

His compositions are mainly of sacred music, including the oratorios *Gideon* (1865) and *The Crucifixion* (1887), and the cantata *The Story of the Cross* (1893), all extremely popular to the present day.

Stamitz, Carl (1745-1801) Czech violinist and composer, son of Johann Wenzel **Stamitz**. He entered the Mannheim orchestra as second violinist (1762) and in 1770 he went to Paris where he achieved great success both as a violinist and as a composer. From 1777 he travelled widely until in 1794 he settled in Jena as musical director at the university. He wrote more than 50 symphonies, 38 *symphonies concertantes* and a great deal of chamber music.

Stamitz, (Johann) Anton (1754-*c*1809) Czech violinist and composer and brother of Carl **Stamitz**, a pupil of his father and **Cannabich**. Together with his brother he went to Paris (1770), where he settled as a violinist in the court orchestra. His works included 12 symphonies, and concertos for violin, viola, flute and oboe.

Stamitz, Johann Wenzel (1717-1757) Czech violinist and composer who received his early teaching from his father. He was appointed to the Mannheim court in 1741 as violin virtuoso and later (1750) as music director. Under him the Mannheim orchestra became the most famous in Europe. He was also founder and the most important member of the Mannheim School. His works included 74 symphonies and concertos for violin, harpsichord, flute, oboe and clarinet.

Standford, Patric (1939-) English composer who was a pupil of Rubbra, **Malipiero** and **Lutoslawski**. Some of his compositions occasionally use aleatoric techniques. His works include *Christus-Requiem*, for narrator, child and adult voices and orchestra, two symphonies, two string quartets and a sonata for unaccompanied violin.

Stanford, Sir Charles Villiers (1852-1924) English composer, teacher, conductor and organist who studied at Queen's College, Cambridge (1870-1873), and was appointed organist of Trinity College (1873-1882). Between 1874 and 1876 he studied with Reinecke in Leipzig and Kiel in Berlin, and in 1873 he conducted the Cambridge University Musical Society for which he composed *The Resurrection* (1875) and other works. Having achieved success as a composer and conductor, Stanford's reputation was further advanced when Tennyson asked him to write the incidental music for *Queen Mary* (1876). When the Royal College of Music opened in 1883 he was made professor of composition, and from 1885 to 1902 he was conductor of the London Bach Choir. In 1887 he was elected professor of music at Cambridge, and in 1902 knighted. Among his pupils were **Vaughan Williams, Holst, Howells, Ireland, Bridge** and **Bliss**. He was a prolific composer and is particularly known for his sacred music, such as the morning, Communion and evening services in B♭ (1879), anthems and motets. Some of his finest oratorios and cantatas include *The Three Holy Children* (1885), *The Revenge* (1886), *Songs of the Sea* (1904) and the *Stabat Mater* (1907). Stanford had a passionate interest in opera and composed 10 works, including *Shamus O'Brien* (1896), *Much Ado About Nothing* (1908) and *The Travelling Companion* (1925), which was performed posthumously. His instrumental music included seven symphonies, three piano concertos, two violin concertos, string and piano quartets and two cello sonatas.

Stanley, (Charles) John (1712-1786) English composer and organist who was blind from the age of two, but became a pupil of **Greene** and held various organist posts in London. In 1779 he succeeded Boyce as Master of the King's Music. He became famous for his organ voluntaries, and in addition he wrote 12 cantatas, six concertos for strings, the dramatic pastoral *Arcadia* (1761) and keyboard and chamber works.

Starker, Janos (1924-) Hungarian cellist who studied at Budapest Academy of Music, becoming first cello in the Budapest Opera orchestra. In 1948 he settled in the United States where he rapidly achieved fame playing for the Dallas Symphony Orchestra, the orchestra of the New York Metropolitan, and the Chicago Symphony Orchestra. He has toured widely in Europe and the United States as a soloist.

Starokadomsky, Mikhail (1901-1954) Russian composer who studied under Vassilenko, **Miaskovsky** and Catoire at the Moscow Conservatoire. Among his works was an organ concerto (rare in Soviet music), an opera, *Sot*, an oratorio, *Simon Proshakov*, two string quartets and a piano sonata.

steel band (Caribbean) Trinidadian ensemble, associated with Carnival, whose music is often referred to as pan calypso. Tempered steel drums are made in families from oil drums and are tuned by beating the top into a concave shape and hammering segments to the appropriate pitch. Adjacent sections are generally at an interval of a 3rd, 4th, 5th or 6th. In each band there are bass pans, rhythm pans (including double second pans, double guitar pans, treble guitar pans and cello pans), and tenor pans. During carnival processions players often retain the spirit of carnival combat by dressing in recognizable costumes, e.g. as soldiers or sailors. See also **calypso**.

Stefano, Giuseppe di (1921-) Italian tenor who became prominent at La Scala, Milan, from 1947 and has since appeared elsewhere in Europe.

Steffani, Agostini (1654-1728) Italian composer, clergyman and diplomat who learned music as a choirboy at Padua and later in Munich, where he studied under Kerl. Following further studies in Rome (1673-1674), he returned to Munich and became court organist in 1675. After studying theology he was ordained a priest (1680), and then served the Duke of Hanover (1688) and the Elector Palatine (1703) as musical director and diplomat. He was appointed ambassador to Brussels (1698). In 1706 he was elected Bishop of Spiga and Apostolic Vicar in 1709.

Steffani's works include operas, some of which were much admired in their day, vocal duets, madrigals, chamber sonatas for two violins, viola and double-bass, and motets.

Steinberg, Maximillian (1883-1946) Russian composer who studied at the Moscow Conservatoire as a pupil of **Rimsky-Korsakov**, and also of **Lyadov** and **Glazunov**. Steinberg later (1934) became director of the Leningrad Conservatoire. He wrote five symphonies, the ballets *Midas* and *Till Eulenspiegel*, a dramatic fantasy on Ibsen's *Brand*, two string quartets and a violin concerto.

Steinberg, William (1899-1978) German-born conductor who later settled in the United States. He studied in Cologne and in 1920 became **Klemperer**'s assistant at the Cologne Opera. In 1925 he went to the German Theatre in Prague and in 1929 became the musical director of the Frankfurt Opera, where he conducted the premiere of **Schoenberg's** *Von Heute auf Morgen* (1930). In 1933 he was removed from his post by the Nazis and became associated with the Jewish Culture League, and from 1936 to 1938 conducted the Palestine Symphony Orchestra. After his move to the United States, he conducted the NBC Symphony Orchestra (1938), the Buffalo Philharmonic Orchestra (from 1945) and from 1952 the Pittsburg Symphony Orchestra. His performances of **Verdi, Wagner** and **Strauss** were widely praised.

steinspiel (Ger.) Original term for **stone chimes**.

Steinway & Sons Firm of piano makers, founded by Heinrich Steinweg (later Henry Steinway, 1797-1871) in Brunswick (1836). He emigrated to the United States with his five sons in 1850, and by 1853 had established his firm, which in time expanded to include branches in London (1875) and Hamburg (1880).

Stenhammar, (Karl) Wilhelm (Eugen) (1871-1927) Swedish composer, conductor and pianist who was a pupil of his father and also studied the piano in Berlin (1892-1893) with Barth. He had a successful career as a conductor with the Stockholm Philharmonic Society (1897-1900), the New Philharmonic Society (1904-1906) and the Götesborg Orkesterforening (1906-1922). His works were influenced by **Wagner**'s music, but he also drew on Swedish folk music. He wrote two operas (*The Feast of Solhaug* and *Tirfing*), two symphonies, two piano concertos and many songs.

Stern, Isaac (1920-) American violinist of Soviet origin who studied in San Francisco where he made his debut in 1935. He has travelled widely, performing not only as a soloist but also in a successful trio with Istomin and **Rose**. Stern has a wide repertory, ranging from **Bach** to **Bartók**, and is considered among the most musical and successful of modern violin virtuosi.

Stevenson, Ronald (1928-) English composer and pianist whose work makes use of Scottish literary and musical sources. His compositions include piano works, such as *Passacaglia on DSCH* (the initials representing **Shostakovich**), two piano concertos and chamber music.

sthāyī/astāī (India) First section of a vocal composition which is set in a particular mode (**rāga**) and rhythm (**tāla**), and used as the basis for subsequent improvisation. Its main theme often recurs during improvised passages as a refrain, or framing device. See also **antarā**.

Still, William Grant (1895-1978) American composer who was educated at Wilberforce University and studied music at Oberlin Conservatoire and later at Boston with **Chadwick** and **Varèse**. He was the first black American to compose a successful symphony (*Afro-American Symphony*, 1931) and to conduct a major symphony orchestra. His other works

Isaac Stern

include an opera, *Blue Steel*, the ballets *La Guiablesse* and *Sahdji*, songs and chamber music.

stochastic music Theory of music evolved by Iannis **Xenakis**, based on mathematical laws of chance and computer indeterminacy. His compositions are given the prefix ST, followed by a number indicating how many performers are required. His string quartet ST4 (1956-1962) is an example.

Stockhausen, Karlheinz (1928-) German composer who studied at the Cologne Conservatoire (1947-1951) and in Paris with **Messiaen** and **Milhaud**. Since 1953 Stockhausen has worked at the electronic music studio for West German Radio, Cologne, and at the same time has studied phonetics at Bonn, which has influenced his composition. Much of his music combines live performers with pre-recorded sound, but he has also written music for the traditional media. Since 1958 he has travelled widely as a performer, conductor and lecturer when, on occasions, he can be seen sitting at a console in the middle of an auditorium, manipulating a mixing desk to control and transform live musical performance into a new electronic-sound product. Some of his electronic music includes *Gesang der Jünglinge* (1955-1956), *Kontakte* (1959-1960), *Telemusik* (1966) and *Hymnen* (1966). In addition, Stockhausen elaborated group compositions such as *Kontrapunkte* (1953), *Zeitmasze* (1956) and *Gruppen* (1957), the last work consisting of three orchestras and three conductors. Another example of his music is the composition *Zyklus* (1959) for one percussionist, where the performer begins at a point of his or her own choosing and then goes through the score, finishing at the same point.

Stokowski, Leopold (Antonin Stanislaw Boleslawowicz) (1882-1977) British-born conductor of Polish descent, who took American citizenship in 1915. He studied at the Royal College of Music, and in 1900 became organist at St James's Church,

Leopold Stokowski

Piccadilly. In 1909 he became conductor of the Cincinnati Symphony Orchestra and of the Philadelphia Orchestra in 1912, where he introduced much modern music and also experimented with the physical layout of the orchestra. His other appointments included conducting the NBC Symphony Orchestra (1942-1943) with **Toscanini**, and in 1945 he founded the Hollywood Bowl Symphony Orchestra. Stokowski also conducted the American Symphony Orchestra (1961), and the Houston Symphony Orchestra (1955-1960). From the early 1970s he continued to conduct in Europe and the United States, but was mainly resident in Britain.

Stolz, Robert (1880-1975) Austrain composer who was a pupil of **Humperdinck**. He lived in the United States (1940-1946), and is chiefly known for his operettas, such as *Wild Violets* and *White Horse Inn*. Stolz also wrote a large number of songs and film music.

stone chimes Ancient Chinese percussion instrument which consisted of 16 stone slabs of different thicknesses. Modern stone chimes have been used by **Orff** in his operas. In German the instrument is known as *steinspiel*.

stop Device by which the registration of the organ can be regulated and altered.

stopping Act of placing the (usually left-hand) fingers on the strings of stringed instruments in order to change the pitch of the notes of the open strings.

Storace, Stephen (1762-1796) British composer who studied at the Conservatoire of Saint Onfrio in Naples, and later went to Vienna, where he became friendly with **Mozart**. Returning to London in 1787, he conducted Italian operas at Drury Lane (1792-1793). His works included several operas, such as *The Haunted Tower* (1789) and *The Pirates* (1792), and also a ballet, *Venus and Adonis*.

Stradella, Alessandro (1644-1682) Italian singer, violinist and composer. He composed operas and oratorios and in 1658 became singer to Queen Christina of Sweden, in whose service he remained for several years. He later returned to Rome where he composed sacred music, but he was forced to leave in 1677 and travelled to Genoa.

Stradivari (or **Stradivarius**), **Antonio** (c1644-1737) Italian violin maker based in Cremona who was a pupil of Nicolo **Amati**. He is acknowledged as the finest maker of violins in the world, and this applies especially during the period 1700-1725. His two sons Francesco and Omobono continued the business after their father's death.

strathspey Scottish folk dance in quadruple time whose name is derived from the strath (valley) of the River Spey in the 18th-century. It is characterized by the use of a dotted quaver-semiquaver and its retrograde (commonly known as the 'Scotch snap').

Strauss, Johann (the Elder, 1804-1849) Austrian violinist, conductor and composer. The son of an innkeeper, he was apprenticed to a bookbinder, although he learned the violin and the viola and was allowed to study with Seyfried. He joined **Lanner's** band, of which he became deputy conductor, but in 1825 he formed his own orchestra for which he composed 150 waltzes, 28 galops, 19 marches and 14 polkas. With dances being so popular at that time – especially the waltz – Strauss travelled widely in Europe, and while in Paris added the **quadrille** to the music of the Viennese ballrooms. His best-known composition is the *Radetzky March* (1848).

Strauss, Johann (the Younger, 1825-1899) Son of Johann Strauss, the Elder, who was discouraged from following his father's profession, but studied the violin secretly with Drechsler. At the age of 19 he formed his own orchestra, and in time his fame rivalled that of his father. When Strauss the Elder died, the two orchestras amalgamated.

Following a meeting with **Offenbach** in 1863, Strauss was encouraged to write operettas, and in the same year he was

Johann Strauss

appointed director of the Imperial Court Balls in Vienna.

His operettas include *Die Fledermaus* (1874), *Eine Nacht in Venedig* (1883) and *Zigeunerbaron (The Gypsy Baron*, 1885). Among his many famous waltzes are *Blue Danube Waltz* (1867) and *Tales from the Vienna Woods* (1868). He also wrote the ballet *Aschenbrodel* and many marches and polkas.

Strauss, Richard (1864-1949) German composer and conductor whose father was principal horn player at the Munich opera house. He himself began piano lessons at the age of four, and when he was 12 had his first composition (*Festmarch*, for orchestra, Op. 1) published. He studied philosophy and aesthetics at the University of Munich (1882), and in 1884 was made assistant musical director of the Meiningen Court Orchestra. His conducting career continued with posts in Weimar and Berlin, and from 1919 to 1924 was director of the State Opera in Vienna. Strauss's reputation as a conductor in German opera was supreme, both in his own music and that of other composers, especially **Mozart**'s.

He became the most celebrated German composer of his generation, with a career that covers two distinct periods: the first in which the **tone poem** (1886-1903) was a prominent feature of his work, and the second in which he concentrated on opera (1900-1942). He composed songs throughout his life. His tone poems include *Macbeth* (1886-1890), *Don Juan* (1888), *Till Eulenspiegel* (1895) and *Ein Heldenleben* (1898). The influence of **Wagner** is apparent among some of his early operas, such as *Salomé* (1905), *Elektra* (1906-1908) and *Der Rosenkavalier* (1909-1910). The later operas were in a more romantic style, and included *Ariadne auf Naxos* (1912), *Intermezzo* (1922-1923) and *Capriccio* (1940-1941).

Among his other works were a violin concerto (1881-1882), two horn concertos (1882-1883 and 1942), an oboe concerto, and the ballet *Josephs-Legend* (1914). Due to his relationship with Stefan Zweig (a Jew), he caused some displeasure with the Nazis and Strauss resigned as president of the Reichs-Musikkammer.

Richard Strauss

Stravinsky, Igor Feodorovich (1882-1971) Russian-born composer whose father was a singer at the Imperial Opera. His parents refused to allow him to pursue a musical career, so he studied law at St Petersberg University. In 1907 he became a pupil of **Rimsky-Korsakov** who showed some of Stravinsky's work to **Diaghilev**. As a result, Diaghilev commissioned *Firebird* (1910) and other ballets followed. Leaving Russia in 1914, Stravinsky lived in Switzerland (1914-1920), in France (1920-1939) and finally in 1939 settled in the United States, where he became a naturalized citizen in 1945. In 1962 he visited the Soviet Union for the first time since 1914. His early ballet music, such as *Firebird*, *Petrushka* (1911) and *The Rite of Spring* (1913), are nationalistic in subject and style, whereas after World War I he developed a **neo-Classical** idiom as in *Apollo musagete* (1928) and in a fine Violin Concerto (1931), and in his Piano Concerto with wind instruments (1924). Some of his other

Igor Stravinsky

works included the melodrama *Persephone* (1933); the music-theatre pieces *The Soldier's Tale* (1918) and *The Flood* (1961–1962); *Dumbarton Oaks Concerto* (1938); the operas *Oedipus Rex* (1927) and *The Rake's Progress* (1951); and sacred music, such as *Symphony of Psalms* (1930) and *Requiem Canticles* (1966).

street piano Alternative term for **barrel organ**.

stretto (It.) Overlapping of entries of a **fugue** subject. The subject begins in one voice before the preceding voice has finished singing it. It is also a direction that a passage should accelerate or become intensified.

strict counterpoint Traditional name for **counterpoint** written according to the rules of the **species**.

Striggio, Alessandro (c1540–1592) Italian organist, lutenist, violinist and composer who was in the service of Cosimo de' Medici at Florence during the 1560s. He subsequently visited several European courts and became a virtuoso performer on the **lira da gamba**. His works included a 40-part setting of *Ecce beatam* (1568) for 10 four-part choirs, and many madrigals.

stringed instruments Instruments in which the sound is produced by the vibration of stretched strings. Such instruments may be bowed or plucked. Although the sound produced by the harp and piano is made by their vibrating strings, they are not normally considered to be stringed instruments.

Stringed instruments may be fretted (lute, cittern, mandolin, guitar, ukulele and banjo), or unfretted (violin, viola, cello and double-bass).

stringendo (It.) Indication that a passage is to be performed with increasing speed and intensification.

strophic Song in which each verse is sung to the same tune, rather than being **through-composed**.

Stuart, Leslie (1866-1928) British composer whose real name was Thomas A. Barrett. He composed several musical comedies such as *Florodora*, and the song *Lily of Laguna*.

student's counterpoint Alternative term for **strict counterpoint**.

study Instrumental piece, usually for a single instrument, written for the purpose of technical exercise and display. Some pieces have an artistic value too, such as the 27 studies for piano written by **Chopin** which are often performed as concert works. Studies are more often known by the French *étude*.

subdominant Fourth **degree** of the major or minor scale. For example, F is the subdominant in the key of C major.

subito (It.) At once, immediately.

subject Musical theme which is of distinct structural importance. See also **fugue**.

submediant Sixth **degree** of the major or minor scale above the **tonic**. For example, A is the submediant in the key of C major.

Subotnick, Morton (1933-) American composer who was a pupil of **Milhaud** and **Kirchner** and has become very active in electronic music. He has produced some pure **tape** works, multimedia and theatre pieces, and also 'sound-environments' for shops and offices. His composition, *Silver Apples of the Moon* (1967), is thought to be the first electronic work composed for issue as a gramophone record. Some of his other works include *Electric Christmas* (1967), *Before the Butterfly* (1976) and *A Sky of Cloudless Sulphur* (1980).

suite Instrumental composition consisting of a sequence of stylized dances. In the late 17th century a tradition was established of including four regular dance movements: the allemande, courante, sarabande and gigue. They were written in the same **key**, probably because suites were often written for lutes, which had to be newly tuned for each key. Other dances such as the gavotte, bourée, minuet, loure, polonaise, rigaudon and passepied were included between the sarabande and the gigue, and they could all be preceded by a prelude.

J.S. **Bach** was a prolific composer of suites, especially his English and French suites and **partitas** (suites in groups of six).

The suite declined in the second half of the 18th century, although at the end of the 19th century it re-emerged in a freer form in such compositions as **Rimsky-Korsakov**'s *Schéhérezade* (1888), **Tchaikovsky**'s *Nutcracker Suite* (1892) and **Grieg**'s *Peer Gynt Suite* (1875).

Suk, Joseph (1874-1935) Czech composer and violinist who entered Prague Conservatoire in 1885, graduated in 1891 but stayed on for a further year to study with **Dvorák**. He was a prominent member of the Czech String Quartet, and in 1922 was appointed professor of composition at the Prague Conservatoire.

Some of Suk's works contain elements of Bohemian folk music. Among his compositions are two symphonies (1899 and 1904), the Piano Quintet in B Minor (1893), the symphonic poems *A Summer Tale* (1907) and *Harvestide* (1917), and a Mass in B♭ major (1931).

suling (Indonesia) Bamboo, end-blown vertical flute in several sizes, with four to six finger-holes and a rattan band which helps to direct the air. It is used in a wide variety of ensembles including the 'soft style' of Javanese **gamelan** playing. The *suling gambuh* is the largest version and is found in the **gambuh** theatre ensemble of Bali.

Sullivan, Sir Arthur (Seymour) (1842-1900) British composer and conductor who was a chorister at the Chapel Royal and in 1856 gained the **Mendelssohn** scholarship at the Royal Academy of Music, where he studied under Sterndale **Bennett** and Goss. He also took further studies at Leipzig Conservatoire (1858-1861).

In 1869 he was introduced to W.S. Gilbert and in 1875 Gilbert commissioned Sullivan to set to music *Trial By Jury*. This was the beginning of a very successful partnership between the two. Their success compelled Richard D'Oyly Carte to lease the Opéra-Comique Theatre, London, in which to perform their operettas. There performances of such operettas as *The Sorcerer* (1877), *HMS Pinafore* (1878) and *The Pirates of Penzance* (1879) took place, and during the production of *Patience* (1881) they moved to the the newly-built Savoy Theatre.

In 1883 Sullivan was knighted, and from 1885 to 1887 he was conductor of the Philharmonic Society concerts. Throughout the period of their many successes, the relationship between Gilbert and Sullivan was professional rather than social, and at times it was rather strained. Their highly successful comic operas include *Iolanthe* (1882), *Princess Ida* (1884), *The Mikado* (1885), *Ruddigore* (1887), *The Yeoman of the Guard* (1888), *The Gondoliers* (1889), *Utopia Limited* (1893) and the *Grand Duke* (1896). Sullivan's other works included the opera *Ivanhoe* (1891), anthems, chamber music and hymns, such as the ever-popular *Onward Christian Soldiers*.

summation tone In acoustics, one of two **resultant tones** heard when two notes are sounded loud together. The summation tone is the higher of these two notes, and represents the sum of the frequencies of the two original notes. The lower of the resultant tones is known as the **difference tone**.

supertonic Second **degree** of the major or minor scale above the **tonic**. For example, D is the supertonic in the key of C major or minor.

Suppé, Franz von (Francesco Ezechiel Ermengildo Cavaliere, Suppe Demelli) (1819-1895) Austrian composer who studied law at the University of Padua, going on to Vienna to study music with Sechter and Seyfried. In 1840 he became third conductor of the Theater in der Josefstadt. Other appointments in Vienna were *Kapellmeister* of the Theater an der Wien (1862-1865), the Kaitheater (1862-1865) and the Carltheater (1865-1882).

Suppe's main compositions were of operas, operettas and incidental music. Some of his greatest successes in Viennese operetta were *Die schöne Galatea* (1865), which was influenced by **Offenbach**'s parodies, and *Die leichte Kavallerie* (1866). Probably his masterpiece was *Boccaccio* (1879), which is the nearest he came to true opera. He also wrote the overture *Poet and Peasant* (1846) as well as choral and orchestral works.

surbahār (India) Large, plucked lute-type instrument from northern India, effectively a bass **sitār**, tuned a fourth or fifth lower than the *sitār*, invented in the early 19th century for playing the older **rāga** style. It is constructed in virtually the same way as the *sitār*, but for its larger dimensions, and is played with a similar technique. Usually it is used with *sitār* players alongside, or in place of the normal *sitār*. There are a few great masters of the instrument, notably Imrat Khan.

Surinach, Carlos (1915-) Spanish-born composer and conductor who became an American citizen in 1959. His works include three symphonies, *Symphonic Variations* for orchestra, *Songs of the Soul*, for chorus, *Flamenco meditations* for voices and piano, and ballet scores.

Susato, Tielman (*c*1500-*c*1561) Dutch music publisher, editor and composer who worked in Antwerp and was the most outstanding Dutch music publisher of his time. He published Dutch songs and dances, and volumes of masses, motets and chansons by the leading composers of the day, including some of his own works.

suspension Device in harmony whereby a note is sounded as part of a **chord** and held over while a second chord is sounded, and resolved downwards by step on to a note of the second chord. The suspension is prepared on a weak beat, held over a strong beat, and resolved on the next weak beat. In a retardation the resolution is obtained by rising one note on the scale.

Susskind, Walter (1913-1980) British conductor of Czech origin who made his debut at the German Opera House, Prague, in 1932. From 1942 to 1945 he conducted with the Carl Rosa Opera Company, and then at **Sadler's Wells** in 1946. He was also conductor with the Scottish National Orchestra (1946-1952), the Toronto Symphony Orchestra (1956-1964) and the St Louis Symphony Orchestra (1968-1975).

Sutermeister, Heinrich (1910-) Swiss composer who entered the Basle Conservatoire and later studied with Courvoisier and **Pfitzner**. In 1934 he settled in Berne as operatic coach at the local municipal theatre. He became professor of composition in 1963 at the *Hochschule für Musik* in Hanover. Sutermeister's works include the opera *Romeo and Julia* (based on Shakespeare), the ballet *Das Dorf unter dem Gletscher*, orchestral works and chamber music.

Sutherland, Dame Joan (1926-) Australian soprano who initially studied in Australia and then at the Royal College of Music with Clive Carey. She made her London debut in 1952 at Covent Garden and in 1959 she sang the title role in **Donizetti's** *Lucia di Lammermoor*, in which she was received with international acclaim. She has established herself as one of the leading dramatic coloraturas of the day, which has led to appearances in Italy, France, Austria and the United States in the Rossini-Bellini-Donizetti repertory. Most of her performances are conducted by her husband, Richard **Bonynge**. She was made a DBE in 1979.

Joan Sutherland

Svendsen, Johan (Severin) (1840-1911) Norwegian composer, violinist and conductor who studied with Hauptmann, **David**, **Richter** and **Reinecke** at Leipzig Conservatoire. He formed friendships with **Liszt** and **Wagner**, and in 1872 he played at Bayreuth at the inauguration of the Festival Theatre. As the most prominent Norwegian conductor in his day, Svendsen toured Europe, and in 1883 was appointed conductor of the Royal Opera, Copenhagen. His compositions include two symphonies, *Carnival in Paris* (1872), violin and cello concertos, *Norwegian Rhapsodies*, chamber and piano music.

Sweelinck, Jan Pieterszoon (1562-1621) Dutch composer, organist and teacher who studied under his father, the organist at the Oude Kerk, Amsterdam, and whom he succeeded in the post. He taught many pupils, including Samuel **Scheidt** and Heinrich **Scheidemann**. Sweelinck was a celebrated organist and a highly skilled harpsichordist. His works consisted mainly of vocal pieces, but also included fantasias, toccatas and motets.

swell Device on an organ for increasing and diminishing the volume of sound. It is also found on certain 18th-century harpsichords.

swell organ One of the manuals of an organ, the pipes being enclosed in the swell box.

swing **Jazz** style, popular in the 1930s. Swing bands consisted of independent sections of trumpets, trombones, saxophones and percussion. Swing bands played carefully orchestrated melodies with little or no improvisation, except in the solo sections. Some prominent swing bands were led by such names as Duke **Ellington**, Benny Goodman, Tommy Dorsey, Harry James, Count Basie, Woody Herman and Glenn Miller. Each band had its own distinctive style of playing.

Swingle Singers French vocal group founded by Ward Lemar Swingle. It gave a distinctive rendering of vocal arrangements of Baroque and Classical instrumental music, especially that of **Bach**, and achieved wide popularity. Swingle II, a British vocal group founded in 1973 by Swingle after the Swingle Singers was disbanded, has followed the same style, but with a wider repertory.

sympathetic strings Set of strings in certain types of bowed instruments which vibrate and sound in accord with those actually touched by the bow.

symphonia In some contexts, the same as **symphony**. Richard **Strauss** in his work *Symphonia domestica* (1904) used it to describe his domestic life in musical terms.

symphonic band Alternative term for **concert band**.

symphonic poem Alternative term for **tone poem**.

symphonic study A term not in standard use, but has been related to an orchestral work similar to a **tone poem**. It is said that the term was invented by **Elgar** for his *Falstaff* (1913).

symphony The major form of orchestral composition, structurally identified with the sonata, but almost invariably in four movements.

The prototype of the Classical symphony was the Italian **overture** form called **sinfonia**, which was developed by **Scarlatti** in the mid-18th century. The familiar pattern of four movements consisted of an opening allegro in **sonata form**, a lyrical slow movement, a minuet and trio, and a fast finale in rondo or sonata-rondo form. By the end of the 18th century the symphony orchestra consisted of four woodwind instruments in pairs (flutes, oboes, clarinets and bassoons); trumpets, horns and timpani, also in pairs; and a string choir consisting of first and second violins, and string basses.

The early symphonies of **Haydn** and **Mozart** were severely restricted in the choice of key and lasted about 15 or 20 minutes. Nevertheless, their output was considerable; Haydn wrote more than 100 and Mozart 41. Some of the symphonies of **Beethoven** and **Brahms** have a wide range of keys. Beethoven composed nine symphonies, including the first programmatic symphony (No. 6, *The Pastoral*, 1809) and No. 9 (*Choral*, 1817), which departed still further from the Classical tradition by scoring for additional instruments (piccolo, contrabassoon, triangle, cymbals and bass drum), and for solo voices and chorus in the finale.

Other composers who made major contributions to the symphony were **Schubert, Schumann, Berlioz, Liszt, Bruckner, Borodin, Tchaikovsky, Dvořák, Mahler** and **Sibelius**. In the early 20th century the English symphonic tradition emerged, which included works by **Elgar, Stanford, Vaughan Williams, Walton, Britten** and **Tippett**. The Russian composers **Prokofiev, Shostakovich** and **Stravinsky** provided symphonies of outstanding merit, with the first two composers both providing light-hearted works such as Symphony No. 1 (1916) and Symphony No. 9 (1945), respectively.

syncopation Deliberate changing of the normal accent from the strong beat of a bar to one that usually carries a weak beat. This can be achieved by placing a stress on the weak beats, by putting rests on the strong beats, or by holding over a note that first occurs on a weak beat to an accented position. It is a device widely used, especially in jazz music.

synthesizer Electronic device (often with keyboard, but sometimes in the form of an electronic guitar) that creates musical sounds through a complex of oscillators, circuits, filters and magnetic tape recorders. Through a complicated process of modification, mixing, amplification, envelope variations and serialization, the final result is a series of composite sounds which are recorded directly on multiple-track magnetic tape.

The first syntheizer was produced in 1955, and in 1969 a more complex machine was invented by Robert **Moog** and is known as the Moog synthesizer, which is controlled by a piano-type keyboard.

Szell, George (1897-1970) Hungarian-born American conductor who turned the Cleveland Orchestra into an outstanding body of musicians of internationally acclaimed excellence. Born in Budapest, Szell first showed himself to be a child prodigy as a pianist, studying with Max Reger and appearing with the Vienna Symphony Orchestra at the age of 10. Later turning to conducting, he directed the Berlin Philharmonic Orchestra in one of his own compositions when he was only 17. He impressed Richard **Strauss**, who in 1915 appointed him to the staff of the Berlin Staatsoper. He later held conducting posts in Strasbourg, Prague, Darmstadt, Berlin and Prague again. In 1936 be became conductor of the Scottish Orchestra, retaining the job until 1939.

In 1931 he had already made his US debut, with the St Louis Symphony and had become a regular visitor. With the outbreak of World War II, he moved to the United States permanently and in 1946 took up US citizenship. During the war he conducted at New York's Metropolitan Opera.

From 1946 until his death, Szell conducted the Cleveland Orchestra, pushing up its standard of playing and leading it on international tours that brought it fame and critical applause. A man with prodigious memory for musical detail as well as a mordant wit, Szell was noted for his attention to sound balance and for the chamber-like clarity of his orchestra in performance. He was a well-known interpreter of **Wagner**, **Strauss** and **Mahler** as well as the classics, and outside the United States he made guest appearances with the Amsterdam Concertgebouw and at the Salzburg Festival.

Szeryng, Henrik (1918-) Polish-born violinist who studied with Flesch in Berlin before settling in Mexico, where he became naturalized in 1946. He has toured internationally since the mid-1950s and has been active in the performance of contemporary Mexican music.

Szigeti, Joseph (1892-1973) Hungarian-born violinist who settled in the United States in 1926. He studied in Budapest with Hubay and was also helped by **Busoni** and **Joachim**. He made his debut in 1902, and has since made extensive European tours. He also gave the first performances of the violin concertos by **Busoni** and **Bloch**.

Szokolay, Sandor (1931-) Hungarian composer who was a pupil of Farkas. Most of his music is vocal and choral, and shows the influence of primitive and folk music. His works include concertos for violin (1956), piano (1958) and trumpet (1968), and the oratorios *The Power of Music* (1969), *Blood Wedding* (1964) and *Samson* (1973).

Szymanowski, Karol (1882-1927) Polish

composer who learned music as a child and composed a set of piano preludes by the age of eight. He studied in Warsaw with Noskowski and later in Berlin. His work was much influenced by **Beethoven**, **Wagner**, **Chopin**, Richard **Strauss**, and later by **Stravinsky**. After World War I, he went to Warsaw where he became professor of composition and director of the state conservatoire. His works include three symphonies (1907, 1909 and 1915-1916), two violin concertos (1917 and 1932-1933), the operas *Hagith* (1912-1913) and *King Roger* (1920-1924), *Stabat Mater* (1928), chamber music and piano pieces.

T

tablā (India) Pair of single-headed drums used extensively throughout northern India. It more specifically refers to the right-hand drum used with the **bāyān**, and is tuned to the tonic (Sa) of the **rāga** by hammering small wooden chocks, which are wedged between the body of the drum and goathide laces, connected to the upper and lower rims, to tighten or relax the skin-head.

tablature System of writing down music not in notes, but by means of letters or numbers. Originally it was used for the **lute**, but the only modern instruments for which tablature notation is now normally in use are the **ukulele** and **guitars**.

table piano Alternative term for **square piano**.

tabor Small hand-held drum with two heads made of animal skin, often used in Britain to play folk music.

Tabor

Taburot, Jehan Pen-name of Thoinot **Arbeau**.

tacet Direction indicating that an instrument or performer is to be silent for a time, for example, for the duration of a movement.

taekum See **taegŭm**.

taegŭm/taekeum (Korea) Transverse flute, used in both court and folk music. It has six finger holes and an additional hole covered with a membrane which produces its characteristic nasal tone. The largest of the Korean flute family.

Tailleferre, Germaine (1892-1983) French composer, a pupil of **Ravel** and a member of Les **Six**. Her work was generally lightweight in style with only occasional excursions into the **serial** and **polytonal** modes of composition. Concertos for piano, harp and full orchestra are among her compositions, together with many operas. The best known of these are *Marchand d'Oiseaux* (1923) and *Parisiana* (1955).

tailpiece Fan-shaped piece at the opposite end to the **peg box** where the strings of instruments such as a **fiddle, viol** or **violin** are attached.

Takemitsu, Toru (1930-) Japanese composer, largely self-taught and a leading member of the Japanese avant-garde. The influence of **Schoenberg** and *musique* concrète together with a brief period of study under Kiyose led Takemitsu to blend traditional Japanese and European avant-garde styles of music. His work relies heavily on experimental procedures, such as the use of tape-machines, and has been praised in particular for its exploration of **timbre**.

Takemitsu's better-known compositions include *Coral Island* (1962), *Quatrain* (1975) and *A Flock Descends into the Pentagonal Garden* (1977, for full orchestra). Takemitsu has organized experimental workshops and was art director of the Space Theatre, Osaka, for EXPO 71.

tāla (India) System of rhythmic cycles, characterized by a repeating pattern of four to 16 or more beats (**mātras**) subdivided into groups. In addition to a stress on the first beat (or **sam**) of the cycle, the first matra of each group is also emphasized. As an example, the most popular *tāla*, *tīntāl*, comprises 16 beats grouped 4 + 4 + 4 + 4.

Talich, Václav (1883-1961) Czech conductor, violinist and art director of the Prague National Opera from 1935-1945. Talich studied the violin under Sevcik and conducting under **Nikisch**, before going on to conduct various minor European orchestras. Talich's later fame derives from his work with the Czech Philharmonic Orchestra (1919-41) and his re-orchestrations of several of **Janáček**'s operas. After the annexing of Czechoslovakia in 1945 he was frequently dismissed for his dissent and just as frequently reinstated for his talent. Talich retired in 1956.

Tallis, Thomas (*c*1505-1585) English composer and organist at Waltham Abbey until its dissolution in 1540. Tallis's early compositions were influenced by composers such as **Fayrfax**, whose work he surpassed in both scale and complexity. His works include masses, motets, anthems, many works for the keyboard and two of the earliest known **plainsong** settings. His achievements were recognized by Elizabeth I when she granted Tallis and his pupil **Byrd** the lucrative music-printing monopoly in 1575.

His best-known works are the forty-voice motet *Spem in Alium* and his second *Lamentation*, with its innovative use of **modulation**. Tallis is often thought of as a typically English composer and has influenced **Vaughan Williams** among many others.

Talma, Louise (1906-) American composer, born in France. Talma studied in Paris under Nadia **Boulanger** and in New York with Howard Brockway, before taking a teaching post at Hunter College, New York, where she has lived since 1928. Her various works include an opera, *The Alcestiad* (performed in Frankfurt, 1962), as well as an oratorio, *The Divine Flame* (1948) and many smaller pieces. She was made professor of music at Hunter College in 1952, and has collected many awards and prizes.

talon (Fr.) Heel of the **bow** of a stringed instrument.

Talvela, Martti (1935-) Finnish bass. Talvela's powerful voice and stage presence have made him ideally suited for the grand roles in the operas of **Verdi** and **Wagner**.

He studied in Stockholm and has performed in many of the major European operatic centres including **Bayreuth**, Salzburg, Berlin and Milan. He was art director of the Savonlinna Opera Festival from 1972 to 1980.

tambour (Fr.) Alternative term for **drum**.

tambourine Small **drum** with a single skin stretched over the edge of one side of its rim, into which jingles are set to add to the sound when the skin is struck or rubbed by the hand. The drum can also be shaken to obtain the jingling sound. The tambourine is of Arab origin.

tāmbūra (India) Vertically held, plucked tube-zither with a gourd-bowl as its base, often mistakenly referred to as a member of the lute family. It has four open metal strings, usually tuned in the order of a fifth, a pair of upper tonics and a lower tonic. These are gently plucked throughout most genres of Indian music to provide the **drone**, emphasizing the relationship between the tonic of the **rāga** and the solo melody.

tamtam Alternative term for **gong**. Sometimes also spelled tam-tam.

tān (India) Rapid melodic patterns used in both vocal and instrumental improvisations. They are used to brilliant effect in **khyāl**, usually sung to an open vowel 'a'.

Taneyev, Alexander Sergeyevich (1850-1918) Russian composer and uncle of the more famous Sergey Ivanovich **Taneyev**. Alexander Sergeyevich graduated from St Petersburg University and subsequently pursued a successful career in the civil service alongside his activities as a composer. He studied with **Rimsky-Korsakov** and Petrov. One of his best-known works, the Symphony No. 2, was an attempt to write a specifically Russian composition and was not a great success. His talents were more evident in his lighter pieces, which included bagatelles, serenades and mazurkas.

Taneyev, Sergey Ivanovich (1856-1915) Russian composer, pianist and teacher. Taneyev was educated at the Moscow Conservatoire studying composition under **Tchaikovsky**. The two were later to become close friends.

The 1880s saw Taneyev increasingly involved in the Conservatoire, reluctantly accepting a series of posts until he was made director in 1885. **Scriabin** and **Rachmaninov** were among his pupils at this time. Taneyev's own music was at first a closely-guarded secret between Tchaikovsky and himself, but successful performances of his cantata *John of Damascus* (1884) and his Symphony in D minor (1885) made him less reticent. His most ambitious work was his opera *The Oresteia* (performed in 1895), while his most successful instrumental work was his symphony in C minor (1898).

tangak (Korea) Literally 'Tang music', a term used to distinguish secular court music of Chinese origin from native music or **hyangak**. Although the repertory constitutes a rare survival of medieval Chinese music, the only two remaining examples (excluding some additional dances) are actually instrumental versions of love songs dating from the Sung era (960-1279). Originally sung with instruments, they are now played by a more native orchestra including **taegŭm**, **haegŭm**, **p'iri**, bell-chimes, stone chimes, barrel drum, bowed **zither** and wooden clapper.

tangent One of a series of small pieces of metal used to strike the strings of a **clavichord**.

tango Dance of Argentinian origin, closely resembling the Cuban habanera. It is a fairly slow dance in 2/4 time with a syncopated rhythm. The tango became popular during and immediately after World War I.

Tansman, Alexandre (1897-) French composer, conductor and pianist. Born in Poland and educated at Lódz Conservatoire, Tansman moved to Paris in 1919 where he has since lived. He toured with the Boston Symphony Orchestra as pianist in 1927 and later began to conduct his own works. Early influences included **Chopin**, **Ravel** and **Stravinsky**; the latter was a close friend whose death inspired Tansman's best-known work, the elegiac *Stele* (1972). Tansman has written many large and smaller-scale works, and is as at home with **serial** and **polytonal** methods of composition, as well as with more conventional techniques.

tanto (It.) So much. For example, *allegro ma non tanto*, fast but not too fast.

tape Magnetic tape that is used to record sound. It is now used in a variety of ways. The most widespread use is in the recording of musicians either in the studio or at a concert, for mass production by the record industry. More innovative uses include the production and recording of electronically-produced sounds to be used as backing for a live performance or, indeed, to constitute a performance in itself.

tarogato Hungarian single-reed **woodwind instrument** now fitted with a **saxophone** mouthpiece. It is sometimes used for the shepherd's call in **Wagner's** *Tristan und Isolde*.

Tárrega (y Eixea), Francisco (1852-1909) Spanish guitarist and composer. Trained in both guitar and piano, Tárrega played a prominent role in revitalizing the guitar as a serious musical instrument.

He studied at the Madrid Conservatoire in the 1870s and during the 1880s was giving recitals throughout the capitals of Europe. As well as composing, he arranged for the guitar many works by **Chopin, Mendelssohn** and **Thalberg**. Through his teaching he has had an enormous influence on 20th-century guitar-players, his pupils including Pujol and Robledo.

Tartini, Giuseppe (1692-1770) Italian composer, violinist and teacher. Tartini studied law in Padua before fleeing the city and taking refuge in a monastery of Assisi because of disapproval of his marriage. Returning in 1715, he played in the orchestra there and, after an interval of several years spent in Prague, founded a school of violin-playing in 1728. He described **resultant tones** (only fully understood by Helmholtz much later) and a new type of violin bow. His compositions include various religious vocal works, many canzone and sonatas, the most famous of these being the *Devil's Trill* sonata, probably composed after 1745.

tasto (It.) The **key** of an instrument. For example, *tasto solo* is a direction to a keyboard **continuo** player to play only the **bass** notes. It also means the **fingerboard** of a stringed instrument.

Tate, Phyllis Margaret (1911-1987) English composer of operatic, choral and children's music. Tate studied at the Royal Academy of Music but has discarded all her work from this period. Her best-known works are the *Sonata for Clarinet and Cello* (first performed in 1947) and, more spectacularly, her opera *The Lodger*, which was produced in 1960. Tate is not a prolific composer and is generally more at home with smaller-scale compositions.

Tauber, Richard (1892-1948) Tenor, born in Austria, later a naturalized Briton. Tauber came from an operatic family and studied with Carl Beines at Freiburg. His debut, in 1913 in *The Magic Flute*, was an immediate success and he sang most of the great tenor parts during the next five years. However it was in lighter operas and operettas that he found greatest fame, especially in **Lehár**'s *Das Land des Lächelns*, which played in Drury Lane in 1931.

Tausig, Carl (1841-1871) Polish pianist and composer, a favourite pupil of **Liszt**, whom he accompanied on many of his tours (and who later described his technique as infallible). Tausig gave wild, virtuoso performances in many German cities which were only partly understood by contemporary critics. His playing was passionate, strident and extravagant. His compositions are negligible for the most part, although a piano exercise, *Tägliche Studien*, is still used today.

Tavener, John Kenneth (1944-) English composer educated at the Royal Academy of Music. While still a student, along with **Berkeley** and **Lumsdaine**, Tavener composed two religious cantatas of which one, *The Whale* (1965), was later recorded by the Beatles' company, Apple Records. Much of his work has a religious theme and his strongest affinity is with the late **Stravinsky** of *A Narrative and a Prayer*. His most ambitious work is his multi-layered *Celtic Requiem* (1969), which draws on children's games, poetry and church music.

Taverner, John (*c*1490-1545) Foremost

English composer of the early 16th century. Taverner's early life remains a mystery, but by 1525 he was first instructor of the choir at Cardinal College, Oxford, and in 1530 held a similar position in Boston, Lincolnshire. It is likely that most of his works were composed in the 1520s and 1530s, at the time Wolsey was fostering the development of English music. All of Taverner's music was composed for the church and he excelled in the composition of ambitious, large-scale masses and magnificats (of which he wrote three). His works draw on the best elements of the florid style of the era and prepared the way for **Tallis, Tye** and **Sheppard** in the 1540s and after.

Tchaikovsky, Piotr Ilyich (1840-1893) Russian composer and teacher, the foremost musical figure of his generation. Tchaikovsky trained at the St Petersburg Conservatoire, and was employed at first at the Moscow Conservatoire by Nikolay Rubinstein, later to become an important advocate of his work. In 1867 he met **Berlioz, Balakirev** and other members of The Five, with whom he discussed his first masterpiece, *Romeo and Juliet* (1870). Tchaikovsky's nationalist sympathies are evident in his use of Russian folk songs throughout his work, especially *The Oprichnik* (1870) and in the subject matter of *Eugene Onegin* (1878). However, he never sought to use material from Russian folk music to the same extent as some of his contemporaries.

A disastrous marriage in 1877 caused his nervous collapse in the same year and a period of low creativity that was to last until 1884. The last nine years of his life saw the composition of the ballets *Sleeping Beauty*, first performed in 1890, and *The Nutcracker* (1892).

Tchaikovsky's work ranges widely from the popular, such as *Swan Lake* (1876) and the *1812 Overture* (1880), to more difficult creations such as the challenging sixth symphony, written in the year of his death. His oeuvre covers the symphony (of which he wrote six), symphonic poems, concertos for piano and violin, ballet music, string quartets and piano music. Tchaikovsky's influence on Russian music has been immense and the popularity his works enjoy has ensured their frequent performance and recording, not only in his native country, but also in Europe and the United States.

Tcherepnin, Alexander (Nikolayevich) (1899-1977) Composer, pianist, conductor and the son of Nikolay **Tcherepnin**. Tcherepnin was a precocious composer and pianist. He studied at the St Petersburg Conservatoire but fled the Soviet Union with his family in 1921 as the political climate turned against them. His music, composed in Paris, London and the United States, is traditional with some evident influence from **Prokofiev**. His works include ballets, operas and many smaller pieces, but his best works are probably his Symphony No. 2 (1951) and Symphony No. 4 (1957).

Tcherepnin, Nikolay (Nikolayevich) (1873-1945) Russian conductor and composer. A pupil of **Rimsky-Korsakov** at the St Petersburg Conservatoire, Tcherepnin concentrated his energies on music for ballet, collaborating with **Diaghilev** for the first season of the *Ballets Russes* in Paris in 1909. He moved permanently to Paris in 1921 (after a successful career in his homeland) and there produced works combining his Russian idiom with the latest French style. Two later works, the operas *Swat* (1930) and *Vanka* (1932), mark a return to the Russian style and perhaps reflect his personal sense of exile.

te Seventh note of a major scale when using the **tonic sol-fa** system. In French and Italian, spelled as *si*.

Tear, Robert (1939-) Welsh tenor. Tear was a choral scholar at King's College, Cambridge. He joined the St Paul's Cathedral Choir in 1961, and in 1963 the English National Opera. His voice is more suited to the delicate operatic and choral roles such as the Evangelist in **Bach**'s

Passions. He has a very wide operatic repertory and has made several recordings of English songs, as well as music by **Rachmaninov** and **Weber**.

Tebaldi, Renata (1922-) Italian soprano and former pupil of Carmen Melis. Chosen by **Toscanini** to sing at the re-opening of La Scala in 1946, Tebaldi has since gone on to sing in England, North and South America and throughout her native Italy. Her voice was judged to be close to perfection, and the improvement of her dramatic technique has established her as one of the world's greatest sopranos.

Te Deum Laudamus We praise thee, O God. Latin hymn of thanksgiving to God used by many Christian churches. It may be sung either to a traditional **plainsong** setting or to settings with orchestral accompaniment, such as those by **Haydn** and **Berlioz**.

tegotomono (Japan) Important type of **koto** music of the *jiuta* genre, so-called because of its use of *tegoto* (instrumental interludes). Its basic form is *maeti* (fore-song), *tegoto* and *atouta* (after-song), and may be extended to include further alternating songs and instrumental interludes.

Te Kanawa, Dame Kiri See **Kanawa, Dame Kiri Te**

Telemann, Georg Philipp (1681-1767) Hugely prolific German composer, theoretician and writer. Without any formal training, Telemann had composed arias, motets and an opera by the age of 12. He studied law at Leipzig but was soon spending more time, and gaining more success, at his music. He subsequently held posts at Soren, Eisenach (where he probably met J.S. **Bach**) and Hamburg. In the age supposedly dominated by Bach, Telemann's output was greater and he was probably far better known. During his life he produced both secular and religious music: of the latter the **cantata**-cycle *Tafelmusik* stands out. Other works include more than 40 operas and over 600 overtures.

temperament System of tuning whereby compromises are made in order to produce a series of notes which, although mostly a fraction out of perfect tuning, are nonetheless acceptable to the ear, avoid awkward gaps between tones, and allow modulation to any **key** without difficulty.

Equal temperament is the division of the **octave** into twelve equal **semitones**. In this system the amount that each note gives and takes from its perfect tuning is slight enough to deceive the ear, which will accept, for example, C♯ and D♭ as identical, although when perfectly in tune they are different notes. J.S. **Bach**'s collection of preludes and fugues, *The Well-Tempered Clavier* (Book I – 1722, Book II – 1744), demonstrates this system.

temple block Percussion instrument in the shape of a hollow wooden box that produces a dry, rapping sound when tapped. It can be in various sizes, giving different pitches, although not tuned to any one clear note.

Templeton, Alec (1909-1963) Welsh composer and pianist, born blind. After a period as a radio entertainer in London, Templeton left to work in the United States. He has written many pieces for orchestra and solo piano, but his most famous work is probably his pastiche of **Bach**, *Bach goes to Town*.

tempo Speed at which a composition is played. Some indication is usually given at the head of the music, such as **allegro**, **adagio** or andante. A more accurate indication of speed is given by using a **metronome** mark, annotated in terms of beats per minute.

The word tempo is also used with other words to give more precise speed markings. For example, *tempo giusto* (in strict time), *tempo ordinario* (common time, moderate speed) and *tempo primo* (at the original pace).

tenor Highest-pitched adult male voice produced naturally, apart from **alto** which uses falsetto. It is derived from the Latin word *teneo* (I hold) because it held the **plainsong** theme in early **polyphonic** compositions using a **cantus firmus**. It is also used to describe instruments with a range comparable to that of the tenor voice, for example tenor saxophone and tenor drum.

tenor clef **Clef** that is now almost obsolete, in which the note C is positioned on the second line down. Instruments that would play from the tenor clef include the tenor trombone, cello and bassoon.

tenor drum Drum of indefinite pitch that is half-way between the **snare drum** and **bass drum** in size. It has no snares. In a marching band, the instrument is held at the side of the player's body. The tenor drum is usually to be found in a modern drum kit, but rarely in orchestras.

tenor tuba Alternative term for **euphonium**.

tenuto Direction indicating that a note is to be fully sustained, up to and sometimes slightly longer than its strict time value.

ternary form Vocal or instrumental piece in three distinct sections, the third of which is a repetition of the first. The three sections are commonly designated as ABA. The middle section is usually a contrast, sometimes based on similar but more often on different, thematic material, but always relevant in style if not in mood. Examples of ternary form may be found in the da capo **aria**, and in minuets or scherzos with trios.

Tertis, Lionel (1876-1975) English viola player and pioneer soloist on that instrument. Tertis studied violin at Leipzig and the Royal Academy of Music in London, where he was urged to take up the viola. He toured Europe and the United States giving recitals, much of his music being specially commissioned by him from composers such as **McEwen, Bax** and **Bridge**. Tertis used a larger than normal viola designed for him by Arthur Richardson. From 1936 he spent his time promoting interest in and encouraging students of the viola, and made many transcriptions for the instrument.

tessitura (It.) Prevailing range of a composition or voice part. It may be high, low or normal for the voice or instrument concerned.

tetrachord Term with two meanings.

First, it is the sequence of notes within a perfect fourth, consisting of two tones and a **semitone**, but not necessarily in that order.

Second, it is an ancient Greek four-tringed instrument also called a tetrachordon.

Lower tetrachord Upper tetrachord

Tetrazzini, Luisa (1871-1940) Italian soprano who made her debut in her native Florence as Inés in *L'Africaine* in 1890, and quickly established herself as the greatest **coloratura** soprano of her time. Her reputation abroad was as high as in her native Italy, with her triumphs extending from St Petersburg to Buenos Aires. From 1908 she sang mostly in the United States, appearing at **Hammerstein**'s Manhattan Opera House.

Tetrazzini's technical skills were astonishing and her voice strong, even in the higher registers. In later years she taught in Milan, her pupils including Lina Paglinghi.

Teyte, Dame Margaret (1888-1976) English soprano also known as Margaret Tate. Teyte's operatic career began at the age of 17 with her appearance at the 1906

Mozart Festival. From 1908 she sang in **Debussy**'s opera company in Paris, a formative influence on her career. She sang in all the operatic centres of the world and in the 1940s made a great many recordings of songs by **Fauré** and **Debussy**. Her final performance was in 1955 at the London Festival Hall.

Thalben-Ball, George Thomas (1896-) British organist and international recitalist who studied at the Royal College of Music, becoming a fellow of the Royal College of Organists at the age of 16. He performed at the Henry Wood Promenade Concerts for many years, and more recently advised the BBC Music Department.

Thalberg, Sigismond Fortune François (1812-1871) Austrian pianist and composer. Thalberg was perhaps the greatest virtuoso pianist in an age of virtuosi. Studying under Sechter and **Hummel**, then later with Pixis and Kalkbrenner, he evolved a technical command of his instrument rivalled only by **Liszt**, with whom he conducted a good-natured contest throughout the 1830s. He toured Europe and the United States, finally retiring to Naples in 1863. His compositions are mostly negligible, written more as showcases for his ability than as works in their own right.

thāt (India) Mode type or parent scale in Indian musical theory. In the classification system of Hindustani **rāgas** devised by Bhatkhande (1860-1936), there are ten *thāts*, grouping together those *rāgas* which share the same basic scale. The *thāt* of a *rāga* corresponds to the mode to which the instrument is tuned.

theatre organ Alternative term for **cinema organ**.

thekā (India) Set rhythmic pattern extending over a complete time cycle (**tāla**), played on the **tablā** drums. Such patterns, of which there are several for each *tāla*, are learned using the mnemonic system of **bols**. In performance, a *thekā* is repeated continuously as a time-keeper, while also serving as a point of departure for rhythmic interplay with the soloist.

theme Musical idea that forms an essential structural part of a composition. It is a passage that returns in one form or other throughout a piece of music. A theme is generally complete in itself, whereas a **motif** is a (usually shorter) figure which contributes something to a larger conception. In a **fugue** the theme is also known as the **subject**. See also **theme song**; **variations**.

theme song Song or some other musical theme that recurs in a musical play in association with a particular character. See also **leitmotiv**.

theorbo One of the largest members of the **lute** family. The theorbo has a double peg-box with one set of strings passing over the fingerboard and stopped in the normal fashion. The second set of strings does not have a fingerboard and they are played open.

thérémin Electronic instrument invented by Lev Thérémin (1896-) in Russia in 1920 and originally known as the etherophone. It consists of an upright pole through which a high-frequency electric current is passed. The proximity of any object (such as a hand) changes the rate of oscillation of the current and thus is able to produce different tones. The first composition to be written for the instrument was First Airphonic Suite by Joseph Schillinger.

Theodorakis, Mikis (1925-) Greek composer. Theodorakis supplemented early influences from Byzantine and Cretan folk music with a course at the Paris Conservatoire in the 1950s, where he began to compose in earnest. With the credential of having his first opera, *Antigone*, produced at Covent Garden in 1959, Theodorakis returned to Greece to launch an impassioned attack on the conservative musical establishment there.

The 1960s saw an increase in his revolutionary activities and when a right-wing government gained power he was imprisoned, 1967-1970. As well as operas, he has composed ballets, oratorios and film scores, all of which touch on the issues of Greek history and national character.

Thibaud, Jacques (1880-1953) French violinist and child prodigy. Thibaud made his first public recital at the age of eight in Bordeaux. Engaged by Edward Colonne in 1889, his appearances in the *Concerts Colonne* launched his career. His partnership in a trio with **Cortot** and **Casals** in the 1920s and 1930s resulted in their famed recording of **Schumann**'s Piano Trio in B♭, 1926. Thibaud maintained a highly polished tone in his playing and excelled in works by **Mozart** and the French Romantics.

Thiman, Eric Harding (1900-1975) English composer and organist, largely self-taught. A professor at the Royal Academy of Music from 1932, Thiman's career was committed to music education for all. His compositions are appropriately simple and direct, finding great popularity among amateur musicians. His choral works have proved more successful than those for orchestra, and the former include *The Last Supper* (1930) and *The Temptations of Christ* (1952).

third **Interval** of three notes of the scale, counting both the first and the last notes, being four semitones for a major third (C-E) and three semitones for a minor third (C-E♭). A diminished third (C-E♭♭) is equivalent to a major second.

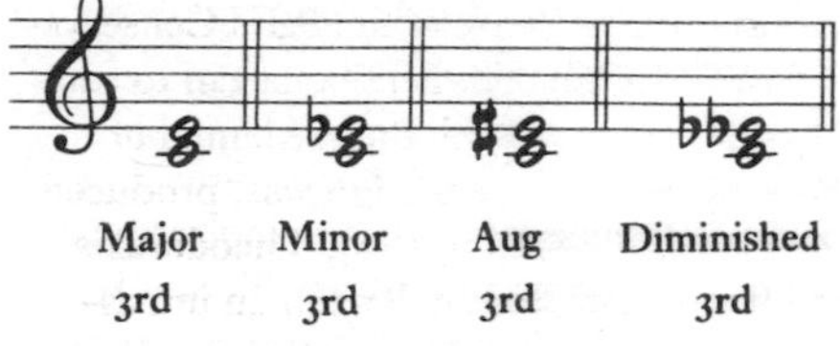

thirty-second note Alternative name for **demisemiquaver**.

Thomas, (Charles Louis) Ambroise (1811-1896) French composer of operas. His early education at the Paris Conservatoire under Bernd **Zimmermann** and Dourlen was completed privately under Kalkbrenner (for piano) and Barbereau (for harmony). After a stay in Rome, where he forged a friendship with Ingres, he returned to Paris and began producing the comic operas which were to ensure his fame. Chief among these are *Hamlet* (1868) and *Mignon* (1866), the latter receiving more than 1,000 performances at the Opéra- Comique during the following 30 years. Eclectic in his influences and, some say, bland in style, Thomas's works (apart from the above) are now rarely performed.

Thomas, Arthur Goring (1850-1892) English composer. Trained as a civil servant, it was not until 1873 that Thomas took up music seriously. He studied under Emile Durand in Paris, then **Sullivan** and Prout at the Royal Academy of Music before completing his first opera, *The Light of the Harem*, performed 1879. He wrote several other operas and some choral works, but few are of popular interest now.

Thomson, Virgil (1896-) American composer, pianist, critic and collaborator with Gertrude Stein. Thomson learned to play the piano at five, studied it further at Harvard in 1919 and in 1921 toured Europe with the Glee Club. In Paris he met Cocteau, Les **Six** and was introduced to **Satie**. Meeting Gertrude Stein in 1926, they conceived the bizarre opera *Four Saints in Three Acts*, eventually performed 1934.

Returning to the United States, he worked as a music critic from 1940 and after 1950 toured the country lecturing and occasionally conducting. Of his numerous avant-garde compositions, the most successful is probably the opera *Lord Byron*, first performed in New York in 1972.

thorough bass Alternative term for **continuo**.

Three Choirs Festival One of the oldest English festivals, dating back to 1724, when it was a means of raising funds for cathedral charities. It has been held annually since then at one of the cathedral cities of Gloucester, Hereford and Worcester, taken in rotation. It originally consisted of performances of liturgical music and anthems, and this practice still continues. The festival encouraged the performance of new English works, and in particular those by **Sullivan, Parry** and **Elgar**. Among the premiere performances played there were **Vaughan Williams'** *Fantasia on a Theme of Thomas Tallis* (1910), **Bliss's** *A Colour Symphony,* **Holst's** *Choral Fantasia* (1931) and **Howell's** *Hymnus Paradisi* (1950).

through-composed song Song in which each verse is set to different music. From the German, *durchkomponiert*, through-composed.

thumrī (India) Light, classical, vocal genre usually sung by women's voices. It is characteristically graceful with romantic lyrics. Developed during the 19th century, it is still popular and is one of the freest forms in northern Indian music. It may mix **rāgas**, folk tunes and popular song, providing the emotional intensity is not lost.

thundersheet Sheet of flexible metal used to simulate thunder in certain compositions. It is suspended from a wooden pole and shaken or struck with a soft **drumstick**.

ti (China) Transverse bamboo **flute**, usually with six finger-holes, a blowing hole, and one further hole covered with a membrane which when caused to vibrate produces the distinctive tone of this popular instrument. It also has two decorative holes at the lower end holding silk string tassels.

tie Musical notation in the form of an arching stroke, used to connect two notes of the same **pitch**, or a group of such notes in chords, indicating that the second note of the pair is not to be sounded.

Tie

tierce de Picardie (Fr.) Picardy third. In a musical piece composed in a minor key, a device that ends the piece on a major chord. For example, if the piece is in C minor the *tierce de picardie* would be the chord of C-E-G, rather than C-E♭-G.

Tilson Thomas, Michael (1944-) American conductor and pianist. Tilson Thomas studied at the University of California, then in Bayreuth and England before taking up a post with the Boston Symphony Orchestra in 1969. He worked as the music director of the Buffalo Philharmonic throughout the 1970s.
He was made principal conductor of the LSO in 1988.

timbale (Fr.) Alternative term for **kettledrum**.

timbre Alternative term for **tone colour**.

timbrel Ancient form of **tambourine**.

time The time of a piece of music is its division into units of two, three, four or more beats per bar. The speed at which the music moves does not affect its time, but only its **tempo**. The time remains constant (duple, triple, quadruple) until there is a change of **time signature**.

time signature Sign at the beginning of a composition or movement to indicate the kind and number of beats in the bar. It consists of two figures written one above the other. The lower figure is the unit of the note values into which each bar is divided, and the upper number represents the number of such note values contained in a bar. For example, a lower 2 indicates **minims** (half notes) and a 4 indicates **crotchets** (quarter notes). Therefore 4/4, known as common time, indicates that there are four crotchets to the bar. The symbol for this particular time signature (also known as common time) is a broken circle resembling a C. See also **compound time; simple time**.

timpani Alternative term for **kettledrums**.

tin whistle Simple, rudimentary pipe of the **fife** or **recorder** type, which has a small range of high notes controlled by six finger-holes. Also called a penny whistle or flageolet.

Tippett, Sir Michael (Kemp) (1905-) One of Britain's foremost 20th-century composers. Coming to music at the relatively late age of 18, Tippett studied at the Royal Academy of Music from 1926, but his dislike of the teaching methods there meant that he was to a large degree self-taught. During World War II he registered as a conscientious objector and was jailed for three months in 1942. His first acknowledged work (String Quartet No. 1) was not produced until 1925, and he achieved little recognition for the next ten years. Tippett's early lyrical period produced the oratorio *A Child of Our Time* (1941) and his first opera *The Midsummer Marriage* (1952). Thereafter his work grew more disjunct and difficult, this second style culminating in the choral work *The Vision of Saint Augustine* (1965). Tippett's work generally incorporates personal feeling with a larger social awareness, and in his later years his work has taken a more popular, sometimes naive, turn.

Sir Michael Tippett

toccata Single-movement keyboard work of free or sectional form which usually lays stress on brilliance and rapid execution alone. Claudio **Merulo** (1533-1604) was responsible for organizing and developing the toccata in its sectional form, which usually consisted of five sections, alternately free and fugal, the former of a brilliant character. Modern toccatas are works in an essentially rhapsodic style.

Toch, Ernst (1887-1964) Austrian-born composer, teacher and pianist who became a naturalized American. Entirely self-taught, Toch was heavily influenced by **Mozart**'s string quartets in his youth and remained primarily a composer of chamber music. Toch taught and composed in Berlin, London and then in the United States from 1934. His compositions are **neo-Classical** in style (although some of his work verges on **atonality**) and include symphonies, choral works, song cycles and film music. Toch's early work remains his most accomplished, from which his piano piece *Kleinstadtbilder* of 1929 might be singled out.

todī (India) One of the ten parent scales (**thāt**) in Hindustani music, corresponding to C, D♭, E♭, F♯, G, A♭, B, C′.

Toeschi, Carl Joseph (1731-1788) German composer, violinist and a member of the

Mannheim School. A member of the Mannheim Court Orchestra from 1752, he led it from 1759 and moved to Munich with the orchestra in 1778. Toeschi composed more than 60 symphonies and 30 ballets, many influenced by J.W. **Stamitz** and Filtz. He was regarded as a leading German composer at the time and some of **Mozart**'s work, notably the *Paris Symphony*, bears traces of his influence. His chamber piece, *Quatuor Dialogués* (1766), was important in defining the different instrumental roles in that genre.

Tōgaku (Japan) 'Music of the left', or that of Chinese origin, in **gagaku** court music, as distinguished from 'music of the right' (**komagaku**), being that of Korean and Manchurian influence. In addition to wind and percussion instruments, the orchestra employs two stringed instruments (lute and zither), except when accompanying **bugaku** dance.

Togni, Camillo (1922-) Italian composer and pianist, influenced by **serialism**. A pupil of Margola and **Casella**, Togni graduated in the piano, music aesthetics and philosophy. He worked as a pianist until 1953 but has concentrated chiefly on composition since then. Togni was one of the first Italian composers to abandon **neo-Classicism** for the complexities of **twelve-note** serialism in 1940. Heavily influenced by **Schoenberg**'s work, Togni's most successful compositions are his *Piano Capriccios* (1954-1957), which aim to widen the expressive scope of serial music.

Tomášek, Václav (1774-1850) Czech composer and teacher. An early post as tutor and composer to Count Buquoy (1806-1822) eventually enabled Tomášek to establish his reputation as a composer and teacher in Prague. Forming the social centre of the Czech music world, Tomášek nevertheless travelled widely, meeting **Haydn** and **Beethoven**. His work lies between the Classical and Romantic traditions, and includes influences from the nationalist compositions favoured by his pupil, Jan **Voříšek**. Among his operas, symphonies and piano works are a great number of German and Czech songs, of which *Nähe des Geliebten* (1815) is probably the best known.

Tomasi, Henri Fredien (1901-1971) French composer and conductor. Tomasi studied the piano, counterpoint and composition at the Paris Conservatoire before making his reputation with the opera *L'Atlantide* in 1954 and consolidating it with *Miguel de Manara* in 1956. Influenced by **Ravel**, Tomasi's music is elaborate and intense in feeling. He also wrote many orchestral pieces which showed his considerable abilities as an orchestrator.

tombeau In 17th-century French music, a memorial work. An example is **Ravel's** *Tombeau de Couperin* (1920), a suite for piano such as Couperin may have composed, but resembling him in spirit rather than in style.

Tomkins, Thomas (1572-1656) English composer in the school of **Byrd**. An early appointment as instructor of the choir at Worcester Cathedral was succeeded by the post of organist at the Chapel Royal in 1621. Little is known of his life after 1628. Tomkins wrote a huge number of anthems and services, together with several madrigals and a large volume of instrumental works, chiefly for the keyboard. He was jointly responsible for the music at the coronation of Charles I, but is principally remembered now for his madrigals, *Songs of 3, 4, 5 and 6 parts* (1622), about whose worth opinions still differ sharply.

Tommasini, Vincenzo (1878-1950) Italian composer whose personal fortune enabled him to compose free from financial constraints. After studying at Rome and under **Bruch** in Berlin, Tommasini travelled widely. Influenced by **Debussy**, about whom he wrote an important article, Tommasini's francophilia did not stop him associating himself with **Casella**'s *Società Italiana di Musica* during its existence from

1917-1919. Tommasini wrote operas, music for ballets (mostly unperformed), many orchestral pieces and piano sonatas. His music is praised for its impressionistic interpretations of Debussian techniques, although most of it remains little known even today. The orchestral diptych, *Chiari di Luna* (1914), is probably his best-known work.

tomtom High-pitched **drum**, an imitation of an African drum, used in dance bands and occasionally in the orchestra.

tonada (Sp.) Type of ballad that originated in the 16th century. The Chilean composer Humberto **Allende** (1885-) revived it by composing 12 tonadas for piano.

tonadilla (Sp.) Stage interlude for singers derived from the **tonada** and introduced into Spain during the 18th century.

tonality In short, the use of a **major** or **minor key** in a musical composition or passage and the piece's coherent adherence to that key. See also **atonality**; **polytonality**.

tone Term with five meanings.

First, it is the interval of a major second between two notes on the **diatonic scale**. See also **scales**; **temperament**.

Second, it is one of the eight melodic formulae to which a **psalm** was sung in **plainsong**. Also known as a Gregorian tone.

Third, it is the quality of musical sound produced by an instrument and a record player.

Fourth, it is a pure note from which **overtones** have been omitted.

Fifth, it is the American term for note.

tone colour Quality or sound characteristic of a particular instrument or voice. The tone colour of a **note** makes it possible to distinguish between various instruments playing the same tune. The characteristic **frequency** of a note is only the **fundamental** of a series of other notes which are simultaneously present over the basic one. Such additional notes, known as **overtones**, are not distinctly audible because their intensity is less than that of the fundamental. They are important because they determine the quality of a note and they also give brilliance to **tone**. Tone colour is also known as timbre.

tone poem Also known as symphonic poem, a large-scale orchestral work, usually in one movement, with a descriptive title and based on some literary work, legend or scene. The term was first introduced by **Liszt** in the mid-1850s with his *Prometheus* (1850). Altogether, Liszt wrote eight such compositions. Other symphonic poems include *Má Vlast* (1874) by **Smetana**, *Danse macabre* (1874) by **Saint-Saëns**, *The Sorcerer's Apprentice* by **Dukas** (1897) and *Till Eulenspiegel* by Richard **Strauss** (1895).

tonguing Articulation on a **wind instrument** by use of the tongue to produce notes that are separate from each other and well-defined. This may be done by the forming of the sound 'T', 'T-K' (double tonguing) or 'T-K-T' (triple tonguing).

tonic First note (keynote) of a **scale**. For example, the tonic of the key of G major or G minor is G.

tonic sol-fa English system of notation introduced in the 1840s by John Curwen (1816-1880). The principle of the system is that each note of the scale is given a singing syllable. The eight notes of the scale become doh, ray, me, fah, soh, lah, te, doh. The system is now used with a movable doh so that, in the key of E♭ major, doh is E♭ and soh (the **dominant**) is B♭, whereas in the key of C, doh is C and soh is G. In minor keys the lah of the major key becomes the tonic and me the dominant.

tonus (Lat.) Term with three meanings.

First, it is an alternative term for **Gregorian tone**.

Second, it is an alternative term for **mode**.

Paul Tortelier

Arturo Toscanini

Third, it is shorthand for **tonus peregrinus**.

tonus peregrinus (Lat.) Medieval name for the **Aeolian mode**, now applied to an Anglican **chant** based on **plainsong** in that mode.

Torelli, Giuseppe (1658-1709) Veronese composer and violinist, remembered mostly as the developer of the instrumental **cantata**. Torelli worked in various small orchestras in Italy before moving to the court of the Margrave of Brandenburg in 1697. Within two years he was performing in Italy again and by the time of his death was among the best-known violinists of his age. He composed sonatas, sinfonias and concertos, but it is the latter form for which he is best known. Works such as his *Concerti grossi con una pastorale*, published in 1709, redefined the structure of the concerto (in particular the role of the *ritornello*) for subsequent composers.

Tortelier, Paul (1914-) French cellist and composer. Tortelier made his debut at the Concerts Lamoreux and went on to play as soloist with the Boston Symphony Orchestra in 1937. He has since become one of the world's best-known soloists and teachers, numbering Lamasse and Jacqueline **du Pré** among his pupils. His compositions include *Israel Symphony* (1956) and *Offrande* (1971), based on the works of **Bach**.

Toscanini, Arturo (1867-1957) Italian conductor, cellist and director of La Scala (1898-1903 and 1920-1929). Toscanini studied cello and piano at the Paloma Conservatoire and conducted for the first time in Rio de Janeiro at the age of 19. The opera was *Aïda* and Toscanini's success was the springboard for his subsequent career. In a working life spanning 70 years he brought his considerable energies to bear on having opera taken as a serious art form in Italy and elsewhere. His conducting was superb and earned him the famous commendation from **Verdi**, "Grazie, grazie, grazie". His hatred of Mussolini led him to leave Italy for the United States in the 1930s, but his work at La Scala remained the focal point of his career.

Tosti, Sir (Francesco) Paulo (1846-1916) Italian composer of songs and singing teacher. Tosti studied violin under Pinto and composition under **Mercadante** before moving to Rome and composing the songs which made his reputation. He was taken on as a singing teacher by Princess Marghenta of Savoy, and his popularity enabled him to take a similar position with the British Royal Family in 1880. He was a prolific composer of songs, which were very popular in England, France and Italy. Tosti was knighted in 1908.

total serialism See **serialism**.

touch Manner in which a pianist strikes the keys of a piano. The impact of the fingers upon the piano can effect only the loudness or softness of a note, although different pianists are able to make differences to the sounds produced as a result of their touch.

touche (Fr.) **Fingerboard** of a stringed instrument.

Tournemire, Charles Arnould (1870-1939) French organist and composer. Organist at St Pierre in Bordeaux at the age of eleven and later at St Seurin, Tournemire studied under **Bériot** at the Paris Conservatoire. His mysticism ill-equipped Tournemire for the materialist age in which he lived and his works stand as records of his faith. His *L'Orgue Mystique* is an organ work of immense scale composed over five years from 1927 to 1932.

Tourte bow Designed by François Tourte (1747-1835), the Tourte bow is concave in shape – previous bows were convex. It is now in common use for the violin, viola and cello. Most English double-bass players also favour the Tourte bow. See also **bow**.

Tovey, Sir Donald Francis (1875-1940) Scholar of English music, pianist and composer. Educated under Sophie Weisse, who exerted her influence over much of his life, Tovey played as pianist with **Joachim**'s quartet before his appointment to the chair of music at Edinburgh University in 1914. His early works were performed in the 1900s, but after 1914 his only major composition was an opera *The Bride of Dionysus* (1929). Tovey's critical essays are still read, although his music has fallen into relative obscurity.

toy Old English term for a composition of a light, playful character. Also spelled toye.

toye Alternative spelling of **toy**.

toy symphony Symphony scored for strings, and sometimes a piano, and augumented with toy instruments such as a cuckoo, quail and nightingale. An example was attributed to **Haydn**, but was probably composed by Leopold **Mozart**. Toy symphonies have also been written by **Mendelssohn** and Malcolm **Arnold**.

traditional jazz Form of **jazz** that was popular between the late 1940s until the early 1960s and includes the original **New Orleans style** and **Dixieland**. The craze spread from the United States to Britain, where Humphrey Lyttleton and Chris Barber were among its main exponents.

Traetta, Tommaso (1727-1779) Italian composer of operas. Traetta trained in Naples under Porpora and **Durante** before coming under the influence of **Jommelli** in 1753. With his appointment to the court at Parma in 1758 he began to write many full-scale operas, but dwindling funds and enthusiasm drove him to Venice in 1765 where he completed his one acknowledged masterpiece, the opera *Antigone* (1772). He was popularly acclaimed almost everywhere in Europe, except London, many of his compositions anticipating works by **Benda** and **Mozart** (especially *Idomeneo*).

transcription Term with two meanings.

First, it is the act of arranging a composition for different instruments to the original.

Second, it is the act of translating music from one notational form into another.

transposing instrument Musical instrument pitched in a **key** other than C major, for which music is written down as if its basic **scale** were C major. For example, a **clarinet** in B♭ automatically plays the scale of that key when the music is written in C major. If it is to play a piece in F major, the music must be written in G major. The most common transposing instruments in an orchestra are French horns, clarinets and trumpets.

transposition Performing music in a different **key** than written, or the subsequent written appearance of music in other than its original key.

transverse flute **Flute** that is blown from the side, as opposed to one that is blown from the end. End-blown flutes are members of the **recorder** family, whereas side-blown flutes are members of the flute family.

trascinando (It.) Holding back the speed, from the Italian word meaning dragging.

Traubel, Helen (1899-1972) American soprano, particularly of **Wagnerian** roles.

Helen Traubel

She studied with Vetta Karst and made her debut in St Louis in 1926. Traubel became America's greatest Wagnerian, rivalled only by Helen Flagstad whom she replaced at the Metropolitan Opera, New York in 1941. She retired from opera to write mystery novels after 1953, making occasional appearances in films and television shows.

Travis, Roy (Elihu) (1922-) American avant-garde composer. Travis studied at the Juilliard School from 1947 to 1950, later in Paris and at Columbia University. He has worked as a teacher at the University of California. His compositions are mostly of electronic music and include most notably an opera, *The Passion of Oedipus* (1965).

treble Highest voice in a vocal composition in several parts. The term is derived from the Latin word *triplum*, which was the top part in the earliest three-part **motets**. It is also the term for a boy's voice that has not yet 'broken'.

treble clef Highest pitched **clef** in modern musical notation. It is known as a fixed clef in that the middle C is fixed on the first **leger line** below the stave.

Treble clef

Tremblay, George Amédée (1911-1982) Canadian composer and pianist. Tremblay studied with **Schoenberg** in 1936 and after his move to the United States in 1919 gained a reputation as an important performer of avant-garde work. In 1965 he founded a school to further investigate **serial** composition techniques. He has written various works of orchestral and chamber music, including three symphonies written in 1949, 1952 and 1973.

tremolo Rapid repetition of a single note to produce a tremulous effect, especially associated with bowed instruments when very fast bowing is executed. A tremolo can also be produced on **kettledrums**, and on a wind instrument by control of the breath.

tremulant Mechanical device on an **organ**, operated by a draw-stop, that causes the sound to fluctuate in pitch and power to produce a **vibrato** effect.

trepak Russian dance of Cossack origin in animated 2/4 time.

triad **Chord** that has three notes sounding simultaneously. The lowest note of the triad is known as its root. The second and third notes are known as the third and the fifth, respectively. A triad may be major or minor, depending on whether the third is a major or minor third. Augmented and diminished triads are distinguished by the interval between the root and the fifth. If this interval is augmented, the triad is said to be augmented; if it is diminished, then the triad is said to be diminished.

Triads may be built on any note of the scale. They may also be found in any position. For example, the triad in the key of C major of C-E-G is in root position (that is, the root is the lowest note). If it were changed to E-G-C, it would be in the first inversion. If the chord appeared in the form G-C-E, it would be in the second inversion.

To produce a harmony in four parts rather than three, one of the notes of the triad is doubled. The note doubled is usually either the root or the fifth. To double the third is less common because it tends to weaken the chord.

The use of the triad was introduced in the late 15th century and came to fore in the 16th century. It was used as the basis of harmony until around 1900. See also **harmony**.

triangle Cylindrical steel bar bent into a triangle shape. The sound is produced by striking it with a metal beater. The tinkling sound of the triangle is of indefinite pitch. It was first introduced into orchestras and military bands in the mid-18th century.

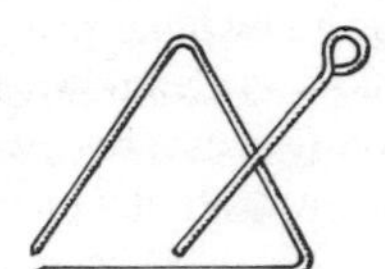

Triangle

trill **Ornament** consisting of the rapid alteration of the note written down with the **note** a **semitone** or a whole tone above it. Also known as a shake.

Trill

trio Chamber work for three voices or instruments, or a group that performs such a composition. For example, a piano trio is a piece for a piano, violin and cello; a string trio usually consists of a violin, viola and cello. **Haydn** achieved considerable fame with his piano trios and altogether composed 31. He also produced 20 string trios.

The middle section of a minuet or march was also known as a trio because it was scored for three instrumental parts. By the 18th century this became an established tradition when a central trio section was included in the minuet movements of suites, sonatas and symphonies.

trio sonata Type of composition played from the late 17th century to the early 18th century by an ensemble consisting of two violins and one cello, or bass viol, with an accompaniment supplied by a harpsichord played from a **figured bass** part. See also **sonata**.

triple concerto **Concerto** for three solo instruments. The most famous example is **Beethoven's** Triple Concerto in C major for piano, violin, cello and orchestra (1804).

triple counterpoint Form of **invertible counterpoint** in which three voices may change positions without significantly affecting the integrity of the composition. See also **counterpoint**.

triplet Group of three notes played in the time of two of the same value. They are written tied together with a small figure 3 placed above or below the tie.

triple time Time signature in which there are three beats in a bar. For example, 3/4 indicates three **crotchets** (known as **simple time**), and 9/8 indicates nine **quavers** in three groups of three (known as **compound time**). See also **duple time**.

tritone Alternative term for the **diabolus in musica**.

tromba (It.) Alternative term for **trumpet**.

tromba marina (It.) Stringed instrument with a single string and played with a **bow**, measuring more than 2m (6ft) long. The instrument was used in Europe between the 12th and 18th centuries. It has acquired a variety of names, such as the German names *Nonnengeige* (nun's fiddle), *Turmmscheit* (drum log) and *Brummscheit* (humming wood). Its nautical name is said to come from Italy because of the instrument's resemblance to the speaking trumpets on Italian ships.

trombone Brass wind instrument developed in the 15th century from the **sackbut**. It is similar to the **trumpet** but it has a **slide** for lengthening and shortening the tube, and also a **mouthpiece** that is both larger and deeper. There are seven positions of the slide so that all the notes of the **chromatic scale** can be produced. The most commonly used trombones are the tenor and bass, both of which are non-**transposing instruments**. The tenor trombone has a range of about two and a half **octaves** from E below the bass stave, and the bass trombone has a similar range from the B below the tenor's E. Other trombones include the alto and double bass, and the valve trombone, which has valves added to produce more notes without using the slide.

The trombone is an important member of the orchestral brass section, and is also used in **jazz** and **dance bands** as well as **military** and **brass bands**.

Music for trombone includes a trio by Karl Bamberg, **Beethoven's** *Equali*, a concerto by **Rimsky-Korsakov**, and sonatas by **Hindemith** and Schroen.

Trombone

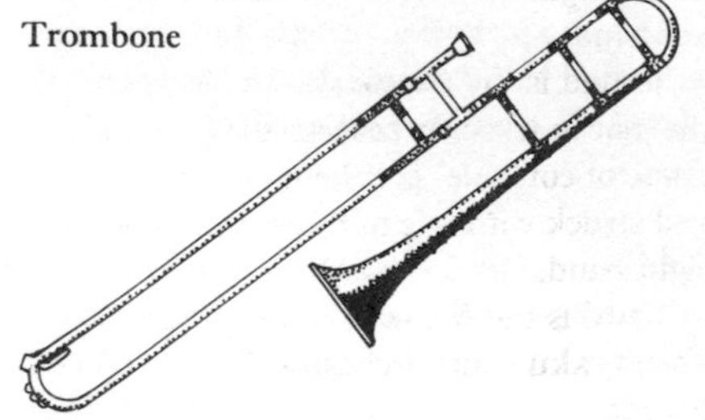

Trombonicino, Bartolomeo (*c*1470-*c*1535) Italian composer and developer of **frottola**. A native of Mantua, Trombonicino was a well-known composer in that town even before his murder of his wife and her lover made him a notorious one. He seems to have spent the years between 1502 and 1508 in the service of Lucrezia Borgia, and after that moved to Venice.

His most important work was in secular music, particularly the large number of frottola he composed. Together with Cara, he was the most significant innovator in this form.

trompong (Indonesia) Row of ten small, horizontally-mounted, knobbed gongs with a range of two octaves. *Trompongs* are always played in pairs, the *trompong pengarep* being the larger leading version, while the *trompong barangan* is pitched an octave higher and follows.

tronco (It.) Direction indicating that a note or chord is to cease abruptly.

trope Interpolation into a liturgical chant, dating from the 8th or 9th century. At first tropes were vocalized as musical **ornaments** or sung (sometimes as melismas) on syllables of certain words. Later they became so important that special words were newly written for them.

troppo (It.) Too much, a musical direction that is often used in the negative, such as *non troppo*, not too much.

troubadour (Fr.) Poet-musician from Provence in the south of France, active from about the 12th century until the 14th century. Some *troubadours* were of noble birth, and some of humble origins, but most were attached to courts or noble families and most were well educated. The *troubadours* (along with the later **trouvères**) provided a huge input into French secular music at this time. Many of their poems and melodies still survive, and these include love poems, satirical poems, laments, pastorals, ballads and chronicles. Among the musical forms used by the troubadours are the *ballade*, *rondeau* and *virelai*. Notable *troubadours* include Bertrand de Born and Marcabru of Gascony.

trouvère (Fr.) Poet-musician of northern France in the 12th and 13th centuries whose form of art was similar to that of the **troubadour**. Notable *trouvères* include Adam de **la Hale** and Quesnes de Béthune.

trumpet **Brass instrument** that has evolved from the primitive version in the form of a hollowed-out piece of wood. The trumpet has a cylindrical bore and a cupped **mouthpiece**. Until the introduction of valves in the 19th century with which to change the length of the tube, the trumpet (the natural trumpet, that is) could produce only natural harmonics.

Modern trumpets are usually pitched in B♭ or A, although instruments in C and F are still used. The present orchestral trumpets are about as half as long as the 18th century version.

Because early instruments were without valves, their notational range was limited. As used in fanfares by J.S. **Bach** or by

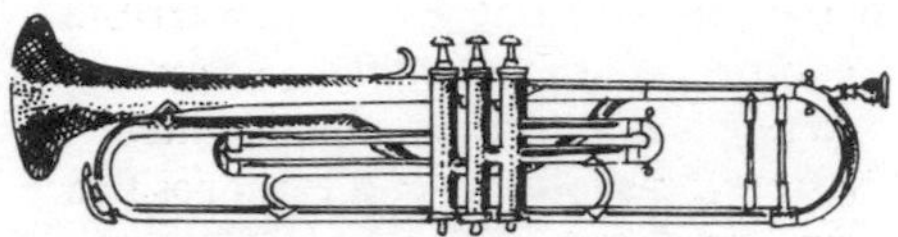

Trumpet

Handel (notably in *The Trumpet Shall Sound* from *Messiah*), the writing had to make use of the simple harmonics of which the instrument was capable. As a result, such pieces were difficult to play. **Haydn** was the first major composer to write a concerto (Trumpet Concerto in E♭ major, 1796) for the instrument.

The trumpet is now widely used in orchestral music, **jazz** and dance music. By using a **mute**, the tone of the trumpet may be altered, especially in **dance bands**.

trumpet voluntary Composition for the **organ**, and not for the **trumpet** as the title would suggest. The tune is played on the **trumpet stop** of the organ. For many years the work known as *The Trumpet Voluntary*, made famous by Henry **Wood**'s arrangement, was wrongly attributed to **Purcell**. However, it was established as having been composed by Jeremiah Clarke (*c*1673-1707) and originally entitled *The Prince of Denmark's March*.

tsuzumi (Japan) Hourglass-shaped drum with two lashed heads of skin, of which there are three main types.

First is the *Ko-tsuzumi*, the smallest of the three, and the most important in the **hayashi** ensemble of the **noh** drama. It has horsehide heads stretched over iron rings, with a smaller ring of lacquered deerskin on the back to dampen reverberation. It is held on the right shoulder and struck with the left hand.

Second is the *Ō-tsuzumi*, the larger of the pair in the **noh** ensemble, with heads made of cowhide. It is held on the left hip and struck with one to three fingers of the right hand.

Third is the *San-no-tsuzumi*, used in the **komagaku** court orchestra. It is played on its side.

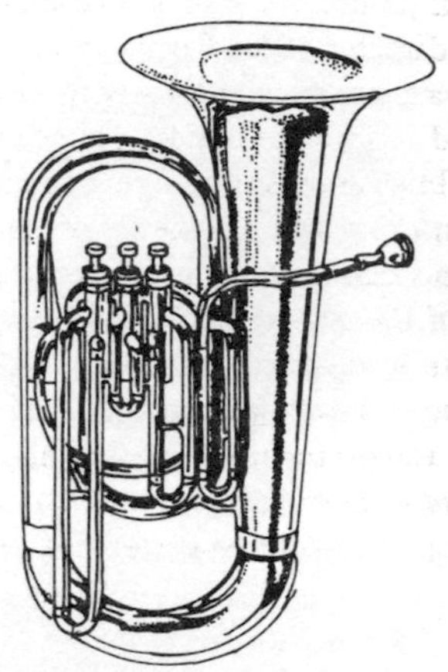

Tuba

tuba Deep-toned **brass instrument** now used in orchestras and in brass bands. The tuba first appeared in Germany in 1835. The instrument has a conical bore like the **horn**, and a cupped **mouthpiece**, similar to that of the **trumpet**.

There are various types of tuba. Sometimes it is made so that the instrument encircles the player (the circular brass or **helicon**), or in other instances the bell points upwards above the player's head (the **sousaphone**). The tenor tuba is generally known as the **euphonium**, which is used in **brass bands**, mostly in the United States. The tuba was invented in Germany in 1843.

A notable solo piece for the tuba is **Vaughan Williams'** Concerto for bass tuba and orchestra in F minor (1954).

tubular bells Series of metal tubes hung on an upright frame and struck with a hammer to produce a bell-like sound. Tubular bells are tuned and are in sets usually covering an octave. The most common tuning is in the diatonic scale of E♭, but chromatic sets are also made.

Tuckwell, Barry (Emmanuel) (1931-) Australian horn player. Tuckwell played with the Melbourne and Sydney Symphony Orchestras before going to Britain in 1950. He was chairman of the London Symphony Orchestra from 1959 to 1968, since when he has played in the Tuckwell Wind Quintet and the London Sinfonietta. The foremost horn player of his generation, his repertory is very wide and includes a large number of contemporary works.

Tudor, David (1926-) American pianist, avant-garde composer and joint inventor of 'happenings' with John **Cage**. From the late 1940s, Tudor has been associated with Cage, **Feldman** and **Wolff**, his virtuoso piano-playing proving ideal for the performance of their work. He taught at the Black Mountain College with Cage in the 1950s and has been very active in the composition and performance of electronic and mixed-media works. Among these are *Cartridge* (1966, in collaboration with Cage), *Bandoneon!* (1966) and *Reunion* (1968), which accompanies a chess game played between Cage and Marcel Duchamp.

Tunder, Franz (1614-1667) German composer of church music and organist. Born in Bannesdorf, Tunder was appointed court organist at Gottorf in 1632 and travelled to Florence some time after – the origin of an Italianate influence in his work.

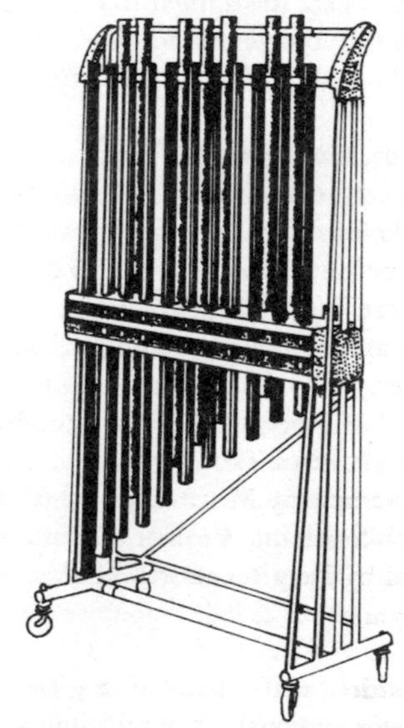

Tubular bells

He held a later position in Lübeck from 1641 until his death.

Although little of Tunder's music has survived, his **preludes** and choral arrangements can be heard as influences in **Buxtehude**'s later development of them. His choral cantatas began another line of development which was to culminate in the work of **Bach**.

tune Term with three meanings.

First, it is loosely applied to the melody of a piece.

Second, it is used to describe the pitch of a sound, in that it is said to be either in tune (correct) or out of tune (incorrect).

Third, as a verb, it means to adjust the pitch of an instrument until it is correct.

tung-hsiao (China) Vertical bamboo flute (originally made of jade and occasionally found in copper or marble), with a blowing hole at the top and five finger-holes on top and one behind. It has two additional decorative holes at the lower end which hold silk string tassels.

tuning fork Two-pronged metal instrument which when struck produces a sound that serves to check the **pitch** of instruments and to give the pitch to voices. It is said to have been invented by John Shore in 1711.

tupan Large, double-headed drum used to accompany the dance music of Yugoslavia, Bulgaria, Greece and Turkey. It is suspended over the player's left shoulder and is struck by the left hand with a small drumstick and by the right hand with a large beater.

turca, alla (It.) In a Turkish style, direction used for example by **Mozart** for the finale of his Piano Sonata in A major, K331 (1778), and by **Beethoven** in *The Ruins of Athens* (1824).

Turchi, Guido (1916-) Italian composer, administrator and critic. Turchi studied at the Rome Conservatoire and later under **Pizzetti**, joining the staff at Rome in 1941. He was director of the Parma and Florence Conservatoires simultaneously from 1967 to 1972 and has written for several newspapers. His compositions figure prominently in the post-war renewal of Italian music and demonstrate a consistent rejection of the formal innovations of the European avant-garde. Although most of his music is purely instrumental, his greatest achievement is probably his opera *The Good Soldier Schweik* which, a decade in the making, was first performed in Milan in 1962.

Turina (y Pérez), Joaquín (1882-1949) Spanish composer, often paired with **Falla**. Born in Seville, to which his music frequently alludes, Turina travelled to Madrid (where he first met Falla) and to Paris, where he was influenced to some extent by **Debussy**. Turina's first major success came in Madrid with the performance of his symphonic poem *La Procession del Rocio* in 1913. He wrote a great number of works for the piano and several for orchestra including the acclaimed *Sinfonia Sevillana* of 1920.

turn **Ornament** that entails the playing of a group of four notes instead of a single **note** if the turn sign is placed above the single note. If the sign follows the single note, the group is played after it.

Turn

tutti Passage in which all performers play. It also applies where all passages of a concerto, for example, are played by the entire orchestra, and in a choral work it indicates the full participation by the chorus.

twelve-note composition Original standard form of **serialism**. The basic principle is that all twelve chromatic notes have an equal value. The traditional predominance of tonic, dominant and subdominant notes, both in establishing of scales and tonality, is rejected. A note row, consisting of twelve chromatic notes in whatever order the composer desires, replaces the traditional tonal centres as a 'gravitational force'.

In the strictest form of twelve-note music, no note may be repeated until the other eleven have been sounded. Having established the note row, the music is developed by submitting the row to a series of mutations. It may be used vertically to form chords, or in its horizontal form may be transposed, used in diminution, augmentation, inversion, cancrizans, or in a combination of these.

The three classical figures in twelve-note composition are **Schoenberg** (*Serenade*, for septet and baritone, 1923), **Berg** (*Lulu*, opera, 1928-1934) and **Webern** (Symphony, Op. 21, 1928, and Concerto, 1934).

Tye, Christopher (*c*1505-*c*1572) English composer of whose life little is known. Tye first appears as a lay clerk in King's College, Cambridge, in 1537. He was introduced at court before 1550, served as master of the choir at Ely Cathedral, later becoming a deacon. Little of his music has survived intact, but his compositions include a mass, *Euge Bone*, and a choral work, *The Acts of the Apostles*, published in 1553.

Tyrwhitt-Wilson, Gerald Hugh See **Berners, Lord**

U

'ud Short-necked, plucked **lute** of the Arab world, and forerunner of the Western lute. It was probably of Persian origin, but was adopted by the Arabs in the 7th century and became widespread throughout Muslim lands from Spain to India.

Although the *'ud* is no longer found in Iran, it is still common in parts of North Africa and the Near East. From early Arabic and Persian texts which demonstrate the importance of the 'ud in Middle Eastern musical theory, it is known that the instrument once had four strings and frets, but is now generally fretless with five, six or seven strings.

uillean pipes (Ireland) Literally 'elbow' pipes. The air bag of this form of **bagpipe** is filled by bellows held under the arm and pressed against the body by the elbow. The chanter has a range of two octaves, while two closed chanters may provide tonic and dominant chords when the keys are depressed with the wrist. There are three drones. Also (incorrectly) called **union pipes**.

ukulele Small four-stringed **guitar** developed in Hawaii by the Portuguese in the 19th century. It may be played from a notation resembling the old lute **tablature**. The word ukulele literally means 'the jumping flea'. A version with a skin-covered, metal-framed body is called the ukulele-banjo. See **banjo**.

una corda Direction in **piano** music to indicate the use of the **damping pedal**, which shifts the action so that only one string is struck by the hammers instead of two or three.

undulating stop Organ stop that controls a rank of pipes deliberately tuned marginally sharp or flat to produce a regular beating when used in conjunction with another stop.

union pipes Irish **bagpipes** consisting of a chanter and three **drone** pipes. They are also incorrectly known as **uillean pipes**.

unison Two notes sounding together at the same **pitch**. It also applies to the singing of the same tune by men and women an **octave** apart. In the latter sense, the expression 'singing in unison' is used.

unit organ Compact pipe organ in which the number of pipes required is reduced by a process of borrowing. For example, an eight-foot stop and a four-foot stop shares pipes for the part of their range that overlaps, instead of having completely separate sets of pipes as in a normal organ. **Cinema organs** are built on this principle.

unprepared dissonance See **preparation**.

upbeat Movement of a conductor's baton in an upward direction, and the beat that this represents (usually the beat before an accented beat). See also **downbeat**.

upbow Motion of a **bow** in the playing of stringed instruments in the direction from the **point** to the **heel**, that is, the player is pushing the bow. The opposite is downbow.

upper mordent Ornament that indicates that three notes are to be played in the time-value of the principal note, consisting of the principal note, plus the note above it, returning to the principal note again. See also **double mordent; inverted mordent.**

upper partial Alternative term for **overtone.**

upright piano Piano that is built in such a way that its strings are in a vertical position, rather than in a horizontal one, as on a **grand piano**. *See also* **piano.**

V

va. Abbreviation of **viola**.

vādī (India) Principal tone (*sonant*), besides the tonic, in a **rāga**, and the note that occurs most frequently in the melody. Depending on its relation to the tonic (Sa), the *vadi* is said to evoke the characteristic mood (**rasa**) of the *rāga*. See also **samvādī**.

Valen, Fartein (Olav) (1887-1952) Norwegian composer who studied in Germany and was influenced by the twelve-note system of **Schoenberg**. His compositions include four completed symphonies, a violin concerto, a piano concerto and other orchestral and chamber works.

valse (Ger.) Alternative term for **waltz**.

valve Keys added to brass wind instruments, invented in the early 19th century, which make it possible for **horns, trumpets** and **cornets** to produce the complete **chromatic scale** instead of only the natural harmonics. Valves are fitted to all members of the **saxhorn** family and have also been used for the **trombone** as a substitue for the **slide**. See also **acoustics**.

vamp To improvise an instrumental accompaniment or introduction, (for example, to a song).

Vanhal, Johann Baptist (1793-1813) Bohemian composer, a friend of both **Haydn** and **Mozart**, who contributed to the Classical period with many symphonies and string quartets, as well as sacred music. An alternative spelling of the name is Wanhal.

Varèse, Edgard (1883-1965) French-born composer who settled in the United States, where he founded several organizations for the promotion of new music. He was a pioneer in the creation of new and unusual instrumental sounds, and in the use of tapes and electronic devices. His works include *Amériques* (with a part for a police siren), *Ionization* for percussion and *Density 21.5* for solo flute (taking its name from the specific gravity of platinum).

variation Musical form, consisting usually of a theme followed by various treatments of it, with sometimes a restatement of the original theme at the end.

The variation was one of the earliest means of producing an extended composition, and first emerged in England and Spain during the 16th century. At first melodic and harmonic characteristics were followed in each variation, but in time much freer treatment was given to the variations themselves. In the **chaconne** and **passacaglia** there is found a persistent theme in one of the parts, often in the **bass**. Variations can change the theme in many ways including **melody**, figuration, texture, **harmony** and **rhythm**, but the form is much more than an exercise in ingenuity; at its best it treats the theme as a source of inspiration for further composition.

The English composers William **Byrd** (1543-1623) and John **Bull** (*c*1562-1628) composed variations for virginals and for lute, sometimes called divisions, and the form was extended by J.S. **Bach** (*Goldberg Variations*, 1742) and **Handel**. **Beethoven** in his *Diabelli Variations* used the form for a major piano work and **Brahms** showed his mastery of form in variations for orchestra as in his *Variations on a Theme of Haydn* (1873). Both **Beethoven** and **Brahms** used variations in their symphonies.

Modern composers have adapted the principle of variations in large-scale works such as *Don Quixote* (Richard **Strauss**, 1890) and *Enigma Variations* (**Elgar**, 1898).

Varnay, Astrid (1918-) Swedish-born soprano, resident in the United States for most of her life, specializing in the operas of **Wagner** and Richard **Strauss** and performing regularly at the Metropolitan Opera New York, Covent Garden and at Bayreuth.

Varviso, Silvio (1924-) Swiss conductor, primarily of opera, appearing at the Metropolitan Opera, the Stockholm Opera, Covent Garden, Glyndebourne and Bayreuth. He was appointed musical director at the Paris Opéra in 1981.

Vásáry, Tamás (1933-) Hungarian pianist and conductor who made his piano debut at eight years old, then studied with his compatriot **Kodály**. He made his London and New York debuts in 1961 and has since established himself as a specialist in the music of **Liszt**.

vaudeville Satirical French song which is thought to have originated in the valley of Vire in Normandy, the home of Oliver Basselin (*c*1400-1450). Similar songs were used to conclude a play, and the term also came to be used to mean a play with such songs interspersed. **Mozart** used this device at the end of *Il Seraglio* (1782).

Stage performances featuring songs and dances became known as vaudeville in France in the 19th century, and the term was also used for the same type of entertainment in the United States, which in England is usually known as music hall.

Vaughan Williams, Ralph (1872-1958) English composer whose generally Romantic but highly personal idiom is derived from his researches into English folk song and dance and his love of Tudor music. His works include nine symphonies, (notably No.1. *A Sea Symphony* with chorus, No.2 *A London Symphony*, No.3 *A Pastoral Symphony*, No.7 *Sinfonia Antartica*, based on his music for the film *Scott of the Antarctic*); an overture *The Wasps*; *On Wenlock Edge*, song cycle with string quartet and piano; *Fantasia on a theme by Thomas Tallis* for strings; *The Lark Ascending* for violin and orchestra; *Job*; *Fantasia on Greensleeves*; *Serenade to Music* for voices and orchestra; tuba concerto. He was active also as a teacher at the Royal College of Music and as a conductor. He was awarded the Order of Merit in 1935.

Ralph Vaughan Williams

Vautor, Thomas (*c*1580-?) English composer and one of the last of the school of madrigalists. *Sweet Suffolk Owl* is his best-known piece.

Vecchi, Orazio (1550-1605) Italian composer, choirmaster and priest. He composed masses, motets and *L'Amfiparnaso* (The Slopes of Parnassus), a dramatic sequence of madrigals, not intended for the stage, but generally considered to be a link to early opera.

vedic chant (India) Hymns of the four sacred Hindu scriptures (*Rig Veda, Sāma Veda, Yajur Veda, Athārvā Veda*) which are said to have been received by divine revelation in prehistoric times (first millennium BC). In Indian music history, the highly ornamented tunes of the *Sāma Veda*, as preserved by a few Brahmans, are thought to be the fount of the Sanskritic tradition of Indian music.

veenā (India) See **vīnā**.

Végh, Sándor (1912-) Hungarian violinist, founder of the Végh String Quartet, famous for its interpretations of the **Bartók** quartets.

veloce (It.) Indicates uninterrupted smoothness of performance rather than increase in speed.

vent (Fr.) Wind. For example, *instruments à vent*, wind instruments.

Ventadorn, Bernart de (*c*1135-1195) French troubadour, poet and composer, one of the circle attached to the court of Eleanor of Aquitaine. He may have visited England when she married Henry Plantaganet (later Henry II) in 1152. A few of his poems and melodies have survived.

Veracini, Francesco Maria (*c*1690-1750) Italian violinist and composer of the High Baroque, noted for his violin sonatas and for operas, including *Rosalinda*, based on Shakespeare's play *As You Like It*.

verbunkos 18th-century Hungarian recruiting dance for soldiers, who performed it in full uniform with swords and spurs. It had a slow introductory section called a *lassu*, and a quick (*friss*) section. *Verbunkos* were included in some works such as **Liszt's** *Hungarian Rhapsody* No. 2 (1852), **Bartók's** *Rhapsodies for Violin and Orchestra* (1928), and the **intermezzo** from **Kodály's** *Háry János* (1926).

Verdelot, Philippe (*c*1475-1550) Flemish composer, singer and choirmaster, who spent most of his life in Italy, and is chiefly remembered for his madrigals.

Verdi, Giuseppe (Fortunino Francesco) (1813-1901) Italian composer whose 26 operas include many of the most famous ever written. His music is highly expressive and noble in character, but without frills. Verdi's exceptionally long career spanned most of the 19th century, and it is customary to divide his work into periods. His early operas, including *Nabucco*, *I Lombardi*, *Ernani*, *I due Foscari* and *Macbeth*, are influenced by the *bel canto* tradition of Italian opera. His middle period operas are richer, both musically and dramatically. These include *Rigoletto*, *Il Trovatore*, *La Traviata*, *Simon Boccanegra*, *Un Ballo in Maschera*, *La Forza del Destino*, *Don Carlos* and *Aïda*. His last two operas, *Otello* and *Falstaff*, come close to **Wagner** in their integration of music and drama. He also composed a highly dramatic setting of the Requiem Mass.

The historical background to Verdi's life is also important. He lived during the period of the 'Risorgimento' – the movement for Italian Unity and independence – and many of his operas reflect these political ideals. He was, and remains, a national hero.

Veress, Sándor (1907-) Hungarian composer and teacher and colleague of **Bartók** in the study of Hungarian and Romanian folk music. His own compositions include *Homage to Paul Klee* for two pianos and strings, symphonies, concertos and chamber works.

verismo (It.) Classification of a form of Italian opera with a libretto based on realistic contemporary events, some of which included violent plots amid sordid surroundings. The writers of such operas included **Puccini, Mascagni** and **Leoncavallo.**

verse In Anglican church music, a service or piece (such as an anthem) that makes use of a solo voice (as opposed to a full choir) for some passages. The verse **anthem** features such passages.

verset Short organ piece containing some reference to a given **plainsong** tune. The name is derived from an arrangement used in the Roman Catholic Church of replacing very other sung verse of **psalms** by interludes on the organ to relieve the supposed monotony of plainsong.

Viadana, Lodovico Grosso da (1560-1630) Italian composer and monk who adopted his name from his birthplace. He wrote madrigals, songs and a large collection of instrumental *concerti ecclesiastici.*

vibraphone Percussion instrument, similar to the **marimba,** in which the resonating lids are made to vibrate by means of electric motors, and thus produce a bell-like sound. The vibraphone has been used in the modern orchestra by a number of composers including **Britten, Berg** (*Lulu,* 1934) and **Messiaen** (*Trois Petites de la Presence Divine,* 1944).

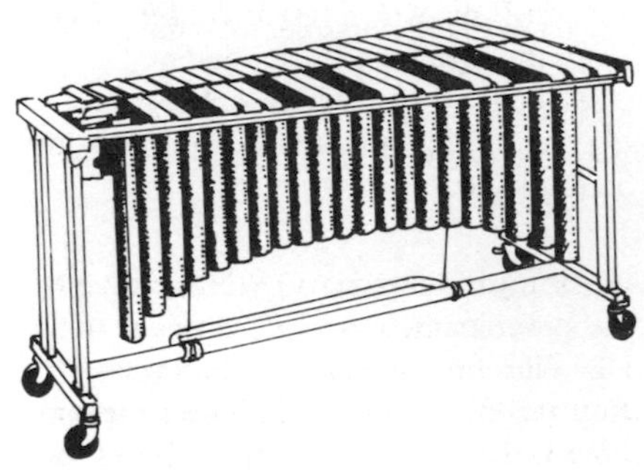

Vibraphone

vibrato (It.) Shaken, indicating a rapid but mute fluctuation in pitch which is used to improve tone. It is now almost universally used in violin and cello playing and is produced by a rapid movement of the left hand. In wind instruments the effect can be obtained by a rapid interruption of the air supply.

With singing the practice is often much over-used, even by reputable singers, and seems too often to affect long, held, loud notes to the extent of harming their intonation.

Vicentino, Nicolà (1511-1572) Italian Renaissance composer and scholar, interested in the revival of ancient Greek music. He also composed madrigals.

Vickers, Jon (Jonathan Stewart) (1926-) Canadian tenor, noted for his versatility in major operatic roles by **Wagner, Verdi, Britten** and others. He has made many appearances at Covent Garden, the Metropolitan Opera, New York, Bayreuth and elsewhere.

Victoria, Thomás Luis de (*c*1548-1611) Spanish composer of the High Renaissance who spent many years as organist and choirmaster in Rome (hence the alternative spelling of his name as Vittoria). He wrote a large body of choral church music – masses (including a requiem), magnificats, motets, hymns, psalms in the polyphonic style of his time, but charged with a degree of drama and passion that distinguishes it from the music of his older contemporary **Palestrina.**

Victory, Gerard (1921-) Assumed name of Irish composer and conductor Alan Loraine. Among his works are several operas, in English or Gaelic. He has also acted as director of music for Radio Telefis Eireann.

Vienna Boys' Choir Austrian choir founded in 1498 when it was part of the chapel of the former Austrian imperial court. It is internationally known for its secular performances. It sometimes includes adult male voices and performs with the Vienna State Opera.

Vienna Philharmonic Orchestra (German name *Wiener Philharmoniker*) Austrian orchestra of high international repute. Founded in 1842 under the composer/conductor Otto Nicolai, its activities were cut short by the 1848 Revolution and did not resume on a regular basis until 1860. The Vienna Philharmonic is one of the world's greatest orchestras. Its principal conductors have included many legendary musicians and interpreters of the classics, notably Hans **Richter**, Gustave **Mahler**, Felix Weingartner, Wilhelm **Furtwängler**, Bruno **Walter**, Herbert von **Karajan** and Claudio **Abbado**. The great conductor Karl **Böhm** is one of a select band who have formed a special relationship with the orchestra. The Vienna Philharmonic Orchestra is an autonomous organization and plays for the Vienna State Opera.

Vierne, Louis (1870-1937) French organist who studied with **Franck** and **Widor**, and organist at Notre Dame Cathedral, Paris, until his death and professor of that instrument at the Schola Cantorum. His works include five organ symphonies. Vierne was blind from birth.

Vieuxtemps, Henri (Joseph François) (1820-1881) Belgian violinist and composer who made his debut aged six and toured Europe and the United States as one of the greatest violin virtuosi of his time. He was also violin professor in St Petersburg and Brussels. His six concertos for the instrument are notable additions to the Romantic concerto repertory.

vif (Fr.) Lively. Sometimes appears as *vivement*, in a lively way.

vihuela (Sp.) Spanish **lute**, made in the shape of a **guitar**. It dates back to at least the 13th century, but became obsolete in about the 16th century.

Villa-Lobos, Heitor (1887-1959) Brazilian composer, the first Latin American one to enjoy international fame. He wrote operas, ballets, symphonies and many other orchestral, instrumental and vocal works. His best known compositions are *Chôros*, a group of pieces inspired by South American native and popular music, and *Bachianas Brasileiras*, pieces combining the styles of J.S. **Bach** and Brazilian musical idioms (including the descriptive 'Little Train of the Caipira'). Villa-Lobos' preludes and studies for guitar are probably among his most popular and enduring works.

villancio (Sp.) Term with two meanings.
First, it is a 16th-century Spanish song made up of several verses with refrains between them.
Second, it is a 17th-century Spanish term for an extended **cantata** with orchestra, often sung at Christmas.

villanella (It.) Part-song of the mid-16th century, set to rustic words and light in character.

villanelle (Fr.) Vocal setting of a poem which consists of stanzas of three lines, the first and third lines of the opening stanza being repeated alternately as the third line of the succeeding stanzas. It is similar to the Italian **villanella**, but not identical.

vīnā/veenā (India) Ancient name associated with several types of harp and lute in India. It now refers to the plucked lute of southern India which resembles the **bīn** of the north, having fixed frets and no sympathetic strings. There is, however, only one small gourd, attached to the upper end of the neck.

viol Family of bowed stringed instruments. The Italian name was *viola da gamba* (leg viol). Viols first appeared in the 15th century and were in use until near the end of the 17th century when, apart from the bass viol, they disappeared. The most common viols were the **treble**, **tenor** and

Viol

bass. The lowest string of the treble was tuned to D below middle C, the other strings being tuned at intervals of a fourth or a third (D, G, C, E, A, D). The tenor viol was tuned a fourth below the treble instrument (D, D, G, B, E, A); and the bass viol was tuned an octave below the treble viol.

Also in the viol family were the *viola da braccio* (known as the arm viola), and the double-bass viol (or *violone*), which was tuned an octave below the bass viol.

There has been a revival in the use of viols during the 20th century, associated with the interest in reproducing authentic sounds.

viola Bowed four-stringed instrument that is the tenor member of the **violin** family. Its strings are tuned at intervals of a fifth, the lowest being C below middle C (C, G, D, A). It has a range of four octaves and a lower pitch than the violin. The viola is the regular middle part in the string section of the orchestra and in the string quartet. The string quartets of **Haydn** and **Mozart** featured the viola in a prominent way, and other composers such as **Berlioz**, **Glinka**, Richard **Strauss** and **Hindemith** also included it in their repertories.

viola da gamba See viol

viola d'amore Bowed **stringed instrument** of the **viol** type, but not related to the viol family, which is played like a **violin**. The *viola d'amore* has seven bowed

Viola

strings and from seven to fourteen sympathetic strings not touched by the **bow**, but vibrated with those actually played. It was a popular instrument of the 18th century.

violin Principal modern bowed stringed instrument, to whose family belong also the viola and cello. The strings of the violin are tuned at intervals of a fifth, the lowest being tuned to G below middle C (G, D, A, E). It has a range of four octaves.

Violins were first made in Italy during the middle of the 16th century. They evolved from the fiddle and the *lira da braccio*.

The master violin makers came from three families in Cremona, the most famous members of which were Nicolo **Amati** (1596-1684), Giuseppe Bartolomeo **Guarneri** (1698-1744) and Antonio **Stradivari** (1644-1737).

With the increasing importance of strings in the orchestra and the emergence of the string quartet as a medium for chamber music, came the virtual eclipse of the **viol** in the 18th century and its replacement by

Violin

the violin and other members of its family. Since the time of Stradivari the design of the violin has not changed, except for the introduction of thinner strings and a higher bridge in the 19th century.

The violin is a prominent member of an orchestra, where the players are normally divided into two sections, the first and second violins. A section usually corresponds to higher and lower pitched parts. The violin section is led by a member of the first section, called the leader, who dictates such things as bowing.

The brilliance of the violin encouraged the writing of solo concertos from the 18th century onwards. Among the vast number of works for violin are concertos by **Bach**, **Beethoven**, **Brahms**, **Bruch**, **Berg**, **Mendelssohn**, **Tchaikovsky** and **Vivaldi**.

violoncello Original name for the tenor member of the violin family, held between the knees, and now more commonly known by the shortened form of cello.

violone Alternative term for the double-bass **viol**.

virginal Earliest form of **harpsichord**.

virtuoso Term with two meanings.

First, it is a musician (an instrumental player or singer) who has achieved complete mastery over the instrument he or she plays. It is not an attribute that a musician is born with, but something that begins with a basic talent and is gradually developed by an obsessive dedication to practice.

Second, it is a piece written to display the technical ability of a performer.

Vitali, Giovanni Battista (*c*1632-1692) Italian violinist and composer, both a church and court musician who is said to have been a pioneer of the Baroque trio sonata.

Vitali, Tommaso Antonio (1663-1745) Italian violinist and composer, son of Giovani Battista **Vitali**. A famous chaconne for violin is attributed to him.

Vitry, Phillippe de (1291-1361) French composer, priest and courtier. Little of his own music has survived, but he is important in musical history for his treatises on **ars nova**, which marked a link between the music of the Middle Ages and that of the Renaissance.

Vittorio, Thomás Luis de Alternative spelling of Thomás Luis de **Victoria**.

vivace (It.) Direction that a piece of music should be played in a lively, animated manner.

Vivaldi, Antonio (1678-1741) Italian composer, violinist and priest (known as *il prete rosso*, 'the red priest' on account of his hair). Vivaldi supervised the music at a girls' orphanage in Venice for many years, but he also travelled widely. His output, of great importance to Baroque music, was prodigious: more than 400 works in the concerto grosso style, of which the four known as *Le quattro stagioni* (The Four Seasons) are the most famous; many more sonatas for various instruments, also operas and oratorios. J.S. **Bach** admired his music and made many transcriptions of it.

vivo (It.) Lively, little-used as an instruction. The more common term is **vivace**.

Vlad, Roman (1919-) Romanian composer, scholar and teacher, who has worked mainly in Italy. His works include the ballet *La Dama delle Camelie*, and *Variatizione Concertanti* for piano and orchestra, extracted from a theme in **Mozart**'s *Don Giovanni*.

Vladigerov, Pancho (1899-1978) Bulgarian composer and pianist, whose works include the opera *Tsar Kaloyan*. His son, Alexander (born 1933) is also a composer and conductor.

vocalize To sing a piece without words, but on one single vowel.

Vocalizing was used by such composers as Bach and Handel to express deep emotions of all varieties.

vocal score **Score** that gives the vocal parts in full, reducing the orchestral score to a piano part only. The alternative American term is piano-vocal score.

voce (It.) Voice. The direction *colla voce* (with the voice), indicates that the accompaniment should allow the vocal part some freedom and follow accordingly.

Vogelwiede, Walther von der (*c*1170-1230) German *Minnesinger*. Only about eight of his melodies have survived, but he is an important figure in medieval music. He features in **Wagner**'s *Tannhäuser* and *Die Meistersinger von Nürnberg*.

Vogler, Georg Joseph (1749-1814) German composer, pianist, organist and teacher. He held many teaching posts, numbering **Meyerbeer** and **Weber** among his pupils. He composed operas, sacred music and organ works.

voice The sound of the human voice is produced by the vibration of the two vocal chords which are stretched across the larynx of the throat. The chords are set into vibration by air as it leaves the lungs, forced out by relaxation of the diaphragm. The **pitch** of the sound produced depends on the tension of the vocal chords. The mouth and the area behind the face act as a resonating chamber.

Human voices are classified by range, and by tone. There are three main categories of male voices: bass, baritone and tenor. These may be divided to indicate tone, using such terms as heroic (heroic tenor). The female voices are contralto (or alto), mezzo-soprano and soprano. Tone is indicated with terms such as coloratura (coloratura soprano).

The average human voice has a range of about two octaves, the pitch of the male voice being an octave lower than the corresponding female voice. Boys who have not yet reached puberty have voices corresponding in range to a soprano (often known as treble voices), and the range of a man's falsetto voice lies between that of a female voice and his natural voice.

voice leading (US) Part-writing, from the German *Stimmführung*.

voix celeste 8ft organ stop with two pipes to each note, one tuned slightly sharper than the other, so that they produce an ethereal wavering quality.

volante (It.) Fast and light, from the Italian, flying.

Volkonsky, Andrei (1933-) Swiss born composer who worked in the Soviet Union before emigrating to Israel. Compositions, influenced by **Schoenberg**, include the cantata *Dead Souls* and *Serenade to an insect*, for small orchestra.

volles Werk (Ger.) Full organ.

volta (It.) Time. For example, *prima volta* – first time, *seconda volta* – second time and *ancora una volta* – once again.

volti subito (It.) Indication that a quick turn of the page of a score is necessary, in order to be ready for what follows on the next page.

voluntary Organ music intended for use in the church, but not part of the service. It is played at the beginning of the service and especially at the end when the congregation leaves. See also **trumpet voluntary**.

Vorísek, Jan (1791-1825) Bohemian composer, pianist and organist, and friend of **Hummel** and **Moscheles**. He wrote symphonies, concertos, sonatas and a group of piano pieces entitled *Impromptus*.

Vorspiel (Ger.) Prelude or overture.

Vranicky, Anton (1766-1820) Moravian composer and violinist who studied with **Haydn** and **Mozart** and served Prince Maximilian Lobkowitz (**Beethoven**'s patron). His works include symphonies and violin concertos. The German spelling of his name is Wranitzky.

Vranicky, Paul (1756-1808) Moravian composer and violinist, brother of Anton **Vranicky**. He played in the Esterházy Orchestra under **Haydn**. He composed operas, symphonies and string quartets. The German spelling of his name is Wranitzky.

vuota (It.) Direction to string players to play a note or notes on an open string.

W

Waart, Edo de (1941-) Dutch conductor and oboist, musical director of The Netherlands Wind Ensemble, principal conductor of the Rotterdam Philharmonic Orchestra, and a frequent guest conductor elsewhere in Europe and the United States.

Wagenseil, Georg Christoph (1715-1777) Austrian composer and music master to the Empress Maria Theresa. He composed numerous operas, symphonies and instrumental pieces that mark a transition from the Baroque to the Classical style.

Wagner-Régeny, Rudolf (1903-1969) German composer and conductor, active mainly in Berlin before and after World War II. His works, primarily operas and ballets, were influenced by the music of Kurt **Weill** and **Schoenberg**.

Wagner, Richard (1813-1883) German composer who is said to have revolutionized opera. He was born in Leipzig and after years of struggle, including a period of political exile, built his own theatre at Bayreuth, for the staging of his works. Wagner's work epitomized the romantic spirit of the 19th century in seeking a union of music, poetry and drama to create a new art form. To this end he wrote all his own libretti, based for the most part on myth and legend. He dispensed with traditional recitative and aria in favour of a type of vocal declamation and he created a continuous flow of music by his use of motto themes (leading motifs or *Leitmotiven*). Harmony and orchestration were equally important parts of this process.

Wagner's three early operas, *Die Feen, Das Liebesverbot* and *Rienzi* are uncharacteristic works. He began working towards his ideal of music-drama with *Der Fliegende Holländer*, *Tannhäuser* and *Lohengrin*. He realized it in *Tristan und Isolde*, *Die Meistersinger von Nürnberg*, *Der Ring des Nibelungen* (in four parts) and *Parsifal*. His influence, not just on music but on literature, art and aesthetics as a whole, has been immense.

Wagner, Siegfried (1869-1930) German composer and conductor, the son of Richard and Cosima **Wagner**. He studied with **Humperdinck** and became artistic director of the Bayreuth Festival. He also composed operas, symphonic poems and other works.

Wagner tuba Brass wind instruments designed to Wagner's specifications for use

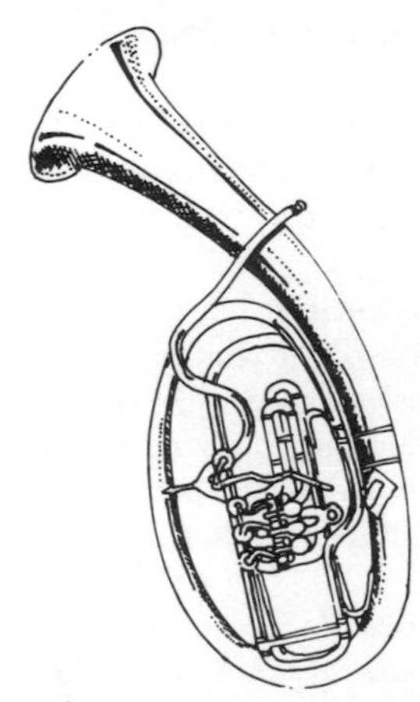

Wagner tuba

in his *Ring des Nibelungen*. They are in B♭ and F, with the same range as the horns in these pitches. The B♭ instrument, called a **tenor tuba**, and the F instrument, called a bass tuba, are more related to the horn than the tuba. The instruments have also been used by Richard **Strauss** and **Bruckner**.

Wagner, Wieland (1917-1966) German opera producer and director, the son of Siegfried **Wagner**. He was active in the Bayreuth Festival before World War II; but his most important work was done after the war, when he became co-director of the Festival with his brother, Wolfgang. Their revolutionary productions marked an exciting new chapter in the Festival's history, and helped to purge it of Nazi associations.

wagon (Japan) Six-stringed **zither**, with the strings passing over inverted V-shaped bridges placed to provide its fixed open-string tuning. Its musical function is generally to play set stereotyped patterns. The wagon is indigenous to Japan and is used in *kagura shinto* music and **gagaku** court music.

Walcha, Helmuth (1907-) German organist, blind since youth, who studied in Leipzig and has held important posts, as organist and teacher, throughout Germany. Also a composer of organ works, and probably the greatest living authority on the organ music of J.S. **Bach**.

waldhorn (Ger.) Forest horn or hunting horn. It is a natural horn, consisting of a single, coiled tube without valves.

Waldteufel, Emil (1837-1915) Alsatian-French pianist, who studied at the Paris Conservatoire, served at the court of the Empress Eugénie, and wrote many dances, including the well-known waltz *Les Patineurs* (Skaters' Waltz).

Walker, Ernest (1870-1949) English composer and musical scholar, who studied at Oxford University, then became music director at Balliol College. His compositions include a *Stabat Mater*. Walker also wrote, with Sir Jack **Westrup**, *A History of Music in England*.

Wallace, Vincent (1812-1865) Irish composer, who played the organ and violin as a boy, emigrated to Australia, then returned to London, where he composed *Maritana* and other operas. Wallace's works gained great popularity in Victorian England.

Wallace, William (1860-1940) Scottish composer and musical scholar, who practised medicine before embarking on a career in music. He wrote symphonic poems, probably the first by a British composer, was a professor at the Royal Academy of Music, and wrote a book, *A Study of Wagner*.

Walmisley, Thomas Attwood (1814-1856) English organist, principally at Cambridge University, where he was also professor of music and composer of church choral and organ music. He did much to revive interest in the music of J. S. **Bach**. He was also a noted mathematician.

Walter, Bruno (1876-1962) German-born conductor of the Leipzig Gewandhaus Orchestra, and musical director of the Vienna State Opera, until penalized by the Nazis as a Jew. He moved, first to France and then to the United States, taking American citizenship. He was noted for his warmly expressive interpretations of the Viennese classics – **Mozart, Beethoven** and **Schubert** – and also for his performances of **Mahler**, whom he knew well, and of Richard **Strauss**. Walter's real name was Schlesinger.

Walton, Sir William (Turner) (1902-1983) English composer, who was largely self-taught and developed a distinctive style, noted for clear, bright orchestration and certain affinities with jazz music. He created an early sensation with *Façade*, settings of satirical poems by Edith Sitwell

Sir William Walton

(better known today in the form of two orchestral suites or as a ballet), and with his overture *Portsmouth Point*. More substantial works are: two symphonies, concertos for viola, violin and cello, the oratorio *Belshazzar's Feast*, and the opera *Troilus and Cressida*. He also composed much film music, including that for Sir Laurence Olivier's *Henry V*, *Hamlet* and *Richard III*; and two ceremonial marches, *Crown Imperial* and *Orb and Sceptre*. Knighted in 1951, Walton was awarded the Order of Merit in 1968.

waltz Dance in 3/4 time, which can be slow or fast. The origin of the waltz is said to have been the German *Landler* in the late 18th century. The name is taken from the German *waltzen*, meaning to turn. An early form, consisting of two sections of eight bars, may be found in the works of **Mozart** and **Beethoven**, and it was developed by **Schubert** and **Weber**, the first composer to adopt the waltz as a purely instrumental form.

At the beginning of the 19th century the waltz spread to France and England where it became a popular ballroom dance. The compositions of the **Lanner** and **Strauss** families achieved immense popularity. Waltzes not intended for the ballroom have been written by many composers, other than those already mentioned, including **Chopin's** 14 piano waltzes.

Wanhal, Johann Alternative spelling of the name of **Johann Vanhal**.

Ward, John (1571-1638) English composer, representative of late Renaissance and Tudor music with his output of madrigals and many other pieces for viols and the virginal.

Warlock, Peter (1894-1930) Assumed name of Philip Heseltine, English composer and writer on music, a friend of **Delius**, **Moeran**, **Lambert** and other leading British musicians of his generation. As a composer he is noted, above all, for his songs, including the song cycle *The Curlew* for tenor with instrumental accompaniment. Warlock also wrote the popular *Capriol Suite* for strings, based on old French dances.

water organ Alternative term for **hydraulis**.

Watkins, Michael Blake (1948-) English composer, who studied with Elizabeth Lutyens and Richard Rodney **Bennett**, and has made a special study of the guitar and lute, which feature in some of his works. His Double Concerto for oboe and guitar won the Menuhin Composition Prize in 1975.

Watts, Helen (1927-) Welsh contralto, who sang in the Glyndebourne chorus and took many operatic roles, but is noted primarily for her performances in oratorio, especially of **Bach**, **Handel** and **Elgar**. She was awarded the CBE in 1978.

wayang kulit (Indonesia) Shadow play with leather puppets which are operated by a single puppeteer or *dalang* and used at temple festivals, cremation and purification ceremonies, and generally performed late at night. The texts are based on the *Mahābhārata*. In Bali it is accompanied by the *gendèr wayang*, a quartet of two pairs of ten-keyed **gendèr**. For dramatic or battle scenes from the *Rāmāyana*, drums, gongs and cymbals are added.

Webbe, Samuel (1740-1816) English organist and composer of a wide range of church and vocal music, from masses and motets to secular songs and choruses. His son Samuel also wrote vocal music and music textbooks.

Weber, Carl Maria von (1786-1826) German composer, conductor and pianist, taught by Michael **Haydn** as a boy, and later holder of various musical posts in Prague, Dresden and elsewhere. Weber was a key figure in the development of German Romantic opera, his three finest operas, *Der Freischütz*, *Euryanthe* and *Oberon*, having a considerable influence on **Wagner**. The overtures to these are concert favourites. Weber applied his same distinctive style, by turns strong, rhythmically vigorous and lyrical, to a number of distinguished orchestral and instrumental works, including two clarinet concertos, and the famous *Invitation to the Dance*, originally for piano and later orchestrated. He died in London, but on Wagner's initiative his body was later taken back to Germany.

Webern, Anton von (1883-1945) Austrian composer and conductor, a pupil of **Schoenberg** and exponent of the latter's dodecaphonic or **twelve-note** method of composition. Webern combined this with a study of the relationship between tone quality and individual notes leading, in such works as the *Five Pieces for Orchestra*, to music of extreme economy and brevity. Other works include two symphonies, and three pieces for string quartet. Webern's music much influenced **Stravinsky**, **Stockhausen** and **Boulez**.

Weckerlin, Jean-Baptiste Théodore (1821-1910) Alsatian-French composer of operas, oratorios and songs; also librarian at the Paris Conservatoire, and editor of collections of old French music.

Weelkes, Thomas (*c*1575-1623) English composer of some of the finest madrigals, noted for their daring harmonies and expressiveness, contributing to the famous madrigal collection *The Triumphs of Oriana*. He was also organist at Winchester College and Chichester Cathedral, and composed much church music.

weighted scale Basic analytical method used primarily for determining the pitch characteristics of a **monody**. Various criteria for investigation can be chosen, for example the frequency or the total duration of particular notes in a melody. Results are presented in the form of a written scale, generally that of the melody studied, with its tones being assigned relative duration values, e.g. crotchet, quaver, etc., according to the data obtained.

Weigl, Joseph (1766-1846) Austrian composer, a godson of **Haydn**, who studied with **Salieri** in Vienna. Weigl held several court appointments, and wrote operas in the prevailing German and Italian styles, which were very popular in his lifetime.

Weill, Kurt (1900-1950) German composer who studied with **Humperdinck** and **Busoni** and composed symphonies and other instrumental and vocal works. He is best known for his collaboration with the dramatist Bertold Brecht, resulting in their brilliantly satirical, jazz-influenced operas *Die Dreigroschenoper* and *Aufstieg und Fall der Stadt Mahogonny*, among others. Attacked by the Nazis, Weill resumed his career in the United States, writing sophisticated music for several stage musicals. He married the singer Lotte Lenya.

Weinberger, Jaromir (1896-1967) Czech composer who lived and worked for many years in the United States. He achieved fame with his folk opera *Svanda Dudák*, a dance from which remains a popular concert piece. Other works include the orchestral variations and fugue on *Under the Spreading Chestnut Tree*.

Weiner, Leo (1885-1960) Hungarian composer and teacher who studied in Budapest, Berlin, Vienna and Liepzig, and was professor of composition at Budapest State Academy. Compositions include two violin concertos, a Hungarian folk dance suite for orchestra and three string quartets.

Weir, Gillian (1941-) New Zealand organist who studied at the Royal Academy, and is internationally acclaimed for her performances, notably of the music of **Messiaen**. She also plays the harpsichord.

Weisgall, Hugo (1912-) Czech-born American composer who studied at the Curtis Institute and with Roger **Sessions**. He later taught at the Juilliard School of Music. He has composed several operas, including *Six Characters in Search of an Author* (after the play by Pirandello).

Weiss, Sylvius Leopold (1686-1750) German composer and associate of J.S. **Bach, Fux** and **Quantz**, who held court appointments in Dresden, Prague and Rome. He was noted primarily as a lutenist, composing more than 600 pieces for the instrument.

Weissenberg, Alexis (1929-) Bulgarian-born pianist who studied at the Juilliard School of Music and has since played with most of the world's leading orchestras, noted for his virtuoso style and his wide repertory.

Weldon, John (1676-1736) English composer and organist. He was a pupil of **Purcell**, organist at New College Oxford and the Chapel Royal, and composer of operas, masques and incidental music to Shakespeare's *The Tempest*, formerly attributed to **Purcell**.

Weller, Walter (1939-) Austrian violinist and conductor, leader of the Vienna Philharmonic Orchestra, founder of the Weller String Quartet and principal conductor of the Royal Liverpool Philharmonic and other British orchestras.

Wellesz, Egon (1885-1974) Austrian-born composer who studied with **Schoenberg**, became a professor at Vienna University, then moved to England (taking British citizenship) and to a post at Oxford University. His compositions, including operas, ballets and nine symphonies, are varied in style, ranging from Schoenberg's twelve-note method to much more traditional idioms. He was also an authority on medieval music.

Well-Tempered Clavier, The See **Wohltemperierte Clavier, Das**

Werle, Lars Johan (1926-) Swedish composer who studied at Uppsala University and joined the staff of Swedish Radio. His best known work to date is the opera *Dreaming about Thérèse*, designed to be performed theatrically 'in the round', with the orchestra surrounding the audience.

Werner, Gregor Joseph (1693-1766) Austrian composer and **Haydn**'s predecessor as *Kapellmeister* to Prince Nikolaus Esterházy. He composed mainly masses and oratorios.

Wert, Giaches de (1553-1596) Flemish composer who went to Italy as a boy and served at the court of Mantua, where he influenced **Monteverdi**, especially in the composition of madrigals.

Wesley, Samuel (1766-1837) English composer related to John Wesley, the founder of Methodism, but who became a Roman Catholic and wrote mainly sacred music. He was also a celebrated organist who helped to revive the music of J.S. **Bach**.

Wesley, Samuel Sebastian (1810-1876) English composer and organist, illegitimate son of Samuel Wesley. He was organist at Hereford, Exeter, Winchester and Gloucester Cathedrals and professor of that instrument at the Royal Academy of Music.

He raised the standard of Anglican church music with his many fine anthems and hymns.

Westrup, Sir Jack Allan (1904-1975) English musical scholar and teacher who studied at Oxford University and held teaching posts at the Royal Academy of Music, Birmingham and Oxford Universities and elsewhere. He was also a well known writer and critic and was knighted in 1960.

White, Robert (*c*1535-1574) English composer. As organist and choirmaster at Westminster Abbey he wrote mainly church choral music in the rich polyphonic style of the Tudor period. His name is also sometimes spelled Whyte.

whole note Alternative term for **semibreve**.

whole-tone scale Scale that progresses by steps of whole tones only. No more than two such scales are possible, one beginning on C and the other on C sharp (or its enharmonic D♭), but each can begin at any point because there is no keynote. The whole-tone scale has six different notes, the one beginning on C being C-D-E-F♯-G♯-A♯-C. The use of this scale is very much associated with the compositions of **Debussy** and **Liszt**.

Whyte, Robert Alternative spelling of the name of Robert **White**.

Whythorne, Thomas (*c*1528-1595) English composer of many secular part songs and pieces for viola and other instruments. He travelled widely in Italy and his rediscovered autobiography, written in a form of shorthand, was published in 1961. His name is also sometimes spelled Withorne.

Widor, Charles Marie (1844-1937) French composer and organist at the parish church of St Sulpice, Paris. He was professor of organ and composition at the Paris Conservatoire, produced with Albert Schweitzer a complete edition of J.S. **Bach**'s organ works, and published a treatise on orchestration. Widor composed operas, symphonic poems and concertos, but his best known works are ten organ symphonies and two orchestral symphonies with organ.

Wieniawski, Henryk (1835-1880) Polish composer and one of the most famous violin virtuosi of the 19th century. He began his studies at the Paris Conservatoire aged eight, was appointed violinist to the Tsar of Russia and taught at the St Petersburg and Brussels conservatoires. He also made a concert tour of the United States with Anton **Rubinstein**. Among his compositions are two violin concertos, the second of which is quite well known.

Wieniawski, Józef (1837-1912) Polish pianist and composer, younger brother of Henryk **Wieniawski**. He studied with Alkan at the Paris Conservatoire and with **Liszt** at Weimar. He later taught at the Moscow and Brussels conservatoires. He performed with his brother, and composed a concerto and other piano works.

Wilbye, John (1574-1638) English composer of some of the finest madrigals, which he published in two volumes. He also contributed to the celebrated madrigal collection *The Triumphs of Oriana*.

Wild, Earl (1915-) American pianist who studied with Egon Petri, performed with **Toscanini** and is celebrated for his interpretations of **Liszt**. His own compositions include an oratorio and a ballet.

Wilde, David (1935-) English pianist who studied with Nadia **Boulanger** and has been professor of music at the Royal Academy of Music and the Royal Manchester College of Music. A specialist in the music of **Liszt** and **Bartók**.

Wilkinson, Marc (1929-) French-born Australian composer and conductor who studied with **Messiaen** and **Varèse**. He has worked with the Royal Shakespeare

Company and the National Theatre and written music for many plays (works by Osborne, Stoppard and Schaffer among them) and films.

Willaert, Adriaan (1490-1562) Flemish composer who first studied law, then abandoned this for music, travelling to Bohemia and Italy and becoming choirmaster at St Mark's, Venice. In that capacity he wrote much church music, but was also one of the finest composers of madrigals.

Willan, Healey (1880-1968) English organist and composer who settled in Canada, holding academic posts at Toronto University and composing an opera, orchestral and organ music and some choral pieces. He was also an authority on medieval plainsong.

Willcocks, Sir David (1919-) English organist and conductor who studied at the Royal College of Music and King's College, Cambridge. As a cathedral organist, teacher at Cambridge University and conductor of such groups as the Bach Choir, he has been at the centre of English musical life for many years, specialising both in choral and in English music, and composing some church and choral music of his own. He was knighted in 1977.

Williams, Grace (1906-1977) Welsh composer who studied with **Vaughan Williams** at the Royal College of Music and with Egon **Wellesz**. Her compositions include *Penillion* for orchestra, based on a traditional form of Welsh bardic singing, and other works with Welsh associations.

Williams, John (1941-) Australian guitarist who studied at the Royal College of Music and with **Segovia**. He has made many tours, some with fellow guitarist Julian **Bream**, and has done much to bridge the gap between concert and popular music, especially by his association with the pop group Sky. Several works have also been written for him. He was awarded the OBE in 1980.

John Towner Williams

Williams, John Towner (1932-) American composer who studied with **Castelnuovo-Tedesco** and at the Juilliard School of Music, and began his career as a pianist in the Hollywood studios of 20th Century Fox. He has since produced many scores for films and television, and composed some concert works.

Williamson, Malcolm (1931-) Australian composer who succeeded Sir Arthur **Bliss** as Master of the Queen's Music in 1975. He studied with Eugène **Goossens** in Sydney and with Elizabeth **Lutyens** and Erwin Stein in London and has since held posts at Westminster Choir School and Princeton University. His own style owes something to **Messiaen, Britten** and jazz, and like Britten he has also written music for children. His compositions include the operas *Our Man in Havana* (based on the novel by Graham Greene) and *The Happy Prince* (based on the fairy tale by Oscar Wilde), the *Mass of Christ the King*, also symphonies, concertos, piano and organ works and songs.

Wilson, John (1595-1674) English musician

whose versatile gifts as singer, lutenist, viol player and composer earned him the posts of court musician to both Charles I and Charles II and a professorship at Oxford University. He may also have acted in Shakespeare's company of players, as well as setting many of Shakespeare's verses to music.

wind band Band comprised of mixed woodwind and brass instruments, usually with percussion. In England the term **military band** is preferred, as opposed to **brass band** (which is made up only of brass instruments).

Windgassen, Wolfgang (1914-1974) German operatic tenor, prominent at the Bayreuth Festival in such great **Wagnerian** roles as Siegfried, Tristan and Parsifal. He was also artistic director of the Stuttgart Opera.

wind instruments Musical instruments in which the sound is produced by the vibration of air in a tube. **Organs** and **accordians** do not come into this category, because it is usual to restrict it to instruments blown by the player. Wind instruments in an orchestra are commonly divided into brass (horn, trumpet, trombone and tuba) and woodwind (flute, clarinet, oboe, bassoon, piccolo, cor anglais and saxophone).

wire brush Drumstick with a head of several stiff wires used on side drums and cymbals by drummers in dance and pop music. It produces a characteristic brushing sound.

Wirén, Dag (1905-) Swedish composer, many of whose works are based on the idea of the evolution or development of a single musical motif or 'cell'. They include symphonies, concertos, a serenade for strings, and stage and film music. He has also been a music critic and journalist.

Wise, Michael (1648-1687) English organist and choirmaster at Salisbury Cathedral, and composer of anthems and other church music and part-songs.

Wishart, Peter (1921-) English composer and teacher who studied with Nadia **Boulanger** and has held teaching posts at the Guildhall School of Music and Drama, King's College, London, and elsewhere. He has composed *Klytemnestra, the Captive* and other operas, symphonies, concertos and choral pieces.

Withorne, Thomas Alternative spelling of the name of Thomas **Whythorne**.

Witt, Jeremias Friedrich (1771-1837) German composer and violinist, famous as the composer of the so-called *Jena Symphony*, formerly attributed to **Beethoven**. He also composed operas and oratorios, as well as much instrumental music.

Wittgenstein, Paul (1887-1961) Austrian pianist, a pupil of Leschetizky, who lost his right arm in World War I. Subsequently several major composers wrote pieces especially for him, most notably **Ravel** (*Concerto for the Left Hand*), Richard **Strauss**, **Prokofiev** and **Britten**.

Wohltempierte Clavier, Das Two sets of **preludes** and **fugues** by J.S. **Bach** for keyboard (BWV 846-893). In this instance the word *clavier* means any keyboard instrument, and not just the clavichord. The collection is made up of two sets, each consisting of 24 works, and was published in 1722 and 1744 respectively. The preludes and fugues are in major and minor keys in ascending order. The two sets are commonly known as *The Forty-Eight*. The English translation of the title is *The Well-Tempered Clavier*.

Wolff, Christian (1934-) French-born American composer, a prominent scholar, but largely self-taught. His works, influenced by **Varèse** and **Cage** among others, make use of electronics and the 'prepared piano', and he has also evolved his own system of notation.

Wolf-Ferrari, Ermanno (1876-1948) Italian composer who composed mainly operas, generally light and tuneful with bright, accomplished orchestration, of which *The School for Fathers (I Quattro Rusteghi*, after Goldoni), *Susanna's Secret* (*Il segreto di Susanna*) and *The Jewels of the Madonna* (*I Gioielli della Madonna*) remain the best known on account of their overtures.

Wolf, Hugo (1860-1903) Austrian composer, mainly of songs, by which he is considered one of the greatest masters of the German Romantic *Lied*, welding vocal lines and piano accompaniment into an indivisible means of expression. His three most celebrated groups of songs are the *Mörike-Lieder* (settings of the German Poet Eduard Mörike) and the *Spanisches Liederbuch* and *Italienisches Liederbuch* (settings of Spanish and Italian poems in German translation). Other works include the opera *Der Corregidor* (based on the same story as **Falla**'s ballet *The Three-Cornered Hat*), and the charming *Italian Serenade*, originally for string quartet and then orchestrated. Wolf was also an outspoken music critic, especially in support of **Wagner**.

wolf note Jarring sound produced between certain intervals on keyboard instruments tuned in **mean-tone temperament**, or on stringed instruments by defective vibration on a certain note or notes.

Wolpe, Stefan (1902-1972) German-born composer who studied with **Busoni** and **Webern**, collaborated with the dramatist Bertold Brecht, and after a period of work in Palestine, settled in the United States, becoming an American citizen. His compositions – operas, ballets, orchestral and instrumental works and songs – use his own special kind of serialism and are influenced also by traditional Jewish music.

Wolstenholme, William (1865-1931) English organist and composer, blind from birth, given instruction and help from **Elgar**. He composed mainly organ music.

Wood, Charles (1866-1926) Irish teacher and composer, who studied at the Royal College of Music, then taught there and at Cambridge University, **Vaughan Williams** being among his pupils. His compositions include the opera *The Pickwick Papers*, choral and instrumental pieces and much church music.

Wood, Haydn (1882-1959) English composer of orchestral and instrumental works, but chiefly remembered today for his songs, tinged with a gentle sentimentality, including *A Brown Bird Singing* and *Roses of Picardy*.

woodland flute Organ stop controlling a 4ft or 8ft pipe with inverted mouths producing a sound similar to the claribel stop.

Wood, Sir Henry Joseph (1869-1944) English conductor and organist who studied at the Royal Academy of Music, began conducting opera, and in 1895 was engaged by the impresario Robert Newman

Sir Henry Wood

to direct a new series of Promenade Concerts in London (originally so named because the audience could walk about). His career and his name were thenceforth associated with these famous concerts. Wood also conducted at many other British music festivals, and was a champion of new music by, among others, **Mahler, Scriabin, Debussy, Sibelius** and **Schoenberg. Vaughan Williams'** *Serenade to Music* was written in his honour. He also made several orchestral transcriptions and arrangements, including the *Fantasia on British Sea Songs*, still a popular feature on the Last Night of the Proms. He was knighted in 1911 and made a Companion of Honour in the year of his death.

Wood, Hugh (1932-) English composer who studied at Oxford University and with Mátyás **Seiber**, and has since held teaching posts at the Royal Academy of Music and Morley College, London, at Liverpool University and elsewhere. His compositions, fairly advanced in style, include *Scenes from Comus* for soprano, tenor and orchestra, orchestral and chamber works and songs.

Wood, Thomas (*c*1530-1592) Scottish churchman who compiled an interesting and valuable collection of mainly Scottish vocal and instrumental music, widely known as the *St Andrew Psalter* or *Thomas Wode's Part Books*. Additions to his collection were made by others in the following century.

Wood, Thomas (1892-1950) English composer who travelled to Australia and did much to popularize the song *Waltzing Matilda*. His own compositions include the cantatas *Chanticleer* and *The Rainbow*.

woodwind instruments Musical instruments generally made of wood, in which a column of air is made to vibrate by one or two reeds, or through a blow hole. Woodwind instruments are made to produce the notes of the scale by opening holes in the side wall of the tube. Opening holes in succession has the effect of temporarily shortening the air column and so raising the pitch of the **fundamental** obtained, by scalewise **degrees**. The woodwind instruments of the orchestra are the flute, clarinet, oboe, bassoon, piccolo, cor anglais and saxophone.

Wordsworth, William Brocklesby (1908-) English composer, related to the poet, who studied in Edinburgh and has lived for many years in Scotland. His compositions, in a generally traditional style, include six symphonies, six string quartets and other chamber works and songs.

working out Alternative term for **development**.

Wotquenne, Alfred (1867-1939) Belgian musicologist and scholar, best remembered today for his catalogue of the works of **Gluck** and of C.P.E. **Bach** (whose compositions are usually quoted with their Wq number).

Wq. Abbreviation of Wotquenne. Alfred Wotquenne (1867-1939) compiled a catalogue (1905) of C.P.E. **Bach**'s works, and used Wq as a prefix to indicate the number of a piece in the catalogue.

Wranitzky Alternative spelling of the name of Anton and Paul **Vranicky**.

Wuorinen, Charles (1938-) American composer, pianist and teacher. He studied at Columbia University, taught there in his turn and has also been active in the promotion of new music. His own works encompass a wide range of forms and styles, tonal, serial and electronic.

Wurlitzer American firm of instrument makers founded in 1858 by Franz Wurlitzer (1831-1914). It achieved fame through its production of electric and electronic pianos and organs. In addition, the firm became world famous for its rare **violin** collection.

X

Xenakis, Iannis (1922–) Composer of Greek parentage who studied in Paris with **Honegger**, **Milhaud** and **Messiaen**, and adopted French citizenship. He is one of the most innovative composers of his time, employing among other things, a method called by the Greek word *stochastic* whereby the mathematics of probability are applied to the form of a piece of music (not to be confused with **aleatory music**). In this connection he founded a School of Mathematical and Automated Music in Paris. His works are mostly for large or unusual instrumental ensembles, or for tapes and other electronic devices. Xenakis has also been an engineer and architect, working with Le Corbusier.

xiao (China) See **hsiao**.

xoomij/chöömij (Mongolia) Vocal form distinguished by its use of multiphonics. The male singer simultaneously produces two notes by forcing air through his vocal chords, emitting a low drone rich enough in harmonics so that, by tensing his cheek and tongue muscles, he can select high tones to form a whistle-like melody. Thus there are no words to these songs, but only vowel sounds produced by manipulation of the mouth cavity.

xylophone Percussion instrument consisting of a number of resonant wooden bars laid horizontally and struck with beaters. It has a range of three to four octaves. The xylophone probably originated in southeast Asia, although primitive types can be found among some African tribes today. The first time it was used in a modern orchestra was by **Saint-Saëns** in *Danse Macabre* (1874) and later by **Walton** in *Belshazzar's Feast* (1931).

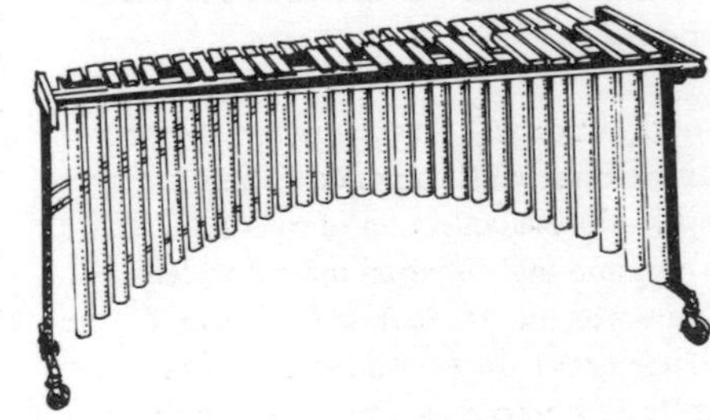

Xylophone

xylorimba Percussion instrument (combining the names of **xylophone** and **marimba**) with a range of five octaves.

Y

Yamash'ta Stomu (1947-) Japanese musician who studied at Kyoto Music Academy and in the United States, and has achieved world fame as a virtuoso percussionist, playing both jazz and concert music. Among his own compositions is *Prisms* for solo percussion, also some film scores. He also directs the Red Buddha theatre and dance company.

Yepes, Narcisco (1927-) Spanish guitarist who has done much to revive the repertory of guitar music of his own country, but has also recorded all the lute music of J.S. **Bach**. He often plays a ten-string guitar of his own design.

yo (Japan) One of the two principal scales of folk origin. See **Japanese scales**.

yodel Type of singing without words that is practised in alpine countries. It is usually sung by men in falsetto, with rapid changes to **chest voice**, very free in rhythm and metre. Normally it uses the restricted scale of the natural harmonics of instruments such as the alphorn.

Yonge, Nicholas (*c*1550-1619) English chorister who is famous for editing and publishing *Musica Transalpina*, two volumes of Italian madrigals translated into English. He is thus credited with having introduced the madrigal to England and ushering in a golden age of English music.

Young, Alexander (1920-) English tenor who studied at the Royal College of Music; he has taught at the Royal Northern College and founded the Jubilate Choir. His exceptionally wide repertory has encompassed opera from **Handel** to **Stravinsky**, and German *Lieder*.

Young, La Monte (1935-) American composer who studied with **Stockhausen**. His own work has something of the same novelty of thinking about it. He describes one of his pieces as 'building a fire in front of the audience', and another as 'draw a straight line and follow it'. *The Tortoise, his Dreams and Journeys* calls for voices and electronics.

Young, William (?-1671) English flautist, violinist and composer who travelled widely in Europe and was a pioneer in the development of the Baroque **trio sonata**. After the English Restoration he returned home and joined the King's Band.

Ysaÿe, Eugène (1858-1931) Belgian violinist and composer. He studied with **Wieniawski** and **Vieuxtemps**, was professor of violin at the Brussels Conservatoire and founded the Ysaÿe concert society. As one of the greatest virtuosi of his time he toured Europe and the United States, introducing many new works. As a composer he wrote violin concertos and sonatas, and an opera in Walloon.

yüeh-ch'in (China) Instrument known as the 'moon guitar' after the shape of its body. It has a short neck and ten frets and is plucked with a small plectrum. A single-stringed version is used in the Chinese opera, whereas in the Chinese orchestra a two- to four-stringed version is used, often in pairs to increase the volume.

Yun, Isang (1917-) Korean composer, who studied in his own country and Japan and then in Europe. He has also taught in Berlin. His works, combining Western **serialism** with traditional Korean musical idioms, include the operas *The Dream of Liu-Tung* and *The Butterfly's Widow*, orchestral and instrumental works.

Z

Zabaleta, Nicanor (1907-) Spanish harpist who studied in Madrid and Paris. As well as reviving much old music for the harp he has commissioned new works for the instrument from, among others, **Milhaud** and **Krenek**.

Zachau, Friedrich Wilhelm (1663-1712) German composer and organist. As organist at the Liebfrauenkirche, Halle, he became **Handel**'s first important teacher, for which he is chiefly remembered today.

Zacher, Gerd (1929-) German composer who studied with **Messiaen**, **Boulez** and **Stockhausen**. He is also a noted organist, giving the first performance of several new works for that instrument and featuring it in his own compositions.

zampogna (It.) Bagpipe from the Calabrian region of Italy, consisting of an air-filled bag, a chanter and four drones, two of which have finger-holes to allow variation of the notes accompanying the melody.

Zandonai, Riccardo (1883-1944) Italian composer who studied with **Mascagni** and wrote operas, mainly in the prevailing *verismo* style, including *Francesca da Rimini*; also orchestral and choral works.

zapateado (Sp.) Dance for a single performer in 3/4 time and with the rhythmic accents marked by the stamping of the heels, rather than by **castanets**.

Zarlino, Gioseffe (1517-1590) Italian monk and musical theorist who studied with **Willaert** in Venice and succeeded him as choirmaster at St Mark's. In his musical treatises Zarlino proposed the system of tuning for keyboard instruments known as equal temperament, which has been of tremendous significance in the development of Western music.

zarzuela (Sp.) Light musical or comic opera, generally of a satirical nature. The libretto has spoken dialogue and allows for improvisation, in which even the audience joins in.

Zelenka, Jan Dismas (1679-1745) Bohemian composer and double-bass player, active in the musical life of Dresden, composing masses, oratorios and many instrumental works in the Baroque style of the time.

Zelter, Carl Friedrich (1758-1832) German composer who lived and worked for most of his life in Berlin, teaching mainly vocal and church music, and composing choral works and songs. One of his pupils was **Mendelssohn**, with whom he joined in reviving the music of J.S. **Bach**.

Zemlinsky, Alexander von (1872-1942) Austrian-born composer and conductor, of Polish parentage, at the centre of Austro-German musical life in the early years of the 20th century and a close friend of both **Mahler** and **Schoenberg**. His own compositions, operas, symphonies, songs with orchestra and chamber works, share some aspects of their aims and styles.

Efrem Zimbalist

Zimbalist, Efrem (1889-1985) Russian-born violinist who studied at the St Petersburg Conservatoire with Leopold Auer and made concert tours of Europe before settling in the United States and taking American citizenship. There he became director of the Curtis Institute. He also composed a concerto and other works for the violin.

Zimmerman, Franklin Bershir (1923-) American musical scholar who has produced a full catalogue of the music of **Purcell**.

Zimmermann, Bernd Alois (1918-1970) German composer and teacher, mainly in Cologne after the World War II. His compositions cover a wide range of styles and techniques, incorporating serialism, jazz and electronic music. They include the opera *Die Soldaten*, also symphonies, concertos, choral and instrumental pieces.

Zingarelli, Niccolò Antonio (1752-1837) Italian composer and violinist, also choirmaster at Milan Cathedral and St Peter's, Rome, and teacher of **Bellini**. He composed many operas and sacred music.

zither Generic name for an ubiquitous instrument – a plucked chordophone, which has a box or tube resonator and strings over frets or bridges. The zither was developed during the 18th century from the **cittern**, from which it took its name. It consists of a shallow box with no neck but with either two curved sides or one curved and one straight side. There are usually five melody strings stretched over a fretted **keyboard**, with up to 40 accompanying strings in addition. It is played with the fingers, the bass strings alone being struck with a **plectrum** fixed to the thumb by a ring.

Other more primitive zithers exist, such as the trough zither, the Indian vina (a stick zither) and the long zithers of China and Japan (**koto** and **qin**). The Arabian *qanun* derives from these instruments.

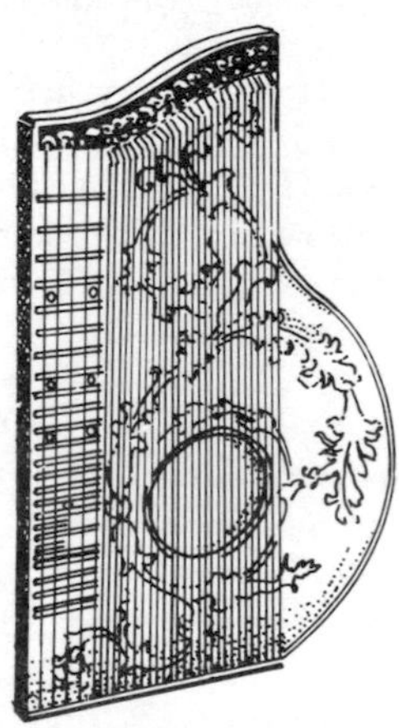

Zither

The zither gained world-wide popularity when it was featured in the film *The Third Man* (1949), with music written and played by Anton Karas.

zoppa, alla (It.) Music played in a syncopated rhythm.

Zukerman, Pinchas (1948-) Israeli violinist and viola player who studied in

Israel and at the Juilliard School. He is acclaimed both as a soloist and chamber musician, and has had a close association with the English Chamber Orchestra.

zurna General term for various kinds of oboe of ancient origin which occur throughout Asia and south-eastern Europe. The name is Persian ('festival flute'), although local names are commonly used (*ghayta* in North Africa (see **gaida**), *shehnai* in India and *sarunai* in Malaysia). The instrument consists of a conical wooden pipe flared at the lower end. A mouthpipe holds a double reed, at the base of which there is usually (but not in Iraq, Turkey or India) a surrounding metal disc, placed against the player's lips. It is normally played outdoors in ensembles with drums, for use in dances, games, processions and village festivals. Some members of the ensemble may play drones, often using circular breathing.

zydeco (US) Modern, black, Cajun music of the French-speaking bayou region of Louisiana. It is characterized by rhythmic accompaniment of accordian, fiddle and/or steel-stringed guitar. Contemporary groups add drums and amplification.

Picture Credits

The publishers would like to thank the following for permission to reproduce the illustrations on the pages indicated.
Mansell Collection: 41 bottom, 45, 56, 76, 89 top, 92, 97, 133, 155, 174, 188, 298, 301, 410, 411. Popperfoto: 1, 19, 28, 35, 38, 41 top, 44, 49, 51, 52, 62, 63, 67, 69, 70, 80, 88, 89 bottom, 101, 115, 116, 128, 136, 137, 138, 144, 146, 166, 184, 194, 196, 207, 210, 211, 223, 231, 239, 241, 245, 247, 255, 265, 266, 274, 282 right, 284, 307, 310, 315, 320, 322, 331, 339, 340, 343, 347, 350, 354, 358, 363, 373, 375, 382, 383, 386, 389, 390, 393, 394, 399, 400, 408, 409, 412, 415, 432 left, 432 right, 434, 455, 459, 461. Royal Festival Hall: 365 top. Royal Opera House: 365 bottom. Topham: 22, 50, 130, 212, 220, 250, 263, 277, 282 left, 329, 341, 342, 357, 429, 444, 468.